MARY MacSWINEY

MARY MacSWINEY

LEEANN LANE

UNIVERSITY COLLEGE DUBLIN PRESS
PREAS CHOLÁISTE OLLSCOILE BHAILE ÁTHA CLIATH
2025

First published 2025
by University College Dublin Press
UCD Humanities Institute, Room H103,
Belfield,
Dublin 4

www.ucdpress.ie

ISBN 978-1-7390863-8-1

CIP data available from the British Library

Typeset in Dublin by Gough Typesetting Limited
Text design by Lyn Davies
Printed in England on acid-free paper by
CPI Antony Rowe, Chippenham, Wiltshire.

Contents

Acknowledgements

In writing this book I have accrued numerous debts of gratitude. Many people have encouraged and supported me.

I would like to first acknowledge the staff in the various archives consulted including the National Archives of Ireland, the National Library of Ireland and UCD Archives. I would particularly like to thank Kate Manning in UCD Archives for her support and help. Catherine and Cathal Brugha were so generous in welcoming me into their home and allowing me to consult private papers in their possession.

Thank you to my colleagues in the School of History and Geography, particularly Professor James Kelly, Professor William Murphy and Professor Daithí Ó Corráin who have been unfailing in their support. Dr Catriona Crowe encouraged this biography from the beginning of the project. I am very grateful for her invaluable feedback to draft chapters and encouragement throughout the process.

Thank you also to Dr Síobhra Aiken, Hayley Brabazon, Professor Catherine Cox, Cecile Chemin, Dani Martini, Professor Tom Dunne, Professor Lindsey Earner-Byrne, Professor Diarmaid Ferriter, Dr Deirdre Foley, Rachel Granville, Caroline Heafey, Molly Hennigan, Kevin Hickey, Dr Sinéad Kennedy, Dr Mary McAuliffe, Dr David McCullagh, Dr Gerri O'Neill, Professor Micheal O'Riordain, Professor Paul Rouse, Dr Angela Veale and Dr Margaret Ward.

I would like to express my sincere thanks to the staff in UCD Press for their professionalism and expert work at all stages in the process. I would particularly like to thank Noelle Moran who has once again unfailingly supported me and who believed in the project and my ability to execute it – and who patiently tried to keep me to deadlines. I could not ask for a better editor; I am very grateful. Also, thanks are due to other key team members from the Press including: Fiachra McCarthy, Shane Gough, Yvonne Reddin, Caitlin O'Neill, Jane Rogers and Nigel Carré.

Thank you to my father, Dr Pat Lane, my sister Niamh and my brother-in-law, Philipp Prince. Finally, in memory of my mother, Renée Lane.

Leeann Lane
Dublin, February 2025

Introduction

Mary MacSwiney was one of the most uncompromising opponents of the Anglo-Irish Treaty. Her unyielding adherence to the ideal of full republican independence was a stance she maintained during the Civil War and after the Sinn Féin split in 1926, right down to her death from heart failure in 1942. To this day she is viewed as politically one dimensional. MacSwiney was not, however, merely a cipher for the extreme element within republicanism during the Treaty debates. She was a woman who suffered ultimate loss in Brixton Jail in 1920 as her brother Terence starved to death on hunger strike. Her witnessing of, in the words of her sister Annie, scenes that were 'agonising beyond anything I could describe', changed the trajectory of her life.[1] Her brother's 'agony' would never, as she wrote to de Valera, 'have been endured to the end for anything less than absolute and entire Separation'; this determined her unyielding rejection of the Anglo-Irish Treaty, 1921.[2] Terence's high-profile death to advance the cause of full republican independence also meant that MacSwiney was not able to countenance, as de Valera was, re-entry into parliamentary politics in 1926.

In her lifetime MacSwiney was not, however, just a one-dimensional caricature of extreme republicanism but rather a multi-faceted individual. Relatively unusual for a woman born in 1872, she was educated to third level and in 1916 established the first Catholic lay school for girls in Cork. While St Ita's School struggled financially, it was successful pedagogically. Initially a supporter of female suffrage, MacSwiney moved to prioritise the national cause in the second decade of the twentieth century. She was elected TD for Cork in 1921, a seat she held until the first general election in 1927. This study argues that she had political influence particularly in the period 1920–3. Indeed, even up until the Sinn Féin split in 1926, her voice was powerful on the republican side. It is notable that de Valera chose to confide to MacSwiney his deepest unease as to the course of the Civil War and to tease out their respective positions on the Treaty in a very intimate political correspondence.

The only biography of MacSwiney was published nearly 40 years ago and is almost solely based on her papers in the archives of University College Dublin.[3] Using a wider range of primary sources, including the Home Office files and medical notes on Terence MacSwiney's hunger strike in Brixton in 1920, this study seeks not just to understand the trajectory of Mary's[4] political life.[5] Rather than merely dismiss her as one dimensional in her opposition to the Treaty and in her continued political intractability, it is necessary to understand why she was increasingly viewed as a virago. She was a woman who had suffered extreme loss as she witnessed the protracted death of her brother in Brixton Jail in

1920. Moreover, the perception of her political extremism was heightened by the fact that she was a woman.

From an early age Mary assumed a sense of responsibility for her younger siblings, taking over as head of the family in 1904 on the death of her mother. It was Mary, not Terence, who assumed the role of head of the household on the 1911 census form, despite the latter being 32 years old.[6] Her biography cannot be written without sustained reference to the importance of family; in particular, her politics must be understood with reference to the politics of Terence both in his life and in the aftermath of his death. That is not to deny Mary individual political agency or to suggest that she was anything other than the strong and principled woman that she was. A recognition of the centrality of her siblings to Mary's life is instead a testament to familial love and the influence of such on a political level. A holistic analysis of an individual life cannot isolate the private persona from that of the public. Moreover, as Joan Scott states, information about women in the past is 'necessarily information about men … one implies the study of the other'.[7]

Mary's commitment to the wellbeing of her siblings is key to an understanding of her personal and political decisions. Her sister Kit offered the following vignette of family life in Cork around the turn of the twentieth century. The siblings returned late one evening after a tea party with relatives:

> We went straight to Mamma and said 'Mamma, there is nothing like the home cup'. I wonder if that expression has the same meaning now that it had once 60 years ago? Then it meant Tea en famille … our dear mother's face lit up with a lovely smile. It showed so well our love for home.[8]

Agnes Maillot writes that Mary's 'political trajectory could be seen as one of dedicated idealism characterised by a lack of political realism'.[9] This is true to a point, but the statement fails to offer that deeper analysis that draws on the centrality of family to Mary and the trauma she experienced in Brixton as her brother endured a long-drawn-out and painful hunger strike to death. Irish historiography has placed a focus on the Irish wife and mother.[10] A review of the play *Hunger-strike* set during the Civil War, published by Máirín Cregan in 1931, drew the following praise in the *Catholic Bulletin*. The play – based on the hunger strike of Cregan's husband, James Ryan, in 1923 – the reviewer stated, placed 'in her proper setting and due prominence, the Irish wife and Irish mother in the particular phase of the struggle for Irish Freedom'.[11] Historiography has, by contrast, paid little attention to the Irish sister. Rather than stating that Mary lacked political pragmatism, the reasons why that became increasingly the case need to be analysed and understood.

In 2001 Paul Lerner and Mark S. Micale noted that 'the study of trauma has begun to inspire a rapidly growing historical dimension'.[12] Graham Dawson does identify certain issues with 'trauma theory' within the Humanities. In his work on post-conflict Northern Ireland he makes 'a case for shifting the frame for investigation of subjective experiences and psychological legacies of the conflict, away from trauma and towards the history and memory of emotions'.[13] This study is concerned with the emotional response of Mary to her brother's death and the fact that it did not manifest as pathology but rather in an impetus to ensure that the cause of full independence for which he had given his life was achieved. The American Psychiatric Association defines PTSD, recognised since the 1980s, as 'an event out of the range of ordinary human experience in which one's life or the lives of one's family are endangered'.[14] Hunger strikes and their potential consequences were not extraordinary events for Mary. As a suffrage activist she was familiar with the hunger strikes that began in England in 1909 and in Ireland in 1912. When Thomas Ashe died on hunger strike in Mountjoy in September 1917, Terence was in Cork Prison. Stating she did not want to see a similar tragedy occur in Cork, Mary demanded that those prisoners be granted the status achieved by the men in Mountjoy.[15] Yet, there was something 'unspeakable' in Mary's experience of her brother's Brixton hunger strike because he, and his family, believed that he would be released. As William Murphy writes of April and May 1920:

> Prison, as it had two years earlier, appeared to be on the verge of worthlessness as a weapon against the IRA. The hunger strikers of Cork, including Terence MacSwiney, therefore had good reason to believe that they would not be obliged to choose between abandoning their strike and death.[16]

On 25 September 1920, Terence was discussing the possibility of moving to a nursing home should the government release him.[17] Two days earlier Mary expressed her 'confidence and willingness ... should his release be ordered' to have him remain in Brixton under Dr Higson's care 'until he was fit to be moved'.[18] That her brother was not released but instead died after such agonising suffering elevated the hunger strike to something 'extraordinary' in her experience.

During the debates on the Treaty delegation Mary indirectly called on her register of suffering in Brixton when she declared her political stance as one of the 'strong uncompromising minority' who:

> refuse allegiance direct or indirect to the British Crown ... There was always an element who did not want to suffer but those who suffered most realised they suffered for nothing less than the Republic.[19]

In her reference to an 'uncompromising minority' and the necessity to suffer to bring forth the Republic, she was not just drawing on her own experience of trauma at watching her brother endure a protracted and agonising death, she was also bearing witness to his political beliefs. Following her brother's death Mary sought to promote a political and moral culture in Ireland that validated and memorialised the self sacrifice of her brother, her own suffering and that of the wider MacSwiney family. The appropriate way to record and to remember his traumatic death was the establishment of that for which he had died – a separatist republic. She would be, she declared in the Dáil on 21 December, the 'first and most deliberate and irreconcilable rebel' if the country 'should be so false to itself as to adopt the so-called Treaty'.[20] Mary witnessed an intimate act of self sacrifice which bound her to a belief that her task was to continue her brother's fidelity to a separatist republic for which he had given his life. When she declared in the Dáil that Ireland had 'stood on a noble and spiritual ideal for the last three years' she was referring to the sacrifices of men such as her brother.[21] Betrayal of the republic, for her, would have meant betrayal of a brother she loved and admired, and it would have been almost impossible for her to think and feel in any other way.

The dominant gender roles of the period are an important context for understanding attitudes to Mary's politics after 1920. Despite her high-profile uncompromising stance during the Treaty debates, Mary was not alone in her opposition to the Articles of Agreement signed by the Irish delegates. Republicans during the Civil War held the belief that what had been achieved during the peace talks was not sufficient to offset the sacrifices and deaths during 1916 and the War of Independence. Men and women fought on the anti-Treaty side and there was large scale imprisonment. While only republican men were executed, women and men used the weapon of hunger strike in the period 1922–3. However, there was a gendered dimension to the derision and scorn that Mary experienced, particularly from 1921 onwards. She became for many on the pro-Treaty side a symbol of all that was aberrant on a republican side who refused to accept the will of the people. During the Civil War, W. T. Cosgrave described her as a 'female fanatic'.[22] Her ambition was, he declared, 'to be Queen of Ireland'.[23] When the Irish public had the 'bad taste to decline her proffered gift and dispute her authority, like the Queen in "Alice in Wonderland" her cry is, "Off with their heads"'.[24] In February 1923, the *Freeman's Journal* described her as 'on the warpath' and 'capable of a rebellion of her own'.[25] Campaigning during the Sligo-Leitrim by election in 1925 Kevin O'Higgins declared, to howls of laughter, that Mary had 'a Republic in her vanity bag'.[26] Speaking on behalf of T. F. Healy's candidature in the by election in Dublin the following year, O'Higgins stated that the Irish Free State had 'vindicated democracy' and that 'their necks would be no longer under Miss MacSwiney's heel'.[27] No republican man was derided as Mary was. The *Belfast Newsletter* described her as falling on those with whom she disagreed 'with every tooth bared, drops of clotted venom suspended from every outstretched fang'.[28] Even some contemporary writers engage in caricature. Describing the Sinn Féin Party after the 1926 split the journalist Brian Feeney described Mary in a different way to her male colleagues, drawing attention to her physical demeanour:

> The same names recur: J. J. O'Kelly or 'Scelig' as he was commonly known, 'Ceann Comhairle' of the Second Dáil and later President of Sinn Féin; Mary MacSwiney, sister of Terence, grim, implacable, with a black cloche hat crammed on her head; Brian O'Higgins, purest of pure republicans... [29]

As a strong woman who could be strident and who refused to bow to pressure to dilute her republican message, Mary did not conform to the gender roles of the period. She was a single, unmarried woman in her mid-40s when Terence died, propelling her into republican politics in an increasingly central role. As an unmarried woman she existed outside the domestic paradigm of woman as wife and married mother within the confines of the home. She was not submissive or deferential to any form of patriarchal authority. Her dominant presence within republicanism after the Treaty split was used by Cumann na nGaedheal to emasculate de Valera. That he was subject to 'henpecking' by Mary was a repeated jibe.[30] That she featured so heavily in the anti-republican propaganda and comments of the pro-Treaty side was, of course, testament to her political influence. She could not be ignored, instead humour was used to denigrate her and those like de Valera who refused to accept the Treaty and worked to destabilise the state in formation from 1922.

Counter to the one-dimensional caricature that formed over Mary was a much more nuanced human reality. She was loved by her family and close friends. She had many colleagues who both liked and respected her. Kathleen Lynn described her as very 'steadfast' and developed a close working relationship with her after the Civil War.[31] In an interview with Dr Margaret Ward, Máire Comerford was asked to describe Mary. Tellingly she noted the way she was vilified as a woman who spoke her mind:

> She was a most tolerant and kind person but she had great courage in confronting every situation. But the men … they made a harridan of her. But she wasn't at all. But men won't face up to a woman if they be in the wrong you know, and she was one person above all they couldn't face.[32]

However, like all who were politically influential during the revolutionary period and beyond, Mary had detractors, many of whom were male. Her political weight during the period of the Treaty debates and the Civil War, and to a lesser extent up to 1926, coupled with her gender, meant that she was subjected to a degree of vitriol not meted out to men on the anti-Treaty side who also preached violence and refused to compromise.

Chapter One situates Mary within her family background. The socio-economic hardships faced by the family at end of the nineteenth century and the way that Mary, as the eldest, assumed responsibility for younger siblings is outlined. The commitment of the family to education for all members is discussed. The cultural values and aspirations of the MacSwiney family in the period before 1916 are analysed: notably their commitment to the ideals of Irish Ireland and their move towards advanced nationalism in the period before 1916.

Chapter Two examines the failure of Cork to rise in 1916. In the lead up to the rebellion Mary, as most republican women, was involved in gendered work. Unlike women in Cumann na mBan and the Irish Citizen Army in Dublin where the rising did take place, women in Cork had no opportunity to expand their involvement in republican politics during Easter week. Mary, as the founder of Cumann na mBan in Cork, was centrally involved in all the discussions and recriminations that took place in the city. Terence's position as deputy leader of the Irish Volunteers in Cork meant that the MacSwiney home in the suburb of Blackrock was the locus for many of those who delivered the series of messages, often contradictory, from members of the military council of the Irish Republican Brotherhood in Dublin. After the Rising Mary began what would become a lifelong pattern of defending the actions of Terence. Riddled with anguish about the failure of Cork to rise, Terence's sufferings were also Mary's. From this period, she sought to explain and rationalise his actions in pursuit of an Irish republic. It is important to also underscore that Mary was a firm republican in her own right. The MacSwiney siblings operated as republican family unit.

In the period after the Rising, Mary was involved in prisoner aid. This form of activism was, as Chapter Three discusses, both personal and political. Terence was interned after 1916 and repeatedly re-arrested until his death in October 1920. However, Mary was also committed to ensuring the welfare of all republican prisoners with a particular focus on those incarcerated in England and Wales in the aftermath of the Rising. While she was still involved in gendered activism, she began to establish a name for herself within republican circles, working, for example, with the London-based Art O'Brien in prisoner support through the Irish National Aid Association, later the Irish National Aid and Volunteer

Dependents' Fund. She finally joined Sinn Féin when the newly re-organised party declared itself in favour of an Irish republic at the Ard Fheis in October 1917. In later life she emphasised that no member of her family had joined until the party committed itself to securing full independence. This chapter engages also with the position of Cork Cumann na mBan in the period up to 1920. Mary's strident personality did cause tensions in the organisation in the city, hostilities that manifested at certain flash points, notably during the split in Cumann na mBan after the Treaty debates.

Mary's life changed exponentially in October 1920. Chapter Four details the arrest of Terence in August of that year and his protracted hunger strike in Brixton Jail, leading to his death on 24 October. The chapter focuses on the experience and feelings of Mary and the wider MacSwiney family as they watched day after day as their beloved brother became weaker and inched towards death. Terence's medical notes show the suffering he endured but they also illuminate the trauma experienced by Mary, his wife Muriel, and his other siblings as they watched him slowly die. Mary was not just a passive observer: she was to the forefront in the attempt to have Terence unconditionally released. She engaged with British officials and his doctors. She negotiated to ensure that the correct information was disseminated to the press. She attempted to garner the support of trade unionists and high-ranking church men. She verbally denounced anyone who suggested that Terence was committing suicide. With these actions she cemented the reputation she gained amongst British officialdom when Terence was interned after 1916. Assertive in demanding rights for her brother, she was labelled a difficult woman who did not know her place.

Mary experienced trauma in Brixton in 1920 and entered into a cycle of repetition compulsion that revolved around making meaningful the death of her brother. Chapter Five discusses the testimony she gave to the American Commission on Conditions in Ireland in December 1920 and her decision to remain in the US to conduct an extensive speaking tour. Brief statements in her testimony in Washington give an insight to the pain and extreme suffering she endured in Brixton. She noted how medical and official appeals encouraging Terence to take food were made less to Muriel than to her and Annie, continuing:

> They had the grace to leave his wife alone. I think her youth and beauty appealed to them. Perhaps they thought we were not feeling it so much. But we got the brunt of it to bear, and it was not easy.[33]

There was, Mary stated, 'a limit to human endurance, and some of us have had to go quite close to it.'[34]

At considerable personal expense Mary resolved to spend time away from her grieving family and her management of St Ita's school as she travelled across America in 1921. In her speeches in cities across the US, she represented Ireland as one of the small nations whose freedom had justified the allied response to the outbreak of the First World War; she referred repeatedly to President Woodrow Wilson's statements on national self determination as an American war aim.

Mary returned to Ireland in August 1921 having been elected as a TD for Cork in the June elections of that year. The months before the Treaty debates were agonising for her as she both feared that the plenipotentiaries would compromise but simultaneously could not conceive that such a betrayal could take place. She had existed in a liminal space in Brixton in 1920, waiting for Terence to die yet not being able to conceptualise that it would happen. Chapter Six discusses how this pattern played out again between August and December 1921. Speaking for over two and half hours against the Treaty on 21 December, her anguish was palpably on show when she appealed to the House in response to sneering on the pro-Treaty side at the length of her speech. She claimed her right to 'speak for the honour of my nation' based on what she 'went through for 74 days at Brixton'.[35] Her distress was also patently evident in her correspondence with de Valera in this period.

During the Civil War Mary, described by the British government as one of 'the most extreme and dangerous women in Ireland', endured two gruelling hunger strikes: in November 1922 in Mountjoy Jail and again in April 1923 in Kilmainham Jail.[36] Chapter Seven analyses Mary's willingness during her imprisonments to stand in opposition to the Bishops' Joint Pastoral of October 1922. Yet again, she was a woman who refused to be silenced or defer to what she deemed inappropriate authority, in this case the right of the Catholic Church to make political statements. The chapter also considers the strong political relationship Mary had with de Valera during the Civil War and her increasing concern that he stand firm as rumours of, and overtures to, republican surrender grew in 1923. That de Valera explained his political choices and leanings to Mary is noteworthy and testifies to her political centrality in the period of the war.

Chapter Eight considers the period from the conclusion of the Civil War until the establishment of Fianna Fáil in 1926. De Valera's imprisonment from 15 August 1923 to 16 July 1924 facilitated Mary's uncompromising stance and masked her growing irrelevance. Her voice dominated at the higher echelons of Sinn Féin during his imprisonment. She reiterated the need for republicans not to compromise. De Valera, by contrast, was much more questioning, inching arguably towards finding a path to re-establish parliamentary involvement which he achieved with the establishment of Fianna Fáil in 1926. De Valera's correspondence with Mary in the period up to 1926 shows his desire to find his way out of what he viewed as the arid political cul-de-sac of parliamentary abstentionism. She, by contrast, exhorted him to stand firm on the bedrock of republican principle.

The period 1926 until her death in 1942 was one of political disillusionment for Mary. Her political position become progressively divorced from political realities. By the mid 1920s, having determined that entry back into parliamentary politics was essential to realise the republic by alternative means, de Valera's letters to Mary were increasingly curt and irascible. Chapter Nine discusses the increasing fractures and splits within the Fourth Sinn Féin Party which emerged from the 1926 split and within Cumann na mBan in the later 1920s and early 1930s. Yet as Mary's political life became increasingly fractious and irrelevant, there was happiness in her personal life as Terence's daughter, Máire Óg, came to Cork in 1932 to live with her; a fitting reminder that an individual life should never be reduced to a single dimension.

Chapter One

A Republican Family Unit

Mary MacSwiney was born on 27 March in 1872 in St Olave, Bermondsey in London, the eldest child of John MacSwiney and his English wife Mary, née Wilkinson. The economic background of the MacSwiney family is more complex and nuanced than has been represented. Charlotte Fallon refers to the 'austerity and modesty' that prevailed within the family.[1] However, the family initially experienced the rising expectations of upwardly mobile Catholics in the post-Famine period. The middle-class aspirations of Mary's family were evident from their educational and lifestyle choices. The occupations of John MacSwiney's siblings also reflect the rising middle-class status of the extended family. Even though the household experienced economic difficulties as Mary grew to adulthood, a focus on the value of education prevailed. The family maintained cultural middle-class status through participation in what Ciaran O'Neill refers to as the 'credentialist revolution'.[2]

In later life Kit MacSwiney recalled that she never remembered Mary playing with dolls as a child, but she remembered 'her vividly playing "School"'. A bookcase in the parlour contained volumes of Shakespeare which she read voraciously.[3] Voicing opinions, political and literary, was core to the way in which members of the MacSwiney family interacted together and in society. As the oldest sibling, Mary assumed familial duties at an early age due to the economic difficulties experienced by the family in the late nineteenth century. Such responsibilities did not, however, preclude her growing involvement in the suffrage campaign and in cultural nationalist and separatist politics in the early twentieth century.

Mary's father John, the son of a small farmer, was born *c.*1835 in Kilmurray near Crookstown, County Cork. His father, also John, married twice; in 1823 and again in 1831.[4] Just before the Famine, John MacSwiney's family moved to Bandon.[5] On the death of his father, the household moved yet again, this time to 26 Great George's Street, Cork city.[6]

This was a relatively affluent street in the centre of the city, although it is not clear whether the family shared the premises. The 1901 census indicates that number 26 was a first-class house occupied by the McGrath family who were members of the Church of Ireland; the house had 12 windows in front and 13 or more rooms. The McGrath household comprised eight children in addition to the parents, a lodger and two female servants. William F. McGrath gave his occupation as a manager of a boot shop.[7] When John MacSwiney's family moved to the city in the mid nineteenth century, number 26 operated as commercial premises. While in 1870 it was the location of J. Rearden & Son, grocers, wine and spirit merchants.[8]

Many of John MacSwiney's siblings and half-siblings were socio-economically upwardly mobile. His brother Eugene spent some time in Maynooth training for the priesthood but, lacking a vocation, he emigrated to Australia where he became a successful hotel owner.[9] In 1870 his half-brother, Terence, was listed as the proprietor of a grocery business at 119 Patrick's Street; by 1881 he was designated a wine and spirit merchant at the same premises in addition to managing commercial ventures at numbers 25 and 26 Drawbridge Street.[10]

Terence's son, Paul MacSwiney, became a composer. His opera, *Amergen*, was staged in the Cork Opera House in February 1881 with a further production in May of that year.[11] Munster had, the *Cork Examiner*, declared, 'a right to be proud of such musical composers as Mr M'Swiney of Cork'.[12] Paul later emigrated to England before moving to New York in 1883, becoming musical director for the Society for the Preservation of the Irish Language in the city.[13] The *New York Daily Tribune* described 'An Bárd 'Gus an Fó' as the 'first Gaelic musical work composed in the United States'.[14] Peter, another brother of John MacSwiney, was on the staff of the *Cork Examiner*.[15]

According to his daughter Annie, John MacSwiney left Ireland for Rome joining the Papal Zouaves. In the late 1850s Pope Pius IX, fearful of the annexation of the Papal States during the Italian unification campaign, called on Catholics across Europe to join an army to defend his territorial interests. By March 1860 papal emissaries were in Dublin negotiating the raising of an Irish Battalion, while across the country priests were encouraging Irish men to enlist. Discussing the manner in which Cardinal Paul Cullen brought the Irish Catholic church into line with Rome after the Famine, Colin Barr writes that in the period until the establishment of the Home Government Association in 1870 'love of the papacy and fear for its fate became the outstanding public cause of Catholic Ireland'.[16] Men enlisted for religious reasons but also on the basis of anti-British sentiment, the latter a response to the strong anti-papal contingent within the British establishment.[17] Catholicism and nationalist sentiment would similarly be amongst the defining features of the life of John MacSwiney's daughter, Mary.

From Italy, John went to England and worked in some area of education. According to his daughter Annie, writing in later life, he was the 'first catholic on the Board of Education in London'.[18] In 1871 he married Mary Wilkinson, an English woman whose Irish connections were alleged to extend to three grandparents.[19] While Fallon argues that the family circumstances in England were often straitened, consequent on the 'low, sometimes unreliable' income of John, his daughter Annie recalled that there was 'a nurse for the three children, Maire, Catherine (Kit) and Peter'.[20] John and his growing family returned to Ireland in 1879 on the urging of his youngest sister Mary, whose husband, a manager in a 'large' tobacco factory in Cork city, 'had a wide knowledge of the business and conceived [sic] the idea of establishing such a factory for himself'.[21]

By the late nineteenth century Cork was 'a city in decline'. Its importance as a centre of trade in the early nineteenth century had progressively contracted. There were high rates of poverty and established slums. The lack of urban growth was reflected in the city's static population; this despite, as Patrick Maume discusses, high rates of migration throughout the century from the surrounding areas.[22] However, although almost all the raw material was imported, tobacco manufacturing was, according to the 1907 census of production, one of the country's biggest industries.[23] John and his brother-in-law, John Buckley, went into partnership, establishing a business, with a premises at 48 King Street, where the family also resided. The business also had two retail outlets on Great George's Street and North Main Street, while John's sister Mary 'herself owned a Cigar Divan in Patrick Street'.[24]

King Street was a bustling street in the centre of Cork city comprising residential dwellings and commercial units. Family life in Ireland began well: 'there were many happy days.' John MacSwiney was 'overjoyed to be in Ireland again' and the family immersed themselves in the nationalist politics and culture of the city.[25] Mary recalled:

> watching for the great Parnell processions in Cork and cheering and waving from a window as they passed … I remember two such processions, and I can still feel the thrill of excitement they caused us youngsters though I doubt if we had any clearer idea of what it all meant than that Parnell was going to drive the English out of Ireland.[26]

In discussing her sister's upbringing, Annie MacSwiney refers to the strong nationalist leanings of her father. John was an Irish speaker and he loved to hear his eldest child recite rebel Irish poems: 'the more "rebelly" the poem the more he liked it.'[27] The children learned the poems of T. D. Sullivan and Thomas Davis and Mary recalled 'getting a bright new sixpence' when she recited 'The Death of Owen Roe O'Neill'.[28] She also emphasised that she 'never learned one line of Irish history' at school in Cork. What an individual learned of the Irish past, she stated in America in 1920, 'depended upon what sort of a family you came from – what England would call a rebellious strain'.[29] Several of John MacSwiney's generation of the family were involved in the nationalist politics of the later nineteenth century. Terence MacSwiney, Mary's half-uncle, was 'a great Parnellite and a member of the City Council, always to the fore in welcoming and entertaining the "chief" Parnell, when he came to Cork'.[30] Parnell held his parliamentary seat for Cork in the period 1880–91 and spoke at meetings in support of the Land League and Home Rule.[31] In the early 1880s Terence MacSwiney was co-treasurer of the Political Prisoners Maintenance Fund in the city.[32] Many of the prisoners supported would have been interned without trial as a result of Land League activities.[33] At a meeting of Cork Corporation in advance of Parnell's visit to the city on 3 October 1880, Terence defended the latter against charges that he had called on tenants to pay no rent. The landlord was, Terence argued, entitled to his rent 'but it should not be 100 per cent more than the unfortunate man could realise out of his bit of land'.[34]

Uniquely for the time, the MacSwiney parents valued education for both female and male members. New opportunities for female education emerged in the later nineteenth century. The Intermediate Education (Ireland) Act, 1878, allowed females to take state examinations at second level. As Raftery and Parkes state, these examinations facilitated women to get better-paid jobs and, in some instances, to go on to third-level education.[35] Mary and her sister Kit were sent to St Maires of the Isle, a national school founded in 1839 by the Sisters of Mercy. When St Angela's High School was opened by the Ursuline order in 1887 the two transferred, attending 'from the first day of its opening'.[36] In 1890 St Angela's began to offer classes to facilitate students to sit third-level exams under the University Education (Ireland) Act, 1879; the name of the establishment was changed to St Angela's College and High School to reflect this expansion in educational provision.[37] St Angela's High School had been established at the request of the Bishop of Cork, Dr Thomas O'Callaghan, with the intention of counteracting 'the great evil of the day, the pursuit of learning unaccompanied by religious training'. The decision of the school to offer classes at third level was taken 'to keep pace with the changes in education, to develop the mental faculties of [the] pupils so that they could better grasp and understand the truths of Religion and keep their place among the highly educated of the world'.[38] Catholicism formed a strong part of Mary's identity throughout her life as did a commitment to education, the duality of purpose in the establishment of the Catholic female schools and colleges in this period represented a vital influence in her intellectual formation.

Mary Wilkinson had been a teacher in England when she met her future husband and their daughter Annie later emphasised her mother's commitment to the education of her growing family.[39] 'No matter how busy she was she was always ready to help us, answering our questions about our schoolwork'. Her daughter Mary was a dedicated student. Staying up late to study in a shared bedroom, she recited Latin verbs and poetry as her sister Kit tried to sleep.[40] In this period of her life she experienced life-changing health issues. An untreated injury to her foot on the day of her first communion resulted at a later point in the amputation of her big toe, necessitating a lengthy and difficult hospital stay. Annie wrote:

> Great delicacy ... resulted from the infection, and at one period she spent almost a year in hospital ... For months she lay with covered eyes, and night after night had terrifying nightmares.

At aged 18, after several 'years of suffering', Mary's foot had to be amputated from the ankle joint. At times her pain was 'excruciating'.[41] The only extant information on her injury and the ensuing medical procedures is in the retrospective memoir by her sister Annie. It is likely that the amputation carried out on her toe was the result of a delay in treating a septic wound.[42] Studies on amputation during the First World War, discuss the lengthy hospital stay required and, in many cases, the 'intense' pain. Historians of the war also increasingly focus on the traumatic nature of amputation.[43] Mary's operations took place before 'the dramatic development in orthopaedic surgery' during the First World War and concomitant attempts by some doctors to understand the 'mental trauma associated with amputation'.[44] Yet, she persevered with study and on 11 August 1890 she was listed in the *Cork Examiner* as one of two girls from St Angela's High School who had passed the Royal University Matriculation Examination.[45]

In the 1880s the MacSwiney family's economic situation deteriorated rapidly. The tobacco factory which seemed to begin in a promising manner was afflicted with poor financial management and structures. Lacking the backing of a capital fund, the factory was not able to compete with more established firms in the city. Bielenberg and Johnson note that the leading Irish tobacco companies of the late nineteenth century were well-established by the mid-century. Expertise in blending and controlling moisture content gave 'established businesses an advantage over less experienced rivals'.[46] The partnership between John MacSwiney and his brother-in-law was dissolved and for a time the former ran a solo business from the 48 King Street premises.[47] In July 1883 his firm was offering a trial of cigars to the trade at manufacturer's prices.[48] According to Annie, her father lacked a business instinct and with the collapse of the enterprise he decided to emigrate to Australia in 1885 with the intention of sending for his family once he established himself.

Suffering from asthma and sciatica he also believed that the Australian climate would be more conducive to his health. His brother Eugene had a successful hotel business in that country while his cousin, Dr Daniel Murphy, was the bishop of Hobart in Tasmania since 1866.[49]

John MacSwiney failed to thrive in Australia and died in Melbourne in 1895.[50] In that year he was hoping to 'get into one of the hospitals' as 'the proper place for me for a few weeks'. The hospitals were, however, 'full and in debt'.[51] Less than a month later, on 17 October, he passed away.[52] His son Terence wrote that when he arrived in Australia 'everything … was at a very low ebb – Banks smashing … and he was not able to reap the success hoped for'.[53] In Cork his wife assumed responsibility. As the ramifications of the loss of the tobacco business and her husband's absence impacted heavily on the family, she was obliged to make difficult decisions. Indeed, she was pregnant when her husband left, giving birth to Seán MacSwiney six months later.[54] In the words of Annie 'it was a grim struggle'. The family were forced to vacate their premises at number 48 King Street where houses in the 1901 census fell largely into the first-class category. Staying on the same side of the river Lee, they moved to the infinitely less salubrious Blarney Street to take over the running of a shop, 'it's cheapness was its attraction'. Like the tobacco business, this shop also failed, and the family moved further down the street. The writer and republican Frank O'Connor (1903–66), who lived in Blarney Street until he was five years old, summed up the prevailing wretchedness in his memoir, *An Only Child*: 'It begins at the foot of Shandon Street, near the riverbank, in sordidness, and ascends the hill to something like squalor.'[55] Houses in Blarney Street in the 1901 census fell into the second-class category. However, the MacSwiney family were not able to rent an entire house but rather a premises in a three-flat house.[56] Annie recalled the extreme poverty of the family in a letter to Étienette Beuque:

> I can remember being hungry at times when mother had to ration our share of bread, I can remember having to remain indoors for weeks, away from school, because my shoes had fallen to pieces, & mother could not buy me others.[57]

Consequent on the family's quite extreme decline in socio-economic circumstances, several the siblings were forced to jettison any aspirations towards further education through the usual trajectory. Peter left school at aged fourteen taking a job as a boot operative in Dwyer's Factory. George's Street.[58] In 1908 he emigrated to Canada. From there he went to the United States, becoming a naturalised citizen in 1916.[59] Kit, who was older, left St Angela's High School going to France to work as a governess before entering a convent. Terence, at school in the Christian Brothers' North Monastery, was an excellent student winning exhibitions at preparatory, junior and middle grades in the Intermediate examinations.[60] He too, however, was forced to leave education before the senior grade examinations 'because of the ever-growing financial need'. He also entered Dwyer's Factory to work in the Counting House.[61] In a family that prized education for all members regardless of gender, Mary, as the eldest child, was more fortunate than younger males in the family, particularly the scholarly Terence. Her education was more advanced than his at the point when the family experienced economic decline. In 'normal times', she stated, and 'in less strenuous conditions, as far as money went, he would have remained at school and entered a college course'.[62] The younger siblings, like Annie, were able to pursue third-level degrees as the older members of the family began in paid employment.

The focus of Mary's mother on the wellbeing of her family facilitated an *esprit de corps* within the unit. It allowed family members to transcend many of the obstacles of economic hardship. Terence wrote of Mary senior that she was more 'bound up in the work of every one of us than we were ourselves – rejoicing in our successes and feeling more our reversals'. He continued:

> God willed she should be heavily laden with trouble ... Some of us who were younger sometimes sounded a despondent note, but she never – the trouble will soon be over, if not soon, some time, when God wills it. That was her firm belief.[63]

Studying at home, Terence continued his education while working long hours in Dwyer's Counting House.[64] In 1907 he graduated from the Royal University with a BA in 'Mental and Moral Science'.[65] A touching vignette of family life written in later years by Mary underscores the manner in which both females and males in the family prized and participated in education to a high level. Terence worked early in the morning having gone to bed at 8pm. In this he:

> differed from his sisters, who always preferred to work at night, and for a long time, it was a practice for his younger sister – who was studying for First Arts examinations at the time – to put on a kettle to make Terry a cup of tea and call him at 2 am when she was preparing to go to bed herself...[66]

The Royal University was an examining body only and Terence studied without a tutor or formal intellectual guidance. Moirin Chavasse notes that Mary, having already graduated, was able to offer help in certain subjects.[67] What is vital to note is how bound the family members were to each other. The closeness of the family members was something that would bind and sustain them in later life. In 1903 Terence wrote of the potential break-up of the family unit as members left to pursue their life choices:

> Next year Maggie will be the second to leave the Home circle [sic] and I suppose we may expect to see it gradually grow thinner as we all follow our different paths. It is surely sad to see the old home circle begin to break up...[68]

As the family's financial situation worsened, Mary applied for tutoring jobs. She was in London in 1895 looking for a 'situation'. Her father wrote to his wife that the news of her 'stopping in London has completely unnerved me'.[69] Through an educational agency, Mary found a teaching position in a private school in England, moving from there to Bordeaux in France. Financially able to help her family through such work, she also continued in formal education with the help of a loan from the Students' Aid Society.[70] She graduated with a diploma from the Cambridge Teaching Training College in 1900. She was considered a 'bright, energetic and enthusiastic' teacher and secured a job in Hillside Convent in Farnborough.[71] Her name appeared on the First Arts pass list of the Royal University of Ireland.[72]

Such educational achievements notwithstanding, from the period of her father's departure to Australia Mary had to shoulder obligations that devolved to her as the eldest child. In her memoir, Annie declared: 'Máire was only fifteen years old when Papa left home, and though so young, she seemed, even then, to rise to meet and bridge the loneliness in Mama's life'.[73] Such sentimental retrospection aside, Mary's assumption of responsibility for family members was a key pattern in her life from this point, influencing both personal and political choices going forward. Kit recalled that when the youngest member of the family, Seán, did something wrong, Mary took him to 'her side reasoning with him, advising him, instructing him'.[74] Taking on tutoring work, her sister Annie remembered: 'Máire was much stronger now, and happy in being able to shoulder definitely and regularly financial responsibility – as she had always shouldered responsibility in thought and guidance'.[75]

The family's economic situation improved as a result of the entry into employment of the older siblings facilitating a move to No. 5 St Mary's Terrace. Like Blarney and Shandon Street, the address was still part of Cork Urban No. 4 census district. The family had, however, moved up the socio-economic scale. The house comprised six rooms, with three windows in front.[76] The occupations of neighbours ranged from cattle dealer[77] to RIC policeman,[78] situating the MacSwiney family in an upper-working-class area. Mary senior had no recorded occupation. Peter and Terence were respectively listed as a boot cutter and an accountant; Margaret, Anne and Seán were designated scholars. Mary herself was not recorded as she was teaching outside Ireland.[79]

In 1904, just as Mary accepted a new post in the Benedictine Convent in Ventnor, Isle of Wight, news of her mother's impending death reached her. This was a difficult time for the closely knit family, Terence describing it as their 'great trouble'.[80] Kit wrote to Mary lamenting the loss. What, she said, 'is home without her'.[81] Terence noted that Mary was the first one to cry as those present stood around the recently deceased body of their mother. [82] She immediately assumed the role of head of the family, a role that she would maintain throughout her life:

> in the home Mama had left Maire [sic] took charge of everything. From the first moment she stepped into Mama's place. As the Summer [sic] days passed she planned the year ahead for us all...[83]

She organised the educational plans for all relevant siblings before returning to her post in Ventnor. She remained in this position for two years while keeping her 'hands on the reins' and 'her finger on the pulse of the home life'. 'She might', Annie wrote, 'really have been at home, so closely was she knit to us.' After two years she 'determined to be with us altogether'.[84] Kit, who had not yet taken her religious vows did state that she would return to help the family if needed. The home, she wrote, 'must be kept together'.[85] An entry in Terence's diary in December 1905 is interesting in his presumption that Mary, affectionately referred to as Min or Minnie, was now in charge of the household; there is almost a suggestion that her individual needs and desires were to be subordinated to this role:

> On home matters – we have had considerable discussion as to whether Minnie will remain at home for good after Xmas, and the matter is not settled yet. ... It would be an undoubted advantage to have her with us ... the only argument the other way being a financial one. Clearing off outstanding debts makes money necessary and for this reason only would she go away ... If Min stays at home the 'clearing up' process would be delayed a little. So she has a

> choice of alternatives – to remain at home and supervise things that she can best attend to or go away and help to put us speedily in a more even financial condition.[86]

This role as head of the MacSwiney family and her 'direction of the home life'[87] influenced Mary's lifelong response to Terence's death on hunger strike in October 1920 discussed in Chapter Four. It also in part explains the power differential in her relationship with her younger sister Annie as they both operated within the arena of republican politics and in the running of St Ita's school which they established in 1916, as discussed in Chapter Two. Terence wrote that Mary's return to Ireland in 1906 was a 'great thing on account of A[nnie] who is not well'.[88] Her position as head of the household extended to a consideration of the marital prospects of family members. In his diary Terence discussed the concern he and Mary had for Peter after he emigrated to Canada. There was an attempt to arrange a marriage with a Mary Riordan in Cork:

> there was a temptation to throw our influence into the scale & get Peter to make the match. He would be married & settled down – pretty comfortably as far as we might judge & he would no longer be a responsibility to us. That would be a burden off us. It seems a strange thing that Peter should be in anyway still a burden – tho' he has cost us nothing while away. To send him to Canada meant giving him towards his outfit over £7 pounds worth of things. As long as he is not settled at home ... we feel some effort to fix him...

When Riordan set up a public house to make a living for herself, Mary's approval for the match plummeted, Terence writing that she 'feared this a temptation for Peter'.[89] The issue for Mary in the case of the mooted marriage between Peter and Riordan was arguably not disapproval of a woman establishing her own business but rather the fear that an environment around alcohol would not be good for Peter. There is no evidence regarding Peter's relationship to alcohol but certainly Mary believed in female equality, becoming involved in the suffrage movement in Cork. As a woman with a career herself, it was arguably the nature of Riordan's business that was of concern.

On return to Cork in 1906, Mary took up a teaching position in St Angela's High School while completing Second and Third Arts, graduating from University College, Cork in 1912.[90] Her initial political involvement in this period centred on her belief in gender equality enunciated through the suffrage movement. The establishment by Hanna Sheehy Skeffington and Margaret Cousins of the Irish Women's Franchise League (IWFL) in 1908 marked a shift in the campaign in Ireland. Influenced by the establishment of the Women's Social and Political Union (WSPU) by Emmeline Pankhurst in 1903, the IWFL was the first militant Irish suffrage society. The publication from 1907 of *Votes for Women* by Pankhurst and Frederick Pethick-Lawrence was, Margaret Ward states, 'immensely important in introducing ideas of the militant suffrage movement to an audience far removed from British centres of activity'.[91] A Cork branch of the IWFL was formed in 1910. However, less than a year later, some members broke away to form the separate and non-militant Munster Women's Franchise League (MWFL), stating that local tactics had to suit local conditions.[92] Mary joined this organisation established in Cork in February 1911. At the annual general meeting in November of that year she occupied the chair emphasising that the small turnout was due to the inclement weather.[93]

The MWFL was affiliated to the non-militant, non-party umbrella organisation, the Irish Women's Suffrage Federation created in 1910. Members were opposed to the IWFL's 'insistence on arguing for votes for women in the tense period when the Home Rule bill was going through parliament'.[94] Relations between the Cork branch of the IWFL and the MWFL were less than amicable.[95] Moreover, there were fissures even within the latter organisation. Mary's discussion of the organisation in later life suggests that the issue of militancy within the Cork branch of the MWFL continued to create tensions. Some of the members wanted to adopt the tactics of the WSPU:

> a course which the few of us who were national in the Cork branch opposed on the ground that those mainly responsible for the injustice perpetuated against women were the parliament & people of England. Even if every member of the Irish Party was in favour of votes for women, they could not affect the issue ... Every now and then a fresh burst of admiration for the women in England putting up such a gallant fight would bring forth again an ardent desire to do something similar.[96]

An address and a discussion entitled 'Has Militancy Advanced the Cause of Woman [sic] Suffrage' was held by the MWFL on 11 November 1911.[97] At this point in her life, Mary believed that women needed the vote to be respected as equals.[98] However, she judged that there were both men and women who were 'not fitted to exercise the responsibility of the vote'. To rectify this, she argued for 'an educational basis for the franchise':

> Before leaving school every boy and girl should attend a compulsory course of lessons in elementary civics. The duties and responsibilities of citizenship should be explained, and the value and significance of the vote, among innumerable other things, should be carefully taught and properly understood. All who were unable to learn or understand this course in elementary civics should be excluded from the franchise as being unfit to exercise the duties and responsibilities of citizenship.[99]

Mary must be situated within the aspirational middle-class concept of education, her own experience. While clearly such a civics course could be included in a modified school curriculum aimed at the middle classes, she failed to expand on how this might work in practice on a wider class level. Of course, when she made the statement in 1914, women were looking for the vote based on the property qualification that determined the male franchise. It would be middle-class women who would benefit. Moreover, universal male suffrage was not granted until four years later under the Representation of the People Act, 1918.

Mary admired strong and determined activist women. On 28 March 1914, she extolled the tenacity of a 'Lady Guardian' in Cork who five times in the previous year, in the face of '44 children suffering from different infectious diseases sleeping in 25 beds', proposed an extension to the Cork Union hospital. Repeatedly defeated by 'a majority of men, because it would mean a farthing more on the rates', she nevertheless persisted and 'won her long fight'.[100] Mary was referring to Suzanne Day. The MWFL established a special committee of women 'who had knowledge of Workhouse affairs' with the intention of canvassing for the appointment of women Poor Law Guardians.[101] Day was appointed as one of Cork's first female Poor Law Union Guardians and was prominent in the MWFL. She believed that it was increasingly necessary to emphasise the non-militant stance of the organisation.

The Home Rule Bill of 1912 failed to include a provision for votes for women and the IWFL responded by engaging in its first act of militancy. Sheehy Skeffington and seven other women were arrested for throwing stones at government buildings in Dublin. Day argued that such actions by the IWFL 'would be construed as "an anti-home rule policy" and that this might prove "fatal" to the Irish women's movement'.[102] While Day was non-party she still recognised that Home Rule was, in her words, 'a sentiment, bone of the people's bone, and flesh of their flesh' and that '[w]oman suffrage cannot yet be said to have attained that degree of intensity'.[103]

Such statements by Day are noteworthy in the context of the priorities of Mary whose growing correspondence in the newspapers on the need for Irish women to prioritise the campaign for independence was quite nuanced. In May 1914, she felt it incumbent on her to stress that Irishwomen had to prioritise the issue of Home Rule, but she did not feel it necessary at that point to leave the MWFL because it adopted a non-militant stance, officially at least.[104] Her focus was instead on the potential damage the militancy of the IWFL could bring to bear on the nationalist campaign. Developments within Irish nationalism, however, brought to the fore Mary's core commitment to securing Irish independence.

In 1914, when Mary prioritised national independence over female suffrage, the Irish Volunteers had been in existence since November of the previous year. While the ostensible concern of the organisation on foundation was the passage into law of the Third Home Rule Bill, 1912 against the trenchant opposition of Ulster Unionists, there were within the organisation a minority of advanced nationalists. Terence MacSwiney argued that the Irish Volunteers were established 'to win and hold Ireland's liberty'. He referred to men 'trained in what is called the moderate school' by comparison with those 'trained to a daring course'.[105] As early as 1902 he recorded in his diary that 'a home parliament under the English flag … is not the full measure of our rights'. To state such to a constitutional nationalist, he wrote, labelled one an 'extremist'.[106] By September 1914 this cleavage within the Irish Volunteers emerged to the surface; advanced nationalists committed to a rebellion to achieve full independence. Terence was to the vanguard of such a political trajectory in Cork, as was Mary.

The politics of Terence are important to understand when considering Mary's increasing alignment with advanced nationalism in the period before 1916 and the manner in which her commitment to suffrage became less immediately important. In later life she wrote: 'I found my time in the Cork branch of the Suffrage movement most interesting but more important issues were demanding attention and Ireland was [sic].'[107] According to Cornelius Murphy, Quartermaster of the B Company Irish Volunteers in 1916, the numbers who participated in the politics of the Gaelic revival in Cork were small:

> The whole movement for National revival in Cork between 1900 and the organisation of the Volunteers started with, and depended upon, the activities of from twelve to twenty families. Even after the start of the Volunteers that organisation depended mainly upon the same people for leadership, policy and morale. They went into everything that looked like being national – the Gaelic League, the GAA, the Fianna, the Celtic Literary Society, the Industrial Development Association and the AOH American Alliance.[108]

Similarly, Patrick Higgins, Cork Brigade IV, wrote:

> The whole Volunteer movement in Cork and the position it created grew out of the activities of a relatively small group of men and women who had been working in different ways to promote various aspects of the Irish Ireland movement.[109]

In the late nineteenth century, the city of Cork, according to Daniel Corkery, was devoid of 'intellectual life'. He drew attention to the lack of public institutions to facilitate cultural expression and edification and the staid intellectual milieu that enervated the city ether.[110] In *The Threshold of Quiet*, he described the 'quiet desperation' of lower middle-class life in Cork. In the novel Cork is described as a city that 'keeps busy – mostly about nothing'.[111] In 1914 Terence noted that the 'Cork book buying public is not large'.[112] Higgins identified a 'small group …active and forward in every activity' who worked to stimulate the cultural life of the city.[113]

The MacSwiney family were centrally located in this nexus of cultural nationalism in Cork city. In 1899 Terence – described by Corkery as a 'genuine idealist' and a man of 'earnest clay' – immersed himself in the ethos and organisation of Irish culture with 'great zest'.[114] In 1904 the heavily political Keating Brach of the Gaelic League established a teacher training college in the Ballingeary, Co. Cork.[115] Terence, a member of the North Parish branch of the League, regularly attended summer courses in the east coast village from 1907.[116] The importance of the Gaelic League summer colleges R. F. Foster declares 'lay in bringing together the likeminded and suggesting the possibility of a new way of life'.[117] It was in this Gaeltacht area that Corkery and Terence forged a friendship that would last until the latter's death on a hunger strike in 1920 while Mary and Annie increasingly spent Easter and summer holidays in the area.[118] Speaking of the period around 1910 Corkery stated that the Gaelic League was 'the biggest thing in our lives'.[119] In his foreword to Moirin Chavasse's biography of Terence MacSwiney he noted that members of the revolutionary generation, in encountering the Irish language movement came into contact 'with their own country spiritually instead of merely, and mostly wrongly, politically. They really came upon the rock from which they had been hewn; came upon their deeper selves'.[120] Writing in December 1920 after Terence's death, Corkery noted: 'it is many years since we ceased to speak English to each other'.[121]

Terence MacSwiney and Corkery were also key playwrights in the Cork Dramatic Society founded in November 1908. Liam de Róiste noted that the foundation of the Abbey Theatre in 1904 'had aroused interest in the production of Irish plays and we doubted not but that there was local talent capable of writing and producing plays of a similar type to those of the Abbey'.[122] In the four years after 1909 the CDS staged 18 plays by Cork playwrights. Terence was the second-most prolific playwright being responsible for four of the 18 scripts produced.[123] Mary and other members of the family were also involved. She was a member of the theatre orchestra while Seán had the leading part of Cuchulainn in *The Wooing of Emer* written by Terence and produced in December 1911.[124] Theatre and playwriting was very important to Terence and even after he assumed an organisational position with the Irish Volunteers he was considering a move to America. He asked his brother Peter 'for some information about American theatres, actors and plays'. He wrote to his sister Peg: 'I want an opening – oh how badly!'[125] Writing in December 1914 de Róiste foresaw Terence making 'a name for himself some day' as a playwright.[126]

During the literary revival a multitude of cultural organisations emerged, particularly in Dublin, but also in the smaller cities across the country. Terence was a key member of the Celtic Literary Society founded on 2 January 1901.[127] The society was described by J. J. Horgan, a Captain in the National Volunteers in Cork, as more 'revolutionary than literary', affiliated as it was with Cumann na nGaedheal.[128] The latter was established in 1900 by Arthur Griffith and William Rooney as an umbrella organisation to link the activities of the various advanced nationalist bodies in existence. [129] De Róiste stated that to 'ensure there would be no ambiguity regarding its aim', the Cork Celtic Literary Society 'put as its object "TO STRIVE FOR THE ESTABLISHMENT OF AN IRISH REPUBLIC"'.[130] He clarified that what was meant by this was full separation from England but that the 'form of Government in a completely independent Ireland, we are not so very sure about'. That would be, he stated, 'a matter for the future'.[131] Terence was recorded as Chairman in the minute book on 5 March 1905.[132] During the visit of Edward VII to Ireland in 1903 the society sent a letter written by Terence to all councils and public bodies protesting his presence.[133] When George V visited Ireland in 1911, a national vigilance committee was set up to try to prevent the presentation of a loyal address by Cork Corporation. It was Terence who wrote 'many of the important letters and manifestos'. Despite such efforts, the Corporation voted to present the address at which point another MacSwiney brother – Seán – was among the men who 'hoisted a big black flag on two poles ... drawing it across the Council Chamber'.[134] A black flag was also placed on the national monument to the dead patriots of the period 1798–1867 on the Grand Parade.[135]

P. J. Murphy stated that it was the Celtic Literary Society that launched 'the first branch of the Sinn Féin movement' in the city.[136] The CLS by late 1905 had become, according to de Róiste, 'hidebound'. He referred to the idea of starting a branch of Sinn Féin:

> There is room for a society in Cork for all who believe that the salvation of our nation must be worked out in Ireland itself and not 'on the floor' of the House in Westminster; whether they be strict and pledged Republicans or not.[137]

A Cork branch of the organisation was in existence from 1906 to 1911, emerging not just from the CLS but also from Inghinidhe na hÉireann and the Cork Young Ireland Society. The establishment of the branch did not come about, Borgonovo argues, without 'considerable debate about Arthur Griffith's dual-monarchy programme'.[138] Mary noted that her brother did not join 'Arthur Griffith's Sinn Fein Society because it was not primarily for Republican independence'.[139] It was for that reason also, Terence stated, that he left the Cork Young Ireland society.[140] Mary likewise refused to become a member of Sinn Féin when it was established in the city although in later life she wrote that she supported their economic policy of 'self-reliance'.[141] She noted that in this period several of her friends 'joined the Sinn Féin movement but I never felt any inclination to bind myself to an organisation that was based on the so-called Grattan's Parliament of 1782'.[142] With this she statement she referred to Griffith's concept of dual monarchy. He argued that the Act of Union, 1800, should not be recognised; Irish MPs should withdraw from the House of Commons and establish an independent Irish parliament with the two islands linked through a common monarch.[143]

Terence's idealism and cultural activism were key influences in his sister's developing political outlook in this period up to 1916. It was Mary, who as head of the household, filled out the 1911 census form in Irish, reflecting the family's commitment to the language and cultural nationalist ideals.[144] The political and cultural interests of brother and sister aligned and solidified in the years before 1916.[145] By this date, the family had moved residence once again. No 66 Knockrea was a second-class house comprising eight rooms inhabited in 1911 by Mary, Terence and Seán.[146] In the late nineteenth century the suburb of Blackrock diversified. Facilitated by the introduction of the electric tramway system in 1898 which allowed people to commute cheaply to the city centre, Blackrock witnessed the construction of terraced houses on the estate land of the larger houses built early in the century.[147] From this residence Mary and Terence travelled in and out of the city, to work and to attend various cultural and political meetings. The Blackrock to Tivoli tram line brought the former from her residence in the south side of the river Lee to her place of work on St Patrick's Hill on the north. In the years after Mary's return to Cork in 1906 numerous family members left the home. Seán attended university. However, disliking the teaching job he secured with the De La Salle Brothers in Waterford, he decided to emigrate to Canada.[148] Peter, as noted, went also to Canada before moving on to America; Annie was in Ventnor teaching while Margaret and Kit had both entered convents. Kit joined the Parisian Order of St Maur while Margaret founded St Genevieve's College in North Carolina in 1912. 'The family circle was now very small, just Máire and Terry'.[149]

Mary was criticised by friends and acquaintances in Sinn Féin for her involvement in the MWFL:

> How, they asked, could I ally myself with a lot of unionists to get a vote which I declared I should not use if I had it for a foreign parliament. But my reasons were quite clear to me if they failed to satisfy others.
>
> ...
>
> Membership was a protest against a manifest injustice which had nothing to do with Irish nationality. I believed that if Ireland were free women would get the vote.[150]

Increasingly, however, Mary, although still a committed believer in a woman's right to vote, prioritised the campaign for national independence. Of the MWFL she wrote in a draft memoir: 'London was really the centre of their universe, even if they did not realise it'.[151] In November 1914 she resigned her membership of the MWFL, citing the pro-war stance of the Cork branch. In that month the organisation voted to raise funds to send an ambulance to the front to aid 'sick soldiers'.[152] On 5 December this vehicle was handed over to Colonel Morris, Principal Medical Officer of the Forces, Cork District.[153] In response to the pro-war stance of the MWFL, Mary declared that she was, an 'Irishwoman who puts the needs of her own country before those of the British Empire' and she could not allow her name 'to be connected with any society which put England first'. She continued:

> I understand that many of the committee are anxious to banish the Irish Citizen from the Office simply because it is Anti-War. While it was merely Anti-Home-Rule-till-Woman-Suffrage-is granted, there was no such proposal. I disagreed totally with your attitude on the Home Rule question, but it did not strike me as fair play to suggest the banishment of the only Irish Suffrage paper because I disagreed with its attitude.
>
> The conclusion has been forced on me – very much against my will – that the majority of

> the members of the committee ... are Britons first, suffragists second, and Irishwomen perhaps a bad third. As the reversal of that order is, to my mind, the only right one, our co-operation was no longer possible.[154]

Mary reminded the editors of the *Irish Citizen* that when she had argued previously for 'Home Rule first' she had stated her belief that:

> if trouble arose between England and Germany, English suffragists would sink their claims before the National need, and that Christabel Pankhurst herself would be the first to do so. Let Irishwomen learn the patriotic lesson and put Ireland first and Ireland only, till Ireland is free.[155]

When she resigned from the MWFL Mary was a member of Cumann na mBan, an organisation which, as discussed below, had by September 1914 moved beyond Home Rule as a solution to the Irish national question and was committed to securing full independence.

Despite the dwindling unit, the MacSwiney home was the scene of many literary and political meetings which progressed into impassioned, at times fractious, debates as to the future political configuration of Ireland. If, as the maternal figure within the family, Mary played the role of hostess at literary and political gatherings in the home, her own political stance and priorities were developing and hardening. On 25 November 1913, the Irish Volunteers were established at a public meeting and enrolment rally at the Rotunda in Dublin. Confronted with the strident and clamorous opposition by Ulster Unionists and the establishment of the Ulster Volunteers in January of that year, the Irish Volunteers pledged to ensure the passage into law of the third Home Rule Bill. Three weeks later, on 14 December 1914, a public meeting was held in Cork City Hall to establish a branch of the organisation in the city. Those who convened the meeting were part of that nexus of advanced nationalism in which Terence and now increasingly, Mary, were centrally immersed:

> The initiative in calling the meeting was taken by a group of men interested in Gaelic League and Irish Ireland activities, the IRB, Fianna Eireann, the Industrial Development Association and anti-British activities. They had premises in An Dún in Queen Street.[156]

Over 400 men enrolled at that first meeting; an initial drill class took place a week later.[157]

On 2 April 1914 Cumann na mBan was established at a meeting in Wynn's Hotel, Dublin, as the female auxiliary to the Irish Volunteers. Margaret Ward discusses the restraints of the organisation's constitutional imperative to 'assist' the Irish Volunteers in their fight for freedom.[158] Senia Pašeta notes that many women were offended by accusations that in accepting an auxiliary role to the Irish Volunteers they had betrayed their sex. Mary believed as Pašeta states, that there could be no national freedom without the freedom of women. However, she argued that waiting a few years to gain the female vote from an Irish parliament 'will not hurt us'.[159] Two months after the establishment of Cumann na mBan in Dublin the Cork branch was formally launched.[160] Prior to this a branch of Inghinidhe na hÉireann was in existence in Cork, meeting over Kelleher's shop in Great George's Street where 'they held dances, socials and meetings'.[161] Founded by Maud Gonne in

1902, the branch was, de Róiste states, 'identical ... in aims and objects' to the Cork Celtic Literary Society. The aims of Inghinidhe na hÉireann were both cultural and political. The focus was an independent Ireland and support for such manifested in commitment to the Irish language and in an anti-recruitment campaign in opposition to the Boer War.

Mary recalled that prior to 1914 she had 'no connection' with politics but had an interest 'in every forward movement'. Testament to the manner in which the MacSwiney home was a hub for increasingly radical politics in the period up to 1916, a meeting to discuss the establishment of Cumann na mBan in Cork was held in that domestic space. Reading of its establishment in Dublin in the *Irish Citizen* Mary wrote to Sheehy Skeffington and then invited Madeline O'Hegarty, Alice Cashel, Nora O'Brien and Bridie Conway to her home in Blackrock. They arranged a meeting with Inghinidhe na hÉireann in the rooms of the Gaelic League on Queen Street and determined to form a Cork branch of Cumann na mBan.[162] She noted that she had 'little knowledge of Inghinidhe na hÉireann prior to this'.[163]

In the lead up to the inaugural meeting of Cork Cumann na mBan in the City Hall on 8 June 1914, Tomás MacCurtain wrote that the 'Executive of Cork Volunteers desire to give every possible assistance' to the organisation.[164] In billing the meeting as 'non-party', the organisers recognised, and hoped to circumvent, the acrimonious O'Brienite/Redmonite split in the city which had resulted in disruption and violence at the inaugural Irish Volunteer meeting.[165] Mary, however, made clear that while Cumann na mBan in Cork 'was not a party movement ... at the same time, they didn't hold with the attitude of the man who said he would not touch politics with a forty-foot pole'.[166]

The *Cork Examiner* of 5 June 1914 listed the speakers. Agnes O'Farrelly, elected President of Cumann na mBan at the meeting in Wynn's hotel, headed the bill while others included the O'Rahilly, Bulmer Hobson, J. J. Walsh and the Cork Volunteer Commander, Maurice-Talbot Crosbie. [167] The gallery, the *Cork Examiner* reported, was 'reserved for ladies'.[168] This segregation of women was a strange anomaly in the context of the establishment of a female organisation but reflected the norm in the House of Commons where female visitors had to watch proceedings from what was known as the Ladies Cage.[169] The concealment of women in this manner underscored the male nature of parliament before 1918. Mary chaired the meeting, writing to Annie of her 'anxiety to be equal to the occasion, and play her part well and worthily'.[170] That she did was reflected in her election as President.[171] The letter to Annie, however, indicates that on a private level she expressed the usual human emotions of apprehension and nervousness.

Cork Cumann na mBan was presented in newspaper coverage as fulfilling an auxiliary role to the Irish Volunteers. The *Cork Examiner* declared after the inaugural meeting in June 1914 that the 'Cork ladies who have come forward to help the National Volunteers by assisting to collect the necessary funds for their equipment deserve the highest praise'.[172] This issue of the supplementary status of Cumann na mBan was one that generated debate from its establishment in Dublin in April 1914. Sheehy Skeffington was ejected from the inaugural meeting in Wynn's Hotel as she heckled and vehemently voiced her objection to the unequal status of women within nationalist organisations.[173] Mary engaged in the debate and took issue with the editors of the *Irish Citizen* who criticised women in Cumann na mBan for accepting a supportive role to the male organisation:

> I should suggest that the editor, for his own sake, adopt a more respectful tone towards his opponents. 'Slaves' and 'camp followers' and such choice epithets can only degrade the man who uses them towards the women whose pride it is to help their country in her fight for freedom.[174]

There were those like Rosamond Jacob who agreed with her. 'It was a great pity,' Jacob wrote, 'for F. Sheehy-Skeffington [sic] to permit himself to talk such nonsense as he does in his leading article on "Slave Women".'[175]

Members of Cork Cumann na mBan met in 'An Grianan' on Queen Street; their activities included first aid lectures and drills. Examinations in first aid were held under the auspices of the Department of Agriculture and Technical Instruction for Ireland.[176] They held collections outside churches and went house-to-house across the city seeking donations to equip the Irish Volunteers.[177] Following the Howth gunrunning on 26 July 1914, a general parade of the Cork corps of the Irish Volunteers took place in the Cornmarket in a show of 'appreciation'. '[B]ringing up the rear, behind the pipe band, 'a party of ladies belonging to the Ambulance Corps marched'.[178] In her evidence to the American Commission on Conditions in Ireland in December 1920 Mary stated that the role of Cumann na mBan was 'to train the minds of the people to know what the Republican movement meant'. Their 'chief work', she declared, 'was to support the Irish Volunteers by every means possible in their fight for the independence of Ireland.'[179]

The outbreak of World War I in August 1914 precipitated a train of events in Ireland that facilitated advanced nationalists to make their generation's statement in arms. In September 1914, John Redmond, speaking in Woodenbridge, County Wicklow, called on the Irish Volunteers to support the British war effort. In the aftermath of the split that ensued, Cork Cumann na mBan held a meeting. The following resolution was 'proposed and carried by a very large majority':

> That we, of the 'Cork' Branch of Cumann na mBan are determined to stand loyally by the original Provisional Committee and recognise that our duty in the present crisis is to Ireland and Ireland alone.[180]

Peg Duggan recalled that the branch lost 'quite a few members' although the officers remained unchanged.[181] This mirrored the split in the Cork branch of the Irish Volunteers. Those who rejected Redmond's war policy, Borgonovo states, 'returned to the familiar margins of Cork's body politic, though [the Irish Volunteers] retained a clear message and most of the militia's committed officers'.[182] Membership of Cork Cumann na mBan at this point was around 100.[183] Weekly parades, fundraising and first aid instruction continued to inform the activities of the branch. In January 1915 a concert and tableaux were deemed an 'unbounded success in the representations shown, in the numbers present and the enthusiasm'. [184] In the context of first aid, the members took advantage of a British government scheme implemented during the period of the First World War; a grant was provided to those who successfully completed a course in first aid leading to certification. Margaret Lucey noted: '[p]ractically every one of us qualified for the required certificate and was awarded the grant which we passed on to Cumann na mBan funds'.[185] Mary's name appeared on the report from the Department of Agriculture and Technical Instruction for Ireland on 24 July 1915 which included a list of students who completed a course in 'First

Aid to the Injured & Hygiene & Emergency Nursing'.[186] Margaret Skinnider similarly took advantage of the rifle clubs set up by the government to train women in the use of arms to aid the defence of Britain during the First World War. She fully intended to use the skills gained in Glasgow 'to defend my own country'.[187]

Cork newspapers reported on increased food prices consequent on the outbreak of World War I.[188] Mary represented Cumann na mBan on the committee of the Cork Consumers League established at a meeting on 14 August 1914 by the Cork branch of the Irish Industrial Development Association. The Cork Celtic Literary Society was, Liam de Róiste stated, influential in the foundation of the latter association. Members of the former 'were interested in every phase of national life'.[189] The League was founded because of concern for the 'poorer classes' in the context of spiralling prices and food shortages in the city.[190] It was 'formed for the purpose of giving the public the right to live' and to fight unscrupulous profiteering.[191] Mary viewed such activism through the prism of national politics. Cork Cumann na mBan issued a manifesto and appeal signed by Mary and Madeline O'Hegarty: 'At the present juncture we are concerned that the food of Ireland shall be conserved for the people of Ireland, and so prevent a repetition of the Black Famine of '47.'[192] The reference to the worst year of the Famine of 1845–50 was one utilised by many Cork public officials and Sinn Féin.[193]

The objectives of the League were to conserve food supplies and to impress on manufacturers and producers the necessity to maintain output 'so that distress through unemployment may not become general in the community'. Consumers were urged to 'give a preference to local and Irish made' goods, while the League desired to 'impress upon Government Departments' the need to extend land under cultivation 'so that the food supply of the nation may be increased'.[194] During a potato shortage in the period February – March 1917 the city authorities encouraged the Local Government Board's urban tillage initiative and provided allotments, tools and seeds to encourage the public to grow their own food. However, lack of sufficient land hampered the full success of the programme.[195] Focus was also placed on the housing of the working classes and on the provision of meals for necessitous school children, although in the case of the latter Mary felt that the 'first duty of the League was to conserve the food supply of the nation'.[196] She formed part of a subcommittee appointed to 'draft rules for the guidance and governance of the League' and to recommend the minimum subscription fee required from members.[197] Still a member of the MWFL at this point, she outlined the aims of the Cork Consumers League at a meeting of that organisation on 4 September 1914. She was also a member of the Cork Ladies Committee of the Irish Industrial Association, from which the Cork Consumers League emerged: 'it was the duty of every true citizen of Ireland ... to strengthen and enrich Ireland by buying Irish goods and supporting Irish industrial and commercial enterprises'.[198]

Mary acted as Vice Chairman of the League until her resignation from the position in January 1915, although she continued to hold membership.[199] It is likely that her involvement in Cumann na mBan determined her decision to resign from the committee. Her days had become 'minute-crammed with work' after the inauguration of the Cork branch of that organisation. She taught in St Angela's until 3pm at which point she devoted herself to:

> many duties connected with the activities of Cumann na mBan and the Volunteers.... Her pen was always busy advocating the Principles of Freedom and Justice, and exposing the hypocrisy and insincerity of those who clothed its denial in the cloudy phrases of subterfuge.[200]

Mary travelled to Dublin with Annie to attend the O'Donovan Rossa funeral on 1 August 1915 which, as Ward writes, brought nationalist Ireland together 'in tremendous strength'.[201] There was optimism within the ranks of those involved in advanced nationalism in Cork as 1915 gave way to 1916. It was, Annie recalled, 'a glorious time', a time 'full of a rising fire and enthusiasm'.[202] The MacSwiney family operated as a collective political unit; galvanised with similar aims and mutually supportive. In 1914 Terence established *Fianna Fáil*. A paper preaching separatism, it was intended, as the by-line stated, as journal for 'Militant Ireland'. It was printed in Dublin as the Cork printer initially contracted 'got "afraid of his customers" to continue it'.[203] The first issue appeared on 19 September; the next day John Redmond gave his speech in Woodenbridge, County Wicklow, calling on the Irish Volunteers to join the British war effort.[204] This call was denounced by *Fianna Fáil* as a 'betrayal'. The goal was not 'Ireland within the Empire, not even Ireland moulding and ruling the Empire! We despise and repudiate it.'[205]

When Mary and Annie discovered Terence was selling his books to fund the paper, they also sacrificed theirs. Terence's collection was extensive and included, for example, full sets of Molière and Ibsen. Daniel Corkery noted that the only copy of Aristotle's *Poetics* that he read he had on loan from Terence. Corkery conversed with Terence on what he meant to him to have to sell his library; however, all he essentially cared about was that 'the great work was going ahead like wildfire'.[206] Although the paper was suppressed on 5 December after the eleventh issue, Corkery wrote that Terence was 'exultant' in the period after the establishment of the Irish Volunteers.[207] In 1915 he gave up the teaching position he held from 1911 in the Cork School of Commerce and became a full-time organiser for the Irish Volunteers:

> The city, then the county Cork, was his province; he would push his bicycle twenty, thirty, forty miles against a windy rain to speak brave words to some little hamlet or other hidden in the hills. Then there were frequent journeys to and from Dublin. And all the time he was writing – the noblest propaganda that perhaps ever was written.[208]

The resignation of Terence from his teaching position meant a less secure wage in terms of the household budget but the commitment of the family to republicanism was absolute, and the mood was one of buoyancy and expectation.

Chapter Two

Cork: 1916

Cork city and county experienced 'phenomenal' rainfall on Easter Sunday and Monday.[1] Annie MacSwiney recalled Seán O'Hegarty's return from Kealkill to where the MacSwiney sisters were staying with his family in Ballingeary. The men had failed to retrieve German guns and they entered the cottage as water 'literally poured from them as if from an open tap'.[2] Almost in reflection of the weather, the demeanour of republican Cork was increasingly one of 'dark feeling' during the week of the Easter rebellion, a *volte-face* from the optimism of 1915. Mary MacSwiney's refusal to provide a Bureau of Military History witness statement facilitates an initial reading that she was not as actively involved as some of the other women in Cork Cumann na mBan in the period 1916–20. This was not the case. Charlotte Fallon argues that she was content to acquiesce in military matters to republican men, in her case to her brother Terence.[3] However, this is to miss the complexity of her involvement in republican politics in the period up to and including 1916. Members of Cork Cumann na mBan, as most members elsewhere, operated within a certain set of parameters. Their work was in the immediate years after establishment largely gendered; it was not until the aftermath of 1916 that women's roles within republicanism expanded and diversified. Writing to Terence in prison in July 1916 Annie recounted a ditty that was in circulation:

> Here's to the Sinn Feiners [sic]. The Sinn Feiners are men. If I were a boy, I would Sinn Fein with them. As I'm a girl, I must lead a girl's life. But I'll do my best to be a Sinn Feiner's wife.[4]

The gender roles that operated in the period notwithstanding, Mary was as centrally involved in the 1916 rebellion as any member of Cumann na mBan in the city. She was trusted by both Tomás MacCurtain and her brother, and she was immersed in the feelings of despair and humiliation when the Irish Volunteers in Cork did not take up arms during Easter week.

Confusion around order and counter-order meant that the 1916 rising was largely confined to Dublin. Members of Cumann na mBan and women in the Irish Citizen Army carried the IRB Military Council's counter-order to rise on Easter Monday to Irish Volunteer units outside the capital. However, lack of clarity and information predominated in Cork. For the remainder of his life Terence, deputy leader of the Cork Volunteers,[5] sought to explain and justify the lack of rebel action in the city and county. Mary continued to explain his decisions after his death in October 1920. Moreover, the failure of Cork to rise meant that opportunities were denied women like Mary that were available to those who went out in Dublin.

The events of Easter week 1916 indicate Mary's overwhelming support for her brother, to the point of looking for scapegoats for Cork's failure to rise, to an extreme extent that surpassed his own rationale. Mary lost her position in St Angela's in April 1916 as a result of her involvement in republican politics. While this was distressing on a personal and financial level, she established St Ita's High School in the September after the rising. The first lay Catholic school for girls in the city, it was also intended to educate the future citizens of the republic. This was achieved while she visited Terence and other prisoners in internment camps and jail across England and Wales.

Within the specific context of Cork republicanism in 1916, Mary was central, and not just because of her brother's leadership position within the Irish Volunteers. As stated, the family operated as a republican unit. From early 1916 they experienced increasing anxiety and fear as Terence entered a cycle of arrest, release and re-arrest that dominated his life until his death on hunger strike on 25 October 1920. The shared republican goal of the MacSwiney unit was summed up by Seán, imprisoned in Canada in 1918 for refusal to enlist:

> The future is surely full of promise for Ireland and it is a pleasant thought that your family will grow to take their place in that new Ireland which shall once again become a leader among the nations.[6]

In another letter his declaration echoed the views of the entire MacSwiney family: 'Self-determination' is worth going to jail for, or dying for it if need be. Only we must do the determining.'[7]

Sheila Wallace testified that in the lead up to the rising in 1916 officers of the Cork No. 1 Brigade held meetings in her city-centre premises. Dispatches were delivered to the address while she herself oversaw 'communications'.[8] Martin Corry, a member of the Mourneabbey Company of the Irish Volunteers in 1916, stated before the Military Service Pensions Board that he received instructions regarding Easter Week from Wallace who had a shop in Brunswick Street in Cork.[9] This was a backstreet between two central city arteries: the Grand Parade and the South Main Street. This pivotal location meant that the shop become 'a rallying ground for city & co. men … and the natural selection as a carrying house for despatches'.[10] While the MacSwiney home in the suburb of Blackrock had not the same 'natural situation', Mary was, as Seán O'Hegarty described the Wallace sisters, 'the right stuff' and she did very similar work in the lead up to, and during, the 1916 rebellion.[11] Mary's home was at the disposal of the Irish Volunteers and, like Annie Walsh, MacCurtain's sister-in-law, she was entrusted with confidential duties.[12]

By this point the family were still living in the suburb of Blackrock but had moved to 4 Grand View Terrace, Victoria Road, a four-room, second-class dwelling as per the 1911 census.[13] Their home was raided repeatedly from early 1916. On 13 January 1916 Terence was arrested under the Defence of the Realm Act, in the words of *The Irish Volunteer*, 'at five o'clock in the darkness of a mid-winter morning and cast into Cork Jail'.[14] Together with Tomás Ceannt from Fermoy, he was arrested for seditious speeches delivered at Ballynoe, Co. Cork, on 2 January. Mary also made reference to the fact that letters were found in the family home from their brother Seán who was living in Berlin, Ontario. She claimed the word 'Berlin' on the letter was the basis of Terence's arrest. Seán was simultaneously arrested in Canada and 'informed that he and his brother were in a German plot to invade' that country.[15] In prison, Terence refused to see any visitors as he would 'have to meet people in the ordinary room … that is, through a grating'.[16] That prisoners were held in a wire cage during visits was a common grievance of Sinn Féin,[17] although Terence at this point was still not a member of the organisation. He refused, Liam de Róiste wrote, 'to have anything to do with legal defence', adding that such a stance 'was in keeping with his ideas'. He wanted to undergo a trial or to be released. He did agree that 'a public agitation' might 'be got up for his immediate trial'.[18]

With this arrest in January 1916, Mary entered what would become a common pattern when her brother was imprisoned. She corresponded with the relevant authorities for information on Terence's condition and the charges against him.[19] She called 'frequently'; to the office of Cork solicitor and Crown Prosecutor, Henry Arthur Wynne, and wired Laurence Ginnell and William O'Brien, MPs for Cork.[20] The former took up the case in Parliament, enquiring as to how many 'British born subjects' were being kept in jail without charge.[21]

While agitating on behalf of her brother, Mary maintained a central presence within Cork Cumann na mBan. In late January 1916 the Cork Volunteer Officers' training school was held. Cumann na mBan held a ceilidh to entertain those who attended, Mary giving the welcome address. She was described in *The Irish Volunteer* as 'sister of our felon comrade'.[22] In the first week of February she received a communication from General Friend that Terence's trial was imminent.[23] With no further details forthcoming, and anxious that this would preclude mounting a legal defence, on 14 February she went to Wynne who informed her that only an hour's notice might be given. She hired Frank Healy, a solicitor from Queenstown and brother of Timothy Healy, Irish Parliamentary Party MP; she made representations to 'popular Justices of the Peace'.[24] Terence's trial took place on that day. All members of the MacSwiney family resident in Cork were in attendance in the 'crowded' courtroom.[25] Liam Ruiséal recalled that 'a big crowd of us, who were free, practically took over the Bridewell. Songs were sung and loud cheering …'[26] Terence was granted bail until the following Monday on which date he was fined a shilling despite the seven-hour proceedings.[27]

While the MacSwiney house, some remove from the city centre, was less central than the shop run by the Wallace sisters, it was still a locus for dispatches and messages. Annie recalled that in the period before the rising there was 'an air of increasing and intense, though always most quiet, activity'.[28] Mary continued her work with Cumann na mBan while Terence was involved in creating a well-organised Volunteer force in the county.

In 'the telling of the Easter 1916 story, Cork appears only on the margins'.[29] Charles Townshend states that the Irish Volunteers were 'decapitated by the 1916 rebellion'.[30] Borgonovo argues, however, that the failure of the organisation to rise in Cork, facilitated their rapid expansion when public opinion shifted to embrace republicanism in 1917; their 'structures, personnel and operational practices' were still in place.[31] The Irish Volunteers in Cork were, he states, 'motivated to clear the cloud hanging over their organisation', manifesting an 'aggressive spirit and a desire to start fighting as soon as possible'.[32] Yet, the impact of the failure to mobilise must also be considered in terms of human emotions. That failure became 'for some at least, a source of abiding regret that bordered on embarrassment'.[33] This regret permeated entire families and such emotions were not solely the preserve of the male Volunteer leadership in the city. The Volunteers had surrendered their arms without a shot being fired. Terence's anguish at the failure to rise instigated a pattern whereby his sister Mary began a protracted and vehement defence of his position and actions. In the context of the MacSwiney family as a republican unit, she assumed co-responsibility for her brother's decisions; she absorbed and experienced the emotions that emanated from their consequences.

The confusion within the Irish Volunteers in Cork in the context of the rebellion is mirrored in the accounts written. Retrospective in nature, they reflect failing memory but also the fact that no one within the Irish Volunteers and Cumann na mBan in Cork was fully cognisant of the trajectory of events during Easter week outside the city. The accounts highlight the role that rumour played throughout the week and underscore the misunderstandings generated by contradictory orders. On the Wednesday before the rebellion Annie went to Dublin to arrange a meeting the following day for Terence with Thomas Clarke, James Connolly and Seán MacDiarmada. On 17 April Breeid Foley, Dublin Cumann na mBan, delivered a sealed dispatch to MacCurtain and MacSwiney. The contents of the missive are unknown, but the latter determined to send Annie to Dublin to arrange the meeting.[34] Terence believed that it would not be advisable for him to remain in Dublin overnight given the political climate. Annie was unaware of the purpose of the meeting, later learning that it was to 'ensure that a miscarriage of plans would not occur'. Terence was concerned at the lack of unity of purpose between the IRB and the Irish Volunteers. Annie stated that as she boarded the train to Dublin 'she had not the slightest inkling that a Rising was contemplated so soon'. She continued:

> My sister and I always, as in this case, co-operated with the Volunteer Leaders without asking for any explanations. Terry did not discuss Volunteer matters with us in such as manner as to give us any intimate knowledge of policy or intentions, except in a general way. We had both arranged, my sister and I, to go to Tuirin Dubh in Ballingeary for the Easter holidays, and when we mentioned this to Terry early in the week he advised us not to go there … Later, we learned that all that district was to be in the line of action of the Volunteers from Easter Sunday on …[35]

However, if Mary did not know that the rising was planned for Easter Sunday, she had been approached by MacCurtain in her capacity of President of Cumann na mBan in Cork. According to Annie, he informed her that:

> the Brigade Headquarters would entrust to Cumann na mBan, the care and maintenance of the dependents of the Volunteers 'in the event of their having to leave the City. We'll be easy in our minds if we know they are in your care,' he said. But he gave no hint as to when their leaving might come.[36]

Indeed, Annie wrote that the primary reason for Terence's relief when Mary agreed not to go to Ballingeary was not her safety. He 'wanted to feel that at all times Máire would be in the City as a safe place of contact, and be primarily responsible for the dependents of the Volunteers'.[37] This was clearly gendered work and, indeed, Terence had published an article on the role of women in revolutionary movements in *Irish Freedom* in November 1911, declaring: 'if it be admitted that there is to be a fight to-morrow, then there are some things to be settled to-day. How is the woman training for to-morrow?'[38]

Nora Daly Dore wrote that on the second day of the rising she was asked by Seán MacDermott to deliver a verbal message to Terence informing him that the Dublin rebels were 'in action'. She noted how she only had his 'private address'.[39] During Easter week Mary opened her house to women such as Daly Dore who travelled from Dublin and was logistically involved in the line of communications between her brother and other members of Cork city and county Volunteers. At points she was followed by the police and operated in a city that was 'full of military'.[40] Notwithstanding that Mary was engaged in gendered activities, it was still work that had the potential to result in arrest or injury.

As Borgonovo writes, 'events in Dublin and Kerry overtook Cork republicans'.[41] Costello states that Terence and the other leaders of the Irish Volunteers in Cork were themselves in a state of ignorance as to the decision by the Military Council of the IRB to stage the rising on Easter Sunday. Diarmuid Lynch, who was the Munster representative on the IRB supreme council, was not informed until the Thursday before Easter Sunday.[42] MacSwiney and MacCurtain were, however, aware of a shipment of arms arriving from Germany.[43] Annie recalled:

> There was nothing said about a general Rising, or about what the rest of the country was doing. The landing of arms was the operation talked of, though of course all realised this could lead to a general fight ... [44]

Knowledge of the imminent arrival of arms led MacSwiney and MacCurtain to act on 'the theory that something "was on" for Easter Sunday' and the Volunteers under their command were mobilised.[45] Pat Higgins who was a member of Cork Brigade IV stated that, under orders from Dublin, they were to occupy positions along the Cork/Kerry border from Newmarket Southwest to allow for the landing of arms. He noted that it may have been that 'the Brigade had no orders beyond these'.[46] Florence O'Donoghue was much more definite and recalled that MacSwiney and MacCurtain 'were aware that the Easter Sunday mobilisation was for the purpose of insurrection'.[47]

Members of the Irish Volunteers in Cork city were mindful that something was in the offing in the week before Easter Sunday. Liam Ruiséal recalled that there was 'feverish activity' in his bookshop on the Grand Parade with people in and out the Saturday of Holy week.[48] Both MacCurtain and Terence MacSwiney slept in Volunteer Hall in Sheares Street during that week.[49] Cornelius Murphy stated that the Volunteers 'were told to go to Confession'.[50] On 20 April de Róiste, however, wrote in his diary that his belief was that:

> no rising, insurrection or 'trouble' will take place unless the Castle authorities force the issue; as the attitude of most of those at headquarters of the Volunteers seems definitely to be to wait until attacked.[51]

On 21 April de Roiste was 'disgruntled' at orders to go out with his Volunteer Company on Sunday, having been told that they might not return to the city until at least Monday night. If 'serious action' was intended, he would not mind missing the committee meeting of Coláiste na Mumhan on Monday night but 'no one can tell me what is intended'.[52]

Also on Friday 21 April, Ginger O'Connell travelled from Dublin and asked to meet Tomás MacCurtain in Mallow. O'Connell was dispatched by Eoin MacNeill to carry his order that the Irish Volunteers were to take defensive measures only.[53] As there was no suitable train from Cork to Mallow on Good Friday, MacCurtain asked Mary to hire a car and driver. Gender roles apart, tasking her with such a job does indicate that she was within the republican core in Cork in the lead up to Easter 1916. She had to wrangle to acquire a car as the military had issued orders about their hire. Picking up MacCurtain enroute in Blackpool, the MacSwiney sisters drove to Mallow with 'every Police Station en route ... on the watch for us'. In keeping with the general confusion of Easter week, when they arrived at Mallow, they discovered O'Connell had already left for Cork. That night at the MacSwiney home he delivered the order from Eoin MacNeill.[54]

Mary was not appraised of the details of that meeting held in her home in Blackrock. O'Connell, MacCurtain, Seán O'Sullivan and Terence were 'closeted together for a consultation' while Mary and Annie, joined later by Alice Cashel, 'fell to speculation'.[55] When the men left later that night, Terence told his sisters not to wait up; they said the rosary and went to bed.[56] On Easter Saturday there was a stream of callers with messages and reports.[57] Despite their lack of full knowledge of transpiring events, Mary and Annie were sent to Ballingeary by Terence – despite his earlier desire that they avoid holidaying in the area – with an 'urgent dispatch for Seán O'Hegarty', who was head of the Cork IRB.[58] On Easter Tuesday they woke up to news of the rising in Dublin; Mary left for Cork immediately.[59]

Ginger O'Connell's order from MacNeill was followed by an order from the IRB Military Council; the Cork Volunteers were to 'proceed with their previous plans'.[60] However, when Eoin MacNeill learned of the premature arrival of the Aud carrying German arms and the resultant scuttling of the ship, he issued an order in the press calling off the manoeuvres planned for Easter Sunday. James Ryan was despatched to Cork with the new order for MacCurtain.[61] However, the Cork Volunteers, acting on the previous order, were instructed to proceed with their plans for Easter Sunday.[62] Their function was connected to the expected landing of German arms.[63] De Róiste travelled straight to Macroom on Sunday; other Volunteer members arrived at the town via Crookstown. They were then dismissed and told to return to the city on the next train, MacCurtain having received the latest order carried by Ryan.[64] De Róiste states that many were: 'dissatisfied, loud-complaining, a few angry and loudly critical. They felt they had been fooled, in some way or other; they had expected a different ending to the Easter "manoeuvres".'[65]

Rumours abounded in Cork on Easter Monday. There were no Dublin papers and the trains had stopped. De Róiste believed that the Irish Citizen Army had risen in Dublin. Fred Cronin informed him that James Connolly had 'forced the pace':

> 'The "better men" were against the rising. Pearse and others have gone over to the "Connolly crowd". The men here had decided to obey Eoin MacNeill'. (Terence MacSwiney and Tomas MacCurtain were understood as the 'men here'). Their decision explained the cancellation of our 'manoeuvres' on Sunday.[66]

Seán O'Hegarty spoke to Terence and MacCurtain in Ballingeary on Easter Monday noting that they were 'upset' about the 'confusion from conflicting orders'.[67] Annie later recalled that her brother claimed that there had been 'seven contradictory despatches from Holy Thursday to Easter Monday'.[68] Ruiséal wrote:

> During those fateful days nine separate dispatches arrived in Cork, some contradictory or countermanding, others affirming previous orders. It can well be understood how bewildering the situation was, and how unenviable was the position of the Cork command.[69]

O'Hegarty expanded on his memory of his conversation with Terence and MacCurtain in Ballingeary:

> They told me they had received a number of conflicting messages during the week. But the one from Seán MacDiarmada on Friday (brought by Dr Jim Ryan), stating that the differences in Dublin had been resolved and that they were all together now, appeared to them to indicate that any subsequent orders would represent the views and instructions of both the IRA and the Volunteer authorities in Dublin. Consequently when they received MacNeill's order on Sunday they assumed that it represented a united decision to postpone the Rising.[70]

However, O'Hegarty made no reference to the order delivered by Ginger O'Connell. When the two men arrived back to Cork from Ballingeary to news of the rising in Dublin they were, Higgins writes, 'in a terrible mood, frustrated, puzzled and anxious'.[71] Men such as Higgins testified to 'tension and uncertainty'.[72] By this point, Cork was surrounded by the British military, precluding the Volunteers from taking action to create a diversion as requested in a message from MacDiarmada and Clarke.[73] Higgins stated that Terence and MacCurtain had determined not 'to call out the men again and that they were justifying that decision by a recapitulation of all the arguments against such a course'.[74] Nora Daly Dore's Bureau of Military History Witness Statement suggests that both men felt that they were following the correct chain of command in not acting in Easter week:

> I told them what had been done in Dublin and that Seán McDermott sent me to deliver a verbal message 'Tell Terry McSweeney [sic] we are in action and I know he will follow us'. They both seemed to think Dublin was wrong and they were right. They said they had documents to prove they were right.[75]

De Róiste wrote in May 1916: 'Dublin was left [to] fight practically alone. Cork failed. Over which much heartburnings'.[76]

In the Volunteer Hall the men hunkered down defensively. They were prepared to resist any effort by the authorities to disarm them. MacCurtain recorded in his diary that he felt this to be the best decision:

> We had previously agreed that under no circumstance would we leave the Volunteer Hall, as we were convinced that the Soldier [sic] would surround us and we were prepared to die that week, satisfied to know that no one would have it to say that we ran away from the fight.[77]

Women from Cork Cumann na mBan entered and left the building bringing food and carrying despatches. Many of these women were on full-time duty in the Cork Cumann na mBan headquarters in Great George's Street. Margaret Lucey testified to having first aid material in 'readiness'.[78] Although Mary was not informed as to the outbreak of the rising, it was she, in the absence of Terence from the city on Easter Monday, who received communications from Dublin. Peg Duggan, a member of Cork Cumann na mBan, noted that on that day a Miss Foley arrived in the city with a message from Pearse which she delivered to Mary. Breeid Foley, who had travelled to Cork three times during the previous week, had been sent by MacDiarmada. The car in which she was travelling was detained by the military in Dunkettle on Easter Sunday, so she did not arrive in Cork until the next day. Duggan testified to the confusion and lack of knowledge but also declared that Cumann na mBan in the city:

> were prepared to 'go to the hills' if necessary during that period of the Easter Rising 1916. We were equipped with strong boots, ground sheets and first aid equipment in case of emergency, but we were not called on to take part.[79]

On 3 May Terence was arrested at the house of Robert Hales, Knocknacarra, Bandon. He had travelled from Cork in a landau provided by Fred Cronin, concealed under a rug.[80] From Bandon Military Barracks he was sent to Cork Jail. On 9 May was he taken by train with 'a large number of other prisoners' and lodged in Richmond Barracks, Dublin. His two sisters and Muriel Murphy visited him before he was deported.[81] In deciding to travel to Dublin, Mary and Annie believed that there was the 'possibility that we might never see him again'. The sisters stayed in the Four Seasons Hotel where the other guests gave them their 'first graphic description of life in Dublin during Easter Week'.[82]

Terence was one of 74 separatists taken up by the authorities in County Cork after the rebellion.[83] Uncertainty as to the intentions of the British must have weighed heavily on Mary and the other members of his family. The executions followed the rising were not confined to Dublin; Thomas Kent was shot in Victoria Barracks in Cork on the 9 May. De Róiste wrote in response: 'Still the orgy of blood continues. Still the "rounding up of Sinn Feiners, Volunteers and sympathisers".'[84] Borgonovo notes that during the War of Independence ten of the 20 IRA men executed by the British were members of the Cork Volunteers, shot in Victoria Barracks.[85] This was the atmosphere of uncertainty and fear in which Mary lived in the immediate aftermath of the rising. Costello states that Terence's 'increasingly regular periods of incarceration during the years 1916–20 were readily accepted by his brothers and sisters'.[86] This statement is too bald; the family accepted that imprisonment was in the service of the republic. Their set of beliefs were the same as his; they were part of the same republican family unit. Annie wrote to him in 1916: '[w]e'll have a lot of interesting literature in the near future from "Irish Rebels in English Prisons"'.[87] However, the family's belief in Terence's political decisions did not mean that Mary did not worry about her brother's health and agitate to her utmost to ensure his rights within British sites of incarceration. At a very fundamental human level Mary worried intensely about Terence.

The immediate aftermath of the rising was a difficult time for Mary as she tried to penetrate the secrecy of the internment process through communication with various military officers and offices. When she called to the office of the Crown Prosecutor during the period of Terence's first incarceration in January 1916, she was told that the 'charge was exceedingly grave – investigations were being made – it was very probable the death penalty might be involved'. Annie wrote that rumours 'were rife all over the City that Terry was going to be shot as a German spy'. It was a 'demeanour – meant to frighten'.[88] Such a 'demeanour' also prevailed after the rising. Cork City Council held a special meeting 'to consider the present situation in Ireland' and Mary wrote stating 'that relatives were not informed of their place of detention or allowed to send them necessities'.[89]

From the outset Mary adopted a confrontational approach with the authorities. On arrival in the capital in May 1916 the sisters were sent from Dublin Castle to the General Military Headquarters in Parkgate Street only to be ordered to return once again to the former site. From there they travelled to Richmond Barracks. While much has been written about the deprivation internees suffered after 1916, the effect on family members has been less considered. As Lil Conlon wrote:

> Mothers, wives, sisters, sweet-hearts – all were dragged into that cauldron of self-sacrifice … No neon lights emblazoned the lives of those faithful individuals, who risked all, aye, even life itself at times, to prove that sex was no deterrent in the National fight.[90]

The two sisters had travelled to Dublin with no knowledge of where their brother was. They were clearly tired. Having returned from the fruitless journey to Parkgate street, Annie recalled Richmond Barracks 'was a long way off' from Dublin Castle:

> … we were feeling our endurance rather tried. On reaching the gate, we found that it was to be tested further. A sentry on duty refused to let us pass. In vain we protested that we had been twice to Dublin Castle and Park Gate, and had come on the instructions of Lord Powerscourt. His orders were not to let anyone pass and Lord Powerscourt meant nothing to him. We insisted, so did he, and he had a gun.[91]

The MacSwiney sisters and Kathleen McDonnell[92] were not to be deterred and they determined that they would enter the barracks. Transgressing gender norms as they faced the patriarchal authority of the state in the person of the sentry they determined:

> In we were going, somehow, sometime. We made several attempts to rush past him when he moved, but the space was narrow, and he was truculent. At last our chance came. A big lorry came along, and he had to open the gate. As he swung back one side, we slipped behind the lorry, and ran, and as he could not leave the lorry at the gate, we eluded his guard, and made our way across the barrack yard to a block of buildings facing us.[93]

The sisters were finally permitted a half hour interview with their brother.[94]

On 22 May Terence was deported to Frongoch in Wales. The next month Mary travelled to North Wales but was denied entry to the internment camp. This necessitated more correspondence and waiting for replies. On 25 June she received a letter from Brigadier General Byers informing her that the Irish prisoners in Frongoch were 'no longer under the jurisdiction of the War Office, and any permission to visit them must be obtained from the Commandant of the Camp, who in this matter, is acting under the instructions of the Home Office'.[95] That same day she was issued a visiting order by Colonel Commandant Heygate Lambert; she was granted 15 minutes to see her brother on 27 June. She was also permitted to visit Tomas MacCurtain for 15 minutes.[96] Mary never confined her prison visits to Terence; she saw her role as providing support to all who were part of what Townshend described as 'the imagined state'.[97] Nancy Wyse Power wrote admiringly to her in July: 'If you have visited all the Irish Rebels in the English prisons you're great!'[98] Immediately on Terence's arrest in May 1916 Mary became involved in providing necessities to Irish internees across British jails and internment camps, establishing a support committee in Liverpool.[99] She visited Wakefield, Stafford and Lewes with the intention of reporting 'on conditions of prisons and prisoners'. In this capacity she interviewed General Childs who was, Annie later wrote, disgusted at the executions, and wanted to alleviate conditions in the jails and facilitate visitor access.[100] Mary's reputation in the field of prisoner support reached Bishop Cohalan of Cork who referred individuals to her when they sought information on how to visit loved ones.[101]

Having visited her brother, Mary wrote to the Home Office declaring in the context of visits that it was 'barbarous to confine a prisoner to one quarter of an hour a month'.[102] She also issued a similar letter to the Home Secretary, the Right Honourable Herbert Samuel, stating that she had been led to believe that relatives were permitted to visit twice a month.[103] In another letter she drew attention to the 'conditions prevailing at Frongoch Camp' and requested permission to see Terence again.[104] She stated that she had private business in connection with the sale of a property to agree with her brother:

> '[t]he other party to the agreement apparently is taking advantage of the prisoners [sic] detention and Miss MacSwiney wants to discuss with her brother course of action etc.'

M. L. Waller, the Under Secretary at the Home Office, agreed to allow her to visit her brother for a further fifteen minutes. She was, he wrote, 'most grateful' but he stressed that 'NO written permit was given to her'.[105]

However, Colonel Lambert, commander of the camp at Frongoch, wrote to Waller detailing the reasons why Mary could not be permitted entry. On her visit to the camp on 27 and 29 June to see Stephen Collins and Henry Dixon, she had clearly not adopted a sufficiently supplicant or submissive tone. She was there to ensure her brother's wellbeing and she made her feelings clear. To Samuel she wrote that Terence:

> had as much right to be an Irish Volunteer as Sir Edward Carson had to be an Ulster Volunteer and he maintained that right. You English talk a great deal about justice and fair play. If you had <u>practiced</u> it a little more you would not have created the present situation in Ireland.[106]

She queried with 'on what grounds <u>untried</u> prisoners are treated with regard to their visitors on the same footing as men sentence to penal servitude'. Insistently she declared that she 'should be glad to know from you at your earliest convenience also how soon you will kindly have these regulations altered'. In retort to Samuel's statement in the House of Commons that the sanitary inspector found prison conditions acceptable, she wrote 'I should suggest his testing his verdict by personal experiences'.[107] Such a willingness to assert her opinions and demand rights for her brother was perceived as an affront to the military authorities; she was a woman who was willing to engage directly with them and assert her republican rights and position. Lambert wrote:

> She was reported as being a great mischief-maker and having used language which, had she been a man and not a woman, would have resulted in her being handed over to the police under the Defence of the Realm Act.
>
> I had given instructions, in view of this that she was not to receive another pass for some time.[108]

Mary continued to be deeply concerned about her brother's health. Towards the end of July 1916, she wrote to Kate Kelly[109] about a rumour that the internees were to be released.

She noted that the bad ventilation in the camps 'told rather badly' on the prisoners: 'It certainly did on my brother who looked ten years older and horribly sallow and ill looking the day I saw him'.[110] Indeed, the Irish National Aid Association noted that they had received a statement that 'German prisoners were removed from Frongoch because the place was condemned by the American Ambassador as being unfit for human habitation on account of improper ventilation and unsanitary arrangements'.[111] Muriel, who visited Terence and the other Cork prisoners in Wakefield in June 1916, testified that the men were 'in a frightful state. They literally had no food except what we brought them'.[112] In a letter to Samuel, Mary denounced the fact that Terence was 'obliged to sleep in a room which was never built for human habitation'. She also noted that she had travelled from Cork. Visitors from Ireland cannot be, she wrote, 'so frequent' and she expressed her anguish as she declared: 'I trust you will send me permission to see my brother again before going home. I shall not be able to return again for a very long time if you keep him there'.[113]

Mary was not just concerned about Terence's physical wellbeing as she travelled back and forth to visit him in prison; she was troubled about his feelings on the failure of Cork to rise and his own culpability. When Bishop Cohalan of Cork called on the Volunteers in the city to surrender their arms, Terence and MacCurtain conditionally agreed. The understanding was that the arms, if surrendered to Cohalan, or to the Lord Mayor, Thomas Butterfield, would not be handed over to the British. Terence also naively believed that the arms would be returned.[114] While in Richmond Barracks in May 1916 he returned to the issue in what he described as a 'short diary'. Important points 'from our point of view require', he wrote, 'to be corrected'. The agreement, or what he described as the 'Cork Treaty', did not 'mean a surrender on the part of the Volunteers'.[115]

Peter Hart writes that the inaction of the Cork Volunteers in Easter week 'haunted' the officers 'for the rest of their lives'.[116] Townshend refers to the 'atmosphere of guilt' that hung heavily.[117] However, this has not been analysed at any personal or familial level. The confusion of Easter week in Cork and the failure of the Cork Volunteers to rise caused Terence immense anguish. Townshend states that the purpose of the issue of a commemorative certificate of participation in the rising to Cork City Battalion members was to: 'assert that the ordinary rank and file bore no responsibility for what happened, or failed to happen ... The (unstated) implication is that they were let down by somebody.'[118] What Borgonovo says of MacCurtain can also be applied to Terence. In the week after Easter Monday MacCurtain:

> struggled with a terrible choice: to pit his poorly armed men against professional British soldiers, without benefit of surprise and in support of the Dublin Volunteers acting on their initiative; or to sit out a once-in-a-generation patriotic fight, and face accusations of cowardice.[119]

De Róiste described Terence as 'very serious, very perturbed and strained-looking' on Tuesday morning.[120] He tasked de Róiste with taking a message to Seán Hales in Ballinadee telling him to take no action. There was criticism within the Volunteers in Cork at such instructions given by Terence and MacCurtain. De Róiste wrote that he 'personally did not agree with a policy of inaction, but was obeying orders'. He reported Hales as declaring: 'It will be as in '98 when Wexford fought and got no help'.[121]

After the confused events of Easter week in Cork Mary was concerned to vindicate her brother's actions. An injury to one member of the family was an injury to all. She immediately began to apportion blame. On 30 April she described Casement as 'a traitor' to members of Cork Cumann na mBan, continuing that it was only 'the scum of Dublin, Larkin's crowd' who were engaged in the fighting. De Róiste stated that some of the women 'resented' her remarks, but most members were 'influenced by Miss MacS'.[122] She denounced the Dublin leaders for leaving Cork unarmed, describing them, to the anger of Kathleen Clarke, as murderers.[123] Clarke recalled the incident. She had invited Mary and Annie to stay with her when they travelled to visit Terence, imprisoned in Dublin, after the rising. She suggested to the sisters that Dublin hotels might be reluctant to take them on account of their connection to the rebellion. Arriving back from Limerick, Clarke found Mary and Annie on her doorstep, ready to leave for Richmond Barracks. In Clarke's recollection, the atmosphere quickly became tense:

> I was shocked and surprised when Mary, without preliminary, started to denounce the men who had been executed. She said they were nothing short of murderers. I said, 'Come back to the house and explain what you mean, Miss MacSwiney.' In the house she repeated her accusation. She asserted that all the arms had been kept in Dublin, and that Cork was left unarmed, helpless to defend herself. ... No matter what I said, she persisted in her accusation and her denunciation.
>
> Finally I said to her, 'Miss MacSwiney, after all you have said, and the charges you have made against those who are dead and therefore cannot defend themselves, or refute your charges, I do not wish to have anything more to do with you'.[124]

Clarke wrote that despite this encounter she allowed the sisters to remain in her home until Terence was transferred to England, although she refused to spend time with them.[125] However, Annie's unpublished memoir of her sister makes no mention of staying in Clarke's home but states that they resided in the Four Seasons Hotel for the duration of the time in Dublin.[126] Clarke also stated that Mary came to see her in Limerick a few months after the Dublin incident. Even though Clarke was ill, Mary repeated her charges causing her much distress. Clarke claims that when she recounted the incidents to Terence after his release from prison, he asked her to 'make allowances' for his sister as she had been 'in a terrible state of mind over his arrest'.[127]

In *Revolutionary Women* Clarke's criticism of the actions of the Cork Volunteer leaders is easily inferred, possibly a response to Mary stance. Clarke noted that when Cork Volunteer leaders stated that it was 'impossible' to do anything, the city being surrounded, her sister, Nora Daly Dore was: 'very disappointed; she had arrived so full of hope. From what Seán had said about Terence MacSwiney, she had thought that if she got to him everything would be alright.'[128] Moreover, in her memoir Clarke arguably constructed her first meeting with Mary in the period before the rising through the lens of the latter's comments after the executions. She claimed that Mary denounced the idea of German aid prior to 1916:

> I lived in Germany and I dislike the Germans. They are a tyrannical people, and if we accept their help we will be under the rule ... It was no use continuing; she had her views and I had mine, and we both held on to them and parted in no friendly frame of mind. I thought her stupid and narrow.[129]

For Mary to have uttered such sentiments would have placed her at odds with Terence's viewpoint about German aid and attitudes to Ireland. On 5 December 1914 he discussed in *Fianna Fáil* the importance of Germany's declaration of good will towards Ireland:

> The German manifesto to Ireland is the most significant document in modern Irish history. It practically amounts to the recognition of an independent Irish State: it is drawn up in the assumption that such an outcome is a possibility of the present world-war; and in anticipation it gives expression to German good-will and guarantees on behalf of Germany the recognition of Irish independence.[130]

Moreover, Mary had never lived in Germany so Clarke either confused her with another woman who said such things or, as is possible, re-imagined her first meeting with her to cast her in a negative light on the basis of the real hurt she felt at her crass remarks after 1916; her 'complete lack of sympathy with the sorrows of my family'.[131] Mary's cruel remarks to a woman who lost her husband and brother to execution and had also lost an unborn child very recently have to be viewed in the light of her need to defend her brother against all charges of cowardice and accountability in the failure of Cork to rise during Easter 1916.

The actions, or lack of them, of the Cork Volunteers during the six days of the rising continued to be of concern to the MacSwiney family throughout their lifetimes. In 1954 Annie wrote to Florence O'Donoghue regarding Moirin Chavasse's biography of Terence:

> … I felt from some of what she said to me that in her desire for truth in her picture of any 'incompetency', or inaction … that she did not want to paint Toms [sic] and Terry doing the right thing, when they did the wrong thing … she seemed to me to have a very odd picture of the happenings of Easter week.[132]

In the immediate aftermath of the rebellion, Mary was concerned to update family members living outside Ireland of the events from the perspective of Terence's decisions. She continued to apportion blame and nefarious intentions to the Dublin leaders of the Irish Volunteers. Cork officers did not, she wrote to her brother Peter in America, receive Pearse's order until late on Monday evening as they had been 'making a tour of inspection' through the county:

> Militarism was out of the question that night and by Tuesday morning the city was surrounded on all sides. The men could not have got out even if they had ammunition in tons and guns in hundreds which they did not. It seemed to us that Dublin had made a criminal mistake. We have since learned that it was 'come out & fight' or 'be disarmed on Tuesday morning' – but we did not know that at the time. We thought, and still think, that the Inner Council were not justified in keeping MacNeill in the dark so long …[133]

What is notable in this letter is how centrally implicated Mary was. The use of the words 'we' and 'us' are noteworthy. She may not have been aware when the rising was to take place but once it did, she presented herself as fully invested and involved. In explaining the record of Cork in the rebellion she repeatedly referred to how central planning had created a division between what she referred to as the 'Provinces' and Dublin:

> The Provinces did not wish to be left out the affair but there certainly was a woeful disregard of the Provincial Conditions [sic] on the part of Dublin. They were well supplied with rifles and

> ammunition; the Provinces were not, and Dublin had been told again and again that without help in arms &c, the Counties could do nothing.[134]

Mary would return to this concern to defend her brother's actions in 1916 following his death on hunger strike in Brixton Jail in October 1920. In 1922 she wrote to Cathal Brugha who, together with Diarmuid Lynch and Con Collins, represented the Dublin General Headquarters in the inquiry held in Cork as to the actions of the Cork command in 1916. Cork could not, Brugha wrote to her, 'have acted other than they did'.[135] In May 1916, however, Mary was faced with the more immediate consequences of her central position in Cork Cumann na mBan and wider republican politics.

On 3 May 1916 Mary lost her position in St Angela's College. The previous day she was arrested; taken from her classroom and brought to Cork jail. Nora O'Brien, the secretary of Cork Cumann na mBan, was also arrested that day.[136] While in prison Mary wrote to Annie with details on managing the house in her absence.[137] The latter, home alone in Victoria Road, was 'rushed' at by three policemen looking for Terence. When she refused to divulge any information, the men ran into the kitchen and 'roughly dragged into the sitting-room a young daily maid, quite new to the house, who knew nothing of our comings or goings'.[138] Due to the intervention of Bishop Cohalan, Mary and O'Brien were released later that day, both of them 'laughing and excitedly recounting their experiences' in the MacSwiney home.[139] Excitement was tempered, however, with worry about Terence.[140]

The following day Mary arrived to work early with the intention of telling the head mistress 'how grieved I was at the unwarrantable action of the authorities in having me arrested at the school'.[141] The head mistress was inured to any apology and informed her that, on the authority of the Reverend Mother, 'she was not on any account to enter the school again'. Mary's response was confrontational: 'I asked if Rev. Mother was under the impression that I had committed theft or forgery & the reply of the head mistress was that she knew that was exactly what I would say'. She made clear that she was aware that the Ursuline Order had already taken steps to ensure her dismissal. On 28 March 1916 she had received a letter informing her that due to 'changes that will take place in the Community' the order could not 'promise to retain her as a teacher … for the Scholastic year 1916–17'.[142] According to Annie all the lay teachers received a similar letter but displayed no sense of being perturbed in the 'teachers [sic] room'. Mary believed that 'they had been told quietly that the notice did not apply to them'. She determined to confront the Reverend Mother. The following is Annie's account of the conversation:

> I am the oldest teacher on the staff. I am the best qualified. You say yourself, I am the best teacher, and I am not getting a penny more than anyone else, therefore, if I am dismissed, it can be for no other reason but my political convictions.[143]

Despite her strong Catholicism, Mary was never submissive in the face of religious authority. She let it be known that she was aware that the order had determined to dismiss her because of her politics even before the rebellion took place:

> You know Mother you are only doing now openly what you have already done under cover of 'changes in the Community'. Everyone knows that the notices of dismissals given to teachers at the end of last term were really aimed at getting rid of me on account of my politics.

Mary succeeded in forcing the headmistress to concede that the Reverend Mother could not 'hand on all that trouble about politics to her successor'.[144]

Mary was known to the police in Cork; she was not seen as merely an adjunct to her brother. On 10 October 1916 District Inspector C. F. Walsh was asked to give his opinion as to the suitability of the release from custody of 'interned rebels' from Cork. His report on Terence declared him to be 'an extremist ... possessed with a fanatical hatred of all things British'. 'An able and dangerous man', Walsh stated that he should on 'no account ... be released until the termination of the war'. In this report Walsh noted that 'his sisters share his views and are prominent members of the Cumann na mBan'.[145] Walsh had clearly formed this view of Mary some time before he wrote this report. He had an ongoing issue with her position as a teacher in the school. On the return of staff and students to school following the Easter break, his ten-year-old daughter Cecily walked out of the classroom when Mary entered; this was done, she contended 'at the bidding of her parents and had been permitted by the head mistress'.[146] According to Annie, Walsh went to the school even before the events of 1916 unfolded and 'remonstrated with Rev. Mother for having a teacher like Máire, and had, either suggested, or demanded, that she be dismissed'.[147]

Prior to Mary's arrest on 2 May, members of the religious community showed their 'disapproval' of the 'Dublin Insurrection to her'. She had, she declared, 'a perfect right to my own opinions and I consider the attitudes adopted by the people in question as great an impertinence as a similar action on my part towards them would be'.[148] Seeking help from the trade union, the Association of Secondary Teachers Ireland, she compiled a report on her dismissal. What emerges in her account of her conversation with the headmistress is her strong political and moral principles.

Mary's unwillingness to compromise or be conciliatory was a facet of her personality that informed her politics long before the death of her brother in 1920 or the Treaty debates in 1921–2. Expressing anxiety at the events of 1916, the headmistress in St Angela's asked her 'what has been happening', declaring that the nuns could not sleep the previous night having been told 'the city was to be shelled'. Mary informed her that the city was spared and that the nuns 'might thank the Cork Volunteers' who had been involved in 'negotiations ... all the week'. She did not get angry with the headmistress during the discussion on her politics until the latter made allegations that she and other members of the family were in receipt of 'incomes from the volunteer organisation ... so we were not badly off'. The impact of this statement on Mary was evidence of the core of principle and personal sacrifice that defined her lifelong commitment to republican politics: 'This echo of corrupt politicians, who not knowing the meaning of sacrifice themselves cannot understand sacrifice for a sacred ideal on the part of others, was base slander.' Hearing these allegations from 'those who have known me since my childhood did affect me'. It was at this point that she 'lost [her] temper'.[149] The events that unfolded in St Angela's in the immediate aftermath of the rebellion did impact on Mary on an emotional level. When she returned home on 3 May, she 'dropped her attache [sic] case of books on the floor' and 'sank on to a sofa'. 'Chucked' she declared to Annie. As she recounted the confrontation in the school 'tears rose to her eyes':

> It was not the thought that she had 'lost her job,' but the thought that the Convent she had always valued, where she had enjoyed her work, and felt really happy and at home, had done this thing.[150]

On the day of Mary's dismissal, the executions began in Dublin adding to the sisters' concern for their brother. Annie recalled:

> As night came on – we were alone – we sat wondering when, and how, we should get news of Terry. Executions had sent a shiver of coming evil through all – and the uncertainty of Terry's whereabouts heightened it for us.

As they began to say the rosary in anticipation of going to bed, they heard a knock on the window. Outside were Miss O'Mahony and a man named Allman who delivered a message from MacCurtain stating that those who were released in Cork were to be rearrested. Mary was told to go 'on the run' while Annie was to go to Miss O'Mahony's house in Parnell Place as it would not be safe for her to remain alone in case the family home was raided once again. Mary declared that she 'could not go hiding and jumping over hedges and ditches'. In the end, she agreed to leave for one night 'just to obey the order'. The occupants of the safe house, however, concluded she was not coming and there was no answer to the pressing of the bell. She went on with Annie to Miss O'Mahony's house. The next day Annie went to MacCurtain who looked in 'amazement' as she recounted the story of the previous night. He had heard of no re-arrests and had issued no orders. He concurred that '"going on the run" was out of the question for Máire'.[151]

In her conversation with the headmistress of St Angela's, Mary noted that she had kept her promise that she would 'not talk politics in school'.[152] However, Annie later wrote that in teaching the 1641 Irish Catholic rebellion Mary had:

> pointed out how striking was the parallel between that period and 1914-18, in Ireland. Owen Roe and his army paralleled by Sinn Fein and the Irish Volunteers, Redmond and the Irish Party, by Ormond and Preston, and the Unionists and anti-Irish Freedom groups by Cromwell and his Ironsides. It was historically a very exact parallel, but would not commend itself to those who throbbed with zeal for England and her Allies.[153]

R. F. Foster states that education in Ireland had 'always taken on a political and religious complexion'.[154] In discussing politics, the headmistress of St Angela's stated that Mary did not 'allow for their difficulties or see their point of view & they had to consider the parents'. In response she stated that she:

> quite saw their point of view but she [the head mistress] lost sight of the fact that St A's was a public school: that the nuns considered only one section of the parents: they kow-towed to the British element and ignored the Irish element which existed also.[155]

In a letter to Dr Mannix, the Archbishop of Melbourne, in January 1928, Mary noted that when the First World War broke out, she was told by the nuns in St Angela's that she was 'too Irish' in her teaching of history. In her letter to Mannix, she noted that female schools 'in which a better class of education was given, and in which the refinements of life were taught … were hopelessly shoneen'. Referring to male education, D. P. Moran stated that schools 'vie with one another in offering to the *Irish* nation what they call a "sound *English* eductation"'.[156] Girls' schools, Mary stated, were 'even worse in this respect' than those that catered for boys.[157] The nuns in St Angela's, she claimed, viewed those who 'believed in the freedom of their country, in its language and culture' as 'the rowdy element'. On more than one occasion, they expressed 'surprise that I should find myself "dans cette galère"'.[158] Foster discusses the 'suburban values' that prevailed in the elite Catholic male schools in the early twentieth century; Mary found herself in opposition to a similar outlook in St Angela's.[159] She was told that she was 'making the pupils in my class Sinn Féiners'.[160] *An Claidheamh Soluis*, the journal of the Gaelic League, denounced those who ran girls' schools for 'conniving at an Anglicizing approach'.[161]

Under severe financial pressure after losing her job, Mary made a momentous decision to open her own school in which she could put into practice her ideas about modern education. As Peter MacSwiney stated, the 'school venture is an undertaking that requires character and courage to make it succeed but Minnie has both'.[162] The establishment of St Ita's in September 1916 was influenced by both idealistic and economic factors. The school was designed to 'eradicate the slave mind from Ireland'. A verse on a fundraising leaflet *c.*1927 declared: 'By "education" fools are still raised. For they believe because they are so bred.'[163] Mary set herself 'the task of killing the "shoneen" mentality':

> We were able to give the children who came to us, at least as much of culture, refinement and good manners, as well as the training in the secondary school subjects, they could get in any shoneen school. We did not 'talk politics' in school, but we succeeded in getting a normal, healthy, Irish atmosphere, where the study and speaking of Irish was taken for granted, and Irish history was studied in the same spirit as French children would study the history of France.[164]

There were also financial imperatives. On finding herself without employment after the Easter rebellion and unsuccessfully defended by ASTI,[165] Mary was faced with difficult decisions. Muriel MacSwiney described her husband's family as 'very poor'.[166] Of course, Muriel as the daughter of Nicholas Murphy, the owner of Cork Distilleries Co. Ltd., would have experienced an affluent life growing up that was very different to that lived by members of the MacSwiney family. The Murphy family were, in the words of Máire MacSwiney Brugha, 'surrounded by luxury'.[167] Such different economic perspectives notwithstanding, Mary's job was vital to the family budget, particularly as Terence had given up his position as a teacher in the Cork School of Commerce to become a full-time Volunteer organiser in 1915.[168] Although he received a small stipend towards expenses, he was Annie recalled, 'determined to accept no salary for his services to Ireland'.[169] Moreover, when Mary lost her job in St Angela's, Terence was imprisoned and, indeed, the future of the Irish Volunteers was not clear. As Annie wrote: '[w]e had to live, she and I, and it behoved us to plan a means of doing so'.[170] Mary opened St Ita's 'with the intention of making a living without having to leave Cork'. She was 'determined', she wrote later, 'not to be driven out of my own city by the pro-British element'. She knew that she would not get a position in another school having been dismissed from St Angela's 'for my national opinions'. All Cork schools were, she stated, 'equally pro-British'.[171] Giving testimony to the American Commission on Conditions in Ireland in Washington in 1920 she denounced nuns who ran second-level schools in Ireland:

> The system in those schools was English. It was an anglicizing influence entirely. I am sorry to say that it was largely carried on by religious denominations, by the nuns, who were afraid. They were very timid, and were afraid to be anything except conventional.[172]

St Ita's comprised a Kindergarten and a High School and prepared female students for university entrance exams with most going to University College, Cork, established as a co-educational constituent college of the National University of Ireland under the Irish Universities Act, 1908. The school opened at 4 Belgrave Place and the MacSwiney family moved from Victoria Road to live on the rented premises. The advertisement in the *Cork Examiner* on Saturday 2 September detailing the imminent opening of the school appeared just above that giving particulars of the new term in St Angela's.[173] Boys up to the age of ten years were also accepted as pupils.[174] Annie, who had been teaching in Ventnor in the Isle of Wight, returned to Cork to teach in St Ita's, graduating from UCC with a BA.[175] However, it was Mary who led the project to get it established.[176] This necessitated locating a suitable premises, advertising, hiring teachers, and organising timetables. She enquired as to the possibility of acquiring the furniture from St Enda's school from Mrs Pearse if she did not intend to keep the school in operation.[177] As principal all enquires were directed to her.[178] Annie wrote, 'innumerable things attendant on the great venture, had to be dealt with daily'.[179] Indeed Mary, in apology to Art O'Brien for a delay in correspondence about prisoner aid, noted that the 'start here took up all our time and energy'.[180] All this she achieved while travelling back and forth to Britain advocating for her incarcerated brother. Later in life Annie recalled:

> Máire, as Principal, was most meticulous in her attention to all school duties – always at her post – always at the disposal of the children's parents for discussions and advice about the children, while at the same time, she was always at work for the National cause. Her days were spent in the school-room … her evenings were given to the work of the Nation, either in the Cumann na mBan or National Aid Organisation.[181]

The establishment of St Ita's was a fraught economic venture; the school was not in receipt of any public grant and the fees charged were not sufficient, leading to potential closure at various points after its establishment.[182] This was also an issue for Louise Gavan Duffy when she, together with Annie McHugh, established Scoil Bhríde in Dublin the following year. The two women met when studying in UCD; both were committed members of the Gaelic League.[183] However, Gavan Duffy was financially able to make a loan of £400 to Mary to facilitate the opening of St Ita's in September 1916.[184] The latter was optimistic about her ability to make a success of the new educational venture when she wrote to O'Brien in September 1916, but she also indicated that pupils 'must be much more numerous to make the school a financial success'.[185] The *Cork Examiner* noted the congruence between St Ita's and Scoil Bhríde. Gavan Duffy stayed with the MacSwiney family during the Christmas period of 1916 so the two women would have had the opportunity to converse on their pedagogical vision.[186] Indeed, they had conversed earlier via letter and continued to do so with Gavan Duffy recommending 'first rate Irish scholars' when Mary was looking to fill positions. [187] Gavan Duffy hoped that the two women would have 'large flourishing schools which have proved themselves absolutely necessary to the educational welfare of the country'.[188]

In both establishments education was 'essentially Gaelic' and the schools were 'met with marked success and appreciation'.[189] However, the *Cork Examiner* noted that the 'expenses entailed on the individual proprietors have been very great'.[190] The two women communicated on matters to do with the Irish language but also on the availability of possible grants.[191] Muriel MacSwiney contributed to the finances of St Ita's, providing, for example, £10 in April 1918.[192] She came into her inheritance on her 25th birthday, the day before she married Terence on 9 June 1917. She continued to contribute to the running of the school. After Mary's visit to Terence in Dundalk jail in July 1918 he wrote to Muriel:

> Min is very despondent over School. Things have not turned out well. She even talks of giving up. I said we wouldn't have that for a year or two at least – till we see if there wasn't a chance of pulling it through. I explained any help we give is not a mere personal matter. That we both think work of greatest importance.[193]

However, Terence and Muriel worried about their own finances so their support for the school was not guaranteed.[194]

In the early period of the school's establishment, Mary supplemented her income with other teaching work. In September 1916 a meeting of the Cork Borough Committee of Technical Instruction appointed her to the 'lectureship of English' at the Cork Municipal College of Commerce.[195] Nearly four years later it was decided to register St Ita's as a co-operative society to 'obviate any risk of having to close down'. It was described by the Irish Self-Determination League as 'the only Secondary School in Ireland ... which was really National in tone, while giving a general education second to none in the country'.[196] A similar co-operative society was formed in the case of Scoil Bhríde. Despite this change, the 'internal organisation' of St Ita's would 'be conducted as usual' with Mary as principal.[197] This decision to establish St Ita's Educational Association in the Spring of 1920 resulted in an increase in student numbers.[198] Those 'interested in Education imbued with Gaelic ideas' were invited to become members. At this point Mary believed that this solution was merely required 'pending the time when DAIL EIREANN [sic] would be ready to take over the control of Education throughout the country'.[199]

The historiography of advances in female education in Ireland is heavily focused on the campaigns of the nineteenth century and the opening of university education to women in the first decade of the twentieth. These campaigns were conducted in the 'context of the Protestant liberal-humanitarian tradition of social justice' in nineteenth-century Ireland.[200] As the *Cork Examiner* noted in 1920 St Ita's 'marked a new departure in education in Cork as it was the first lay Catholic high school'.[201] The school reflected the value Mary placed on third-level education for females. She herself embodied the way in which women were, albeit slowly, able to forge meaningful lives outside of marriage and motherhood. She was proud that in the first 12 years after the school's opening pupils had gone on to become doctors, teachers and business owners, while one was completing studies in law.[202] From 1919–23 she sat on the governing board of University College, Cork as a graduate representative.[203] As a member of the Cork County Teachers Association, she was interested in equality for female teachers. She was in attendance at a branch meeting on 4 November 1916 during which members discussed the war bonus and pledged 'to take practical steps' to ensure 'an equal increase for male and female teachers'.[204]

In considering her pedagogical mission, Mary noted that men were better educated and knew more about the Irish past than women because of decisions taken by the Christian Brothers who refused to come under the auspices of the National Education Board in the nineteenth century:

> The Christian Brothers refused it because you had to confine religious education in schools to one-half hour a day, and you had to use books appointed by the national board, and those books omitted all mention of Irish history, about Irish heroes, or a single word about a martyr or a saint whatever. And the Christian Brothers would not have that system, and they adopted books of their own, which are very fine books. And perhaps the reason that the men of Ireland are better educated and know more about the history of their land than the women do, is that the men have been educated by the Christian Brothers and the women have been educated in the national schools or anglicizing secondary schools.[205]

Of course she failed to note that males who were not educated by the Christian Brothers were in the same position as female students. The education that Daniel Corkery received at the Presentation Brothers South Monastery School in Cork did not involve heroes of his nationalist upbringing.[206]

Catholic female education was dominated by nuns and Mary was aware that she faced potential criticism from the Catholic hierarchy in opening St Ita's. There was, she wrote, 'a tendency … to imply that such training [religious] cannot be efficiently given by lay teachers'.[207] In 1917 she sent a letter to an unidentified member of the hierarchy, probably Cohalan, the Bishop of Cork, outlining the work accomplished in the first year of the school's opening and assuring him that they aimed:

> at combining careful moral and religious training with a high standard of intellectual work and assure the parents that utmost care is given to the religious training (and preparation for the sacraments).
>
> We wish to emphasise this point of the Religious training in St Ita's.[208]

St Ita's was supported by Cohalan and the clergy in the city. In August 1916 the former wrote wondering if she had filled all her staff requirements. He recommended Peg Tobin from Macroom who would 'prefer an Irish appointment' to an 'English appointment under which she could not teach Irish history properly'.[209] Later that month Cohalan advised her on the procedure to have St Ita's blessed on first opening. He was glad to hear, he wrote, that 'a good number of pupils' had enrolled and looked forward to paying the school a visit.[210] The bishop distributed prizes at the school beginning in 1917.[211] In December 1919 Cohalan, together with local priests, watched as students performed four plays in Father Mathew Hall. One of the plays was wholly in Irish while the fourth entitled *The Wisdom of Foolishness* had as its theme the execution of Sir Thomas More due to his refusal to convert to Protestantism during the Reformation. Mary read the annual report following the performances and noted the increasing number of students the school was attracting. She outlined one of the core principles in the school namely that students were not obliged to sit state examinations:

> In St Ita's they were of the opinion that the system of examination was a cramping one and did not leave sufficient time to enable any broad educational work to be done. Miss MacSweeny [sic] then referred to the pressing need of educational reform and pointed out that the parents,

> as well as the clergy and teachers, should closely examine any new Education Bill and see that as well as safeguarding religious teaching, it makes Ireland the centre of the Universe for Irish children and her language and interests their chief study. This was the aim of St Ita's to make the school as thoroughly Irish as Eton or Stonyhurst is English. Already Irish was spoken in class and in the school and they hoped before long to see St Ita's bilingual.[212]

In her approach to the state curriculum, Mary echoed Patrick Pearse's view of traditional education as a 'murder machine'.[213] Indeed, when Pearse moved St Enda's from Cullenwood House to Rathfarnham in 1910, St Ita's school for girls took over the premises. Pearse acted as 'an arms-length proprietor' in the short-lived school which closed in June 1912.[214] That Mary chose the same name for her Cork school can hardly have been a coincidence. As Charles Townshend notes, Patrick Pearse's commitment to the Irish language 'made him a dedicated educator'. [215] The language was also core to Mary's educational pedagogy as it was integral to her politics. Despite the adamant desire of Douglas Hyde and Eoin MacNeill that the Gaelic League be non-political, increasingly after 1893 the 'threatened loss of the language was seen as a British initiative'.[216] In diary entries in 1916 de Róiste noted arrests of people for speaking Irish; in March Padraig Ó Conaire was arrested in Donegal at the house of Mrs Gavan Duffy for speaking Irish to a member of the Royal Irish Constabulary (RIC).[217] In June 1917, Terence gave a speech declaring that Irish must be the language of the republic.[218] He received honours in Celtic, as the Intermediate Board described the Irish language, when a student with the Christian Brothers and he taught in St Ita's in Cork for period.[219] The republican activist Michael Hales wrote: 'Irish was and remains a token of separateness, of our instinctive nationhood'.[220] Conlon noted that at meetings of the Cork District Council of Cumann na mBan, the President Margaret O'Leary 'emphasised that all should endeavour to make Ireland Gaelic as well as free and that Irish should be spoken as much as possible'.[221] At an executive meeting of the organisation Mary called on members to take up 'Irish in earnest':

> There is not one of you who could not master the Irish [sic] inside of twelve months, and if you really believe in Irish freedom you will take up the language of Ireland which will give you an Irish mentality sooner than anything else will.[222]

By 1922 St Ita's provided 'suitable lodgings' for pupils 'from the country, especially from the Irish-Speaking districts'.[223] In his address at the December 1919 prize-giving, Cohalan noted that that the school was finding increasing favour among parents in Cork, offering as it did an education 'thoroughly Catholic and thoroughly Irish'. However, he noted approvingly that the school did not confine itself to Irish subjects and that pupils received 'the widest possible education'.[224] Indeed, Foster notes that St Ita's was popular with parents who did not hold Mary's 'uncompromising republican values, simply because it was a good school'.[225]

Such a rounded education included sports, with an emphasis on Irish games. Students participated in the Camogie Schools Cup in Cork.[226] They also participated in various philanthropic and fundraising events in the city. St Ita's was very much in the tradition of schools like Alexandra College in that regard.[227] A flag day in support of the Cork Poor School Children Meals Fund meals was held on 1 February 1919. Mary and the St Ita's students managed the collection from King Street to Glanmire train station.[228] As the collection did not have a permit, fines were issued, drawing Mary's ire. She wrote to the School Meals Committee protesting the use of money collected 'being paid as fines to the English government'.[229] For Mary the professional – in this case her work as an educator – was political.

St Ita's was very much a school linked to the political movement. Alice Cashel, another Cork Cumann na mBan member, became a teacher in the school in January 1917.[230] Geraldine O'Sullivan, bridesmaid at Terence's wedding, also taught in the school. She later married Seán Neeson, interned after 1916. Kathleen Murray was another member of Cumann na mBan who taught in the school.[231] The degree of personal sacrifice for the political cause was encapsulated in a memo by the Irish Self-Determination League which noted that staff 'for a long time were teaching for much less than the salary to which they were entitled'.[232] The location became a receiving point for correspondence; Muriel and Terence used the address while he was imprisoned at various times.[233] The former recalled that when Terence was arrested in Dublin in March 1918 and sent to Belfast, she returned to Cork carrying a suitcase of arms which she brought to St Ita's for collection by Seán O'Hegarty.[234] The building was subject to raids, and this must have had an impact on the school's viability. The home of Agnes Gallagher, Westport Cumann na mBan, was 'used as a station for dispatches and procuring supplies ... under her own supervision during both wars'. Gallagher testified to the closure of her music academy during the War of Independence: 'all pupils were prevented from attending ... through hold-ups and searches of girl pupils. My premises thus having to close down and forfeit my means of livelihood [sic].'[235] Pupils would, Gallagher testified, 'be kept standing in the hall and searched'; the 'children were afraid to come in.'[236]

Planning over the summer of 1916 for the opening of St Ita's took place as Mary simultaneously worked to find information as to the whereabouts and condition of Terence within the British internment system. This brought her into contact with men like Art O' Brien in London who founded the Irish National Aid Fund in the immediate aftermath of the rising, discussed in Chapter Three. Travelling back and forth to England and Wales also added to the financial concerns as she dealt with the loss of her position in St Angela's. In a letter in July to the Home Secretary from the Queen Hotel in Chester she noted the 'expense' of waiting in England to hear news of Terence which she could, she declared, 'badly afford'.[237] Three days later Mary was still paying to stay in the Queen Hotel and heard that her permission to visit her brother was cancelled.[238] She railed at the delay and the financial outflow.

Despite Mary's optimism about releases in July 1916 it would be close to six months before Terence was released.[239] He arrived back in Cork on Christmas Day having been released from Reading Jail on 24 December. That Christmas Peter MacSwiney was also back in Cork from America.[240] Such a 'great and unexpected treat' did not stop Mary from considering the men still interned. In early January 1917 she wrote to O'Brien on behalf of the Cork Committee of the Irish National Aid and Volunteer Dependents' Fund asking if they would be allowed to send parcels into Lewes and to Countess Markievicz in Alysbury.[241]

In June 1916 Mary wrote to Peter thanking him for his money order. She noted that she gave half of it to Seán, 'as I know it will be a boon to him'. She had received no news from her sister Peg and asked him 'to let her know we are alright'. She then turned to detail the conditions in Wakefield prison where Terence was in solitary confinement. Having got personal matters out of the way, she turned to political plans. She assumed a position of authority. This mirrored the way women filled the vacuum created because of male internment post-1916 and kept the ideals of the rising alive through propaganda work and fundraising.[242] The press, Mary declared to Peter was 'under the thumb of the authorities and not a single word in any paper can be relied on'. She requested that Peter contact John Devoy and 'let him know that all the chief men in Dublin who were not shot are in prison' together with the 'prominent men' from other counties.

Mary then moved her attention to the 'present state of affairs', illuminating Peter as to future planning. She declared that 'whatever opinions there were before Easter, practically the whole county is right now'.[243] Echoing Terence's concept that those who suffered would prevail, she argued that the imposition of martial law, the executions, the arrests 'have acted as a tonic'. At this point Mary contemplated the possibility of a future armed engagement with the British. She noted that despite the lack of sufficient arms in the county there was the will to ensure full independence: they would not, she wrote, be 'cowed down' by the 'fact that they contemplate giving what they call a "measure of Home Rule" at once'. Martial law, she contended, prevented any political statement of opposition to proposals to exclude six Ulster counties.[244] The British government, indeed, did fear a second rising and, Hart writes, engaged in policy shifts in fear of provoking one throughout 1917 and 1918.[245]

Mary stated that she had many 'intimate talks' with Tom Clarke before 1916 and inferred that he had confided confidential information to her. He: 'told me of a certain document in our favor [sic]. I do not want to particularize more than that but John Devoy will understand. What we need now is to get in touch with America if possible.' Martial law and General Maxwell, she wrote, would be better than having Ireland represented at the Peace Conference by John Redmond.[246] Waiting for a future call to arms, Mary meanwhile busied herself with propaganda and prisoner support.

Chapter Three

Cork: May 1916–August 1920

Like so many republicans in the aftermath of the Rising, Mary MacSwiney experienced what Charles Townshend describes as the 'revolutionary psychological dynamic'.[1] In the words of Todd Andrews there was a sense of 'belonging to an exclusive club or to any group of conspirators'.[2] Discussing Cork's 'evolving politics', Borgonovo notes that 'the political ground was shifting beneath the Irish Party'. Anti-British sentiments in the city became louder.[3] Annie MacSwiney wrote of Cork after the rebellion and into 1917 that a 'surging life' was 'athrob everywhere':

> One very noticeable feature of that time was the enthistiastic [sic] greeting of Republican prisoners by the people everywhere. A lorry load of prisoners was the signal for outbursts of cheering along the streets, waving handkerchiefs, and rushes to the gaol to cheer them on.[4]

Women in Cork were centrally involved in the street theatre of an increasingly visible republicanism and the creation of a counter state in the city. In her account of Cumann na mBan, Lil Conlon repeatedly referred to the wearing of Sinn Féin badges by men and women across the county.[5] On 15 April 1917 male and female members of Sinn Féin held a demonstration at the National Monument on the Grand Parade following mass in St Peter and Paul's church in memory of those who died in 1916. The RIC intervened and ordered the attendees to disperse. The result was:

> Loud bursts of alternative cheering and hissing, led by the female section, added a little commotion to the scene, and individual attacks by the young women on policemen, some of whom were knocked down, was followed by the order for the drawing of batons to clear the streets ...[6]

A month later, Teresa O'Donovan of Evergreen Street was charged with an assault on a Constable Farrell using her umbrella as a weapon. She was sent to jail for refusing to pay the fine.[7] Female counter-cultural activism continued in Cork city during the War of Independence. On 13 May 1919 magisterial proceedings against six young women for the distribution of seditious literature on the treatment of prisoners saw friends and sympathisers turn up in large numbers. There was 'great excitement and interest' and for some time before the hearing commenced 'the prisoners' voices could be plainly heard singing *The Soldier's Song* and other National Airs'. The women refused to recognise the court, having previously refused to give their names in English. They 'sang all the way to the Female Prison in Sunday's Well', to 'tumultuous cheering from the crowd'.[8] When Cumann na mBan was refused permits to hold fundraising events they subverted the ban by moving the venue.[9] The flu-pandemic, of course, also interrupted certain events planned by the organisation. The Cork District Council of Cumann na mBan organised volunteers to assist those suffering from the flu.[10]

Mary was not involved in any street fighting but she was an increasingly central presence in Cork republican politics after the rebellion; a driving force within the MacSwiney political family unit. In early January 1917 Dublin Castle reported on the 'disloyal character of the McSweeney [sic] family' to the Home Office, noting that Mary and Annie shared Terence's political views and were leading members of the Cork branch of Cumann na mBan.[11] Members of the Irish Volunteers and Cumann na mBan were committed to establishing as a political reality the Republic declared in the 1916 Proclamation. Republican women, through the Irish National Aid and Volunteers Dependents' Fund (INA&VDF), raised funds and distributed relief to the families of interned men. This was Mary's area of concentration in the immediate aftermath of the rebellion. The INA&VDF was, as Caoimhe Nic Dháibhéid argues, central to the reorganisation of the advanced nationalist movement after the rising; it provided 'a focus'. Moreover, the organisation developed as 'an administrator of political – or politicized – welfare'[12] For Mary prisoner aid was political; it was also personal as her brother Terence was repeatedly incarcerated in the period from early 1916 until his death in October 1920. Her brother Seán was also imprisoned in Canada from March 1918–March 1919.

Involvement in prisoner aid brought Mary into contact with key figures in the revolutionary movement in Ireland and in London, notably Art O'Brien who founded the Irish National Aid Fund and who was president of Sinn Féin in England and Wales. Extending her political network, she was laying the groundwork for her more prominent role in the revolutionary moment after October 1920. In the period after 1916 Mary's unwillingness to compromise on her political principles became more apparent. There were those, particularly within Cork Cumann na mBan, who perceived her as strident and overbearing. Meetings of the organisation in the city became fractious and personality driven leading to an outright breach in 1917.

Mary had much responsibility. The success or otherwise of St Ita's rested with her. She genuinely wanted the school to triumph on an academic level and as an educational manifestation of Irish Ireland principles. She also needed the school to succeed to ensure the financial independence of herself and Annie. Added to such concerns, she dealt with constant anxiety as Terence was repeatedly imprisoned after 1916. She, like him, genuinely believed in the republican cause; she did not have time for niceties and in many cases bluntly spoke her mind, causing offence within Cork Cumann na mBan as discussed below.

On 6 June 1916 a public meeting was convened by the Lord Mayor of Cork, T. C. Butterfield, in the Council Chamber, Municipal Building, to promote a flag day to augment the Mansion House Fund in Dublin established in the previous month. The intention of the fund was, the *Cork Examiner* stated, to relieve shop assistants who had lost their positions due to fire and other damage caused to premises during the rebellion. Dissension arose: Mary spoke saying that the fund was not intended to benefit soldiers' dependents or shop assistants.[13] She noted that she had recently been in Dublin and was very interested in the work carried out by the Irish National Aid Association (INAA). Nic Dháibhéid states that the INAA 'operated a broad-based appeal from the outset' of its foundation at the end of May 1916.[14] MacSwiney testified that she had seen large numbers of people queuing for the relief administered by the association. According to the *Cork Examiner* she stated that 95 per cent of distress in Dublin was experienced by the families of interned men. Civilian casualties of the rising were not mentioned. The men, she declared, had 'fought for an ideal' and it was 'now the duty of the Irish nation to support their wives and children'. She called for the funds from the Cork flag day to be divided between the Lord Mayor's fund and the Irish National Aid Association.[15] It was decided, however, that the proceeds would solely benefit the former.[16]

There was some co-operation between the fund established by the Dublin Lord Mayor and the INAA. A letter on 19 June from the secretary of the former to the INAA expressed 'regret if there were anything in my letter to lead you to suppose that my committee were not desirous of any proposal as to co-operation between our two committees'.[17] However, the Lord Mayor's Fund was short-lived, but branches of the INAA were established rapidly around the country.[18] On 29 June a Cork branch of the INAA was established at a meeting in the City Hall. Both Mary and Annie were in attendance.[19] At the meeting Donal O'Callaghan, Liam de Róiste and Seán O'Sullivan were elected as honorary secretaries.[20] Mary was elected a member of the branch committee, her name appearing first on the letterhead of the branch.[21] The inaugural meeting was held as news that Roger Casement had been found guilty of high treason and sentenced to death circulated in Cork.[22] In a letter to her brother Peter in that same month of June 1916 Mary was overt in her criticism of the operation and focus of the Lord Mayor's fund and indicated her support, by contrast, for the INAA. Discussing funds coming from America she wrote that the money:

> was sent to the Lord Mayor of Dublin. He is devoting it to the relief of shop assistants and others thrown out of work owing to the destruction of property &c. He proposed getting a grant from the Prince of Wales Fund for the dependents of soldiers and amalgamating the two. Of course no dependent of a Volunteer would touch money coming from the Prince of Wales Fund, and it was felt that the present Lord Mayor was not the person to be trusted in a matter like this. The Irish National Aid Association was formed. The Committee is representative, but the controlling element is right.[23]

With this statement Mary refered to the diverse nature of the first committee of the INAA comprised as it was of members of the Irish Parliamentary Party such as Lorcan Sherlock and members of the IRB such as Fred Allan. Louise Gavan Duffy, who Mary was in correspondence with regarding the setting up of St Ita's, was also on the first committee.[24] Mary made it clear to Peter that all monies coming from America should bypass the Lord Mayor of Dublin and be sent directly to the INAA.[25]

Supporting the INAA, Mary was critical of Kathleen Clarke's establishment of the Irish Volunteers Dependants' Fund (IVDF), established also in May 1916. Clarke was adamantly opposed to what she viewed as the Irish Parliamentary bias of the INAA's committee.[26] Nancy Wyse Power recalled:

> The National Aid Association had been formed on a very broad basis and Mrs. Clarke objected to the admission to it of persons who had not been friendly to the Volunteer movement before the Rising. Further, her fund was intended solely for the dependants of members of the Volunteers while the National Aid Association were prepared to help all who had been arrested, even if they had not been concerned in the Rising.[27]

Discord between Mary and Clarke over how prisoner aid should be organised and who should receive it illuminates the familial cost of the rebellion. The latter lost her husband, Tom, and her brother, Edward, in 1916. Both men were amongst the 15 executed in the immediate aftermath of the rebellion while she herself suffered a miscarriage. Mary's brother was imprisoned, while her own short incarceration led to the loss of her teaching position. Moreover, she, as discussed, absorbed her brother's distress at the failure of Cork to participate in the events of Easter week. To Peter she wrote:

> Now I want to touch on a rather delicate subject. Mrs Tom Clarke naturally enough feels very bitterly about the situation. She has lost her husband – a man whose loss we all feel deeply – and her brother. She makes no allowance for the difficulties of other counties, and thinks they should have supported Dublin. As a result she is making a separate appeal for funds for the dependents of those who actually fought. ...As Ireland from all parts was only anxious to do its utmost, and it was no fault of the counties that plans went wrong, and the men here are penalised solely and entirely because they were ready to stand for Ireland against the Empire and fight and die for Ireland, it seems hard that their dependents should not be helped.[28]

Mary did note that she was sure that an outright 'clash' would not occur and was hopeful that the 'difficulty will ... disappear in a little while' as both funds were 'devoted to those suffering for Ireland'.[29] In reality, the IVDF, as Kitty O'Doherty recalled, was willing to support the relatives of both executed and imprisoned Volunteers.[30] In August 1916 the two organisations merged to become the Irish National Aid and Volunteer Dependents' Fund organisation at the urging of an American delegation of Friends of Irish Freedom who were not willing to countenance two rival organisations.[31] Nic Dháibhéid notes that the Cork branch of the INA&VDF were 'sensitive to perceived slights to their honour' because of their failure to rise in 1916. This manifested in resentment at perceived handouts to individuals from Dublin.[32] As a solution, O' Callaghan was informed in a letter from Michael Collins on 9 March 1917 that future cheques would be sent directly to the branch for distribution.[33] Yet 'over-zealous territoriality continued to bubble away sporadically throughout the INA&VDF's existence'.[34]

In mid-August 1916 the Cork branch noted the amalgamation of the National Aid Association and the Irish Volunteer Dependants Fund; at that same meeting Mary undertook to arrange collections at 'sports meetings and such public gatherings'.[35] The renewed arrest of members of Sinn Féin in 1917 and again in 1918 led to appeals for funds to enable those looking after the prisoners in Cork Gaol and other sites of incarceration to provide 'proper food'. Prisoners also needed to be 'free from worry of the helplessness of their families ... left without support'.[36] A letter from Tadg O'Shea of the Cork branch of the INA&VDF to Michael Collins on 30 September 1917 referred to the case of Mrs Liddy in Cooraclare, Ennis. Her son, Seán, had been sentenced by court martial at Cork to 12 months imprisonment for drilling local Volunteers. Mrs Liddy requested help 'to pay the wages of a man whom she had to employ to work a farm in place of her son'. O'Shea noted that the matter had been brought to the attention of the Cork committee 'thro' Miss M'Swiney'.[37]

Prisoner aid was political; in aiding detainees and their families the republican ideal was disseminated across Cork city and county 'at a time when government repression made it difficult to do so'.[38] Mary was centrally immersed in such politics. She eschewed any suggestion that the INA&VDF was solely philanthropic. Prisoner aid was, she outlined to her brother Peter: 'solely for the dependents of the men who were shot, sentenced to Penal Servitude, imprisoned or deported in consequence of the late Rising. None others are to benefit.'[39] A decision was reached at central level to close the INA&VDF on 1 November 1919. At a meeting of the Cork branch on 22 August the Executive was asked to reconsider given the 'large and increasing number of arrests'. Moreover, they believed that county branches should have been consulted.[40] With no rescindment of the decision the Cork branch of INA&VDF closed on 9 November 1919.[41] Mary was still on the committee when the fund closed. She was also by that date on the committee of the Cork branch of the Irish Republican Prisoners Dependants' Fund (IRPDF).[42] This organisation was 'unashamedly an adjunct of Sinn Féin, operating out of the party's headquarters and promoted by members'. By 1917 Mary was, as discussed below, a member of Sinn Féin. The IRPDF, as William Murphy, writes, 'maintained none of the INA&VDF's pretensions to the purely philanthropic' and as such fully appealed to Mary.[43]

Mary considered prisoner aid through the lens of familial concern for her brother. Terence was arrested twice during 1917. In the early hours of the morning of 23 February he was arrested together with MacCurtain and Shaun Nolan under the Defence of the Realm Act and imprisoned in Bromyard Gaol.[44] On 9 June he married Muriel Murphy, one week before the general release. The decision to wed came despite Terence's earlier musing that he was not 'shaped for marriage'.[45] He wrote to his Aunt Kate that:

> All the conventions that seem to go to the making of a suitable and admirable married man are just the things that I can't stand. For example that prosperity and comfort are the two chief things.[46]

He noted that in the case of people who were 'ruled by any higher idea that might entail sacrifice for the man', there would be 'trouble for the woman and destitution for the children'. That, he stated, 'would seem nothing short of a crime and a very great crime'.[47] These sentiments were expressed as he was writing *The Revolutionist*. He continued:

> ... if 'a good match' had just been made for me and I were married to a girl with a good fortune and if the fortune were swallowed up because of my patriotic activities – what do you think the people-in law would say? Not to me the girl herself! ... You may say I could only get a girl as foolish as myself! That would be a dream![48]

While he does say that the 'girl is not at hand' he had at the time of writing the letter met Muriel.

Muriel wrote that she first saw Terence in 1915 at a public meeting in honour of the Manchester Martyrs held on the Grand Parade, Cork. She stated that she was interested in the Sinn Féin movement at this point. She presented her nationalist conversion as a form of youthful rebellion. Her family were 'Imperialist, conservative, capitalist and roman catholic [sic]'. The children were sent to school in England as they were not to mix with the 'common people'. The youngest of six children, there was a large gap between her and the next oldest sibling; her childhood was, she wrote, 'isolated'. By contrast, with her family, those she met in the Irish-Ireland and advanced nationalist circles in Cork were people of 'wonderful principles and high moral standing'.[49]

Muriel's family were opposed to her courtship and subsequent marriage. Terence referred to the 'coldness of her relatives'.[50] They looked on the Irish Volunteers as 'criminals and murderers'.[51] However, Terence stated that the efforts of Muriel's mother to 'draw you away from me, only discovered for me more beauties in your love'.[52] The two conversed on art.[53] As she learned Irish, he wrote to her in the language with a dictionary of Irish words on the back of the page.[54] In the lead up to the wedding he described her as 'so beautiful', declaring that she would be 'such a perfect wife'.[55] After marriage he referred to holding 'her body in reverence'.[56]

The wedding ceremony, in Irish, was held at the open prison.[57] Both Mary and Annie were in attendance and the pupils of St Ita's gave a silver dish made by the Cork silversmith, William Egan.[58] Muriel's dress reflected the 'green, white and, yellow colours adopted by the Sinn Feiners'[59] Arriving back to Cork on 23 June Terence and the other released men from the city and country were greeted with a demonstration of welcome, Muriel riding in a wagonette with her husband. The Sinn Féin welcome reception resulted in street riots as women whose husbands were serving on the front clashed with republican supporters. One man lost his life.[60]

Muriel and Terence were frequently apart after their marriage due to his political work and repeated arrests. She stated that she knew before the marriage that her husband's work 'naturally came before everything else'.[61] When apart the two carried on a loving correspondence. Writing from Mary's home in July 1917 he spoke of their reunion the next day when he would 'take you in my arms'.[62] However, from an early point he worried about her health. In early December 1917 he advised her to stay in bed if the 'pain' was still bad.[63] Muriel suffered from Terence's absences and suffered from depression. Her 'unhappiness', he wrote to her from prison, was his and he was glad she had confided in him. He wrote that her acceptance of his politics and the resultant arrests had reminded him of the self-sacrificing nature of Wolfe Tone's wife. However, the news that 'things may not be well with you is worse than any jail punishment'.[64] He told her to 'be an infant with me whenever you like' as he encouraged her to talk about how she felt when she had a 'nerve attack'.[65]

Terence was arrested again on 30 October 1917 and sent to Cork Gaol, having taken part in an Irish Volunteers route march and parade the previous Sunday while illegally wearing a military uniform.[66] He was sentenced to six months with hard labour.[67] By this date Thomas Ashe had died in Mountjoy prison having been forcibly fed while on hunger strike. The strike which was started on 20 September by 40 DORA prisoners was in pursuit of political prisoner status. As a result of Ashe's death on 25 September the demands of the prisoners on hunger strike were granted. On 29 September the government conceded '*de facto* political status, in the form of improved conditions'.[68] There was heightened tension in Cork in the immediate aftermath of Ashe's death resulting in an increased police presence. De Róiste wrote:

> 'respectable citizens' are warned off the city streets at night time – the police are abroad with bayonets and loaded carbines and batons … people are thrown down, bruised, beaten, batoned. Stones are thrown at the police.[69]

Such a climate of fear and violence did not deter Mary from attending the usual round of meetings. Walking down Patrick's Hill across Patrick's Bridge and into the city she was in the thick of such potential violence. The *Freeman's Journal* reported on a meeting of Cork Corporation on 12 October and the attendance of a deputation from the Cork branch of the INA&VDF. The Council was asked to pass a resolution that the prisoners in Cork Gaol, tried and untried, be treated as prisoners of war. A letter from Mary was noted. As the paper put it, 'she did not wish a repetition of the Ashe tragedy in Cork'. Those prisoners were, she wrote, 'entitled to the status won by the men in Mountjoy'.[70]

After a three-day hunger strike in Cork gaol beginning on 10 November Terence was released under the Temporary Discharge for Ill Health Act, 1913.[71] In March 1918 he was arrested again to complete the remainder of his sentence.[72] He was sent to Belfast and from there to Dundalk; after a six-week period he was returned to Belfast before being released on 4 September.[73] During this period Mary became an aunt for the first time. In her witness statement Muriel MacSwiney stated that she knew she was pregnant on the day Terence was arrested in October 1917. He was in jail in Belfast in 1918 when she gave birth to Máire Óg and his first meeting with their two-month-old daughter involved Muriel making the long journey to a prison in Belfast in August 1918 and staying in that city for several weeks.[74]

When Muriel was pregnant, Terence talked about the necessity for him to help her further with her Irish so that they could have an 'Irish speaking home'.[75] He was 'building dreams' he stated at the thoughts of the new baby which he believed would be a boy.[76] Despite the arrival of a girl in June 1918 the two were overjoyed although Muriel did suffer issues with breastfeeding.[77] Terence also referred to matters of managing visits from Mary and Annie in the immediate aftermath of the birth of Máire Óg. He stated that the sisters wondered about staying with Muriel on the Douglas Road where she and Terence had established a home. He wondered how she felt about this.[78] In the event Mary and Annie did stay with her until 12 August.[79] Terence also encouraged Muriel to show her mother 'every possible consideration as she loves you very much & all her interest is concern for you'.[80]

On 5 July 1916 Cumann na mBan was declared an illegal organisation by the British government. In her witness statement Peg Duggan is confused and dates this declaration to late November 1916. She stated that in response a special meeting of the Cork Cumann was held. Mary addressed the meeting. Duggan recalled that she 'put it to the members to decide whether we should carry on, in view of the fact that our organisation had now been declared illegal and members would be liable to arrest and imprisonment'. The majority were determined to 'carry on under the name Cumann na mBan, Craobh Corcaigh'. Members made scarves and gloves for prisoners and gathered 'other comforts'. Celidhs were held to raise funds. When republican prisoners were released members of Cork Cumann na mBan arranged reception committees, providing 'meals, accommodation and clothes'.[81] Some accounts from released men detail Mary's kindness. Laurence Garvey, an Irish Volunteer from East Galway, stated that when he was released from Frongoch in August 1916 he had 'no pocket money'. Mary, who he believed was on the same boat back to Ireland, 'treated us to tea and cigarettes in Dublin'.[82]

Mary's strident personality caused tension within the Cork branch of Cumann na mBan resulting in a split in 1917. Simmering tensions reached a critical point over the issue of whether it was acceptable to hold a céili on St Patrick's day, which in 1917 fell on the eve of Passion Sunday. Mary was in favour of holding the fundraising event 'and was very annoyed at her wishes being questioned by others in the organisation'. She demanded a new election of officers which was duly held. Together with Nora O'Brien and Madeline O'Hegarty, she was removed from office. Mary's response was to go directly to Cumann na mBan headquarters in Dublin where she received permission to set up 'a branch of her own', naming the new branch Craobh Poblacht na hÉireann.[83] In 1943 Nora O'Brien would testify that the branch became the biggest outside Dublin comprising between 120 and 140 members, although such figures were disputed by the Brigade Committee.[84]

In mid-1917, as part of the reorganisation of the Irish Volunteers, it was determined that each Volunteer company should have a Cumann na mBan unit attached. The Craobh Corcaigh branch began organisation on these lines in the city and suburbs. Margaret O'Leary was appointed organiser for the city and county.[85] Duggan estimated that branches 'averaged about 50 each in number and, in all, totalled approximately 700'.[86] The Shandon Branch of Cumann na mBan was formed in January 1918 by May Conlon.[87] The typing work in connection with the extension of Cumann na mBan in the city was divided between members. Margaret Lucey notes that she typed during her hours of work in Crosse and Blackwell, jam manufacturers and fruit canners. The work was also carried out in Mary's home.[88] A District Council of Cumann na mBan in Cork city was then formed under instructions from Dublin headquarters. The Council comprised two delegates from each branch who elected a president, secretary, and treasurer. According to Duggan, 'Dublin H. Q. recognised this District Council was the properly constituted authority governing Cumann na mBan affairs in Cork city'.[89] The Craobh Poblacht na hÉireann branch sent two delegates. Duggan rather pointedly recalled that Mary was not one and that neither was she 'of course … an officer of the Council'.[90] However, the minutes of the inaugural meeting of the Cork District Council in the City Hall on 3 February 1918 listed Mary and Nora O'Brien as the two Craobh Poblacht na hÉireann delegates. At that meeting, Mary proposed Madeline O'Hegarty for the position of chairman. In the vote that followed, she lost to Margaret O' Leary.[91] At the meeting on 3 March 1918 the chairman, speaking in Irish, stated that:

> this was a time for practical work for all branches of Cumann na m-ban [sic]. She advised all branches to do practical route marching and arranged for some marches between country branches.
>
> It was also recommended that each member of each branch should supply herself with a first aid outfit.[92]

At the end of 1919 the District Council represented 19 branches, an increase of three from the previous year.[93]

The split in Cumann na mBan in Cork continued to simmer in 1918 and caused tensions within the Irish Volunteers as family loyalties came to the fore. Florence O'Donoghue recalled a 'clash' between MacCurtain and Madeline O' Hegarty's husband, Seán, at a Cork Brigade meeting. O' Donoghue described it as:

> a stupid row precipitated in Cumann na mBan by two groups of jealous women, relatives of almost everyone on the council except myself. I do not remember the details of that row now, nor had I much interest in it at the time, but it was unpleasant and it took several months to patch up.[94]

Mary wrote to MacCurtain berating him for his handling of the dispute:

> The question was bound to affect our men all over Cork county and perhaps split us in two. As far as the two Branches of Cumann na mBan are concerned they don't seem to care what happens so long as they can continue to fight out this dispute irrespective of what harm they may do to the fine spirit of comradeship which always existed between the Volunteers. The position is certainly deplorable and is undoubtedly affecting in a small way the work of the Volunteers. ... Perhaps you will say why should it effect the men? Whenever or wherever a split occurs in a National organisation, it is bound to effect everybody working in the same grooves. If it only affected or tended to affect Cumann na mBan you may feel assured I wouldn't interfere ...Your action in refusing to discuss the matter with us is perfectly inexcusable and to it may be traced the subsequent regrettable developments.[95]

There was resentment at Mary's domineering and confrontational manner. The Cumann na mBan executive in Dublin dispatched Áine Ceannt to the city on 15 September 'for the purpose of settling the Cork dispute'; a special meeting was convened.[96] In November the delegates from the Shandon Branch reported that 'their work in connection with the election was interfered with by the P. na hÉireann Branch'. It was decided to send a letter to the Blarney Street Sinn Féin club 'pointing out to them that the District Council had allocated the district covered by this S. F. club to the Shandon Branch of C. na mb'.[97] In early December 1918 de Róiste described the 'friction' between the two sections as 'vindictive': 'one led by Miss MacS ... and by Mrs. Seán O'H. The other is the more popular section and contains most of the ordinary workers of C.na mb'.[98] In January 1919 six members of Cumann na mBan in Cork, including O' Leary, were suspended by the executive for fomenting conflict within the organisation.[99] The six women took a case before the Dáil courts in 1920 against Mary, Markievicz and Jennie Wyse Power, charging them with 'slander and victimisation' and demanding 'restitution'.[100]

Despite local friction, Mary, as a member of the executive, represented Cork Cumann na mBan.[101] In this capacity she attended, together with Madeline O'Hegarty, the national assembly on 19 April 1917 convened by Count George Noble Plunkett, father of Joseph Mary Plunkett executed as one of the 1916 leaders.[102] In 1917 the separatist movement was reorganised; the North Roscommon by-election of February 1917 facilitated this development, despite the differences between 'the groups and individuals' who campaigned and voted for Plunkett.[103] However, as Laffan states, all 'parties and individuals shared the ideal of creating a united and widely based party which would coincide with the unorganized "Sinn Féin" or separatist movement and all were anxious to end the multiplicity of factions which had characterised separatism before the Easter Rising'.[104] Plunkett's circular calling for a national assembly was ignored for the most part by the Redmondite-dominated local government boards; at a meeting of the Cashel Rural District Council, the 'manifesto was thrown aside'.[105] However, the assembly was attended by Sinn Féin clubs, 11 trade boards, divisions of the Ancient Order of Hibernians and delegates from literary and labour clubs. Nineteen branches of Cumann na mBan were represented.[106] Members of the clergy were also invited.[107] Plunkett conceived the April conference as a forum to initiate a national policy.[108] Laffan states the convention 'came close to splitting the separatist movement in two'.[109] At the convention Plunkett launched the Liberty League, a body intended to oppose the Irish Parliamentary Party. The League would, however, 'duplicate the work done by Griffith's Sinn Féin, and it would either replace his party or else challenge it for the political leadership of radical nationalists'.[110] To avoid an outright split, it was decided that all separatist organisations would maintain their different identities but work together through, what Laffan describes as, an 'organising committee'. This committee would 'represent the two rival factions': Arthur Griffith and Count Plunkett.[111]

A branch of Sinn Féin had been re-established in Cork on 3 December 1916 and following the convention there was a marked increase in membership.[112] *Irish Nationality* stated that every ward in Cork city had a branch with all reporting growing membership figures.[113] Sinn Féin, Laffan writes, 'was the fad or the craze of 1917'.[114] Contrary to this trend, Mary aligned with Plunkett. During her speech on the Anglo-Irish Treaty on 21 December 1921 she stated defiantly that she, and all 'belonging to me ... absolutely refused to join Sinn Féin until Sinn Féin became Republican'.[115] De Valera wrote from Lewes prison rejecting the idea that separatists should contest the South Longford by election in 1917. He noted that aspects of Sinn Féin's 'old ... political policy' had the effect of alienating individuals.[116] Mary and her family were amongst such people. Griffith's promotion of the concept of dual monarchy was the antithesis of their concept of how the national question should be resolved. Even before Terence's death in 1920, Mary refused to countenance any compromise on the republican ideal. Annie wrote that in the period before 1916 Alice Cashel took issue with Mary for her willingness to join a suffrage society but not Sinn Féin. Mary in response pointed out:

> the Womens' Suffrage League [sic] was an international organisation to assert woman's [sic] right to vote – whereas Sinn Fein [sic] was an Irish political organisation for the Restoration of Grattan's Parliament – King, Lords and Commons of Ireland, a position she would never accept, as she would never recognise the right of the overlordship of the King of England in Ireland. For that reason she would never join Sinn Fein.[117]

On 26 May 1917 Plunkett requested that Mary attend a meeting to establish branches of the Liberty League in Cork city and county.[118] Laffan notes that Plunkett's 'genuine distaste for any sort of compromise with Britain' made him 'the temporary spokesman of the radical republicans'. He states that bonds were forged during the Roscommon by-election campaign between Plunkett, Father Michael O'Flanagan and J. J. Kelly, 'who over the next two decades would come to represent irreconcilable, fundamentalist republicanism'.[119] To that triumvirate the name of Mary MacSwiney must be added. However, Fallon's statement that Mary responded with 'enthusiasm' to Plunkett's invitation should be more nuanced.[120] She replied to Plunkett that she 'need hardly say what pleasure it will give me to attend any meeting called by you', but she informed him that an 'independent Ireland must be sought – in Cork anyhow – in the ranks of the Volunteers and Cumann na mBan'. She stated that unless the executive of the Liberty League was 'composed mainly of them and controlled by them it cannot succeed'.[121] She wrote, she declared, 'to warn' him, asking that he treat her communication as 'confidential'. Throughout the letter, for the length of which she apologised, Mary berated Plunkett, insisting that he should attend a meeting in Cork on 3 June to demand 'Prisoners of War treatment for the men in Lewes and in respect of the imprisonment of Markievicz':

> We think this matter very urgent and do not feel that it ought to be placed only as a secondary resolution after the magnificent meeting called by Cumann na mBan in Dublin for that purpose specially.[122]

At that public meeting held in the City Hall a resolution was passed calling on 'foreign powers' to note the treatment of Irish prisoners in English convict prisons with reference to the case of Countess Markievicz.[123] The latter was in Aylesbury Prison having been transferred from Mountjoy in August 1916. Markieviciz felt her isolation from her revolutionary colleagues and repeatedly denounced the fact that she was held with star-class convict women who were, she alleged, dissolute and immoral.[124] At the Cork public meeting, Mary stated that it was their intention to send the resolution to the Pope, to President Wilson and Kerensky of Russia.[125] She stated, in the words of the *Cork Examiner* editorial that the Irish had to 'help themselves by making English misgovernment of the country impossible'.[126] On Markeviciz's release eight days later, the paper repeated the claim that she had been forced to associate with 'characters of the vilest class, including, according to her own statement a baby murderer'.[127]

Mary's focus on prisoner support and the need for the Irish Volunteers and Cumann na mBan to control any emerging political party indicates that her priorities lay on the military side of republicanism in the period after 1916. Laffan notes that when the Sinn Féin Convention in October 1917 'ratified and consolidated the new united party which had developed during the previous six months', the Irish Volunteers and Cumann na mBan 'embodied the military wing'.[128] At a meeting of the Volunteers in Cork on 4 January 1917 Terence and MacCurtain spoke, de Róiste noting that the 'attitude towards Sinn Féin was entirely friendly'. However, 'it was explained' that those who had high ranking positions in the Volunteers in the city' had 'enough to do to carry out their duties efficiently and so are unable to devote time to the Sinn Féin organisation'. De Róiste was critical:

> It seems to me, however, that 'military work', in the minds of some, is regarded as much more important than political work and that this is the real cause of partial withdrawal from Sinn Féin.[129]

Terence, of course, can be described as an intellectual republican rather than a soldier; the issue for the MacSwiney family was full commitment to a republican solution to the Irish national question.[130] At the Sinn Féin Ard Fheis in October the party committed itself to securing a republic. De Valera emphatically declared 'we want an Irish Republic', although it was agreed that at a later point 'the people could choose between a monarchy and a republic'.[131]

It was only from this point in October 1917 that Mary, Terence, and other members of the family entered the political arena and embraced Sinn Féin. The fortunes of this newly reconstituted party were to be advanced six months later when the British government attempted to subject Ireland to conscription.

Conscription was introduced for England, Scotland and Wales in January 1916. It was considered expedient not to extend compulsory military service to Ireland at that point; the political environment in the country was considered too volatile. As de Róiste noted in his diary: 'even English newspapers recognise a national distinctiveness between the two countries. The matter of conscription emphasises the distinction'.[132] On 12 January 1916 a public meeting was held in the City Hall in Cork 'to protest Cork Employers applying economic Conscription to their employees'. Women from Cumann na mBan sold flags in the vestibule 'on which the words "We won't have Conscription" were printed'.[133] De Róiste contended that the presence of armed Volunteers and 'the national sentiment of the people' were the reasons why the Military Service Act, 1916, excluded Ireland.[134] By 1918 such 'national sentiment' was even more potent; Sinn Féin, representing the separatist ideal, increasingly held the support of most Irish nationalists.

The surrender of the Bolshevik army in December 1917 enabled the German Ludendorff offensive on the Western Front in the Spring of 1918, forcing the British to reconsider the issue of conscription for Ireland. A serious manpower shortage in the armed forces placed attention squarely on the latter country. As the age of exemption was raised from 48 to 51, there were those who argued that 'Irishmen's immunity' was 'glaring and unjust'.[135] The Military Service Act extending conscription to Ireland became law on 18 April 1918. On that day a meeting was held in the Mansion House. Called by the Lord Mayor of Dublin, Laurence O'Neill, it was attended by members of Sinn Féin, the Irish Parliamentary Party and the Labour Party, *inter alia*. A resistance policy was formulated. On the same day a meeting of the Catholic hierarchy in Maynooth discussed the matter. These meetings, Townshend writes, 'signalled an unprecedented fusion of Irish national opinion'. This was augmented by the withdrawal of the Irish Party from Westminster.[136] On 21 April people across Ireland signed the anti-conscription pledge. The previous day, the Irish Trades Union Congress and the Labour Party called a general strike for 24 April.[137]

Across Cork there was immediate denunciation of the Military Service Act; many prominent public servants resigned or offered their resignation, including the City High Sheriff and the Cork Crown Prosecutor. With four unionist exceptions, all members of Cork public bodies repudiated the imposition of conscription.[138] On 15 April 'an impromptu public demonstration' in Cork city saw thousands march to the National Monument.[139] Mary was once again central to republican campaigns as they developed, emerging to the fore of the anti-conscription campaign in Cork. This was not opportunistic but reflected her holistic republican vision. Her opposition to enforced military service predated 1918. In June 1916 she declared: 'One thing is certain. Recruiting for the B. Army is dead in Ireland. I doubt it they have got a half a dozen in the whole country since Easter.'[140] Enlistment to the British Army in Cork, already declining before the rebellion, was dramatically reduced after Easter 1916. On a national level, recruitment was in sharp decline in 1917.[141] In her letter to her brother Peter in the immediate aftermath of the rising, she noted that Lloyd George wanted to extend conscription to Ireland and that Redmond 'would gladly give it if he dares' in exchange for Home Rule even at the cost of the exclusion of six Ulster counties.[142]

On 11 April 1918 the Executive of Cumann na mBan issued a resolution. As the 'largest women's society in Ireland', they protested on behalf of Irish women 'against any attempt to impose conscription on Ireland'. As an executive member, Mary was fully behind such a statement. Branches were instructed to 'use every means in their power to prevent such a measure becoming operative'.[143] Mary travelled to various parts of the county to administer the women's pledge, addressing, for example a meeting in Castletownbere, Co. Cork.[144] According to Malcolm Bickle, the newly arrived English pension officer in town, she declared that 'the police were worms – no decent girl would walk on the same side of the road as one of "em"'.[145] Townshend discusses how the process of alienating the police from local communities that had begun in 1917 was 'decisively accelerated by the conscription crisis'.[146]

On 23 April 1918 many Cork businesses shut their doors in support of the national protest. This development was organised by the Cork Districts Trade and Labour Council. The *Cork Examiner* announced that there would be no bread deliveries in the city that day.[147] On that evening there was a demonstration of up to 30,000 people, the 'largest protest in city history'.[148] Cumann na mBan collected anti-conscription pledges in the afternoon.[149] This was a role that Cork Cumann mBan fulfilled throughout the conscription crisis. Margaret Lucey noted that the women:

> were allotted the task of taking charge of registers in which the citizens of Cork recorded their names as protesting against the imposition of the Act. Various halls in Cork city were used for this purpose in which our members worked long hours in connection with these registers.[150]

At four o'clock that same day, a meeting of Cork women against conscription was held in the City Hall.[151] The *Cork Examiner* noted that the hall, galleries, passages and platform were 'thronged'. As a result, some of the speakers convened a 'second meeting' in the vestibule. Mary was one the of speakers at the 'overflow' meeting'.[152] The previous January, the US President, Woodrow Wilson had issued the 'fourteen points' which were to form the basis of the post-war world order. As Townshend writes their 'most resonant concept was national self-determination'.[153] Both the Cork Lady Mayoress, Helen Butterfield, and Mary referred to the idea of self-determination at the women's meeting on 23 April. The former decried the 'mockery' of Britain fighting a war 'for the benefit of small nationalities and for the liberty of all the people in the world and then they impose compulsory military service on Ireland'. Mary sounded a note of warning: the 'question of Ireland would come before the Peace Conference and England was terrified'. It was for that reason, she asserted, that England was so anxious to settle the issue of Home Rule.[154] She stated that only an Irish Parliament had the right to decide whether the people were to be conscripted. She denounced the idea of Home Rule as a solution to the Irish national question. They had, she glibly stated, been hearing about it for thirty years; it was 'Home Rule with England the top dog'.[155]

Despite the unity of purpose against conscription, tensions in Cork Cumann na mBan continued to simmer. On 28 April a 'further public meeting of women' was held in the City Hall, again under the auspices of the Cork Districts Trade and Labour Council. The two 'feuding wings of Cumann na mBan were represented by Mary and Margaret O'Leary'.[156] Mary proposed a resolution 'against the threatened industrial conscription of women'.[157] On 9 June 1918 Lá na mBan saw women from Cumann na mBan, the Irish Women Workers Union and other female activist organisations register their opposition to conscription, the imposition of which they described as 'tyranny'. Members of the different organisations pledged that they would not 'fill the places of men deprived of their work through refusing enforced military service'. They undertook to 'do all in their power to help the families of men' who were victimised for standing against conscription.[158] Local circumstances saw women in other areas of the country hold their own Lá na mBan after 9 June.[159] On 3 July 1918 Cumann na mBan, the Irish Volunteers, Sinn Féin and the Gaelic League were proscribed. A public assembly ban was also implemented. According to Lil Conlon a Lá na mBan demonstration planned for Cork on 7 July had to be cancelled following the proclamation against all republican organisations. However, Cork women were on duty outside churches and 'provided tables and chairs to assist the signing of the Pledge by all Women'.[160]

The co-ordinated opposition within Ireland to conscription forced the British government to shelve the Military Service Act, 1918, but 'they decided to take action against those groups which they blamed for their humiliation'.[161] They also made clear that conscription was still a possibility.[162] On the night of 17–18 May arrests of prominent members of Sinn Féin were carried out with further members deported under the Defence of the Realm Act in the days that followed.[163] A proclamation issued by the Lord Lieutenant Viscount French stated that Sinn Féin leaders had been engaged in treasonous communication with Germany. Mary travelled to Dublin to attend a protest meeting in the Mansion House under the auspices of Cumann na mBan on 27 September and made a speech in support of the Sinn Féin prisoners.[164] Yet again the political resonated on a personal level for her. Terence was in jail in Belfast at the time of the 'German plot' arrests. On his release in September, he was, however, promptly re-arrested and sent to Lincoln Gaol.[165] From jail he was nominated as a Sinn Féin candidate for the mid-Cork constituency.

Mary was also concerned for her brother Seán, who was arrested in 1918 for refusal to enlist in the British Army. He would not agree to fight for other small nations while Ireland was unfree.[166] He was sentenced to two years hard labour in Kingston penitentiary in Canada.[167] Peter MacSwiney visited him during the 1918 Christmas period and reported:

> He was subjected to very brutal treatment some time ago because he would not put on the English uniform and fight for the Freedom of every small Nation in the world except his own.[168]

P. H. O' Meara who had previously been imprisoned with Seán wrote to Peter that his brother was 'roughly handled'.[169] He was also 'inoculated forcibly'.[170] Peter had to inform Mary that her letters did not reach Seán in prison as there was 'too much politics in them'.[171] As she did every time Terence was arrested, Mary conducted a letter writing campaign to secure information about Seán.[172] Released by March 1919, Seán wrote that he had received the box of shamrocks sent to him by Mary and Annie for St Patrick's Day.[173] Peter, based in New York, received a similar gift of shamrocks; the family unit in evidence even when members were separated.[174] Seán stated that they would 'certainly have a great talk-fest when he returned home'.[175]

The Representation of the People Act, 1918, extended the vote to women over the age of 30 with certain qualifications. A woman had to be a graduate or be a householder, the wife of a householder, or hold property, not being a dwelling house, worth £5 per annum. Mary was a graduate, a householder, and a woman over the age of 30. Her brother Peter wrote from New York after the election that he was 'very glad' that she was able 'to record your vote'.[176] On 11 December a meeting 'by women, for women, concerning women' was held at the Grand Parade in support of the candidates.[177] Addressing the meeting Mary referenced her long-time support for women's suffrage but crucially this was linked to her desire to establish an Irish Republic. The *Cork Examiner* report of her speech noted that she: 'could not say how proud and happy she felt that the power of voting was theirs for the first time, to vote for an Irish Republic.'[178] Rosamond Jacob believed that Irish suffragists should be working to get female candidates selected.[179] By contrast, Mary's focus was on using the female vote to secure full independence; the gender of the Sinn Féin candidates was immaterial, what mattered was winning seats. Margaret Ward discusses how the feminist movement 'continued to be marginalised' in this context of the selection of candidates to stand in the 1918 election.[180] Despite her initial apparently feminist statement, Mary moved to draw on her brother's gendered ideas on the role of women in revolutionary times. In 'Womanhood' Terence discussed how Wolfe Tone's wife did not hold him back with 'clinging arms'.[181] Mary similarly: 'asked the women to lift up their hearts and be brave – help the men: do as Wolfe Tone's wife did when she said: "Think not of me and of the children".'[182]

Yet despite such gendered language, Mary was visible on the streets of Cork in the lead up to the election as she actively canvassed for Sinn Féin. By invitation she visited the mid-Cork constituency for which her brother stood unopposed.[183] She supported the two city Sinn Féin candidates, J. J. Walsh and Liam de Róiste, who faced unionist and Irish Parliamentary Party opposition. Annie testified to a 'vibrant' republican life in Cork in the period before the election. She recalled 'glowing faces, eyes alight with pride and victory, marching cheering crowds'. The 'flame of enthusiasm that lit the land', she wrote, 'cannot be exaggerated'.[184] Every quarter of Cork city had its republican election centre where printing presses turned out propaganda leaflets for Sinn Féin to be despatched to every voter. Mary, her sister recalled, 'was immersed in work with her great gift for organisation. She bent to the task with the keenest zeal.[185]

As early as March 1918 the Cork District Council of Cumann na mBan placed attention on 'organising the women's vote on the register'. In May the chairman 'urged necessity for getting every Republican vote available on the register'. All branches were to work with their local Sinn Féin clubs to prepare lists.[186] On 1 December, at a meeting at which Mary was not present, the names of Cumann na mBan officers in charge of polling stations were submitted and approved by the District Council. A discussion followed about the work on polling day and 'stress was laid on the advisability of providing C. na mb help to enable women to absent themselves from their homes to record their vote'. The help took the form of looking after children.[187] The Shandon branch also gave the names of typists who would give service during the election if required.[188] On the day of the election over 100 Volunteers entered the city. Women from Cumann na mBan provided meals to them, while food was also brought around to the 'Peace Patrols and the polling booths by car'.[189] Terence's win saw him gain one of the 73 party seats in the landslide victory that decimated the Irish Parliamentary Party.[190]

Terence and Muriel established a home at 5 Eldred Terrace on the Douglas Road in 1917. Under constant threat of arrest, his home was the first place the authorities looked for him. Mary's home and school was also a target for potential raids and attacks due to her own increasingly prominent position within Cork's republican politics. St Ita's was situated near three RIC barracks.[191] The area around the school, which was close to the city centre, was also subject to raids by both sides. Michael Murphy testified to a raid on a grammar school on Wellington Road, a few minutes' walk from Belgrave Square, in September 1917. There was a military cadet corps in the school and rifles were stored there.[192]

Through all disruption and political concerns, family life and work life continued, all taking place in 1918–19 against the backdrop of the Spanish flu pandemic. In January 1919 Mary wrote to Terence in Lincoln jail. She had a bad cold and worried that she was getting the flu. She was due to go to Dublin, but Annie went in her place. This brought its own issues: the 'double duty in school for the past two days did not tend to improve my head but it could not be helped'.[193] On 17 February the *Cork Examiner* reported that the flu had again 'made its appearance in Cork, and within the past week developed with a rapidity and to an extent that is somewhat disconcerting'.[194] In late February St Ita's was forced to close for three weeks as the flu pandemic worsened, Mary noting that a similar order was given to theatres and to the Free Library amongst other bodies.[195] On his release from jail in Canada in March 1919 Seán wrote that he was glad all his family 'escaped the flu', noting that Cork was 'particularly unfortunate with three visitations'.[196] He noted the prevalence of the virus in the Canadian prison camps in which he was held.[197] Muriel, however, testified that she came down with the virus in March 1919.[198]

An unsanctioned ambush of RIC men at Soloheadbeg, Co. Tipperary is considered in hindsight as the first shots in the War of Independence. This occurred on 21 January 1919, the same day as Dáil Éireann met for the first time in the Mansion House in Dublin. While the Soloheadbeg ambush did not 'signal the beginnings of outright hostilities', when these did commence the country was engulfed with violence.[199] The British government introduced new troops in a bid to counter the guerilla warfare waged by the IRA. From January 1920 the Black and Tans and the mobile auxiliary unit were recruited to augment the RIC. Speaking of the War of Independence in Cork Annie wrote: '[a]rrest, imprisonments and shootings were the order of the day, with increasing tension on both sides.'[200] Peter Hart wrote of Cork after the 1916 rising and throughout the War of Independence:

> The political arena was transformed into a nightmare world of anonymous killers and victims, of disappearances, massacres, midnight executions, bullets in the back of the head, bodies dumped in fields or ditches.[201]

In the period 1917–23 Cork was 'by far the most violent county of Ireland'.[202] Citizens of the city, Borgonovo states:

> grew accustomed to street ambushes, prison escapes, shootings of suspected prison informers, executions of IRA prisoners, and arson and assassination reprisals carried out by Crown forces.[203]

De Róiste wrote of raids across the city on 11 May 1919 stating that police and soldiers 'routed people out of bed, locked them into one room while searching other rooms, showed no respect for age or sex'.[204] He continued to record instances of raiding and violence as 1919 progressed into 1920.[205] All police leave in Cork during Christmas 1919 was stopped.[206] On 17 March, Professor Stockley, University College, Cork, was shot at midnight as he travelled from the Metropole Hotel to his home in Tivoli.[207] The next day 'arrests and raids for arrests' continued across the city. 'Surely, surely', de Róiste confided to his diary, 'this condition of affairs cannot continue'.[208] Stockley was a close friend of the MacSwiney family. His 'miraculous escape' as he was shot directly with a bullet from a revolver must have been a source of immense relief. This was, however, a short-lived respite as tragedy struck in a dreadful and high-profile manner three days later.

On 20 March 1920 the Lord Mayor of Cork, Tomás MacCurtain, was murdered in his home at Thomas Davis Street by members of the Royal Irish Constabulary. That night Terence was sleeping in Belgrave Place; Muriel, being unwell, was staying at her mother's home. When news of the murder was brought to him in the early hours of the morning he came, Annie wrote, 'immediately to both of us'.[209] The relationship between Terence and MacCurtain was political but was also one of friendship. Terence was godfather to Tomás Óg MacCurtain.[210] Mary and Annie awoke to find Terence standing by their bedroom door 'looking strained and stunned'. He determined to go to the MacCurtain home; Mary's immediate response was '[w]e'll follow' while she voiced her sympathy for MacCurtain's wife and children.[211] Mary and Annie listened as Annie Walshe, MacCurtain's sister-in-law, recounted the details of the murder:

> the demon faces – the shots – the screaming children awakened from their sleep by the shots and cries. She made us spectators as she spoke. And as she ceased, we felt again the great silence that clamoured to be heard – what could speech say?[212]

The inquest of MacCurtain handed down a verdict of murder in April 1920. District Inspector Swanzy who had complained of the presence of Mary on the staff of St Angela's College was one of the RIC officers named. The jury stated that the murder was 'organised by the R.I.C.'[213] The ramifications of this verdict was far-reaching. After the murder of MacCurtain, Swanzy had been transferred to Lisburn. On 22 August he was killed in an IRA reprisal. Swanzy's murder in turn resulted in a violent loyalist counter reprisal. Looting and arson was carried out against the minority Catholic population in Lisburn, forcing many to flee to Belfast, Newry and Dundalk.[214]

In Cork, Terence assumed MacCurtain's position of Commandant of the No. 1 Brigade. Days after the murder he was elected Lord Mayor. On the day he assumed his new position, Mary attended a public meeting in the City Hall to inaugurate a memorial fund for MacCurtain's widow and children.[215] This memorial, as Collins wrote to Terence, was a political statement as much as an act of personal solidarity with the MacCurtain family. Every subscriber gave 'proof that he or she knows that the late Lord Mayor of Cork died for Ireland, and signifies belief that he was murdered by the agents of England'.[216]

Annie recalled that life in Cork became increasingly tense after the murder of MacCurtain; 'raids and arrests were on the increase – murder was in the air'. Across the island, everyday brought 'its own tale of outrages'.[217] Rumours abounded. Hundreds of extra police were drafted into the city. Raids on shops and other premises were conducted.[218] De Róiste wrote that Terence viewed the position of Lord Mayor as a '"gap of danger" and to be in such a position gives him pleasure'.[219] As Foster states, for Terence 'the notion of a righteous war of liberation was a desiderium from early youth'.[220] Indeed, on 17 May a man approached de Róiste to say that 'it was overheard at a funeral in a country place not far from the city that Terry MacS is in danger of being shot by the police'.[221] Terence, and other prominent republicans in the city, 'moved in groups. They acted as a sort of bodyguard to one another'. Annie remembered seeing her brother from the top of a tram as he walked alone on the Western Road. A 'throb of fear surged' through her; Mary was also clearly troubled when she was told.[222]

For some time after he assumed office, Terence spent many nights in safe houses across the city although he always attempted to come for breakfast to Belgrave Place on Sundays. However, one night he realised that the occupiers of one such alleged safe house had no idea who he was and merely assumed he was 'hard up for a bed'. He was angry at the 'disaster that might have come on their home' and determined to sleep in the home of his sisters going forward.[223]. Annie recalled that he declared: 'My own home is ready to face whatever's coming'.[224] She witnessed him draw his revolver twice in St Ita's when he 'thought the British were at the door'.[225] Peter Hart has discussed the exhaustion and difficulties experienced by republican men on the run in Cork after 1916. He quotes Liam Deasy who remembered that it was a life that 'was considered very difficult and trying by many of my comrades'.[226] The impact on wider family members of the men on the run also needs to be considered. The guerilla nature of the War of Independence meant that the domestic space of the home had the potential to become a battleground. The Military Service Pensions Collection includes many accounts by women of the violation of the home by British soldiers and the Black and Tans.[227] When Eilís MacCurtain opened the front door of her home on the morning of 20 March 1920 she was forcibly detained downstairs while her husband was murdered in his bedroom. Shoved against the door, she heard the shots that killed her husband and on leaving, the murderers pushed her out onto the street.[228] Notably, when Terence referred to sleeping at home, he was not referring to the home he shared with Muriel. Annie wrote: 'Naturally Máire and I agreed with him, but, naturally too, we dreaded the night, and all future nights more now.'[229] 'We felt so helpless', Annie wrote, 'in the event of an attack.'[230]

The anxiety experienced within the MacSwiney family must have been heightened by Terence's need to prove the commitment of the Cork Volunteers after the events of Easter week. Muriel recalled that during 1917 he went to Dublin once a month attending meetings of the Gaelic League Coiste Gnótha. He also attended what she referred to as private meetings of the Irish Volunteers. Muriel claimed that Terence brought munitions back to Cork from Dublin monthly in this period, making the War of Independence in the south of the country 'possible, unlike the '16 Rising when they had nothing'.[231] Annie wrote that a constant refrain for Terence was: 'Dublin won the first battle; Cork will win the second'.[232] He was frustrated, as MacCurtain had been, with the limited pace of IRA activity in the county. The two men had suggested to GHQ a plan to stage multiple risings around Ireland but had been vetoed.[233] Terence engaged in actions that brought him, and by extension, his family into conflict with the military.

The day after the first attempt on the King Street Barracks in Cork city on the 30 June 1920,[234] a policeman came to Belgrave Place. Mary was informed that any further attack on the barracks would result in the military seizure of St Ita's. Professor Stockley received a similar notification that his home would be seized in respect of the attack on the barracks on the Lower Road.[235] A third visit was paid to a man who lived with his family in the working-class suburb of Blackpool. He was ordered to leave his home immediately. Terence was furious at the different treatment meted out to the latter believing that he had been targeted more severely because direct attack on St Ita's or on the residence of Professor Stockley would 'create too much sensation'.[236] Yet, the incident also shows the constant threat Mary lived under in this period. De Róiste received a comparable warning that if the barracks in the process of vacation near to him was destroyed his house would be commandeered by the military within 24 hours. He believed that this threat had greater ramifications for him as he owned his home while Mary rented hers. He believed that the destruction of barracks by the Irish Volunteers was 'a waste of violence'.[237] While by contrast Mary supported attacks on barracks, that did not make the threat of the seizure of her home and business any less mentally burdensome than that felt by de Róiste. On 11 July 1920 a report in the *Irish Independent* read:

> The police barracks at MacCurtain St, Lower Road, and St Luke's, Cork, which had just been vacated, were set on fire simultaneously yesterday morning ...Threats were made last week by the police that if the two other buildings were destroyed the residences of Professor Stockley and Miss M'Swiney would be commandeered.[238]

On 18 July there was further violence centred on the King Street Barracks and surrounding areas resulting in causalities.[239] Belgrave Place was just off Wellington Road so almost parallel to King Street, meaning that Mary's residence was within the epicentre of the furore; within striking distance of the 'armoured cars [that] dashed through the streets, shots being fired at intervals'.[240] According to Annie, that night the MacSwiney's home was surrounded by 20 armed republicans. As the threat to take over St Ita's had been 'emphatic', it was decided to 'resist'. While the house was subjected to raids no attempt was made to take possession of it.[241] However, the violence of 18 July was not precipitated by the Irish Volunteers but, according to de Róiste, was an internecine dispute between soldiers and ex-servicemen, so this resistance to the potential seizure of Mary's home may have occurred earlier in the month.[242]

Before one of the attacks on the barracks Mary tried to convince Terence to attend a piano recital at the home of Professor Stockley. He was clearly anxious to know what time his sisters would be returning home from the event as the strike was planned for that evening. To prevent the Stockleys' guests walking into the explosion he was forced to confide in his sisters that there would be 'trouble' and request that they delay their leaving until after seven thirty. Concern for her brother, however, meant that Mary could not sit at the recital and slipped away, feeling that 'it necessary to be home within reach'.[243]

During the War of Independence Mary became increasingly cognisant of the importance of propaganda. She was present on the platform at the public meeting in Cork when the American Commission on Irish Independence delegation came to the city as part of their ten-day tour of Ireland in April and May 1919.[244] The purpose of the visit was to facilitate the safe travel of Sinn Féin leaders attending the Paris Peace Conference to present their case for Irish self-determination. A special meeting of the Cork District Council was held in May in response to the call on Cumann na mBan by the Sinn Féin Executive to help 'towards making the reception of the delegates a success'.[245] Mary was conscious of the necessity of effectively presenting Ireland's case for independence to an American audience. Madge Lucey testified that during the War of Independence, she did the necessary typing in respect of the propaganda aimed at the American press 'handled' by Mary.[246]

For Mary the landslide election of Sinn Féin in 1918 and the establishment of the first Dáil Éireann on 21 January 1919 would come to represent the high mark of republicanism.

She would return during the Treaty debates to the principles of the first Dáil. In early 1920, however, she believed that the future trajectory of full republican independence was achievable. Others felt similarly. When the hunger striking men in Mountjoy were released on 14 April 1920 de Róiste declared: 'The forces that won yesterday can win the complete victory … A united people, urged by the three great forces of religion, nationality and democracy, can achieve the final victory.'[247]

The death on hunger strike of her closest brother in October 1920 would fundamentally change the nature of Mary 's republican activism. While her role as member of Cumann na mBan in Cork and her crusading work in the area of prisoner support up to this point was an important link in the republican chain, it was peripheral relative to the activism of those within the Dáil and in the upper echelons of the IRA. By 1921, however, she was increasingly located within the nexus of republicanism at the level of influence and even, up to 1923, if not 1925, within the circles of decision-making. After October 1920 when Terence died for the 'Declaration of Independence of January 1919', life would never be the same for the remaining MacSwiney siblings.[248] As discussed in the following chapter, it is essential to recognise the trauma of what Mary suffered, as she witnessed her beloved brother die an agonising death, to fully comprehend her political and personal choices from 1921 onwards.

Chapter Four

1920: Trauma and the Brixton Hunger Strike, 1920

All death, for the most part, produces varying degrees of distress for those left behind. A sudden death is conceptualised by many in the context of what Joan Didion describes as 'the ordinary nature of everything preceding the event'.[1] The sentiment expressed by Liam de Róiste about daily affairs in Cork during the War of Independence is apposite: '[s]till, life goes on and men laugh and joke and work.'[2] Mary MacSwiney, like all republican activists, was living prior to her brother's arrest in August 1920 in a situation where 'death and terror and violence surround us'.[3] Terence's death was not sudden but rather a protracted spectacle. Yet it was, paradoxically, an unexpected death as the family believed that he would ultimately be released. The death of her beloved younger brother in a high-profile hunger strike on 25 October 1920 was a watershed moment for Mary; the everyday nature of her life as she carried out her teaching and political activities was viscerally sundered.

In her article on killing in the Irish War of Independence, Anne Dolan states that 'the soldiers' voices have long been the obvious ones'. She 'makes the case instead' for wider 'tales' of 'trauma and victimhood':

> ...for the witnesses who saw and stood by, for those who watched, for those who identified corpses, who went from wives to widows in the space of a few words before a coroner or a military court, for those who witnessed Ireland's kind of war but not as soldiers or combatants or victims or participants in the sense that the history of killing has become accustomed to.[4]

In discussing civilian accounts of violence Dolan is concerned to 'introduce another set of voices, the voices of those who were often the first to set the terms of how violence was understood ... but who went back after the inquests to whatever lives, occupations, households that their testimony gave only fleeting glimpses of'.[5] Mary did not fall 'out of the historical record' as did the individuals that Dolan discusses. She did not return to her life as before her brother's death, but still Dolan's argument is pertinent in considering her experience as a witness of a certain form of violent death during the War of Independence, the death of a brother on hunger strike.

Ian Miller writes that the hunger strikes of the revolutionary period could be 'construed as a form of violence being used by a government who had alternative options available such as recommending early release [or] granting concessions'.[6] The MacSwiney family were, in the words of Donal O'Callaghan, Deputy Lord Mayor of Cork, 'watchers'; over a prolonged period, they bore witness to Terence's excruciating death.[7] Mary experienced vicarious trauma as day by day she watched her brother transform into a skeletal shadow of his former self.[8] It was 'agonising', Annie wrote of Terence's last week, 'to see all the pain and struggle ... to see him helpless in their hands, being subject to such torture'.[9]

Diarmaid Ferriter writes that historians are 'much better placed to do emotion justice' due, *inter alia*, to the opening up of new archival sources and a 'growing interest in the depths of personal history'.[10] Annie's declaration that 'none of us will ever forget the horror of that place [Brixton jail]'[11] is vital in understanding the response of Mary to the Anglo-Irish Treaty, 1921, and in critiquing her political stance from October 1920. Ferriter states that 'personal trauma, both internalised and externalised' is one of the 'underwritten themes' of the Civil War.[12] This chapter considers the trauma experienced by Mary in Brixton jail in 1920. What should animate the historian, Ferriter aptly states, 'is what was felt at the time'.[13] What should also be considered is the enduring legacy of the experience of trauma. Síobhra Aiken notes that trauma 'though possibly disruptive and dissociative, is not always pathological'.[14]

It is necessary to make the case for understanding the emotions experienced by Mary, how she 'made sense' of, and gave meaning to, her brother's death.[15] Orla Muldoon states that the dominant way of thinking about trauma in the western world 'is that traumatised people are a clinical concern and that modern medicine, psychiatry or clinical psychology might be able to provide a "treatment" for affected people'.[16] To a large extent Mary subverted the contemporary gendered understanding of how trauma manifested. The Military Service Pensions Board saw mental breakdown in response as a female illness.[17] Muldoon argues that anger, a functional emotion, can be a response to trauma and in turn may precipitate political action.[18] Mary did not succumb to any form of nervous illness; her response was to bear witness to her brother's death through her own political position on the necessity to gain full republican independence and her anger at any suggestion of compromise.

Terence MacSwiney was 5ft, 9 and a half inches tall and weighed 136 pounds on arrival in Brixton prison; in his coffin his body appeared 'like that of a child of twelve'.[19] Florence O'Donoghue similarly noted in respect of Michael Fitzgerald, who died in the same month on hunger strike in Cork: 'He had been a burly lad: now I could lift his poor body as if it was that of a little child. His face too was childlike...'[20] On Thursday 12 August 1920 Terence left Belgrave Place where he had tea with his sisters at half past five. He then took the six-minute walk across the north and south channels of the River Lee to the City Hall. Violence in Cork was high so Mary must have experienced some anxiety for his welfare when he departed. 9 August, De Róiste wrote, was 'another night of terror: volleys of rifle fire in many districts; bullets entering houses; shops broken into and looted by the English soldiery'.[21] Terence, along with ten other men, was arrested in the City Hall less than two hours after he left Mary's home.[22] He was on the premises to attend a meeting of staff of the Cork No. 1 Brigade. A sitting of the Republican Courts took place in the same hall while a meeting of Institutional Review Board (IRB) officers from another area was also scheduled in the venue.[23] The arrests were described by the *Evening Herald* as a 'sensational military swoop'.[24] At midnight the home of the MacSwiney sisters was raided. Earlier Mary had opened a letter addressed to herself and Terence purporting to be from a member of the Irish Volunteers and discussing the necessity to shoot a policeman named Quinn who was 'causing a great deal of trouble'. She burned it, believing it to be 'manufactured evidence'.[25]

The next day the men were taken 'under a strong escort' to Cork Gaol from the Victoria Cross Military Barracks. There they joined the hunger strike which had begun two days earlier, spearheaded by Michael Fitzgerald, IRA Commandant OC, First Battalion, Cork No. 2 Brigade.[26] The strike was for immediate release. In the light of the decisions of the government in the case of the August hunger strike de Róiste's comments were prescient: 'I doubt that hunger striking will accomplish their release and they will probably be tortured'.[27] On Saturday Mary travelled to the seaside town of Youghal, 30 miles outside the city, to inform Muriel who was on holiday with her daughter. Before she left the city, she saw Terence in Cork Gaol and had her 'first intimation that he was hunger striking'.[28] Mary remained with her niece while Muriel returned to Cork.[29]

On 16 August Terence was tried by court martial at Victoria Barracks, Cork. Mary, in Youghal with Máire Óg, was not present at the trial.[30] He was charged under Regulation 224 of the Defence of the Realm Act with possession of an RIC cipher and under Regulation 27 with possession of two documents 'likely to cause disaffection to His Majesty'.[31] Found guilty, he was given a two-year sentence.[32] The other men who were arrested on 12 August were released due to the British Army failing to understand their status.[33] Michael Murphy recalled 'great amazement' as the British discharged Michael Leahy, O/C 4th Battalion and Dan Donovan, O/C 1st Battalion along with the other men arrested on 12 August.[34] On his sentencing Terence issued a challenge to the court, stating that he had 'decided the terms of my detention'. As he was on hunger strike, he declared that he would be, 'free, alive or dead, within a month'.[35] He made it clear that it would be futile for the government to apply the Prisoners (Temporary Discharge for Ill Health) Act, 1913, as he would only eat if unconditionally released. He declared the proceedings of the Court illegal. Its officials and the wider government would 'shortly have to realise that the Irish Republic exists'.[36]

Following the court martial Terence was detained in the military barracks and not conveyed back to the Cork Gaol as was the usual custom. At half past two in the morning of the 17 August he was transferred to London in line with the government's 'new hard line' policy aimed at repressing IRA violence.[37] This was a policy implemented from mid-1920, including, as Murphy discusses, the attempt by the British government 'to re-establish the credibility of imprisonment as a weapon'. The power of the authorities to keep republicans in prison, 'in tatters, following the release of large numbers of prisoners on hunger strike in English and Irish prisons from early May 1920, needed to be restored'.[38] Continuing his hunger strike, Terence was placed in the prison hospital in Brixton jail. Mary saw her brother briefly before he was transferred to England; he was 'wrapped in a big coat and evidently feeling badly'.[39]

Mary's telegrams to the Governor of Brixton prison and to her brother on 19 August yielded no replies.[40] She was also in communication with Art O'Brien, head of the Irish Self-Determination League of Great Britain.[41] In March of the previous year O'Brien, at the behest of de Valera, had established the League to 'capitalise on the popularity of the Wilsonian concept of "self-determination" in world political and diplomatic discourses'.[42] Mary, of course, already knew O'Brien from her work in prisoner aid. She then sent a telegram to the Home Office, receiving the reply that as her brother was continuing to refuse food, he was beginning to 'show signs of consequent weakness'.[43] On that same day she left for England.

When Mary reached Brixton her brother had passed the seven-day period without food after which, as Miller discusses, emotional changes become evident.[44] Gallagher stated that at the seven-day mark during the hunger strike in Mountjoy in 1920, some of the men were 'almost unconscious'.[45] During the strike in the Gormanstown internment camp in October and November 1923, a number of men were ordered not to strike but to be ready to provide nursing and other care as those that were on strike became weakened. Seán Prendergast's record of the effect of the strike on men as they entered the second week can be used to gauge what Mary witnessed when, following an overnight cross channel journey, she first saw her brother in Brixton:

> … the awful pathos, the cruel drama, the immense tragedy that hunger striking effort manifested. 'A drink please' from the parched lips of one who was growing weaker with the passing of time conveyed a message that meant more than the words implied – the owner was losing his grip on life and moving slowly yet steadily on the ebb tide.[46]

On 20 August, the day of her arrival in Brixton, Mary stated that she 'did not think he could live a week'.[47] On that same day, the *Times* reported that the hunger strikers in Cork 'have fasted since Thursday, August 12, and are now too weak to leave their beds'.[48] Indeed, the *Freeman's Journal* reported that at the time of his court martial, after only four days on hunger strike, Terence was 'accommodated with an armchair' flanked by two soldiers with rifles and 'showed signs of the ordeal he was going through'.[49]

It must also be remembered that Terence had been transported to England on board the British naval destroyer, *Salmon*. This voyage forcibly undertaken while he was on hunger strike may have expedited his decline. Thomas Treacy describes his passage from Belfast in April 1920 when he, together with upwards of 100 men, was transferred to Wormwood Scrubs:

> The sea voyage on hunger-strike was a big ordeal. We were handcuffed in pairs and nearly all, including myself, got seasick. The empty retching under these circumstances was much more racking than ordinary seasickness.[50]

Maurice Crowe, who was transferred to Winchester Jail from Cork in August 1920, around the same time as Terence was transferred to Brixton, stated that the prisoners 'were not given even a drink of water during the voyage'. When they arrived at Pembroke after an 18-hour journey some of the men were so weak that they had to be 'taken on stretchers' to the awaiting train.[51] Fr Dominic noted that Terence had been on hunger strike 'more than 107 hours' when 'he was placed on board a British Government Naval sloop and transported to England'.[52] He arrived in Brixton Prison at 4 am on 18 August.[53] O'Brien referred to the effects of 'the long sea journey' in a memo to Michael Collins, noting also that Terence was 'a man starting with all the disadvantages of a run-down system'.[54] Similarly, W. D. Higson, one of the medical officers attached to Brixton, stated that Terence:

> complained of headaches, weakness and fatigue from the journey. He is not of good physique, is of sallow complexion with an icteric tinge of skin and conjunctivitis. Prisoner states that he suffered from Pleurisy when a youth and also saw a doctor on two occasions for heart trouble.[55]

A Home Office minute stated that on his arrival, the newly-designated Prisoner No. 6794 'appears to be in the early stage of pulmonary phlebitis & is not a fit subject for feeding'.[56] Indeed, when Mary and Annie saw Terence in the Prison Governor's office in Cork Gaol on 14 August the latter recalled:

> He was looking very badly as his health had been in a very poor state, owing to strain & overwork, for some time previous – he had been told by more than one doctor that he would have a big breakdown if he did not take a long rest, & he had planned to take a fortnight off at the first available moment.[57]

On 20 August, the day of Mary's arrival, Higson wrote: 'the prisoner is now showing definite signs of exhaustion from his refusal to take food'.[58] A headline in the *Freeman's Journal* that same day read: 'Mayor Faces Death' and stated that Muriel had received 'a brief letter from her husband asking her to be ready to cross to England on short notice'.[59] The 'shadow of a great tragedy is surely deepening' the paper declared.[60] As Miller notes, '[m]any still believed that death could occur in a matter of days of hunger striking'.[61] By the end of August Terence had developed neuritis in his arms and Mary declared that the 'end may come at any moment'.[62] On 6 September Dr Griffiths expressed his astonishment that Terence's 'body does not seem to waste as one would expect'.[63]

Mary saw her brother twice on 20 August.[64] The *Freeman's Journal* reported that when she first saw him, she could barely comprehend what he was saying, so weak was he. She was obliged to conclude her visit after 15 minutes.[65] His condition was, she declared, 'even worse than I expected'.[66] Fr Dominic recalled that she sent a telegram to her sister-in-law stating that her husband was in 'a grave condition' and that she should 'cross to England without delay'; he accompanied Muriel across the channel that night, Mary meeting them in Paddington station.[67] On that same day, in the company of O'Brien, Mary also called to see the Secretary of State but was instead given an audience with Sir Ernley Blackwell, Legal Assistant and Under Secretary of State at the Home Office.

Mary's response to the distress of seeing her brother so physically debilitated was to turn to action. Murphy states that the 20 August 'was a frantic day when both sides staked out their fatal positions'.[68] The centrality of Mary in this context has been underestimated. Blackwell stated that at the meeting she 'used very violent language against the Government and the Secretary of State', while it is noteworthy that he also stated that 'Mr O'Brien said very little'. Mary, by contrast, trenchantly asked Blackwell 'whether the Government were going to murder the Lord Mayor as they had murdered his predecessor.'[69] Following this meeting Mary wrote to the Home Secretary, Sir Edward Shortt, noting that Blackwell had informed her 'that it is the final decision of the British Government to let my brother … and his comrades die in prison'. Her tone in the letter was assertive and to the point. She requested an interview and stated that before she saw him, she wanted to impress certain matters on him. It was Mary, not Art O'Brien, who laid out Terence's position:

> If you let my brother – or any of his comrades – die in prison, we shall hold you personally responsible for murder. We are not accustomed to bluff. What we say we mean. So if you imagine that any of these men is bluffing and will take food at the end, you are mistaken.[70]

As a woman, Mary's challenges to officialdom was not without precedent. As Ward discusses Hanna Sheehy Skeffington was determined to get justice for the murder of her husband Francis by Captain John Bowen-Colthurst during the 1916 rebellion. She insisted on a full government inquiry. Ward states that she 'wrested a great deal from a government possessing immense powers under wartime conditions'.[71] Both Mary and Sheehy Skeffington had university degrees, they were both used to public speaking and had confidence in challenging politicians.

O'Brien was 'the leading activist in the prosecution of the Irish revolution' in London.[72] As the London envoy of Dáil Éireann, he was seen as the crucial point of mediation as Mary sought to secure the release of her brother and to ensure maximum publicity for his political statement. As Irish envoy he 'co-ordinated activity in relation to intelligence, accounts, international trade, [and] propaganda for Sinn Féin'.[73] It is important to note MacDiarmada's statement that O'Brien saw much more than 'propaganda value in MacSwiney's struggle'; he was genuinely concerned for the man himself and, indeed, his family, as they arrived one by one to London.[74] He opened his home in Ealing to both Mary and Muriel.[75] O'Brien provided regular updates on Terence's deteriorating condition to Michael Collins, while the ISDL issued regular public statements. However, although O'Brien had the political contacts and presence in London, it was Mary who spearheaded the campaign to support Terence and garner maximum publicity with a view to affecting his release.

In the context of the gender roles of the period, Mary's refusal to adopt a supplicatory position in her dealings with prison staff, the medical officers who attended her brother, and government officials such as Blackwell and Shortt, meant that she came across as a difficult woman who did not know her place. Griffiths, a medical officer in Brixton, did note after an interview with her on 18 September that she 'seemed from her general conversation to have a bitterly anti-British bias – and talked of "fools who went to war for freedom"'.[76] Anti-British language was typical of Mary's lexicon but how far she engaged in violent language needs to be interrogated through the lens of gender. According to her sister Annie, she spoke 'warmly of General Childs and others she came in contact with' during her tour of prisons in May 1916. She found Childs 'anxious to facilitate her in every way'. Annie continued: 'Over and over again in our dealings with the British Officers, we have met courtesy and appreciation of our point of view'.[77] After her first meeting with Terence in Brixton on 20 August Mary reported that the warder and the doctor were 'very kind'.[78] She praised Dr Higson. Before the American Commission on Conditions in Ireland she said that she had 'nothing to say but good' of him, although she believed that he should have resigned his position in protest at the 'inhumanity' of the government.[79] However, when she met with hostility and experienced a refusal by government and other officials to engage with her, she spoke her mind; then she was labelled a difficult woman. In his medical report on 23 October Griffiths wrote: 'Miss Mary MacSwiney asked to see me last night and behaved in an extremely unpleasant and disorderly manner in my room'. She was, he wrote, 'troublesome'.[80]

A core element of Mary's campaign to have her brother unconditionally released was to instigate and sustain a propaganda drive. This involved briefing the press while she scoured the papers to ensure that she refuted any negative responses to her brother's protest. She initiated the campaign also with a view to amplifying what Terence himself described as the revulsion against his imprisonment 'throughout the civilised world'.[81] On 17 September the family issued a statement that no further information would be given to the British press as updates were 'distorted from their proper meaning' at the behest of the government.[82] Information continued to be supplied to the foreign press.[83] It was Mary who in late September hired Sir Norman Moore, President of the Royal College of Physicians, to make a public statement 'that my brother was not getting any food in his medicine'.[84] It was she who smuggled out a sample of his medicine in an empty perfume bottle and had it tested in a laboratory to prove that that he was not being secretly fed.[85] Writing on O'Donovan Rossa on the occasion of his death in 1915, Terence dwelt on Rossa's discussion of the manner in which the British government can 'lie like Hell'. Terence wrote that in prison Rossa:

> must have felt ... that not only his body and his life, but his very character itself was at the mercy of unscrupulous enemies. It nerved him to persevere till he at last reached the world. Something got in the press, then came the exposure, the Commission of Inquiry, and revelations.

Mary echoed similar sentiments, on the manner in which the British government resorted to falsehood, in conversation with Dr Griffiths in Brixton. As Terence developed scurvy toward the end, Griffiths attempted to convince Mary that lime juice was not the equivalent of his taking food. She replied angrily: '"You English all tell lies from the Government downwards", and entered into a long tirade on the Government and Englishmen generally'.[86] It was Mary who took the lead in ensuring that the political demands that Terence was striking for 'reached the world', that no 'Master Lie' that he 'yielded at the end' be allowed to circulate at the command of the government.[87]

The media campaign to achieve the release of Terence meant that Mary was directly involved in a combative relationship with leading British politicians. On 25 August the British cabinet discussed Terence's case, most notably the question of his release or otherwise. As Mary noted in a letter of 20 September her brother's 'protest' was 'not against the kind or degree of treatment meted out to him; it is a protest against the act of imprisoning him'.[88] The stakes were consequently raised on both sides. While there were those at the cabinet meeting who noted the public demand for Terence's release, Arthur Balfour argued that to do so would mean 'paralysis of the law'.[89] To release him would 'open the way to any person imprisoned for any similar offense to use the case of the Lord Mayor as a precedent, with good hopes of securing a release and the opportunity to repeat the acts which led to his incarceration'.[90] Balfour reiterated Shortt's assertation that that if Terence's hunger strike resulted in death it would be his 'deliberate choice'.[91] Lloyd George sent a telegram to Mary stating that it was 'impossible' to make any exception in the case of her brother: 'Were they to do so it would break down the administration of law in the United Kingdom for all prisoners would claim the same privilege'.[92]

To describe, as she did, Lloyd George's answer to her telegram of 24 August indicting the British government in the event of Terence's death, as one of 'impertinence' displayed an assertiveness not usual in a woman. She asked for no exception to be made for her brother, she retorted. Her demands for his release were also demands for the similar release of the hunger strikers in Cork.[93] As Murphy discusses, the protests in Cork and Brixton were undertaken in defiance of the IRA policy of hunger strike in pursuit of political prisoner status rather than as a demand for release.[94] In what became increasingly a war of words concerning the fate of Terence, a woman – his sister – took a leading role. While other members of the family, including Muriel and Annie, spoke to the press, it was Mary who orchestrated the campaign. Astutely she noted that by incarcerating her brother in Brixton in the centre of London 'he was in the spot where newspaper reporters of all quarters of the world are'.[95]

Stating her position in her letter to Shortt, Mary made very clear that there was no gender divide within republican families in terms of support for her brother's hunger strike and that of the prisoners in Cork jail:

> I judge you are ... counting that that the mothers and sisters and wives of these men will urge their surrender.
>
> In that you are ... mistaken. We are as true to principle as our men folk, and even if we played the coward they would not listen.[96]

Muriel did, however, provide an alternative and more traditional female response. She was delicate and much less assertive than her sister-in-law, Mary. Terence worried about her even before his 1920 incarceration. In letters to her from Cork Gaol in November 1917 he was 'so anxious' as she was 'not looking well'.[97] He referred to her desire to 'go away into some hole & hide yourself' and noted her depression.[98] In her testimony to the American Commission on Conditions in Ireland in 1920 Muriel noted that she was ill after Terence was released in December 1916. She was also incapacitated at the time of the general election in 1918.[99] In March 1919 Terence was granted a week's parole to see his 'sick wife'.[100] Muriel was again unwell when Tomas MacCurtain was murdered in 1920 and she recalled that due to her illness she had no discussion with her husband when he decided to stand for Lord Mayor.[101] As late as May 1920 de Róiste noted in his diary the 'domestic troubles' experienced by Terence which might have been a reference to Muriel's mental health problems.[102]

During the ordeal of 1920, Muriel was at times more amiable to the suggestion that she encourage her husband to give up his hunger strike. In her Bureau of Military History witness statement, she wrote: 'I naturally tried to save Terry's life'. She 'did not resent' but rather 'understood' the assistant prison doctor who asked her to encourage her husband to take food. Indeed, she wrote to Richard Mulcahy and Cathal Brugha, amongst other high-ranking members of the Irish Volunteers, urging them to 'order' her husband to give up his hunger strike.[103] Her stance was not that of her two sisters-in-law. Neither Mary nor Annie was willing to encourage their brother to end the strike. When the former informed the doctor that her brother's fate was in 'God's hands', Beddard sharply retorted that 'it was not, it was in ours'.[104] In the middle of September Dr Griffiths noted that Muriel stated 'quite definitely' that she would not induce her husband to take food; clearly she prevaricated on the matter, possibly influenced by the stronger willed Mary.[105]

Mary understood that the failure of Cork to respond to the rising in Dublin continued to weigh heavily on Terence's mind. Ernest Blythe recalled how he talked to him about the surrender of arms in Cork during Easter week when both men were imprisoned in Dundalk in 1918. The issue, Blythe wrote, 'preyed' on MacSwiney and it appears he dissembled in his account of what occurred:

> I may say that the account he gave me of the affair, struck me as not being quite candid. It was the only time that I can remember Terence MacSwiney telling me something which I took to be false. ... His remarks to me in Dundalk Gaol came forcibly back to my mind when Annie MacSwiney told me of his last message to Cathal Brugha a day or to before he died on hunger-strike. The message, as far as I remember, ran something like the following: 'Cathal, this blots out the bitterness of Easter Week'.[106]

The issue of the decisions of the Cork Irish Volunteer leadership in 1916 intruded on politics in the city even in the last months of Terence's life. De Róiste recorded his annoyance with Terence over the management of the Dáil loan in Cork. He stated that the latter had sent Michael Collins a letter that amounted to a 'bitter attack and complaint on myself'. Attempting to explain Terence's animosity he wondered if it was partly rooted in 'my attitude over his word and actions in 1916'.[107] Annie wrote: '[a]lways the thought was with him: "Dublin won the first battle; Cork will win the second".'[108] He adhered to the ideal of a second rising, although as Hart states he had 'little contact with the gunmen and never participated in any operations; he thought of violence in romantic terms, as gesture and self-sacrifice'.[109] Mary recognised that Terence's hunger strike in 1920 was part of the continuum of his politics since 1916. When news of Michael Fitzgerald's death in Cork was brought to Terence he was 'very sad ... He would have wished to be the first & hoped he could save the lives of the others'.[110] Mary was clear, however that she could not encourage Terence to come off the strike on the basis also of her own political beliefs. She informed the reporter from the *Daily Express* in early September:

> 'The prison doctor has asked me if something could not be done for him,' said Miss McSwiney [sic] yesterday. 'I said that it was impossible to ask my brother to surrender his principles – in fact, it would be against my principles to make such a suggestion.'[111]

During the visit of Sir Norman Moore to Brixton he had a private interview with Mary and Annie. In his medical report Griffiths wrote:

> He told me afterwards that he found them quite obdurate in their determination not to attempt to influence MacSwiney to take food. In his own words 'they seemed even more determined if possible than he was'.[112]

Griffiths held his own interview with Mary a week previously which again indicated her absolute belief in the political statement being made by her brother:

> I then pointed out to her that as she had the opportunity of doing something to induce him to take food, at some future time she might reproach herself with her part and public opinion generally might consider her family partly responsible for her brother's death. She said that she was not careful of the opinion of Englishmen, that opinion in Ireland and on the Continent would be with her and she entirely declined to take any steps to induce her brother to take food.[113]

As doctors urged the family to intervene to halt the hunger strike, Muriel's malleability facilitated the demonisation of Mary as truculent and problematic as she negotiated to have her brother released – on his terms. It is important to remember that a person may experience grief and distress even if they do not outwardly show it. Aiken discusses the tensions in Máirín Cregan's play *Hunger-strike* (1929). Nano grapples with the conflict between her public stoicism and private suffering as she watches her husband deteriorate on hunger strike during the Civil War.[114] Indeed, Mary stated: '[w]hile we were in England, it was a point of honour to us that the enemy should never see us cry'. Mary noted, however, that showing no emotion before the enemy did not 'mean that the women of Ireland do not have to cry sometimes in secret'.[115] This was very much also the sentiment of the Kathleen Clarke and her sisters, Madge and Laura when they visited their brother Ned in Kilmainham before his execution in 1916. Lucy McDiarmid writes:

> The primary concern of all the women enduring the 'Kilmainham farewell' is the maintenance of an attitude they variously called 'holding up', 'bearing up' or 'not breaking down' – in other words, hiding their emotions from the men they encounter.

Those men were not just their relatives but also the soldiers and other officials they engaged with.[116] Mary noted that the appeals to Terence's relatives to urge him to take food were 'very painful'. It was, she said, 'heartrending enough' for them 'to have to witness the slow agony he is enduring'.[117] In her memoir of her sister, Annie discussed the establishment of the paper *Fianna Fáil* by Terence in 1915. As discussed in Chapter One, the only way in which he could raise the necessary funds was to sell his library. He believed that newspapers 'were necessary to put the Nation's principles before the people'. Terence framed his decision in terms of personal sacrifice: '[i]f sacrifice had to be made to get the minds of the people – begin with yourself'.[118] When Mary failed to dissuade him, she determined that the books of all family members would be sold. Using the imagery of death, Annie constructed the event in later life with reference to Terence's ultimate sacrifice in 1920; all family members were centrally involved in the sacrifice in 1915 as they would be again in 1920.

As Aiken states in her discussion of the testimony of the Irish revolutionary generation, 'personal memory is always "multigenerational".'[119] For the MacSwiney family, bearing witness and testimony was also cross generational. The reference to the silence that the distress at the selling of their books generated amongst the MacSwiney siblings in Annie's account is significant. After the auctioneer's men had finished packing up, the family: 'went into the dining-room, and the sight was unbearable. The empty shelves were as the death bed from which a loved form had just been moved – and the cases as the coffin. With one accord and without a word, we left the room – nor did we speak of it again.'[120] Mary would speak of Terence's hunger strike and death – again and again. What she would not do was to express her own personal distress other than in asides. As a woman, Mary was expected to nurture and care in terms of the understanding of gender in the period. Prendergast writes that as the strikers fell prey to emaciation and hallucinations in Gormanstown internment camp in October 1923:

> 'Stick it out, boys! Stick it out!' was a commonplace slogan in use during that period and had been so for quite a long time. It held meaning for us in those days when our endurance was tested. 'Stick it out, boys' became a watchword a password [sic], a virtual slogan of defiance.[121]

Michael O'Donoghue, IRA, Cork, 2nd Battalion recalled that during the Cork hunger strike in 1920 crowds in their thousands assembled nightly outside the prison, 'and prayed and sang to strengthen the spirits of the men refusing food within'.[122] Mary, in her unwillingness to encourage her brother to give up his hunger strike, was centrally located in this discourse of republican solidarity and defiance. However, inferred criticism was levelled at her in a way that it was not at Peter or Seán MacSwiney because as a woman she was expected to nurture; she was not expected to situate herself actively within the nexus of potential death for political reasons. Yet, as she stated, Terence's principles were those of his sisters and his wife.[123] Mary was also perceptive enough to note that her stance was problematic also because the British did not view the republican struggle as legitimate:

> Meantime one wonders what the English people would have thought of any woman, if in the recent War, she urged her soldier brother to throw down his arms in the face of the enemy to save his life.[124]

Shortt's letter to Mary on 21 August made clear the British government's position. Terence MacSwiney would not be released. 'For any consequence that may ensue from his refusal to take food' he 'alone' was responsible.[125] A statement by Terence to Shortt that same day noted that he had been informed that 'the consequence of my refusing to take food would rest with myself'. His rejoinder was that 'the consequence will rest with you'.[126] He declared that he was 'prepared to die'.[127] Murphy states, however, that, 'despite the rhetoric of death', Terence believed that he would be released at the last moment. Mary and other members of his family worked to try to affect that. It is important to imagine the traumatic effects for the family as they existed in a liminal space between Terence's release or death; expecting his demise and yet not believing that it would occur. Or as Aiken states about the ending of Cregan's *Hunger-strike*: 'there is a sense that the certainty of death would bring as much relief as the unknowability of survival'.[128] In America Peter MacSwiney's distress caused Liam Mellows to write to John J. Hearn:

> It is painful to watch poor Peter feverishly watching the papers for a gleam of hope – hoping against hope, prepared to face the worst, proud of his wonderful brother, torn with love but enduring an agony of anguish at the thought of the latters [sic] suffering. Oh dear! How small do we all appear in the face of this terrible tragedy.[129]

Mary and Annie read aloud passages from *The Imitation of Christ*, Terence choosing, as he became weaker, to hear the section entitled 'Thoughts on Death' from the fifteenth century text by Thomas à Kempis.[130] This was the book MacCurtain recalled as a 'great comfort' when he was imprisoned after the 1916 rebellion.[131]

O'Brien visited Terence on 2 September and was 'very much alarmed at his appearance' and was amazed that he 'should have hope of lasting another week'.[132] In early September, although conscious, Terence was reported to be 'unable to converse with his relatives'.[133] On 7 September Fr Dominic reported that he was suffering extreme pain on the left-hand side of his abdomen and heart.[134] By 9 September both his arms were bandaged as his skin atrophied.[135] To ease his pain, he was placed on an air bed.[136] Griffiths reported on 12 September that the 'skin over the bony prominence of his body is becoming dry and rough from pressure'.[137] Annie reported that on the previous day, for the first time, she could not read to her brother while he 'had to think for a while before he could answer'. She declared that he had 'reached his worst point'.[138]

The protracted suffering of both Terence and his family was to continue for another six weeks. The medical report on 23 September noted that Terence was being sprayed with Eau de Cologne about the head and face, in an attempt to prevent the dehydration of his skin, Griffiths commenting that 'no doubt the absorption by the mouth of the spirit vapour is having a good effect'.[139] By the end of the month, however, both Drs Griffiths and Beddard agreed that 'the patient had almost got to the end of his reserve of fat' and 'had gone down in physical condition a good deal as compared with the previous week'.[140]

As her brother continued to deteriorate, Mary's days in London were busy. Her role was not that of a passive sister sitting by her brother as he lay on his prison bed. Family and close friends established a rota to ensure that Terence was not alone. For Mary, prison visits were combined with visits to government officials and embassies; she lobbied trade union officials and the medical officers in Brixton. This cannot have been anything other than tiring and stressful, particularly as the days passed and Terence inched closer to death. Moreover, there was still St Ita's to worry about. An advertisement in the *Cork Examiner* on 28 August noted that in 'the unavoidable absence of the Misses MacSwiney, a substitute has been appointed' who would interview prospective parents in advance of the reopening on 6 September.[141]

By early September the key British newspapers were increasingly sympathetic to the plight of Terence while Lloyd George, on holiday in Lucerne, received several death threats based on his continuing failure to release him.[142] 'The Premier of England is on the Alpine Hills', de Róiste wrote, 'while the Saviour of Men is behind prison bars in London'.[143] These positive developments from the point of view of the family were testament to the success of the propaganda campaign orchestrated by Mary. On 4 September, accompanied by Muriel, she visited the American, French, Spanish, Italian and Belgian embassies to ask them to make representations to their governments. 'None of the ambassadors was in town' although the two women did meet the Belgian secretary.[144] Mary also targeted the support of prominent churchmen from different denominations. In late September she sent letters to Cardinal Bourne of Westminster calling him to issue a statement on behalf of the English hierarchy condemning the actions of British government towards her brother. She sent a similar request to the Protestant Archbishop of Canterbury.[145] Meanwhile in Cork masses were offered up 'publicly' for the release of Terence and the hunger strikers in the city.[146]

On 9 September Mary arrived at the Trades Union Congress in Portsmouth intending to issue an address on behalf of her brother.[147] A week previously Congress had sent a telegram to Lloyd George calling for the release of Terence. Bonar Law, Chancellor of the Exchequer in the Coalition Government, detailed his objections to the appeal. To release him would be a 'betrayal' of the 15 officers who had 'been brutally and treacherously done to death' in Ireland since MacSwiney's arrest and an affront to their 'bereaved widows and families'.[148] In seeking to present an address, Mary did not hope to influence the Congress to declare a general strike in support of her brother. 'I did not want to urge direct action ... I desired only to have three minutes plain talk with the representatives of six and half million of workmen in England'.[149] However, J. H. Thomas, the President of the Congress, stated, in the words of a New York paper, that in 'view of the great strain Miss MacSwiney had undergone in the last two weeks … it would be madness to allow her to address the conference'. Instead, another telegram was sent to Lloyd George demanding Terence's release.[150]

Mary was critical of the 'red tape and procedure' that meant she was denied 'the five minutes' straight talk I wanted'. She was particularly scathing of Thomas's condescending approach to her. She knew that he had worked to frustrate her request to address Congress based on the pretence of gendered perceptions of her fragility as a woman:

> Finally they agreed to put the question to Congress, but note how Mr Thomas does it. He talks pathetically and suggests to Congress that it would not be fair to ask Miss MacSwiney to appear before them at the present time, etc., etc. Personally I am surprised that the united intelligence of the Congress did not suffice to suggest to them that no one had asked Miss MacSwiney to appear there, and if she wished to speak to them she was the best judge of what was fair to herself and her feelings.
>
> Mr. Thomas's manner of putting her request was, she said, unmitigated humbug. … they camouflaged their refusal under a pretended consideration to my feelings.[151]

The *Daily Mail* described her attempts to 'interrupt' the Congress as a 'pathetic appeal … to save her brother's life'.[152]

Mary was particularly concerned to target American support. In September she issued a statement calling on American businessmen, both individuals and companies, to withdraw economic support from English investments if the government did not release her brother and the hunger strikers in Cork prison.[153] 'We do not ask you', she stated, 'to go to war with England: we do ask you to act at once, before it is too late, by exerting economic pressure'.[154] Later that month she wrote to the Home Office:

> America really did fight for Freedom for all small nations, and the American people are asking themselves seriously why Ireland should be denied the freedom which is freely given to Belgium, Poland and Czecho-Slovakia.[155]

In making this claim MacSwiney situated herself within the context of the discussion which developed within Irish republicanism based on Woodrow Wilson's apparent commitment to self-determination in the period before the signing of the Versailles Peace Treaty in June 1919. In this discourse Ireland's position was like that of 'the Czechs, Slovaks, Jugoslavs, Poles, Belgians Serbians and others not enjoying national self-determination'.[156] During the 'Self-Determination of Ireland' week in America on 8–15 December 1918 Cardinal William O'Connell of Boston declared that the war could only be 'justified by the universal application of the principles of self-determination'. 'Let that application,' he declared, 'begin with Ireland.'[157] In August 1920 Peter MacSwiney, still in America, and Margaret MacSwiney in North Carolina, separately wrote to members of the Wilson administration asking them to intervene with Britain to prevent Terence's death. Margaret declared that intervention would be forthcoming if 'America was sincere in her war aims'.[158] In early September Peter appealed to Wilson himself.[159] The reality, of course, as Bernadette Whelan discusses, was that Wilson, while sympathetic to Irish claims, would not allow them to jeopardise US-British relations which were central to the success of the Versailles peace conference.[160] As Mel Farrell states, satisfying the aspiration of Irish republicans was 'complicated by virtue of the fact that Britain was a victorious ally of the United States'.[161]

As discussed in further detail in Chapter Five, Ireland's expectations from the post-war settlement were frustrated as the country was deemed not to be a nation and consequently peace settlement principles did not apply.

By early September Terence's health was rapidly deteriorating. On 4 September Griffiths medical report stated that he is 'liable to collapse at any time and if the deterioration in health progresses in the same ratio as comparing to-day with yesterday death is probable in a few days'.[162] In the early days of this month, his doctors repeatedly expressed surprise that Terence was able to maintain his strength.[163] In early September the *New York Tribute* quoted Annie MacSwiney:

> As to his condition ... that changes from hour to hour. Sometimes one would think he would die in a few hours and then he rallies. The prison doctor cannot decide how long he will last, as the doctor has no criterion by which to judge.[164]

On 11 September O'Brien wrote to Michael Collins stating that Terence was 'very bad, indeed, and we have to face the position that at any moment the end may come'.[165] The family experienced a type of paradox. They lived with the sense that death was imminent; yet they experienced this perception over a protracted time period. In mid-September Mary was in discussion with Richard Mulcahy who informed her that a uniformed guard would be sent to accompany the body back to Ireland on her brother's death.[166] On 15 September O'Brien described him as 'almost completely wasted away'.[167] Geoffrey Whiskard, Assistant Secretary at Dublin Castle, wrote to the Home Office on 22 September 1920 in respect of 'the legal questions which will arise as to the custody and ownership of the body'.[168] By late September O'Brien had provided the sculptor, Albert Power, with photographs to create a bust of MacSwiney.[169] While the family desired independent medical advice to counter suggestions and rumours that Terence was being given nourishment, both Mary and Annie, O'Brien stated, also wanted some clarity 'with regard to how long he may last'. In the event Dr Moore would not give an estimate as to how long he would live.[170] The attitude of Terence himself to his impending death had both a public and a private dimension. In a petition to the government dictated by him on 20 August 1920 he declared:

> Knowing the revolution of opinion that will be thereby caused throughout the civilised world and the consequent accession of support to Ireland in her hour of trial, I am reconciled to a premature grave.
>
> I am prepared to die.[171]

On 12 September he responded to the usual medical request as to whether he would take food that he was 'here as a matter of duty and my example is a good one for those in Cork'.[172] These political statement were belied on a more human level as Terence asked Dr Griffiths on 26 September: 'I wonder how much longer it is going to be until the end'.[173] This was also the response of Gallagher on hunger strike in Mountjoy the previous April.[174]

Mary was to the fore in ensuring that Terence's political stance reached out into the world. Friends and wider family members began to promote the idea of Terence's cheerfulness as he faced death. On 28 August Bishop Cohalan of Cork, Liam de Róiste and Professor Stockley were amongst those who visited Terence. The former two men, who comprised an official Cork Corporation deputation, gave a statement emphasising the cheerfulness of the man on hunger strike:[175] 'Terence MacSwiney is as calm, as thoughtful for others, as affectionate in his friendliness as of yore, and he does not forget the Irish work going on in world ...'[176] Yet, only a short time before Terence was arrested de Róiste was heavily critical of his role in Dáil proceedings:

> In the evening T. Mac. S was [moved?] to the chair, as 'Scelig' had to leave and his autocratic attitude created general protest and 'feeling' ... Mac S. had brought anger into the atmosphere ...[177]

Mary, other members of the family, and, indeed, his doctors witnessed the less public human frailty of a dying man; this was often not pleasant. The medical reports increasingly referred to Terence as 'depressed', 'sullen' and 'anxious'.[178] Griffith's medical report on 22 September summed up the reality of illness and death and the fraught emotions generated:

> He has become more depressed and irritable during the last few days and his relatives are extremely irritable. They still come to me to argue out the justice of the matter and appear quite unable to appreciate the fact that we are doing nothing to him and that the whole thing can be terminated by his taking the nourishment which is handy at his bedside day and night. They urge that it is a matter of principle with them and him to starve and seem quite unable to appreciate and to be unable to entertain the ideas of others on the subject.[179]

On 14 October Griffiths once again referred to Terence as 'depressed' continuing that the nurse on duty thought it 'may be due to some family discussion which went on yesterday'.[180] As discussed, from an early point in their marriage Terence worried about Muriel's ill-health. Concern for her and for his young daughter must have weighted heavily on him. According to Máire MacSwiney Brugha her father had appointed Mary her joint guardian as early as January 1920.[181]

In mid-September Mary and Muriel, together with O'Brien, moved into the Jermyn Court Hotel in central London to be close to the prison in the event of a deterioration in Terence's condition. Patrick Moylett testified to the fact that Peter was also staying in the hotel.[182] In October Terence requested that O'Brien bring the family 'under one roof' as he had been 'worrying a lot about his wife and sisters', notably that they were scattered in 'different houses and hotels'.[183] Higson's medical report on 26 August had noted that MacSwiney 'became excited on the visit of his brother and a second sister'.[184] This was a reference to Annie and Seán. The latter arrived back in Cork in June 1920. Unwilling to apply for a British passport he had travelled from Canada as a stowaway.[185] In early October Peter MacSwiney, a shoe cutter in New York, visited Terence who, according to the *Topeka State Journal*, he had not seen in 20 years. He expected, the paper reported, to find his brother dead and wanted to attend his funeral service.[186]

On 16 October Muriel sat for an interview with Forbes W. Fairbairn, a London correspondent for the Universal Service.[187] The American *Irish Press*, founded in 1918 by Joseph McGarrity, reproduced the interview which exposed the brutality of Terence's impending death. His skin was so drawn he appeared to be baring his teeth. The very touch of his bed clothes caused him horrendous pain:

> If it wasn't for his eyes and fingers one might think he was dead. Once in while he moves his

> head sideways but that for him is a great effort. When he wants water the message comes with his eyes.[188]

Annie maintained a diary of the last week of her brother's hunger strike. Margaret Lucey, who gave a copy to the Bureau of Military History stated that it would 'convey some idea of the courage and devotion shown by members of his family who were close by him during the final days of his martyrdom'.[189] Miller states that '[h]unger striking is an intensely personal act involving a body in distress'.[190] The hunger strike of Terence can also be described as a familial act, as his wife and siblings bore witness and, in the context of the latter, encouraged him to persevere to the end. In the last week of his hunger strike his family watched as he became 'quite unlike himself'. Dr Beddard, one of the three doctors who attended him, told Mary that Terence was 'developing scurvy' and advised lime juice. Other physical manifestations of malnutrition included weakening eyesight.[191] When he became unconscious, Annie wrote: 'the fact for us was that Terry would not be released'. Any attempt to administer food to him while he was in an unconscious state was to 'torture him'.[192]

On the Tuesday before his death, Terence became 'very excited' and was talking 'wildly'; he was, Annie wrote, 'very disturbed mentally'. She alleged that Dr Griffiths talked to her brother 'in a very brow-beating way. The result on Terry was fatal'. Annie stated that the 'terror of the doctor's threat had completely turned his brain'.[193] Dr Higson noted that Terence was 'in a state of acute delirium, he was violently restless, talking incoherently and at times screaming out'. Mary requested that he administer morphine.[194] In a letter she stated that all day on that last Tuesday her brother was 'more or less excited from the effort of combating' 'an attack in words' by the doctor.[195] The reality was that 'mental deterioration' and 'loss of competence' manifested in the final stages of a hunger strike.[196] Gallagher began to 'experience paranoia about the prison staff' on the 13th day of his strike in Mountjoy in April 1920.[197] However, Miller discusses how the treatment of Terence was very different to that experienced by the prisoners on strike in Cork where 'prisoner doctors had shown greater respect for the wishes of the prisoners and their families'.[198]

On his last Wednesday he was, Annie recorded, 'on the verge of delirium', constantly struggling against the fear that he would be at the doctors' 'mercy' and given sustenance if unconscious. He became transfixed by knocking in the prison yard, interpreting it in his increasingly delirium as the doctor's 'new treatment'; it was evidence of 'international importance'. The family witnessed him 'striking out' at those who came near to him. He was 'shouting loudly' and trying to get out of bed. So 'emaciated was he, however, that it was an easy thing to overcome him'. Fessler discusses 'aggressivity and anger attacks' in various contexts around dietary constriction.[199] Writing of the general hunger strike in the Gormanstown camp in 1923 Prendergast referred to the 'poor emaciated frames that were once strong bodies, once healthy active human beings'. Prendergast referred to the 'strain' on, and the 'anxiety' experienced by the men who helped those on strike. Indeed, he stated: '[w]e, who tended them ... were perhaps most disturbed.'[200] Hunger strikers became 'disfigured' as their bodies fall prey to extreme malnutrition; 'descent into death' was slow and painful.[201] The effect on those family members and others waiting or watching cannot be underestimated. Gallagher wrote: 'That is the real pain of hunger striking ... to know that those outside endure so much ... that it is a load upon their hearts. They imagine ten times more agony than is here and, imagining, feel it …' Gallagher saw 'suppressed agony' in his father's eyes when he visited.[202]

As Prendergast wrote: '[t]he painful scenes that we witnessed then were enough to affect one's nerves'.[203] Prendergast wrote of the 'dread shadow of death' that 'hung close to many participants' after the strikers passed 15 days.[204] If Prendergast was at the 'limit of … endurance' at that point, the distress experienced by the MacSwiney family must have been so much the greater as Terence neared 70 days without food. Indeed, earlier in September O'Brien had written to Collins of the horror witnessed by the family as Terence succumbed to delirium and violent outburst:

> I need not relate to you the effect on his wife and sisters of witnessing these terrible paroxysms of delirium, in which he says the most violent things, and added to which is terrible screaming and shrieking.[205]

Notwithstanding the gendered nature of O'Brien's letter in considering only the distress of female members of Terence's family, it is important to foreground the mental toll of expecting death at any moment; this was the reality the family sustained over many months.

The first two hours of Terence's descent in delirium on his final Wednesday was, Annie MacSwiney wrote, 'beyond the imagination of anyone who did not witness it'. The inability to fully conceptualise the horror of the slow death of Terence without having been present is a repeated theme in her account of his last week. Contradicting her earlier requests, Mary alleged that he had been given morphine without the consent of the family facilitating feeding while he was unconscious. Griffiths made clear to the family that in feeding him while unconscious, the doctors were acting as they had previously told Terence they would.[206] He could not, she declared, 'have been fed in the wild delirium; the stupor of the morphine made it possible'.[207] On Thursday a nurse administered two teaspoons of meat juice to Terence causing him distress with the result that 'all the stuff they gave him came up again'. Two hours later he was given brandy and milk after which he 'vomited more than a half of basin full – a green liquid'. The 'cruelty of it all', Annie wrote, 'was and is beyond description'.[208] The word 'is' should be noted. Writing her account decades later language could still not adequately transmit the horror of the experience. Joseph Lennon states that writers 'conscious of contributing to the formation of culture wrestle with how to represent hunger, if at all'.[209]

Tensions were understandably high. On Thursday of the final week Peter MacSwiney turned 'angrily' on the nurse who was attempting to administer sustenance and had to be stopped by Muriel.[210] That night Annie, Seán and Fr Dominic took the night shift, remaining one hour at a time in the passage before relieving each other.[211] On Friday Terence remained unconscious all morning but, according to the Irish Self-Determination League Bulletin, he recognised Mary.[212] On Saturday morning she was refused entry past the outer gate of the prison to relieve Seán.[213] According to the Home Office this was to ensure that she did not interfere with attempts by the doctors to feed her brother while he was unconscious.[214] In answer to a parliamentary question as to why Mary and her sister were refused entry to see Terence, Shortt apportioned the blame to them. They were denied entry 'because of the extremely bad effects they had on the condition of their brother'.[215] This was a repeated trope in the government's dealings with Mary. According to Shortt's statement of 20 August she used 'violent language' while he listened 'courteously'.[216] On the 19 October Dr Griffiths wrote that Terence's: 'people seem to have no more common sense on the subject than he has ... It seems useless to try and explain anything to them. They all seem obstinate and ignorant.'[217] Denied entry to see her brother Mary wrote a statement of events as they unfolded.[218] This statement also comprised instructions to O' Brien, taken to him by Seán. She determined to remain there on hunger strike until she was granted admittance telling the latter that he 'must make the most of it for propaganda purposes':

> We must make it as uncomfortable as possible for them. I think my way is the best but I would not go against your wishes only remember it is publicity we want, to save Terry from lies & leave my convenience out of count in your judgement. I shall feel I am doing something anyhow to top the lies.[219]

Basic human needs still had to be attended to by the family; Mary instructed O'Brien to have Annie bring to her a 'big coat' while she organised that Seán get breakfast as he left his stint by Terence's bedside.[220] The banality of such details brings into relief the horror that the family were enduring. Later that day she was joined by Annie who, according to the *Topeka State Journal* became 'hysterical' on being denied entry.[221] Both sisters remained in the waiting room all day, Mary accosting the passing doctors, asking 'each one individually was he responsible for the brutality'.[222] Dr Griffiths, Mary wrote, 'ran away' from her; 'literally ran'.[223] When she spoke to the prison Governor, he 'hectored & bullied a bit'.[224] At 10 pm an attempt was made to remove the two women. Failing to persuade them to depart, three policemen 'laid their hands on our shoulders'. At that point, Mary and her sister departed 'as we did not mean to let them drag us out'.[225] Dr Griffiths made a note of the impasse in his medical report writing:

> The two sisters who had becamped themselves in the waiting room near the gate were prevailed upon to leave yesterday evening after almost half an hour's argument. Police were called in to make a show of force in the background, but no force was actually used, nor did the Police touch them.[226]

The sisters reached their hotel just before 11 pm, Mary having been at the prison since 8.30 am.[227]

The next day the sisters arrived at the prison at 12.30 following mass, ready for the day's 'vigil'. Once again not allowed entry, they were faced with a strong police presence that mobilised when anyone exited from the prison as if, Annie wrote, 'we were going to fight our way in'.[228] One of the inspectors noted that the latter looked unwell, but Mary declared: '[i]f my sister falls I'll look after her'. Annie's account of the day gives an insight into the hardship, both physical and mental, that the sisters continued to endure:

> I wondered at the police shivering with cold, stamping up & down, waving their hands & blowing on their fingers to try & keep warm, & grumbling all the time, while Min & I stood there feeling nothing – I suppose we felt so much mentally that we knew nothing of physical feelings. We never moved from the spot, though several times we were asked to leave just to get a cup of tea.[229]

Despite the propagandist nature of the statement, the bulletin issued by the Irish Self-Determination League did speak to the human toll of the decision by the Home Office to deny entry to the sisters:

> The additional strain is also telling on the Misses MacSwiney. They tasted no food during their long vigil in the cold prison waiting room from an early hour yesterday morning until nearly 11 pm last night. Their friends are extremely anxious on their behalf. The pain caused to them by total exclusion from their brother during his dying hours is terrible to contemplate.[230]

It was, the League stated, 'an inhuman and senseless embargo'.[231] When the two finally left by taxi at 10 pm, Annie addressed the police, declaring 'you seem very miserable & cold, we are sorry but the misery & cold are worse for us, & unfortunately this will go on till we see our brother'.[232]

On Monday 25 October at 5.40 am Terence MacSwiney died. It was some hours before Mary, Annie and Muriel were informed by O'Brien knocking at their door. At the prison 'the family group stoical and dry-eyed, prayed over the body as it lay on the cot'.[233] They took turns by his bedside in Brixton jail. Annie noted that the night vigil maintained by her brother Peter and Fred Cronin 'was a dreadful one in every way'.[234] Although Annie's account of the final week in Brixton was retrospective, she was, as noted, still not able to articulate the full extent and depth of the feelings of family members who had borne witness to the protracted death of Terence:

> I am here just stating facts – our feelings are beyond power of words. Terry was dead. And we had been kept from him. We got to the prison at 9 o'c ... We saw Terry, at peace after his long agony, safe from his torturers, a victor in his battle – but Terry – dead. Never again would he speak to us, never again smile in the old way...[235]

She was 'only going to write what happened here'; she could not adequately convey the emotions of family members.[236]

While Peter and Seán left to 'go into town' Mary and Annie remained with the body. When the warders entered to bring the body to the morgue, they attempted to stop them until the rest of the family returned. They were not 'going to have his body desecrated by those wretches', despite O'Brien informing them that it was usual practice in institutions to speedily remove a dead body. When the body was finally removed, clothed in the habit of the Franciscan Order, Annie again highlighted the limited power of language in conveying the family's horror and distress:

> No words could describe the awfulness of that place – four stone walls – a stone floor, & a stone step in the centre on which Terry's body was laid. The place was icy cold & we were locked in every time & there was no way of communicating with a warder if you wanted to go out.[237]

Moreover, despite the appalling vista that was the death of her brother – or maybe because of it – Mary continued to assert his case before the government. On 21 October in the House of Commons Shortt had referred to the fact that in his unconscious state Terence had been fed with 'liquid food'.[238] Even as Terence's death was imminent, and despite the evidence of his medial notes, Mary continued to engage with the government to refute such allegations. Mary's grief was mediated through action. Shortt was, she declared, guilty of 'another lie'.[239]

The inquest was held on Wednesday, Annie emphasising that the 'English coroner could not sneer away the declaration that Terence's occupation was that of an Irish Volunteer' and was forced to note it down. At that point the issue of the place of burial ignited further distress for the family. The Crown Solicitor declared that the coroner had no power to release the body to be buried outside of England.[240] While Muriel and O'Brien went to the Home Office to attempt to expedite the situation, Mary and Annie remained with Terence in the morgue.[241] As the *Irish Independent* declared: '[a]ll through the day members of the family kept watch and prayed at the bier which temporarily rested in the prison mortuary, and until the last moment they remained beside it'.[242] For nearly six hours Mary and her sister 'watched by his dead body in that awful place'. As 'the day wore on the darkness came'. Annie's account framed their response to their brother's death by foreshadowing their need to supplement and carry on his sacrifice for Irish freedom: 'Our one thought was that he was beyond their power; they could hurt him no longer, much as they wished to do so, and for ourselves – well, whatever Ireland asks she will get.'[243]

Having represented the family at the inquest, Muriel then collapsed; O'Brien issued a statement referring to the effects of the 'strain and anxiety of the martyrdom of her husband'.[244] It was Mary who organised matters relating to the funerals. While relations between her and her sister-in-law had in no way broken down at this point, Mary was both allowed, and forced, to assume the role of head of the family in the immediate aftermath of Terence's death. Many years later she wrote to Etienette Beuque: 'Poor Muriel could not be expected to be a stoic like the MacSwineys all were'.[245] Mary believed that Muriel had not the inner stoicism of the MacSwineys. To the American Commission on Conditions in Ireland Mary stated that Muriel was 'very young, and she was not used to fightings things out as we were'.[246] While the former gave into her grief, Mary took on a performative political role which necessitated the repression of her own personal feelings. The psychological toll on her of assuming the key familial duty of transmitting the necessary narrative of Terence's death in the days and months after Brixton must be understood.

Prostrate with grief and exhaustion, Muriel was not able to attend the funeral service in Southwark Cathedral.[247] Neither was she well enough to travel to Ireland with her husband's body. As the world-wide press reported on the funeral proceedings in England and Ireland it was Mary who represented the family and who constructed the chronicle of a good death that would, in the words of her brother to Dr Griffiths 'do Ireland great good and "this Government" much harm'.[248] Indeed, she had been clear from an early point as to how she wanted the funeral proceedings conducted. Although MacDiarmada states that O'Brien 'managed the hunger strike and death of MacSwiney to effect the maximum publicity and sympathy for both MacSwiney and the Irish independence cause',[249] Mary was an active, if not the, dominant agent in the management of her brother's funeral and reputation. In late September the papers reported that no funeral processions would be permitted in Ireland. She had, even before Terence's death, approached O'Brien about the matter and was 'emphatic' that the body should not be temporarily buried in England but taken to Cork 'at once'.[250]

In Cork, all theatres and 'places of amusement' closed on news of Terence's death.[251] A day of national mourning was called for 29 October with the suspension of all business in

Cork.[252] Public bodies closed across Ireland.[253] Terence was removed from, in the words of Annie, 'that vile place where he had been tortured to the peace of Southwark Cathedral'.[254] On Thursday 28 October, requiem mass was held at 11 am, the cathedral being 'quite inadequate to accommodate the thousands who wished to attend the service'. A large queue of those who wished to pay respects developed from an early hour; during the service police had to link arms to keep the swelling throng back.[255] Terence's body was then transferred to Euston station for removal to Dublin at 6.20 pm; thousands following the coffin.[256] When the train passed Crewe a letter from the Irish Chief Secretary, Sir Hamar Greenwood, was handed to Seán MacSwiney to open in the absence of Muriel who, ill, had remained in London; the body was to go straight to Cork 'owing to the possibility of trouble'.[257]

The railway contract had been to bring the body via Kingstown to Cork, the family-purpose being, as Murphy states, to extract 'the maximum publicity for their loss'.[258] Following a procession through the city, requiem mass was planned in the Pro-Cathedral at 12.30 pm with the train to depart for Cork at 2 pm.[259] Mary and Annie had 'just turned down the light in our compartment … when this new shock came'.[260] As Murphy notes, discussions had been initiated by Sir Edward Troup, Permanent Under Secretary at the Home Office, as early as 8 September as to how the body of Terence would be dealt with.[261] On 22 of that month Whiskard wrote to the Home Office:

> With a view however, to avoid so far as possible any demonstration which might inflame public feeling, I am to express Their Excellencies' earnest desire that, if in Mr Shortt's opinion such a course is in any way possible, such measures shall be taken as will ensure that the body shall be sent direct by sea to Queenstown or Cork and shall not be permitted to be sent to Dublin or to any other port in Ireland other than Queenstown or Cork.[262]

On the 4 September the *Topeka State Journal* had reported that his end was imminent and declared that his supporters and sympathetic Irish newspapers were 'planning to capitalize the dramatic settings of MacSwiney's imprisonment and … death'.[263] In his diary de Róiste wondered if the Southwick funeral mass 'frightened or annoyed' the government into the decision not to allow the body to travel to Dublin:

> The funeral itself in London was large – the attitude of the hundreds of thousands looking on was reverent and respectful. It was in striking contrast, I learn, – the attitude of the London crowds – to the meanness, spite, hatred, vindictiveness of their rulers.[264]

The family determined to remain in Holyhead until Muriel had been informed of the new development; simultaneously they grappled with the possibility that Terence's body would be taken by force. They were compelled to make the difficult decision not to accompany the body if that occurred. Again, this was to extract 'a further propaganda tariff by ensuring that the police had to carry out their instructions by force'.[265] However, the mental and physical toll of this resistance to comply with the decisions of the government on Mary and her family cannot be underestimated.

At Holyhead Mary and Annie assumed a position at either side of the coffin. Negotiations ensued to no avail and the family and supporters 'joined hands around the coffin', Mary and her brother Seán at the end nearest to the entrance to the van. Railway men entered and removed the van but were forbidden by the family to touch the coffin.[266] According to the *Evening Echo* Mary vehemently responded to the statement by the stationmaster's superintendent that he was merely carrying out his duty: 'My God, what duty? You shall not take him. You shall only take my brother away over my dead body'.[267] Emotions were understandably high; at that point the situation escalated and police 'rushed forward and were on us'. According to Annie, Mary and Seán endured the 'brunt' of the violence:

> they were dragged from the coffin; Min was lifted off her feet and thrown out of the van. Seán tried to protect her; he had his arm around her, and three huge police attacked him in front; one of them struck Min in the face, while a military officer jumped at him from behind, caught him by the collar and tried to choke him.[268]

Fr Dominic described Mary as being 'cast from the wagon, causing her to fall'.[269] Another account stated that she was 'removed by force'.[270] It was, the *Evening Echo* declared, 'a terrible scene to be forced on the relatives in the death chamber'.[271] News of the violence directed at Mary and others within the family reached the wider world within a short period, de Róiste recording in his diary that Terence's relatives were 'assaulted and hustled'.[272] As the SS Rathmore, carrying Terence's body, left the shore Mary and other members of the MacSwiney family, the *Evening Herald* reported, 'remained on the pier for a while weighed down with sorrow and horror'.[273]

Annie described her brother's body as being 'under arrest again'.[274] As the ship steamed out of the harbour, she recorded that the family: 'knelt and said the Rosary in Irish and watched all that was left of Terry being carried off across the sea to the land he died for, and carried off a prisoner, dead.'[275] The family travelled to Kingstown and assisted at High Mass after which they left for Cork, travelling in procession behind an empty hearse to Knightsbridge train station.[276] Fr Augustine Hayden, one of the assisting priests, came to the Pro-Cathedral directly from his last meeting with the 18-year-old Kevin Barry, scheduled for execution in Mountjoy Jail on 1 November.[277] Arriving in Cork the MacSwiney siblings 'felt dulled to everything' but were forced to go to the Customs House at 10 pm to take Terence's body; if they failed to do so, it would be returned to Queenstown. They travelled behind the Volunteers who bore the coffin to the City Hall, the building from which Terence had been arrested three months previously.[278] A tragic loop was closed.

Past and present students of St Ita's assembled outside the school on the morning of Terence MacSwiney's funeral and 'went in a body to assist at the Requiem Mass of our Heroic Lord Mayor'.[279] Throughout the period of his hunger strike students in the school had followed his ordeal; on 22 September eight o'clock mass in St Patrick's Church was offered for 'the Lord Mayor and his fellow-prisoners at the request of the Children of St Ita's High School'.[280]

Ian Miller states that hunger strikers 'inflict pain and suffering upon their healthy bodies and refuse medical intervention; they manipulate and damage their own bodies for a broader political purpose'.[281] Michael O'Donoghue described Terence's body as it lay in state in a coffin in the Cork City Hall. O'Donoghue formed part of the rotating IRA six-man guard of honour and recalled:

> Beneath the glass cover lay the shrunken corpse ... the face small, pinched, but very serene. The most striking feature of the body was its smallness, like that of a child of twelve. The folds of the uniform piteously accentuated the mummy-like contour of the corpse. From the

> parchment pallor of the face and hands it seemed as if the whole body had not alone been drained of blood, but dehydrated as well.[282]

De Róiste, who visited the hunger strikers in Cork in early October, described Seán Hennessy as looking like 'a child of eleven or twelve years'.[283] A prison official in Cork discussed the effect of hunger strike when Michael Fitzgerald died that same October:

> They are slowly eating themselves up … They go along for several days without visible alteration, then suddenly seem to strike a new stage and drop down. The skin is now drawn over their faces as tight as a drum, and all of them are hollow-eyed.[284]

In *The Revolutionist*, Terence depicted the smile and composure of a dead hero as family and friends stood over the coffin of Hugh O'Neil.[285] This was a depiction of political martyrdom. The human reality experienced by Mary was expressed in the depictions by O'Donoghue and de Róiste of the dead hunger strikers in October 1920.

Mary continued to function after the death of her brother, unlike Terence's wife Muriel. She continued to teach; she maintained her position as head of the family. She witnessed not just a brother's death but the suffering of one to whom she had assumed a maternal role. It was Mary, not Terence, who assumed the role of head of the family on the 1911 census form despite the latter being 32 years old.[286] The family vigil at Terence's bedside in Brixton Jail was, as his wife stated, 'unceasing'.[287] Terence acknowledged the closeness of the household, writing to Mary and Annie in 1917: 'there were never brothers and sisters more loyal to one another'.[288] Terence's daughter, born on 23 June 1918, was named Máire after his eldest sister.[289]

Mary noted that during Terence's hunger strike she and other members of the family had to 'keep two sides of us alive': We have had the personal sorrow … we have also had to fight day and night the English propaganda that was carried out to discredit him with the world.'[290] Giving testimony before the American Commission on Conditions in Ireland in December 1920 Mary emphasised that she was not going 'to touch on' personal sorrow.[291] This conscious elision in her testimony to the Commission is noteworthy. Referring to the first week she spent in Brixton she stated: '[y]ou can understand what his sufferings were, and therefore I do not want to linger on that point.'[292]

Frank O'Connor recalled that he attended the MacSwiney funeral in Cork with his mother, emphasising how in a matter of months, 'the long, dark, masochistic face' he had seen conversing with Daniel Corkery by the New Bridge, lay dead in the City Hall.[293] The world marvelled as Terence clung to life past medical understanding. His body was, as his chaplain, Fr Dominic, stated, consuming itself to stay alive: 'the system, in its search for food' came 'on some nutritious portion of itself'.[294] He was immediately elevated to the status of republican martyr, despite, as William Murphy discusses, the almost simultaneous deaths of Michael Fitzgerald and Joseph Murphy on hunger strike in Cork prison that same October. Terence's position as the lone hunger striking prisoner in an alien country accorded him the heroic status denied the two other men. As Murphy states: 'the group at Cork was rendered almost faceless by its collective action'. He continues: '[t]hose like MacSwiney, who have been elevated to the status of martyr … endure a form of condescension from posterity. In their martyrdom they come to exist outside time, joining an ahistorical elite or tradition within Irish nationalism'.[295] Terence's apotheosis as republican martyr became the defining narrative after his death. Mary was central to ensuring that this version of her brother's death prevailed.

Despite the deification of republican martyrs such as Terence MacSwiney, the historiography of hunger striking during the revolutionary period has paid scant attention to the effect on family members, to the way they experienced the death on an emotional level. By contrast with historians, contemporaries did refer to the suffering of families as they watched their loved ones become malnourished, emaciated and, often, delirious. Lloyd George's statement on 26 August 1920 made it clear that Terence had made a 'deliberate choice' to starve, inflicting that suffering 'not only on himself but on his relations and friends'.[296] A telegram sent by him to Mary referred to 'the pain inflicted upon you by the determination of your brother to starve himself.[297] Terence himself noted that the his family's 'part in the suffering was ever so much harder than his, because it is always harder to see one you love suffer than to suffer yourself'.[298]

Mary's emotional responses to the horror she witnessed caused that 'discomfort' to others that Dolan writes of. Bearing witness to the death of her brother goes some way to explain why she was never easy to listen to and was perceived as shrill. As discussed in Chapter Three, she had a tendency towards gruffness even before Terence's death; in the aftermath such stridency became more pronounced. Many kept her, to use Dolan's phrase, 'at arm's length'.[299] She was considered too extreme by several and was often subject to ridicule. The derision she was subject to had, of course, a gendered dimension; the perception of her political extremism was heightened by the fact that she was a woman. Expounding extreme political principles was behaviour acceptable in a man; it was less so in a woman. Mary was not, however, merely a cipher for the doctrinaire element within republicanism during the Treaty debates and later; she was a woman who had suffered ultimate loss and witnessed, in the words of her sister Annie, scenes that were 'agonising beyond anything I could describe'.[300] Discussing the Cork and Brixton hunger strikes Murphy writes that by September 1920, 'the question had changed from whether the men would die to what would be the manner and meaning of their death'.[301] An understanding of her emotional response to Terence's death allows a more holistic view of Mary's politics from 1920 onwards.

The families of the hunger strikers in Cork and Brixton prisons in 1920 'shared the near universal desire ... that the story of their deaths should be told in ways that offered meaning and solace, and in ways that evoked admiration and condemnation'.[302] Historians like William Murphy have focused on the contemporary competing narratives and constructions of the deaths of Fitzgerald, Murphy and MacSwiney in October 1920.[303] He details how the inquest into the death of Terence, and the military inquiries held in lieu of same in the cases of Fitzgerald and Murphy, were 'fora where the authorities attempted to disrupt the narrative of a good death that the men and their supporters wished to construct'; they were 'determined that a verdict of suicide should be returned'.[304] The manner in which the need to maintain the narrative of a 'good death' shaped the later lives of the relatives of those who died in October 1920 has not been examined in any similar detail. Mary devoted the remainder of her life to ensuring that the death of her brother had political meaning. His death further radicalised her and rendered her – particularly from the viewpoint of her opponents – politically one-dimensional. She did not merely seek to shape and influence how her brother would be remembered as a grieving sister within a familial setting. Instead, she maintained his legacy and honoured his sacrifice by becoming centrally involved in republican politics in a way that she had not been to this point. She assumed the political voice of the MacSwiney family.

The treatment of those who died on hunger strike during the revolutionary period has focused on the political capital produced by republican martyrs. Murphy writes of Thomas Ashe's death from forcible feeding in September 1917:

> Sinn Féin had a prison martyr, providing a fresh emotional charge to the movement and further hastening the demise of the Irish Party. His funeral and inquest proved enormous propaganda opportunities ...[305]

Miller discusses the 'physical and emotional consequences of hunger striking' but with a focus on the individuals on strike and the relationship between Irish doctors and hunger strikers; there is no sustained discussion of the family as witness to the resultant physical and mental decline.[306] Murphy in discussing Terence, does note the 'stress on the family' and the fact that the death of men on hunger strike 'and very often their lives, tend to be stripped of all other meaning, unmoored from the complexity of context'.[307] A key component of that context is the emotional and psychological consequences of those deaths on family members as they bore witness to the slow, excruciating passing of close family members.

Joanna Bourke writes: 'Historians have been more comfortable analysing "utilities" or "moral economies" than studying the ebb and flow of anger, hatred and fear.'[308] Yet, those emotions come to light when one examines in detail the horror experienced by the family members of hunger strikers in Cork and Brixton from August to October 1920; when the reality of death by starvation was laid bare in all the messiness of the breakdown of bodily functions, alternating states of despair, hope and elation, delirium and, finally, the end itself. The medical report on Terence for 2 September noted that he had 'the bedpan twice but nothing was passed by the bowels. He is reported to have seemed exhausted after these attempts at defecation'.[309] As he neared the end of his life, he suffered intestinal distension as a result of flatulence and was passing 'his urine into the bed'.[310] Samples of his faeces were tested to see if they showed signs of his consuming food.[311] This was the sordid actuality and increasing dreadfulness that Mary witnessed.

Bourke writes that the 'act of narrating emotions – to oneself as much as to others – is dependent upon the ordering mechanisms of grammar, plot and genre'.[312] Each person who witnessed a family member on hunger strike narrated their emotions in different ways. Joseph Murphy's mother wrote that his father 'through his death died of a broken heart'.[313] On his application for a dependent's allowance Timothy Murphy declared that had been 'suffering from an ulcerating stomach' since his son's death despite being under 60 years of age.[314] Frank Gallagher, on hunger strike in Mountjoy in April 1920, worried about the effect of his death on his Aunt Margaret: 'she will go mad ... No ... It will be deeper than that'.[315]

Her brother's death was the defining moment in Mary's life. From this point onwards she engaged in a compulsive 'repeating [of the] tale' to use the language of theories of cultural trauma.[316] Roger Luckhurst describes Freud's 'highly speculative' *Beyond the Pleasure Principle* (1920) as his:

> attempt to understand what he termed [the] repetition compulsion. In essence, the psyche constantly returned to scenes of unpleasure because, by restaging the traumatic moment over and over again, it hoped belatedly to process the unassimilable material, to find ways of mastering the trauma retroactively.[317]

Luckhurst continues:

> Repetition compulsion has become a cultural shorthand for the consequences of traumatic events: individuals, collectives and nations risk trapping themselves in cycles of uncomprehending repetition unless the traumatic event is translated from repetition to the healthy analytic process of 'working through'.[318]

Mary's mind narrowed itself around the trauma of her brother's hunger strike and her need to ensure that his demise continued to be viewed as a 'good death'. This became an *idée fixe*. In *Spiritual Wounds* Aiken discusses the lifelong 'imperative to tell' engendered in many by the trauma of the Civil War.[319] Mary's testimonial urgency dated to the death of her brother on hunger strike. On the day before he died, she worried to O'Brien that a rumour that Terence had been secretly fed would sully his sacrifice:

> Perhaps leaflets could be got ready at once. If this lasts a few days something must be done ... if they succeed or even half succeed in libelling Terry now – it would be ruinous for the Cause, so just at the moment I feel it is the most important Republican duty ever.[320]

Terence's motive was not, she asserted to Fr Bernard Vaughan, 'self-murder' and she continued:

> He will do more by his single death to destroy the evil thing which is the British Government in Ireland, than if he led a whole army into battle and lost the lives of his men as well as his own. ...
>
> To die for a greater principle is a noble death ... [321]

Mary sought to impose a political and moral culture in Ireland that validated and memorialised the self-sacrifice of her brother, her own suffering and that of the wider family. The appropriate way to record and remember his traumatic death was the establishment of that for which he had died – a separatist republic. In 1922, at a meeting held under the auspices of the Irish Self-Determination League and the Roger Casement Sinn Féin Club in Essex Hall, London, Mary declared that she accepted the invitation to speak to 'carry on the work of him who died this night two years'.[322]

Mary MacSwiney lost her beloved brother in Brixton on 25 October 1920. This death was to determine the future course of her political life. When news of the death of Michael Fitzgerald on hunger strike in Cork reached the MacSwiney family, Annie wrote: 'it has brought the end so much nearer'.[323] Fitzgerald, the *Washington Herald* stated, 'had been without food about thirty hours longer than Terence MacSwiney'.[324] His death on 17 October was a 'shock to us all', Annie MacSwiney wrote, because the family still 'hoped' for the release of the hunger strikers.[325] According to O'Brien, who visited Brixton on 8

October, Terence believed that God would intervene to facilitate his release 'as by doing so the victory over the enemies of his country would be greater'. Terence spoke to O'Brien 'about a possible nursing home'.[326] The death of Fitzgerald made it clear that MacSwiney had 'not the slightest chance of release and death is the only alternative'.[327] The death of the hunger striker marked 'a glorious end to their fight' Annie MacSwiney stated but, she continued: '[f]or us who have watched this agony & who will witness their death, it is hard'. Ireland, however, she declared, 'cannot be freed without suffering'.[328] In this she echoed the words of Nora, Hugh's wife following his death in Terence MacSwiney's *The Revolutionist*: ''Tis we who are troubled and frightened. There is no fear on his face.'[329]

Mary's determination to ensure that her brother's death was not in vain manifested itself in her absolute unwillingness to compromise on the republican ideal even to the point of her death and the death of others. This willingness to shed blood was not a stance she had always maintained. Ernest Blythe recalled a meeting in Limerick in the months before the rebellion. The Cumann na mBan branch in the city invited Mary to speak. For Blythe she spoke outside her remit:

> At the time there were stories going around that someday the British forces were going to surround the Volunteers, while they were out on some route march, and disarm them. Mary MacSwiney, who had no business to deal with such matters, proceeded in her speech to urge the Volunteers not to fight but to give up their arms peacefully if surrounded, as while arms could be replaced lives could not be replaced. There was great indignation against her, and rightly so, at the time.[330]

Clearly, this statement reflects Blythe's problematic attitude to female activists. Blythe had, as David Fitzpatrick argues, a 'contempt for women'.[331] More pertinently the incident offers an insight into the manner in which Mary's political stance shifted and solidified consequent on the trauma she experienced during her brother's hunger strike and death.

Chapter Five

America: December 1920–August 1921

Mary MacSwiney displayed no outward signs of trauma after Terence's death. Indeed, she travelled the length and breadth of America from late December 1920 until early August 1921, having been tasked by de Valera with continuing the US propaganda tour in the context of the bond drive following his return to Ireland.[1] This role saw her undertake numerous long train journeys. She met with Irish American politicians and members of the Catholic hierarchy and spoke at large meetings, all the time corresponding with de Valera and Harry Boland, US envoy of the Dáil and, indeed, the person 'in control of every facet of the American mission'.[2] Mary was also in constant communication with first, James O'Mara, and, later, Stephen O'Mara, successive financial organisers in respect of the American bond drive.

However, as Lerner and Micale note '[e]vents considered "traumatic" provoke a spectrum of responses'. They continue: 'trauma turns out to be not an event per se but rather the *experiencing* or *remembering* of an event in the mind of an individual'.[3] Terence's death was the fulcrum around which Mary's political activities revolved. This is not to deny her own absolute commitment to the republic. However, it is arguably unlikely that her commitment would have taken the shape it did but for his death on hunger strike. It is doubtful that she would have pledged herself to a long sojourn in America, away from her family and St Ita's school, had she not wanted to intensify and diversify tactics to bring about the republic for which her brother had given his life. She believed that American money and support was crucial to the winning of the republic for which her brother had given his life.

Irish republican supporters in America, as in other countries, mobilised in response to death of Terence MacSwiney. On 7 November 1920 sympathisers marched in single file for an hour around the White House in Washington. The march, the leaders declared, was to be repeated each night for 74 days, the duration of MacSwiney's fast.[4] De Valera had been in America since 11 June 1919 and his tour of the major cities made real the struggle for Irish independence for the American people while putting him 'centre stage'.[5] Mary stated that she ' looked at America from one point of view only and that was what America could or would not do for Ireland'.[6]

After the collective republican outpouring of horror at the martyrdom of Terence MacSwiney and the high-publicity funerals, Mary was left to deal with her raw emotions as she attempted to return to her daily life in Cork. Gavan Duffy encouraged Art O'Brien to take a holiday after the high-profile death in Brixton. Acknowledging the stress O'Brien had endured during the protracted hunger strike, he wrote: 'you have gone through more than any man should be asked to undergo ... in working and constant anxiety'.[7] Mary had no such luxury as a holiday. She had to turn her attention to St Ita's, the running of which had been left to the other teachers during her absence in England. Indeed, in Easter 1920 the school was faced with closure. Supporters of St Ita's, however, formed a committee to place it 'on a paying basis pending the time when DAIL EIREANN would be ready to take over the control of Education throughout the country'. St Ita's Educational Association 'invited those interested in Education imbued with Gaelic ideals to become members'.[8] Shareholders subscribed up to £600 and 'the number of pupils greatly increased'.[9] Yet, at the very point that the school was saved from imminent closure Mary had to be absent from its running as she endured the ordeal in Brixton. She had to face the impact of such absenteeism immediately after her brother's death. The escalation of the violence of the War of Independence in Cork also impacted on the school:

> The troubled year that Cork has had naturally hampered the work of the School. Many of the pupils were sent to boarding Schools for safety, or removed to schools less closely identified with the Republican Cause. The result has been a much larger deficit on the working of the School than was anticipated.[10]

Other schools fared similarly. The South Presentation convent school was 'struck' during a night of violence in the city on 6 October 1920.[11] Of course, the nuns had resources and government grants that were not at the disposal of St Ita's. Disruption to the workings of the latter school continued because of Black and Tan activities in the city into 1921.[12]

Mary's growing stature within republican politics after the death of Terence meant that even more than previously, she had to balance republican activism with management of the school while also concerned for the wellbeing of her siblings. as they struggled to come to terms with the horror of their brother's death. On 6 October 1921, following over seven months of political work in America from December 1920, she wrote to Eileen and John J. Hearne that the school had 'suffered considerably from my absence and occupation in the evenings on political matters in some shape or form and on Sundays dragged out to make speeches so you see there is no rest for the wicked'.[13]

On 4 November 1920 Cork Corporation elected a new Lord Mayor. Councillor Donal O'Callaghan, the Deputy Lord Mayor, was unanimously elected; the 'Republican position' was 'that they absolutely refused to be terrorised'.[14] Mary was centrally immersed in such politics of resistance. Despite strong words of defiance, terror and violence continued in Cork and across Ireland. As Terence lay dying in Brixton the City Hall in Cork was bombed on 9 October.[15] On 10 November Christopher Lucey, a medical student who had been on hunger strike in Mountjoy in April 1920, was shot in Túirín Dubh, Ballingeary. During his service in Cork two days later, members of the police 'in motor vehicles passed through the funeral procession, firing shots from their rifles when they got in front'.[16] In the city persons with Irish names over their shop fronts were targeted by the police and notices in the language were ordered to be taken down.[17] At midnight on 20 November de Róiste wrote: '[t]he past few days and nights have indeed been days and nights of terror in Cork'.[18]

Within a short time, Mary left the city once again, travelling to America on 24 November in the company of Muriel, both women designated as witnesses before the American Commission to Investigate Atrocities in Ireland established by the journalist

Oswald Garrison Villard, editor of the journal *The Nation*, a paper which supported the concept of self-government for Ireland. Both sides in the War of Independence were invited to give evidence although the New York doctor and republican propagandist, W. J. A. Moloney, who conceived the idea declared that the 'main object to be kept in mind is that the Commission is merely a mask to place the Irish case before the tribunal of the civilized world'.[19] He called all US senators, governors and mayors of large cities to come together with newspaper editors, members of the different religions and well known individuals to establish a 'Committee of One Hundred'. This committee was tasked with the establishment of an eight-member commission to inquire into conditions in Ireland. Professor William MacDonald, formerly of Brown University who had visited Ireland in his capacity as a journalist earlier in 1920, headed the commission.[20] Private individuals from both sides of the conflict were asked to give details of their experiences. Those travelling from Ireland received transportation and accommodation costs.[21] The British ambassador to the US, Sir Auckland Geddes, recognised that the Commission was intended to embarrass their side and the Foreign Office determined that there would be no assistance.[22] Mary and Muriel were amongst several republicans who travelled from Cork to give evidence.

By her own admission Mary was no longer a young woman when her brother died.[23] Yet it was in this period that she began to assume a progressively more important role in Irish politics; tentatively at first as many of the male politicians only saw her as a mourning sister, while others were circumspect about the merits of women in the political arena. Máire Comerford stated that Mary and her sister Annie 'became known to me, as to all the people, in newspaper reports at the time of Terence's hunger strike to death'.[24] A somewhat hyperbolic report on her reception by Americans during the period of her 1920–1 tour stated:

> Miss MacSwiney has risen during the few months she has been in America from comparative obscurity to one of the most widely known women in the count[r]y and has been accorded receptions in nearly a hundred American cities that can be compared only with those given great world leaders. When Miss MacSwiney came to America several months ago, following the death in Brixton Prison of her brother, the late Lord Mayor Terence MacSwiney of Cork, little was known of her.[25]

The *Boston Globe* similarly reported on the relative anonymity of Mary on her arrival in Boston other than as the sister of the 'Martyred Mayor of Cork'. However, once she began to speak to the Commission she cemented her presence and political weight as an activist in her own right:

> Miss MacSwiney made a speech which those in the hall will long remember because of the impressive manner in which it was delivered and the unusual character of the address itself. It was a great surprise, for there were few in that vast audience who realised – knew anything of this remarkable woman – knew anything of her great power as a speaker; her remarkable diction and the comprehensive knowledge of the woman on every phase of American history in relation to Ireland. ... It was the utter unexpectedness of the thing that made it so dramatic ...[26]

The invitation by the Commission was issued in the first instance to Muriel, even before she was strong enough to return to Cork.[27] As Terence's widow she clearly had emotive appeal. Most of the messages of sympathy on Terence's death were to her, although some

Cumann na mBan branches sent telegrams also to Mary.[28] Tomás MacCurtain's wife, another high-profile widow, was also invited to give evidence before the Commission.[29] However, she declined. Unlike Mary's response to Terence's death, Éilís MacCurtain displayed outward signs of the trauma she experienced as witness to the shooting dead of her husband. De Róiste noted in his diary that he met her in August 1920. While the two engaged in conversation some members of the police passed and 'she spoke of them in a tone that betokened hysterics almost'.[30] Éilís's two sisters, Anna, and Susanna Walsh, did attend the Commission to give testimony.

Prior to departure the Irish newspapers' interest lay in Muriel, not Mary. The *Cork Examiner* noted her arrival in 'Cove' on 24 November to embark for New York on the SS Celtic; no mention was made of Mary.[31] While the *Irish Independent* noted that the latter sailed for America on 26 November, it reported that it was her sister-in-law that would give evidence.[32] *The Liberator (Tralee)*, indeed, incorrectly recorded that Muriel was accompanied by Annie MacSwiney.[33] Due to fog, the ship, due to dock on 3 December, was delayed. However, Reuters international news agency reported that a special tug would be sent by Irish sympathisers to transport Muriel ashore to attend a reception while a parade of motor cars along Fifth Avenue was planned as a 'demonstration of sympathy in her recent bereavement'. Again, no mention was made of her sister-in-law.[34] In the event, due to quarantine regulations which doctors refused to break, none of the MacSwiney party were allowed to land until the next morning. On board the ship rival anthems were bellowed out. *The Soldier's Song* emanated from second class. When 'fervent strains' of *God Save the King* emerged in response from first class, the women's committee on board the patrol tug circling the ship took up the tune with the words of the *My Country 'Tis of Thee*:

> Then an unidentified member of the black gang stuck a grimy head out of one of the portholes near to the water's edge and with lusty voice shouted, 'To hell with MacSwiney!' The challenge was quickly taken up by one of the Irishmen in the second cabin who bellowed back with equal force, 'To hell with Lloyd George!'[35]

Although Mary's role in America was initially perceived as that of companion to her sister-in-law, positions quickly began to shift. Muriel clearly had political value as the widow of a republican martyr. Her youth and glamourous bearing drew attention from the newspapers. *The New York Tribune* described her as 'appearing much younger than the twenty-eight years she admitted'.[36] The *Evening Star (Washington DC)* devoted some time to her appearance on her arrival in New York:

> There was little about the appearance of Mrs. MacSwiney to suggest the tragic purpose of her visit to America. A mere girl of the pure Celtic type, with her brilliant eyes, quick and engaging, and a strong well-shaped mouth, containing a perfect set of teeth, this Irishwoman, who patiently watched for seventy-two days while her husband starved, smiled to the onlookers as the long parade wended its way from the station ...[37]

The *Evening World (New York NY)* wrote in a similar vein emphasising Muriel's physical appearance and feminine vulnerability:

> There was a flush on the hitherto pale face of the widow and her smile was the bewildered one of a child, while a tear sparkled in her eyes. She lifted her widow's veil at the request of

> the camera men and gave them a rosy smile, revealing [sic] two perfect rows of beautiful white teeth.

An image accompanying the report showed a beaming and youthful Muriel and a middle-aged, dowdy Mary.[38]

It was to the former that Mary McWhorter, the Chicago-based president of the Ladies Auxiliary of the Ancient Order of Hibernians, addressed her reception letter. She wished to welcome her to America 'in my own name and also in the name of the American women of Irish blood whom I represent'. McWhorter was present on the boat which circled the SS Celtic and she saw Muriel 'at a distance'. Her heart, she wrote, 'aches in sympathy with yours'. McWhorter detailed her own speaking itinerary on behalf of Irish independence and hoped that when she returned to New York she would see Muriel 'for a few minutes'. McWhorter was sure that Ireland, 'will ever be grateful for the sacrifice you have made. You will always be a shining star among the women of Ireland'. Mary was only briefly mentioned in the closing line of the letter.[39] As a widow of an Irish republican martyr, Muriel had propaganda value. She had fulfilled the traditional role of women within Irish republicanism; she had sacrificed her husband. Peter MacSwiney wrote in this vein to her while Terence was on hunger strike: 'Everyone here is talking of the great sacrifice you have made in agreeing to the Hunger Strike. Being Terry's wife you could do nothing else.'[40]

The situation quickly changed, and Mary's profile grew as that of her sister-in-law waned. Muriel suffered ill-health during the voyage and on arrival. Increasingly Mary took over speaking duties showing from the outset a large degree of political acumen and leadership qualities. In that way Muriel and Mary represented two images associated with republican women. Muriel was the grieving widow, felled emotionally and physically by the tragedy she suffered. Mary, by contrast, displayed what Aiken describes as the 'stoicism and composure popularly associated with republican women'.[41] The American papers were quick to also note the gravitas she displayed. The *New York Tribune*, describing the arrival and first speeches noted that Mary talked for a half an hour 'answering or cleverly evading questions as she saw fit'.[42] A report in the *Boston Globe* of a meeting held in the Mechanic's Hall in Boston on 19 December 1920 stated that an 'immense' crowd stood 'patiently' outside to 'catch a glimpse' of the two women:

> They were somewhat disappointed, however, as Mrs. MacSwiney did not go to the hall. She did not feel equal to the strain of such a meeting. Miss Mary MacSwiney came, and she more than made good for the disappointment which Mrs. MacSwiney's absence caused those in the hall.[43]

A brief meeting was held with de Valera on the day after arrival in New York. However, at this point he was both 'wary of women' and unaware of Mary's political abilities so the meeting was merely one of courtesy.[44] From New York Mary and Muriel travelled to Washington, appearing before the Commission on the next day.

Muriel was supposed to speak to the Commission before Mary; on the day the speaking order was changed, most likely due to the former's ill health.[45] Mary began giving evidence in the morning of 8 December 1920 and continued to do so after the noon recess. She began by briefly describing her family background before she went on to 'sketch the republican movement'. Her opinions at this point in her life were clearly solidifying and becoming absolute. There 'had never been a rebellion in Ireland', she declared, distinguishing for the benefit of her American audience, the difference between a rebellion and an insurrection. The former was 'an uprising against lawfully constituted authority … England's authority in Ireland was never lawfully constituted – it was an usurpation maintained by the sword'.[46] Mary was concerned to make clear that the republican movement in Ireland comprised both Protestants and Catholics. Emphasising that there 'is no religious difficulty in Ireland of serious importance' she stated that the republican movement was entirely one 'for political freedom'.[47] Her breath of knowledge of Irish history came through in her testimony; she was, of course, a history teacher and one who felt strongly aggrieved, as discussed in Chapter Two, that in so many Irish schools pupils were not taught their own history.

She ranged from the Nine Years War, 1593–1603, through Grattan's Parliament, 1782–1800, moving on to the 1798 rebellion and the Act of Union before discussing the famine and the failed rebellions of the nineteenth century. She discussed in depth the land struggle and the Home Rule movement, representing Charles Stewart Parnell as someone for whom a domestic parliament was merely the first step to full independence. Continuing with her testimony she moved onto the revolutionary period, explaining why the Irish Volunteers did not mobilise in Cork during the 1916 rebellion. To make this point was vital in her mind as the failure to rise preoccupied Terence in the years after 1916. She detailed the victory of republicans over 'parliamentarians' in the 1918 election, the transfer of allegiance by 'ninety one percent'[48] of county and municipal councils to the Irish republic and the establishment of a parallel state with the establishment of the first Dáil Éireann and the republican courts. She made special reference to the way the revolutionary period impacted children. This was because 'today in Ireland women take their stand by the men and yield not to them one iota in their power of endurance'. However, she added, 'it is hard to see the children suffer'.[49] She drew parallels with the American War of Independence declaring that the next winter would be 'Ireland's Valley Forge': 'The British have destroyed our crops, our supplies of food. The men can get on, the women can stand the suffering. But it is for the children I plead. We must have help this winter.'[50]

The range of her testimony was somewhat of a surprise to the commissioners while the length of her testimony, comprising ten hours, prefigured her lengthy speech against the Anglo-Irish Treaty in December 1921. Towards the end of the first day Chairman Howe attempted to draw proceedings to a close declaring: 'It is now ten minutes to six, and perhaps we should stop now before you branch out into any new subject.[51] An unsigned report on Mary's appearance before the Commission testified to the manner in which she did not merely recount events from the perspective of a sister who aided her brother's revolutionary activities; she firmly established herself for her listeners within the revolutionary narrative she described:

> However, MacSwiney had been on the witness stand in Washington but a few minutes before Chairman Frederick C. Howe, Miss Jane Addams and the other commissioners realized that they were interrogating the most unusual witness that had been called to the stand. The commissioners and spectators marvelled [sic] at Miss MacSwiney's brilliancy, her world knowledge and her intimacy not only with Irish history but with American history as well.
>
> It had been planned to ask Miss MacSwiney a few questions regarding her late brother's activities and then excuse her. However, her first few answers to questions put by the

> Commission indicated the extra ordinary character of the witness and she was kept on the witness stand for ten hours. It was said by the commission afterwards that: no witness from Ireland had given such a clear recital of facts or had shed so much light on the Irish position as Miss MacSwiney.[52]

The *Topeka State Journal* described how Mary, clad in 'a deep black with a heavy black veil thrown back from her ruddy face', appeared nervous at first 'but gained confidence as she swept into an arraignment of British rule'.[53] Her education to third level was remarked on by several of the American newspapers. Twice the *Topeka State Journal* noted that she had been elected to the governing body of University College Cork.[54] She addressed the College Women's Club in Washington during the first month of her stay, the *Washington Herald* writing: 'Miss MacSwiney is in a sense a member of the sorority, being enrolled in the College Women's Club of Ireland'.[55]

Mary alluded to the factions and tensions within Irish American politics during her deposition to the Commission and firmly supported de Valera's position, notably his statement that Irish foreign policy in respect of Britain could mirror that between the United States and Cuba. When he arrived in America in 1919 Irish American politics was riven with faction and division. During his 18 months in the United States de Valera supported Joe McGarrity, Clan na Gael, against the rival faction, Friends of Irish Freedom established in 1916, which was led by the Fenian John Devoy and Judge Daniel Cohalan of the New York Supreme Court.[56] On 6 February 1920 the *New York Globe* issued an abridged account of an interview de Valera had given for publication in the *Westminster Gazette* the following day. In it he stated that an independent Ireland could follow the United States Platt Amendment in respect of Cuba and not enter a treaty with a foreign power that would be detrimental to British security. Although as McCullagh states, de Valera's 'comments didn't suggest subservience but neutrality', the declaration brought forth charges that the head of the Irish republic was curtailing the country's sovereignty, accusations that were reiterated by Devoy and Cohalan.[57] In late 1920 de Valera established the American Association for the Recognition of the Irish Republic in the context of Irish American factional disputes, most notably over the interpretation of self-determination and 'whether republican principle should give way to a more accommodating interpretation' of the term.[58] The Association was under de Valera's control and was intended as a counter to the Friends of Irish Freedom and the criticism of him by Devoy and Cohalan as regards his reference to US Cuban relations.[59] The name of the new organisation, while clunky, meant that, as McCullagh, states, 'there would be no ambiguity about aims or control'.[60]

In her evidence to the Commission Mary made direct reference to de Valera's interview in the *Westminster Gazette*:

> Our President took lately the first paragraph of the new agreement made with Cuba by the United States. It is a guarantee that the ports of Cuba will not be given to any foreign power or used in any way that would injure the United States. … we are perfectly willing to give a promise that we will not let any other foreign power, or any power, use our ports as a war base.

When pressed by Senator Walsh as to whether she expressly referred to 'Great Britain' she replied in the affirmative. However, she did make clear that Ireland was not going to adopt a submissive relationship with Britain:

> Neither will we allow our ports to be used by one big nation that wants to make war on another big nation. England says that is not enough. If it is not enough, she will have to do without. She is not going to keep us perpetually in slavery. England will have to be satisfied with what is right from us. She will have to be satisfied with justice to our interests as well as hers. ... If, as Lloyd George said some time ago, England will never agree to an Irish Republic until England is beaten to the ground, well, I am very sorry, because England will have to be beaten to the ground.[61]

Mary also echoed Terence in this context. On 19 September 1914 he wrote of the outbreak of World War I in *Fianna Fáil*, stating that the Irish Volunteers would: 'hold Ireland, for Ireland, against all comers ... And we guarantee to England that this country will not be used as a base against her. She is entitled to this – no more. On our side we demand the recognition of our independence. We will take no less.'[62] Mary continued to maintain this position on foreign affairs between Britain and a putative independent Ireland in the period before the Treaty split. In a letter to Eileen and John J. Hearn in October 1921 she declared:

> Keep on [working hard] & when the negotiations break down – as I feel pretty sure they will – remember the point to stress is that Ireland is willing to give England every guarantee for her safety but will not any longer submit to English domination.[63]

As Mary continued to talk over the course of 8 December, she described to the Commission the suffering her brother endured on hunger strike. The issue of whether he was forcibly fed was raised: '[w]e took away some of the medicines in the hospital to see if it contained nourishment but there were no traces of any in the samples which we got'.[64] She also spoke to the violence against republicans during the War of Independence, describing how MacCurtain was killed. Responding to Senators Walshe and Norris, she stated, eliding events such as Soloheadbeg, that the Irish only turned from passive resistance when unarmed men were shot and the workings of the Republican Courts and the work of members of Dáil Éireann was interfered with. She expressed her fear that the British government would not permit herself and Muriel to return to Ireland.[65] The *Evening Star (Washington DC)* described her testimony as 'clean cut and precise. She presented her views with a fluency and a command of language that never left her at a loss for a word'.[66] The *Washington Herald* stated that for several hours Mary held in 'alternative suspense and applause a throng that that filled every available space in Old Fellows' Hall'.[67]

Muriel gave evidence on 9 December. Her testimony was much more personal than that of her sister-in-law and revolved around her relationship with her husband. She persisted in her statements that the British authorities had fed Terence against his will and in contradiction of the express wishes of his family.[68] On several occasions, however, she was forced to defer to the better knowledge of Mary. Repeatedly she testified to being ill at crucial times during her husband's hunger strike. Consequently, her account was much less strong and hard-hitting than that of her sister-in-law. Mary had to intervene to clarify how many members of Sinn Féin were elected in December 1918 and to give details on the election of Terence as Lord Mayor.[69] Quite quickly the commissioners recognised the relative weight of the two testimonies. When questioned as to the murder of Tomás MacCurtain and as to whether she was at the inquest Muriel MacSwiney responded: 'I was in Cork, but I was very ill at the time'. The commissioner pointedly replied: 'So you had better leave that to your sister-in-law?'[70]

Three days before Mary left Ireland for America the attack and counter attacks of Bloody Sunday on 21 November occurred. Three days after she gave testimony, on the night of 11 and 12 of December the burning of Cork took place. She stated before the Commission that she did 'not know the details' of the attack carried out on British officers on the morning of 21 November but vehemently asserted that they were 'English secret service men who had the clews [sic] of the machinery of our government'. They would, she stated, have 'been shot justly and after warning'; if they had left the country 'they would be safe'.[71] Mary argued that the killing of British spies by the IRA was justified in the context of war. This was also the way de Valera responded to the murders on the morning of Bloody Sunday. In the *New York Times* on 23 November 1920, he declared that of all human beings 'enemy spies ... rightly deserved death ... for they provide the alien government with knowledge and the strength to persecute and inflict misery upon a whole nation'.[72] This was the received republican version of the murders. In discussing the men who carried out the shootings Anne Dolan states that 'the dead had to be spies because if they were not, then their killers were the murderers and assassins that British propaganda always said they were'.[73] On 16 January 1921 Cumann na mBan issued a leaflet endorsing 'the right of ours as of all armies in self-defence to shoot all Spies'.[74] In her letter on 30 December 1920 to the bishops who attacked IRA tactics Annie also brought up the question of the shooting of spies. This was something, she stated, that was carried out in any war situation, citing the First World War as an example. Maybe to display her adherence to received gender roles in her correspondence with the hierarchy, she alleged that she knew 'no more of the working of the Irish Republican Army than the sister of an English soldier would know about the deliberations of their Army Councils'. However, she asserted that she was 'sufficiently acquainted' with those in the republican government to 'know that no man is shot by its orders unless he is proved, up the hilt, guilty of black treachery to his Country, or if he an Englishman, guilty of being actively engaged in bringing about the ruin of our land'.[75]

Throughout her eight months in America, Mary fretted to hear news of events in Ireland. At the end of January 1921, she wrote to Harry Boland, Dáil Éireann representative to the US, about the 'absolute dearth of interesting news about Irish affairs ... in their local papers'.[76] However, just over a week following her arrival she received news that was distressing, both on a political and on a personal level as Cork was subjected to an 'orgy of destruction and ruin'.[77] The result was a 'wildness of ruin and debris in the main area around Patrick's Street'.[78] The burning of Cork was the culmination of arson attacks on shops and republican clubs across the city in the previous months. The Lord Mayor giving evidence to the American Commission on Conditions in Ireland on 13 and 14 January 1921 estimated the destruction before the events of the 11 and 12 December at over a million pounds.[79] On the evening of 11 December, the A Company, 1st Battalion of the 1st Cork Brigade mounted an attack on the K Company of the Auxiliaries on the north side of the city near to Victoria Barracks. The death of one of the Auxiliaries and the injury to others resulted in reprisals on the inhabitants of Dillon's Cross with six houses burned to the ground.[80] Another reason for the actions of the crown forces in Cork on 11-12 December may have been the death of 17 members of the RIC Auxiliaries during the IRA ambush at Kilmichael on 28 November. The response of the government was to proclaim martial law in counties Cork, Kerry, Limerick and Tipperary on 10 December.[81] After the attacks in Dillon's Cross, further reprisals were carried out in the city centre. The inquiry by the Irish Labour Party noted that this occurred when the city was under the curfew issued on 20 July 1920; all the main streets were deserted after 10 pm.[82] Lil Conlon wrote:

> In all parts of the city and suburbs the whole population was disturbed by rifle and revolver firing, bomb explosions, the smashing of windows and extensive outbreaks of fire. Most of the leading business houses were reduced to ruins.[83]

With limited initial details as to what had occurred, with no small degree of narcissism, Mary conflated the events in Cork with the testimony she and Muriel had just given in Washington. The *Washington Herald* wrote:

> Miss MacSwiney ... is quoted as declaring that the great fire in Cork may have been set by the Black and Tans in reprisal for the testimony she and Mrs. Muriel MacSwiney gave before the unofficial American commission investigating conditions in Ireland.

The paper continued: 'In an interview yesterday she compared the destruction of a large section of Cork to Germany's devastation of Louvain and Rheims.'[84]

Privately she asked if 'any of Cork' would be 'left' when she went home. Having wired for news and received none, she expressed her worry about Annie. While Belgrave Place was toward the top of Patrick's Hill and therefore out of the line of the fire spreading in Patrick's Street, it was still sufficiently close to the main events of the night; it fell within the three-mile radius of the General Post Office on Pembroke Street subject to curfew.[85] Dillon's Cross was within walking distance of Belgrave Place and auxiliaries travelling from there into the city would have traversed King Street turning left down to Patrick's Bridge. The Lord Mayor of Cork, Donal O'Callaghan stated that 'shortly before nine o'clock military cars drove through the town very wildly and recklessly and a number of shots were fired'.[86] A priest from St Peter and Paul's church testified to taking the northbound tram from Father Matthew Station on Patrick's Street at 9 pm on 11 December. At Summerhill the tram was surrounded and boarded by armed men. Amongst those who were assaulted, one woman 'was knocked to the ground and kicked by a uniformed man as she lay helpless and screaming'.[87] At the corner of Patrick's Hill and Coburg Street, a university student was fired upon. He escaped the bullet and making his way along Wellington Road he saw 'about twelve "Black and Tans", each with a girl, going towards town'.[88] Belgrave Place was one of the smaller roads off Wellington Road. While Mary would not have known such specific details as news filtered to her in America, she was broadly aware that St Ita's school and the family home were very much in the immediate radius of the events of the night of the 11 and 12 of December. Political horror at the actions of the Black and Tans and personal fear for her sister coalesced. Indeed, Conlon estimated that the:

> total area destroyed amounted roughly to 5 acres and the total number of premises destroyed was between 40 and 60. A very considerable amount of looting had been carried out.[89]

Stephen Powell, the Managing Director of Mangan's Jewellers at numbers 3 and 4 St Patrick Street, was held up at gunpoint and the shop safe looted. Powell, who gave evidence to the Strickland Inquiry into the events of the 11 and 12 December referred to the fact that his wife was on the premises and was 'nervous'.[90] The city hall where Terence had been arrested, and the Carnegie Library on Anglesea Street were also burned. According to O'Callaghan 15,000 books in the library were burned while all city records were destroyed.[91] In some cases people were rendered homeless: the 20 or 25 'girls' who lived over the Munster Arcade department store 'came out with a considerable amount of distress and alarm'.[92] Florrie O'Donoghue estimated that somewhere between 1,500 and 2,000 people 'were thrown out of work' due to the destruction of businesses.[93] Testimony gathered by the Irish Labour Party referred to drunkenness as 'a general characteristic of the Crown forces' on the night.[94] Mary was, she wrote, 'very uneasy. I don't mind them burning the house [St Ita's] if their lives are saved'.[95]

Mary left Washington on 16 December to conduct a tour of other 'larger cities' in the US under auspices of the AARIR.[96] Taking his place in 'leading the bond drive' was at the special request of de Valera, as she reminded him in July 1921.[97] Recalling the request, she stated that she 'obeyed' as a 'soldier of Ireland, though only a woman'.[98] There was a family symmetry in her work to raise money for the Republic; in the period 1919 until his arrest in August 1920, Terence had been involved with Michael Collins in the collection of the Dáil Loan in Cork.[99] That de Valera accorded her the role was also evidence of her growing stature within Irish republicanism as an activist in her own right, as a person who could hold her own politically. She hoped she was, she declared to de Valera, 'as good a solider as the next'.[100] It had quickly become clear that Mary impressed the Commission on Conditions in Ireland, and this was likely to have filtered through to de Valera. As the report on her impact stated: 'No thought of sending MacSwiney through the country on a speaking tour was entertained when she came from Ireland. But the story of her brilliancy and her oratorical ability soon become known …'[101] Mary accepted the request to carry out an American tour because she believed:

> with all my heart and soul that America meant what she said when she entered this great World's [sic] War. … if the world were made free for democracy Ireland was free, because democracy means government of the people, of a country, by the people of that country, and for the people of that country.

However, she believed that America had failed Ireland. Despite fighting for the freedom of small nations, America 'left Ireland, the biggest and oldest of small nations, a slave'.[102]

Mary and Muriel spent Christmas 1920 at the Clinton, Massachusetts home of Senator David J. Walsh, travelling from there to Worcester where the former addressed meetings.[103] On 30 December Muriel received the Freedom of New York, the first woman to receive the honour. [104] Before she left for Ireland, she visited Terence's sister Margaret in Asherville convent, North Carolina.[105] Leaving the US in early January, she arrived at Tilbury in England in the middle of the month with Kathleen O'Connell, the ship not being permitted to call at Queenstown.[106] Writing to Fred Cronin in early February, Art O'Brien noted that Muriel was still in London, continuing: ' [s]he was rather exhausted on her return from the States , and I think she felt the strain of it much more than she herself realised'.[107] On 4 January 1921 Mary's brother Peter arrived in New York, together with O'Callaghan, both stowaways on board the steamer the West Cannon. The two were duly detained by immigration. Peter was released when he showed his passport issued by an American consul.[108]

De Valera was not the only one who required Mary to exercise her voice in the US. On 29 January 1921 the Honorary Secretary of the central branch of Cumann na mBan wrote to her. Cumann na mBan believed that it was necessary that the 'American people should learn the exact attitude of Irishwomen toward the present warfare in Ireland' and they wanted her to speak in America on behalf of 'the largest organised body of women in Ireland'. Cumann na mBan wanted Mary to follow in the 'wake' of the deputation of the 'International Women's League' in America. Although the latter 'mean well', they may, the letter stated, 'give the impression that we, the women of Ireland, want peace at any price'. 'We want you to emphasise everywhere the fact that our attitude is NOT a pacifist one'.[109]

In the period between January and August 1921 Mary travelled to 58 cities and spoke at over 300 meetings.[110] She paid a 'visit of courtesy' to every bishop whose episcopal city she visited.[111] The bishop of Columbus she described as a 'narrow type', adding that 'he and I did not quite hit it off'. Crucially, the bishop 'set himself in opposition to the full demand' for a republic, drawing Mary's ire.[112] The AARIR facilitated her some degree of support, appointing Catherine Flanagan from Hartford, Connecticut, as her secretary.[113] She reported directly in America to Harry Boland, James O'Mara and from July 1921 Stephen O'Mara who assumed the position of special envoy and fundraiser on the latter's return to Ireland. Unlike de Valera who, certainly in the early period of his American tour, read prepared speeches due to fear of being misquoted in the press, Mary's speeches were spontaneously given from rough notes.[114] She, however, was also cautious of how she was presented in the press:

> In case you were thinking of publishing a speech of mine, do not publish that one. You know I do not prepare my speeches and they are not models of style. I shall revise one for printing if you wire me you want one.[115]

The speeches Mary gave across America in late 1920 and in 1921 took the format of the evidence she gave before the Commission on Conditions in Ireland. She drew parallels between the Irish struggle for a republic and the American war of Independence. She made clear the similarities but also the way the two struggles diverged. The Americans were rebels; the Irish were not:

> I have said that you were rebels, because you called England your mother country. You took her laws and her constitution, and it was only when the government of England became a tyranny and an oppression that you felt justified in throwing off English rule and setting up an independent republic. We are not rebels, because one cannot be a rebel except against lawfully constituted authority, and the authority of England in Ireland was never lawful, and has never been constituted by the Irish people.[116]

Several of the speeches appeared later in pamphlet form.[117] Souvenir publications also appeared.[118] In Cleveland the local committee: 'got out a card showing Terence MacSwiney's picture on one side and Miss MacSwiney's on the other, and the end of the card was perforated so that it could be torn off as a membership card.'[119] In Hoboken, New Jersey, she was given the freedom of the city engrossed in sheepskin.[120]

The focus of de Valera's period in America was the raising of a loan of $10 million; the floating of this bond would also, he believed, 'help the concurrent propaganda campaign in favour of the recognition of the Republic'.[121] Mary seamlessly saw her aims in America in 1921 as similar. The twin planks of her work in the United States in this period were the linked causes of the Dáil bond and the education of America in republican principles in pursuit of the recognition of the Irish Republic. The latter was to be achieved through rousing speeches and the dissemination of propaganda. Indeed, Mary was not just concerned to appeal to Irish America, she targeted all Americans, waging a propaganda war on tour. She stated that she was followed by 'English propagandists ... trying to undo the work we had been doing'. They aimed, she declared, to represent her as 'an extremist'.[122] She claimed that 'the impression created by the truth about Ireland's case was so great' that while touring the South she was followed by the British Ambassador to the United States, Sir Auckland Geddes.[123] While she sometimes responded through the press her *modus operandi* was to 'reply to propagandist criticism from the public platform'.[124] Mary's position was 'that Ireland already had a Republic and meant to keep it'. All she asked of Americans was 'to get your government to recognise an existing fact'.[125]

Mary's interviews and speeches in America were sharply focused. In this period republicans situated Ireland in the context of the small nations whose freedom had justified the allied response to the outbreak of the First World War. America 'commanded the attention' of Irish republicans because of 'President Woodrow Wilson's commitment to national self-determination as an American war aim'. From November 1918 de Valera, Fanning writes, 'saw his own role as best played on the American stage'.[126] Mary in her testimony to the American Commission on Conditions in Ireland referred to Wilson's commitment and continued: 'If you say "all people" you must count us'.[127] She declared that 'what was done to Belgium is not one-hundredth of what is happening in Ireland today ... And America went to war for Belgium!' Ireland, she stated, did not ask any country to take up arms. 'All we ask is recognition. Ireland has a functioning government and only one government'.[128] Earlier, in Washington in December, she declared: 'We Irish are no domestic problem of England ... We are an international problem'.[129]

In the US, Donal O'Callaghan called on the American Red Cross to send relief to Cork following the burning of the city in December. This was not initially forthcoming, as there were concerns about sparking an international incident but calls for humanitarian aid for women and children across Ireland who suffered hunger and displacement consequent on the political violence continued to emanate from Sinn Féin. The American Red Cross did, however, donate $100,000 to the American Committee for Relief in Ireland in March 1921.[130]

In drawing an analogy between the situation in Ireland and that in Valley Forge where food shortages beset the encampment of the Continental Army under George Washington in 1778–9, Mary reflected tropes within Irish American politics of the period. The three members of the American Commission on Irish Independence who addressed a public meeting of the Dáil on 8 May 1919 referred to the Irish and American struggles for independence.[131] Supporters of Irish republicanism in America also drew attention to the parallels. On 8 April 1921 Rev P. J. O'Connor wrote to her where she was staying in Chicago from Renville, Minnesota, stating that what 'America needs is to be brought back to fundamentals'. He suggested the writing of a book on 'Ireland's case from an American standpoint':

> Take the American Declaration of Independence and write a paragraph of it in one column of a page and parallel with it Ireland's Case and show paragraph by paragraph that here is an exact parallel in Ireland today in the objections of the colonists against English rule, and present-day conditions in Ireland. In a third column on same page you could show that the same England is hitting back at American institutions today .... In that way you will be hinging the whole issue on American principles. And by proving that recognition of right & justice is the foundation of democracy, you will be forcing on the American people the conviction that it is America's duty to recognise the Irish Republic.[132]

Mary desired to reach a wider audience than the Irish American cohort within the US. In a speech in Galveston, Texas, on 23 February 1921 she made clear that she wanted to appeal not to 'hyphenated Americans' but to '100 per cent Americans'. She appealed to the latter:

> who love and revere the fathers of this great republic, who stand for the ideals which George Washington, Thomas Jefferson, Daniel Webster and Patrick Henry stood ... It is to you, Citizens of America, that I have come to tell Ireland's story. To tell you what it is we ask, what it is we are striving for, and to ask you for the recognition of the Republic of Ireland by this great sister Republic of the West.
>
> It is not so very long ago in the history of the world since your fathers were fighting the same fight as we fight today, and against the same enemy.[133]

De Róiste referred to an article in the *Irish Independent* detailing a convention held under the auspices of the AARIR in Chicago in April at which Mary, Boland and O'Callaghan spoke. He expressly noted that non-Irish Americans also spoke 'including a Jewish Rabbi'.[134] Mary was proud that on the tour she succeeded, as she claimed, 'in winning over a record number of non-Irish and non-Catholic Americans'. She believed that women came to hear her as a fellow female speaker and because 'she was interested in women's suffrage'.[135] She also drew parallels between the American Civil War, 1861–5, and the republican opposition to the creation of the Northern Irish state under the Government of Ireland Act, 1920. In her testimony to the American Commission, she declared:

> A parallel with your war of secession is the parallel between Ulster and the rest of Ireland today. And if you maintain that you were justified in waging a long war of five years which nearly broke President Lincoln's heart, if you were justified in fighting that war rather than let a part of your country secede, then you must admit that we are justified in fighting for a century, if need be, rather than let a part of Ireland secede. The parallel is between north and south as far as Ulster and the rest of Ireland are concerned. But between England and Ireland your Revolutionary War is the parallel.[136]

Throughout this period Mary continued to draw analogies between the history of Ireland's struggle for freedom and that of the United States. Visiting Denver in March 1921, she sent a telegram to Joseph McGarrity wishing him a happy Easter and anticipating that America would 'hold out the hand of recognition and friendship to her sister republic across the sea'.[137]

Some newspapers were critical of Mary's creation of analogies between the War of Independence and that of America in the eighteenth century. The *Bamberg Herald (SC)* stated:

> America did not attempt to get her freedom by the indiscriminate murder of British officers, and she did not carry on any secret warfare, such as has characterized recent Irish activities. Neither did America have its Ulster, opposed almost unanimously to separation from the mother country.[138]

In February 1921 the Nebraska Legislature voted 48 to 44 to deny Mary the right to speak in Lincoln on the basis that 'her mission to this country was not of importance to the people of Nebraska'. However, her 'eloquence attracted over 40,000 persons to hear her' in Oklahoma.[139]

Family affairs in Ireland continued to be a priority for Mary. On 15 February 1921 she was in Topeka, Kansas, where she was due to give three speeches. On arrival she received news of Seán's arrest in a house in Whitechurch, Co Cork, for possession of arms and ammunition.[140] Giving an interview in her hotel room she noted that 'it is very likely they will kill my brother if it is true that he had firearms'. However, she added: '[p]erhaps they will hardly dare to do so ...after what they have already done to our family'.[141] This would be an idea that would become part of Mary's arsenal from this point onwards; the martyrdom of her brother rendered the family invincible. While in Washington in December 1920 she expressed her belief that the death of her brother had advanced the republican cause, bringing into disrepute leading British politicians. She described a series of telegraphs exchanged with Lloyd George to determine who was responsible for her brother's sentence and 'the treatment he and his relatives had been accorded by the British government'. 'The result of this exchange of telegraphs ... made me feel that Lloyd George was responsible before God and man for the death of my brother. I shall continue to feel that way and I shall continue to spread truth of that situation throughout all of Ireland.'[142]

Seán MacSwiney returned to Ireland from Canada in June 1919, having been released from jail the previous March.[143] Living in Cork he worked in Henry Ford & Son until January when he took sick leave.[144] He had, of course, been absent from his employment during the later weeks of Terence's hunger strike in 1920 and it is not unlikely that his sickleave was related to the trauma he experienced – like his sister and other family members – in Brixton. Cross-generational trauma impacted on the lives of the MacSwiney family in different ways. While Mary took refuge in political activism other members of the family experienced ill health. Art O'Brien referred to the fact that Annie was 'very ill' from the beginning of 1921, quite likely a response to what she had witnessed in Brixton.[145] Muriel referred to the ill health of both the incarcerated Seán and the anxious Annie: 'I have only just heard about Jack [Seán]; it is too bad especially as he is not strong, poor Annie must be very upset, ill & all as she is.'[146] Seán was a private in the Cork No. 1 Brigade of the Irish Volunteers when he was arrested on 8 February in a 'general round up'.[147] He claimed that having gone out for a walk and traversed five to six miles, he realised that he would be unable to reach the city before the curfew and he took a 'shakedown' in the home of Mrs M'Kay, Rahanisky House, in Whitchurch.[148] The trial of the 14 men opened before a military court in Victoria Barracks, Cork, on 22 February; Seán's address was listed as that of Mary's home and school at Belgrave Place.[149] He claimed that he carried a weapon for self-defence as he received 'definite information' before and after Christmas 1920 that 'what were known as the murder gang of the Black and Tans were after me'.[150] O'Brien, however, claimed that none of the men arrested had arms in their possession. When Annie received news of the arrest two days later, she went to the military barracks but was sent away without being allowed to see her brother. She returned later that day, waiting an hour and half before being given a permit to see Seán. Going to the block of buildings in which he was incarcerated she was then told there was a mistake, and she could not be admitted. O'Brien noted the toll that all this took on Annie. She was 'too poorly' to return to the barracks to further negotiate for admittance.[151] On 27 February she wrote to Fred Cronin asking him to send a car to allow her to travel to the barracks the next morning as she couldn't walk.[152] Her next step was to write to General Strickland demanding an explanation for the refusal to allow her to see Seán.[153] In her letter to the latter, she drew attention to the fact that her brother was left without sufficient clothes.[154] Annie continued to write emphasising the inappropriate treatment of Seán and those arrested with him. When the lorry containing the men passed through the streets of Cork:

> a rain-storm was raging, none of the men had any head-gear, many of them had nothing on but their shirts, my brother had not even that. Some of them were attached by halters around their necks to the side of the lorries, others were roped together to the back of the lorries or attached by the ropes to the cross beams overhead. My brother's hands were tied behind his back, and a rope halter was passed round his neck and tied to the tope that bound his hands behind him. His feet were tied together, and he was thrown face downwards, to the bottom of the lorry.[155]

As well as details of such brutality, Annie alleged that a gold watch and £4 that Seán had in his possession were stolen. These allegations were the subjection of questions in the House of Commons.[156] More worrying was the fact that he appeared to be targeted for special hatred by the arresting officers because he was Terence MacSwiney's brother:

> ... the Military officer who arrested my brother recognised him, and asked him was he the Lord Mayor's brother. On his answering 'yes' the officer replied 'WELL WE FINISHED HIM AND WE WON' T BE LONG IN FINISHING YOU'.[157]

When questioned at the trial the officer claimed that this allegation was an 'exaggeration': 'I said his brother had died through his own fault and that he would probably die through being shot for consorting with rebels'.[158] O'Brien summed up the state of fear that the family must have experienced on Seán's arrest. He stated that the:

> English authorities have shown such spleen against the MacSwiney family that it is generally feared in Cork that, following the precedent in the case of Cornelius Murphy, the military may convict Seán MacSwiney of the possession of arms, sentence him to death, and shoot him, and make an announcement of his sentence and execution after the event.[159]

Cornelius Murphy, a 31-year-old farmer from Rathmore, Co. Kerry, was executed on 1 February 1921 at Victoria Barracks, Cork, for illegal possession of a revolver. The result of the trial was made known only after the date of his execution.[160] De Róiste referred in his diary to 'killings and shootings legal and illegal' in the context of Murphy's execution.

He further noted that so-called rebels 'found with arms are executed whether engaged in conflict or not'.[161] Cornelius Murphy's execution, he declared, 'is probably the beginning of a large number of executions'.[162] Mary can only have been too aware of this when news of Seán's arrest reached her.

While there are no extant letters to Mary from family members on the topic of Seán's arrest, it is more than probable that that Annie wrote of her distressing negotiations with the British military. Indeed, she referred to cabling both Mary and Peter.[163] Peter also cabled Padraic Fleming in West Virginia. If Fleming knew where in America Mary was, he requested that he wire her about Seán's situation.[164] Such statements from Annie as she negotiated around Seán's arrest must have caused Mary intense anguish, a fact compounded by her distance from her family: 'If Seán has to die, he'll know how to – but stop it if you can'.[165] Annie also feared that the MacSwiney home would be subject to a raid following Seán's arrest.[166] Peter MacSwiney, who did not give testimony before the American Commission on Conditions in Ireland but who made himself available for questions, stated that when he briefly lived in Cork after Terence's death Mary was nervous about him sleeping at Belgrave place. While there 'was a time when a man used to be protection in the house' such became a liability as the War of Independence continued.[167]

Violence in Cork was intense. De Róiste detailed a bomb explosion in the city that wounded civilians including a woman on 28 February while that same night five unarmed soldiers were shot dead and 11 wounded.[168] Mary's concern for Annie was not unfounded. Cork city was, de Róiste stated, 'now indeed the city of a war zone'. By this date the 9 pm curfew was changed to 6 pm while hold-ups and searching of individuals on the streets were a daily occurrence.[169]

Mary and other family members worried about Annie long before the events of February 1921. In his diary in April 1903 Terence wrote of a conversation he had with his sister Kit:

> A [Annie] we agreed was most need of anxiety [sic]. She is likely to be the only girl in the family who will not become a nun, for she appears to have her mind made up in this point, and we were naturally puzzled as to what her future course might be; for a girl setting out on the road of Life is generally in more need for care and guidance than a boy, and we considered A's case more likely to cause anxiety than P [Peter] or J's [Seán].[170]

Mary described Annie as 'intensely sensitive' and later in 1921 had to intervene from America in a dispute between her and other staff in St Ita's, a situation made worse by Annie's continued illness.[171]

Despite Seán's arrest and her concerns for Annie, Mary kept her itinerary of scheduled talks. The *Topeka State Journal* described her demeanour:

> No loud blazing zeal for her cause is apparent about Miss MacSwiney. Her manner has a quiet firmness that is more appealing and sincere than that of the ranting crusaders. Her eyes are 'Irish blue,' one perceives at first glance and frequently show an Irish flash of feeling. Her brown hair has become partly gray [sic]. Her severely simple black silk gown, probably worn in mourning for her late brother, is becoming to her type.[172]

While she spoke, Mary, 'fingered letters in her lap', reading extracts from them describing the worsening violence in Cork, the nationwide curfew and the way people were living in a war zone. O'Brien wrote to Fred Cronin about the situation in Cork that Mary described:

'[i]t is a wonder to us here how you all stand so well the terrible strain of the present conditions'.[173] Mary's was not an abstract speech; it was not even solely mediated through the experience of Terence's death. It was even more immediate; Seán, and by extension, Annie, were fully caught in the maelstrom of the aggression and hostility of life in Cork. De Róiste writing about the trial of the men taken near Whitecross noted that Seán stated that he had a revolver for self-defence. That, he continued 'is now a capital offence: and, unless some change occurs speedily, he is liable to be shot'.[174] Under martial law imposed the previous December a person found carrying a weapon was subject to execution.[175] On 28 February six men in Cork Jail were executed.[176] On 4 March, the *Evening Herald* stated that it was 'unofficially understood' that Seán had been sentenced to 15 years penal servitude.[177] One result of MacSwiney's speeches in Topeka in February 1921 was the establishment of the Kansas Association for the Recognition of the Irish Republic.[178] Such political successes were particularly noteworthy, achieved as they were when she knew that Seán faced uncertainty and brutality in Victoria Barracks in Cork.

Mary's first American tour illuminated structural issues and problems within the AARIR. In a letter to James O' Mara, Catherine Flanagan stated:

> Miss MacSwiney is creating the most favourable impression – and the enthusiasm is unbounded, but I do not see what we are going to do about organisation. We spoke to over ten thousand people in Tennessee and yet we have no organisation – not one card of membership was handed out.[179]

Mary herself voiced criticism about the lack of embedded infrastructure at the local level within the AARIR. Some organisers suggested that her presence was necessary to stimulate organisational development:

> A telegram has come in signed 'Isaac' about Miss MacSwiney's complaint that organisers are unfit. Since leaving Buffalo she has only seen of our organisers Monteith and Cotter, and both are doing just what the telegram says is not being done, namely setting up machinery to realize on this enthusiasm.
>
> ... Quite possibly there is justification for her complaint against local people. She does not seem to realize that in Tennessee she is the pioneer and that her going was necessary to produce the organisation.[180]

Mary wrote to O'Mara that there were '[c]omplaints everywhere of want of direction, no idea how to set to work'.[181] From New Orleans she chided him at the dearth of propagandist literature: '[h]ave you nothing to send out to the people'.[182] Mary voiced frustration to Harry Boland. She felt that he and O' Mara were 'treating me very badly'. In the letter she outlined her understanding of what needed to change:

> I have been watching, noting, comparing everywhere we went, and I am coming now to say that if we are to have any chance of success, it must be through a complete change of tactics. You must both find the money to finance this thing for the next two months on a big scale. I have waited till half my journey was over, I have questioned everyone, noted everything and you can't say I was in too great a hurry to give you any advice.
>
> Now I say unhesitatingly, that we have a great chance of success if you will only do things on a big scale within the next two months. You told me the President had left plenty of money for this. For Ireland's sake, Harry, spend it... get organisers 2 or 3 or 4 in every state. ... Let us get plenty of women with faith and confidence.[183]

In particular, she asked for Kathleen O'Brennan and Mrs Corless. They would be, she wrote, 'most useful and they are brainy and live wires. Some of the people organising are half asleep. I feel like sticking pins in them'.[184] For all her sense of exasperation with Boland and O'Mara's organisational tactics the letter was signed Min, indicating the degree of familiarity between the two; they were both after all on the same political side. She signed off: '[w]rite to me like a good Boy [sic] and tell me you will be a brick and shell out generously.'[185] To O'Mara she joked that he would never have the patience to read her long letters.[186] Yet, as Fitzpatrick writes, in 'the absence of a master plan, demarcation disputes continued to generate resentment and bickering between members of the mission'.[187]

In the letter to Boland she declared:

> ... I am dead earnest about the immediate Recognition [sic]. I have met and talked with many important men on my travels and they all agree that a big drive on Congress, especially after Mar. 4th. may bring immediate results. Easter Monday this year happens to fall on Terry's birthday. I do not know any date more suitable and so I am urging that date for the U. S. Recognition, with the suggestion that I might be able to wait till April 24th but no later. My latest slogan is U.S. Recognition March 28th Easter Monday. Recognition by the other countries will follow by April 24th.[188]

Mary similarly sought to galvanise O'Mara into further action. As early as 2 February she wrote that some of the 'best workers are hampered for want of money'. She noted that many who gave of their time were not well off and should be paid salaries and expenses. Mary felt that there were many young women who could be harnessed to organise the cause across America if proper financial structures were put in place.[189] Later in February she exhorted him to get the Dáil to consent to the necessary expenditure to organise 'literature, speakers and organisers go leor'. It was necessary, she wrote, to take advantage of the 'enthusiasm which our visits are arousing', exhorting him to 'lay aside the doubting Thomas attitude'.[190] She wanted 'the Recognition by April, & if we don't get it, it will be for want of real live efficient and optimistic organisation'.[191] A few months later in May, she indicated that she had requested de Valera to sanction money towards the propagandist efforts in America but noted that she had done so before she learned 'directives have been received from you necessitating retrenchment':

> I wrote you a few weeks ago suggesting, among other things – that Mrs Michael O'Callaghan and few more women of the same type should be asked to come out here to help. I also took the liberty of suggesting that it would be 'spoiling the ship for a ha'porth of tar' to stint organisers now.[192]

De Valera, however, was determined to, as O'Mara put it, 'force through' his imprimatur to cut spending on organisation in America as the campaigns in Ireland 'are more extensive than you could imagine'.[193] In March 1921 he wrote that propaganda 'should henceforth be done mainly by the American organisations'.[194] This decision, O'Mara declared, drew the 'unanimous condemnation of the Irish mission in America'. He tended his resignation and Mary's calls for increased expenditure yielded no results.[195] O'Mara expressed his lack of confidence in de Valera's judgement 'in American affairs' to Boland but there was no similar condemnation from Mary.[196]

Mary's need to see the republic for which her brother had died realised meant that her sense of realpolitik was lacking. People cannot, she declared to de Valera, 'be said to have done our part fully till Ireland is free or we are dead'.[197] De Valera had she believed been in a 'rather pessimistic frame of mind' about achieving US recognition as early as his return to Ireland December 1920.[198] As always for Mary the political was personal; in an aside in the middle of the letter to O'Mara she noted that she had no news of Seán's trial. By the end of the letter, she had received a cable telling her that he had been found guilty but that the sentence had not yet been handed down.[199]

Whelan discusses how the new Congress and administration under President Harding, inaugurated on 4 March 1921, transformed the expectations of activists that US recognition of the republic could be achieved.[200] An AARIR convention in Chicago in April resolved to 'ask President Harding to treat with Ireland as one of the "most favoured nations"'.[201] Mary and other republicans in the US were furnished with the names of men in Washington who should be contacted.[202] Despite the optimism as displayed by MacSwiney the reality was more complex. Most of Congress, Whelan argues, feared jeopardizing US-British diplomatic relations, while the Irish question was viewed by many as an internal British matter.[203] Other republicans were more realistic than Mary. De Róiste wrote on 22 March:

> The war declarations of 'freedom for small nations' and the like are all reduced to hypocrisy and cant by the major States of the world ... Of sympathy and resolutions there is plenty: of acts that would change the course of the English Government there are none that we can see.[204]

On 20 May Mary noted to de Valera that she had tried to secure an interview with the US Secretary of State, Charles Hughes, but failed. He had made it 'a rule not to see non Americans on political matters'. She did get an interview with State Department official Robert Bliss, making clear to him that republicans would agree to no compromise with the British and could hold out for the next four years. She noted to de Valera that the 'significance of the four years and its effect on future elections did not pass unnoticed'. Ireland would, she wrote, continue to be a factor in US politics, despite Cohalan's attempts to represent Sinn Féin as 'only a faction'.[205] President Harding did meet Mary and Flanagan.[206] De Róiste was scathing at the fact that she received an interview while simultaneously Donal Óg O'Callaghan 'has been ordered to leave the States after addressing many large meetings'.[207] Mary's attempts at a follow up meeting-were rebuffed, Harding taking advice from Hughes. The latter stated that the State Department desired that foreign persons should be presented only by the diplomatic representative of their country.[208] When Mary was informed that she could only secure an official meeting with the President through the British ambassador she made clear that she would not engage with the 'representatives of my brother's murderers and my country's enemy'.[209]

On 13 November 1920 the *Irish Independent* noted a statement from Dorothea Jacob calling for the electors of Cork to choose a woman to fill one of the two constituency vacancies to Dáil Éireann. She continued to add:

> Surely it would be only a fitting tribute to the memory of Terence MacSwiney to elect his heroic sister, Miss Mary MacSwiney, B. A., in his place. Cork owes the MacSwiney family a debt of gratitude for the noble work they have done within the last few months and this might

be one way in which this gratitude could be expressed. I write as a native of Cork who worked with Miss MacSwiney at one time and learned to appreciate her admirable public qualities.[210]

Dorothea knew Mary as a fellow member of the Munster Women's Franchise League. By early April 1921 selection candidates were being made in Cork although on 18 of the month de Róiste recorded that there were doubts if any elections would take place outside the six northern Irish counties as there were calls for postponement.[211] Mary was one of four Sinn Féin candidates for Cork city, nominated with J. J. Walshe, Liam de Róiste and Donal Óg O'Callaghan. Internally there was some disagreement as to what candidates should be selected in Cork, de Róiste stating that while the standing committee of Cork Sinn Féin urged his candidacy the 'Óglaigh' objected to him.[212] In the event the objectives of the representatives of the Irish Volunteers to de Róiste were overruled with de Valera apparently intervening; all four candidates were nominated on 13 May 1921.[213] All candidates were elected unopposed; the result in the South of the country was a 'foregone conclusion' with no election 'excitement'. The day of nomination meant 'the day of election'.[214] Mary was elected while still in America, one of six 'lady members' as the *Irish Independent* declared.[215] Before the Sinn Féin nominations in Cork were finalised de Róiste noted that: 'the new candidates to be put forward will be Volunteer leaders. This means the election will be a 'war election', such as occurs in all countries during a period of fighting.'[216] Mary clearly did not fall into this category but her work in America meant that despite her gender she was increasingly viewed as part of the republican leadership; her connection to her dead brother, of course, was also influential in her nomination. Seán MacSwiney also won a seat in the Cork Mid, North, South, South-West, and West eight-seater constituency for which Terence had been elected in 1918.[217] He had been rescued from Spike Island prison in April 1921 together with two other prisoners.[218]

Jason Knirck argues that 'many' of six women in the second Dáil 'felt the need to justify their place ... and their right to speak'. He writes that 'only Countess Markievicz had substantial military experience; the others felt the need to establish another clear basis of legitimacy'.[219] The situation is more nuanced in the case of Mary MacSwiney. While certainly her nomination as a Sinn Féin candidate was based on her familial relationship with Terence, she had proved herself in America, first through her testimony to the American Commission on Conditions in Ireland and then through a comprehensive and gruelling tour across US states. When she was due to return to Ireland, Vivien Pierce, AARIR, stated that she hoped 'they realize over there all you have done over here'.[220] She spoke before large audiences, in that way showing the numerical strength of support for republican independence in America. Her secretary, Flanagan, wrote to O' Mara about her reception in Pittsburgh:

> The ballroom of the Wm. Penn hotel has been hired. It holds 6000. The auditorium of Kaufmann's store in the near vicinity was hired. This was not enough. The 10th and 11th floors of the hotels were crowded as were the extra halls in Kaufmann's. In all, Miss MacSwiney spoke 4 times to 19,000 people. She even spoke from the balcony of the hotel to 2,000 people in the lobby who could not get upstairs. Practically the entire hotel ceased to function for over 2 hrs ... [221]

Less than two weeks after her letter from Des Moines, Flanagan wrote again to O'Mara, this time about the reception in Galveston, Texas: 'I am enclosing the front page story of our meeting last evening. We are told that this is the first time a front page story has ever been given in this paper to the Irish cause.'[222]

Perceptively Mary recognised that initially some local organisers did not feel that she had the same drawing power as a male activist. In February she wrote to Boland from Des Moines, Iowa:

> ...Had a very successful day here. Four speeches. (1) Big girls' Academy and nuns from various quarters. (2) Reception in ballroom very good. (3) College women. Mass meeting, not more than 2000. The asses could have got the large hall if they had thought a woman could fill it![223]

Mary was aware that as a woman she at times directed her political attention differently than did the male activists in the US. Her activism in the suffrage campaign and within Cumann na mBan meant that she understood the necessity to appeal to women as well as men. She wrote to O'Mara:

> I enclose Miss O'Toole's card. She has undertaken to give me letters of introduction to the heads of all Suffrage Clubs, to the Business and Professional womens' [sic] clubs and probably to the Women Lawyers. Between her introductions and those I hope to get after Wednesday's meeting, I shall probably be able to accomplish some of the work suggested by Senator Walsh.
>
> Please tell him if you see him that some of the Washington men to whom I suggested that I would probably confine my attentions to women, have protested indignantly against the suggestion.[224]

She was also aware that the prevailing gender roles where women were considered as wives and mothers in the domestic sphere meant that she sometimes had to assert herself. She wrote to O'Mara about Joseph J. Castellini of Cincinnati's attitude to women:

> He seems to have taken a dislike to the State Secretary Miss Madden and I am afraid is going to work to get her supplanted at the State Convention. She is a very capable girl and has done excellent service. The person he has in mind to put in her place is not capable is [sic] a married woman with a family and not the type to be able to give of her best, nor would her best be very good, to the cause ... Castellini himself is the type of man that likes to have nice obedient women about him, a confessed opponent of woman suffrage [sic] which you will think probably has me prejudiced against him, well it is not that but the type of woman he wants to put in Miss Madden's place is not the type of woman we want.[225]

There were those, however, who saw Mary as well placed to harness the power of female pressure groups. Frank P. Walsh, one of the key American supporters of Ireland, wrote:

> The best canvass that I have ever known to have been made of Congress was that made by the National Women's Party. Without any suggestion from any other source, one of Major Kinkead's first proposals was, that we should try to get in touch with Miss Alice Paul, and see if we could not duplicate the National Women's Party effort. ... Miss MacSwiney ... would be the ideal person to get up this organization.[226]

Paul and other suffrage activists known as the silent sentinels picketed the White House and protested in Layfette Square during the Presidency of Woodrow Wilson, resulting in the passing of the Nineteenth Amendment to the US constitution in the House of Representatives on 21 May and in the Senate on 4 June 1919.[227] The Amendment granted the right to vote to white women in the US. Walsh's statement to O'Mara shows an increased understanding of the efficacy of the role of women in both American and Irish politics and placed Mary centrally in this nexus. Fully aware of the emotive power of the discourse of female sacrifice in pursuit of the republic, she advised making visible 'the Mothers and the sisters of men who lost their lives in the War for Small Nations, on the style of the Suffrage pickets'.[228]

Mary was still in the US when the truce in the Anglo-Irish War was declared on 9 July 1921, coming into effect two days later. In a letter to de Valera she noted that it was nearly eight months since she 'took up, at your special request the task of touring this country'. She was 'longing for a peep at the inside negotiations'.[229] She stated that if 'there should be a question of putting the matter before the Country' she would return home immediately to 'add my voice to the "No Surrender" side'.[230] She also made that point clear to Boland telling him that she had informed de Valera that if there was any 'question of an election of the basis of a compromise' she would leave for Ireland at once.[231] Writing in the later 1920s she stated that she 'did not feel happy about the Truce; still less about the vagueness surrounding the procedure'. She was anxious at the fact that moving, as she was, from city to city in America she could not get regular or immediate news from 'Headquarters'. She wrote that she was certain that there 'could be no question of compromising the Republic, or accepting anything less'.[232] In 1921 Mary clearly respected the republican hierarchy and docilely declared to de Valera: 'Otherwise I shall await your orders and I would be glad if you would tell me plainly what you wish me to do'. She was anxious to be allocated a role 'where I can be most use'. She continued in this submissive vein. She did, however, indicate her lack of enthusiasm for continued involvement in the Bond drive, declaring that 'Americans like to be flattered and I don't flatter them'. Not 'much good as a beggar' she preferred the role of speaking on behalf of 'Recognition' and letting her audience 'infer the necessity for supplying the sinews of war'.[233]

In the early paragraphs of a long letter to de Valera written over several days in July 1921, Mary was optimistic that the treaty talks would yield acknowledgement of 'our Republic at once'. Lloyd George, as 'a clever man', she declared, recognised that 'in view of England's big troubles all over the World' to do so was 'the wisest course'. However, as the missive progressed, she referred to the possibility of a recommencement of 'the fighting'. She expressed her worry that if the republic was not achieved, she would find herself in jail on return to Ireland where she could be of no use. At this point Mary still believed in the possibility of the recognition of the republic by the United States and declared that 'it was only a question of months if England does not give it first'.[234] Despite her personal desire to be back in Ireland, she was open to being asked to remain in the United States. In the event of the failure of the negotiations she believed that it would be important to 'have some of us on the spot' in Washington. In the case of that eventuality, she suggested the organisation of 'pickets of the men of Irish birth or decent – especially those who were wounded if possible'.[235]

Continuing the letter on 24 July she outlined for de Valera her dealings with the Friends of the Irish Republic, notably her two interviews with Bishop Michael Gallagher in Michigan and the rumours and machinations at the Ancient Order of Hibernians

Conference to which she had been invited to speak to the Ladies Auxiliary by McWhorter. There was 'insinuation everywhere that you were going to compromise'. When she went to Detroit, she 'found that the whole men's Convention had been captured by the Friends of Irish Freedom (FOIF) and they planned a cablegram which would have been an insult if they had succeeded in sending it'.[236] What emerges strongly from this letter is the manner in which Mary clearly saw herself as aligned to de Valera in this period and in absolute support of his position amid the factions within Irish America. She assumed this position from the outset of her tour. A headline in the *Freeman's Journal* on 21 January 1921 read: 'Miss MacSwiney Resents Attacks on De Valera'. Telegrams from members of the Friends of Irish Freedom, an Irish American nationalist organisation founded in 1916, calling on de Valera to use the bond drive money openly for relief in Ireland, were, she declared, 'couched in terms offensive to Ireland's President – an insult to the man of whom we are so proud, and who alone is entitled to speak to America with Ireland's voice'. At this point, as discussed earlier, de Valera had founded the rival American Association for the Recognition of the Irish Republic. Using the money openly would, Mary argued, render it liable to seizure by the British.[237] She continued to support de Valera's position throughout her period in the US. Discussing the Ancient Order of Hibernians Conference she wrote:

> A Resolution from the West asking that the Representative of the Irish Republic and myself be invited to attend was turned down. However, I was there by Mrs. McWhorter's invitation and by management on her part spoke to a joint session. Some of the Cohalan people tried to spoil the meeting but as they did not dare do it openly we had a splendid meeting. … In view of the welcome they gave you two years ago, it would have been very bad if they had succeeded in belittling your efforts this year. They got their ticket elected but that does not matter two pins.[238]

In August 1920 Bishop Gallagher was elected President of FOIF and used the opportunity of his acceptance speech to deliver criticisms of de Valera. Mary wrote to Gallagher when she arrived in Detroit, reminding him that he had informed her that 'he was not a willing party to the attacks on you and your representative in this country'. The attacks hinged around the suggestion that de Valera in entering discussions with Britain was 'compromising'. Since the 'attacks still continued' Gallagher had to, Mary informed him, 'publicly repudiate them or resign'. In her dealings with the bishop in defence of de Valera, MacSwiney used what she believed was her most effective weapon. She told Gallagher at a further meeting that 'if I and all the others whose martyrs had died for a Republic were convinced we could trust our President and government, it was rather cool impudence [for] any American to distrust them'.[239]

Mary discussed how from the outset of her period in the United States she was 'courted and flattered by those within the Friends of Irish Freedom' who stated that she should speak for all factions within Irish America as she was a 'National character'. She wrote of how 'the suggestions have become insistent that it is my place – my duty in fact – to reunite both parties'. She denounced the audacity of Cohalan, Devoy and Gallagher in their attempt to dictate to de Valera as President of the Republic and wrote: 'it is hard to make these people – even our own friends – take in the reality and dignity of the Irish Republic. Slave Mind rampant everywhere'.[240] Again, deferring to de Valera, she stated that although she 'spoke without consultation with anyone or indeed without premeditation, I was and am convinced that I spoke the opinions of you and the Government'.[241]

On 28 July she continued her 'disconnected effusion' asking de Valera to let her know in good time if hostilities in Ireland recommenced and whether nurses are 'really needed from this side'. A letter from Mary Donegan, president of the of the American Auxiliary of the Irish White Cross, to Archbishop Hayes of New York, on 6 July 1921, discussed the suggestion and approval 'by Members of the Irish Republican Government' of the establishment of centres by the American Auxiliary White Cross nurses in Dublin, Cork and Belfast initially and then with an extension to the 'different martial law cities'. In such 'community centres' the 'poor could get at least one nourishing meal a day' while clothes could be distributed. The nurses 'could keep in touch with prominent women and give advice, and help where needed'. The suggestion was that about 20 nurses should be sent to Ireland in groups of two or three. There was to be no publicity until the women had arrived and the centres established with the help of the women of the Irish White Cross. Donegan stated that the presence of 'American women in Ireland will be a great moral support to the whole population'.[242] Mary was opposed to this plan on the grounds of the expense given that there were 'nurses go léor in Ireland, as well as Cumann na mBan, and strangers would only be a nuisance'. She requested confirmation as to whether Miss Donegan's suggestions 'are really official'. Again, bringing up the factionalism within Irish American politics, she declared that the some of the proposed women had 'been creating quite a lot of trouble'. They were 'a mixed lot, some old FOIF's among them and a few people who are always difficult to harness'.[243]

Mary wrote to Boland on the same matter on 19 July and his response was to take her position over that of Donegan's. He gave a her a series of suggestions as to how to deal tactfully with the latter. She was to say that he had had long despatches from de Valera 'without mention of her visit'. He advised Mary to 'band' all the American women 'together working in close co-operation with H.Q. in Ireland'.[244] Taking control of the situation with Boland's imprimatur, she wrote a diplomatic yet direct letter to Donegan. Nothing could be done, she told the latter, until 'definite instructions from home were received'. In the meantime she would be happy to work with her 'in every way possible to band the women together so that we may have strong financial and moral support on this side working in close cooperation with Cumann na mBan headquarters in Dublin. Mary firmly put the authority in her own hands. She was one of the executive officers of Cumann na mBan and in 'close contact' with all the work they did. In this capacity, and in co-operation with Boland, she would co-operate with the American women's organisations 'in carrying out the wishes of the Government in Dublin'.[245]

The last section of Mary's post-truce letter to de Valera was written on 4 August and she declared her total faith in him and the republican government in a statement that almost prefigured the breaking points that would emerge in the treaty negotiations. Using the possessive case, she declared: 'I know we can trust you all to have no Compromise. We will not haul down our flag or acknowledge allegiance to the King of England or the Empire directly or indirectly'. She hoped there would be no election 'because there is no doubt that there would be found weaklings who might reduce our majority'. In an argument that she would make throughout the Treaty debates, she declared that Dáil Éireann had 'its mandate and can answer for the Nation'.[246] In writing this letter to de Valera Mary sought the advice of Boland. Clearly the issue of a potential compromise was on her mind but also, she did not want to antagonise de Valera. Boland replied to her: 'Do not worry yourself in writing to de Valera under this head there can be no compromise between Ireland and England and there will be none, needless to say I will send on any letter you may forward to me, so send it along!'[247] She expressed her political fears to Boland in the context of the Truce and upcoming negotiations. While she believed that the majority of the Dáil could be trusted 'to have no compromise ... S. O'M. [sic] 'leaves me with an uneasy feeling'. Compromise in any form, she wrote, 'would be the unforgiveable sin now'. While she would guarantee neutrality of Ireland's shores to England and possibly be willing 'not to build up a navy' ... 'beyond that nothing':

> Not a red cent in money – not an English official in our country, not a trace of God Save the King or Union Jackism, and no attempt to quarter any imperial emblem on our flag. We want no election or referendum over it. The Dáil has been given its mandate clearly enough.[248]

'Harry a Croide,' she wrote, 'let me have news from home the minute you get it, good, or bad, or indifferent'. She reiterated her loyalty to him, declaring 'how could I be disloyal to anyone so loyal to Ireland'.[249]

The respect Mary had for Boland was reciprocal. In the period after the death of her brother and before the Treaty debates, she increasingly garnered the high opinion of those within the republican leadership. She, herself, was increasingly deemed one of those elite not just because of her brother's death but progressively because of her unstinting work while in America. Frank P. Walsh writing to Boland stated that outside of de Valera, 'she is undoubtedly our greatest propagandist'.[250] Her reputation, however, as someone with strong principles who was not afraid to voice them was growing. Boland referred to her meetings with Bishop Gallagher and declared: 'I can imagine Doctor Gallagher wince under your cross examination. I congratulate you and pity him: as I would pity any wrongdoer who might fall in your way'. In her diary, Agnes O'Mara referred to tensions and factions at the AARIR national convention in Chicago:

> Big row at the end. Very unfortunate. Tactless handling of the situation by Ginnell and Min MacSwiney led to slight soreness on Harry's part and open resentment on Jim's [O'Mara]. He lashed at M. MacS. And a sad scene ensued ... However all made peace by night.[251]

Yet Boland's letter to her on 26 July 1921 shows the esteem in which she was held. It also shows once again the way she respected the authority of those who held republican office. Boland declared that in the past he was 'very direct and honest both in thought and speech'. His time in America had, however, made him 'cynical and doubting in my dealings with people'. Recognising this, he wrote:

> I must be careful that I deal with you in the manner you deserve – frankly, honestly and without reserve, you have been so good and true to me during your stay in this country that I would be an ingrate did I not say how highly I regard you not alone for the wonderful work you have given to Ireland but also the loyal manner in which you have supported me in my work as Envoy of the Republic.[252]

Boland and Mary were well matched, both given to extreme sentiments. In early 1920 the *New York Times* quoted the former at a speech in Madison Square Gardens, New York, as referring to a 'RACE VENDETTA'.[253] Although Boland claimed afterwards that he was 'misquoted', it was Mary who was more conciliatory as she stood by his side during this speech, assuring the listeners that the Irish were not calling on the US to go to war with Britain to support Irish claims.[254]

By early August 1921 Mary and Boland were the 'sole remaining members' of the Second Dáil in the United States. Boland stated that he would remain until he was 'recalled or replaced' but added 'God speed the happy date'. He outlined the two choices that Mary had. She could remain in America to assist Stephen O'Mara in raising the new loan or she could return home. Boland wrote: 'I know your answer will be, in whatsoever way you can best serve Ireland!'. He thought she could be 'of more service' staying in America 'assisting in the work of Education and raising of money'.[255]

'Eight months to-day since I landed in New York. I little though I should be away so long' began Mary's letter to de Valera on 4 August 1921.[256] She was weary: 'Am very tired but Meeting [sic] was wonderful and my voice succeeded in carrying but I confess I do feel in need of a rest, so do not let J. C. pile on more meetings after March 30th till I see how I am feeling.'[257] Those around her commented on the toll on her physically:

> Miss MacSwiney swept Los Angeles as no other visitor from the east or from Ireland even has ever done. Her argument is the most intellectual convincing [sic] and persuasive outside of your own robust self we have ever heard down here. The poor woman is pretty tired physically, although wonderfully alert mentally.[258]

Flanagan's letter to James O'Mara from St Louis in early February gave details of the gruelling nature of the itinerary:

> Yesterday Miss MacSwiney spoke 7 times. To-day we travelled all day from 6.40 this morning to 4.45 this afternoon – dinner, then a magnificent meeting. To-day a State Convention was held … The meeting to-night was most inspiring and Miss MacSwiney spoke to over 200 delegates after the evening meeting.[259]

In California in March she 'planned to rest' but 'it was impossible'. Flanagan continued to note the way the extensive tour impacted on Mary's health: 'Miss MacSwiney is holding out beautifully. She is frightfully tired however and I do not believe another trip should be planned until she has had a good rest.'[260] Moreover, Mary disliked the formality and etiquette of itinerary and meetings: '[h]olding people's hands for the next 2 hours or so does not appeal to me, But [sic] I suppose it has its uses', she declared to James O'Mara.[261]

Mary was homesick. She wrote to Boland describing herself as a 'lonely colleague'.[262] To the Committee of St Ita's she declared: 'I just long to be home with you all again'.[263] She was worried about the school which, as discussed, was in financial trouble. Money, Annie wrote to Fred Cronin, 'was needed' and she wondered if it would be timely to publish Terence's *Principles of Freedom* which would generate income. She pressed on Cronin that he should send his children to St Ita's:

> Fred, will you send us your kiddies? You know if we had thousands, I should love to have yours, because of everything, but, too, the Committee said yesterday if we didn't get more

> pupils we'd have to close & that we haven't enough pupils to pay salaries. We have 92 & we need at least 120.

From the letter it appears as if there had been a falling out with the MacCurtain family whose children had left the school.[264] The handling of the financial issues of St Ita's in the Spring of 1921 caused Annie to threaten to resign. This caused Mary distress; she had, she wrote, 'begged Annie to withdraw her resignation for my sake and St. Ita's. It would break my heart to have the school go now'. She wrote urgently to the school committee evincing a tone of criticism:

> The gloomy predictions – in and out of Committee – of impending disaster, and the airy declaration then of shoals of money sure to come, and flouting the idea of reductions! It was most unfair both to her [Annie] and to Mr. Conran. I understand your position of leaving it to the businessmen of the Committee, but the businessmen should not have behaved as if all the rest of you – including Annie – were slackers who needed to be goaded by threats into doing your best.[265]

Mary worried about money when she was in America. She made it clear to de Valera that she was 'not in a position to pay my own expenses' while also stating that she would 'not consent to receive a salary from any Americans for doing Ireland's work'.[266] She wondered to de Valera if this was a gendered issue: '[p]erhaps men are less sensitive about these matters than we are'.[267] However, like Mary, Boland did not believe that the expenses of Irish workers in America 'should be paid by American organisations. Republicans must, he wrote, preserve their "Independence"'.[268]

Mary's financial worries were compounded by the expenses that arose from the family's lengthy stay in Brixton. Although the funeral expenses were paid by the Irish Self Determination League, it was clear that the family had money worries in the immediate aftermath of their return to Cork after Terence's death.[269] Fred Cronin, the executor of Terence's will and who managed Muriel's finances together with the solicitor Barry Galvin, referred to money required by Annie for unpaid bills.[270] A statement of accounts shows that £300 pounds was paid by Muriel to the Misses MacSwiney in June 1921.[271] Muriel wrote to Cronin on 11 February 1921 asking if Annie had received the money she 'wanted'. As Annie was 'rather touchy' on the subject she did not like to ask her directly.[272]

Relations with Muriel were also a source of concern for Mary in America. Before the two women left Ireland Muriel came up with the idea of a biography of Terence. Her belief was that this had to be written by P. S. O'Hegarty; no one else would do her husband justice. She noted that she wrote to 'Máire about what I wished regarding it but I think she must have been too upset to have paid full attention to my letter'.[273] This may very well have been the case. However, Mary began to worry about the future of her niece, Máire Óg. It is noteworthy that Muriel returned to Ireland from London in February 1921 for the opening night in the Abbey Theatre of Terence's play, *The Revolutionist*.[274] However, she did not travel to Cork to see her daughter: 'I won't be going to Cork at all, she declared to Cronin in a letter about financial matters'.[275] In this period O'Brien was forced to deny an announcement in the *London Star* that he was engaged to Muriel.[276] Earlier in the year Annie wrote to Cronin about Terence's wishes for his daughter as there was talk of Muriel wanting to bring her to London:

> You remember you said you would find out ... what powers, if any, you as Terry's executor would have to stop it & what powers Min as Máire's guardian with Muriel would have to stop it.[277]

Following the truce Mary was keen to return to Ireland. Politically she wanted to be at the centre of events as moves were made towards peace talks. On a personal level she missed Cork and was worried about her family and St Ita's. Yet, despite her physical exhaustion and her family and financial worries she expressed optimism that full republican independence was in the offing. She did not believe that the treaty talks would immediately bring about a republic believing that this would be wrested slowly from Britain with possibly the necessity to return to violence.[278] What she certainly did not envisage as she set sail from America was the possibility that republicans would countenance anything less than the republic for which her brother had died. However, she returned to an Ireland replete with, as she saw it, talk of compromise. This, not the actions of the British government, was for her the great tragedy in the making.

Chapter Six

Truce to Treaty Split

Mary MacSwiney left New York on 13 August 1921 on board the Olympic. Fellow passengers included Kathleen O'Connell and Harry Boland.[1] The latter paid her passage from Irish American funds underscoring the humiliation she had earlier confided to de Valera concerning her precarious financial position.[2] On 16 August the second Dáil met in the Mansion House in Dawson Street. Four republican TDs were noted as absent including Mary and Boland who were at sea.[3] In the same week as the Dáil first met the Talbot Press issued *Principles of Freedom*, the last work of Terence MacSwiney, a collection of essays dedicated to the 'soldiers of freedom in every land'.[4] The Fountain bookshop on the Grand Parade in Cork offered it for sale at a price of five shillings.[5] During the period of the Truce Terence's death on hunger strike was used by republicans as they toured Ireland making speeches. In Tullamore, Co. Offaly, Patrick McCartan stated that he had not given his life 'heart-beat after heart-beat in an English prison' for 'Dominion Home Rule or a Dual Monarchy'.[6]

The Ireland Mary returned to in August 1921 was different in many respects to the one she had left in late November 1920. Arriving back in Dublin, she outwardly expressed her 'satisfaction with the way in which Irish propaganda in the States was progressing', noting that de Valera's tour 'had done enormous good'.[7] In answer to questions from the press, she declared that she was hopeful about the Treaty negotiations, stating that the British government, 'had recognised the Irish Republic no matter what they said':

> In the first place, the truce was a recognition of the Republic; the release of Commandant McKeown from prison was a further recognition; and, finally, they recognised Mr Boland and herself by giving them a safe conduct, so they had not to apply for British passports.
>
> And we travelled on the boat ... not as British subjects, but as citizens of the Irish Republic.[8]

She was, however, concerned to strengthen the resolve of those she addressed in her homecoming speeches to the real likelihood that the war with Britain would recommence. Privately Mary wrote of the 'nasty atmosphere which nearly choked me when I came home – a regular English fog of compromising cugger [sic] mugger'.[9] Speaking in the debate on the Treaty in December she declared that she came back from America 'straight into an atmosphere of what I can only call compromise'.[10] Discussing the truce with Boland on board ship as they returned to Ireland she outlined her sense of unease; she feared that 'they seemed at home to be behaving as if this cessation of hostilities meant complete victory'. She claimed that she 'considered it a deadly blunder that our Government had permitted the opening of the Belfast Parliament so quietly'.[11]

The months after her return saw Mary exist in a state of political limbo. In early September she declared to de Valera that if a renewal of the war occurred, she would, despite 'difficulties' at home 'be ready at your call to leave everything' to return to the US. She hoped renewal 'is coming now' as:

> it does not look as if the enemy were willing to concede our independence and we must not compromise on that.
>
> In one of his plays Terry makes his hero say 'What is the use of being alive if we give in now?' In his name I repeat it.[12]

On 6 October 1921 she wrote to Eileen and John J. Hearn informing them that her plans were uncertain and hinged on 'the realisation' that Lloyd George: 'manages to acquire … of our state of mind. Up to the present I think he thinks we are "bluffing". If so he has another guess coming as you say.'[13] Her unwillingness to even consider compromise was based on a bedrock of hardened principle, her republican convictions were solidified by the death of her brother. To de Valera she stated: 'I feel as if the world as well as the Country will realise the impossibility of betrayal of the cause for which Brixton was endured'.[14] It must be remembered that Mary in watching her brother die 'endured' a trauma. It is from this period onwards that her reputation as an extremist began to crystallise. This was something she recognised herself, noting in the Dáil on the first day of Treaty talks held in private that she spoke as 'one of the die-hards' of the chamber. 'I am', she declared, 'a doctrinaire republican if you like'.[15]

On 22 August Mary was present to see Leslie Price marry Tom Barry in St Joseph's Church, Berkeley Road, Dublin, with the wedding breakfast held at Vaughan's hotel.[16] The following day she attended her first meeting of the Dáil, arriving in a taxi with de Valera, Collins and Markievicz. She and Boland received 'a cordial reception'.[17] During this period of political anticipation and speech making, Mary was also busy with St Ita's which had 'suffered considerably' from her absence while she began to attend meeting of the UCC governing body.[18] Her days were taken up with the school, with her evenings devoted to 'political matters'. On Sundays she was, she wrote to John and Eileen Hearn 'dragged out to make speeches so you see there is no rest for the wicked'.[19]

On 14 September Mary supported de Valera's decision in the Dáil not to attend the Peace Conference:

> … if the President had a clear inkling that Lloyd George would not go as far as insisted upon then the mere fact of the President going over would give him to understand that the Cabinet had agreed to give in.[20]

During the debate on the plenipotentiaries, she referred to the possibly of the renewal of warfare. In her reference to an 'uncompromising minority' and the necessity to suffer to bring forth the Republic, she was not just drawing on her own experience of trauma at watching her brother endure a protracted and agonising death; she was also bearing witness to his beliefs. Terence wrote of 'the men who held the breach' who 'knew they stood for the Truth, against which nothing can prevail, and if they had to endure struggle, suffering and pain, they had the finer knowledge born of these things'.[21] Her fear of compromise was to the fore and she sought guarantees against such an outcome in London. De Róiste wrote that during the debate she 'was chief in insisting that the hands of the plenips [sic] be tied before going, but Dev would not accept that under any circumstances'.[22] Yet, she praised de Valera's talk at the Sinn Féin Ard Fheis in October and declared his speech in Clare to be 'A.1'. Speaking in Ennis, he had in the words of de Róiste declared that 'his principles and Ireland's principles are the same now as they were during the past four years and we face all future stress with the same courage as we faced stress in the past'.[23] De Valera's view that the Ard Fheis was 'a meeting in miniature of the nation' was a concept that aligned with Mary's politics.[24] He requested that the Press withdraw so that those 'who were responsible for the direction of the nation's policy' could discuss matters in an unhampered fashion.[25] Two days earlier Mary, together with Annie and Seán, attended the Requiem High Mass in Cork Cathedral on the first anniversary of Terence's death and the deaths of Michael Fitzgerald and Joseph Murphy. Silk badges bearing Terence's image were worn by those who attended and, indeed, by citizens across Cork city.[26] Invited to speak in Liverpool on 11 December she wrote to de Valera asking if he wished her to go. When he replied in the affirmative, she arranged to meet him en route 'hoping to get some news'.[27]

From September onwards many TDs made speeches across Ireland and visited their constituencies; some, like Mary, for the first time since election to the Second Dáil. On 7 September she, together with Boland and others, attended a meeting in Athlone at which the focus of attention was the reluctant release of McKeown who had been sentenced to death in June, charged with shooting dead RIC District Inspector, T. J. McGrath.[28] However, her first major meeting on her return was at the republican aeridheacht in Youghal on 2 October.[29] Her speech laid bare the tenets of her political stance and the manner in which it was formed. She had, she stated, 'looked forward to retiring into private life but until the fight was won and the enemy cleared out they must still consider themselves soldiers'. At this point she did not believe that the treaty talks would yield a republic; she 'fervently urged' her listeners to maintain a fighting stance 'for they might have to begin again':[30]

> It will probably take many hard knocks before we have convinced these people [the British government] that we mean every word and every syllable that we say … But let there be no weakness, no talk of compromise in our ranks. If there is such a thing as a slave-minded Irishman in this country to-day who would be willing to accept less than a Republic he will not get it. The people of Ireland will stand out, and it is the extremists who count in this thing … it is the extremists who will carry this fight to a finish until the last English soldier and the last vestige of English rule are driven from our country. Above all do not let people frighten you with the thought of what foul things the English will do to us if they begin war again.[31]

She called on the people of Youghal to 'drive out' from their acquaintance any man who was not a member of the IRA, 'unless he becomes a soldier tomorrow'.[32] Her brother and the other 'martyrs' had not given their lives for 'Dominion Home Rule'; the 'tragedy of Brixton must not result in allegiance to the British Crown'.[33] There were those like de Róiste who were condemnatory of her militant tone in Youghal and sceptical of her belief that Ireland 'can win in the military sense'.[34] Giving these speeches Mary paid no attention to the reality of the depleted position of the IRA. During the Treaty debates Seán Mac Eoin, vice O/C 1st Battalion, Longford Brigade, IRA, stated that there was only one rifle for every 50 men.[35] By marshalling TDs such as Mac Eoin, Seán Hales, Richard Mulcahy and Eoin O'Duffy who spoke not as politicians but as military men, Collins intended to show the Dáil the true state of military position of the IRA.[36] Yet, if Mary was to be true to her brother's death she could not countenance compromise. She told John and Eileen Hearn in October 1921 that she hoped to see them in Ireland but that was contingent on whether the country 'was back to war again'. She was 'pretty sure', she wrote, that the peace negotiations would 'break down'.[37] To de Róiste she confided her belief that the peace conference would collapse after three days.[38]

Mary's speech in Youghal was interesting in its delineation of a desire for social equality in the purported republic. There was, she declared, no country in the world 'really free', not even the United States, 'for there the poor are ground by the rich': 'In Ireland, thank God, we have no multimillionaires, and we do not want them. We want a country where all the people will have enough, and that is now within our grasp.'[39] The Republic should be a country 'founded on the ideals of Christianity'. Freedom was, she contended, 'possible without injustice to others'.[40]

Despite the fighting tone of many of the speeches, the republican aeridheacht held during the period of the Truce were convivial events, comprising, 'musical, vocal and dance items' from local people together with athletic events. A marathon race from Passage to Ballinahassig, Co Cork, was put on in honour of the aeridheaecht in the latter venue. Speaking at the interval Mary lamented that they had to speak in English as so many would not understand her if she attempted to converse in the Irish language; this would change, she asserted, once the republic was achieved.[41] She believed that it was necessary for her to speak to those who were yet to be convinced of the republican position. Nevertheless, she saw such events as the Ballinahassig aeridheacht as an opportunity for the republican faithful to come together 'to renew their baptismal vows' and to remember the sacrifice of 'our martyrs'. She believed that the imminent treaty talks would 'not last very long' and she encouraged her listeners to understand 'that before long our country will be at war again'.[42] If the Irish accepted anything less than a republic, within two years the British would have eroded even the meagre rights gained on the basis that 'the things we considered necessary for Irish advancement were against our oath of allegiance to the Crown'.[43]

In this period Mary outlined and solidified a political position that she would maintain throughout the rest of her life. Normal democratic principles of majority rule were not admissible until the republic had been achieved:

> She was told that the majority of the population didn't want war again, but let her remind them it wasn't the majority of the country that fought for Ireland during Easter Week; it was the minority that fought, and if necessary the minority would carry the fight through now … they should remember that the tragedies of Cork and Brixton were not undergone for Dominion Home Rule but for a Republic and nothing else.[44]

There were those who even at this point before the Treaty split objected to her viewpoints as undemocratic. Liam de Róiste, who confided to his diary his belief that Mary disliked him, took issue with her statement that 'if the people in any country were consulted there would be no war'. 'What a term Democracy is!' he wrote.[45] 'We will not', she declared, 'lower the flag for which our martyrs have died'.[46] As she had pronounced on several occasions in America, she stated that once Ireland had full freedom, England would be given 'guarantees that they would not join with any of her enemies'.[47] However, such guarantees, she declared in the Dáil could only be provided it they 'did not involve directly or indirectly allegiance in any shape or form to the British Crown'.[48] She concluded her speech by reading out verses written by her brother 'at a time when there was talk of Devolution and making peace with England'; her final words were his – 'No compromise'.[49] This was a political stance that she enunciated repeatedly in the months after the Treaty split. All that Arthur Griffith had written in criticism about the Irish Parliamentary Party could, she argued, be levelled against him in the context of the Treaty. The *Cork Examiner* reporter, paraphrasing her words, wrote:

> He now spoke about the majority of the people ruling, but he said not long ago that Irish Nationality had always been saved by the intelligent minority. He was one of the intelligent minority then. He was one of the stupid majority now ... It was a minority who proclaimed the Republic, fought for it, and the minority if necessary would maintain it.[50]

For those like Mary, so centrally invested in the outcome of the Anglo-Irish peace talks, the period was one of heightened tensions as propaganda was disseminated, speeches were made, and rumours circulated. Although her political reputation had been secured in the eyes of many, including de Valera, by the way she negotiated and spoke in America, there were those who increasingly adopted a dismissive tone and attitude towards her. Ernest Blythe recalled how he met her in Louise Gavan Duffy's house before the ratification of the plenipotentiaries. He wrote that he spent most of the evening 'arguing' with her:

> Miss MacSwiney asked me about the prospects of a recognition of the republic by the British. I told her that in my opinion the prospect was nil. She brought out the theoretical argument that nobody had the right to abandon or disestablish the existing republic. The next day in the Dáil, when the plenipotentiaries were being nominated, she made a speech in which she declared that they were being sent to England for one sole purpose – to obtain British recognition of the Irish Republic. She wound up pointing her finger directly at me and saying 'If anyone here has a contrary opinion, let him speak now or be forever silent'. I only laughed at her.[51]

Austin Stack's wife, Una, recalled the speech without the supercilious attitude of Blythe but does infer that Mary was amongst the most vocal in attempts to force agreement in the Dáil that no compromise would be accepted in London:

> ... a meeting was held of the Dáil which ratified the appointment of the Plenipotentiaries.
>
> I cannot say whether or not that it was at this meeting that a discussion arose on 'compromise'. It came up at some meeting anyhow and, unless I mistake it, was raised by Miss MacSwiney. She referred to rumours afloat and an inexplicable atmosphere of compromise. Where did it originate? Who was responsible? Did it come from any man or section of men in the Dáil? And then she challenged any member who thought we should accept less than our sovereign rights 'to speak now, or to remain forever silent'. No one accepted her challenge.[52]

On 15 October representatives from the American Red Cross were in Cork. They inspected 'the scenes of the recent Cork burnings' and paid a visit to the Bishop of Cork, Dr Cohalan. Later in the day they visited the prison in Spike Island to meet with Cornelius Conroy who was serving a sentence of 15 years 'in connection with the round-up at White's Cross' Conroy had been rounded up with Seán MacSwiney in Whitechurch not White's Cross, as the *Cork Examiner* stated. That evening Mary was among the guests at the dinner for the delegates in the B and C restaurant, Prince's Street.[53] During the after-dinner speeches, Mr France, a member of the delegation, referred to 'one of the best classics which had ever been written' and added that it was a great pleasure to speak in the presence of the author's sister. Mary was 'enthusiastically cheered' when she stood up to speak. Referring to her brother's writings she declared that 'it would teach the world that the great spiritual ideals for which they in Ireland were fighting so long would not possibly be overcome by brutal material force'. It was 'impossible' to believe that 'a great and magnificent fight such as Ireland's had been, could fail'. As she had done on many occasions during her American tour, she drew analogies with the American War of Independence: '[t]he Americans had refused compromise, and so should Ireland'.[54]

On 11 October 1921, the first day of the Anglo-Irish peace conference, crowds of Irish sympathisers assembled on the end of the Downing Street first approached by Irish delegates. Hymns were sung, the rosary was recited, and flags were waved in 'scenes of wild enthusiasm'. As the crowd shouted out the names of 'prominent Irishmen', Terence was 'spoken of reverently'.[55] Simultaneously with the opening of the peace talks, the Abbey Theatre staged *The Revolutionist* published and set in 1914.[56] Prophetically the play's central theme was the necessity for individual self-sacrifice in the form of death to bring about national unity. A special performance on 16 October was in aid of the Irish Republican Prisoners Dependants' Fund.[57] On that same day Mary delivered a lecture at the Cork Opera House entitled 'Ireland in America' which was followed by a 'high-class concert', all proceeds going also to the fund.[58] Professor Stockley, who presided over the occasion, stated that Terence's 'spirit was over them that evening'. Stockley outlined the immorality of internment without charge.[59]

Mary claimed that she was alerted in the initial period of the Truce to the possibility that the Dáil leadership might be willing to compromise on the republic as result of what Patrick Maume describes as 'some cryptically expressed misgivings by Seán Etchingham'.[60] In letters – pages long – to de Valera, she betrayed an emotional response. Adopting a supplicatory tone, she requested 'that he would not be angry with her for writing to him in the way she has'. She implored him for guarantees: 'Don't you think it would be nice of you to show me you are magnanimous by sending me a line of assurance – just for me – that our Envoys will not come back with any plan of Ireland inside the Empire directly or indirectly'.[61] Speaking in the Dáil she noted that she had 'worried' de Valera 'out with letters' on the argument that the act of sending delegates to London indicated a willingness to compromise.[62] Mary was not the only individual who displayed anxiety about the peace talks. The Dáil envoy in Paris, Seán T. O'Kelly, returned to Ireland in November to remonstrate with de Valera about the way that the negotiations were being conducted by Collins and Griffith. Received coldly, there is a sense that de Valera believed that he could manage the course and outcome of the talks.[63]

Mary enclosed poems written by her brother and *Principles of Freedom* with marked passages which she implored de Valera to read. Her brother 'had earned the right to speak'.[64] She was adamant that there could be no compromise on the republic that her brother had died to defend but was conscious that her stridency might make de Valera 'cross':

> These are anxious days for us all. I wish I could feel happier than I do about the 'Conference' and its outcome.

> You and A. G. [Arthur Griffith] are the only people of the innermost circle to whom I have spoken and I cannot say I derived comfort from either of you. And yet the issue is so simple.
>
> I know you have read Principles of Freedom. Will you forgive me asking you to re-read the pages I have marked on the enclosed slips, especially the passages on Separation and what he says on page 110 ... about a Split. A Split would be a real disaster now, but there would be worse things. There can be no final peace while there is any formal link of dependence and there must be no camouflage about it.

Mary clearly asserted her right to have an opinion on the outcome of the peace talks based on her brother's death and on the trauma and agony endured by the wider family:

> I claim that the daily torture of unspeakable suffering gives me a claim to speak for mo dherfoire and myself ... There must be no link formal or otherwise: no allegiance to anything but the Republic: no flag to fly in our Country but the flag of that Republic.[65]

Mary vehemently downplayed the idea that the general population would not 'stand for another and a worse fight'. The people, she declared, 'will stand behind you if you stand by the oath we have all sworn'. If he faltered, others would too but not 'the best', not those 'who have suffered: not those who have faith in the justice of their cause, and regard for the honour of their Dead'. She declared that the rights of the minority, referring to unionists, can be considered 'when we have driven the enemy out'. De Valera had, she told him, 'no mandate to consider them now'. He was chosen as President, she stated, because he 'at least would have no compromise'. He had the ability, she asserted, to 'keep us all together or you can break our unit'. She herself, she wrote, was 'a practical idealist with the emphasis perhaps more on the practical'[66] Adopting a tone of conciliation, she accepted the 'responsibility' that rested on de Valera and requested that he would not be angry with her for writing to him in the way she had.[67]

Mary solidified her reputation as one of the key doctrinaire republicans during the Treaty debates; this status would be augmented by her imprisonments and hunger strikes during the Civil War (see Chapter Seven). In her Bureau of Military History witness statement, Elizabeth Brennan, secretary to Art O'Brien until late 1921, underestimated Mary's strength of conviction. Brennan clearly despised O'Brien, describing him as a 'very difficult person' who was 'more concerned with the official dignity attached to his position than to the national cause'. She stated that during the negotiations on the Treaty O'Brien was 'active in intriguing against the proposed articles' and continued: 'I know that Mary McSwiney [sic] spent several hours with him and I would imagine that he poisoned her mind against it'.[68] No one 'poisoned' Mary's mind. The moment the reality of the compromise that was the Treaty became known her response could only be vehement rejection. Her mind had narrowed itself around the trauma of her brother's hunger strike. She engaged in a 'repetition compulsion'; her need to repeat and find meaning in 'the tale' of Brixton 1920 meant that her response to the Treaty was predetermined.

At 2.15 am on 6 December the five Irish delegates signed the Articles for Agreement for a Treaty between Great Britain and Ireland without referral back to Dublin.[69] Mary was not the only person horrified. De Valera's sense of his own position as leader was highly inflated in this period and he could not conceive of the situation in which the plenipotentiaries would, as they did, sign and then publish the wording of the Treaty without consulting him.

This was, he declared, an 'act of disloyalty to their President ... without parallel in history'.[70] The Treaty established the new Irish Free State within the British Commonwealth of Nations with same constitutional status as Canada, Australia, New Zealand and South Africa. The 'de facto' partition of country, established under the Government of Ireland Act, 1920, was agreed. Lloyd George's promise of a boundary commission to consider the matter with due reference to the wishes of the inhabitants allowed the Irish delegates to believe that the southern state would regain Fermanagh, Tyrone and sections of Armagh essentially rendering the Northern Irish state unviable.[71] All Dáil deputies had to take an oath of allegiance to the monarch who was represented in the person of the Governor General. This was not the republic for which Terence MacSwiney had given his life. The excruciating ebb of his existence watched over by Mary and other members of his family. Dorothy Macardle described the atmosphere in the Mansion House on evening of the 6 December where de Valera spoke at an event organised by the Arts and Culture Minister, Count Plunkett, to commemorate the 600th anniversary of the death of the poet Dante:

> The people who filled the hall knew nothing but what the papers had reported and were told nothing from the platform. De Valera presided with a stony formality, unlike the manner they knew. In an atmosphere of oppressive constraint and tension the lectures on Dante went on. Of the elation and comradeship that had characterised Republican reunions there was no sign.[72]

On 8 December the Cabinet voted to accept the Treaty. Mary travelled to Dublin, meeting with de Valera the following day.[73] That the latter was 'aiming his plans at the more Republican end of the spectrum, rather than trying to win the middle ground' must have given her some initial degree of hope. As McCullagh states: '[d]e Valera's stance inevitably encouraged opposition to the Treaty'.[74] Mary saw a version of Document No. 2 positing external association whereby Ireland would be part of an association with the king as head but not monarch of the country, before the meeting of the Dáil commenced. Kathleen Clarke recalled that when the 'Articles of Agreement' for a Treaty were published:

> they caused a howl of indignation from one section of the people, and approval from another. De Valera issued a statement to the press saying that he was summoning a meeting of the Dáil to discuss the proposed Treaty, and that he saw a way of settling our differences. As the wording seemed ambiguous to me, I felt I must ask him to clarify it before the meeting of the Dáil, and I went to the Mansion House, which was then his headquarters, to see him. I met Miss MacSwiney at the door, and she told me she was there for the same purpose. He said he was very glad we had come, and handed each of us a document to read which he said he was going to propose at the meeting.
>
> Miss MacSwiney said she would like to study it before giving an opinion...[75]

Staying in the Standard Hotel in Harcourt Street, Mary wrote to de Valera: 'on consideration I do not think an alternative policy would be wise'. She did not believe she could support the proposal as it would mean compromise. She was 'sure others would feel similarly though it is not so bad as the "Treaty"':

> It is better for you to stand firmly against the Treaty pointing out that Ireland at least got her case before the world by the Conference & our object was to see how far L. G. [Lloyd George] would go & then we would have the world's sympathy (including England's perhaps) if we had to break on the principle.[76]

She wrote to him, as she put it, hoping to have an opportunity of speaking to him before the Dáil session opened in the Council Chambers in University College Dublin on Earlsfort Terrace. This letter illuminates the political stasis in which Mary was increasingly mired from this period onwards. She argued that the value of the peace talks was that they presented Ireland's case for republican independence 'before the world' and garnered sympathy. The letter was tinged with a desperate optimistic belief based on limited realpolitik particularly in this instance in her discussion of the creation of a republican counter state that would render the Treaty impotent. She concluded the letter with a list of 'Essentials'. That government must, she wrote, be chosen by the members of the Second Dáil who have remained true to the Republic' and 'the members nominated to fill the places of those who have died or been killed'. All citizens who declared allegiance to the republic should be levied with a tax and no income or direct taxes should be paid. In the case of the latter, she made an exception for doctors, hospitals and charitable institutions. She recommended that the citizens of the republic 'should set up and maintain arbitration courts'. Her key message was, as she underlined, that the republican government must be kept 'in being'.[77]

Administrative and procedural matters dominated the first day's proceedings when the Dáil met to debate the Treaty, most notably the question of whether to convene in private session. The thorny issue of whether a document had been submitted to the Cabinet before the Treaty was signed also emerged on that first day, exposing the tensions and fault lines that had been forming since the delegates returned to Ireland. While the rage of male deputies such as Collins at de Valera's reading out the instructions given to the plenipotentiaries has been discussed[78] there has been little or no discussion of the intervention of female deputies on such procedural matters. Mary's vehemence in calling for every document to be produced is noteworthy.[79] Of the six female deputies she was the first to contribute to the debate and from the outset presented her position as 'a doctrinaire republican' and one of the 'die-hards of the Dáil'. On that first day of the debate she stated her belief that it would be necessary to 'go back to war again'. With that in mind the relevant documents needed to be produced to allow a discussion relating to the army and finance in a private session.[80] The question of whether the Treaty was ratified under international law also emerged on the first day of proceedings; a committee of inquiry on the matter was established with Mary, Professor Stockley, Patrick McCartan, Patrick Hogan and Micheál Ó hAodha proposed by Richard Mulchahy. The committee was to go through the 'documents necessary to find out the relations between our own Cabinet and the delegation'.[81]

Standing up to speak again on 17 December, Mary began by asking for 'forgiveness if I speak too long'. She stood, she declared, 'in the name of the dead'.[82] The issue was 'not between peace and war; it is between right and wrong'.[83] She noted that she asked Terence on his deathbed, 'was it worth the cost'.[84] It behoved her now to ensure that his death had meaning. The atmosphere at the Dáil sessions was increasingly impassioned and fractious: 'bitter words passing, taunts and insinuations. Passions aroused: quelled by the good sense of the great body: to arise again'.[85] In this hothouse atmosphere Mary emerged as the bête noire for many who would vote for the Treaty. De Róiste wrote:

> I am morally certain now that the small section of the army in Cork who sent us a notice

> equivalent to a death warrant if we vote for the Treaty – expressing the opinion that if we do this we are traitors – were inspired by Miss MacSwiney.[86]

Mary rose to speak again at 4.25pm on 21 December. Concluding at 'exactly 7 o'clock' she addressed the chamber, as the contemporary *Irish Independent* journalist Padraig de Burca noted, for 'precisely the same length of time as the five Plenipotentiaries had taken with their combined speeches'.[87] She was aware of the growing mood of frustration within the chamber, but she defied the irritation of her audience: 'I care not and apologise not if I take more of your time than you are willing to give'.[88] There were those who praised her. Seán T. O'Kelly declared that her address 'not only vindicates the far-flung movement for women's rights but places Miss MacSwiney in the highest ranks of the greatest orators of our race'.[89] Describing her speech as 'epoch making', Kathleen Lynn wrote in her diary that Mary 'wiped the floor with Cosgrave & all opponents'.[90] James E. Campion, a member of the Roger Casement branch of the AARIR in Boston wrote to her on 27 December 1921: 'I have just read the speeches in the Dail for the second time. Your speech easily over tops all the others, and makes you the leader of the new revolution against the Irish Free State in case the treaty should be adopted.' She was, he declared, 'splendid' in exposing the recusancy of the Treaty delegates and 'in case of their failure, you, and the woman of Ireland would carry on the war'.[91] At a later date Macardle described MacSwiney's speech as 'a masterpiece of logic and eloquence'.[92] On the other side of the growing political divide Piaras Béaslaí denounced her belief that the Irish people would be behind renewed warfare.[93] During the Christmas recess that separated the Treaty talks de Róiste noted in his diary a conversation with a member of Sinn Féin in Cork who alleged that there was a 'general feeling against the selection of Miss MacSwiney' as a Dáil candidate in May 1921.[94]

As Caoimhe Nic Dháibhéid has stated 'the most oft-noted feature of the Treaty debates was the tenor of the exchanges'.[95] In Mary's case she was subjected to derision and scorn but then so were others. Markievicz scathingly referred to the pro-Treaty side on 7 January as 'Lloyd'.[96] De Valera referred to the sneering that Document No. 2 received by deputies on the pro-Treaty side.[97] De Róiste described him on 6 January 1922 as feeling 'very sensitive'.[98] Mary was also well able to retort to criticism; on 6 January she described those who voted for the Treaty as 'traitors', de Róiste describing her as giving 'another lecture' on that day.[99] She was not, however, merely a cipher for the extreme element within republicanism during the Treaty debates. Notwithstanding de Burca's statement that she never once mentioned the name of Terence MacSwiney, she was a woman who had suffered ultimate loss. Indeed, she did mention her brother's name during her earlier speech on 17 December as she drew her listeners attention to *Principles of Freedom*.[100] Terence's political life and death reverberated through her speech even if his name was not explicitly uttered. Indeed, Mary inferred a hierarchy of grief, placing herself at the top of the pyramid; she laid bare the trauma she had experienced:

> I consider myself in a different position from most of those who have suffered, for every other person who lost one near and dear to her lost him suddenly, I did not … let me tell you in 74 days you have much time for thinking. I weighed the cost, I weighed every thought. I am not a fool though I have been told I was a fool if I thought this Dáil did not mean to compromise. I do not think I am a fool and sitting there by that death bed the like of which has never

> been known in the world before I looked at this question which we are facing tonight ... I asked myself, when talking with my dying brother I asked him was it worth the cost, and we decided it was, and one of the last things he ever said to me was, 'Thank God there will be no compromise now'.[101]

Others, however, referred to explicitly to Terence. Seán Etchingham in his anti-Treaty speech stated:

> We cannot get away from the principle that we are in this Dáil standing for the Irish Republic and cannot have different shades of that Republic. We have for instance reference to the uncompromising opportunist shade. I do not conform to that. I may be a die-hard, but it is better the die-hard than soft. Terence MacSwiney died hard, he was over 90 days dying. What did he die for? Did he die for this thing that is before us?

Mary responded with one word: 'No'.[102] De Róiste described de Valera when he spoke in early January as: 'very much under the influence of Terence MacSwiney at present: his attitudes, statements and actions remind me very forcibly of all I knew of Terence in all sorts of meetings, great and small.'[103]

Jason Knirck argues that 'many' of the female deputies felt the 'need to justify' their position as a member of the Dáil and their 'right to speak'. He argues that reference to the dead 'was thus a strategy aimed towards giving the women a more authoritative voice in the debate'.[104] This was not true of Mary. Never did she feel that she needed to supplicate for her right to be heard; her allusions to Terence and to the trauma of Brixton were not used as an approach to assert herself. What she wanted was for Terence's death and the wider familial sacrifice in the service of the republic to have meaning. Her anguish was palpably on show when she appealed to the House 'against the sneers' of Arthur Griffith at the length of her speech, claiming her right to 'speak for the honour of my nation' based on what she 'went through for 74 days at Brixton'.[105] On 3 January 1922 Seán McGarry similarly mocked her. Referring directly to her demand during the debate on the ratification of the plenipotentiaries that they declare their stance on compromise, he continued: '[i]f talking would have got us a Republic we would have it last week (laughter)'.[106] The following day, Deputy McCabe, Leitrim-Sligo, stated that for the sake of principle Mary would have 'the whole population of Ireland wiped out of existence, man, woman and child'. When she objected, he flippantly responded, to laughter, that she would 'not leave us even a grasshopper'. Mary's retort that his understanding of her contributions to the debate showed that intelligence as well as principle belonged on the anti-Treaty side also drew laughter. At that point in the exchange McCabe suggested that she had become unhinged; that her 'mind and outlook' were 'distorted by the terrible experiences she has passed through'. She requested that he 'leave out my experiences', declaring that she 'did not bring anything of my personal experiences into my public speech here'.[107]

The reality, however, was that Mary's unrelenting opposition to the Treaty must be put in the context of what she described in a letter to de Valera as the 'agony' of her family 'this time 12 months'. They had to:

> face and count the cost daily and hourly. There was time for searching analysis – time to explore every avenue of compromise and having rejected them, time to pray that sacrifice might give strength to all others to endure to the end and give our Cause final triumph.[108]

Her brother's 'agony' would never, as she wrote to de Valera, 'have been endured to the end for anything less than absolute and entire Separation'; this determined her response to the Treaty.[109] It is, however, important to also underscore that Mary was a firm republican in her own right. As de Burca noted, those listening to her speech on the Treaty on 21 December 'wondered whether she was the teacher or the disciple of Terence MacSwiney'. In that speech she noted that she, and all 'belonging to me … absolutely refused to join Sinn Fein until Sinn Fein became Republican'.[110]

Mary declared that she spoke as 'a woman … who realises, as only a woman can, the evils of war and the suffering of war'. There were, however, 'evils worse than war'. The Dáil, she announced, had been told that it was a choice between acceptance of 'the document' and war. With 'every sense of deep responsibility', she stated, 'let us take war'. In her speech she offered herself to the 'other side' of the House as 'one of the first and most deliberate and irreconcilable rebels' if 'this country should be so false to itself to adopt the so-called Treaty'. Certainly, as per McCabe's indictment, she sounded a note of fanaticism in her contributions to the debate. If, she declared, England:

> exterminates the men, the women will take their places, and, if she exterminates the women, the children are rising fast; and if she exterminates the men, women and children of this generation, the blades of grass, dyed with their blood, will rise, like the dragon's teeth of old, into armed men and the fight will begin in the next generation.[111]

Her speech on 21 December also, however, hinged on principle. She denounced those who argued that they would accept the Treaty but would not take the oath. This, she argued, was 'cowardice', a defilement of the 'noble and spiritual ideal' of the republic. A person could not, she stated, be 'at the same time faithful and unfaithful'. Moreover, England would not allow any such prevarications. Referring to Lloyd George, she exhorted deputies not to think they could 'get the better of that wizard trickster in Downing Street'.[112]

Mary refused to accept that she was 'either a fool or wilfully blind' in not considering the very act of negotiation as a compromise. She reminded the Dáil that she was vigilant during the discussions around the sending of a delegation: 'I kept my eyes and my ears open to see if compromise was intended'. Michael Collins, she contended, declared to her that he was no 'compromiser'. Collins was pragmatic; Mary was an ideologue. Dolan and Murphy discuss the nuanced approach to the peace negotiations taken by Collins and the subtlety he demonstrated in engaging with Britain's demands during the writing of the new constitution:

> When it had come to making decisions about whether to sign the Treaty and later, whether to accede to British demands that the new constitution include references to the monarch and the oath, Collins concluded that a republic was not on offer. Given this fact, adhering to a particular mode of government was, he would claim, a betrayal of that for which separatists had fought.[113]

Mary and Collins interpreted betrayal differently. Having previously trusted the delegates 'too much', Mary moved in December to indict them for treachery. Childers allowed the propaganda victory that was implicit in bringing England to the negotiating table to 'be given away by the English Press'. She queried why O'Brien, 'the representative of our

Government in London', was not 'consulted as to whether it was a bluff or not' when Lloyd George threatened war.[114] After the Treaty was ratified by the Dáil, she returned to this point in a letter to Joseph Scott, a member of the AARIR in Los Angeles. In this correspondence Mary indicted Griffith specifically, stating that he was 'never a convinced republican' but that Brugha had assured her that 'they were perfectly safe' in trusting him.[115]

The issue of the will of the people was integral to Mary's speech. Her constituents knew what she 'stood for' when she was elected. She had 'not changed' nor would she. Seán MacSwiney in his brief speech made a similar point: he had his 'instructions in my pocket to vote against the Treaty'. Such directives came, he clarified, from the civilian population in his constituency and not the military men.[116] Yet even before the Treaty talks de Róiste noted that fellow TD, J. J. Walsh, told him that he had 'not found a constituent left in Cork who favours war'.[117] The latter reiterated this statement publicly in the Dáil on 3 January 1922 with even more certainty.[118] The issue of the will of her constituents was not considered by Mary unlike Frank Drohan, TD for Waterford-Tipperary East who resigned given his own anti-Treaty position and the desire to accept it amongst his constituents.[119] Mary, moreover, conveniently elided the fact that she, as many of the 124 Sinn Féin candidates, had been elected unopposed to the Second Dáil in May 1921. She stated: 'I love my people, every single one of them' but who exactly those people were was ambivalent given that no individual had actually voted for her.[120] As Weeks and Mícheál Ó Fathartaigh state the 'unelected nature of the Dáil is perhaps its most striking feature; it was a product both of intimidation by Sinn Féin and of the Labour Party's decision not to contest the 1921 election'.[121] What Mary could draw on, however, was that immediately after the signing of the Treaty, brigade and staff officers of the 1st Southern Division IRA under Liam Lynch met in Cork and declared the Articles of Agreement repugnant.[122] Invoking her brother's writing, she declared that it was 'not those who can inflict most but those who can endure most will conquer'. Appealing to the legitimacy of republican martyrs she stated that if Seán Mac Eoin, who seconded the 'abominable document', were her brother 'I would rather he was with Kevin Barry'.[123] A key theme in Terence's *Principles of Freedom* was the concept of a sacrifice that would benefit future generations, the idea that the revolutionary 'spirit ... [passed] breaths on other souls' even as the body is crushed'.[124] This idea of a future enjoyed only by others infused Mary's speech. Denouncing the 'flippancy' of Kevin O'Higgins, she stated, 'I should like to be as young as Deputy O'Higgins is now to carry on the fight for posterity'.[125]

The Dáil decision to go into recess for the Christmas period on 22 December was rancorous, with Arthur Griffith, as noted, drawing attention to the length of Mary's speech the previous day. Griffith's snideness notwithstanding, her protracted contribution as Christmas approached was significant. While de Valera wanted to continue the debate into the night to allow a vote to be taken on the 23 December, 'the pro-Treaty side were not going to allow their speakers to be curtailed' given the latitude allowed Mary. De Valera believed that had the vote been taken on 22 December a small majority against the Treaty might have been achieved.[126] Similarly, J. J. O' Kelly proclaimed: 'If only we had taken the vote on the Treaty before Christmas! At the Christmas recess, ecclesiastical influence was used strongly against us, and people who certainly did go down the country inclined to oppose the Treaty were influenced in that way'.[127] David Fitzpatrick notes that public support for acceptance 'as expressed by local councils, clubs and societies, newspapers, and clergymen of all denominations, was yet more overwhelming after the Christmas break'.[128] Both Mary and her brother Seán voted in favour of Collins's amendment to adjourn until 3 January 1923, as did de Valera.[129]

As the Dáil reconvened on 3 January 1922 the press noted the foundation of the anti-Treaty weekly newspaper in response to the perception amongst republicans 'of the lack of support accorded to them by the Press of Southern Ireland'. *The Republic of Ireland* was launched under the editorship of Liam Mellows with a nine person 'committee of direction' of which Mary was one.[130] As she arrived at the National University, Dublin, on the first day after the Christmas recess 'she was given a most hearty reception'.[131] As de Valera took 'his customary position on the left-hand side of the Speaker's chair' on 3 January she joined him and, as the *Evening Echo* noted, 'engaged in conversation with him for some time'.[132] During the Treaty debates, de Valera was, as McCullagh discusses, 'desperately trying to find a compromise that would preserve unity'.[133] Mary also talked about the need for concord; on 16 December she noted that her name was down to speak but requested to contribute at a later point 'because my speech is mainly an appeal to this Assembly for unity'.[134] However, what she demanded was unity on her intractable terms. Nevertheless, she still deferred to de Valera's presidency and viewed their political positions as aligned. At no point did Mary desire to assume a leadership position unlike de Valera who in this period of the Treaty debates 'believed that the welfare of Ireland would be served by his retention of power'.[135] On 9 January she spoke in the House in defence of de Valera's resignation as President:

> The President was perfectly right in resigning because he was in a minority; and as he was not only the President of the Republic, but leader of the House, he had to resign being in a minority. We have to re-assert here to-day that this is a Republican Government and the Parliament of the Government of the Irish Republic; and we must have a President for that Republic. If the other side wish to elect somebody in opposition to President de Valera let them do so; but how can they be at the one time, or how can any man from their side be President of the Republic and supporter of the Free State? I maintain that and I take great pleasure in supporting the re-election of the President.[136]

Mary's political position in this period was more fluid and nuanced than has been represented. Although, as discussed above, she stated to de Valera before the debates commenced that she could not vote for Document No. 2, by the end of the December she was less adamant. At the very least, she viewed it as less reprehensible than the Treaty. Writing from Cork during the Christmas recess she declared herself 'angry at this dreadful betrayal'. She reproached de Valera for not recalling the Treaty delegates 'when you found what they were like'. The main point in her letter, however, was that if de Valera could get 'the others to back your Document in its latest form we shall back it ... but we want the biggest vote we can get on our side and no camouflage'.[137] De Valera, indeed, informed McGarrity in late December that Mary, amongst others, supported his proposal which he had redrafted over Christmas.[138]

While Mary's position was more nuanced than has been understood when her attitude to Document no. 2 during the Treaty debates is considered, her doctrinaire mind-set was influential at crucial points in determining de Valera's position, forcing him at times into a political place that he had not wanted to find himself in. When the Treaty was passed in the

Dáil on 7 January 1923, Collins called for unity and proposed a type of joint commitment to facilitate it. De Valera, McCullagh argues, 'seemed receptive to Collins's approach, but any hope of unity evaporated when MacSwiney spoke'.[139] Interjecting, she declared:

> I claim my right, before matters go any further, to register my protest, because I look upon this act to-night worse than I look upon the Act of Castlereagh. I, for one, will have neither hand, act, nor part in helping the Irish Free State to carry this nation of ours, this glorious nation that has been betrayed here to-night, into the British Empire ... I register my protest, and not one bit of help that we can give will we give them. The speech we have heard sounded very beautiful—as the late Minister of Finance can do it; he has played up to the gallery in this thing, but I tell you it may sound very beautiful but it will not do. Ireland stands on her Republican Government and that Republican Government cannot touch the pitch of the Free State without being fouled... Therefore, let there be no misunderstanding, no soft talk, no ráiméis at this last moment of the betrayal of our country; no soft talk about union; you cannot unite a spiritual Irish Republic.[140]

De Valera called a meeting of those who had voted against the Treaty for 1 pm the following day.[141] Cumann na Poblachta was duly formed on 8 January 1923. A second meeting later that day comprised de Valera's 'new inner circle': Mary joined Boland, Brugha, Childers, Mellows and Stack. McCullagh notes that this group of six were 'distinctly more hard-line than de Valera'. Four would die in the Civil War and the two survivors MacSwiney and Stack remained in Sinn Féin when he established Fianna Fáil in 1926.[142] Later that evening on the 8 January the six met in de Valera's private quarters in Rathmines and formed the policy committee of the new party.[143]

On 9 January Mary's intransigence once again impacted the politics of the anti-Treaty side. De Valera resigned as President. When the Chamber met the next day to elect a new President, de Valera pressed Griffith on the status of the position. When Griffith assured him that he would, if elected, maintain the Republic until the Treaty was presented to the people, de Valera, McCullagh, states, appeared placated. Once again, however, as on 7 January, Mary's intervention at a crucial point hardened his position.[144] In yet another lengthy speech she accused Collins of suggesting that he and Griffith 'should be calmly allowed to murder the Irish Republic'. She stated that what Griffith was asking the Chamber to do was:

> ...to disestablish Dáil Eireann as the Sovereign Assembly of the Irish Republic, and set up an emasculated thing which will be the Provisional Government and, having done that, then this emasculated Assembly with the best gone from it, will appoint the Provisional Government and set up the Free State. That Assembly will not be Dáil Eireann, because, unless Mr. Griffith definitely gives that solemn promise to-day—that he will not combine the two offices, or, failing to give it, unless he is beaten in this Assembly to-day he and everyone who votes with him is automatically declaring himself guilty of treason, and voting himself out of Dáil Eireann.[145]

The *Freeman's Journal* noted that 'a good deal of excitement followed this speech'.[146] Before her speech, de Valera had been appeased at Griffith's assurance that he would keep the republic in existence until the Treaty was put to the will of the people. Following it, he left the chamber before the vote was taken. This was intended as a stance against the election as President of a man who had led the peace delegation and who was now bound under the terms of the Treaty to establish a state that would overthrow the Irish Republic.[147]

On 11 January 1922 a meeting of the new Cabinet was held in the Mansion House. In another room in the same building de Valera held a simultaneous meeting of his 'chief supporters' amongst whom was Mary.[148] The next day she lost her position following the election of a new standing committee of the Sinn Féin Ard Chomhairle. She was not the only person to fail to be re-elected in a heavy defeat for the anti-Treatyites with only three elected out of 15 members.[149]

The Provisional Government was established on 14 January led by Michael Collins. One week later, Mary attended the Irish Race Congress which opened in Paris at the Hotel Continental on 21 January 1922. The intention of the congress, proposed by Irish nationalists in South Africa, was to garner international support for the Irish Republic; the Irish at home and overseas were to come together to 'share in the great destiny of their motherland'.[150] The political agenda was complemented by an economic and cultural one. However, the idea of the gathering as a manifestation of Irish unity and strength was shattered by the signing of the Anglo-Irish Treaty and the rancorous Dáil debates that ensued.[151] The congress marked the jostling for position and advantage by both sides who were represented by an equal number of delegates in, what Fitzpatrick describes as, 'a futile attempt to present a united front'.[152] Robert Brennan described the atmosphere when he arrived somewhat late to Paris as a 'hot-bed of intrigue'.[153] As Helene O'Keeffe discusses, the fractious nature of the Dáil was replicated in Paris as Seán T. O'Kelly, Dáil envoy to France, was perceived to have snubbed the pro-Treaty delegation. De Valera was invited to make a speech at the opening banquet with no contribution asked from the opposing side.[154] The anti-Treaty side, led by de Valera, comprised Markievicz, Boland, Donal O'Callaghan as well as Mary. That de Valera chose two women should be noted. The choice of Mary as a delegate must have been influenced by her familiarity with republican politics on a world stage consequent on her American tour but it also reflects her solidifying position within the anti-Treaty political elite. Both within and outside the Dáil Mary indicated her continued belief in the importance of international allies and support for the successful resolution of the Irish question.

On 25 January Fine Ghaedheal was established as a world federation of the Irish race to promote Irish culture and trade and to work to ensure that Ireland took its proper place amongst the nations of the world.[155] The question of the objectives of the federation provoked heated discussion. Mary declared that the 'Free State is still born' and argued that it was necessary for the anti-Treaty side to, in the words of Diarmuid Coffey reporting for the Provisional Government, 'get the exclusive support of the organisation, as the Irish Government had government resources to draw upon'.[156] The failure of the anti-Treaty side to prevail during the election of a new-standing committee at the Sinn Féin Ard Chomhairle on 12 January must have also been on her mind. The seven person executive elected on the last day saw victory for Mary's point of view; political benefit appeared to derive to the anti-Treaty side. De Valera was elected president with Eoin MacNeill in the position of vice president; the five other positions went to Republicans.[157] MacNeill bitterly attributed this victory to the late arrival of new partisan delegates with delegates from other countries expressing distaste at the party bias that prevailed.[158]

Mary contributed to the economic discussions in Paris. The *Cork Examiner* reported on her speech on 26 January, noting her argument that the Treaty 'was designed to get an economic hold on Ireland'. The republicans 'looked forward to putting the country on an entirely different economic basis. They wanted to defeat the capitalist system and change it into an economic commonwealth'. They wanted a people who had enough to eat and drink but who also had time for amusement and time to enjoy themselves.[159] Mary's denunciation of a capitalist industrial economy was in harmony with Catholic social teaching. In December of that year Pius XI would deplore the economic inequalities of modern capitalism and the 'war between classes'.[160]

Back in Ireland Mary immersed herself in the rippling consequences of the Treaty split. Cumann na mBan was the first organisation to reject the Articles of Agreement. At a meeting on 11 January 1922, before she left for Paris, the executive reaffirmed the commitment to the republic by 26 votes to 2; all provincial members bar 1 were present.[161] As McCarthy states even before a meeting of the general membership, the leadership of the organisation had declared a position against the Treaty and requested that all work to ensure the success of the anti-Treaty side at the upcoming Sinn Féin Ard Fheis.[162] A special Cumann na mBan convention was held in Dublin on 5 February with Markievicz in the chair. At the animated sessions a resolution was adopted by an overwhelming majority reaffirming 'allegiance to the Irish Republic'.[163] Due to the death of her brother in 1920 and the months she spent in America in 1921 Mary was recorded as attending no meetings of the Executive in those years.[164] At the Special Convention held in Dublin on 5 February 1922 she emerged to assume a central role; she put forward the republican resolution calling for rejection of the Treaty and for the organisation to 'reaffirm' its 'allegiance to the political demands for which Terence had died. The meeting was held in the Mansion House, the *Irish Independent* reporter John F. Boyle, writing: 'It was a woman's day. Girls in smart green uniforms and neat hats to match were sprinkled with elderly women, middle-aged women, intellectual women and city and country women.' During the Treaty debates the six female deputies were similarly described with reference to their dress while the IRA uniform of some male deputies was remarked upon emphasising the direct relationship of the latter to the War of Independence. Markeivicz on the 19 December wore a 'white blouse and black fur', other women were clad in deep black.[165] While Mrs Pearse was described as 'pathetic', Mary was 'firm, earnest and immovable'. Her address, the paper reported, was 'terse, vehement and uncompromising'. Her speech vibrated 'with conviction'.[166] The press media of the period once again delineated women according to their physical appearance and dress with a focus on the emotions they manifested. De Róiste also used the word 'pathetic' to describe Mrs Pearse during the Treaty debates.[167] Margaret Pearse was 64 years of age at this point, on 12 February she was due to turn 65. Her two sons, Patrick and Willie, were executed after 1916. She surely cut a tragic figure as reporters watched the demeanour of the roughly 600 women who attended the convention. Yet, it was she who proposed the resolution that Cumann na mBan would only support candidates that rejected the Treaty at the forthcoming election.[168] This resolution carried, Cumann na mBan did not just reject the Treaty but pledged to actively work against its ratification in the upcoming elections.[169]

Strikes on the railroads in South of Ireland hampered many from that region attending the special convention, Mary rising to state that she had received many telegrams from absent members and branches in the south indicating their support for the proposal.[170] Her Mansion House speech centred around the oath of allegiance to the Republic sworn by the First Dáil; this she elevated to a matter of inalienable principle. It was, of course, that oath that her brother had died to uphold. In the speech the ideal of the republic took precedent over human concerns around the renewal of war. Accepting the Treaty, the Dáil had 'voted for the subversion of the Republic'. Women were, she stated, 'the backbone of the nation' and would not renounce 'their heritage' for an 'Imperial Pottage'. She urged delegates not to be 'led astray by those who talk to you of the Treaty being a step towards the Republic'. The idea that the Treaty was the first step on the path to full independence was, of course, the fulcrum around which Collins advocated for an acceptance of the Articles of Agreement brought back from London.[171] The Republic Mary countered, had been established in 1919. Any lesser form of freedom was a retrograde step: 'If you want to get to the top of the hill and you do get to the very top and somebody asks you to take a step towards the top, would you not say "but I am there already". We have the Republic.' That Republic, she claimed, 'had shown that it is able to govern the Irish people and the Army'. With this statement she was drawing on the attempts by Sinn Féin to establish a counter state from the period of the establishment of the First Dáil. In *The Irish Republic* Macardle emphasised the way the legislature extended institutions of a functioning parallel government during the period 1919–21, referring, for example, to the Republic Courts established in June 1920.[172] The reality was that despite the assertion of Mary and others, the 'amount of success the Dáil government had in establishing its authority has often been exaggerated'.[173]

In Mary's conceptualisation, the Republic transcended personalities; it was more than 'any man or woman'. It was not the duty of Cumann na mBan to:

> shout 'Up De Valera' or 'Up Collins'. If they had jointly turned their backs on the Republic, we Cumann na mBan, would still stand here today and if there was not a man in Ireland to stand for the Republic the women would hold allegiance to it, and work to bring the country back to it. We do not give our allegiance because this man or that man stands for it.[174]

Mary urged those who listened to her to 'think very bravely':

> I do not think the women of Ireland were afraid during the War but it is a terrible thing and we must think seriously before bringing those horrors to our people. There are certain things which you cannot give up for any threat whatever, and one of them is the sacred question of principle ... We must remember the terrible fight we have put up for the last three years.[175]

As the speeches went on the *Irish Independent* reporter commented:

> One was reminded of the Dail [sic] as the debate progressed, only there were a couple of notable differences. In the first place all the speakers in the afternoon session were against the Treaty. In the second place the speeches were brief, concise, and very much to the point.[176]

At the convention Mary seconded the resolution proposed by Min Mulcahy calling for a renewal of the Belfast Boycott unless the prisoners in the north, particularly the three men condemned to death in Derry, were released.[177] These men, Leonard, O'Shea and Johnstone, were due to hang on 9 February for the death of two special constables during an escape attempt from Derry jail on 2 December 1921.[178] Mary's support for Mulcahy's resolution marked a point of co-operation between those members who rejected the Treaty and those who accepted it. The latter was, of course, married to prominent pro-Treaty supporter, Richard Mulcahy. As Ward states of the dissident women who left Cumann na mBan, they 'were obviously all highly political women, well able to determine their own attitudes towards the Treaty, but family loyalities must have played some part in their decision'.[179]

Despite the apparent display of unity, Mary took issue with Jennie Wyse Power's amendment reaffirming allegiance to the Republic while recognising 'that the Treaty signed in London will, if accepted by the Irish people, be a big step along the road to that end'. Wyse Power proposed that Cumann na mBan would not 'work obstructively against those who support the Treaty'.[180] While she paid tribute to Wyse Power's work in the cause of Irish freedom, the *Irish Independent* reported Mary's vehement rebuttal of her amendment to the resolution. Wyse Power noted that the IRA had not yet declared a stance on the Treaty and continued that Cumann na mBan 'would be in a very curious position if they decided on policy that would be different to the policy of the IRA'. She did not want the organisation to go out 'in the open against Irishmen who had fought and nobly worked for the Republic'.[181] This argument held no weight for Mary who vehemently declared that:

> … she was intensely surprised to hear her advocate they should wait for the men. For she was fighting when many of them were in their cradles, for women's right to take their places in the councils of the nation. If the IRA became a Free State army were they going to work for them. (Cries of 'No'). Therefore why wait for the men? Rather let it be their place to give them a lead if they needed it.[182]

Mary's stance was, indeed, like that of Hanna Sheehy Skeffington who denounced the subordinate status of women vis-à-vis male activists when Cumann na mBan was established as an auxiliary organisation to the Irish Volunteers in April 1914.[183] Indeed, as Marie Coleman notes during the Treaty debates Mary made reference to the 'opposition of the "women of Ireland" to "the men that want to surrender"'.[184]

Cumann na mBan rejected the Treaty by 419 votes to 63, the *Irish Independent* reporter stating that Mary 'hurled her "Ní Toil" (against) with vehement emphasis'.[185] Those who accepted the Treaty and the establishment of the Free State left the organisation, a number going on to join Cumann na Saoirse led by Jennie Wyse Power. This organisation established on 12 March 1922 in the Mansion House became the female auxiliary to the Irish Free State army. It was also involved in organisational matters around the June 1922 elections, tasked with distributing posters and leaflets.[186] Members were granted positions on the committee when the pro-Treaty party, Cumann an nGaedheal, was established.[187] In Cork, Cumann na Saoirse worked 'strenuously' distributing such material 'on an intensive scale' and canvassing for the two Treaty candidates on the panel: de Róiste and Walsh.[188]

The rejection of the Treaty at the Special Cumann na mBan Convention caused tensions in Cork. However, it is too bald a statement to make that Mary 'purged the ranks of Cumann na mBan in Cork'.[189] Instead, the fissures and cracks within the organisation in the city, discussed in Chapter Three, emerged further into the open. This reflected what was happening in organisations across Ireland. Of Sinn Féin, Laffan states that divisions 'emerged that had been buried or had lain dormant during the previous four years'.[190] There was, moreover, a strong group within Cumann na mBan in Cork who accepted the Treaty. The Poblachta na hÉireann branch of the organisation tabled a resolution that the Cork District Council reaffirmed its allegiance to the Republic. De Róiste scathingly noted that 'the resolution is such as would be drafted by Miss Mary MacSwiney'. Mary, of course, was in Paris at the Irish Race Congress in this period and he surmised that in her absence Annie put forward the resolution.[191] This 'poll' was rejected by 16 votes to seven at the meeting on 29 January, even before the special convention of the organisation was held.[192] De Róiste believed that it was the reference to the 64 TDs who had voted for the Treaty as 'traitors' and perjurers' that caused the strong vote against the demand to declare allegiance to the republic: 'I am sure that view was resented by the women and girls present. [Miss MacS.' view is tantamount to this – she is the Republic and all should swear allegiance to her!]'[193] Mary sought to sanction those within Cork Cumann na mBan who were pro-Treaty, citing the authority of the executive over the district councils:

> I am in receipt of your reply to my letter and note that you have summoned a special meeting for next Sunday to deal with local matters of urgency. No business is more urgent than the interests of the Republic, and in view of the recent action of Cork District Council, the matter I desire to bring before you cannot be deferred.
>
> You will please note that this is an executive order to which local matters must give place.[194]

She was informed that the District Council would inform her of its decision in due course but, in the words of Conlon, 'instead of abiding by this' she sent circulars to all branches instructing them to send delegates to the meetings.[195] Her imprimatur and her refusal to abide by the protocol laid down by the District Council resulted in a decision to bar her from entry 'pending the decision of Council'; Conlon stated that the members 'were not anxious to be subjected to a two-and-a-half hours' harangue of invective such as was delivered in the Dail'.[196] After some discussion it was unanimously decided that neither now nor at any future date would the delegates care to see her.[197]

A letter was sent to Mary the next day bluntly informing her of this decision.[198] Allegations were made by the Shandon branch that the Poblachta na hÉireann branch sent four rather than the requested one delegate to the special convention while the Cork branch sent two, a note archly declaring: '[y]ou can therefore can see how the Convention obtained its majority'.[199] Each branch was allowed 2 delegates;[200] this statement from the Shandon branch in which the Conlon sisters were key members underscored the internal tensions and recriminations that emerged after the Treaty split. In *Cumann na mBan,* Conlon included an extract of a letter received from Cork TD, J. J. Walsh stating: 'This Cumann na mBan affair was rigged … Our people took no notice whatever of it … We will take immediate steps to organise a Women's Political Association … I suggest that meantime you refuse you refuse to disband your district council.'[201]

Mary was not without supporters in Cork Cumann na mBan as the Treaty split reverberated through the local organisation. Nora O'Brien was suspended from the District Council for her support of the latter.[202] On 12 January Leslie de Barra wrote to the Cork District Council of Cumann na mBan asking for a procession to take place to allow the women of Cork demonstrate to the Dáil that it 'act up to the mandate it received from the people on election'. As the policy of Cumann na mBan was republican, members were 'bound to stand fast to the Republic'.[203] A notice appeared in the *Cork Examiner* on 15 February stating that the meeting of Cumann na mBan to be held that evening in the Cork Courthouse 'had been officially sanctioned' and that two members of the Executive, Mary and de Barra, would conduct it.[204] The meeting, conducted in private, was held in consequence of the acceptance of the Treaty by the Cork District Council of Cumann na mBan.[205] This general meeting was called by Mary to 'place before the members the future policy of Cumann na mBan as outlined at the Convention'.[206]

The issue of ownership of the name Cumann na mBan animated the debate on the Treaty split in Cork. Walsh wrote to Conlon on 18 February affirming that 'our people should retain the name of Cum na mBan', adding that 'you girls have made an excellent start'. In a further letter he suggested that Cork set up an all-Ireland Cumann na mBan, ask for affiliations and retain the headquarters of the organisation in the city.[207] Mary was alert to what she perceived as the misuse of the name by those on the pro-Treaty side. She wrote imperiously to the *Cork Examiner* in March about an advertisement which appeared in the *Evening Echo* on 13 of the month calling on members of Cumann na mBan to assemble outside St Patrick's Church. Such a notice, she wrote, was not issued by official Cumann na mBan. No mention of the organisation should 'be made in your paper as taking part in any proceedings in favour of the Free State'. Should this occur 'proceedings will be taken'.[208] 'Certain persons' were using the name 'illegally' and 'proceedings are to be taken in the courts of the Irish Republic against such action'.[209] Reporting on the letter, the *Freeman's Journal* issued an editorial explanation that 'the majority of the Cumann na mBan in Cork approve of the Treaty and at a meeting some weeks ago passed a resolution to that effect'.[210] On 6 March a notice appeared in the *Cork Examiner*, calling on the secretaries of city and county branches in favour of the Treaty or those anxious to form branches to communicate with the Secretary of the District Council.[211] By early March, according to Conlon, there was co-operation with the pro-Treaty faction of Cumann na mBan in Cork 'as far west as Goleen where 99% of the people were in favour of the Treaty'. While some of the branches changed their name to Cumann na Saoirse, 'the Cork District Council and various branches retained the name of Cumann na mBan'. Conlon wrote that it was decided to severe all ties with Dublin and establish an executive in Cork.[212] However, as McAuliffe notes the executive of Cumann na Saoirse was 'Dublin-centred', 16 of 20 members living in the capital.[213] Internal debates within Cork Cumann na mBan ranged on and similar tensions and arguments emerged within Sinn Féin in Cork between pro and anti-Treaty supporters.

De Róiste was tasked by Griffith at the end of January to visit all Sinn Féin clubs in the city to put pro-Treaty views before the members.[214] Cork city continued to experience high levels of violence. De Róiste believed that Donal Óg O'Callaghan as Lord Mayor was not able to impose law and order and feared shooting and other forms of violence in the lead up to the elections. His desire for a municipal police force in the city to which the IRA would only come to the assistance when called upon was stymied by the 'incitements' to violence against Pro-Treaty supporters issued by Mary, Brugha and other high-profile republicans. O'Callaghan voted against the Treaty but de Róiste alleged internal tensions within the republican camp. He stated that the MacSwiney family had turned against O'Callaghan and accused him in the summer of 1921 of not preventing the arrest of Terence in August 1920, he being privy to information that the military were intending to raid the Cork City Hall. According to de Róiste, Seán MacSwiney successfully objected when de Valera proposed nominating O'Callaghan as deputy speaker of the Dáil.[215] Personal traumas played out in republican politics.

Mary's attention was also on wider political decisions and the objectives of the anti-Treaty side in the immediate aftermath of the ratification of the Treaty by the Dáil. De Valera placed his focus on Cumann na Poblachta established as an anti-Treaty wing of Sinn Féin. The central policy plank of the new party was the rejection of the Treaty 'to the exclusion of socio-economic matters'.[216] The first public meeting of the party was held on 12 February in O'Connell Street, Dublin.[217] A week later a meeting was held in Cork. The advance advertisement called on people to: 'Come and hear the true principles of Nationality enunciated, as preached and practised by Tone, Emmet, Pearse, Tomas MacCurtain, and Terence MacSwiney. Come and hear the truth about the "Treaty".'[218]

The *Freeman's Journal* noted the departure of de Valera, Brugha and Markievicz from Knightsbridge Station in Dublin on 18 February to 'open the wrecking campaign in the Southern Capital'. Mary was part of the welcoming party who met them at the train station as the rain poured down.[219] The next day she presided at no. 2 platform, announcing that they were assembled to 'renew their allegiance to the existing Republic of Ireland'.[220] A repeated demand at the Cork meeting was that the forthcoming constitution had to be put before the people before an election was held.[221] Putting forward the resolutions, Mary declared '[w]e will not go into the British Empire with either our heads or our hands up'.[222] As befitted the venue, Mellows made direct reference to the death of Terence:

> Some of the representatives of the people had stated that they didn't believe the Irish Republic was an existing thing. They meant by that to tell the people that the people when they elected them didn't know what they were doing and that the term Republic was only a political shibboleth. They meant to tell them that the men had been hanged and that people had been put into gaol and tortured to death because they didn't believe in a Republic. They meant to tell the people of Cork that when 40,000 of them knelt on the street when Terence MacSwiney was dying in Brixton, and the other heroes were dying in Cork Gaol, that the people knelt and prayed for them knowing that they were dying for the Republic and yet the people themselves did not believe in the Republic.[223]

That same day Mary, de Valera, Markevicz, Brugha and Mellows visited the republican plot in St Finbarr's cemetery, Cork. The *Cork Examiner* issued a photograph of the visit.

Mary was back in Dublin on 21 February to attend the extraordinary Sinn Fein Ard Fheis summoned by the Ard-Chomhairle on 12 January. There was a 'steady stream' of delegates from 10 am, she one of the first to arrive. The *Cork Examiner* noted that there were 'a large number of priests among the delegates, but a comparatively small number of women'.[224] As in Cork the previous weekend, one of the key issues that dominated the anti-Treaty speeches in the Mansion House was the prospect of a 'rushed election'. She declared in Cork: '[l]et the Irish people insist that there will be no election until the last "i" is dotted and the last "t" crossed and the last comma fixed in that Free State Constitution'.[225] She stated that republicans were asked not to impede the election in the interest of unity. Using the analogy of family loyalty – something dear to her – she asserted that the pro-Treaty side 'might as well tell them not to impede the murderer who stood with the knife at his mother's throat'.[226] Cumann na Poblachta aimed takeover of the central structures of Sinn Féin. It was also concerned to ensure the return of republican candidates in the looming elections, although the postponement of these for three months, a decision reached in February at the extraordinary Sinn Féin Ard Fheis, meant the suspension of the attempt to create partisan election committees.[227] There was a desire at the meeting to achieve a 'temporary' unity within the Sinn Féin organisation.[228]

On 28 February the Dáil met and Griffith announced the handover of power by the British to the Provisional Government and details of the new cabinet.[229] Mary's contribution underscored the confused nature of arrangement between the Provisional Government and Dáil Éireann. On the announcement of Michael Hayes as Minister for Education she reiterated her earlier statement that she 'would absolutely have nothing to do with the Provisional Government or any Government that might arise from it'. Cumann na Saoirse women argued that the Treaty would give 'Irish control of education, with power to restore the language and build up a national culture'.[230] Mary considered no such pedagogical issues; her focus was on the grounds of allegiance to the republic. As head of a school, she asked: 'Now, I want to know, in view of the new arrangement, if he will undertake to deal with the education of Ireland as Minister of Dáil Eireann and not refer me, in any communication I have to make to him, to any other Government than the Government of Dáil Eireann [sic]?'[231]

After the ratification of the Treaty by the Dáil on 7 January 1922 there were months of uncertainty. The Army divided between pro- and anti-Treaty with soldiers in many instances taking political leads from their commanders. On 26 March the anti-Treaty side established a separate Army Executive.[232] That section of the IRA that opposed the Articles of Agreement was increasingly proving itself capable of infrastructural disruption. They conducted raids and were responsible for rail network and print media interruptions.[233] In Mary's opinion, voiced strongly, the responsibility for the increasing prospect of civil war in the months after the Treaty split rested 'solely and entirely on the shoulders of those who signed the Treaty and who support it'.[234] Unlike, for example, Boland, at no point did she countenance 'republican subservience to the popular will'.[235] If victory in the forthcoming election was not achieved then the minority had the right, she asserted, to subvert the will of the people in the interest of the Republic. Fitzpatrick discusses the manner in which Boland negotiated 'for unity and therefore compromise' in the months immediately after the 7 January. Mary saw things very differently. 'A man, she wrote, does not show his devotion to the Republic by killing the Republic'[236] Yet, on a personal level she expressed her sympathy for Boland's attempts: 'Poor Harry … For a long time he believed in Mick; believed that Mick and Dev. could be brought together'.[237] By contrast with Boland, Mary believed, as she declared to Joseph McGarrity, that 'no unity was possible except on one basis'. She indicted McGarrity for trying 'to force unity on any other ground than Principle'. She urged him to send money to the anti-Treaty side despite Collins's imprimatur. If the pro-Treaty leaders believed that 'we would get financial support they would come to terms – such terms as we could accept – here and now'. She informed McGarrity: 'if those of us who are still true to the existing Republic and who mean to remain so have to stand alone against the world we will do so to the end'.[238]

During the confused months after the split Mary attended Dáil sessions during which the likelihood of Civil War was increasingly mentioned. Under the auspices of Cumann na Poblachta she spoke at meetings throughout the country in advance of the impending elections. Her speeches very much followed a pattern. On several occasions she spoke mainly in Irish. This, however, may have been for effect; notably when she wanted to reiterate her point she reverted to English.[239] Indeed, this was a stratagem of a number on the anti-Treaty side in the period. De Valera, as McCullagh discusses, engaged in 'verbal trickery' when opening the debate on the Treaty, declaring in Irish that his grasp of the language was not sufficient to allow him to proceed. In the next sentence he said that he was using English as he believed that many members in the chamber were not sufficiently versed in Irish.[240]

In Ballinahassig, Co. Cork, Mary addressed the question that the result of a rejection of the Treaty would mean be a return to 'immediate and terrible war'. This she denounced as palpably untrue. England would not have conceded as much, the newspaper account of her speech declared, 'if she was not prepared to give everything Ireland demanded'. Moreover, she outlined the way England's difficulties in Egypt and India mitigated against the renewal of war against Ireland. In the words of Deirdre MacMahon: 'Throughout 1919, 1920 and 1921 the gloomy quartet of Ireland, Egypt, Mesopotamia, and India appeared with monotonous regularity on the Cabinet agenda. The fear of a domino effect in each theatre of imperial unrest gripped British ministers as they thrashed around for a solution.' The signing of the Treaty moreover, had 'immediate consequences in the case of both Egypt and India'.[241] If war did recommence, Mary made clear the willingness of the anti-Treaty side to suffer physically, even to the point of death, to maintain allegiance to the Republic. The register of her language was increasingly violent and extreme and based on ideology rather than any military assessment. Her position was also unrepresentative of the country. According to the *Cork Examiner* report:

> If they allowed Michael Collins and Arthur Griffith and the rest of the men who were trying to turn down the Republic to establish a government in this country they would have to imprison, and perhaps to torture and kill the men and women who stood where Tone and Mitchell and Davis and the men of 1916 stood, for these would not go into the British Empire with their heads or their hands up. They were going to remain citizens of the Irish Republic, and they would not allow that to be turned down except on their dead bodies.[242]

Mary constructed the Treaty as a document imposed by a foreign government, the effect of which was to spread acrimony within the Irish nation, sundering a republican family that up to this point had stood together.[243] This stance reflected the belief that many held that Sinn Féin was less a political party than a 'national movement'.[244] Mary declared in the Dáil in the context of formulation the coalition pact in mid-1922:

> I wish to join my protest with that of other Deputies against the use of the word 'politicians' to describe our actions. We stand for the preservation of the existing Republic, which exists in consequence of the Declaration of Independence, no matter how much the Deputies who have foresworn it may choose to sneer at it, and any action that we have taken we have taken on that basis and that basis alone.[245]

In a similar fashion de Valera was impatient of opposition and the introduction of what he termed 'party politics' into the Dáil.[246] McCullagh notes that the way in which de Valera saw all opposition to him as 'the result of bad will, and the working of cabals'. This resulted in a situation where 'no compromise was possible ... the good fight had to be fought to the end'.[247] This was also Mary's position. On 25 January 1922 Gavan Duffy issued a memorandum to all Irish representatives abroad in his capacity as Minister for Publicity. The second point in the memorandum noted that 'national unity' had been broken by the 'emergence of two political parties in the Republican state'. Consequently members of the diplomatic service were 'under the obligation of reflecting faithfully the policy of the Government, whatever their personal opinion in party politics'. There was to be no propaganda 'either for or against the Treaty'.[248] Mary roundly denounced Gavan Duffy's introduction of the concept of party politics. The 'establishment and maintenance of the Republic' transcended party politics. She asked Gavan Duffy if he did 'not realise the fundamental difference between Party politics as practised in England, and Party politics when it means the subversion of the established Republic'. For Mary republicans could not be ordered 'to refrain from expressing their views and opinions on, what is to them a matter of life and death to the nationhood of their country'.[249] Mary repeatedly represented the Republic a type of spiritual ideal which stood above material obstacles and democratic politics. Notably, referring to the 'Treaty party', she stated that one of their strongest arguments was:

> that we were not able to defeat England militarily. Granted – but we beat her morally and we did that because of the reality of the Republic to our people, because of the magnificent stand made by the army and the splendid morale of the civilian population and because of the growing effectiveness of our propaganda abroad.[250]

Towards the end of April 1922 Mary wrote to the Terence MacSwiney Memorial Fund Committee in Cork on behalf of the family, asking them to take no further steps in the matter of a memorial to her brother pending the result of the upcoming election. Her brother had died for a republic and 'there will be no memorial to commemorate that sacrifice while Irishmen give fidelity to an English King and commit themselves British citizens'. The committee complied with the request.[251]

The 1922 election was effectively fought between the two wings of Sinn Féin. In May a committee of army officers representing both sides presented a proposal to the Dáil to contest an agreed election based on the present strength of pro and anti-Treaty Sinn Féin within the chamber. Mary was scathing of this development and laid the blame on McGarrity's attempt to bring the two sides together when he visited Ireland in April. She ended her letter to him, she wrote, 'without much hope' since Dan Breen had signed the proposal and had got others such as Seán Hegarty to do likewise.[252] The result was the establishment of a Dáil peace committee; no settlement resulted but a meeting between de Valera and Collins gave rise to the coalition pact.[253] There was much acrimonious debate on how proportions on the panel would be determined and the composition of the post-election coalition government.[254] As an attempt to circumvent civil war, the pact allowed for a Sinn Féin panel of candidates with each side nominating as many as they had TDs.[255] However, as McCullagh discusses there were 'very different ideas' on either side as to how a coalition government should be established after an agreed election.[256] Mary desired the Dáil committee to 'explore every avenue to a settlement' rather than just consider the situation in connection with the statement by the Army officers. She could not vote for a committee to investigate only the latter but 'if it is a committee set up to explore every possible avenue to a settlement with a view to averting civil war, it will have the approval of the whole House'.[257] When asked if she would submit to an election, she retorted that there could be 'no haggling for seats'.[258] She declared:

> the question of the Coalition was very important because if it could have been arranged – and it could have been arranged, with goodwill on the other side – it would have preserved the unity of Ireland and the independence of Ireland … the independence of Ireland would not be compromised by that Coalition unless the other side insisted, as they evidently mean to insist, on the acceptance of the Treaty.[259]

She called for unity, but on her terms:

> Defy Lloyd George. Call your army together on one united basis. Have a Coalition which will stabilise the country. While we are asked to accept the Treaty there will be no Coalition on that basis … Now why cannot you do that? Why cannot you form a Coalition and say we will leave the Treaty in abeyance?[260]

The Attorney General, Hugh Kennedy, privately clarified that every member of the provisional government had to accept the Treaty in writing. This resulted in protracted meetings of the Dáil committee tasked with arranging the election during which time the pro-Treaty side were, in the words of Kathleen Clarke, 'more concerned with committing us to an acceptance' of the agreement.[261] Evincing her opposition to the pact as formulated Mary continued:

> And if the question was allowed to be reduced to the point of the pro-Treaty side allocating – in their generosity we are told – a certain number of seats to the Republican side, then that would have been the virtual acceptance of the Treaty and, just as there was a virtual acceptance of the Treaty, for ever afterwards they would be able to say we went into it through a backdoor. We are not going to have that Treaty by a back door, by a front door, by a side door, or by any door.[262]

Despite the attempted intervention of Patrick McCartan, Mary contrived to turn the debate on the coalition pact into a statement of the grounds on which civil war would and would not be justified. The Treaty, she argued, was 'not worth' civil war while the Republic was 'a thousand times'. She denounced those who called themselves 'pro-Treaty Republicans':

> Are you going to begin by shooting down every man and woman who stands firm for the Republic now and who will not surrender? You have got to take your choice here and now. If you can only secure your Treaty by shooting those who stood as comrades in arms with you a short time ago is your Treaty worth it? If you believe the statements that are being made, that the Constitution which is being drawn up, is to be a Republican Constitution and that you are asked to fight England if England turns down that Constitution, do you want to kill Republicans first?[263]

She called for transparency on the issue of the constitution:

> Deputy McKeon said that when the members from this side of the Committee asked for the Constitution that it was drawing another red-herring across the tracks. It was not. It was another earnest and sincere desire to see if the people on the Pro-Treaty side really meant to work in the interests of the Republic, as they say they do. Now, this is the time to come out and declare your faith, if you really have it.[264]

The debate briefly turned to Document No. 2 and Mary declared her opposition to the many things 'humiliating to our national pride' contained within it. However, it 'preserves our national independence'. Document No. 2 was explicit in its statement that all power in Ireland derived 'solely from the people of Ireland'. This statement was 'a rejection of the Treaty's implicit acceptance that the British Crown was the source of authority'.[265] As McCullagh discusses, if this principle was enshrined in the constitution, Republicans could in conscience swear allegiance.[266] Mary stated that if asked at that moment to vote in favour of it she would consent:

> I would lay down my life now for the difference between Document No. 2 and the Treaty. It contains no oath and there is no Governor General and it does not pretend to draw up a Republican Constitution which in the far distant future you will fight England on.[267]

W. T. Cosgrave responded to Mary, declaring that it: 'is the first time I have heard any person in Ireland say that they were willing to die for a national humiliation'.[268] When he outlined to TDs the pact proposed by the army officers, Seán O'Hegarty's noted that the Dáil atmosphere was one of 'hostility' with 'personalities indulged in across the room'.[269] Mary exemplified this antagonism in a personalised retort to Cosgrave. With umbrage she declared:

> I would never die for money anyhow but I would die for the principle of national independence. I maintain that that is preserved in Document No. 2. I ask the Deputy, at least, to have the decency not to say that I was going to die for a national humiliation.[270]

Cosgrave stated that he believed his statement was correct but that he was not in a position to 'describe the exact words of the whole of the speech made by any Deputy much less a Deputy who takes such a long time as Deputy Miss McSwiney'.[271] Boland interjected calling on Cosgrave to 'have the decency to withdraw' his criticisms.[272]

The willingness by Mary to continue to distinguish the difference between the Treaty and Document No. 2 is noteworthy particularly when de Valera's statement that the latter 'would not satisfy those who wanted an isolated republic' is considered.[273] It would, he conceded be 'unacceptable to those whose political upbringing had been based on "separatism"'.[274] On 29 April 1922 she discussed the matter in a letter to McGarrity:

> De Valera would have recommended a limited Republic, he acknowledged that he was obliged to give up the idea of complete isolation which we would all have preferred, and he foreshadowed that last August in the formula which meant external association. The difference between those of us who really believe in absolute separation and those who stand for the treaty is roughly this: we might tolerate – reluctantly it is true – a temporary arrangement with England over the ports rather than risk a war of extermination if necessary and in order to save our people further suffering but we would risk any war and any suffering rather than give an oath of allegiance or fidelity to the King of England or have his Governor in our country after once establishing the Republic.

Browning's lines express very well the difference the Treaty and the now famous Document No 2. 'Oh! the little more and how much it is. And the little less and what worlds away'.[275] Mary discussed with McGarrity the rumours circulating about the constitution. She denounced Collins's approach: 'The main point is that Collins declares he is going to have a Republican Constitution and if L. George objects he will fight him on it. Now if he is sincere in that why is he risking Civil War on the acceptance of the Treaty.'[276]

In the four seater Cork City constituency, comprising an electorate of 44,400, Mary and O'Callaghan stood on the anti-Treaty platform with de Róiste and Walsh the panel candidates on the pro-Treaty side.[277] In keeping with the spirit of the pact a 'monster rally' was billed for 11 June at which all four candidates would speak as well as prominent individuals on both sides of the divide, notably de Valera, MacNeill, Stack and Mulcahy.[278] In public Mary supported the pact while simultaneously making clear her political position and her belief that the republic would be established. Speaking in Cork on the 11 June she was adamant that the people were not being asked to vote 'on the one great difficulty that had divided Dail Eireann for the past six months'. The electorate were merely being asked to return to the Third Dáil 'the members that they had sent to the Second Dail in order that the enemy – the common enemy – might see that he would not have the pleasure he desired of disuniting the people'.[279] One of the weakness of the pact agreement from the anti-Treaty perspective was that candidates from other parties were free to contest the election.[280] Duly Mary called on Labour to 'to have patience for a few months longer' noting that the working classes were represented in the Dáil as the majority of its members were 'earning their daily bread'.[281] However, in 'the first big sensation provided by the ballot boxes in an urban constituency', the Labour candidate, Robert Day, secretary of the Irish Transport and General Workers Union in the city, unseated O'Callaghan. Mary and the other panel candidates were elected.[282] Short of the quota, she was the last of the four to be elected.[283] With 4,016 votes she was significantly behind de Róiste who polled 5,657.[284] As the *Belfast Newsletter* gleefully reported, 'the notorious Mary MacSwiney just succeeded in securing election.[285] Her victory depended on O'Callaghan's transfers.[286] The election results indicated the strength of pro-Treaty feeling in Cork City despite her connection to the city's key republican martyr. Although as the *Cork Examiner* noted, 'her personal influence' was about sufficient 'to carry her through'.[287] Indeed, the Southern Unionist candidate, Alderman Beamish polled ahead of O'Callaghan.[288] It should, however, be noted, that only 18 anti-Treaty members of the Second Dáil were returned when seats were contested.[289] Of the six female members of the Second Dáil, all of whom were anti-Treaty, four lost their seat. Markievicz was returned unopposed with Mary, as noted, returned on the last count in a contested election.[290] Seán MacSwiney lost his seat.

Mary's speeches on the eve of the Anglo-Irish peace negotiations and during the Treaty debates solidified her growing reputation as an intransigent republican. On 17 October 1921 the *Belfast Newsletter* declared her speech of the previous night as 'violent'. She firmly asserted that it was only a 'minority of serfs' who would accept anything less than a Republic.[291] Her gender increasingly influenced the way she was represented in the press and within the Dáil. The *Belfast Newsletter* described her as making 'another vitriolic speech' on 9 January 1922.[292] While the *Irish Independent* was more tempered in its response to that speech, describing it as an 'emphatic protest', the byline referred to 'A Lady Deputy's Protest'.[293] Of course, the fact that all the six female deputies in the Second Dáil were anti-Treaty facilitated an anti-female tone. Batt O'Connor suggested that the people 'will not be in a hurry again to elect women' who he described as 'mudslinging and name calling and spitting and frothing to the mouth like angry cats'.[294]

McCullagh observes that there 'was bad temper and intolerance on both sides' during the debates on the Treaty. Fitzpatrick similarly makes reference to the increasingly venomous' nature of the proceedings.[295] However, in analysing the vitriol experienced by Mary, the issue of gender roles has to be taken into account. Certainly she was quick to speak during the debates, often interjecting in her unwillingness to brook any compromise. De Róiste's comments in February 1921 on the 'naïve simplicity' of Terence's view of independence and his 'unwillingness to engage in debate or brook opposition' could also be applied to Mary.[296] That notwithstanding, her position as a strong-willed and outspoken woman was an anathema for many men within the revolutionary generation. The *Freeman's Journal* reported her speech on 7 January as follows:

> In a violent speech Miss Mary MacSwiney, who appeared to be obsessed by a consuming rage, protested that the vote was worse than any act of Castlereagh. It was the grossest act of betrayal Ireland had ever endured. There could never, she uttered vehemently, be any union between representatives of the Irish Republic and the so-called Free State.
>
> Excitement was intensified following this declaration.[297]

Of course, Mary had voted to expel the representatives of the newspaper paper from the Dáil chamber following the editorial of 4 January indicting de Valera's autocratic propensities. The supposed nefarious influence of Childers as an Englishman over de Valera was also cited.[298] However, other Dáil deputies had voted, spoke, and would speak as Mary and were not subject to such invective. She did sound notes of fanaticism declaring that if England 'exterminates the men, the women will take their places, and, if she exterminates the women, the children are rising fast'. This was quite similar in timbre to the speech de Valera would give in Thurles on 17 March 1922:

> If the Volunteers of the future tried to complete the work the Volunteers of the last four years had been attempting, they would have to complete it, not over the bodies of foreign soldiers, but over the dead bodies of their own countrymen. They would have to wade through Irish blood, through the blood of the soldiers of the Irish Government, and through, perhaps, the blood of some of the members of the Government to get Irish freedom.[299]

As McCullagh states, those on the pro-Treaty side accused de Valera of 'inciting violence and raising the tension which led to civil war'.[300] Certainly, Mary was intransigent in her unwillingness to compromise but, again, so were others. Nic Dháibhéid noted that Brugha's personal dislike of Collins 'bled into his political opppisition'.[301] On 7 January 1922 Brugha asserted a return to arms rather than acceptance of the Treaty:

> Why, if instead of being so strong, our last cartridge had been fired, our last shilling had been spent, and our last man were lying on the ground and his enemies howling round him and their bayonets raised, ready to plunge them into his body, that man should say – true to the traditions handed down – if they said to him: 'Now, will you come into our Empire?' – he should say, and he would say: 'No! I will not.[302]

The trope of de Valera as politically in thrall to the more extreme Mary began to emerge in this period. Reflecting on the events of 9 January de Róiste noted that the latter 'seems to lead Dev':

> Dev took up my protest against 'fratricidal strife' and said there would be none. But immediately after, Miss MacS. and others made statements of most determined invective to fratricidal strife, to ill will, to bitterness, to hatred, to violence even.[303]

In the months after January 1922, Mary emerged as one of the most intractable opponents of the Treaty provoking reactions from those on the other side of the political divide.[304] On 11 March 1922 several speeches in support of the Treaty were made in Cork to mark the arrival in the city of Michael Collins. Addressing a gathering at the Berwick Fountain on the Grand Parade Commandant Seán Mac Eoin was reported in several papers as saying that he 'was not going to be dictated to by Miss MacSwiney'.[305] When he was brought to task for his utterance, he wrote to the *Freeman's Journal* stating that he 'made no reference to any person whatever'.[306] The *Skibbereen Eagle* attributed the statement to Fionán Lynch.[307] What this reporting demonstrates is that Mary was becoming a cipher for extreme republicanism. Her gender marked her out in this context. As noted, there were men as uncompromising as her in rejecting the treaty but as a woman she stood out and was labelled strident and obstructionist.

Animosity between Mary and Griffith continued throughout the early months of 1922. On 2 March he asked her not to interrupt. When she retorted that she did not speak to him, he parried with 'Then please don't'.[308] She was aware of how she was increasingly viewed. There were also those on the anti-Treaty side, particularly amongst the military, who believed that she was too outspoken and apt to meddle:

> I am not an admirer of red tape, and I am given to saying rather plainly what I think when it seems necessary. That is probably why I am hated not only by the enemy but more or less – generally more unpopular with your own people in high quarters.[309]

On 2 March discussion in the chamber centred around Griffith's decision not to enfranchise women over the age of 21 until the crucial vote on the Treaty was taken. Mary cried shame, to which Griffith snapped: 'Keep your shame to yourself, Miss MacSwiney'. In response she stated that she was speaking not to him but to the Chair. Irritated, Griffith used her interjection to launch an attack on the way the minority were not willing to adhere to democratic norms: 'These people talk about the will of the Irish people. What are they doing at the present time? By every means of obstruction in their power, they are trying to prevent that will being ascertained'.[310]

Griffith was not the only TD to draw attention to the length of Mary's speeches and comments on the matter continued after the debate on the Treaty concluded. During Dáil question time on 1 March Gavan Duffy responded to her beginning 'In reply to that somewhat long question'.[311] Indeed, reporting on Domhnall Ua Buchalla's speech on the Treaty on 4 January 1922 the *Irish Independent* reporter glibly wrote: 'There was this much to be said for his speech – it was brief'.[312] While not directly a comment on Mary, it is likely her speech on 21 December was in his mind.

That Mary was well able to parry within the Dáil was a continued source of annoyance to male deputies, particularly those on the pro-Treaty side. On 1 March discussion ranged on the appointment of Mr McCarron in the Department of Local Government. Anti-Treaty members claimed that he was responsible for the seizure of property of member of the Balrothery Board of Guardians during the War of Independence, including that of Molly Adrien, a member of Fingal Cumann na mBan. When Cosgrave was asked if he had spoken to the latter, he replied with a rare flash of levity that as he was ill during consultations with Richard Hayes about the appointment he did not think it 'would be quite proper to ask Miss Adrien to come into my bedroom'.[313] Mary sharply retorted: 'Would it not be more worthy of Ministers to answer questions and not to play the buffoon? And to remember what is at stake?'[314] Cosgrave, equally sharply, retorted: '[t]he majority of this House is in a position to express its opinions, and if you are dissatisfied with it, it is your business'.[315]

The escalation of violence and the heated Dáil sessions as Ireland moved apparently inexorably towards Civil War had ramifications for Mary's personal life and her principalship of St Ita's. When it was proposed on 11 May 1922 to adjourn the Dáil until the following Wednesday, she interjected:

> Might I not ask if it would not be possible to meet on Saturday, or at the very latest on Monday, instead of adjourning until Wednesday. If the Joint Committee is to meet again to-morrow they can make up their minds between this and to-morrow whether they can or cannot agree. We can meet on Saturday for the necessary business, and that would leave us until next Wednesday to attend to our much neglected private business. I am sure I am only one of many who have to neglect our private concerns. It seems unnecessary to take us away in the middle of every week. Later, say in the week-end, it would not matter so much. Any teacher would know what it would mean to a class to have one teacher on one day and another teacher on another day. In order that that should not happen I have had to get somebody in my place for the last two weeks.[316]

Six months later, in November 1922, Mary was absent from St Ita's for nearly a month as she began her first civil war imprisonment and hunger strike.

Chapter Seven

The Civil War

> Guy Beiner argues that republican memory is linear as well as cyclical: 'the events are sequenced on an eschatological-millenarian timeline that leads towards future triumph and salvation. Its impetus is a memory of trauma awaiting resolution.'[1]

Up until the Treaty split Mary MacSwiney was working towards the future 'triumph' that would render her brother Terence's death meaningful; the denial of this narrative trajectory in 1922 arguably reinforced the trauma she experienced in 1920. In December 1921 Mary was denied the redemptive conclusion she expected. She was, she wrote, 'heartbroken'.[2] Síobhra Aiken notes that in his preface to Dan Breen's *My Fight for Irish Freedom* (1924), Joseph McGarrity contrasted the 'physical suffering' of Breen during the War of Independence with the 'mental torture' he 'must have endured' as former comrades turned on each other during the civil war.[3] Mary had already experienced mental agony during the War of Independence. This was now compounded as those who had lauded Terence's sacrifice rendered it – as she saw it – futile. The meaning behind his death imploded; was truncated. Mary consequently could not transcend her past sufferings. She was forced to continue what La Capra describes as a 'fidelity to trauma, a feeling that one must somehow keep faith with it'.[4] In discussing the 'bond with the republican dead' in Peadar O'Donnell's memoir *The Gates Flew Open* Aiken writes: 'La Capra further suggests that this 'fidelity' to a traumatic past is often associated with one's 'bond with the dead, especially with dead intimates', as reliving such trauma is seen as 'a painful but necessary commemoration or memorial'.[5] Mary's civil war was one fought to reclaim the worth and meaning of her brother's sacrifice. In the immediate months of the conflict, she travelled across Ireland encouraging republicans to stay firm. She was arrested on four occasions and endured two gruelling and high-profile hunger strikes.

During the civil war Mary was increasingly linked in the press to de Valera. She was perceived as someone whose voice had weight on the republican side. De Valera himself viewed her as someone who had status within the anti-Treaty side; if he did not always agree with her, he respected her politically and the two engaged in detailed correspondence. In private she was willing to discuss and hear de Valera's views while fearful that he would arrange terms that she could not accept and split the anti-Treaty side. In public her speeches were at the extreme end of the republican spectrum. As peace proposals were put forward increasingly from early 1923, her stance appeared to be founded on blind faith rather than any realistic assessment of the military situation.

On the 14 April 1922 Rory O'Connor, the 'most high-profile spokesman' within the anti-Treaty IRA seized the Four Courts. At a press conference on 22 March, he stated that the IRA had the power to prevent the upcoming elections.[6] The official statement by the Director of Publicity, IRA Executive, Four Courts included the following:

> Are the sacrifices of 1916 to be forgotten? Are the soul-rending sufferings of Terry MacSwiney, Kevin Barry, and countless other heroes, only memories of the past, or are they a beacon of lights to guide us on the way they have gone? Rather than compromise their personal honour, their pledged word, the traditions of their comrades, or the cause of the Irish Republic, they stood unflinchingly against all the might of oppression, and why should the Army give way dishonourably on the same issue today?[7]

These words reflected Mary's position on the Treaty and her determination to reject it. Her brother's sacrifice would not be relegated to the past. On the day the Provisional Government moved against the men in the Four Courts, O'Connor referred in his statement to the fact that Fr Dominic, Terence MacSwiney's chaplain in Brixton, was 'with us here'.[8]

The election on 16 June 1922 confirmed the earlier ratification of the Treaty by the Dáil. On the morning of the election the constitution was published. Any 'Republican tone' the document had when it was first presented to the British had been eliminated. In *The Separatist*, a paper established in 1922 to heal the Treaty divisions, P. S. O'Hegarty accused Mary of drawing 'unwarranted interference' by the British:

> Miss MacSwiney insisted in An Dail in discussing the Constitution which was not before the House. She boasted that 'she was letting the cat out of the bag.' Whether she did or not it seems obvious that Messrs Griffith and Collins have submitted the Constitution [to the British], and as a result Mr. Churchill and the British press are belling the cat let loose by Miss MacSwiney.[9]

As McCullagh discusses, although Article 2 stated that all powers of government derived from the people, Article 51 made clear that the executive authority was 'vested' in the King and 'exercised' through the person of the Governor General.[10] Clearly, no one on the anti-Treaty side could consider a post-election coalition even if the very possibility had not been subverted by Michael Collins' speech two days earlier in Cork. Collins stated that he was not 'hampered' by the coalition platform and he called on the Cork electorate to 'vote for the candidates you think the best of'.[11] This statement, so close to the election, meant that there was nothing that the anti-Treaty side could do to mitigate Collins' renunciation of a pact that had allowed the election to take place. Similarly, Collins outmanoeuvred the anti-Treaty side by waiting until the morning of the election to publish the constitution. In that way he minimised 'any negative effects for the pro-Treaty position'.[12] The occupation of the Four Courts together with the assassination four days after the election of Sir Henry Wilson, military advisor to the Northern Irish government, gave the British the opportunity to pressure the provisional government to respond to 'republican fundamentalists'.[13] Moreover, on 26 June, the Deputy Chief-of-Staff of the pro-Treaty IRA, J. J. O'Connell, was kidnapped by those occupying the Four Courts. Duly, the provisional government adhered to Lloyd George's 'demand that the sham government in the Four Courts no longer be tolerated'.[14] The civil war commenced on 28 June; two days later the Four

Courts was taken by the pro-Treaty forces. The most prominent casualty of the opening period of the war was Cathal Brugha who was shot by Free State soldiers on 5 July and died two days later. A note found in his pocket made clear that under no circumstances would he 'come into ... [the] Empire'.[15] Collins on hearing of his death wrote:

> At worst he was a fanatic – though in what has been a noble cause. At best I number him among the very few who have given their all that this country – now torn by civil war – should have its freedom.[16]

Collins's words could equally describe Mary's stance on the Treaty. During the civil war she demonstrated through hunger strike that, like Brugha, she was willing to die, if necessary, rather than compromise on the republic. She believed that the war was necessary if future generations were to be fully liberated. She saw those on the pro-Treaty side as having been co-opted by Britain to continue their imperial war. This was a common trope on the republican side in the period. In *Tragedies of Kerry* (1924), Dorothy Macardle stated that the departing British troops in 1922: 'left in their place an army of Irishmen pledged to the same King ... June came and that army was commanded to complete the Empire's unfinished work.'[17] Like Brugha, Mary became 'a totem for violent republicanism', a reflection of what Ferriter describes as the 'civil war legacy of lost nuance and contortion'.[18]

On 10 July Mary stood at the grave side as Brugha was buried in Glasnevin cemetery.[19] In the months that followed that funeral, further deaths on both sides of the political divide underscored the brutality and toll of the conflict. On 31 July 1922 Boland was shot in Skerries, County Dublin. He died the following day. For Mary this death represented more than the loss of a political colleague as her message of condolence to his mother made clear: 'I counted Harry as a dear friend'.[20] Writing to him in February 1921 the genuine feelings of friendship and affection she had for him shone through: 'I am not writing you now because I love you but because I want work done'.[21] David Fitzpatrick notes how Boland 'used his cachet as a freedom fighter to infatuate a procession of women'.[22] However, Mary, as an older woman, had a much deeper relationship with him on a political level. She had worked closely with him in the United States and the correspondence between them showed a real personal friendship. It was not just male republicans who were – as Kathleen O'Connell described de Valera – 'broken hearted and sad' at Boland's loss.[23] Boland was Mary's colleague and friend as much as he was de Valera's.

On 22 July Mary spoke at a conference in Cork held under the auspices of the People's Rights Association. The event was called to work towards an armistice and to discuss the assembling of the new Dáil. The report on her speech underlined the refusal of republicans to accept the legitimacy of the institutions in the process of creation by those who accepted the Treaty and formed the provisional government:

> She thought it just as well to grasp the nettle honestly and ask what was meant by the Third Dail. The Third Dail to which they were elected was the Third Dail as understood by the pact made on May 25th and broken. That Third Dail was not to be a partition Parliament and no Republican would go to a partition Parliament ... constituencies where elections had not been held will be represented by the present members – that is to safeguard the unity of Ireland.[24]

She was asked if the 'voice of the people' did 'not count in the country' and retorted that she did not understand how that could be drawn from her statement.[25] A further meeting was held on 5 August after which Mary wrote to the *Cork Examiner* to clarify that she had not made a party speech in advocacy of Document No. 2. She continued: 'I am anxious to work for peace if peace can be obtained with honour … United action against the common enemy is the only thing that can save us.[26]

Mary brooked no concept of republican defeat in the civil war to the point of ignoring military realities. In *Allegiance* Robert Brennan recalled that when he went to Cork to 'edit' the *Cork Examiner* and to prepare daily propaganda despatches for Childers he stayed with Mary. She was, he wrote:

> as full of fight as ever. She roundly denounced me for suggesting that the Free State could capture Cork. There was no use in pointing out to her that Waterford had already fallen and our right wing thereby turned, that we had been unable to take the offensive anywhere and that the idea of holding the line with our present forces was hopeless.[27]

After the Battle of Dublin concluded on 5 July, attention turned to the so-called Munster Republic where the anti-Treaty IRA held Limerick, Waterford and Cork. After nine days of fighting, the National Army drove the IRA out of Limerick while in Waterford the latter only held the jail by 21 July.[28] On 8 August seaborne troops were landed in Passage West outside Cork from the *Arvonia* under the command of Emmett Dalton. Free State troops 'evacuated' the city two days later, 'burning barracks as they went'.[29] Pro-Treaty women went to the Imperial Hotel to extend a 'hearty welcome; to the commanding officer while members of Cumann na Saoirse handed out cigarettes and other comforts to the National Army troops billeted at the Cornmarket. Extra attention was meted out to wounded soldiers who were patients in the South Infirmary, pro-Treaty women helping them to write letters home.[30] The MacSwiney home was subjected to raids in this period, four in total according to *Poblacht na hÉireann*. According to the paper, the raiding troops were drunk and threatened violence. They were searching for arms and wanted men. The paper noted Mary's declaration that the raids 'left a heart-ache that preceding raids never left … Their predecessors, the foreign enemy, could make us suffer, but could never make us unhappy'.[31] On 24 January 1923 Constance Murphy was arrested at the MacSwiney home, having been 'dragged from her bed by force'. She had travelled from Dublin to organise Sinn Féin clubs in the city.[32] Mary's home continued to be a target for the National Army throughout the civil war. In mid-February a stencil machine, used to print irregular leaflets and propaganda was captured on the premises.[33] It must be remembered that Belgrave Place was not just the private residence of Mary and Annie; it was also where they ran St Ita's. The stress endured by the sisters must have been immense. In a later period, Annie wrote to Louise Gavan Duffy of the effect of the civil war on the school:

> In September 1921, Scoil Ite was flourishing. We had as many children as the school could accommodate – well over a hundred.
>
> We opened School that autumn [1922] on 12th September, and at a quarter before 10 a. m. there were FIVE pupils in the school, and the five ranged from the age of four to the age of eighteen. The worst enemies of the Republic must have been satisfied. At a quarter after 10, fifteen more had arrived …[34]

During the civil war Mary did not confine her activism to speech making and propaganda.

She was present at the republican outpost in Waterfall, Co. Cork, in mid-August when Liam Lynch took a stand on a 20-mile front from Millstreet to Mallow near the River Blackwater.[35] On 8 September 1922 she travelled to Dublin on board the Lady Kerry. After docking at North Wall, she went to the anti-Treaty headquarters of Sinn Féin in Suffolk Street. The *Irish Independent* reported that she carried a message to de Valera and Stack conveying the attitude of the Anti-Treaty members in the south as to attendance or otherwise at the first meeting of the Provisional Government the following morning.[36] In the event the only anti-Treaty member present was Ginnell who, the *Connaught Tribune* declared, 'must have felt lonely'. The paper noted that 'MacSwiney and the rest, who were known to be in Dublin, have presumably decided to observe a policy of abstention'.[37] This was the parliamentary policy Mary would maintain for the remainder of her political life. She was, however, present six days later when the remains of Thomas Addis Emmet, the grandson of Robert Emmet, were interred in Glasnevin cemetery; at the ceremony both pro- and anti-Treaty politicians gathered.[38]

While in the capital Mary attended a meeting of anti-Treaty Sinn Féin on 14 September.[39] This meeting was referred to within the Dáil by the Minister for Defence, Richard Mulcahy, who used it to argue for the establishment of military courts with the power of punishment by death:

> ... on the 14th September a meeting was held at which were present Count Plunkett, Miss McSwiney, Tomas O'Donoghue, Cathal O Murchadha, Mrs. Clarke, Derrig, Countess Markievicz, J. O'Mahony, Frank Fahy, Dr. Jim Ryan, Brian O'Higgins, and they agreed that the military would take over control and that they as a party – that is, a political party – would co-operate.[40]

In this period hostility to Mary's political stance began to appear in the form of letters to the editors of various newspapers. On 24 September a prisoner in Cork Gaol was shot through the windpipe. Patrick Mangan Jr was one of around 435 anti-Treaty prisoners on hunger strike in the prison. He was shot as sentries attempted to quell a riot. Mangan died the next day in the Mercy hospital.[41] The prisoners in Cork jail were, Mary declared, on hunger strike against ill-treatment. Such strikes, frequent over the previous six years, 'rarely had such justification as under the newest regime'. It was 'murder, pure and simple, to shoot an unarmed prisoner'. She continued, again with a focus on the meaning and intention of the Third Dáil:

> The people of Ireland voted by 94 to 34 for the Third Dail ... The Third Dail was not summoned. Instead war on the soldiers of the Republic was declared by England's direct command, not by the will of the Irish people. The present assembly is *an illegal one – a provisional* partition Parliament called under a British act.[42]

Her letter drew a round of invective. The next day the *Evening Echo* published a letter from 'Clodhopper' who, representing himself as 'an ordinary work-a-day person', feigned ignorance at the what he viewed as the pedantic nature of Mary's arguments. He could not:

> reach the same height of ideality [sic] as those who draw a distinction between the Dail now in session and the Third Dail. If I remember rightly it was not the Third Dail that Miss

> MacSwiney's friends wanted a couple of months ago ... but the Second Dail which they maintained never dissolved itself, and inferentially, could not be dissolved even by the decisive vote of the Irish people.
>
> Perhaps it is a concession that she asks that the Third Dail be summoned. Most of us thought that it met in Dublin weeks ago and is now in session ... It is a point to the good that Miss MacSwiney should have even vaguely indicated the way to 'peace and forgiveness'.[43]

Laffan notes that the disruption of the civil war meant that the summoning of the Third Dáil was postponed on a number of occasions while the Second Dáil never again met in full session, the latter facilitating 'republican fundamentalists' to argue that the legislature chosen in May 1921 'remained the only legitimate Irish parliament'.[44] De Róiste referred to the 'haphazard, unmethodical, illlogical' constitutional anomaly because 'there was no dissolution'.[45]

A letter to the editor of the *Cork Examiner* from *Free State* stated that, 'Miss MacSwiney ... claims to represent Cork City, but ... as everyone knows, misrepresents it'. The writer indicted her for condemning the killing of Mangan while failing to denounce as murder the shooting of an unarmed soldier of the National Army. On the basis of the focus on the effects of republican violence on women and children in the letter it is conceivable that the person who penned it was a woman. Indeed the writer inferred that Mary, unmarried and childless, was an aberrant woman; her normal female nature frustrated, she had engaged in sublimation and turned to violence:

> I have not seen or heard any protest from her against the shooting, by members of her party of innocent non-combatants – women and children – in the streets and houses of Cork. And yet she claims to represent these people too ... She has no sympathy with the distracted mothers, who have to tear their children out of bed in the middle of the night and lie with them on the cold floors to escape the bullets that penetrate the doors and windows. She has no sympathy with the invalids and expectant mothers, who night after night, become hysterical from the nerve-wracking fusillade of Republican gun fire. She utters no protest against the senseless and wanton destruction of property which is throwing thousands of workers out of employment and starving innocent children. She has no children to nurse at night, or support; her contribution to the Irish nation is nothing but bellicose speeches of several hours' duration and incitement to destruction.[46]

De Róiste wrote how the irregular soldiers, who he alleged fled from Cork during the capture of the city by the pro-Treaty forces, had returned by the end of August and were engaged in: 'the meanest form of "warfare" – the throwing of bombs from the cover of crowds, women and children being injured in one instance; the murder of individuals; the terrorising of the people generally.'[47] On 2 September, the irregulars, using 'crude' bullets which resulted in 'horrible wounds' fired on the National troops on the South Mall. As the ambulance was taking the wounded to the Mercy hospital, a bomb was thrown injuring a woman. Another woman was wounded on 5 September, shot through her bedroom window in a gunfight initiated by the republican forces.[48] As the letter to the *Cork Examiner* denouncing Mary's callousness in refusing to consider the economic impact of the conflict, de Róiste referred to the 'state of Cork':

> ... the smashing of communications; resulting in dislocation and disorganisation of business,

> restriction of trade – consequence – less and less employment and less and less hope of employment. The want of means of living touches many homes and many people.[49]

Letters supporting Mary against her critics were also in evidence in the press. *Justice* stated that her 'sin' was 'consistency'. She had made known her position on the Republic 'years ago' and 'because she refuses to be drawn or driven from her position, she is now the object of raillery'.[50] In response *A Poor Woman* suggested that *Justice*, instead of 'taking up the cudgels for Miss MacSwiney (which she is well able to do for herself)', work to stop the destruction in Cork city and focus on 'the starving families'. 'A Poor Woman' stated that MacSwiney did not represent the people of Cork and reminded her of her poor showing in the June election.[51]

On 7 September, at a special meeting of pro-Treaty TDs a new 'National Party' was proposed Ernest Blythe. On 7 December the party was named Cumann na nGaedheal.[52] Macardle wrote that the opening of the Third Dáil on 9 September 1922 showed the assembly to be the 'Provisional Parliament decreed by the British Act'.[53] Anti-Treaty TDs were told by de Valera not to attend.[54] The anti-Treaty side needed, Macardle wrote, 'to find some means to keep the *de jure* Government, Dáil Éireann, in being, even though it might be prevented from functioning.'[55] Laffan discusses de Valera's concern to 're-establish a political base of some sort; without one he was in a weak position *vis-à-vis* the army leaders'.[56] On 17 October the army executive called on him to form a government. Nine days later a statement was issued from Suffolk Street after the meeting of republican TDs called 'to maintain the Republic and to secure the continuity of independent Government for the whole of Ireland'.[57] De Valera was called on to 'resume the Presidency'. A Council of State was elected with Mary as a member.[58] This Council was created to assist de Valera 'in carrying on the government until such time as the Parliament of the Republic is allowed freely to assemble or the people are allowed by free election to decide how they shall be government'.[59] Kathleen O'Callaghan was the other female member on this council of 12. In September 1922 Mary was concerned that compromise might be in the offing and wrote to de Valera:

> One of my reasons for wishing to see you was that the air is thick again with rumours of compromise and secret interviews just as it was 12 months ago and I wanted to know where we stand. There seems no coordination between the military and civil sides of the Republican movement; nor any very clear ideas among some of the Republicans themselves. A peace move is certain to be to be made, and I think that the probability of a split ... should be guarded against.[60]

What Mary referred to here may have been de Valera's meeting in early September with Richard Mulcahy, the Minister for Defence in the Provisional Government. De Valera desired to find a way out of the impasse of the civil war, his solution being a revision of the Treaty. He wanted to make peace on the basis of Document No. 2. While the meeting came to nothing it increased distrust of Mulcahy on part of ministers in the government and indicated to die-hard republicans that de Valera's position was more moderate than they desired.[61]

De Valera, who had been in the ascendant since 1917, failed to get a majority in either the cabinet or in the Dáil for his position on the Treaty. This sudden puncturing of his leadership and influence can only have been politically distressing for him. As Laffan discusses de Valera's 'intransigence was for public consumption, while his moderation and his efforts to avoid civil war were concealed from view'.[62] Mary was accorded insight into his private political thoughts in this period while she voiced her fears of compromise to him as she exhorted him to remain firm. His letters to her during in this period saw him voice his disquiet and unease at the course of events; he made it very clear that he did not hold her doctrinaire position on the inviolate nature of the republic or the means to achieve it. On 11 September 1922 he wrote her 'a letter such as I have never before written to anybody'. Despite the differences in their political positions he used her as a political confidant. The correspondence also makes clear that she was someone whose views had weight within republicanism. He noted that she kept on the plane of 'Faith and Unreason' and that made her 'inaccessible'. In this, she was like Mellows and Plunkett and her stance drove 'all who would reason with you to despair'.[63] De Valera similarly described Rory O'Connor as a man led by 'faith' rather than 'reason'.[64] Unfortunately for me', he wrote, 'Reason rather than Faith has been my master ... I have felt for sometime that this doctrine of mine unfitted me to be leader of the Republican party'. He was not by nature, he stated to Mary, meant to be 'a partisan leader'.[65] In a rather self-pitying tone he lamented that he was sorry that he did not 'insist' that Brugha take over leadership 'when the party was being formed'. He continued:

> For the sake of the cause I allowed myself to be put in a position which it is impossible for one of my outlook and personal bias to fill with effect for the party. I must be the heir to generations of conservatism. Every instinct of mine would indicate that I was meant to be a dyed-in-the-wool Tory or even a Bishop, rather than the leader of a Revolution.[66]

He confessed to 'a civil war going on' in his mind as well as in the country:

> ... the fundamental question is 'the Treaty or not the Treaty' – and we are in a minority on that .... For Republicans the choice is, therefore, between a heart-breaking surrender of what they have repeatedly proofed was dearer to them than life and the repudiation of what they recognise to be the basis of all order in government and the keystone of democracy – majority rule.[67]

In his correspondence with Mary, de Valera gave signals that he was not comfortable with his abstentionist political position; his move out of Sinn Féin to form Fianna Fáil in 1926 was in gestation before he made overt statements at the Ard Fheis in 1925. She was more intimately bound to the concept that the republic was 'dearer ... than life' than he was.[68] While he had witnessed comrades die in pursuit of the republic he had suffered the loss of no close family member; he had not witnessed republican death as had Mary.

While de Valera wrote to MacSwiney that he endeavoured faithfully to discharge the duties of every position and 'to realise the ideals of those who elected him' he had made himself 'a slave at times in order to do so.' He stated that as 'soon as I can do it without injuring the cause, I intend to claim my personal freedom again'. What he meant was his personal political freedom. However, he was not, as she might assume, he wrote, 'in the depths of despair ... to see things as they are is not to despair. There are difficulties for both sides in the struggle, and if I see our own, I see also those of our opponents.'[69] Mary retorted that 'Faith and Unreason are not synonymous terms. I plead guilty to the former. I resent the latter':

> Your misunderstanding of my letters makes my regret at not being able to see you all the keener. My faith is simply that in spite of our temporary setback we are not meant to fail and to accept the Treaty even under duress and protest ... would be failure to all that is best and highest.[70]

Brugha was correct, she argued, in his prediction that an oath of allegiance to the British monarch would divide Ireland:

> For Cathal understood, what others evidently did not, the Spiritual and psychological aspects of the struggle, that men who BELIEVED in the Republic, which they had established, and which they swore to defend against all enemies, foreign and domestic, meant what they said. Theirs was the Faith that moves mountains.[71]

Mary's firm belief that victory could be achieved was not that of all on the anti-Treaty side. Máire Comerford recalled the period after the Battle of the Four Courts stating that the 'temptation to cease operations, to give up, and go home was obvious'. An IRA column was, she wrote, 'now four men, short of ammunition, usually hiding in a dripping dugout'. The anti-Treaty army was 'disintegrating like snow on a sunny day'.[72] As McCullagh states, de Valera's 'default position' on the question of success was 'scepticism'.[73] However, Mary's unflinching political faith should not be dismissed as wholly naïve but should be put, as Ferriter discusses, in the broader European context of the period:

> Politics or ideology as faith in 1922, it seems, came to be something to be despised and even mocked, but that was a poor reading of the mindset of the zealousness of that generation and their declarations, vulnerabilities, pieties, arrogance and aspirations that need to be seen in a broader European context: a product of that 'generation of 1914' who could be almost messianic in their rejection of the established order and very moved by images of martyrdom.[74]

McCullagh states that during the later months of 1922 de Valera's 'repeated references to Document No. 2 .... went down like a lead balloon with those on his own side'.[75] In her discussions with de Valera Mary was willing to find a way towards peace. Although she declared Document No. 2 dead as a solution in public during the Cumann na mBan split in February, she was more nuanced in her private correspondence with de Valera as late as September 1922:

> If a peace could be accepted even now on the same basis I for one would consent provided that (a) the Constitution drawn up should ignore England's existence (b) that England should be obliged to withdraw her forces from Ulster & (c) that the temporary accommodation regarding ports should give her the use not the control of them.
>
> I know that in your document no mention is made of a contribution to the Civil List though it was discussed in the Cabinet. I would consider that as objectionable as the Oath itself. I mention it now because in the event of the question being opened up, it may be alluded to.[76]

McCullagh notes that de Valera was aware that while the more intransigent on the anti-Treaty side disliked Document No. 2, 'the point was that they wouldn't go to war against it'.[77]

On 4 November Mary was arrested in Dublin. A raid on Mrs Humphreys house at 36 Ailesbury Road led to the arrest of Ernie O'Malley. Áine O'Rahilly and a maid in the house were wounded, as were O'Malley and Peter McCarthy, a private in the National Army. Madame O'Rahilly, Miss O'Rahilly, Sighle Humphreys and her mother, Nell, were lodged in Wellington Barracks.[78] A second raid was then conducted on the house of Madame O'Rahilly at 40 Herbert Park; the only occupant was Mary who was taken to Mountjoy prison, accused of delivering seditious speeches.[79] De Róiste concluded that these raids and arrests were in response to the failed raid on the home of Richard Mulcahy on the previous Thursday night.[80] Mary's decision to go on immediate hunger strike was the logical conclusion of her politics since Brixton 1920:

> I have begun a hunger strike and with God's help will carry it through as bravely as my sainted brother did, and for exactly the same cause and with equal justification ... I am offering it all and will offer my death if it comes for the immediate triumph of the Republic ...[81]

Mary, as McConville discusses, already had 'a fearsome reputation as a termagant' consequent on her confrontations with British officialdom during her brother's 1916 internment and his hunger strike in 1920. Accordingly, she held a 'particularly eminent place' within the republican leadership and her refusal of food 'unleashed a great storm'.[82] On 6 November she was joined on the strike by Áine O'Rahilly, Nell and Sighle Humphreys and Honor Murphy.[83] However, these women were quickly 'absolved' from their self-imposed fast' by Mary.[84] She wrote to de Valera that she begged them to 'desist', noting that her case was 'exceptional'. She did not, she stated, 'advocate hunger striking for many people'.[85] Mary was interned without trial and her hunger strike was, according to the *Freeman's Journal*, in protest at her 'illegal detention just as her illustrious brother died in protest against his detention because he represented the civic authorities of his native city'.[86] According to the *Belfast Newsletter*, a letter was found after her arrest in which she stated: 'If I am imprisoned I will go on hunger strike. I do not know whether they will make up their mind to let me die, but if they do you will all pray for me that I may be as brave as those who have gone before me.'[87]

Over 600 women were incarcerated during the Civil War. Members of the new government had fought with the full support of female activists during the War of Independence. They were therefore fully aware of the potential of the women on the anti-Treaty side to subvert and destablise the state in the process of formation. Imprisonment was a conscious attempt to remove the threat posed by so-called deviant women. Mary's civil war arrests and hunger strikes had, however, the highest profile within that female cohort.[88] Daniel Corkery, according to the *Freeman's Journal*, argued that if she did not 'hunger-strike she would have gone back on her brother; her calm toleration of ordinary imprisonment would have made a mock of his passion and death'.[89] However, the press attention was also due to her status as an outspoken anti-Treaty TD. Mary was no Mrs Pearse; she was not merely a mouthpiece for her dead brother. She had, as Ferriter discusses, 'considerable influence'.[90] She conducted her hunger strike in November 1922 with a full understanding of its potential as a propagandist weapon. As Brighid O'Mullane wrote to the *Irish Independent* Mary and the women on sympathetic hunger strike are 'giving us an example of how the fight may be maintained even within prison walls'.[91]

A protest meeting against Mary's arrest was held on 7 November under the auspices of the Women Prisoners' Defence League during which Charlotte Despard suggested that female volunteers picket the homes of those responsible for her incarceration.[92] Rallies organised by the League were heavily policed by pro-Treaty troops, often resulting in violence.[93] In many respects this violence served the anti-Treaty narrative that the Provisional Government was acting in a brutal fashion towards republican women inside and outside their jails. From within the prison Mary wrote letters to the newspapers denouncing her treatment at the hands of the Provisional Government. Others on the anti-Treaty side did likewise while telegrams poured in from America holding Cosgrave 'personally responsible for the murder of Mary MacSwiney if she dies'.[94] The AARIR cabled protesting against her detention.[95] On 11 November, 20 women from the organisation picketed the British Consulate in New York, carrying banners, threatening to continue the picket until her release.[96] Ferriter discusses concerns within the Provisional Government that her hunger strike had revived the AARIR which had become almost moribund.[97] Support for her release was strong in places like Cork where over 1,000 signatures were gathered. The petition forwarded to Cosgrave urged her release on the basis that she was the sister of Terence MacSwiney and 'as an act of mercy'.[98] Republicans in Cork stated that no dances would be permitted while she was still in prison and an attack was made on the Catholic parochial hall in Blackrock on 26 November when the order was defied.[99] Susan Mitchell, who worked with George William Russell in the offices of the *Irish Homestead* noted that she had never written to a head of state before. She asked for Mary's release on the following grounds: 'I can think of no plea that I can justly commend to you except that she is Terence MacSwiney's sister & that the Irish State cannot see her kill herself, thus making two tragedies in that family.'[100] Cumann na mBan sent telegrams to the Cardinal Secretary of State in Rome, to Cardinal Logue and to Archbishop Byrne.[101] A Father O'Gorman, on the opposing side wanted Cosgrave to know that 'Cumann na mBan represents nobody'.[102]

On the same day as the Cumann na mBan telegrams were sent, two young women, Ellen and Elizabeth Merrigan, were before the Police Court charged with writing on the Liffey Wall, Ellis's Quay, the words 'Will Ireland let Mary McSwiney [sic] join Terence McSwiney and Thomas Ashe? 12th day of hunger strike'. The two Merrigan sisters were part of a group of 12 females who were sighted by a Dublin Metropolitan Police Constable; ten of the girls 'ran away'. When asked by the Magistrate if they had anything to say the two women stated that they were 'members of the Irish Republic' and did not recognise the Court.[103] Also on the 15 November, Cork Harbour Commissioners unanimously approved an application from female members of MacSwiney's Dáil constituency that that the Provisional Government release her as a gesture to 'help towards the cessation of fratricidal strife which is slowly destroying the country'. Her release would be an 'act of chivalry'.[104]

What is striking is the manner in which members of the Provisional Government felt the need to respond on a personal level. Many of the members of the newly-formed government lacked political leadership skills; their responses were visceral and raw on many occasions. De Róiste described her as having a sub-normal 'mentality'. He indicted Mary as being – outside of Childers – 'the most hated of that party' which was 'a moral sore on the soul of Ireland'.[105] Cosgrave issued a statement in response to the cablegrams received from members of the AARIR:

> Mr. De Valera, Miss MacSwiney and their associates ... are responsible for the shedding of blood in Ireland ...
>
> We on whom the Irish people have placed the responsibility of asserting their authority will not allow the discharge of that duty to the Nation to be hampered by consideration of any individuals be they who they may.[106]

However, there were those in official positions who supported her or, maybe more accurately, who were opposed to the idea that the Provisional Government might allow her to die. Joseph Connolly resigned his position as Consul-General in the US, writing later to de Valera:

> As you are perhaps aware I resigned my position as Consul-General in the U.S.A. immediately after Miss Mary MacSwiney had gone on Hunger Strike and when it seemed as though her strike would be allowed to continue until the end. My action of course put me out of course with the present Government ...[107]

During her imprisonment Mary was willing to expose what she saw as the hypocrisy of the Catholic hierarchy, in particular, the Archbishop of Dublin, Dr Edward Byrne. She was, as she signed off to Byrne, a 'devoted child of the Holy Church'.[108] However, she made clear that she did not defer to him politically. Cosgrave, in refusing to yield to Cardinal Logue's desire to have her released, was of course, similarly indicating that politicians – on either side of the civil war divide – were not going to yield to their spiritual advisers when they transgressed into temporal affairs:

> I fear your Eminence underestimates the part played by women in the present revolt against the majority will of the nation and against principles on which all civilised government is based. Miss MacSwiney is one of those who worked hardest to bring about the present deplorable conditions in Ireland.[109]

Bishop Cohalan of Cork made clear that Catholics were obliged to adhere to church teachings. A Catholic 'does not set up his own subjective speculations or judgements in opposition to the teachings of the Church or of its pastors, whom he is bound to obey'.[110] His opposition to the stance taken by Mary showed the cleavage that had opened between the two since he had approved her establishment of St Ita's in 1916. It was not, however, out of line with statements he had issued during the War of Independence on republican objectives. As Daithí Ó Corráin states, during the War of Independence, the hierarchy 'were fearful of lending moral sanction to either side and stopped short of formally recognising the underground Dáil'.[111] Cohalan, indeed, voiced criticism of the republican position. In February 1921 he issued what de Róiste described as a 'provokingly argumentative' Lenten pastoral:

> The burden of his general argument is that the declaration of independence by Dáil Éireann does not make Ireland a Republic or a Sovereign Independent State: and he seems to contend that only Sovereign Independent States can lawfully use force for the attainment of their objects.[112]

Given such statements by members of the hierarchy, which became more pronounced and prescriptive during the civil war, Mary's willingness to stand in opposition to the Bishops'

1. Mary MacSwiney: head and shoulders. Copyright courtesy of the National Library of Ireland.

2. (*above*) Mary MacSwiney at the Irish Race Congress, Paris, 1922. Copyright courtesy of the National Library of Ireland.

3. (*below*) Mary MacSwiney during the Anglo-Irish Treaty debates, 1921–2. Copyright courtesy of the National Library of Ireland.

4. Muriel, Mary and Annie MacSwiney (late 1920).

5. Terence MacSwiney funeral: Mary with family members and Father Dominic O'Connor. Copyright courtesy of the National Library of Ireland.

6. Mary and Muriel in America, December 1920. Copyright courtesy of the National Library of Ireland.

Joint Pastoral to the point of critiquing the position of the church in correspondence with Byrne is noteworthy. This pastoral issued on 10 October 1922 declared that the provisional government represented the only legitimate authority in Ireland. The bishops denounced the guerrilla warfare being conducted by the anti-Treaty side.[113] The pastoral described the republican opposition as engaged not in a just war but in a campaign of 'murder and assassination'.[114] Even as early as June 1921 the bishops were reluctant to accede to de Valera's request that they would formally recognise the republic set up in 1919.[115] Indeed, Ferriter states that the lawlessness of the anti-Treaty side had resulted in the Catholic Church's shifting from a neutral stance to one in full support of the Treaty, reflected in the Christmas sermons of 1921.[116]

On the Wednesday prior to his death, Terence had declared to Annie:

> Now, you are my witness I'm a soldier dying for the Irish Republic. Say this after me (I, Annie MacSwiney, do hereby affirm that). I am a soldier dying for the Republic, Now we will swear that. Have you anything I could kiss.[117]

Mary's hunger strike in November was viewed by contemporaries on either side of the Treaty divide against the foil of her brother's earlier and fatal protest. Both sides were aware of the propaganda potential of her protest. O'Mullane, speaking on behalf of Cumann na mBan, stated that the provisional government 'are apparently prepared to let her die, just as the Black-and-Tan government violated their own laws in order to perpetuate the murder of her brother Terence'.[118] On 7 November between 200 and 300 people protested in O'Connell Street against her detention. Gonne who led the speeches called on those present to demonstrate against 'the attempt to murder the sister of Terence MacSwiney'.[119] The *Herald* of 15 November published a message from within the walls of the female section of Mountjoy detailing her 'torture' at the hands of her jailers using the previous experience of her brother as a touchstone: 'Miss MacSwiney has now fasted for 11 days, denied the Sacraments which were her brother's consolation'.[120] During Terence's hunger strike neither the Catholic hierarchy in Ireland or in Rome made a definite statement on his protest. This allowed individual priests to openly support his position while Terence's personal chaplain, Fr Dominic, was a constant presence as his hunger strike progressed.[121] The letter to the *Herald*, signed by 16 of Mary's fellow prison inmates, was not just a denunciation of the provisional government but also of the Catholic Church.

On the second day of her imprisonment in Mountjoy in November 1922 Mary began a correspondence with the Archbishop of Dublin, Edward Byrne. In common with the other political prisoners, she wrote, she had 'put in a request for the privilege of receiving Holy Communion to-morrow the Feast of the Irish Saints'. She detailed how Fr MacMahon had visited her and asked her if she accepted and submitted to the bishops' pastoral and if she would 'refrain from all active participation in the Republican cause'. Her answers not being considered 'satisfactory', she was refused the sacrament. 'I maintain', she wrote to Byrne, 'that he exceeded his duty in so questioning me'. She moved her attention to Byrne himself, excoriating him for denying her the 'consolation' of Holy Communion that was her brother's.[122] Despite Mary's deeply-rooted faith and the fact that being refused the sacrament of communion was 'the hardest part of my suffering and sacrifice', she refused to defer to Byrne.[123] Instead she engaged in a detailed defence of her position, arguing that while the bishops were entitled to take a political side as 'private citizens', they were not, she 'respectfully' protested, 'entitled to claim Infallibility'. Mary continued:

> With all respect I tell Your Grace that I cannot purchase the great privilege of Holy Communion with a lie and it would be a lie to say I believed active participation in the Republican Cause wrong. The morality of the act of war committed by the Republican forces depends on the justice of their fight for freedom.
>
> If our fight is wrong to-day, then every fight ever carried on for freedom in Ireland was wrong. The men of 1916 were the murderers some of the Bishops called them then: my brother was a suicide ...[124]

The issue was Mary contended that the lack of consistency within the hierarchy:

> The last Pope sent my brother his blessing on his deathbed for the same cause, and Arch-Bishops and Bishops united in doing him honour. And yet because you have all changed your minds and we have not I have been kept longer without Holy Communion than I have been any time in fifteen years, except once when I was ill.[125]

She believed that the bishops' joint pastoral meant that she, as conveyed to Annie, was 'likely to have a much worse time of it than Terry had'.[126] She compared herself to Joan of Arc who, having been found guilty of heresy by an ecclesiastical court in 1431, was burned at the stake: 'I can no more deny the justice of my cause than Joan of Arc. The Bishops got her burned as a heretic ... but the church has now declared her one of God's saints.'[127] Mary continued to assert her position to Byrne throughout the correspondence; her unwillingness to adopt a supplicant position is noteworthy given the prevailing position of a rigidly hierarchical Catholic church as the key arbiter of right and morality in Irish society in the period:

> I know this will seem presumption to you, but ... it is not meant so. When one is facing death as I do, one faces all the realities that are to follow. We of the laity claim that we have our rights as well as our duties and one of those rights is that of fighting for the Independence of our Country.[128]

'We are going to win, Your Grace, be assured of that', she declared, and continued, introducing a type of gallows levity into her comments: 'I daresay you will consent to give me Holy Communion in *articulo mortis*, but how do you know I will not die suddenly?' She was, she informed Byrne, going to write to Rome if he continued to refuse her the sacraments, 'but I know Rome is proverbially slow, and would be slower than ever in a matter of this kind and I should probably be dead before an answer came'.[129] Byrne responded to Mary's initial epistle by declaring his love for his country. It pained him 'to say anything that seems unsympathetic, particularly to one in the painful circumstances in which you are placed'. However, he wrote, 'a Bishop's duty to God comes before all else'.[130] From Mountjoy Mary also wrote to de Valera, asking him if something could be done 'to show that our quarrel is still with England & all who stand for her in this country'.[131] She indicted the Catholic hierarchy for aligning with the Provisional Government, the latter the tool of the 'British oppressor'.[132] This unholy collusion between the Catholic church and the anti-Treaty government was made manifest for her when Annie was denied permission to visit her.[133] Kathleen Lynn had earlier tried to visit Mary but was sent from 'pillar to post in vain'.[134] Refused entry to see her sister, Annie began a sympathetic hunger strike outside the walls of the prison. It was, *Éire* declared, 'like some great Greek tragedy, timeless in its anguish'.[135] Provided with a deck chair, Annie sat outside the door of the jail wrapped in a fur coat with a rug on her knees. Friends supplied her with a mattress on which to rest and screens to shelter her from the wind.[136] Annie also wrote to Byrne asking him for his thoughts on the fact that she had been dragged and pushed and a hose turned upon her.[137]

Annie's decision to go on hunger strike came as a 'bombshell' to Mary, causing her no small degree of anguish. Her concern at Annie's hunger strike was twofold. She genuinely feared for the health of a sister she considered frail and mentally less robust than herself. However, she was also concerned to manage the optics and propaganda potential. She wrote to de Valera:

> ... now that she has started there is nothing for it but to continue. I have written to her that when she collapses & has to be taken away she must cease the hunger strike at once. Her two days & nights in the open air are worse than my sixteen days in a well [covered?] bed ... I see no way of her withdrawing now until the collapse comes. Out there it can't be long but I fear she will have damaged her health permanently ...[138]

Having heard that Annie was denied communion, Mary contacted Byrne again, linking her sister and brother in their sacrifice for the Irish Republic and contrasting their nobility and fidelity with the ignominious stance of the Catholic hierarchy:

> My sister has all her life been a daily Communicant, and she and my dead brother were, and are, Christians in a sense the world knows little of to-day. They practised the Christianity that is so often preached by others. They hated hypocrisy and falsehood, with the hatred that causes our saviour to drive the bargainers from the Temple. It would be well, Your Grace, if the priests who, to-day, insult the Blessed Sacrament with their violent political diatribes from the Sanctuary had a fraction of the spirit of Christ, and their love of <u>truth</u> inspired by His Teaching.[139]

This letter was forthright and explicit in her denunciation of the manner in which the clergy implemented the strictures of the bishops' joint pastoral, inferring indeed, a sexual pruriency in the questioning conducted by some priests:

> All the young University girls here who are Republicans were refused absolution at the Annual Retreat. Some of these girls are merely Republicans on Principle – they take no active part in the movement. The priest who gave them their Retreat drew an 'Analogy' for them in the confessional. When the first girl (all are about 20 years of age, some under, some over) explains that her conscience would not let her be false to Principle for the sake of material comfort or avoidance of physical pain – this priest suggested that she might be deceiving herself, that in the same way she might reason herself in committing adultery! That she might convince herself if she were married that she would be unfaithful to her husband, and commit adultery with another man! The girl was struck dumb by this horrible talk but the priest would discuss adultery with her and the other pure souled young Republicans.[140]

A letter to Archbishop Byrne in the handwriting of Dorothy Macardle and signed individually by 17 women in Mountjoy, including Mary, laid out the effect of the refusal of the government to allow Annie to enter the jail:

> Her condition is critical. All last night we kept vigil, fearing a sudden collapse ... The anxiety and distress occasioned to Miss MacSwiney by the refusal to allow her sister ... [visit] has affected her condition disastrously & has at the same time forced her to make the last protest in her power, – she refuses the attendance of nurses or doctors until her sister is admitted.

The female inmates desired Byrne to 'protest against this cold-blooded & barbarous act of tyranny', perpetuated by 'men who profess to be loyal sons of the Church'.[141] He was also visited by a deputation of women headed by Maud Gonne, after which he did intercede with Cosgrave. Byrne felt that his request to the latter was 'reasonable'; 'humanity would dictate that a dying woman (even by her own failing to take necessary nourishment) should be allowed the privilege of a sister's presence'.[142] Cosgrave replied to Cardinal Logue's request that he release Mary on the grounds that she and the other female prisoners were 'doing more harm' within the prison 'than they could do outside'.[143] Murphy discusses how Irish political imprisonment in the period 1912–21 'provided Irish activists with another opportunity to rebel, turning the sites that were supposed to "quell political dissent" into places where resistance, even revolution, was nurtured and enacted'.[144] Mary had participated in use of the prison as a theatre of resistance during Terence's hunger strike in 1920; in November 1922 she was the principal actor as resistance was staged from within the women's wing in Mountjoy.

Mary wrote to the Director of Intelligence condemning the decision to refuse entry to Annie, underscoring her belief in the betrayal of their former principles by those who accepted the Treaty and formed the new government: 'the inhuman brutality of this act on the 17th day of my hunger strike is so appalling that I can hardly believe even yet that Irishmen could be guilty of it'.[145] She wrote that she had informed the Governor of Mountjoy that she 'should see my sister on family and business matters, before I got too weak to deal properly with them'. Only two of her letters, she contended, reached her sister, both 'so heavily mutilated and deleted that there was nothing left to read'. She was, she declared:

> reluctantly forced to the conclusion that the action of your authorities in this matter is one of pure vindictiveness against two women whose spirit you cannot break, any more than you can kill the Republic for which they stand.[146]

A memo from the Provisional Government stated that Mary was in a 'state of revolt against prison discipline' and therefore could 'be accorded the same privileges as if she were amenable to the rules'. Moreover, the visit was not 'one of humanity' but rather the 'request is based on a desire for material for political propaganda'.[147] After Mary was released in late November, Cathal O'Shannon declared in the Dáil that the government had shown neither 'sense nor humanity nor ordinary decency' in refusing her a visit from her sister.[148] Kevin O'Higgins retorted that she was:

> in a state of insubordination. She favoured himself and other persons with rather abusive – even bullying – letters, demanding, not requesting, that her sister should be admitted to see her to deal with purely business matters. She did not base that demand on any extreme illness or any feeling that death was imminent – military prisoners were not allowed that kind of visit.[149]

Mary admitted that Annie, in demanding access to visit her, had spoken her mind 'pretty fully ... that riled them'.[150]

Before he was called on to intercede to facilitate Annie to visit her sister, Archbishop Byrne had written to Cosgrave calling for the release of Mary. Describing her as a 'dangerous woman', he nevertheless felt that it would be imprudent to allow her, an 'untried and unconvicted prisoner', to die. He continued:

> Secondly, she is the sister of Terence MacSwiney and if she dies the same way cannot fail to share some of his 'martyr's' apotheosis. She will not fail to share some his heroism. I do not think it at all wise to make a heroine of this woman. Unthinking people, particularly outside Ireland, will identify the cause for which brother and sister died to discredit the Government.[151]

In turn, Cosgrave wrote, that he was happy to receive Byrne's 'mature advice' but he wondered if he was:

> wholly cognisant of the prominent and destructive part played by women in the present deplorable revolt against the Irish people and against those sacred principles upon which civilization and even Christianity itself is founded. This prisoner is one of those who has worked hardest to bring about the prevailing tragic state of affairs in the country.

Mary was, Cosgrave told Byrne, receiving the 'best of food ... should she choose to eat'.[152] When Terence was in Brixton it was similarly stated that food was 'handy at his bedside day and night' in that way underscoring that he, like Mary, was choosing to die by starvation.[153]

In the early days of her hunger strike Mary wrote to de Valera that 'so far' she was 'wonderfully well' although she was keeping to bed. She continued: 'The first three days have been the worst so far, but I suppose it will follow the same course as Terry's. I am ready and quite happy – if only I were not refused Holy Communion... The fight must go on now. Victory is certain.'[154] At a meeting on 12 November to demand Mary's release, Gonne noted that her brother had been able to survive for over 40 days without food. However, as the *Freeman's Journal* noted Mary had already endured a traumatic event: 'Mary MacSwiney, although she was as brave and noble as her brother, would not be able to last forty days, because she had already been through great trouble, and her heart had been weakened by all she had already suffered.'[155] The mental trauma of Mary's hunger strike needs to be considered in the context of the ordeal she experienced watching her brother die in Brixton in 1920. She was also older than Terence was when he began his fateful strike and she had endured a gruelling six-month republican tour in America. 'I am facing death now', she wrote to Byrne, 'it will not take me as long as it took my brother'.[156] Macardle, who was in Mountjoy at the same time as Mary, portrayed her as braver than Terence, her sacrifice for the Republic greater because, having watched her brother's death, she knew what was ahead of her:

> to go to suffering that is unknown to our imagination is less difficult than to go to suffering of which every hideous moment is known, branded into the imagination and memory as is the suffering of hunger strike into hers.[157]

Knowledge of how the body responds to lack of food was something that the MacSwiney family did not have during the time of Terence's fatal hunger strike. In 1920 there was no familiarity 'with a prolonged hunger strike that did not involve artificial feeding'.[158] Mary noted that the doctors in Brixton, pressed as to how long Terence might survive without food, 'haven't the least idea, never having had a precedent'.[159] Having watched her brother starve himself to death, she was able in November 1922 to predict the way her body would break down as it was increasingly deprived of nutrients. Macardle wrote: 'It is the twenty-first day now. After that … even if a hunger-striker is released it is either death or health broken forever. And now, Miss MacSwiney has said to Noreen, the shrinking of the flesh will begin & the neuralgic pain …'

Macardle documented Mary's increased inability to concentrate as her body fell prey to nutrient deprivation.[160] In a letter in the *Evening Herald* on 10 November O'Mullane stated that she 'was yesterday in so prostrate a condition that she asked for her own medical advisor only to meet with a blunt refusal'. Mary was in a 'critical condition' but was prepared to die.[161] That day M. H. O'Connor, Senior Medical Officer in Mountjoy, reported that she was 'languid'.[162] By 15 November the *Evening Echo* reported her condition as 'serious' with the *Belfast Newsletter* referring to a statement from 'Republican quarters' that she was 'showing signs of collapse and was scarcely able to speak'.[163] The following day she penned a letter calling on National Army soldiers to resign and return to their allegiance to the Republic: 'Remember that every Irishman who supports King George's Irish Government and continues to wear the uniform that Terence MacSwiney lies buried in, is having his share in my death and must accept the responsibility.'[164]

Prison officials and doctors drew attention to the mental state of Mary as she continued her hunger strike. This was something that was discussed by the medical men who oversaw Terence in Brixton. References were made to 'a mental element and that a mental specialist might be added' to the next consultation.[165] On 11 November 1922, the Director of Medical Services, Major-General Hayes recommended Mary's release. She was, he declared, 'entering into the dangerous zone'. He continued: 'Another complication following in this case is the unstable highly strung mentality of the prisoner which renders a mental collapse as likely as a physical one.'[166] While certainly the trauma Mary was carrying must have left her mentally brittle, the medical officers in Mountjoy pathologised her hunger strike. M. H. O'Connor did refer the effect of Brixton on her but he also devoted some time to explaining her state of mind on the basis of what he diagnosed as menopausal symptoms. This reference to Mary being unhinged reflected attitudes to female activists in the period of the civil war. Aiken discusses how the understandings in the period 'of what is now recognised PTSD were strongly informed by gender ideologies, and women's mental welfare was routinely connected to the female reproductive system'.[167] O'Connor stated that Mary had been:

> complaining of headaches, diffuse pains, flushes, etc., for the past three months … In my opinion these symptoms taken in conjunction with her age … and three recent missed periods point definitely to the onset of the menopause. This will have a very important bearing on the duration of her hunger-strike – the climacteric being so commonly a period of great mental and physical instability in so many women. In recent time she must have had severe emotional disturbances. These have certainly affected her mental outlook. I feel it is essential to put on record that this present additional strain of facing a long hunger-strike, combined with her past experience in this same trouble and her present disturbed mental equilibrium from the climacteric may conceivably culminate in inhinging [sic] her mind.

In a handwritten note at the end of the report, the Director of Medical Services agreed with the opinions O'Connor expressed.[168] On a wider level this medical correspondence reproduced the pro-Treaty portrayal of female republicans as abnormal. P. S. O'Hegarty stated that female activists on the anti-Treaty side 'became practically unsexed, their mother's milk blackening to make gunpower, their minds working on nothing save hate and blood'. Women with their 'hysteria', he wrote, make devils of men. O'Hegarty's venom was particularly directed at Mary. He accused her of spreading 'malignancy'.[169] De Róiste wrote that he did not consider republican women as 'normal beings with normal human mentality'. Like O'Hegarty, he singled out Mary and also used the word 'malign' to describe her. He noted that the Labour Party were asking for her release 'because she is Terence MacSwiney's sister and because she is not normal and is also physically disabled'.[170] De Róiste did, however, write to Cosgrave petitioning her release on, as he wrote in his diary, 'the Christian principle of charity'.[171]

The female wing of Mountjoy reverberated with discussion of Mary's hunger strike in November 1922. As Macardle detailed in her jail journal her strike was seen against the backdrop of her brother's earlier protest. Mary's fellow prisoners held vigils at her bedside and understood her anguish at being denied the sacraments.[172] If she was increasingly demonised by the pro-Treaty establishment and press, she was revered and even loved by republican women during the civil war. She was released suddenly on 28 November and taken to the Mater hospital. Within the jail there was a 'hilarious celebration'; her cell was raided for 'souvenirs'.[173]

From the Mater Hospital Mary was transferred to a private nursing home at 62 Eccles Street. No 'sane or unbought person', the anti-Treaty side stated, could see this as an act of '"clemency" on the part of the usurping Colonial "Government"'.[174] Republicans argued that the strength of support for Mary within Irish-American political circles precluded the Cosgrave government from allowing her to die.[175] Yet it is noteworthy that Mary was released in a month that saw the execution of four republicans in Kilmainham jail on 17 November and that of Erskine Childers on 24 of November. Her gender clearly was a factor in her release.

Immediately on release Mary continued to put her position forward through the press. She stated that she had not been denied the sacraments due to being on hunger strike but because she refused to accept, as per the bishops' pastoral, that continuing to fight for the republic was wrong and that those who did so were guilty of murder.[176] She denounced the 'inconsistency' of Bishop Cohalan who officiated at her brother's obsequies in 1920 and two years later declared her guilty of a potential act of 'self murder'. 'My protest is for exactly the same purpose as was my brother's'.[177] De Róiste noted in his diary that when an unnamed person remarked that 'in honour' Mary could not take any other course than that of following her brother's example to hunger strike, Cohalan responded with 'pagan honour'.[178] The prison doctors in Brixton repeatedly emphasised that Terence was responsible for his own death. Cohalan in a sermon during Mary's hunger strike in November echoed these sentiments: 'Are we to have the death in prison of the sister of the dead brother? If she dies she will have only herself to blame.'[179]

Large crowds gathered on Sackville Street on 3 December in expectation that Mary and Annie would make an address, but the former was, the *Cork Examiner* reported, too weak while Annie was in 'rather a low state'.[180] The latter gave an interview in late November and described the loss of any interest she herself experienced in food after three to four days on hunger strike. She stated that feelings of hunger were 'succeeded by an intolerable weakness and a general indifference'. She suffered pains in her limbs and a headache; the weight of the blankets was 'intolerable'.[181]

Mary remained in Dublin until late December. As she recovered, she was 'overwhelmed by the too great kindness of our friends here'. She found it difficult to understand that she was the 'recipient of so much devotion'.[182] She had, particularly since her brother's arrest and death, been forced to battle an increasing degree of vitriol, mostly male. Arguably she was not used to being cared for as she was on her release from Mountjoy and, while grateful, she attempted to explain it: 'I know perfectly well that it is one way of showing ... devotion to the Republic'.[183] On 20 December, the day before she departed for Cork, she attended a meeting in the Mansion House against reprisals, speaking for 20 minutes. Writing to Eileen Hearn she declared, 'you see I am not dead yet'.[184] To Art O'Brien she declared: '[t]hat I am in good form is proved by the fact that I have just returned from addressing a meeting at the Mansion House and if I am not back in Mountjoy for Xmas it is because they are too afraid to put me there.' She thanked Hearn for her 'little gift' which she was going to use to supply 'something for the poor boys in prison'.[185] December 1922 into January 1923 were, however, difficult months. Physically, she was weakened and the determination of the government to eliminate republican opposition weighed heavily on her. On 10 October 1922 the government declared that the military courts established on 28 September had the power to inflict death in the context of anti-Treaty actions. Minister for Defence and Chief of Staff of the National Army, Richard Mulcahy, stated in the Dáil that official execution would prevent unofficial ones by army personnel.[186] The execution of republicans commenced on 17 November with five unknown men who had been caught carrying weapons.[187] This triggered a period of heightened tensions within the female section of Mountjoy during the period in which Mary was imprisoned.[188] Erskine Childers's execution on 24 November was followed later that month by those of prisoners, Joseph Spooner, Patrick Farrell and John Murphy, each charged with possession of arms and bombs. Less than two weeks after Mary's release Rory O'Connor, Liam Mellows, Joseph McKelvey and Richard Barrett were shot as a reprisal for the murder of TD Seán Hales and the wounding of fellow deputy Pádraic Ó Máille. Twelve days later seven republicans captured in a raid were similarly dealt with.[189] Mary wanted something 'drastic [to] be done to stop the executions? It is appalling & the most appalling part is the apathy of the people'.[190] As the actions of the Provisional Government towards prisoners hardened, she was also concerned at the treatment of women within the civil war jails, stating that republicans '<u>must</u> save' Comerford and Humphreys, both were 'too valuable to lose'.[191]

Comerford was arrested in late 1922. She had been tasked, together with Paddy McGrath, with a plan to kidnap Cosgrave in an attempt to halt the further execution of republicans. Sent to Mountjoy, Comerford was involved in the protests against overcrowding and bad conditions in January 1923. *Éire* reported that 'as many as four or five were thrown into one cell'. When 'verbal protests proved unavailing, as a last resort they threw out the extra beds'. Comerford received three months hard labour 'for destroying Government property' and, together with Sighle Humphreys, she was removed to the criminal wing of the prison. The two women 'naturally refused to work with, or to associate with criminals'.[192] They demanded to be treated as political prisoners. Earlier, on 18 January, a National Army soldier fired his weapon and shot Comerford in the leg, narrowly missing Humphreys. Comerford had been 'waving at other women prisoners in the exercise yard and that was forbidden'. She stated that she 'decided to go on hunger strike as a protest against our treatment'.[193] This strike began on 23 January.[194] Comerford had lost blood and became increasingly weak; there was concern that there was no hospital within the prison. *Éire* noted that both women were only aged 21.[195] Yet, despite Mary's concern to 'save' Comerford and Humphreys she 'strongly' opposed the possibility discussed at a Cumann na mBan executive meeting of 'ordering the two off the strike'. It would be 'ruination to stop now'.[196] In the event Mary did not have to worry about a republican climb down on the issue. On 3 February *Poblacht na hÉireann* reported that the two women had come off their hunger strike having won their demand for political status: 'the spirit of two girls has triumphed over the military bullies of Mountjoy'.[197]

On 18 December de Valera wrote to Mary after her release from Mountjoy. He jokingly noted that 'feasts and plum puddings maybe more dangerous than hunger striking' but quickly reverted to seriousness. Again, he sounded a pessimistic note. He saw no likelihood of peace, no 'half-way house'. He did not like to think of 'the results of a prolonged contest of this sort, either in the present or future life of the nation'.[198] Yet, he continued to strategise, and he requested that she take charge of Suffolk Street as the headquarters of Cumann na Poblachta, the anti-Treaty wing of Sinn Féin. This was a significant role. Her salary of £400 per annum reflected this.[199] In reality, as Farrell, states, Cumann na Poblachta was defunct due to the decision of the pro-Treaty side to vacate Sinn Féin.[200] De Valera had been concerned since October to gain control of Sinn Féin. The issue of who should manage party funds was a point of contention between himself and the pro-Treaty wing led by Jennie Wyse Power and Éamonn Duggan.[201] With the establishment of Cumann na nGaedheal in December 1922 de Valera was, as Laffan writes: 'anxious ... to fill the vacuum which supporters of the treaty had created so gratuitously; to take over the old party's name, its image, and as much of its structure and property as possible.'[202] At a conference on 7 December the vote as to whether the nascent pro-Treaty party should retake and re-organise Sinn Féin was heavily defeated.[203] In a statement issued to the organising committee of Sinn Féin in May 1923 de Valera declared:

> ... what we feared most was that our opponents would set out deliberately to get hold of Sinn Fein and try to swamp the Republican element in it. That danger has since been removed practically by the formation of Cumann na Gaedheal which leaves Sinn Fein to us.[204]

Mary's views were similar. In the period after her arrest, she continued to argue that it was necessary for Irish people to unite against Britain. It was, she argued, essential to organise 'not merely Republican opinion, strictly so called, but what might be called "Nationalist" or "Independence" opinion in general'. If the anti-Treaty side did not do this, 'the other side will and the loss will be immense'.[205]

The election of the standing committee of Sinn Féin in January 1922 had been on pro- and anti-Treaty lines resulting in victory for the more moderate element within the party although de Valera was not deposed as leader at the Special Ard Fheis in March.[206] However, as Hopkinson states, Sinn Féin had 'disintegrated' by the time of the pact election in June.[207] De Valera now desired to reanimate the party. In December 1922

Donnelly, the Director of Elections for the newly-organised Sinn Féin, wrote in relation to party treasurers and the holding of an Ard Fheis. The decision should be, he stated, that those: 'who no longer agree with the Constitution of Sinn Féin and who refuse to work for its fulfilment or who have accepted office entailing an oath of allegiance to the King cease to be members.'[208] This was a very similar decision to that taken by Cumann na mBan in February. A circular letter was issued from headquarters which decreed:

> The British Government is at present passing a bill to empower the holding of an election in order to strengthen the hands of those about to pull down the Republic. Any member giving support to a Free State candidate is guilty of treason to the Republic and cannot stay in our organisation.[209]

On 1 January 1923, together with Austin Stack, de Valera issued a circular stating that the Sinn Féin Party headquarters would close and reopen under 'republican management'.[210] Ireland, the circular proclaimed, 'really is ours for the taking'.[211] His desire to re-establish the political machinery shows his priorities. He wrote to Mary of the necessity to establish branches throughout the country:

> We need some point of contact with the public and some responsible person in charge who will be able to give authoritative information, meet representatives of the press, etc., etc. We do not want to allow ourselves to be driven altogether underground. An open centre at which sympathisers from the country could call is as you will realise very necessary.

De Valera stated that she would have to be on the premises 'whole time'.[212] It was important 'not to allow ourselves to be driven altogether underground'. By having an 'open centre' those in sympathy with the anti-Treaty position 'could call'.[213] Despite the onerous commitment and the necessity to leave Cork, she agreed to take on this role, leaving the running of St Ita's to Annie. Branches were furnished with a blueprint on priorities which included a focus on conditions in the Irish Free State jails, particularly the treatment of female prisoners. A prisoners' dependents fund was to be established and a national amnesty demanded.[214] De Valera wrote regularly to advise Mary in this new role. In early February he declared:

> The ARD CHOMAIRLE could be summoned, but I think it would be unwise, in as much as it is composed mainly of the nominees of the other side. We must regard ourselves really as reforming the organisation and the Republican members more or less as a provisional Executive. If the majority of the old ARD CHOMAIRLE were alright, we would be in a splendid position, but I think they are mostly all wrong.[215]

At this point de Valera was on the run and Mary commiserated with him while detailing her plans to commence work in Suffolk Street: 'I am sure you must be feeling the confinement very much. I should imagine being "on the run" would get on one's nerves very soon.' She told him that she would take some personal time in Dublin before she 'gets to work. Then I shall take a room somewhere quietly'.[216]

In the early months of 1923, there were increasingly frequent calls for peace within the anti-Treaty side.[217] By the end of summer 1922, the Provisional Government had succeeded in capturing key strongholds in the west and Limerick, Waterford and Cork in the south. In this they were aided by a successful National Army recruitment drive, British arms and ammunition and civilian support.[218] This pushed the anti-Treaty side back onto the guerilla war tactics of the War of Independence.[219] Writing of Cork in August 1922, de Róiste stated: '… the conflict has developed into sniping, some bomb throwing, destruction of bridges, houses, railways, and isolated attacks and defence-actions between very small parties on either side.'[220]

On 18 January 1923 Liam Deasy, commander of the 1st Southern Division IRA, was arrested. He claimed that he was preparing for peace at the time of his arrest and was granted a stay of execution to allow him to appeal to the IRA to end the conflict. In his letter, received by de Valera on 31 of January, he concluded that the long-term republican cause would be rescued by a move to peace. He referred to the insidious cycle of reprisal and counter-attack, the executions and the loss of popular support for republicans.[221] Mary remonstrated with de Valera at the lack of information she received following the rumours that circulated on Deasy's arrest, particularly given, as she outlined to him, that he had asked her to take on the management of Suffolk Street and that he had given her responsibility as a member of the Council of State. She declared that a 'split in our ranks now – and a slaughter of the best in the country – for that is what a split would mean – would be unforgivable'.[222] De Valera promised her that if: 'there was any marked difference of opinion amongst us you could rest assured that no action committing the nation would be taken behind the backs of the members of the Council of State, who are not on the Executive.'[223]

In the correspondence between the two during the civil war, Mary exhorted de Valera to stand firm: a 'solid unbroken and determined stand now & Victory is ours and soon' she wrote in mid-February.[224] He, by contrast, was much more questioning, inching arguably towards finding a path to peace, although as McCullagh notes he did not use the Deasy surrender to 'move in that direction'.[225] Yet, the correspondence with Mary continued to show him to be quite tortured as to the violence of the civil war and paranoid as to his position as a wanted man. In February 1923 he remonstrated with her for being 'indiscreet' by sending him a message at eight in the morning.[226]

In February, in a tentative step towards brokering a peace, de Valera considered issuing a public statement based on a memorandum sent to Liam Lynch and members of his cabinet calling for disputed issues on the Treaty to be put to a vote, if in turn, the government would recognise the sovereign rights of Ireland. Mary vehemently rejected any idea that republicans had to make concessions, arguing that to grant the principle of submission to majority rule would mean that 'our civil war has no sanction … if it is right now to submit to majority rule ... it was equally right last July. What have the lives been lost for'. She and the other 'incorruptible' republicans perceived de Valera's stance on the Treaty as 'suspiciously moderate'.[227]

On 9 February Mary wrote pleadingly to de Valera to stand firm; not to 'break our hearts':

> I beg and implore of you not to issue any personal statement at this juncture … you will do more to make the Army crumble by issuing a personal statement at this juncture than all the Liam Deasys in the land …
>
> A short time ago you told me you wished you had my faith. Won't you trust to it now a little.?

> Don't issue a personal statement. Consult with the Ministry and issue a joint Governmental statement in conjunction with the Army.
>
> Oh Dev, don't let us down now. I know you don't mean it so but it would be the worst let down we have had. Trust my woman's instinct – my faith if you like but don't do it. We want no man's personal views. Not even yours … [228]

Addressing a Sinn Féin meeting in the Mansion House on the 11 February Mary stated that Deasy's surrender was 'abject'. While he was a 'brave' man, he suffered from a 'want of faith'.[229] In what the *Freeman's Journal* described as a 'long address' she denounced Deasy as a 'deserter' and stated that there 'should be no such thing in the country as ex-IRA men'. She called for the war to continue indicating her belief that loss of life was worth the ultimate victory:

> Knowing that they beat the Free State, as they beat the English for the sake of a few more lives, of a few more hundred lives, or it might be a few more thousand lives – God grant it might not be – but Liam Deasy asked them now to surrender after all they had lost.[230]

This extreme language and lack of regard for individual life exemplified what de Róiste meant when, discussing the Treaty debates, he referred to 'abstract thoughts and ideas, above and apart from the ordinary life of human beings'.[231] Yet on another level, the issue of compromise on the republic was not abstract for Mary. The phrase 'after all they had lost' in her speech on Deasy's surrender is a noteworthy phrase given the ordeal of Terence's death. She believed that it was necessary for de Valera to make a similar statement to that she delivered in the Mansion House. Her brother Seán had informed her that the Deasy surrender would not affect the Cork No. 1, but 'he will affect other Brigades':

> What will probably happen is that some men will fall and go home. They will not give up their arms but they will not fight on. They will always have the feeling that they will 'be let down again'.
>
> I think they are all waiting for a strong statement from the Govt in reply?[232]

However, de Valera was much less extreme and more pragmatic, stating that what:

> 'the men who might fall out' have, is the consciousness that the task we have set ourselves is a task that can only be achieved by a miracle, as I have always said. They don't expect the miracle, and they expect that sooner or later the awakening that came to Deasy will of necessity come to others and that then in the face of the stone wall of realities through which they will not be able to run their heads, they will conceive of some other way out which will be far short of the 'strong statements' that some people are always looking for.

He wrote that he felt it was his 'duty to do my part as I see it, to save the nation from the dangers I see it rushing into, if I can'.[233]

What complicated de Valera's tentative explorative shift towards peace moves was the brief arrest of Mary in mid-February and the capture of correspondence between the two which made its way into the press. The government used captured letters to undermine republicans by leaking incendiary snippets from them.[234] The *Belfast Newsletter* indeed on the basis of the captured letter ran the headline: 'Miss MacSwiney Speaks for Him [de Valera] and Rejects Deasy's Plan'.[235] The *Irish Independent* referred to 'startling disclosures'.[236]

Kathleen Lynn noted that the letters contained 'fine criticism of Dev', adding: '[w]ould God he would heed them'.[237]

The situation that led to the capture of the correspondence was the reopening of the Sinn Féin offices in Suffolk Street, closed since the arrests on 9 November 1922. Mary received members of the Irish, British and American press to reply to Kevin O'Higgins's 'review of the situation in the Free State'.[238] In early January O'Higgins gave an interview to the Hearst American newspaper group, outlining the war against Britain, the peace talks, the acceptance of the Treaty and the manner in which the state under process of establishment was assailed by a 'military and political combination which denied the right of the people to decide the issue, and refused to be bound by the majority will'.[239] Mary had earlier described O'Higgins to de Valera as 'the most sinister figure we have to deal with & E. B. [Ernest Blythe] comes a good second'. Both men were, she wrote 'a bigger danger than either Mulcahy or Cosgrave'.[240] At the interview with the press Mary stated that, although she was a member of the Council of State, which she described as a type of war committee, she was not a member of the republican cabinet; she was then only speaking for herself.[241] However, she claimed that her views were held by 90 per cent of republicans. She described de Valera as moderate in his willingness to contribute financially to the 'King's personal revenue' but she stated that there was 'all the difference in the world' between the Treaty and Document No. 2. The *Belfast Newsletter* reported that she declared that the latter document: '... was no longer under discussion now, and the position was that no peace was possible while the King remained, through his Governor-General, "sprawling all over the Free State Constitution".'[242] Mary rejected the idea that de Valera would surrender on the basis of a 'free election' but stated that 'if he turned against the republic in the morning you would only have a repetition of what you had in 1922'.[243] A bye-line in the *Belfast Newsletter* read 'Mary MacSwiney's veiled threat to De Valera':

> De Valera's continued silence regarding the 'peace' movement in the Free State has given rise to rumours that he is seeking a compromise, and this view receives support from the efforts, renewed yesterday, of Miss Mary MacSwiney, who is one of the most extreme Republicans, to commit him to an irreconcilable attitude.
>
> On Sunday Miss MacSwiney made it appear that De Valera was as extreme as ever. Yesterday her tone was less confident, and her statement contained a veiled threat, meaning that, so long as De Valera remained recalcitrant, the gunmen would support him. [244]

After an hour-long interview Mary was arrested, together with Kathleen Barry, Kathleen Clarke and Rev. Dr P. Browne of Maynooth.[245] Cosgrave described her speech at the press conference as delivered with 'characteristic audacity'. He alleged that her speech was 'a desperate attempt to side track and defeat these "overtures for peace"'. The *Belfast Newsletter* reported on his response to MacSwiney's arrest:

> She of course, anticipated arrest – it was, indeed, planned by her. Miss MacSwiney will doubtless go again on hunger-strike. But she is not the sort of female fanatic to give herself up as she did yesterday unless she had a desperate purpose to serve in doing so. And the only purpose discernible is to stop the peace overtures.[246]

Sent to Kilmainham, she declared to Macardle, that she would have to begin her hunger strike 'all over again'.[247] That she would do so in the event of further arrest she had signalled to de Valera in January.[248] In the event she was released the next morning being, according to Charlotte Despard, 'of no military importance'.[249] However, the letter she had written to de Valera denouncing his overtures towards peace was captured, together with other correspondence, during the arrest and published, as Macardle wrote, 'by the enemy'.[250]

There was recrimination within the republican executive at the potential of the captured correspondence to cause embarrassment. De Valera described Mary's 'carelessness' as 'inexcusable'. He added that the 'capture of these notes of yours may mean a valuable life. They will sure encourage the others to keep on'.[251] P. J. Ruttledge described the situation of the captured correspondence as 'awful' noting that Mary had been told not to keep documents in the office. [252] In a further letter he apportioned blame to himself for sending her the letter in the first place. Ruttledge continued underscoring the fault lines within the republican opposition:

> Miss MacSwiney would probably feel justified in taking the initiative in starting this war. I would not. To me this war is a war of defence – force and unjustifiable methods were used against us, and I think I am not alone in having my attitude determined by this fact. The principal damage the seizure of her note will do is that it will keep the other side 'hoping'. A few more bolts for Kevin O'Higgins to shoot won't matter much.[253]

In the captured letter from Mary to de Valera, she stated that she knew he would 'hate' getting such correspondence from her. While she expressed her sorrow at annoying him, she continued: 'I can't help it. I believe your proposed action ruinous. I must say so and so I am speaking my mind to you as plainly as I did to the Bishops. Forgive me if I have hurt you but Ireland comes first.'[254]

Immediately released from jail, Mary wrote to de Valera apologising for what had occurred and noting that he would be 'relieved' to hear that she was not forced to go on hunger strike; a political intimacy still prevailed between the two.[255] However, once she was subjected to de Valera's ire at the appropriation of the letter she attempted to downplay the situation:

> In spite of your natural disgust with human nature I may at least ask you not to exaggerate the importance of the papers captured. I deny absolutely that the capture of my [criticism] of your statement 'may mean many a valuable life' or 'encourage the others to keep on'. On the contrary the only thing they would show the others was that even if your deserted us <u>we</u> would still keep on.[256]

Mary contended that de Valera was 'cross' more with her 'criticism of your document than the capture of some of the minor criticisms'.[257] She was prescient with this insight; de Valera's style of leadership was one that brooked no opposition.[258] Similarly, she was aware of the lack of experience those on the anti-Treaty side; none of them, she wrote, were 'anything more than the newest amateur in matters of this kind. Our only safety is absolute honesty with each other as with the enemy'. While de Valera was 'wonderful in many ways', she was 'no believer in the divine rights of Presidents any more than of Kings'.[259] She vehemently rejected the idea that he had the authority to issue any statement brokering peace moves without the approval of the anti-Treaty executive.[260] She questioned him as to accountability and in particular the role of the Council of State of which she was a member. She requested clarification as to what exactly the council was: 'What are its duties? its responsibilities?' She suggested that the press and the public 'who think at all' considered the council:

> responsible for Policy, looked upon as the Cabinet really, and would be inevitably involved in any action of the real Cabinet ... Please don't forget that I really want an answer about the Council of State. Am I at liberty to say to anyone who asks, that the said Council was only nominated for the purpose of approving of the Cabinet appointments that it had no other duty and has no further responsibilities? If not, why not?[261]

She wanted all decisions 'dealing with peace or with suggestions for an agreement' to go before the council as well as the executive. They were all 'hemmed in', a result of their wanted status, and consequently were 'apt to lose touch with outside realities and outside points of view'.[262] Her desire for the Council of State to be fully involved in any move to peace was contained in the captured letter published in the press. All statements about peace:

> belong as much to the members of the Council of State as to the Cabinet, for we are all involved in anything that is done ... Would it not be well in view of the Deasy debacle and the trouble it may cause – if at any hazard a joint meeting of the Civil and Military Executive were held, including, I would suggest, the Council of State – and that we faced all the facts of the situation without glamour or exaggeration, and decided on the irreducible minimum of the terms on which, here and now, and to avoid further conflict, we would make peace.[263]

The pro-Treaty press made much of the tensions between Mary and de Valera, emphasising divisions between moderates and the more doctrinaire republicans:

> Miss Mary MacSwiney has discovered that Mr Edward de Valera does not stand for 'the Republic'. It will be interesting to watch this little disagreement gather strength. The opposition of those who make war upon the Irish people has commenced to disintegrate into its constituent fragments of folly.[264]

The *Freeman's Journal* interpreted the captured correspondence as indication that de Valera 'had gone back to' Document No. 2 which would 'not please those with whom he has recently been associated'. Mary was, the paper declared, 'already on the warpath' and was 'capable of a rebellion of her own'.[265] The *Freeman's Journal* represented her as de Valera's nemesis on the republican side. When two girls in their teens were arrested on 21 February carrying petrol, Webley revolvers and ammunition the paper declared:

> Did those who incited them to take an active part in the campaign of violence and bloodshed enlighten them beforehand as to the precise differences between Document No. 2 and the Treaty?
>
> Were they given a clear definition of Mr. de Valera's position as compared with that of Miss MacSwiney?[266]

There was no outright rupture between Mary and de Valera in this period; this was in the future. He determined not to issue any statement signalling peace overtures in February which salved her immediate concerns. The correspondence between the two during the civil war illuminates de Valera's respect for Mary despite her more doctrinaire stance.

Certainly, he snapped at her and admonished her on occasion. He was, however, willing to explain his unease at the course of civil war and violence it engendered. He wrote that he had 'anticipated' her criticism of his potential peace proposals and that his document was 'another case of "thinking aloud"'. He noted that it represented the course he would have taken 'since the "Treaty" was signed if the whole conduct of affairs on our side had been solely a matter of my personal will and judgement'. His course would not be the 'heroic' one, but, he explained, 'it would have avoided the terrible immediate risks into which the nation was being run by the course that has actually been followed'.[267] She was quick to publicly repudiate any suggestion that the captured letter signalled a split in the republican ranks. De Valera, she wrote, 'never surrendered Ireland's sovereign status as the renegade members of his Cabinet and their followers did'. She believed that he would still 'and in a very short time guide the ship of the Republic into the harbour of peace'.[268] Such definitive statements, of course, belied the reality of the military position of the IRA. Ferriter notes that most of the letters in the Ernie O'Malley archive in this period indicate a despondent view of the potential of the IRA to achieve victory.[269]

While correspondence with de Valera over the captured letter continued Mary was forced to engage with an additional, and more personal, concern. On 14 February Annie was arrested at her home along with 28 other women across Cork, 11 of whom were released immediately.[270] A stencil machine used to publish irregular leaflets and literature was captured.[271] On arrest Annie commenced a hunger strike. Immediately Mary set about publicising the treatment of her sister at the hands of the Cumann na nGaedheal government for propaganda purposes; the anti-Treaty press did likewise. There was an emphasis on the substandard conditions in the female wing of Cork Gaol:

> The cells were very dirty – cigarette ends and other remnants strewn on the floor. On Wednesday morning there was no suggestion that any of the girls should wash and no water was provided for them. The majority got no dinner.[272]

Mary was present at the protest meeting against the detention of the Cork women in O'Connell street on 25 February.[273] On a personal level she was concerned for a sister she believed emotionally and physically weaker than she herself. The *Cork Examiner* noted that Annie's health was 'enfeebled' as a result of her hunger strike outside Mountjoy in November.[274] Despard noted Annie's less than robust constitution and reported her on the verge of collapse on the tenth day of her hunger strike in February.[275] In a letter to the press Mary wrote that her sister was 'not as strong as I am, and could not last 24 days'.[276] Mary's role as head of the family came to the fore yet again. She sent a cable to her brother Peter in America and attempted to ease her concern saying :'I suppose if I am "of no military" importance Annie is not either', a reference to her own immediate release on imprisonment earlier in the month.[277] Her anxiety for Annie cannot be overstated; the very real fear of losing another sibling to hunger strike must have been excruciating for Mary to contemplate. Annie wrote to the Archbishop of Dublin echoing Mary's letters to him the previous November. She accused the hierarchy of interference in political matters, referring to the fact that the Pope had ordered the clergy in Italy to avoid involvement in the civil strike caused by the fascist movement. The situation was so different in Ireland, Annie wrote:

> … look at the slander and vilification poured forth from the altars in the Catholic Churches in Ireland today. It has been reported to me on high authority that a Catholic priest in the Kilkenny district, standing in front of the Tabernacle, openly accused the members of Cumann na mBan of being the mothers of illegitimate children of the soldiers of the Republic, and accused the local Commandant of being responsible for ten of them.[278]

Annie's letters to Byrne also reverberated with Terence's ideas of sacrifice for the republican cause:

> I wonder what your Grace thinks of those people that you support. Their Free State will not be secure unless I die? or [sic] they mean to release me, then they are keeping me here to suffer and to see how long I will last. I am indifferent either way. A Free State that can only exist by such means cannot feel very sure of itself.[279]

To see her sister on hunger strike was arguably more difficult for Mary on an emotional level than undergoing a political fast herself. Annie's letters to Byrne had a slightly histrionic edge to them and Mary must have been concerned for the mental as well as the physical health of her sister. After eight days on hunger strike, she reported that Annie was very weak and suffering from neuralgic pains.[280] By day 14 she complained of a cough and a pain in her lung. No outside doctor had seen her. Letters were sent urging her release including one from Mabel Fitzgerald who, according to the *Irish Independent*, 'specially appealed to "Free State Women" to join in the protest'.[281] Annie was, Mary wrote to de Valera, a 'bad subject' for a hunger strike 'especially after her last experience'. She sent a 'special messenger' down to Cork to bring back news. She informed de Valera that she would have to be absent from Dublin 'as long as she is on hunger strike in Cork'. He would 'of course understand' she wrote, as she outlined plans to keep Suffolk Street open in her absence.[282] She also needed to source a substitute teacher to fill in for Annie in St Ita's.[283] A number of days later Annie arrived in Kilmainham Jail, having been conveyed by sea with a number of other women from Cork Gaol, including Connie Murphy who had been arrested at the MacSwiney residence in late January.[284] Conditions on board the ship were, *Poblacht na hEireann* declared, 'shocking'; it was alleged in the *Cork Examiner* that Annie contracted neuralgia as a result.[285]

De Valera, despite the increasingly political acrimony with Mary over the captured letter, was solicitous for Annie's well-being and anxious to help:

> Go down by all means. I am sorry for this new trouble you are in. I am full of remorse. I am afraid I wrote rather harshly today, but don't mind it. I do hope your sister will not go on hungerstrike[sic]. She seemed so frail when I saw her last. Can we help you in any way. [sic] Don't hesitate to let us know.[286]

Mary moved back and forth between personal concern for her sister to the political ramifications of the arrest of the Cumann na mBan women in Cork, noting that it would 'upset all communication with the [IRA] Columns'. In response to de Valera's request that she forgive him his harshness she noted that he asked her 'the same thing when I was in Mountjoy for things that less deserved harshness'.[287] Clearly, there was a depth of friendship and respect between the two during the civil war that could withstand political disagreement. 'I know quite well', she wrote, 'we don't differ on fundamentals. If we did we should have parted company long ago'.[288]

Annie was released on 1 March with her condition described as 'serious'.[289] In early April Mary noted to de Valera that she had 'taken a long time to pull up'.[290] Other family matters also pressed on Mary. The captured letter to de Valera was not the only one that the government leaked to the press to undermine the anti-Treaty side. Another letter on her person was from Hanna Sheehy Skeffington to Áine O'Rahilly concerning the behaviour of Muriel in New York. The former was in America, together with Kathleen Boland and Linda Kearns, at the behest of de Valera. The women travelled across the country under the auspices of the American Committee of the Republican Soldiers and Prisoners' Dependants' Fund. Sheehy Skeffington's arrival in October 1922 overlapped with Muriel's visit to America on the second anniversary of Terence's death.[291]

Attempts had been made, Sheehy Skeffington wrote, to get Muriel to return to Ireland. She had been arrested briefly in Washington on 14 November together with eight other members of the AARIR while marching on the British Embassy to demand her sister-in-law's release from Mountjoy.[292] Letters were sent telling her that her daughter needed her. Muriel refused to return to Cork and was engaged in attempts to get an appointment as Consul in New York. Sheehy Skeffington continued:

> She is with an unscrupulous crowd who use her and exploit her. She turns a deaf ear to all our entreaties and protests, and her general wildness and irresponsibility has done us great harm and caused dangerous comment ... She is very hysterical, and though when she chooses she can be charming and sweet, she can and is also at other times entirely irresponsible and unbalanced – like a spoilt and naughty child ... At times I fear for her an entire mental lapse, and all this sensationalism she is prone to his bad for her mentally.[293]

While in America, Muriel was arrested for her role in the occupation of the Irish consular offices by Laurence Ginnell and Robert Briscoe and forcibly removed by the police.[294] Sheehy Skeffington stated that Mary would 'help us, I think, as she was up against this before, and knows conditions'.[295] John Gibney notes that the republicans involved in the occupation 'may simply have been an isolated faction in an already fragmented world'.[296] Alice Ginnell wrote that 'all the Irish people in New York ... seem to resent L. G. with the exception of Mrs. MacSwiney and Robert Briscoe'.[297] The relationship between the MacSwiney sisters and Muriel became increasingly fraught from the civil war onwards. Muriel was involved in the fighting in Dublin the early days of the civil war, stationed in the Hammam Hotel with other members of Cumann na nmBan before she set sail for America.[298] In her memoir, Máire MacSwiney Brugha stated that she did not see her again for 18 months. Her experience of the civil war was, she recalled, 'the complete disappearance of my mother'.[299] She later learned that her mother had asked some Americans visiting Ireland to bring her daughter back to her in the US. Mary did not permit this to occur. Instead, she continued to reside in the O'Rahilly home in Herbert Park.[300] Muriel, who as discussed in Chapter Four, suffered from depression even before the events of Brixton expressed her trauma differently to Mary. MacSwiney Brugha wrote that her mother 'could not cope with life or its problems'. Her behaviour was 'erratic'.[301] When Muriel returned to Ireland finally in late summer 1923 she was declared herself an atheist and was moving towards joining the Communist party.[302] For Mary, the central issue was the welfare of her niece who Muriel removed from the country in the autumn of 1923 leaving her in a series of boarding schools while she travelled across Europe. MacSwiney Brugha emphasised that her father had made Mary her joint guardian on his deathbed. As discussed in Chapter Nine, Mary acted on her continued concern for the wellbeing of her niece, bringing her to live in Belgrave Place in 1932.[303]

Despite the private fracturing of her relationship with Muriel, Mary denounced the Publicity Department of the Irish Free State in publishing that letter concerning her sister-in-law's behaviour in America. Mary wrote to the press stating that Muriel was not a member of an official delegation. Since she was not 'officially appointed' she could not be 'officially recalled'. She referred to Muriel's state of mind:

> Her health, which has been precarious for the past two years, does not permit any constant work or strain ... If, in the cause for which she has suffered so much, her zeal at times outruns her discretion, your 'Government Publicity Department' must be hard up for weapons to attack the Republic when they use that.[304]

Mary noted that the Free State had also captured Seán MacSwiney's reply to Liam Deasy's surrender; why, she asked, 'do they not publish this'?[305] Indeed, Lynn recorded in her diary that there was '[m]uch disgust' in republican circles at the publication of a 'private letter re. Mrs MacSwiney's health and waywardness'.[306]

On 11 March 1923 Cosgrave stated that 'verbal messages and private letters' expressed a desire for peace despite the 'goading' and 'flamboyant optimism' of the 'so-called "Army Council"'. He outlined the 'four distinct types of opposition' that the government had to deal with: 'First there is the political malcontents, which include Mr. de Valera and Miss MacSwiney. The former took the wrong turn, and is perpetually trying to save his face, while the latter's ambition is, I believe, to be Queen of Ireland.'[307] Two days later Mary gave an interview discussing, amongst other topics, recent ministerial statements. She also referred to the poor financial position of Cumann na mBan. She had no ambition, she retorted to Cosgrave's allegation, to be queen 'here or any place else'. Her ambition was the acknowledgement of the Republic. [308] When that was achieved she would 'sing her "Nunc Dimittis"'; she would depart.[309] A short piece in the *Freeman's Journal* suggested that Mary had power over de Valera. The Irish people would, the paper stated, be relieved that she did not want to be Queen of Ireland but she 'assumes a more than royal prerogative in laying down the law'. When the Irish people have:

> the bad taste to decline her proffered gift and dispute her authority, like the Queen in 'Alice in Wonderland' her cry is, 'Off with their heads'. She had much to say on many subjects yesterday, but she offered no explanation for her policy of 'duress' for the mass of the population who will not accept her as their prophet and as the arbitress of their destinies. Possibly her success in bullying unfortunate Mr. de Valera in scrapping mysterious Principle No. 3 encouraged her to think that she can coerce the rest of Ireland as easily. But if Mr. de Valera is content to be marooned by Miss MacSwiney behind a 'wall of glass,' the average Irishman has no intention of submitting to this sort of dictation. He has no objection, however, to Miss MacSwiney talking, now that the Irish Government has made it clear that it alone has the power to act in this country.[310]

In one of the documents captured by the Free State government, de Valera attested that he had, as the *Belfast Newsletter* stated, 'been compelled to view the tragedy through a wall of glass, being powerless to intervene effectively'.[311] According to the *Freeman's Journal*, it was Mary who bound and paralysed him.

As the Irish Free State government increasingly solidified its institutions and status, the mainstream press sounded a note of derision when discussing the republican opposition. De Valera and MacSwiney were linked in this commentary. The difference was that de Valera was privately questioning the barren political position in which he found himself while Mary still spoke in ideological terms. In early April under the heading 'Futility' the *Freeman's Journal* commented on the blowing up of a railway bridge at Clonsilla by the IRA:

> Their leaders are aware that they have lost the political battle … Though they have abandoned all hope of converting the country, they comfort themselves that they can still punish it for its bad taste in declining to be captivated by their blandishments or terrorised by their threats. Thus, because we will not dance to the piping of Mr. de Valera and Miss MacSwiney, we are not to be permitted to dance at all …[312]

On 14 March Mary responded to the deportation of 110 republicans arrested in Great Britain and their internment in Mountjoy, stating that it would 'retard things a bit, but it won't stop the war'.[313] However, de Valera and other key anti-Treaty individuals, both military and political, concluded in this month that an end to military action had to occur.[314] Mary refused to countenance that Tom Barry had consented to consider peace proposals put forward by Dr Harty, Archbishop of Cashel. She had been informed, she stated, that Barry would take no notice of them, adding that any 'man who wishes can resign, but any man handing in his arms will be severely dealt with'.[315] In the event the peace resolution was defeated at the executive meeting on 24 May by six votes to five, Lynch casting the impeding vote.[316]

Less than a month later Mary was more despondent. Writing to de Valera on 10 April she noted that the newspapers of the previous day made for 'horrible reading'. Republican documents captured were published and exposed a willingness amongst the more militant leaders – Tom Barry in Cork and Humphrey Murphy in Kerry – to move towards negotiated peace, having tested 'the feeling of the rank and file'. Republican leaders were, the *Belfast Newsletter* declared, 'weakening'.[317] The *Irish Independent* referred to the proposal by Barry that the 'in the opinion of the Executive resistance and operations against F. S. Government will not further the cause of independence of the country'. The paper reported that the proposal was defeated by one vote and published extracts from the captured documents, sneeringly describing the republicans as the 'Lord High Tinkerers'.[318] The *Belfast Newsletter* noted that de Valera was looking more favourably on the proposals for peace submitted by Rev Dr Harty and that his '"executive" – excluding, of course, Miss Mary MacSwiney – are urging him to accept it without reservation'.[319] What de Valera described as Mary's blind faith came to the fore as she declared 'We shall win out even if only a few are faithful'. A second letter written at 7 pm that day called for a 'steady intensive campaign to show that it is the cause that matters not the men, will I think have the effect of convincing the enemy that there are enough people with courage and faith enough to carry on'.[320] The *Belfast Newsletter*, noted, however, that Mary was 'amongst the extremists on the other side', referring to a split in the republican ranks. One of the captured documents, it alleged, 'disclose her knowledge of the fact that her influence with the rebel leaders is declining, and she complains that she is not kept informed of the course of events'.[321] As Mary sat writing at length to de Valera on 10 April, Liam Lynch, IRA chief of staff, was fatally shot during an encounter with Irish Free State troops in the Knockmealdown Mountains, Co. Tipperary. Mary declared Lynch a brave patriot. Despite the 'shock after shock' that the week culminating in Lynch's death brought, she still saw wrote of victory, almost in an effort to encourage de Valera to stay stalwart: 'we will only be the more grimly determined. You will not lose heart, sad though it all is'.[322] Yet, de Valera had lost 'heart' unbeknownst fully to Mary. The day previous to Lynch's death, de Valera wrote to Ruttledge: 'To me our duty seems plain – to end the conflict without delay ... The hope of success alone would justify our continuing the fight, and frankly, I see no such hope ...'[323]

Mary was arrested once again on 29 March and released on 1 April.[324] Her brief incarceration did not dampen her willingness to address an anti-Treaty meeting two days later outside the GPO.[325] According to the *Belfast Newsletter* she was joined by other 'wild women', amongst whom were Countess Plunkett and Mrs Pearse.[326] The paper also surmised her attendance at the conference which was the subject of a raid by Irish Free State forces leading to the death of Liam Lynch.[327] This, however, was incorrect; as noted she was writing to de Valera from her base in Dublin when news of Lynch's death reached her. Two days later, on 12 April, she was taken into custody for the fourth time, removed from a train passing through Tipperary town together with Count and Countess Plunkett, Markievicz and Liam Lynch's brother. The five were enroute to Mitchelstown for the funeral of the IRA chief of staff.[328] Transferred to Kilmainham she was consigned, together with Kate O'Callaghan, to 'that awful B wing', both agreeing that 'one night of it would finish us'.[329] She immediately went on hunger strike, believing initially that she and the others arrested would be released after the funeral was over. If that was not the case she would 'go through it to the end'.[330] When the prisoners on A wing discovered that Mary and O'Callaghan were on hunger strike they 'took forcible possession of us and gave us the best quarters at their disposal'.[331] Outside the jail, Annie attended Lynch's funeral with Vivian de Valera while both sisters sent wreaths.[332] From jail Mary described the week of Lynch's funeral as the 'worst yet' for the anti-Treaty side, but, she declared, 'we do not get depressed'. She and the others prisoners could, she wrote to de Valera, face execution or death in prison but they would not surrender. She hoped that he had 'already sent a cheery message out'.[333] Noting that if O'Higgins was 'really in the saddle' the republican side could 'expect bad things', she wondered if they could concentrate on a plot to kidnap him.[334]

There were female prisoners already on hunger strike in Kilmainham when Mary was arrested. On 12 April, the day of her incarceration, Nell Ryan, her sister, Kitty Costello and Annie O'Neill had been on strike in Dublin for 35, 35 and 24 days respectively.[335] Earlier the three women wrote to the Archbishop of Dublin requesting that they be granted the 'privilege of receiving Holy Communion daily until death'.[336] The debate at government level on how to manage such striking women was viewed through the lens of Mary's November 1922 hunger strike and the decision to release her which some saw as encouraging other women to use the weapon. Her presence in Kilmainham and her second hunger strike in April 1923 augmented such ministerial viewpoints.

On 20 of April Patrick McCartan moved in the Dáil for a release of prisoners on hunger strike arguing that it would be 'in the national interest'. He emphasised that female hunger strikers were in danger of death. He himself had never seen a prisoner on hunger strike and he was 'not sure whether a doctor can say when, after a certain period, they are likely to die'.[337] McCartan was, Ferriter states, 'a very reluctant voter for the Treaty'.[338] In the chamber, McCartan referred to the death of Terence MacSwiney; it had 'created a sentiment in the country that it would take some time to get over'. He argued that the war was over: 'We may have a blaze up here and there, but on the whole it is safe to say that it is over, that the Government is in a secure position, that they are the victors, and, being the victors, they can afford to be generous.'[339] Referring to Mary's arrest earlier in April when she was released immediately he stated: 'I cannot see why Miss MacSwiney, who has been very active, was let out as being of no military importance. Why should she have been let out while three women who have not been as active as she was, are allowed to die.'[340] Patrick Hogan by contrast argued that women on hunger strike were part of the republican 'conspiracy' and urged that they should not be released 'because they were adhering to some ideal that they all admired'.[341] Hogan continued:

> There was no analogy whatever between the case of the late Terence MacSwiney and the present case. They heard a lot of talk about the self-respect of people who went on hunger-strike, but he asked those who talked about that to think also of the self-respect of the country.[342]

There were those like Johnson of the Labour Party who drew attention to the fact that the women on strike had not been tried and charged; 'in the absence of any recognition of the ordinary process of law – these women protested in the only way in which it was possible for them to protest'. However, he argued that the form undertaking not to act against the government should be given to them to sign immediately on arrest because as the hunger strike continued the 'mind of these people was unhinged'.[343] O'Higgins pressed the need for strong centralised authority and stated that he had 'no doubt' that the release of Mary in November was 'in the minds of those women who were now on hunger strike'; he did not want to create any further precedents.[344] Cosgrave meanwhile wrote to the Archbishop of Dublin that the 'more serious opposition' to the new state 'comes from the women who apparently are a law to themselves'. Real success in defeating the anti-Treaty side did not occur, he contended, until 'particular attention was directed to women who operated with impunity in every possible way'.[345]

When the debate resumed on 25 April, Darrell Figgis stated that he had not agreed with Terence's hunger strike and 'did not agree with that type of action now'. However, he did believe that some prisoners were in jail on insufficient charges. Costello, he noted was held for possession of *Poblacht na hEireann*, a publication which was not prohibited.[346] O'Higgins again referred to the precedent created by the release of Mary in November. The government, he stated, had been 'taunted' by that action:

> Deputy Miss Mary MacSwiney was given back her life once, and it may be felt that in a way that was due to her family, that a life was owed and she was given back her life, and she has simply proceeded to exhort young people of both sexes throughout the country to continue to fling themselves at the new born State, to drag it down, and to continue to wage a campaign of criminal methods, and now she is in jail again.[347]

The government, as Ferriter discusses, 'gendered the idea of hunger strike'. Women used it as a weapon according to this construction, 'inflicting on themselves the hurt they could not inflict on a man'.[348] McCartan attempted to find a compromise; he withdrew his original motion in favour of the following: 'That, in the opinion of the Dáil, prisoners who decide after the passing of this Resolution, to go on hunger-strike to secure release, should be allowed to take the full consequences of their act.'[349] However, 'rules of order' around what was deemed a new motion rather than an amendment forced McCartan to withdraw his proposal.[350] The republican propaganda sheet, *Éire*, however, continued to draw attention to brutality against incarcerated women. Despard maintained a vigil outside the jail, making arrangements to have 'her bed brought to the prison gates'.[351] However, the *Irish Independent* noted that by 24 April she had left and not returned and certainly there was not the same visible outpouring of support for the striking women as had been during Mary's November imprisonment.[352]

As in November, Mary began correspondence with the Archbishop of Dublin. She requested 'the Privilege which is my right as a faithful daughter of the Catholic church of having Holy Communion brought to my cell'. The issue of confession, she informed him, 'need not arise for some time, unless and until I am brought to the point of death'. She would, she stated, 'answer no political questions from any priest'.[353] On 26 April Nellie Ryan and Annie O'Neill were released in 'grave danger of death'.[354] Gonne and Costello were released in the days that followed. On 28 April Mary was reported as 'weak and inclined to faintness' but refused the attendance of the prison doctor.[355] By the evening of 30 April she was the only female prisoner on hunger strike not released.[356] In later years she referred to this period as 'one of the most horrible memories of my life'. She commended her fellow prisoners for opposing the move from Kilmainham to the North Dublin Union that would leave her at the mercy of her gaolers.[357] Macardle depicted the female inmates as attempting to passively resit their removal by pressing themselves against the railings, forming a human shield of defiance. She depicted the barrage of violence that ensued as women were 'struck', 'pulled downstairs' and 'kicked' in a 'violent' attack.[358] That Mary's fellow inmates determined that to leave her 'alone in the empty jail … was unthinkable' shows her standing amongst republican women.[359] At 6 pm on the following day she was 'removed in a state of collapse' to a private nursing home at 62 Eccles Street having endured a 19-day hunger strike.[360] A bad night's sleep led to her being 'in an almost unconscious condition' on the morning of 2 May.[361]

On 3 May the Dáil passed a resolution that a prisoner being on hunger strike should 'not affect the merits of the question of his detention or release'.[362] From that point warning had been given to republicans that they would be allowed to face the consequences of their decision to hunger strike. The *Belfast Newsletter* discussed what it believed was the weakness of the resolution with reference to the events in Brixton in 1920:

> The only way to draw the hunger-strikers bluff is to let the hunger-striker expire, as the British did with MacSwiney. That effectively knocked hunger-striking on the head at the time, and if some other enthusiasts are permitted to famish themselves into Glasnevin it will be knocked on the head again.
>
> No amount of shouting 'we are going to let you die', whether by the Government or by the Chamber of Deputies, can do the slightest good, because the hunger-strikers will say: 'they are bluffing,' and continue to hunger strike.[363]

The paper did believe that the resolution would mitigate public sympathy for those in the Irish Free State jails. However, the editorial continued: 'Whether the Government is right in fearing as it obviously does fear, that Miss MacSwiney and Madame Gonne MacBride will be able to make hunger-striking fashionable is another question.'[364]

Following her release Mary spent a few days recuperating by the sea in Bray, telling de Valera that she was out of bed much quicker than after her November strike.[365] She was 'starving for news the why and the wherefore of the latest moves'.[366] She was anxious to get fully involved once again in the political fray: 'I think all my friends have come to the conclusion that I was so bad that I should get no news or letters of any kind, but that was not the way to cure me.'[367] On 15 of May she was back in Dublin and desired to 'report for work immediately' although she was under doctor's orders to rest when she felt fatigued and not 'continue to the point of exhaustion'. She requested guidelines from de Valera as to her work in Suffolk Street.[368] Despite such apparent recognition of his leadership, Mary began to conduct an increasingly fractious correspondence with him around the ceasefire on 24 May and the future direction of republican politics.

Chapter Eight

Disillusionment: 1923–26

Despite the cease fire of 24 May 1923 there were over 100,000 prisoners in the Irish Free State's jails.[1] As McConville discusses, the ceasefire was not an unconditional surrender and even if such had been agreed, 'there would have been no immediate opening of the prison gates'. Security concerns dictated the pace of releases.[2] The issue of imprisonment and hunger striking was still a factor in Mary MacSwiney's life in the immediate aftermath of the cessation of the conflict. In November 1923 Seán MacSwiney was arrested in Kerry and participated in the hunger strike that began across Irish jails in October. Kissane notes that at the end of war civilian leaders were dominant on both sides.[3] De Valera, however, was on the run, following the raid at the republican conference in April which led to the death of Liam Lynch. He was arrested on 15 August 1923 on an election platform in Ennis, Co. Clare, and not released until 16 July 1924. In his absence Mary assumed the effective, if not the nominal, leadership of Sinn Féin. De Valera's imprisonment allowed her to pursue her stalwart belief in parliamentary abstentionism and non-engagement with the institutions of the Irish Free State with no strong oppositional or questioning voice within the anti-Treaty side, although as Richard Dunphy notes of de Valera: '... mediating between the various Sinn Féin factions, [he] did much to sustain the myth of the "existing republic".'[4]

De Valera's imprisonment did, however, deflect from Mary's growing political isolation, a fact that would become fully apparent after 1926 when he established Fianna Fáil. That the civil war concluded without a negotiated settlement facilitated Mary in her arguments that the conflict could recommence. Yet by 1923 she was increasingly seen as a political irrelevance as the state established in 1922 garnered the support of most of the Irish population. Her unwillingness to accept the political status quo and to compromise meant that she was viewed as ever more strident and vitriolic. At an anti-Treaty election meeting in Wicklow in August 1923 in support of the candidacy of Robert Barton she was subjected to 'considerable heckling'.[5] Her ideological commitment to the Second Dáil and her repeated statements that no one had the right to vote the republic out of existence had progressively limited political currency. Similarly, with her assertions that the ceasefire was temporary, and that the IRA could and would recommence the war for the republic. Her political elision became particularly evident when de Valera was released and began to move towards establishing a *modus vivendi* with the new state to allow him to participate within its political framework. Mary continued to argue, as she did in Battersea Town Hall in London in April 1924, that 'majority rule did not extend to the sovereignty of the nation'.[6]

In late May 1923 Margaret Collins-O'Driscoll denounced Mary for questioning the political sincerity of her brother, Michael Collins. Mary inferred that the latter had duped the pro-Treaty side when he declared that there would be no oath in the constitution. A faithful adherence to the Pact election criteria would, she argued, have allowed Collins to 'prove his sincerity' and would have facilitated the drawing up of constitution that would have spared the country the horror of the civil war.[7] Collins-O'Driscoll was, of course, a woman who, like Mary, had suffered the trauma of family loss during the violence and brutality of the revolutionary period. She issued a rejoinder to Mary that laid bare the latter's insensitivity on a human level:

> Miss Mary MacSwiney prides herself on her superior virtues, and then proceeds as she had so often done before, to slander my late brother, General Collins, foully slain in his early manhood. Honesty she tells us is the best policy. Had she discovered this on Jan 7 1922 she would not have spent the intervening time as one of the junta who levied war on the Irish people.[8]

Collins-O'Driscoll inferred the political irrelevance of those on the republican side. People were, she stated, 'trying to forget the Stacks, the de Valeras and the Miss MacSwineys'.[9] Collins-O'Driscoll attested to the success of the state that was formed under the Anglo-Irish Treaty of 1921:

> I wonder has it ever occurred to you to ask yourself where would the 'Independent' [the newspaper] be if Miss MacSwiney and de Valera won. I am sure you pretty well realise what the position of the Irish people would have been in that now, happily unlikely contingency.[10]

In the weeks leading up to the ceasefire Mary repeatedly stated that those who did not agree to surrender in 1923 would be 'entitled' to act as they did in 1921–22 against those who accepted the Treaty.[11] De Valera, by contrast, recognised the political realities of military defeat writing on 16 May that it 'may be necessary very soon to change the defence of our national Independence from the plane of arms to that of unarmed effort'.[12] To the republican priest, Thomas Burbage, he wrote:

> From 1916 on Sinn Féin was a very different movement from what it had been before. There is no reason why it should not take on now also a slightly different character to accord with the new phase of the national struggle. Methods to be effective must change with the conditions in which they have to operate ... If any time is lost we shall lose the tide.[13]

This need to adapt to changing political circumstances was not something Mary understood, or at least not something she was willing to countenance; she was an ideologue rather than a politician. To compromise on the Republic would render Terence's 'awful agony' a 'farce'.[14] Speaking in Dundalk in August in support of the candidature of Frank Aiken, she recalled that her last visit to the town was when her brother was imprisoned there, continuing: 'its people were as true to the Republic now as then'.[15] Eoin MacNeill speaking in Clare in the lead up to the 1923 election recognised the growing political tension between Mary and de Valera over the issue of compromise. Republicans, he stated:

> who were seeking to govern the country now were not able to govern an infant school. They were not able to govern themselves. They were as divided as they possibly could be. There

> was Mary MacSwiney and her party, de Valera and his party, and nobody knew who was the real leader.[16]

Cosgrave, speaking in Carlow on 19 August, also alluded to the ideological split that was emerging between the two:

> De Valera is saying now he never stood for destruction. During the last twelve months he never told you that. He has seen the evil of his ways after the hammer blows from the nation. It is a remarkable improvement, and I expect Miss MacSwiney will follow as soon as her temperature goes down.[17]

The republican side also referred to perceptions of a split Mary and de Valera as early as March 1923. This was in the context of de Valera's consideration of peace overtures the previous month. *Éire* sought to minimise the impact of perceptions of conceptual differences within the anti-Treaty ranks:

> The British agents in Ireland are now making all the propaganda they can out of the supposed contrast between the moderation of President de Valera and the strong expression of opinion of Miss Mary MacSwiney ... Whatever differences in opinion amongst Republicans may be spied on, pried into, and betrayed to the public in the pro-British Press ... there is no breach of Republican unity, and there will be none.[18]

Mary did not countenance defeat, despite the declaration of the ceasefire. At a meeting of the Women's Prisoners' Defence League after the ceasefire she declared that the dumping of arms did not mean surrender. That could not occur while any vestige of British authority remained in Ireland.[19] In Kilkenny she stated that republican men 'were getting ready to fight again' and would do so if the people 'attempted to turn down the Irish Republic'. The people had, she asserted, no right to such a course of action..[20] The reality was that from its inception the Irish Free State doggedly solidified its institutions and structures of power. Cumann na nGaedheal's election campaign in 1923 drew the attention of voters to 'the enactment of the constitution, the implementation of universal adult suffrage, the formation of state departments and the establishment of law and order'.[21] Mary, unlike de Valera, was not aligned with the mood of the country. Lil Conlon wrote that after the success of the National Army in taking Cork from the irregulars in August 1922, the latter: 'were forced to admit that the majority of the people were not cooperative and that food and shelter were not forthcoming spontaneously. The Nation wanted to live its own life now.'[22]

Mary and de Valera were on fundamentally different political paths after the ceasefire. At the Kilkenny meeting in June, she declared that the republic was not beaten and would not be 'while Ireland lives'.[23] While this was clearly rhetoric it can still be compared with de Valera's ceasefire message which stated that: 'Military victory must be allowed to rest for the moment with those who have destroyed the Republic'.[24] Moreover, in a letter to her, de Valera stated that the republican government had 'not been functioning and cannot function'.[25] In a later letter he made clear that he was willing to consider ending parliamentary abstention if the oath were removed.[26] Just over a week later de Valera was arrested and Mary assumed the effective leadership within Sinn Féin. This allowed her uncompromising stance to become party rhetoric during his incarceration. The outright breach between the two was temporarily delayed.

On 17 June de Valera announced that the 'general re-organisation of Sinn Fein will be promoted by organisation for a special purpose, such as for the elections'.[27] A conference in the Mansion House in this month marked the establishment of the third Sinn Féin party.[28] Despite tensions between the two, Mary was appointed director of election propaganda. In this role she was tasked with the production and distribution of campaign literature with a particular emphasis on the provision of a 'small election handbook for speakers and canvassers'. The position also involved the holding of public meetings and the personal canvas of voters. Brass bands were to be provided to create a rousing atmosphere.[29] De Valera, however, oscillated on the efficacy of running official republican candidates in the election.[30] Unlike Mary, he was moving towards a pragmatic acceptance of the reality of civil war defeat. For her, the war was merely suspended.

Despite de Valera's prevarication, Sinn Féin launched its election campaign at a meeting in the Mansion House on 17 July. The *Belfast Newsletter* caustically noted that Mary spoke for two hours.[31] Indeed, throughout the 1923 election campaign sneering allusions were made to the length of her speech on the Treaty. At a Cumann na nGaedheal meeting in Ballina on 22 July Charles Bewley, B. L., jeered that 'Miss MacSwiney thought the Republic would be won when she delivered a few hundred more speeches'.[32] In the lead up to the August election, Mary continued to address meetings emphasising the robustness of the republic. In Limerick, she stated that republicans did not want to renew the war but that hinged on removing any reference to the English monarch from the Irish constitution. The Irish people must then, she continued, vote against any person who was willing to take an oath of allegiance.[33] Annie engaged in similar rhetoric. Speaking in Mullingar she stated that 'the rifle would again have to be used' if the 'standard-bearers of Sinn Féin were not placed at the head of the polls'.[34] Although as Farrell states, the election campaign was 'remarkable quiet' despite its 'close proximity to the Civil War', Mary was subjected at times to the threat of violence.[35] At a meeting in Limerick in late July a Crossley tender driven by a National Army soldier carrying four men in civilian clothes attempted to gain passage through the crowd as she spoke. She told her listeners to hold firm and the 'car retired amidst cheers and hisses'.[36] In August she was heckled as she spoke in Castlebar.[37]

There were, however, meetings in which her republican standing still drew the admiration of the crowd. On the 19 June she addressed a republican audience in the Theatre Royal in Waterford. The present government, she stated, must not be allowed to return to power. Paraphrasing her speech, the *Freeman's Journal* noted that she stated that she was 'not out to preach a hymn of hate or vengeance, but it was necessary to realise that the old enemy was still the enemy'.[38] Sinn Féin was, she stated, preparing its election programme and she called for subscriptions.[39] A concert in aid of the prisoners' dependents held in conjunction with her address was, the *Waterford News and Star* reported, so successful that admission had to be refused when the crowd reached capacity. When she came on stage, the paper declared that the audience:

> rose in their seats and cheered like mad for several minutes. From the body of the theatre a

young girl approached the stage and presented to 'the greatest woman in Ireland' an artistic bouquet tied with the Tricolour ribbons.[40]

Mary argued that she had a 'truly democratic heart' but 'she did not grant the right of any majority to give away the independence of the country'. Cheers greeted this statement at the meeting in Waterford.[41] Although on leaving the theatre, she was 'cheered to the echo on the Mall by the large crowds who followed her to her hotel', her speech showed her lack of forward-thinking marking her out from de Valera in this period. Her speech was an apologia for republican decisions from late 1921 as the Treaty was debated and during the civil war. The sneers of the *Belfast Newsletter* later in June illustrated distaste for her based not just on her politics but on her enunciation of the extreme republican position as a woman. No republican man would have been caricatured as the paper did MacSwiney, who was described as falling on those she disagreed with 'with every tooth bared, drops of clotted venom suspended from every outstretched fang'. Such gendered criticism notwithstanding, the editorial did grasp the stagnancy of her political position:

> Miss Mary MacSwiney is still quivering in England's grasp, the powers that be having wisely decided to let her do her quivering in public. The air continues to throb with her tedious litany of wrongs, ancient and modern.[42]

Mary's focus was on the past. De Valera, while similarly publicly committed in this period to the principle of the Second Dáil,[43] was privately looking to extricate himself from the barrenness of the anti-Treaty position. Repeatedly stating that she denied 'the right of majority to give away independence' was a failure to engage with real politick. The Irish Free State was in existence and was supported by most of the Irish people. George William Russell in the *Irish Statesman* wrote of Sinn Féin in December 1923:

> To boast itself, in Miss MacSwiney's phrase, 'the minority eternal' is simply to proclaim its political bankruptcy, for the only alternative it has to offer is so abhorrent as to make the worst mistakes of the Free State appear sound statesmanship by comparison.[44]

Russell allowed Mary a right of response in the 22 December edition of the paper. She accused him of failing to understand the republican position. Underneath her article he inserted his reply:

> No doubt the character of many of Miss MacSwiney's friends has been strengthened by the sacrifices they have made for their ideals. Let them display that character in fields where there is so much to be done, and their cause will gain immeasurably more than if they blew up a thousand houses and bridges, or endured not one month's hunger-strike, but went on even to death.[45]

Russell's comments underscore the way Mary's political position was increasingly anachronistic in the period after the civil war. Richard Mulcahy made a similar point during the election campaign. Indeed, he cited aspects of Terence MacSwiney's political life other than his hunger strike to argue the need for constructive civic duty to allow Irish society to thrive and develop:

> Terence MacSwiney went standing erect as Lord Mayor of Cork doing his civic work without a revolver because he knew it was necessary that civic work should be done ... he knew he had to show in his high example that the sovereignty of the people had to be worked out sitting at a desk at work with the brains and not the wild words or the pulling of triggers.[46]

For Mary, however, the Republic was not an empty symbol. Irish life and culture would, she contended, flourish holistically only within such a polity. Failing to find a pair of Balbriggan stockings in a particular Dublin shop, she concluded that the 'Irish-made goods were gone out of fashion'. She claimed that since the acceptance of the Treaty the 'Irish language had suffered'.[47] However, as Ciara Meehan notes, the statute books relating to the early years of state formation are 'a testament to the flurry of activity and progress'. In 1924 alone 62 measures went through the Oireachtas.[48] 'Common Sense' writing in the *Irish Independent* described Mary's electioneering letters as 'purest flapdoodle', adding that she and the Sinn Féin party: 'even if they should ever attain full power, could not give Ireland either a Republic or peace. They can offer nothing but death, destruction, and permanent partition.'[49] When her name was mentioned on 16 August at a meeting in South Dublin held in support of the Cumann na nGaedheal candidate, the crowd called for her to join de Valera in prison.[50]

Mary wanted republicans to work to achieve the best possible election success and advised de Valera as to how she believed this could be affected. On the 9 August she called on him not to put forward Scelig (J. J. O'Kelly) as well as Aiken as candidates in Louth. The latter's feelings were unimportant, she declared, when weighted against the reality of splitting the vote and losing the seat. She was aware that in the period preceding the election de Valera was renegotiating his position on the oath of allegiance and was alert to any opportunity to bring him fully back into the republican fold. She stated that she could not 'in any circumstances' take her seat after the election 'unless at least it was made the Third Dáil by the inclusion of S. O'Mahony'. Seán O'Mahony had been elected in 1918 and 1920 for Fermanagh and Tyrone. In 1920 the latter constituency was within the purview of the Northern Irish parliament making him the only member of the Second Dáil who was not elected to the southern assembly. The roll for the Third Dáil should also include, Mary unrealistically declared, the second seat de Valera won in 1920 for Down.[51] If she stood for election and then 'made a fuss about that after, in the event of the mere removal of the oath, where would we be'. Recognising, and trying to close the ideological gap emerging between the two of them, she remonstrated with him: 'For Heaven's sake don't start talking of strait jackets again. I am and intend to remain in the strait jacket of the Republic and non partition. No one asks you to get out of it. I want your advice as to the least harmful moment of making that clear now or after the elections.'[52] In Naas on 8 August, she declared that she was happy to 'be an extremist and will be most extreme of the extreme until the Irish Republic is definitely established'.[53]

In the weeks preceding the election Mary discussed the issue of partition in a degree of detail. She believed that de Valera's 'recent pronouncements' had facilitated certain political shifts. She laid out the different approaches Sinn Féin might take after the election:

> ... if the oath were removed either with England's consent, or without it, as a result of the coming election, the Republican deputies would take their seats in the Parliament and work

> inside for the social reform – the amendment or repudiation of the Treaty – the Gaelicisation of Ireland.[54]

The situation of Ulster would be resolved, she continued, by a 'systematic boycott'. She also posited a vague alternative solution that paid no attention to the political reality of the existence of Northern Irish state. She referred to paying salaries to 'higher officials' and instigating 'social reforms' so that most of the population of the 'disaffected Counties' would desire inclusion.[55] She stated that 'much good … can be done like that'. However, her position was that if Republican deputies entered the Dáil on basis of the removal of the oath, that would 'be a political acceptance of Partition'. In early 1924 she announced that Craig and his government were 'Irishmen whether they like or not'. If they wanted to be British they should, she declared, 'go across the Channel'.[56] Moreover, until the position of the Governor General was eliminated, entry to the assembly would mean 'inclusion in the British Empire … [and] many other things which I couldn't accept':

> I see with the President immense possibilities in such a course as I saw immense possibilities in Arthur Griffith's Sinn Féin. But I could not follow the President into such a Parliament any more than I was able as a complete separatist to join Arthur Griffith's Sinn Fein.[57]

Regarding the Governor General, she noted his £40,000 a year salary while the 'Irish people were starving'.[58] She recalled that she had offered to go to America rather than expose divisions within the republican ranks by dropping 'out of things here' or by 'making a statement'. However, she was 'urged' to 'stay and help'. She enclosed a separate sheet in this letter laying out the terms under which it would be possible for her to contest the upcoming election. Republic candidates had to be understood to be standing for election to the government of the republic not the parliament of the Irish Free State. The oath of allegiance had to be abolished and republican candidates successful as candidates in the northern Irish state had to be invited to take their seats in the new republican parliament.[59]

During the election campaign Mary was repeatedly namechecked by members of Cumann na nGaelheal. The tone was scornful and disparaging. O'Higgins described her as 'cooing to the people of Cork'.[60] During the second reading of the Public Safety Bill in the Senate on 26 July, Sir Hutcheson Poe described her as de Valera's 'valiant henchman'.[61] In Thurles Eoin MacNeill pointed out that the republicans 'could claim the moon, but even if Miss MacSwiney were President they could not annex it'.[62] The *Freeman's Journal* referred to her repeating 'her well-known declarations about the Republic' at a meeting in Dun Laoghaire on 7 August.[63] Her message was increasingly one-dimensional and divorced from the prevailing political realities consequent on the end of the civil war. A letter to the editor of the *Irish Independent*, on 11 August from a self-declared republican summed up the way her position was becoming politically anachronous: 'As Miss MacSwiney's words can have no effect on the official Free Staters, and as she knows this, who is she aiming to influence, I would ask.'[64] However, the fact that Mary's name was mentioned by leading politicians in Cumann na nGaedheal during the election campaign indicates that she was still considered to have the potential to destabilise the new state. In Tipperary in August Cosgrave clearly stated that she would have to 'obey the laws of this country, or will leave it or go to jail'.[65] This statement came in a speech which denigrated the activism of republican women and showed Cosgrave's adherence to the ideology of separate spheres; a woman's role was, in his view, within the home as wife and mother:

> Some of you women ought to have your Rosaries in your hands, and others are so young that they ought to be at home knitting. Most of these women are unmarried, and I think for good reason. They have some grudge against mankind and are useless for anything but shouting.[66]

Mary was increasingly the *bête noire* of those on pro-Treaty side and in their employ. Her anti-state profile was enhanced by her gender. When Una Tutty's newspaper shop at 10 High Street, Dublin, was raided in November 1923, the National Army soldiers 'used insulting language about the Republican leaders, and Miss MacSwiney in particular'.[67] She drew the ire of suffragist and pacifist, Louie Bennett. Referring to the 'foreign policy of the Republican Party', she wrote:

> It would appear if Miss MacSwiney voices the views of her party, that they hope for the complete ruin of Germany, the domination of Europe by France and the consequent embarrassment of England. France is to be regarded as Ireland's friend. This is a terrible point of view for any Irishman or woman to put forward, and it is one which every sympathiser with republican principles in the Labour movement ought to repudiate.

Ireland, Bennett stated, needed to recognise the suffering of the German people under the French occupation of the Ruhr, the burden of which had fallen on the workers.[68] Bennett's internationalist approach to politics underscored the increasing insular and island-centred approach of Mary.

During the protracted announcement of parliamentary candidates by the different parties in 1923, a rumour circulated that Mary would stand as a candidate for Carlow-Kilkenny, the constituency in which Cosgrave was seeking re-election.[69] In Cork where she did stand, the election day was marred by the arrest of all working in the Central Ward Sinn Féin Cumann by eight armed men in plain clothes who appeared two hours before the close of the poll. The arrest was based on an allegation of election impersonation. A similar incident occurred in An Grianan in the centre of the Cork city where several girls were involved in catering for election workers. Mary immediately penned a letter to the *Cork Examiner* declaring: 'This is a queer notion of a "free" "normal" election'.[70]

Mary was victorious, claiming one of the 44 seats won by the Sinn Féin party. She was one of only seven women to stand for election. Caitlín Brugha, Lynn and Markievicz were also successful for the party, but Kate O'Callaghan lost her seat. Agnes O'Farrelly standing as an independent for the National University constituency also failed to be elected. Margaret Collins-O'Driscoll was elected in Dublin North for Cumann na nGaedheal. A group of independent women led by the Hon. Mrs Noel Guinness who were to have contested seats in Dublin withdrew at the last minute, as did Mrs Powell, another sister of Michael Collins who was to stand in Cork. She declared that she was not strong enough to do so. Also in Cork, Mrs Mary Lynch, an unofficial candidate in support of the Irish Free State arrived at the sheriff's office with her papers past the deadline and her application to stand was rejected.[71] In Cork City J. J. Walsh topped the poll for Cumann na nGaedheal. The *Irish Independent*, however, noted that many voters who gave Walsh first preference gave second to Mary and vice versa.[72] However, Walsh polled higher than Mary by nearly three to one.[73] Indeed, the *Belfast Newsletter* was determined to make clear that she was only finally declared elected on the tenth count, 'several counts and eliminations being necessary before she reached the quota'.[74]

The 1923 election resulted in an increase in the percentage of the vote for Sinn Féin from 21.5 per cent in 1922 to 27.6 on the 27 August 1923.[75] The anti-Treaty side held a demonstration on O'Connell Street on 2 September and pledged to work for the republic on economic lines.[76] On 16 September a 'Grand Republican Victory Concert' was held in the Mansion House, Mary delivering the address during the interval. Despite the billing of the concert, she stated that she was disappointed in the election result and urged all to participate in Sinn Féin clubs and to remember that 'the Republic still lived'. She emphasised that the election had not expressed the real will of the people while she continued to urge the release of prisoners.[77] On 18 September pro-Treaty deputies met to take the oath of allegiance. That same day a meeting of 11 anti-Treaty deputies was held at which Mary was present. This resulted in the issuing of statement against continued imprisonments and the 'barrier of the oath'. From this point the republican deputies met once a month.[78] Closer to home news reached the family of the earthquake in Japan and the death of four nuns in the community to which Sister Frances Xavier – Kit MacSwiney – belonged. She, however, was declared safe.[79]

At the Sinn Féin Ard Fheis in October Mary presided in the absence of de Valera and P. J. Ruttledge. In proposing her, Lynn stated that 'she felt strongly' that Mary was 'the person who would most nobly fill the position'.[80] By this date party branches had grown to 729 from 65 at the end of July.[81] Mary was elected to the role of vice president of the party in company with Lynn, Father O'Flanagan and Ruttledge.[82] In her address she referred to the absence of 'our beloved President'. There was nobody, she declared, 'but Eamon de Valera himself who can fill the position of Eamon de Valera'.[83] However, his imprisonment allowed her to, in the words of Fallon, wield 'the gavel with dexterity and authority, frequently ruling members out of order and then giving herself the final word on an issue'. She was enabled to 'set the movement back on course', de Valera, as she saw it, having deviated from the republican path in the months prior to his arrest.[84] She stated that the proceedings of the Ard Fheis would 'delight' de Valera but also emphasised that the gathering 'showed the continuity of the Irish Republic proclaimed in 1916, and established in 1919 by the free and unfettered votes of the people of Ireland'.[85] However, it is important to note the bedrock of friendship between Mary and de Valera that still existed. While she did not understand, and feared, his potential for political pragmatism, she respected him as the President and believed that he would see that her course was that of the true republican, which she still considered him to be despite his vacillations. Of course in this she was blinkered but de Valera's ultimate betrayal, as she saw it when he split with Sinn Féin in 1926, was some years away. On the same day, the party Ard Fheis opened the funeral procession of Noel Lemass made its way from the pro-Cathedral in Dublin to Glasnevin Cemetery. Lemass, an intelligence officer for the anti-Treaty side during the civil war, had been kidnapped on 3 July; his skeleton was found in the Dublin mountains on 12 October in a badly beaten state. That such events occurred after the cessation of the war caused 'controversy'.[86] Mary and Maud Gonne headed the 'hundreds of women and girls' who walked in the procession.[87]

At the Ard Fheis delegates agreed that the 25 October, the anniversary of Terence's death, would be observed as a fast day by republicans.[88] This decision was taken against the backdrop of the announcement of a general hunger strike to enforce the demand for unconditional release.[89] Frustration was mounting within the prisons and camps at continued incarceration despite the almost six months that had elapsed since the ceasefire. Allegations were made concerning the degrading conditions experienced by prisoners including beatings, kickings and hosings.[90] The strike, for unconditional release, began in Mountjoy on 14 October and spread to other prisons and internment camps. Mary called for the rosary to be said nightly while the protest continued. She also suggested that everyone should abstain from alcohol for the duration of the strike and to limit cigarettes. Such measures, as well as acting as a show of solidarity, would, she asserted, have a detrimental impact on the Free State economy.[91] On 18 October the government removed 80 men from Mountjoy to the Curragh camp. These were prisoners who were not on strike and according to the republican side they were removed so that they would not be able to nurse those that were. Later that day another 80 men were transferred. Republican women remained outside the jail singing hymns and reciting the rosary. On 19 October in anticipation of further removal of prisoners, Mary headed a group of women who assembled outside the prison carrying parcels of clothing. The women proceeded to kneel in front of 14 lorries carrying 'a strong force of fully armed Free Staters'.[92] On 25 October the government announced that there would be no release of prisoners on hunger strike. Sixty women in the North Dublin Union had joined the strike by this date.[93]

On 22 November Seán MacSwiney was arrested at Kerry Pike in Co. Cork.[94] From Cork Prison he was sent to Newbridge internment camp.[95] As expected, he joined the hunger strike. Yet again Mary was faced with the agonising vista of familial suffering and potential death. As his siblings before him, it was expected that Seán would carry the strike to the point of death. The prisoners' statement issued in Mountjoy on 15 October echoed the words of Terence during his trial in Cork in August 1920: there was no option 'left to the prisoners but to get out of jail alive or dead'.[96] When the strike came to an end on 23 November, Lynn recorded in her diary: 'Sean MacSwiney even off H. Strike'.[97]

Mary was immersed in the discourse of death and sacrifice once again when Seán was arrested. Lynn recorded in her diary on 20 November that she was 'v. distressed'.[98] As McConville states, starvation was 'an extended mental and physical ordeal of the most testing kind'.[99] That mental torment was experienced at one remove by family members. Moreover, Mary found herself dealing with many of the same responses from the government and the Catholic church in November 1923 as she had when she was on hunger strike in Mountjoy in 1922 and in Kilmainham in April 1923. While the Catholic church was less vehement in denouncing Terence's hunger strike in Brixton in 1920, the Irish Free State government appeared in 1923 to be acting as the British government had then in denying familial rights and in allowing strikers to die. Although by the time of Seán's arrest many hunger strikers had dropped off, Mary's fear of the fatality of another sibling was augmented by the deaths of prisoners in later November. On 20 November Denis Barry, commandant of the Cork No. 1 Brigade, died in the Curragh military hospital having been transferred from Newbridge Internment centre. One day after Seán was arrested, Andrew O'Sullivan, another Cork man, died in Mountjoy jail. Earlier, on 18 November, Mary addressed what was billed as a Sinn Féin 'monster demonstration' at

College Green, Dublin.[100] She stated that the government would bear responsibility should any of the prisoners die.[101]

Although McConville states that the Catholic church 'softened its line' vis-à-vis the withholding of the sacraments to striking men and women during the general hunger strike and even though the prison authorities allowed letters and parcels, for Mary the optics appeared very similar to Brixton in 1920 and Mountjoy and Kilmainham during the civil war.[102] The government initially refused to release Barry's body to the family in Cork, fearful that the funeral procession would encourage those still on hunger strike to continue. Following High Court action by the family, the body was released and due for burial in late November. Bishop Cohalan of Cork, however, refused to grant him a Christian burial because of his actions during the civil war. Priests in the dioceses were not permitted to officiate at the funeral.[103] Barry's body was taken to the Headquarters of Sinn Féin at 56 Grand Parade, Cork, and from there to the Republican plot in St Finbarr's cemetery on the 28 November.[104] Mary gave a 'brief' oration while Annie recited the rosary in Irish.[105] Ruttledge's letter of condolence to the Barry family stated that it was 'a fitting coincidence that he who collaborated so tirelessly and so fearlessly with Terence MacSwiney ... should show a like determination and fidelity in upholding their common ideas unto death'.[106] In her graveside address Mary also referred to her brother. She could not 'but remember', she stated, standing in the same place three years ago when Terence was buried. Barry, she told the crowd, 'died in the same cause and the same manner as Terence MacSwiney had died'. However, she continued, at the latter's burial three archbishops, five bishops and hundreds of clergy were in attendance; '[w]hat was right three years ago was not wrong to-day'.[107]

Cohalan denounced republicanism as a 'wicked and insidious attack on the church'.[108] On 28 November, he issued a statement to the *Cork Examiner* explaining his refusal to allow a Christian burial. He was, he stated, 'but enforcing the law of the Church'. Cohalan made explicit reference to Mary in his statement, an indication of the deterioration of the relationship between the family and the hierarchy in the years since Terence's death. Cohalan had officiated at the latter's funeral in Cork; in November 1923 he excoriated Mary, denying her personal political agency, and distorting, and even eliding, her history of republican activism before 1920. He suggested that she had become unhinged by the trauma of her brother's death:

> There are persons who had not been Republicans at all, whose plans had miscarried, who had suffered a serious loss in the miscarriage of their plans: and who then discovered in themselves the theory that they had always been the most extreme of the extremes. The most outstanding example of this class is Miss MacSwiney. She was not a Republican at all in 1916. She prevented the call from Dublin for a rising to reach the Volunteers of Cork. She denounced the rebellion. Later, she gambled on the life of Terry.

Cohalan indicted Mary for encouraging her brother to continue his hunger strike. He claimed that she believed he would be released and that 'she would share in a sunburst of cheap glory'.[109] The later statement was particularly cruel and, indeed, showed a failure to understand that none of the MacSwiney family sought personal glory through politics. Accusing the *Cork Examiner* of publishing 'slanderous and libeilous [sic]' statements about her, Mary responded immediately to Cohalan. She noted that despite the 'unity of Doctrine, and unity of interpretation of that doctrine, regardless of time or space', O'Sullivan who died on hunger strike in the same period as Barry was accorded Christian services in Dublin and Mallow.[110]

The bishop's attack touched Mary on a personal as well as a political level. She was determined to force Cohalan to 'substantiate' his allegations, including the charge she had put pressure on the nuns in Clifton convent to hold money taken by republicans from the customs house. She would, she wrote, 'insist on reparations and repudiations as public as the libels'.

She concluded the letter with a rare personal note:

> Might I suggest to his Lordship the propriety at least in using Terence MacSwiney's name in full when he writes of him in future, and of leaving the familiar diminutive to those who loved him, who believed in his sincerity, and in the cause for which he died.[111]

There were those who came to Mary's defence. Seán O' Hegarty declared: 'anybody knowing the man would know that nobody living had the smallest influence upon his decisions, or could turn him from his purpose once his decision was taken'.[112] O'Hegarty chastised the bishop:

> Insinuations about money are very nasty: and there are a great many people … who believe that his Lordship should be very slow to make such, because they feel that the manner in which his Lordship gained possession, of, and still retains the anti-conscription money, here was of very doubtful morality.[113]

Cohalan's verbal assault on Mary, while particularly personal, must, however, be viewed in the context of her much-stated attacks on the hierarchy during the period of the civil war and in its immediate aftermath. The bishop's statement also reflected the increasingly prevailing public belief that she was the one of the leaders of the extreme republican position and had no compunction in advocating a return to the disorder and bloodshed that had engulfed the country for nearly a decade. On 8 December 1922, the day of the executions of Mellows, O'Connor, Barrett and McKelvey, she had written to all members of the Catholic hierarchy. Penning the letter 'as a woman who has been to death's door unafraid for Ireland's right to her untrammelled Freedom', she called on them to declare their position on the executions. If they did not 'openly condemn' the murder of the four men in Mountjoy 'we count you guilty of this blood'.[114] When she met the Papal Envoy, Monsieur Luzio in March 1923, she told him what she felt about the lack of any condemnation by the hierarchy at the execution in December 1922 of the 'Four Court leaders'. Speaking in Dundalk in August 1923 in support of the candidature of Frank Aiken, she recalled that her last visit to the town was when her brother was imprisoned there, continuing: 'its people were as true to the Republic now as then'.[115] She told her audience in Dundalk that she asked Luzio, 'if she had said one word against Catholic doctrine, and he answered unhesitatingly "No".'[116] Her public statements that death through hunger strike was different from death by suicide placed her in an oppositional position to the hierarchy. In a war of liberation, she wrote, there was no difference between death 'on the battlefield, in the prison cell, or on a Kerry roadside'.[117]

Annie was equally willing to denounce the hierarchy. In Blackrock, Co. Dublin, on 14 August 1923 she declared: 'When the history of the recent times in Ireland came to be written, she said, the Bishops of Ireland would have a sorry place. They would take their place beside Dick Mulcahy and the rest of them'.[118] Annie, like Mary, had written to Archbishop Byrne during her two hunger strikes: outside the walls of Mountjoy in November 1922 and in Kilmainham in February 1923. On her ninth day of hunger strike on 21 February she denounced Byrne for telling her to abide by the wishes of the majority when the hierarchy had 'no respect for the will of the majority in 1920 when the whole of Ireland ... [believed in] the Irish Republic'. She denounced the clergy for 'unpardonable attacks' on Republicans:

> When Priests violate the Sanctuary of the Soul by shouting with vindictive satisfaction that we are all going to be damned, we wonder what master they serve, for assuredly, neither in word nor in deed, do they suggest that they have anything in common with the God of Love and Faith. One would think that those who are supposed to be the disciples of Christ crucified for love would feel sorrow at the thought of souls being damned but on the contrary the convulsed fury in their faces would make me think that their disappointment would be keen if we were not damned.[119]

While Catholics were willing to obey the hierarchy in matters of doctrine they would, Annie wrote, 'defy you when you seek to impose the law of England on us and insist that it is the law of God'.[120] The idea that the hierarchy were interfering in the political domain in a partisan fashion suffused the letters and denunciations of both sisters from the 10 October 1922 when the Bishops' Joint Pastoral was issued. Other republicans expressed their hostility to that statement. Anna O'Rahilly wrote to Byrne demanding an answer as to whether he approved of the actions of the priests in Donnybrook in refusing her communion when she went to the altar. She refuted his answer as 'vague & unsatisfactory' and threatened to submit the matter to the Pope.[121] However, the MacSwiney sisters had publicly challenged the actions of the hierarchy while even in their private correspondence they were willing to debate and refute the bishops' position. The personal attack on Mary by Cohalan following Barry's death should be viewed within that context.

Presiding at the meeting of the Sinn Féin executive in the Mansion House on 29 November, Mary delivered an address on Cohalan's refusal to accord Barry a Christian burial.[122] She noted that, in the words of the *Freeman's Journal*, as a 'Catholic exercising her rights she did not believe that horns were going to grow out of her head'.[123] She continued to spar with members of the Catholic church and, likewise, they felt it necessary to respond to her. On 1 December she replied to the Rev. P Casey, curate in Mallow, Co. Cork, who stated that Andrew O'Sullivan received a Christian burial because he had come off his hunger strike two days before his death. He had not, Mary retorted. O'Sullivan had been: 'fed while unconscious, exactly as Mr. Denis Barry was. This can't be called withdrawal. Both were entitled to Christian burial. One only received it.'[124]

Mary's anxiety for Seán on hunger strike and her further altercation with members of the hierarchy and the clergy came at a time when she was suffering a period of ill-health, quite possibly a legacy of her two gruelling civil war hunger strikes. From late October 1923 Lynn recorded instances of her suffering from tiredness and noted that she needed to spend time in bed. On 27 October, she was 'rather gloomy' and her neuritis was 'bad'.[125]

Although the hunger strike was called off within days of Seán's arrest the family continued to suffer harassment from the National Army. Mary had referred during the Treaty debates to the manner in which during the War of Independence women experienced the terror of raids:

> You men that talk need not talk to us about war. It is the women who suffer, it is the women who suffer the most of the hardships that war brings. You can go out in the excitement of the fight and it brings its own honour and its own glory. We have to sit at home and work in more humble ways, we have to endure the agony, the sunshines, the torture of misery and the privations which war brings, the horror of nightly visitations to our houses and their consequences.[126]

Such horrors continued to be visited on Mary; the MacSwiney home was raided yet again in December 1923.[127]

Although Ruttledge was acting head of Sinn Féin during de Valera's imprisonment, Mary's rhetoric dominated. She assumed the titular position as head of the extreme republican position. At a meeting to commemorate O'Connor, Mellows, Barrett and McKelvey in O'Connell Street in December 1923, she stated that while the civil war was over the fight for the Republic would continue in the press and through elections.[128] However, the political context was different after the ceasefire, and most of the Irish population adhered to the mechanisms of law and order and structures of government established by Cumann na nGaedheal. Endeavours were made by Sinn Féin to create an alternative shadow government as had been attempted in the period after the establishment the first Dáil in January 1919. Mary was given the task of leading the educational drive; this was to comprise of a series of lectures to be delivered across the country. She urged that young engage in discussion at the Sinn Féin clubs. She argued that had people been properly educated the Treaty would not have passed.[129] However, her priority was the establishment of the Republic; the type of society that would develop under it could be worked out at a later point. She was willing to jettison discussion on education at the meeting of Comhairle na dTeachtaí, an alternative republican parliament, on 7–8 August 1924. The issue of education was important but:

> I do feel that it is right for me to say now that it ought to be postponed as the President is back to deal with matters of more urgent importance ... I am quite willing to postpone this until later.[130]

This stance reflected Garvin's comments on the republican 'intellectual tradition' in Ireland. He argues that Irish 'insurrectional republicanism is commonly pre-political in character, representing a somewhat unstructured wish for independence, freedom and change from an uncongenial present to a hazily imagined future rather than a highly organised political blueprint'.[131]

C. S. Andrews referred to the 'drama of the shattered Republic' which played out in the headquarters at Suffolk Street. He recalled Bob Brennan reflecting 'the common feeling that the organisation was threshing about aimlessly'.[132] There is a sense that actors in this drama, unable to learn any new lines, expressed the old ones with increasing stridency almost in a bid to shout down the reality of failure. Mary continued to snipe at the way the new state operated under the terms of the Anglo-Irish Treaty. At a Sinn Féin meeting in Dublin concerning the release of prisoners on 18 November 1923 she criticised the reduction in the old age pension and in teachers' salaries:

> People who were not able to feed their own children adequately had to pay for all the high officials while it was sought to take away a meagre pittance from people who were already starving.[133]

In March 1924 a section of the National Army issued an ultimatum calling for an end to demobilisation and to what they alleged was the preferential treatment given to British ex-officers. This led to the resignation of nine TDs including Mulcahy. The army crisis, Mary argued, was the result of the Treaty; those who 'stood for the King in Ireland were now at each other's throats'. Those who initiated the mutiny had never protested republican deaths during the civil war or the imprisonment of de Valera.[134] The Sinn Féin party was increasingly, as Laffan discusses, 'passive', relying on mistakes made by the Free State government rather than initiating any coherent policy of its own.[135] Andrews stated that the:

> mood of Republicanism was entirely introverted, constantly nursing its hate for the Free State administration and its agencies, the army, the police and the civil service. We had neither social nor political intercourse with them.

The lack of a forward-thinking political programme hampered those who rejected the Treaty within both the IRA and Sinn Féin. Referring to the anti-Treaty IRA executive formed in 1922, Peadar O'Donnell, in later life, declared it 'pathetic': 'All it did was oppose the Treaty it had no policy of its own'.[136]

Mary continued in this negative vein, denouncing, for example, the Tailteann games first introduced in 1924. They could not be a success she argued because 'Aonach Tailteann belonged to a free and united Ireland'.[137] The games were, Mike Cronin states, one of a series of events organised by the new state 'in an attempt to project a fresh and positive self-image'. The government, however, realised that those on the anti-Treaty side would 'not be won over by such events of national unity'. The concern was to show those who had accepted the Treaty 'the positive attributes of the new state', to showcase the 'reality and image of a successful and vibrant independent country'.[138] By contrast with this desire to project a forward image of a developing state, the discourse of those on the anti-Treaty side was defensive and backward-looking. Beginning on 5 January 1924 Mary published a series of weekly articles in *Sinn Féin* entitled 'The Prophecies', outlining a litany of the 'broken promises' of government politicians on how the Treaty would function.[139] The articles involved a partisan dissection of the events of the past; her conclusion was that republicans could not have acted otherwise in rejecting the Treaty:

> All the abuse so plentifully and unjustly lavished on republicans will not alter facts. If we had the time all over again and a vision at the time of voting of all the sorrow that resulted multiplied a hundred fold, those who really believed in the freedom and the HONOUR of our Nation could not and would not have voted for the Treaty.[140]

On a more personal level, Mary exemplified the Sinn Féin party abstentionist and introverted focus in the period immediately after the conclusion of the civil war; the way it became sidelined due to its failure to recognise, and thereby engage with, the institutions of the state.[141] The students in St Ita's did not take the Leaving Certificate, first examined in 1925, or the Intermediate Certificate. Students were highly encouraged to go to third level, but they achieved this through the matriculation examinations.[142] As the school was not under the Department of Education it received no financial support and operated on a year-to-year basis at certain times. In 1923 St Ita's was wound up as a co-operative society and 'the School and its fixtures and liabilities … transferred to the original proprietors – the Misses MacSwiney'.[143] Advice on how to dissolve a co-operative society was secured from Albina Broderick.[144] The dissolution was decided on because 'the scheme was not a financial success'.[145] From this point all liability for the school fell on Mary. In 1925 the former sent a letter to W. J. Stockley and T. J. Murphy, trustees of the school fund. Friends in America who feared the closure of the school 'have insisted on making a private contribution to enable the school to continue for another year at least'. After the fund was initiated, she discovered that there was money in a deposit account and was 'hopeful that by economy we may be enabled to carry on till June 1927'.[146] Teachers were paid from school fees. A statement written in the early 1920s suggesting the involvement of St Ita's in a proposed memorial to Terence MacSwiney by the Irish Self-Determination League noted: 'The school developed more quickly than its founders dared to hope, the number of Pupils [sic] rapidly increased, but this entailed an increased staff, which augmented the expenses of the school.'[147] Mary was forced to make difficult decisions to ensure the school continued to remain open:

> … we are doing without a servant to try to keep on the school as long as possible and the housework has to be done between us. We get a charwoman for the school cleaning but that is all. It takes time and more energy than either of us can well spare with six hours teaching a day.[148]

The focus at the first Sinn Féin Ard Fheis following the ceasefire, chaired by Mary, was, as Rosamond Jacob noted in her diary, on the politics of the past.[149] Released on 21 July 1924 de Valera realised that the party had become sidelined due to its failure to recognise and thereby engage with the institutions of the State. As early as 1923 he had written to Count Plunkett: 'the F. S. people have got behind the shield of popular approval and we must get inside it before we can hope to make any real progress'.[150] As Laffan discusses, the third Sinn Féin party was 'a coalition of different elements … an uneasy combination of extremists and relative moderates'.[151] Fanning states that during de Valera's absence Sinn Féin 'had achieved nothing of moment', failing to capitalise on its gains during the 1923 election.[152] From the period of his release, a fracture line emerged between the idealistic Mary and the more pragmatic de Valera over the issue of parliamentary abstentionism. He noted that the 'Mary MacSwiney view [was] well established'.[153] The correspondence between the two until de Valera broke with the party in 1926 shows his desire to find his way out of what he viewed as the arid political cul-de-sac of parliamentary abstentionism and her refusal to countenance such a move.

Mary's defiant stance was affirmed initially by de Valera's statements at a meeting on 7 August 1924 as he asserted that the structures of republican government should be maintained. This meeting, which included members of the Second Dáil who had subsequently lost their seats, established Comhairle na dTeachtaí intended to function as the 'actual' government of the country.[154] De Valera led the proposal to establish this body which was seconded by Mary.[155] 'We have a government again now' Mary declared.[156] A formal meeting of the Second Dáil met on 8 April, Mary acting secretary on both days.[157] At these meetings in early August, she was quick to remind de Valera that the core issue was not merely a matter of the removal of the oath; that would not suffice to allow the Sinn Féin TDs to enter the Dáil.[158] She emphasised the need for all members of Comhairle na dTeachtaí to speak 'with the same voice': 'It should go out from this body that no speaker should be allowed to say that if the oath were removed we would go into the Free State Parliament. We will only go into Dail Eireann.' In this, Mary was supported by Tom Derrig and David Kent.[159] Her belief that the removal of the oath was not sufficient in itself was something that she had voiced, as noted, the previous year. She penned a letter to Sinn Féin which, she declared, had been sanctioned by de Valera. An understanding had been allowed to develop that:

> if the oath was removed … the Republican deputies would take their seats in the Parliament and work inside for the social reform – the amendment or repudiation of the Treaty – the Gaelicsation of Ireland and the inclusion of Ulster …

While she saw 'much good that can be done like that', the proposal would entail an acceptance of partition and 'would mean inclusion in the British Empire till the Gov General had been removed, it would mean many things which I could not accept'.[160] At the sessions in early August 1924, Mary also spoke to denounce what republicans believed to be the partisan nature of the government in apportioning divided land only amongst its own supporters.[161]

De Valera's commitment in the second half of 1924 to re-organising the party did somewhat salve Mary's apprehension. Together with Kathleen Lynn, Michael Comyn and Eamon Donnelly she travelled with him to Ennis, the party leaving Knightsbridge Station on 14 August to loud and sustained cheering.[162] She shared a room in Ennis with Lynn, both women returning to Dublin on the train the next evening.[163] On 14 September she spoke immediately before de Valera, addressing a 'large' crowd drawn from across Munster on the Grand Parade, Cork.[164] Noting the partitioned status of Ireland, she also declared that Cork was in a state of 'near bankruptcy' because of the machinations of the pro-Treaty side during the Pact election in 1922. Looking toward the next election, she exhorted the city to elect those who stood for the republic.[165] The next day de Valera laid a wreath on the republican plot in St Finbarr's cemetery; Terence remembered amongst other Cork republican dead.[166] Later that evening she hosted a party in Belgrave Place where, according to Macardle, the atmosphere was one of revelry as old republican friends were presented with an opportunity to relax.[167] Mary was, Lynn recorded, jubilant following the success of de Valera's visit to the city.[168] The next month she was nominated for the position of Vice President, Hon. Secretary and Hon. Treasurer of the party but did not allow her name to go forward. Living in Cork, she was aware that she might not be able to attend all meetings.[169] Indeed, the Baltinglass Cumann in Co. Wicklow nominated her as President. She responded quickly requesting that her name be removed from the agenda. She would not, she wrote, 'like any Cumann to nominate me in opposition to the President'.[170]

What is remarkable was Mary's ability to sustain gruelling speaking engagements across Ireland after the conclusion of the civil war, evincing no note of despondency or defeat even in the face of ridicule. At a national banquet attended by government ministers, foreign consuls, business and professional men in the Metropole restaurant in Dublin on 17 March 1924, speeches referred to a 'new era'. O'Higgins, to laughter, declared:

> They might consider they had reached the stage when they could leave it as an interesting and academic subject between Lord Carson on the one hand and Miss MacSwiney on the other, the question of whether there was a shameful surrender by the Irish or the English on Dec. 6, 1922. It was largely a question of angles. He had no doubt that the lady exercising the prerogative of her sex, will insist that her angle was a right angle and he hoped that the noble law lord would be too polite to retort that, on the contrary, it was an obtuse angle.[171]

O'Higgins's ridicule notwithstanding, Mary's rhetoric was increasingly out of kilter with the reality of the institutionalisation of the state and its governmental structures. While she conceded that the Republic was not able to 'function fully', it would, she declared at a meeting in Athlone in January 1924, 'function again' and 'everybody who dared deny its rights, and who did not give it allegiance would be cleared out'. Craig and the Northern Irish government were 'Irishmen whether they like it or not'. They could go across the Irish sea, she stated, if they wanted to be British citizens.[172] Arguing that there would be no 'peace, happiness or stability in the country' under the Free State government, was, however, a refusal of the reality of public support for the new state, something de Valera understood. As an ideologue Mary, unlike de Valera, had no ability or mental room to manoeuvre politically. Consequently, her stance became increasingly calcified. Yet, there were those who understood that her position came from a place of deep belief and family trauma and that her years of campaigning on behalf of the republic, particularly after October 1920 had resulted in a personal toll. A report in the *Nenagh News* in early April summed up the human dimension to her politics in a report on her speech on the first anniversary of the deaths of Matt Ryan and John Sheehy, two Tipperary men killed on 27 March 1923 by National Forces:

> Looking a shade worn, and perhaps a little weary, she held the immense crowd spell bound. Men thought, as they hung on her words, of the grim determination of her family, of the great sacrifice made by her brother, Terence, in his lonely cell in England. Miss MacSwiney's utter sincerity, and her indomitable will, has made her name a household word throughout Ireland. All honour to the brave.[173]

The Sinn Féin party declined in 'strength and influence' between 1924 and 1926. The number of branches declined, and the financial position of the party deteriorated.[174] Yet, two by-election victories out of five held in the period 18–20 November 1924 seemed to suggest the fortunes of the party were improving and allowed the reality of political elision to be ignored by the party faithful. Seán Lemass won in the Dublin South by-election while John Madden was victorious in Mayo North. Indeed, as McCullagh notes, the percentage of the Sinn Féin vote increased in all five constituencies from that achieved in the general election.[175] Mary was to the fore speaking on behalf of candidates.[176] Republicans should, she declared, use the opportunities of the by-elections to demonstrate that the 'tide was turning' as they had done in Roscommon, Clare and Longford in 1917.[177] These victories notwithstanding, there were clear signs in 1924 that the party was faltering. At the meeting of Comhairle na dTeachtaí in July 1924, O'Kelly, in the chair, noted that 33 letters had been sent out 'regretting poor attendance'. Louis O'Dea, elected for Galway in 1923, noted that failure to resolve the issue of travelling expenses may 'have militated against attendance'.[178] A decision was reached to pay the expenses of TDs outside Dublin once a quarter and Mary informed members in advance of the first meeting following de Valera's release that railway fares would be paid. It was hoped, she wrote, 'to have a full attendance'.[179] At that meeting Kate O'Callaghan drew attention to the debts incurred in Limerick at the last by-election. Mary argued that local members of Sinn Féin did not properly participate during the by-election. She believed that a budget should have been drawn up. She stated that 'in the case of elections like everything else the hard work will fall on a few'. Her memory was that many Sinn Féin members came to Limerick 'who did nothing but go into hotels and have their meals supplied there'.[180] She spoke in mid-March in Newcastle West in support of the candidacy of Tadhg Crowley for the Limerick vacancy so was speaking from a position of some authority.[181] De Valera noted that the party faced more than election debts:

> I know a case of a man who had supplied the army in one barracks with goods and showed me an account for £600 ... The Free State people have recommended that he should get £168 ... We have enormous debts like this ... How can we raise the ordinary funds for carrying on?[182]

In early January 1925 Mary left to conduct her second tour of America under the auspices of the AARIR. This was a surprising decision on a personal level. Certainly, she did get to spend time with Peter who indeed spoke at some meetings with her and took on organisational duties due to the illness of Peter Golden of the AARIR and the resignation of other members.[183] However, her tour meant leaving a sister whose mental and physical strength she worried about in charge of St Ita's. Indeed, while Mary was in America Annie suffered from illness.[184] Moreover, the school was, as discussed, a venture on which both she and her sister relied on financially, particularly given that she would not put it under the auspices of the Department of Education. Yet, she determined to go believing that it was necessary to reanimate republicans in the US. On his release from prison in July 1924 de Valera quickly reverted to a belief that funds collected in the US were essential if republicans were to successfully contest elections in Ireland.[185] Considering this, Mary's decision to conduct a second tour of the US was not out of alignment with the views and priorities of the republican leadership in Ireland.

The situation in America had changed considerably from the period of her 1921 tour and there was less media coverage of her arrival and travel across America, as she spoke in Boston, New York, Los Angeles, San Francisco, *inter alia*.[186] During the civil war Mary had received assurance from members of the AARIR that 'friends of the cause in America' recognised that they should 'keep the flag flying' so that 'the cause of Ireland's republicanism may ultimately triumph'.[187] Joseph Scott writing from Los Angeles stated that the 'bitter enemies' of republicans in the US were 'having a happy time of it'. He commiserated with the portrayal of her as 'a virago' consequent on her lengthy Treaty talk and subsequent strident refusal to compromise. He did note that her 'strenuous campaign' across the US in 1921 'left this contemptible criticism ... without any detrimental effect on your legion of friends in this country'.[188] Scott referred to the 'ordeal' of that tour but also the suffering within her 'immediate family and the inspiration which has come from it'.[189] However, on the signing of the Treaty there were those in the AARIR who considered that 'the goals of the organisation had been accomplished'.[190] Linda Kearns, on tour in America from September 1922 wrote to Mary on the issue of fracture within the republican ranks in the US declaring: 'The people who were always true and strong Republicans are with us still, and it is only those who joined us because it was fashionable that have fallen away.'[191] When Mary arrived in America some of those whom she contacted informed her that they no longer 'saw eye to eye on the Irish question with her'.[192] There were those who believed in the Collins's approach; what the Treaty granted was all that could be expected at that point in time and was a springboard to further independence. The Cosgrave-led government was supported by the Coolidge administration. On 7 October 1924 Timothy Smiddy was appointed as the Free State minister plenipotentiary to America. The recognition of the new state was also reflected in the creation of a consulate general office in Dublin; previously the two US consuls based in Dublin and Cobh had been under the jurisdiction of the consul general in London.[193] There were also those like Joseph Scott who were initially happy that Mary was back in America; he declared that 'no one has been quite able to take your place in our hearts since you left'.[194] Yet by the end of her six-month tour Scott had fallen out with her and drew her attention to the feeling within the US that once herself and Boland departed in August 1921, 'it was impossible to get the slightest information from Ireland from anyone'. According to Scott, Peter Yorke, a leader with the AARIR in California, felt he might as well have been 'in Mars. Someone could at least have written a postcard':

> The failure to do it simply crystallised his opinion, in which many others joined, that on the question involving the future of a Republican form of government they were in no mind to listen or accept advice from the United States of America on the question of the adoption of the treaty.

The fact that the vote on the treaty was taken based on a majority decision rather than the two-thirds majority 'as required by the American constitution' was also a point of contention.[195] Mary expressed her dismay that this final letter from Scott was a 'further re-iteration of our past mistakes'; she saw no contradiction in the fact that reiterating a litany of their mistakes was her modus operandi in the US, as at home, when discussing the pro-Treaty party's decisions.[196]

Travelling without an Irish Free State passport, Mary arrived in New York in late January 1925.[197] Her tour was conducted under the 'supervision' of the republican envoy in the US, Seán T. O'Kelly; her 'mission' was 'largely financial'.[198] He wrote to her in February congratulating her on the money collected following her talk in Worcester, Massachusetts, although at other times he expressed disappointment about 'the financial results'.[199] O'Kelly attributed poor contributions in part to the 'apathy and hostility' of the Catholic church in America to the republican cause.[200] Mary believed that a membership drive was necessary and called for the deployment of an organiser who would travel ahead of speakers.[201] The fractured nature of Irish-American politics meant that it was necessary, according to Joe Begley situated in the republican envoy's office in New York, to coax wavering republicans; to engage in 'a little back-rubbing and tender ear-scratching to make them purr and purr effectively'.[202] Begley wrote on a number of occasions forewarning her about divisions and tensions within the Irish-American branches she was to meet with. In Cleveland, he wrote that the state secretary of the AARIR, a Miss Brazell, was 'excellent' but was 'suspicious of everybody's motives and I think a little hysterical'. She had, he continued: 'weird notions about the sinister proclivities of the Clan [na nGael]. If her eggs are not boiled properly for breakfast she blames it on the dark machinations of that innocent body. Here again is a chance for you to case out a few barrels of oil.'[203]

Mary wrote to de Valera of her disappointment at the financial results of her tour but did note that various meetings such as those in California were successful in terms of the 'propaganda effect'.[204] She attended the funeral of Fr Yorke in April. Her presence allowed, as O'Kelly put it, the Republic to be 'properly represented' at the funeral of the 'leader of the Irish and Catholic forces' in the west of America.[205] Mary's purpose on tour was also 'to tell what had happened in Ireland since I was here before' and to 'get all Ireland's friends in this country together for a big final drive against Ireland's age long enemy'.[206] Despite the lack of a welcoming committee on arrival, Mary's talks drew relatively large crowds. She herself noted that the turnout was not as large as in 1921 but places like San Francisco where she spoke in mid-March gave her a 'wonderful reception'.[207] As in 1921 she met prominent churchmen, Cardinal Hayes of New York agreeing to meet her on 27 January.[208] She also communicated with various women's organisations and was in communication with the American suffrage activist Carrie Chapman Cate.[209] Like in 1921 she worked long hours and O'Kelly noted that she at times appeared tired.[210] By April she wanted 'to see a home face and here [sic] some home talk, no matter whether there is news or not'.[211]

Her message, however, represented an account of the failures of the treaty deputation, their perfidy in signing the document without referral back to Dublin. Her focus was one-dimensional; the betrayal of the republic by those who accepted the Treaty and the necessity to overturn such treachery. There was no recognition of the functioning nature of the state in the process of creation by Cosgrave and the other pro-Treaty ministers nor any willingness to accept that the majority supported such a polity. There was no outline of how republicans could create a better state in terms of society and economics. With no irony she noted that many American republicans had visited Ireland in 1922 and 1923 and returned to the US as supporters of the Irish Free State.[212]

By June she expressed frustration to de Valera that he had not responded to her three previous reports, even if he had not replied to her personally, he should, she contended, have acknowledged receipt through the office of O'Kelly. She was, she wrote, 'disappointed'.[213] This was the period, of course, when de Valera was manoeuvring to re-enter parliamentary politics. The nine by-elections in 1925 consequent on the resignation of Cumann na nGaedheal TDs following the army mutiny saw Sinn Féin's share of the vote drop. De Valera, McCullagh states, dated his belief that a policy change was necessary to the failure of the party to win more than two of the seats.[214] In America Mary expressed her dissatisfaction with the results and alleged that in the case of the election in Mayo she was 'perfectly satisfied it was a cheat, we could not have lost Mayo fairly'.[215] At the end of her six-month tour she was 'looking forward to her recall'. She was aware of 'disquieting reports' that reached the US from Ireland. Both she and O'Kelly, she wrote to de Valera, 'should like to be in the thick of whatever is toward. I have heard rumours of a possible removal of the oath'.[216] In the event Mary undertook a further autumn tour as she was concerned about the 'effect on the organisation' in the US if both herself and O'Kelly left.[217] During this latter tour a major point of contention for her was the refusal to allow republican TDs to participate at the 23rd meeting of the Inter-Parliamentary Union in Washington. This organisation, established in 1899, was concerned to promote peace with a focus on parliamentary diplomacy. Mary was informed that:

> no one can be a member and participate in the sessions of the Interparliamentary Union unless he or she is an accredited member of a Parliament or Congress. Mr Lange, the Secretary of the Interparliamentary Union tells me that he has investigated and he is informed by the Irish Government that you have never qualified as a member of the Irish Dail [sic].[218]

Mary's concerns about political change in Ireland were not without foundation. She returned from a less-than-optimal tour of America to a Sinn Féin party that was at a political crossroads and riven by strife and acrimonious debate. Sinn Féin's disastrous showing during the by-elections in March 1925 resulting in changing opinions as to the merits of entering the Dáil.[219] Throughout 1925, as McCullagh discusses, calls for a 'reappraisal' of Sinn Féin's policy on abstention emanated from various sources 'within the political side of the movement'.[220] At the Ard Fheis in November of that year a decision was reached to allow debate of any policy other than 'the acceptance of allegiance to a foreign King and the Partition of Ireland'. As 1925 progressed de Valera was determined to, as he declared to O'Kelly, 'insist on keeping the door open' to changing Sinn Féin policy on the oath and entering the 'Free State parliament'.[221] The decision reached at the Ard Fheis as to what could be discussed by delegates allowed him to open that door to Mary's dismay. Also, in November the republican government was dissolved, and a council was established comprising representatives from the party, the IRA and Comhairle na dTeachtaí. At the Army Convention in mid-November the IRA determined to pursue an independent position, recognising only the authority of the Army Council.[222]

In December 1925 the findings of the Boundary Commission were leaked by the *Morning Post*; the Free State was to be granted less territory than anticipated. Mary supported the protest adopted at a conference of border nationalists at Omagh on 7 December 1925. The agreement, the protesters asserted, cemented partition and abandoned the rights of the minority and republican prisoners in the north.[223] The leaked findings of the Boundary Commission and the resultant decision to jettison the report and to absolve Ireland's financial obligations under Article 5 of the 1921 Treaty heightened discussion and speculation within Sinn Féin on the issue of entry into the Dáil; there were those like Austin Stack who believed that this was the opportunity to do so when 'Irish territorial integrity was at issue and there was a real chance of "the end of the Free State"'.[224] Mary, by contrast, declared:

> the proposed betrayal has not only surrendered – forever as far as the Signatories could effect it – the principle of Partition of our country, but … this new 'Treaty' shamelessly abandons the rights of minorities and the Prisoners in the North.

This shame could only be erased if the Irish people were galvanised to 'show the spirit of patriotism and courage which animated them from 1917 to 1921'. 'Then and then only', she declared, 'can the rights of the Nationalist Minority in the North be secure against English or Orange terrorism'.[225] Macardle discussed how republicans were increasingly 'helpless', 'disfranchised and powerless' in 1925. De Valera was, Macardle wrote, 'a leader without an army, without a voice in Parliament, without funds'.[226] In January of 1926 he indicated his intention to enter the Dáil if a route could be found to do so without taking the oath and called an extraordinary Ard Fheis for March.[227] From this point on Mary and de Valera's relationship fractured and, as the following chapter discusses, her political stance and rhetoric became hollow and had no influence on the wider society.

Chapter Nine

'Holding the Republican Fort'[1]: 1926–42

Mary MacSwiney's political life after the civil war was dominated by her commitment to the Second Dáil. This core pre-occupation resulted in the increasing narrowing of her political options, particularly after the establishment of Fianna Fáil in 1926. By that point de Valera was committed to establishing the republic from within the parliamentary arena. Síobhra Aiken discusses the code of official silence around the civil war, noting that politicians in the Dáil made pleas for reconciliation to allow future progress for the benefit of all.[2] Aiken argues there were a multitude of voices that broke that silence. Mary represented one such voice. She never referred to the civil war as an awful occurrence as, for example, did Sighle Humphreys who declared there was nothing as bad.[3] Mary's 'psychological wounding' – to use Aiken's phrase – occurred earlier than the period of the civil war.[4] Her brother's death was an unassimilated event that haunted her for the remainder of her life; this trauma was expressed politically in her increasingly fruitless unwillingness to engage with the state that formed in the wake of acceptance of the Treaty.

Writing to de Valera and Comhairle na dTeachtaí in October 1925, Mary accepted that republicans could 'no longer stay as we are'. She emphasised the need for a progressive socio-economic programme but reiterated that the committed could 'never recognise a British-controlled Parliament'.[5] She claimed, however, that, 'summoned' home from America to allow her to be present at the Ard Fheis in November 1925 she had no advance knowledge of de Valera's desire to debate the question of what way republicans might enter the Dáil. Neither had the other delegates, she asserted, any expectation of such a development.[6] Due to 'unrest and dissatisfaction' following his announcement in January 1926 of his desire to enter the chamber if the issue of the oath could be circumvented, it was, she wrote, decided to hold an extraordinary Ard Fheis 'to see where the organisation stood'.[7] Yet Eamon Donnelly had written to Annie in July 1925 discussing rumours that a change in party policy regarding abstentionism was being considered in some quarters amongst Sinn Féin in Cork so Mary cannot have been as blindsided as she professed herself to have been:

> Is it true, as is freely rumoured here that efforts are being made to form some kind of new Party whose object is the promulgation of some policy other than that of H. Q. It appears that that in some unexpected quarters the possibility of Republicans entering the Dail is being discussed in a not unfavourable light.[8]

On a personal level Mary claimed to have experienced 'surprise' and 'heartbreak' at de Valera's decision to leave Sinn Féin.[9] The years after 1926 saw her political position become progressively divorced from the reality that the state formed in 1922 had a democratic mandate and was fully functional. Her statements to the effect that 'England's difficulty will still be Ireland's opportunity' and pronouncements that Sinn Féin was 'prepared to begin again and suffer all over again for the cause in which they believed' found an increasingly arid reception.[10] Mary was central to the increasing fractures and splits within the Fourth Sinn Féin Party and within Cumann na mBan in the later 1920s and early 1930s. Indeed, even before the establishment of Fianna Fáil, the Sinn Féin party was isolated by the decision of the IRA to end its allegiance to the Second Dáil in November 1925. The pronouncement 'meant that in the view of the armed organisation, the Second Dáil was not a "properly constituted government", and therefore was not seen as legitimate'.[11] Once again Mary faced the vista of all the ramifications, both personal and political, of party splits as old friends and colleagues found themselves on opposing sides. O'Kelly with whom she had worked closely in the US during her 1925 tour supported de Valera's stance and she wrote a confidential letter to Hearn about the need to appoint a new envoy to America loyal to the party.[12] Dorothy Macardle, whom she had known since imprisonment in Mountjoy in November 1922, sent her a series of cutting letters. While she believed that Mary would 'do a good deal to keep the controversy decent & fair', she wished her 'sense of our moral inferiority did not come out so plainly in spite of yourself'.[13]

As Fianna Fáil's electoral base grew, Mary engaged in invective and criticism, writing reactive letters to newspapers that relied on jaded, politically irrelevant tropes. The anti-democratic basis of her beliefs was increasingly underscored by the success of Fianna Fáil's appeal to the electorate in the early 1930s. This was particularly the case after the party assumed office in 1932 when de Valera set about dismantling the Treaty from within the Dáil. There was something tragically poignant in the spectacle of Mary and her brother Seán continuing to doggedly attend Sinn Féin Standing Committee and other party meetings in Dublin and Cork as de Valera and Fianna Fáil were negotiating and engaging with the reality of Dáil politics and the changing relationship of the state to Britain. After 1926 Mary's language in reference to the Second Dáil and the republic was defensive. In 1927 she described the reduced members of the former as those who took the oath in 1921 and 'faithfully' kept it. In her configuration, members were in a holding pattern; their role was to hold 'the Republic Fort' until, with international recognition, it was able to function freely.[14] The Second Dáil was to act in defence of republicanism at this point rather as an active agent in the realisation of a functioning polity. In letters to de Valera Mary continued to argue that resistance to the Irish Free State was as legitimate in the 1930s as he considered it to be before he broke with Sinn Féin in 1926.

Yet as Mary's political life became increasingly fractious and narrow, there was healing in her personal life. While her relationship with Muriel was damaged beyond repair, the return of Terence's daughter, Máire Óg, to Cork in 1932 brought happiness. The latter's memoir is warm in the sense of familial love between herself and her MacSwiney aunts. The photographs of the family, both in Belgrave Place and summering in Ballyferriter, Co. Kerry, show a warmth and human side to Mary that was so often elided in public due to her politics. In 1937 all four MacSwiney sisters were reunited in Kerry when Kit and Peg came to visit from their convents in Japan and North Carolina respectively.[15] Mary's extreme political stance after 1921 was the based on her need to bear witness to Terence's sacrifice in 1920. Yet, it is noteworthy that she was willing in the 1930s to compromise her refusal to engage with the institutions of the state when to do so was to the benefit of Terence's daughter. Máire Óg recalled that when it 'came to me and my welfare, I came first and the Republic came second'.[16]

De Valera's signalling in November 1925 and again in January 1926 of his desire to allow debate within the Sinn Féin party on the question of parliamentary abstentionism caused Mary dismay. He was adamant, as McCullagh discusses, of the need to take whatever action necessary to realise the Republic. In his mind in late 1925 this did not preclude discussion of how republicans might enter the Dáil.[17] Mary carried on in her usual truculent manner refusing to countenance his willingness to keep 'the door open'.[18] Turning her attention to the upcoming by-elections in early 1926, she stated that she did not believe that they should be fought 'to test the opinion of the country on the Boundary issues':

> ...the wiser course would be that the Standing Committee issue a statement ... that... Sinn Fein does not recognise that the Leix-Offaly seat is vacant, and secondly that as County Dublin is always an Anti-National Constituency we do not consider that contesting it would really reflect the minds of the people on any national question.[19]

In Laois-Offaly, the sitting republican TD, John McGuinness, was disqualified from 28 November 1925 under Section 51 (2) (a) of the Electoral Act 1923, having been sentenced to 18 months imprisonment with hard labour for assaulting and resisting a member of an Garda Síochána. Mary, of course, neither recognised the new civic guard nor any legislation passed by Irish Free State government. She felt that the party could not contest the election 'without acknowledging in some manner the right of the "Free State" to declare one of our nominees a person not fit and person to represent the people'.[20]

De Valera, however, increasingly saw matters differently. Having determined that entry back into parliamentary politics was essential to realise the republic by alternative means, his letters to Mary were increasingly curt and irascible. On 10 February 1926 he wrote to her from Portlaoise; he was canvassing for Art O'Connor in the by-election. She had been trying to rein him in to prevent any further compromising remarks following his January declaration. Initially stating that he would welcome her presence in the constituency in support of O'Connor, as the letter progressed, he began to repeat himself with annoyance at her stance:

> You know Art's and my position. You should know too that this is the first by-election which has taken place since Treaty No. 2 came from London and my ambition is to fight to the death, to defeat the 'Free State' candidate. A Republican victory at present in Leix-Offaly would have far reaching consequences, and it is with that object and with that object alone at the moment that I am concerned. If there is compromise in that, I cannot see it.
>
> There is nobody here, as far as I can see, making any 'compromising speeches'. From 7 in the morning until 1 and 2 next morning the people here are working – this includes the President who is going night and day – canvassing, etc.
>
> No time is wasted on a question which need not be discussed until the Ard Fheis.[21]

In March Mary travelled from Cork to attend the special Ard Fheis held in Rathmines. De Valera's motion was that once the oath of allegiance was removed the issue of entering the Dáil and the Northern Irish Parliament was a matter of policy not one of principle.[22] In advance of the meeting the newspapers identified the fault lines: 'Mr de Valera's movements are considerably hampered by the extremists under the banner of Miss MacSwiney'.[23] For de Valera the matter of going into the Dáil once the oath was removed was one of party policy; it did not, as Mary believed, subvert a core principle.[24]

De Valera chose to interpret the narrow defeat of his proposed policy change at the 1926 Ard Fheis not by viewing the party as 'evenly divided', but as signal to leave Sinn Féin.[25] Mary viewed the fact that he had not achieved a majority vote as victory for the party and their position of no compromise. It was, she grandiosely asserted:

> one of the biggest things that has ever happened in Irish History, that in spite of the great personality of our former President, of our love for, and confidence in him, yet when he suggested a compromise, the majority of organised Republicans did not go with him.
>
> That fact shows a big advance in independent thought.[26]

At the Ard Fheis, she assumed the position of chair during a brief interlude when there was an attempt to maintain a united front to the public. A byline in the *Belfast Newsletter* declared: 'Mary and Eamon urge that there should be "no hasty action"'.[27] Mary proposed that each side appoint a committee and meet separately to discuss their position after which the Ard Fheis should reassemble and find basis for co-operation.[28] However, the mood was tense and fractious with O'Flanagan accusing Mary of forcing a split.[29] Later in March Lynn denounced the former for behaving 'meanly' towards Mary.[30]

Three meetings were held by the two sides during the Ard Fheis 'at which the possibilities of future co-operation were discussed'.[31] At the conclusion of the interlude, it was determined that party unity could not be maintained and the party split. In April Art O'Connor assumed the Presidency of the fourth Sinn Féin party, a columnist in the *Irish Stateman* dryly asking:

> is it treasonable for the rest of us to ask by what right he claims to rule over us? If he could not persuade the voters of Leix-Offaly a few weeks ago to return him as Parliamentary representative, who gave him a mandate to speak for the nation?[32]

The same columnist also alleged that once the severance between the two sides was complete, Mary informed 'her old leader' that the 'descent into hell is easy once the first step has been taken'.[33] Yet in the immediate aftermath of the Ard Fheis she engaged in talks with de Valera; Lynn noted that they had spent the afternoon of 21 March together.[34] Moreover, she was genuinely concerned about his financial situation writing to John J. Hearn:

> I suppose you know that Dev had a paid Executive position. On his resignation he refused to touch another penny, which is natural enough, but as he had not enough to put anything by with his large family I am wondering how he is going to manage till he gets other work. It is a delicate matter but you can understand how those of us, who felt bound to insist on his resignation for the sake of the Republic as we see it, are worried over the undeserved trouble that may fall on him on this account.[35]

On occasions, she denounced those within Sinn Féin who 'who seemed to consider the whole duty of Republicans lay in abuse of de Valera as the source of all our ills'.[36]

Mary returned to Cork after the 1926 Ard Fheis no doubt emotionally drained after what she would later describe as a 'heart-breaking shock'.[37] De Valera's decision to enter the Dáil if the oath were removed was one that republicans refused to consider in 1922.[38] She was not present at St Finbarr's cemetery to commemorate Easter 1916; Seán represented the family.[39] Immediately on her return home she succumbed to a bout of severe flu but she 'fought the doctor' and put her mind to rally an embattled Sinn Féin while looking to secure the support of the AARIR through Hearn.[40] 'Those of us who do base our action on our belief in the principle', she wrote, 'cannot yield to any pragmatic plea of expediency'.[41] While she was personally distraught having maintained a strong political friendship with, and belief in, de Valera, there was, she wrote, 'one consolation':

> In spite of his wonderful personality and all the efforts to propaganda ... the 'extremists' here won. The enemy were prepared to rejoice over the split in Sinn Féin. If Dev had won our position would have been very difficult. Instead we are able to say to England that she has gained nothing. Dáil Éireann has elected a new President. The government of the Republic, the Army, Sinn Féin, Cumann na mBan stand firm. England's difficulty will still be Ireland's opportunity and we will be watching for that difficulty.[42]

For Mary it was 'the act of Jan 1919 and our claim of continuity of that act, which makes F. F. wrong in principle'.[43] There were those who supported her position. Lynn wrote how she 'talked with Mary Mac, she is so strong on continuity of Republic'.[44] When Dan Breen determined to take the oath in 1927, he had, Mary declared, 'broken his mandate'.[45] As Sinn Féin TD for Tipperary, Breen was the first republican to enter the Dáil. He stood as an independent republican candidate in 1927 but was defeated.[46] When Breen's name was shouted out during a republican meeting in response to Mary's refusal to countenance entry into the Dáil she retorted: 'If you turned Protestant tomorrow that's no reason why I should do it. If Dan Breen has turned a National Protestant that's no reason why I should do so.'[47] Breen in turn made clear that he was not going to be brought 'to book' on his 'national actions' by 'anybody, much less Miss MacSwiney'.[48]

In *An Phoblacht* Mary laid out the position of Sinn Féin vis-à-vis the establishment of Fianna Fáil:

> the position of the republic as proclaimed in 1916, and democratically established in 1919, remains; it cannot be compromised by the new departure advocated by Mr. de Valera.
>
> If Fianna Fáil should meet with success in its policy, and by smashing the oath should make it possible for the Republican Government to function fully then the third Dail [sic] could meet and chose its own Executive.
>
> If the new position fails, then the Republican position still holds, and will continue to be maintained as at present, until, through the ballot-box or by force of arms, it is re-instated in its full rights, and internationally recognised.[49]

Yet, as defections to Fianna Fáil increased, Mary sounded a note of despondency coupled, contradictorily, with a refusal to accept defeat. This stance can only have been mentally exhausting:

> It is not easy to be cheerful with these repeated desertions and backslidings but we must go ahead – here and over there [America], those of us who really believe and whose faith may not be shaken.[50]

The biggest danger, she declared, 'is our own discouragement, and it is the hardest enemy to overcome'.[51] However, the pro-Treaty papers were quick to query how the Sinn Féin Party, now in its fourth iteration, could move forward. As the *Donegal News* declared: 'What the followers of Fr. O' Flanagan and Miss MacSwiney intend doing remains a mystery. Outside of the question of finance altogether, they will have absolutely no policy to put before the people save one of pure negation.'[52] Gerry Boland declared: 'let Miss MacSwiney, Scelig and others keep the moribund organisation'.[53]

The foundation of Fianna Fáil, as Maillot states, 'heralded a considerable change, as it presented a credible alternative and a challenge to Cumann na nGaedheal, something which the third Sinn Féin had never succeeded in doing'.[54] Seventeen members of the 37 strong Standing Committee resigned while initially 21 out of 47 Sinn Féin TDs followed de Valera.[55] Those who remained in Sinn Féin struggled to orientate themselves and find a new direction. Dáithí Ó Donnachadha, joint secretary of the party with Austin Stack, commiserated with Mary; it was 'regrettable', he wrote, that things are not as favourable in Cork as we should like. It appears to be the story all over'.[56] Writing to Mary, O'Connor stated that he believed 'a definite cleavage will come upon the issue of fighting elections or the reverse'.

Referring to splits within the party after the secession of de Valera, he referred to the 'majority of the majority party'. He noted that he was unable to get news on what position Sighle Humphreys and 'others' intended to take but he was 'assuming they are all right'.[57] A circular letter to all members of the Standing Committee emphasised the importance of the meeting on 21 May 1926:

> Owing to the extraordinary circumstances that exist at present in the Organisation and owing to the number of secessions which have taken place and the attempts which have been made to weaken the Organisation, it is essential that every delegate who believes in the whole Republican policy should be present at this most important session ...[58]

A rail voucher was issued to each member, arguably to encourage attendance.[59]

The toll of the split told on Mary. In mid-June 1926 she was recovering from an undisclosed accident.[60] In August she took her annual holiday, indicating to her colleagues in the party that she needed a break from politics. Ó Donnachadha encouraged her in this: 'As regards what you say about being out of the world, I think you ought to keep out of it and leave all those old papers on one side, making the most of your holiday while you have the opportunity.'[61] Lynn recorded various instances of Mary's ill health into 1927. In February of that year, she was looking 'badly, fluey'.[62] Mary also had worries about family members. She continued to assume responsibility for her siblings as head of the family as she had done from an early age. In July 1926 Peter accompanied the remains of his second cousin, Peter Golden, from New York.[63] Burial took place in the republican plot in Cork. Mary, Annie, Seán and Peter were all in attendance. De Valera and Mrs Pearse, amongst others, represented Fianna Fáil.[64] Living in America since 1901, Golden was active in the service of republicanism in such organisations as the Irish Relief Fund, 1916, and the AARIR. In 1920 he toured widely for the republican bond drive.[65] Mary wrote that she was 'heartbroken' at the loss to the cause but also 'to his friends personally'.[66] Later that year the family yet again faced the personal anxiety of imprisonment; Seán was arrested, together with nine other men, on a charge of 'conspiring to rob barracks and of murder'. He refused to recognise the court or be professionally represented.[67] Ó Donnachadha wrote to her: 'We are all distressed to hear about Sean [sic]. It is very hard on him considering the severe operation he has just been through. Please God he will be all right.'[68] She was 'upset' not to be able to attend the Standing Committee on 10 December 1926 noting that there were many matters to be discussed. Annie, however, had been unwell all week and 'it is impossible for me to leave her alone while she is ill'.[69]

The Honorary Secretaries of Sinn Féin sent a circular letter to all the party TDs immediately after the split in 1926:

> In order to keep the Organisation intact and to ascertain, as far as possible our strength in the various areas, the Standing Committee has directed us to appeal to the T.Ds to hold conferences in their various constituencies not later than Sunday, the 2nd, of May prox.
>
> To this end we have been instructed to request you to get in touch with 'key' persons in Cork City & County whom you know to be opposed to the new Departure ... [70]

Mary's first address to her constituents after the split did not take place, however, until 30 January 1927. At the Coliseum Cinema on MacCurtain Street, she declared de Valera's new departure 'wrong in principle and futile as a policy'. Even if her constituents gave her a mandate, she could not, she declared: 'enter the Free State Parliament if the oath were removed, because that Parliament was a usurpation, and she could not serve in it and help it to function, and at the same time give allegiance to the true Dail Eireann [sic] – the Government of the Republic.'[71] Democracy had its 'limitations', she stated.[72]

The perilous financial position of Sinn Féin occupied much discussion in the months immediately after the split. This was even more of an issue with an election to be fought – or not – in 1927. To state that Mary wanted Sinn Féin to refrain from contesting the June 1927 elections on the basis that they could not 'hope to secure a majority because of the split within the anti-treaty ranks' is too reductive an assessment of her position.[73] In December 1926 she argued that since the party could not hope to win a 'majority vote this time', it was advisable to only put up one candidate in each constituency. This would ensure that money was not 'thrown away' and could instead be diverted to matters of 'organisation and education'.[74] In February 1927 she wrote to the Standing Committee expressing her fear that the party was losing further momentum:

> If there is a likelihood that the election cannot be contested it should be stated soon. It is no disgrace to be held up for want of money, but the present inertia and failure to put our case before the public will be a disgrace and put us down and out completely if it lasts much longer.[75]

The possibility of creating a common republican platform to contest the general election was considered by Sinn Féin. A special meeting of the Standing Committee was held on 25 June 1926 to consider 'a proposal for co-operation with Republican bodies by way of a national council'. Interestingly provincial members were informed that their attendance was 'not essential if they find it inconvenient to attend'.[76] The issue of a common republican front, however, became more acute with the calling of a general election for June 1927. Mary outlined her position in some detail:

> Fianna Fáil's immediate objective seems to me to be, at its very best, the 'Document No. 2' position, but it is in reality much less. I have never yet heard for instance a public declaration from any of its prominent supporters that they would give Mr Timothy Healy immediate notice to quit.
>
> Sinn Fein … is holding the Republican Fort, and will keep its hands free for the adoption of any and every honourable means – including armed revolution when it seems necessary and expedient – to break all connection with England. Any pact which would involve the surrender of an iota of that position, or any agreement to postpone indefinitely any action in accordance with that position and policy, Sinn Fein could not agree to.[77]

Mary presented Donnelly with a set of points to form a basis for discussion as to the possibility of an election pact. These showed no understanding of the reality of the willingness of de Valera to work within the political system. Instead, she used the language of violence, stating that 'every available weapon' should be utilised to repudiate partition. What she envisaged was a republican coup:

> If we were all tighter and got a majority for the Republic as we well might this time only for this last split, I would have no hesitation in going into 'Merrion St.' to take over control for the Republic, and utilise those buildings till such time as we got others more fitting. It is not the building which could compromise the Republic, but the acceptance … [that] 'the Free State was by law established' …[78]

Mary's attitude to the establishment of Fianna Fáil was initially relatively nuanced. At one level she interpreted the split through the lens of the Treaty divide. Writing to Hearn on the matter of republican supporters in America she stated: '[d]o not let anyone persuade our people there that the division between us is only camouflage, – the same type of propaganda they had about the Treaty'.[79] However, in the immediate aftermath of the split she did not discount the possibility that de Valera and those who left Sinn Féin might be able to establish the republic 'their way'. Other sections of the republican opposition thought similarly. McConville discusses how the reaction of the IRA to de Valera's decision to enter the Dáil in August 1927 was 'rather muted'. This he attributes to the 'hope that, despite all Fianna Fáil's step might simply be a ploy to take the Free State from within'.[80] In many respects Mary did not view what occurred within Sinn Féin in March 1926 as an outright split rather she conceptualised the developments as emanating from the adoption of a new plan by de Valera. She wrote to Hearn about the impact on the AARIR:

> … if there are any considerable numbers … who think that de Valera's plan might be tried with advantage and would wish to help him, could that section continue to work in the organisation and help the main purpose, while earmarking any special collection for de Valera if they liked.[81]

What she wanted to ensure, however, was that Second Dáil continued to function:

> I am considerably worried that de V might try or allow some of his followers to try to have him re-instated as President of an Dáil. That means of course that if he got a majority that we would hold that we alone are Dáil Éireann and the position would be made much worse.
>
> On the other hand there is no reason why they cannot remain under A O'C [Art O'Connor] as a minority Party in the Dáil. If they succeed and get the Republic functioning again their way, we can then constitutionally dissolve and leave it to them. If they fail Dáil Éireann remains and they will be welcomed back.[82]

Speaking in Cork in January 1927, Mary declared that she believed de Valera when he said he would never take the oath and cautioned Sinn Féin members to:

> so bear themselves that no word or act of theirs would make more difficult the re-union of their forces. They wanted the ranks of Sinn Fein [sic] to remain open to receive back those who had gone from them when they would have seen the futility and failure of the Fianna Fáil policy.[83]

Indicting the Sinn Féin TD, Seán O'Farrell, in April 1927, she accused him of putting Fianna Fáil on a level with the traitors who supported the Irish Free State from its inception:

> It seems absurd to ask people to believe that those who are urging the people of Ireland to reject allegiance to England <u>immediately</u> are as guilty of treachery to Ireland as those who have handed the country, over, bound hand and feet to England.[84]

As negotiations on a possible united republican front continued, the political breach between Mary and de Valera remained fluid. In mid-May 1927 she wrote to him stating that she had expected he would call and that she 'would have been glad to have the opportunity of a talk'. She filled him in on developments between the two republican parties during his absence in America.[85] She was aware that a further return of Cumann na nGaedheal to power in 1927 would sanction partition and make it hard 'to convince the outside world that the Free State is not acceptable to the Irish people'.[86] However, she differed from de Valera and those who joined Fianna Fáil in her belief as to the correct way to secure the 'defeat of the present Free State Junta'.[87] Writing before the June 1927 election she argued that if Fianna Fáil entered the Dáil as a minority party the effect would be to 'stabilise the British assembly' while they would 'become as degraded as that of the Irish Party at Westminster just before 1914'. She called on Fianna Fáil to:

> give up the Minority position and let us all arrange safeguards for the Majority position and a sound economic policy, and I for one, believe that the people will by a majority endorse the ignominious dismissal of the traitors and murderers who have disgraced and dishonoured our country.
>
> It is quite possible that a large number of our new secessionists will end up little better than the earlier ones, – evil communications corrupt good morals, – but while they adhere to their declared policy, it surely cannot be said that they are as big renegades as the Free State murder gang, and we only make ourselves ridiculous by saying so.[88]

She was approached from various quarters on the question of finding a basis for united action at the upcoming elections between Sinn Féin and Fianna Fáil. Yet her innate fear of compromise dominated. The danger in proposals for unity was always 'that it is expected that the people who hold the uncompromising position … must give way – and not the compromisers …'[89] While she believed that 'united action could be taken', she did not agree with de Valera's approach:

> … a majority could be secured, provided that the Republican position can be safeguarded. This would involve Fianna Fail giving up the most dangerous part of their policy, – that is, to go into the Free State Parliament as a minority if they can do so without taking an oath. That to me would be disloyalty to the established Republic in which I believe and I could have nothing to do with any agreement which involved the functioning of the Free State.[90]

Mary was aware that she was perceived as a barrier to a united republican front in the aftermath of the split. 'Perhaps I am', she wrote, adding that her opposition was to a 'false unity'.[91] She viewed the question of republican unity against the foil of the 1922 Collins-de Valera pact. This time, de Valera had, in her interpretation, changed sides:

> In effect the policy of Fianna Fail is to do to-day what we refused to do in 1922 – to accept the Treaty position, but not the Treaty, to accept the Free State position, but not the Free State. That is just as inconsistent with Republican allegiance to-day as it was in 1922, to those for who allegiance is a reality, not a formalism.[92]

Her personal sense of despair was obvious: 'I seem these days to be living again through the agony of the early months of 1922. You will remember how anxious everyone was then to bring about a Pact.'[93] Despite the perception that it was Mary who stood firm against republican unity as a vehicle to contest the June elections, others in the party were similarly sceptical. Stack wrote that members of the election organising committee were:

> like yourself in the desire to present a united Republican front at the General Election if it could be done, but so far we have no evidence that Fianna Fail [sic] are willing to come as far as we can go with honour. Possibly they may advance to the point where we can meet them – and I believe they could if the same pressure was brought to bear upon them as has been recently used in the effort to shift Sinn Fein from its position.[94]

Mary's anxiety around political compromise notwithstanding, she supported Peadar O'Donnell's call in April 1927 to hold a meeting between members of Fianna Fáil, Sinn Féin and the Army Council to discuss proposals for unity and if such failed, she supported the suggestion to discuss 'the line to be followed by a Republican majority comprised of both parties in taking over the machinery of government'.[95] This political relationship drew the ire of some members of the party, Lynn describing her in November 1928 as being 'terribly under the thumb' of O'Donnell.[96] The reality was that Mary was grappling to locate solid ground for Sinn Féin and the republican ideal in a changed political environment.

Discussing a potential pact with Donnelly, the Sinn Féin director of elections, she queried how it was proposed 'that the "abolition of the oath" is to be brought about? What is to happen if it is not abolished according to your programme? Details on this are essential'.[97] To de Valera she wrote:

> It has been suggested that a majority is almost a certainty; that we could negotiate for that and make no stipulation about the minority; that if afterwards the minority resulted, and your people did things we could not stand by, we would not be responsible.
>
> That is what I call a Pontius Pilate attitude and I will have nothing to do with it any how.[98]

De Valera's reply was brusque. Having escaped the political wilderness with the foundation of Fianna Fáil, he had no further need to bare his political soul to Mary. There were no longer any soul-searching letters. In May 1927 he wrote that he was not going:

> to give a complete reply because I have explained my position so often before … Knowing your attitude on this question, and being as convinced that I am as right as you are that you right, I feel that we can only agree to differ.

What she called the 'minority' position of Fianna Fáil was, he wrote, 'an essential part of the whole programme, and to give it up would be to cripple the policy as a whole'.[99]

That the establishment of Fianna Fáil changed the political landscape in Ireland became obvious during the run up to the June 1927 election. The new party and in particular de Valera's leadership injected an essential shot of dynamism into the Irish political opposition. It also had the effect of rendering Sinn Féin staid or, in the words of Seán Lemass, 'as a galaxy of cranks'.[100] Members of Cumann na nGaedheal personalised the split in Sinn Féin. Speaking in Dublin at the end of February 1927 O'Higgins declared that Mary's policy was more transparent than that of de Valera:

> Miss MacSwiney's policy was that the Treaty must be set aside, and that policy he thought was more honest and less astute than the policy of those that seceded – if he might put it that way ... Fianna Fail. The policy of the latter party was an insidious one, and he would brand it as a dishonest one. Mr. De Valera went to the electorate, not on a programme of setting aside the Treaty and damning the consequences, but he merely said he disliked the oath of the Treaty.[101]

Cumann na nGaedheal endeavoured to use the split in Sinn Féin to gain political ground in the lead up to the election. In personalising the two sides in the breach, members of the government used a trope in circulation since the Treaty split in a bid to emasculate de Valera. Kathleen Clarke recalled that she kept quiet about her role in the Sinn Féin split and her decision to support de Valera's position:

> My reason for keeping quiet was, in a sense, to shield de Valera. Sometime before, he had been sneered at as being under petticoat government, that Miss MacSwiney was running him. I did not want that sneer repeated, with just a change of petticoat.[102]

George Russell asserted that Mary was the leader of Sinn Féin following the split, no one was, he asserted, taking O'Connor's 'titular headship seriously'.[103] Speaking in Headford, Co. Galway, in April 1927 the Minister for Agriculture, Patrick Hogan, derided both Mary and de Valera, inferring a reversal of normative gender roles. Playing on the fact that de Valera was in America raising funds for the foundation of the *Irish Press*, Hogan declared:

> De Valera is the most unhappy man in the world at present ... He is afraid of his life of Mary MacSwiney. He has been running away from her for the past five years. He is running from her still, and will be running from her until he is gone, and that will not be long.[104]

Speaking in Kilkenny the following month, the Cumann na nGaedheal TD, Denis Gorey, when interrupted with a call of support for de Valera, jokingly replied: '[w]e will put him up on the top of a pole where Mary MacSwiney cannot get at him'.[105] Goulding, presiding over the Cumann na nGaedheal meeting in Ballincollig, Co. Cork, in June referred to the recent speech by Mary in the same place, creating a play on a popular phrase used to encourage children to eat or take medicine.[106] With this he was deploying the caring, domestic role ascribed to women, the inference being that Mary had distorted it in her own case: 'Stripped of all verbiage it meant simply "open your mouth, close your eyes, and see what Mary will send you." If they swallowed the pill that Miss MacSwiney would give them they would be a long time sorry.'

On 10 May a meeting in support of Mary's candidacy was held at North Gate Bridge in Cork. She was only one of 15 candidates fielded by Sinn Féin. As an 'uncompromising republican' she was, she declared, once again looking for the votes of the citizens of Cork. She went on to discuss economic issues, asserting that there could not be economic prosperity and autonomy while there was no political freedom. From the North Gate Bridge, she travelled to Blackpool Bridge to address another crowd.[107] The following day she spoke at Dennehy's Cross in the suburbs followed by a meeting in Capwell on the south side of the city.[108] Despite such frenzied travel back and forth across the city, Mary failed to hold her seat. Indeed, the election saw other key individuals within Sinn Féin suffer losses including Lynn and Art O'Connor although Caitlín Brugha was successful again in Waterford. Writing to those who helped in her campaign, Mary encouraged them not to 'lose heart' even though the overall party results were 'a disappointment'. A note of despondency crept in as her letter progressed: 'It is sad that what the Free Staters failed to do in 1922 and 1923, and what they would have failed to do also in 1927, has been accomplished by those who claim to stand for the Republic.'[109] Her sense of dejection can only have been compounded by the news that Terence's friend, Daniel Corkery, who won a seat as an independent Republican candidate for North Cork, made the decision to 'co-operate' with Fianna Fáil in Leinster House.[110]

The assassination of the Minister for Justice, Kevin O'Higgins by a dissident IRA group on 10 July 1927 created a set of events that cemented the Sinn Féin split and rendered Mary's considerations of the basis for a 'Majority' Republican position defunct. The government responded to the murder by introducing a Public Safety Act under which Dáil candidates would surrender their seats if they did not take the Oath of Allegiance within two months of election. Furthermore, Cosgrave, in removing 'the permissive article' stymied de Valera's attempt to 'exploit the constitution' by raising a petition to have the oath abolished. Under the 1922 Constitution the people had the right to initiate legislation or make constitutional amendments. The first stage in this process was a proposal signed by 50,000 registered votes. De Valera was forced to enter the Dáil or 'give up political action'.[111] Frustrated by the legislation, he came up with the 'empty political formula' solution to the oath facilitating the entry of Fianna Fáil deputies to Dáil Éireann in August 1927. The 'required declaration', de Valera stated, 'is not an oath ... it has no binding significance in conscience or in law'.[112]

For Mary, de Valera's intention to take the oath marked the Rubicon; the decision 'materially altered' the relationship between the two republican parties:

> While they [Fianna Fáil] kept to their proclaimed policy of only entering the Free State parliament if the oath were removed, there was always the chance of getting them back to the Republican position. That is gone now very definitely and they are fast drifting into the same position as the earlier Free Staters.[113]

Moreover, the fact that candidates had to indicate their intent to enter the Dáil under the terms of the Public Safety Act meant that Sinn Féin could not contest the September 1927 election, reinforcing its isolation. The party emphasised, however, that they did not put forward candidates due to the financial restraints.[114] Fianna Fáil, by contrast with Sinn Féin, received large donations from the AARIR and through the exhortations of Cardinal

Mannix in Australia.[115] Mary expressed her horror at the taking of the oath by Fianna Fáil TDs through the lens of Terence's death. She recalled how he had shown her a copy of the republican oath in 1919, asking her opinion of it. She in turn requested of him if he felt that '<u>all</u> members of An Dail [sic] could be trusted not compromise'.[116] This backward-looking approach was in direct contrast to the present-centred political aspirations of republicans who left Sinn Féin to join Fianna Fáil. Maillot describes the way the Sinn Féin party calcified from mid-1927 onwards: 'This downward spiral rapidly transformed Sinn Féin into a ghost-like bureaucratic organisation, more interested in respecting rigid rules than in addressing actual problems. Its decline was rapid and alarming.'[117]

Mary attempted to formulate policy for the fourth Sinn Féin party. Laffan states that de Valera 'appreciated that his republican policy could expect to win the support of no more than a section of the population' and consequently Fianna Fáil concerned itself with economic issues. In this context Laffan cites the issue of the payment of land annuities to Britain and the party's commitment to protect native industries against foreign competition.[118] Accordingly it was the 'politically minded' in Sinn Féin who followed de Valera into Fianna Fáil in 1926.[119] Yet Mary advanced many of the same economic policies that de Valera would implement after 1932. She called for the establishment of 'a second House based on the economic interests of the country rather than chosen on political or class lines'.[120] On 9 April 1927 she issued a letter to the Standing Committee of Sinn Féin in advance of the upcoming meeting. She called for a 'complete embargo on all foreign goods which can be produced immediately in sufficient quantities to supply the needs of the people' and 'graduated protection for other industries'.[121] She also declared that there should be an end to the payment of annuities to the British government. Certainly, there were elements in her proposed economic plan that were unworkable and that would not appeal to voters, notably the emigrant tax of '£10 per head, irrespective of age or sex'. Similarly, her call for the 'repudiation of pensions to non-resident English officials or to persons 'receiving money for services rendered to England' showed her lack of real politick.[122] Moreover, as Eoin Ó Broin notes the Sinn Féin party itself played no role in the land annuities campaign which was very much the focus of the IRA in the period.[123]

In the period after the 1926 split Mary exemplified the obsession with party rules. Her political world became increasingly narrow as she engaged in a series of political disputes. The MacSwiney family remained steadfastly committed to the idea of the republic that their brother had sacrificed his life for, showing no willingness to recognise the changing nature of both public opinion and the Irish polity in the years after the establishment of the Irish Free State. As Kevin Rafter states: abstentionism can be effective only when those adopting the policy are in a majority'.[124] Although he fails to mention Mary, Rafter notes that those within the fourth Sinn Féin party were only willing to use political tools that were 'honed and sharpened in a different era'.[125] Ó Broin, who also notably fails to mention Mary in discussing Sinn Féin in the immediate aftermath of the 1926 split, writes: 'For de Valera's successors at the helm of Sinn Féin – O'Kelly, O'Higgins and O'Flanagan – Sinn Féin was not simply a means to an end, it was an end in itself, to be promoted and preserved no matter what the changes were occurring in the world around it.'[126]

Mary took the issue of non-recognition of the institutions of the state very seriously. As discussed, this stance was at personal expense as St Ita's received no state funds meaning that not just the future of the school but her financial position and that of Annie was never stable. Writing to Louise Gavan Duffy Annie alleged that de Valera's decision to break with Sinn Féin adversely impacted on the school: 'The conditions under which we worked were again adversely affected by Eamon de Valera's betrayal of the Republic, his followers seeming to think it particularly heinous that HE should not be allowed to betray with impunity.'[127] Mary stated that she had been informed by Peter that it was unlikely that any money would be raised in the US for the school because of her opposition to de Valera.[128] However, Elgin Barry went to the US on a fundraising tour in May 1928 in yet another bid to keep the school open as no funds would be requested from the Department of Education.[129] Mary's refusal to engage with the reality of the state in existence and her concern to ensure that Sinn Féin maintained purity on the matter was increasingly an anachronistic stance. Even the most stalwart members of Sinn Féin found themselves at odds with the purist demands of the party as the necessities of day-to-day living forced them to establish a *modus vivendi* with the structures of the state.

In January 1926 Mary wrote to Seán Lemass about the position of republicans on local government boards:

> As we shall be discussing policy at the Ard Fheis it might be well to see how Republicans can remain members of bodies that are obliged to enforce an anti-national test, and conscientiously fulfil their duty to elect the best qualified candidate to public offices. It is, and has been since the advent of the Free State, an impossible position...[130]

In 1927 she supported the forced resignation O'Connor from the presidency of Sinn Féin when, having received a law degree from Trinity College, Dublin, he was called to the bar which necessitated him taking an oath of loyalty to the state. Martin Maguire discusses how the Treaty split impacted on the civil service. As anti-Treaty supporters within the service were seen to pose a challenge to the new state an oath of loyalty was required. Failure to take this could, and did result, in dismissals.[131] Naively Mary stated to Hearn that it never 'occurred to me that he [O'Connor] meant to practice'. She continued, noting the difficulty in electing a successor because those who might be considered eligible were 'still giving the quasi recognition from which the President should be clear'. She offered Count Plunkett as an example, a man who paid taxes and a car license fee and who had applied for a passport the previous year.[132] When she learnt that O'Connor was 'furious' and blamed her for forcing his resignation her response was that he 'should have chosen some other way of making a living'.[133] After the 1927 Ard Fheis Mary put forward a resolution that, while the party supported the ideals of the Gaelic League and the GAA, they could not be expected to attend functions held by the organisations 'in which murderers of Republicans or their servants are permitted to take part'.[134] Such sentiments were increasingly tired and irrelevant in the late 1920s.

Attempts were made to reanimate the Sinn Féin party after 1927. A public meeting was held on O'Connell Street on 20 January 1929 with Mary present on the platform. She declared that Irish people were 'under bondage of the soul and mind, the bondage of those who gave in at the point of a bayonet'.[135] On the same day de Valera spoke in Mallow, Co. Cork to 'an assemblage of fairly large proportions'. While Mary hoped that young men in the IRA would 'not sneak away to America and leave the ranks', de Valera also referred to emigration but with a focus on the economic policies that Fianna Fáil would usher in to effect change. In his speech he focused on the necessity of concentrating on the home market and the abolition of free trade with Britain.[136]

The ever diminishing Second Dáil met on 20 and 21 January 1929. On the second day the chamber met in public session in the Pillar Room of the Rotunda marking the tenth anniversary of the first Dáil. Seventeen members attended.[137] Mary introduced the 'Constitution of the Republic of Ireland' Bill. The 1916 Proclamation, she stated, had to be the foundation of any constitution for the country; the ideals enshrined in it would have been introduced as a founding document of the republic but for acceptance of the Treaty and the split that ensued. The 1929 constitution was dedicated to 'Almighty God' and was heavily sectarian in sections. Ireland was, the document affirmed, a predominately Catholic country, and no anti-Catholic legislation could be permitted including dissolution of marriages. Protestants, Mary stated, could not claim this was a denial of freedom of conscience. No 'godless schools' were to be permitted although children of parents who did not practice would not be obliged to attend religious instruction.[138] Irish was declared as the official language of the Republic. Even though Mary conducted her life through English, that language was to 'be permitted and recognised only so long as may be deemed necessary'. The government was to consist of an elected President, a legislative council and an economic council, the latter with only recommendatory powers.[139] The country was to aim to become self-supporting and while 'drastic measures' might be needed to achieve this 'the co-operation of all citizens must be gained'. Brian Ó hUigínn seconded the bill. However, Stack, while he agreed with the fundamentals, stated that there were articles that would 'require serious investigation'. In particular, he did not agree with Mary's proposal to nationalise landownership.[140]

The condescending tone of *Belfast Newsletter* report on the proceedings of 20 and 21 September underscored how peripheral Mary's position, and that of the other Sinn Féin attendees, was in the context of wider Irish politics. The paper referred to 'Miss MacSwiney and her faithful little band of followers' who 'still kept up their game of pretence'. The report sneered at the 'gravity' with which she introduced the constitution, a document she 'fathered or ought we say mothered'.[141] The paper predicted further splits within Sinn Féin highlighting the ever-decreasing political ground on which Mary attempted ot maintain a foothold:

> We note, however, that although one member of the assembly declared the Articles of the Constitution to be 'as near perfection as they could get,' ... another member took grave exception to a land nationalisation clause. Conceivably another split will still further reduce the ranks of the only original Republicans, and if the process of fissure goes on we shall live to hear of Miss Mary MacSwiney left high and dry on the rock of fidelity to Sinn Fein, proclaiming an Irish dictatorship.[142]

Mary was to the fore in the establishment of Comhairle na Poblachta at the end of 1928 as a response to 'cleavages in the Republican movement' which had undermined the unity of 'those who remained steadfastly loyal to the Republic'. The aim of the council was to co-ordinate republican activities and reunite the Irish people behind the desire to 'overthrow British rule in our midst'. Republicans were called on to 'revive activity in their districts' and to extend membership of organisations. They were to 'continue to repudiate' the dual legislatures of the Irish Free State and Northern Irish State while efforts were to be made to recruit young men to the IRA.[143] Writing in October 1929 on the matter of a proposed conference 'to review the national position', Mary argued that the meetings held under the auspices of Comhairle na Poblachta since its foundation made 'it clear that there is a distinct re-awakening of the National spirit'. At the same time, she noted the necessity to reach young people who had grown up since 1916 while also conceding that there had been little increase in the membership of republican organisations.[144] She was aware that many of the core membership were advancing in years. She outlined the lethargy that had crept into the party: 'The affairs of the Republic are not at the highest level at the moment. People who have been working for many years have perhaps got tired and a bit hopeless. They will not compromise but neither do they seem to have any energy for a forward push.'[145] Comhairle na Poblachta failed to reanimate republicanism; in September 1930 a plaintive letter from the secretaries of Sinn Féin called on all members of the Standing Committee to note that the proposal by Father O'Flanagan had been adopted: 'That each member of the Standing Committee be asked to present to the next meeting a list of five activities in order of their importance, in which the Sinn Fein Organisation as at present constituted may engage with reasonable prospect of success.'[146]

Mary's health declined in the 1930s. In 1932 the secretaries of the party suggested that she not give a speech in Belfast during the Easter commemoration. Apart from the order prohibiting her entering Northern Ireland, 'your state of health and other considerations impel us to frankly give our opinion'.[147] They did, however, request that she deliver the opening lecture at the Sinn Féin Headquarters, 16 Parnell Square, to open Wolfe Tone week commencing on 27 June.[148] That year the party did not attend the annual Bodenstown pilgrimage having 'been refused a guarantee that organisations that have compromised the Republican position will be excluded'. The purist republican demonstration took place a week later.[149] While Mary kept in close contact with the honorary secretaries of Sinn Féin by letter, her attendance at meetings in Dublin was increasingly low. School commitments meant that she was not able to travel other than at the weekend and then not always. In the period 16 October 1931–15 July 1932 she only attended five out of 24 scheduled meetings, although this was more than the number attended by the other provincial members.[150] In the next period her attendance was down to one meeting.[151] Repeated political disappointments as the republic became an increasing chimera, particularly after 1926, must have taken its toll on Mary as it did on other members of the fourth Sinn Féin party. Ó hUigínn wrote to her in 1932: 'I really do not feel I require such a complete rest. If I could bring myself to a point where I would not be too deeply affected by events and keep at that point, I'd be all right. Not work but worry and annoyance it is that upsets me.'[152]

Further dissension and splits dominated Mary's political life in the early years of the 1930s. Ward discusses how Cumann na mBan were stymied in their attempts to recruit new members by their constitutional commitment to the Second Dáil. Younger members 'had barely heard of the Second Dáil'.[153] At the 1933 convention a decision was reached to amend the organisation's constitution. From this point on Cumann na mBan pledged under Article 1 to 'organise and train the women of Ireland to put into effect the ideals and obligations contained in the Proclamation'.[154] Ward notes how this pledge allowed the organisation to recognise and act on Connolly's social radicalism as signalled in the 1916 Proclamation.[155] Eibhlin de Barra proposed an alternative amendment to Article 1 which Mary seconded. Explicit reference was made to the establishment of the republic by the Dáil in 1919. In supporting this amendment, Mary indicated her opposition to the original amendment: 'The meaning of the Resolution was to base allegiance on the Proclamation of 1916 and ignore the result of the Proclamation, namely, the Government lawfully established by the Will of the People in January 1919. Cumann na mBan for the first time in its History was weakening.'[156]

While seven women on the executive were opposed to such changes, three resigned membership: Mary, Eileen Tubbert and Gobnait Ní Bhrudair.[157] The *United Irishman,* while clearly partisan as a paper that supported Cumann na nGaelheal, did highlight Mary's increasing political isolation. Each split left her further denuded of political colleagues:

> Shortly after the ratification of the Treaty, many people who were interested in the political relations of Mr. de Valera and Miss MacSwiney prophesised that the lady would ultimately finish her political career as a member of a party of one. Last week, along with a couple of companions she sailed out of the annual convention of Cumann na mBan because that body made a change in its constitution ... [158]

Mary was genuinely distressed at the decisions reached at the convention writing to Eithne Coyle:

> I would find it hard to put into words the sorrow and disappointment which Saturday's proceedings cause me ... It was bad enough that C. na mBan should give up its allegiance, but that members of whom I had thought highly should have insulted the Declaration of Independence of January 1919 and all that followed from it, passes my understanding.[159]

She took particular issue with the decision to attempt to put into action Connolly's social policies. Her horror shone through her letter to Coyle at what she perceived as the new commitment of the organisation to Marxism. She denounced the decision to 'allow youngsters of two months standing' to vote on issues that most of them 'know nothing about':

> I am informed that a resolution including the adoption of the Social Policy of James Connolly, without any qualification was passed without discussion, and that not one of you took the precaution to point out that James Connolly accepted and preached the principles of Karl Marx; that the principles of Karl Marx are incompatible with Christianity, and that to connect Karl Marx and Connolly now is doing an injustice to Connolly himself, since he died for Ireland – not for the teachings of Karl Marx – and he died a good Catholic.
>
> I have always thought you very level headed, and am therefore making one more effort to beg of you, even if you agree to the turning down of allegiance to the Republic, not to tolerate the teaching of any social programmes based on Karl Marx. We have a big fight before us. I never thought that it would fall to my lot to be on the side opposite the organisation in which my heart was stuck since 1914.[160]

In response Coyle noted that Cumann na mBan was an organisation in existence before that of the Second Dáil while she refuted any suggestion that policy would be formulated on 'anti-Christian teachings'. The organisation's 'conception of the re-construction of a Social System for our country is based on the Encyclical of Pope Leo XIII and on the Christian teachings of Connolly and Mellows'.[161] Mary did emphasis that despite her opposition to the 'newly labelled social policy', it had 'nothing whatever' to do with her resignation.[162] She noted 'glee' amongst certain members in Cork at her resignation in a correspondence with Coyle that became increasingly barbed:

> The present was no time to cause a division in our ranks, and in spite of the practical unanimity of the Executive, I am convinced you have done a real disservice to the Republic.
> I should like to get the names of the branches, if any, and of the members who resigned, after the Convention. It may be you will not be willing to give them to me. If not I shall understand, but it will not be a sign of the strength of conviction will it?[163]

Other key members of the organisation were also indicted as responsible for facilitating a breach. Sighle Humphreys received a stinging invective. In 1931 Humphreys was a founder member of Saor Éire, an organisation which was critical of the refusal of republicans to engage with issues of class. A consideration of class division was, she believed, necessary to link republicanism with the concerns of 'ordinary people'.[164] Saor Éire was concerned to exploit the discontent generated by the economic crisis consequent on the economic decline brought about by the Wall Street crash in 1929. The organisation demanded communal ownership of key resources. Focus was placed on workers, small farmers and traders in a short-lived attempt by a section within the IRA to marry republicanism with the politics of social justice and create a mass popular movement geared to revolutionary action.[165] Opposed to Saor Éire, Mary denounced any Cumann na mBan alignment with its objectives, writing to Humphreys:

> I stand for as much of James Connolly's programme as any of you can stand for, and if your compromise on the Republican issue had not driven me out of Cumann na mBan, it would have been easy, with a few words to make that clause safe from attack ... What I do believe is that the wording of that clause – just like the wording of Saor Eire – is making the enemies of the Republic a present of a stick to beat the Republic with ...What do you really think you have gained by your action. I blame you more than most of them, first because you should have had more appreciation of the uselessness of the change.[166]

Humphreys declared that she had to summon 'courage' to write to Mary. Having done so, she pinpointed the manner in which the latter's politics had become fossilised:

> The real trouble is that you and Eileen Tubbert and a few others look on Dáil Éireann as a fundamental principle. You even said at the Convention that we were about to 'give away our freedom'. I only looked at Dáil Éireann as an episode in the fight for freedom. Taken in conjunction with the military activities, it helped to break down the British administration. But in 1922 when it accepted the 'Treaty' its usefulness was gone. Even in the last day of its power we were very far from freedom so that there was no question, either then or now of giving away what we had not got.[167]

During the recriminations that followed the decisions made at the Cumann na mBan convention in June some members noted Mary's absence from executive meetings in the previous number of years. Humphreys bluntly stated that if she 'had been at our Executive meetings for the last 3 years you would realise why we brought in that change'.[168] As Ward notes, Cumann na mBan had in the years immediately before 1933 become centred around a small group of Dublin-based women.[169] In Mary's case, advancing age and declining health combined with the demands of St Ita's quite likely precluded travel to

Dublin. Increasing references to her health were made in correspondence with the standing committee of Sinn Féin. In January 1932 the honorary secretaries regretted that she had been ill for some days.[170]

On 20 June 1933 Tubbert convened a meeting of members of Cumann na mBan in Dublin who resigned and the question of the establishment of a new republican women's organisation was brought up.[171] Writing to Mary she noted that the Dublin women:

> did not care to be dubbed 'followers of Miss MacSwiney' – not that we had any personal objection to your leadership, but because of the implication conveyed by such a description, namely, that we had been influenced in our action by a great personality and not by principle.

Tubbert, however, desired a nationwide meeting of women who had resigned from Cumann na mBan.[172] Caitleen O'Moore, also from Dublin, wrote to Mary stating that her advice was much sought after and that many: 'would be proud and happy to follow your leadership … I have heard the remark made … If our men were only half as straight, honest and uncompromising as Mary MacSwiney, we should have had the Republic long ago.'[173] In Cork Poblacht na hÉireann resigned as a branch despite the dissension of six members. Writing to Tubbert, Mary stated her belief that this was that most effective approach; that branches rather than individuals resign from Cumann na mBan.[174]

In December 1933 dissident ex-Cumann na mBan members formed Mná na Poblachta.[175] Members pledged to: 'Maintain and defend the Irish Republic proclaimed in Easter 1916 and established by the free will of the people of Ireland on 21st January 1919.' Amongst the aims of the organisation was 'denying the authority and opposing the will of enemy institutions'.[176] In the lead up to the establishment of Mná na Poblachta Mary was in correspondence with Tubbert who criticised the lack of 'help or encouragement from Cork'. The two women discussed potential regulations around the admittance of members. Mention was made of the fact that Comerford and Eibhlin de Barra had voted in Irish Free State elections. Tubbert stated her belief that 'if those of you who opposed voting at "Free State" elections had spoken out more strongly … we would have influenced quite a number of people'.[177]

Mary refused to join the new organisation. It was, she wrote, not just the matter of voting in elections:

> I should like to make it quite clear to you that I do not put Civil Servants in the same category as individuals for whom … special jobs are created. Civil Servants get their posts by competitive examination, and Republicans are quite entitled to hold them, where no declaration of allegiance is involved.
>
> Members of Sinn Fein have spoken with severe disapproval of I.R.A men who took pensions. Yet now, any Free State pensioner may be head of Sinn Fein, or Mna na Poblachta, for all their professed allegiance to Dail Eireann.

Mary did recognise that economic necessity forced republicans to engage with the state. However, she believed that such people could not be elevated to high office within republican organisations:

> I have the greatest pity, and no blame, for people, especially those with families, who have been driven by economic pressure to take jobs or pensions – always granted of course that

> there is no declaration of allegiance – but those who do apply or get jobs or pensions should not be pushed into, or permitted to stand for positions of honour which will compromise the Republican organisations.[178]

Mary's break with Cumann na mBan was not absolute. The organisation still stood for full republican independence and she was one of the speakers at a debate in the Mansion House April 1937 on the motion: 'That only a sovereign republic having no connection with the British Empire will satisfy the aspirations of the Irish people'. The other speakers were The Right Hon. Frank Pakenham, Seán MacBride and Frank McDermot, Fianna Fáil TD. The debate was organised in aid of funds for Cumann na mBan.[179] Mary was a member of the committee established in 1937 to 'arrange and control' the Easter national commemoration. Other members included Maud Gonne MacBride, Margaret Buckley, President of Sinn Féin and the President of Cumann na mBan, Eithne Coyle.[180]

In the same year as she broke with Cumann na mBan, Mary's connection with Sinn Féin began to rupture. As discussed, members of the fourth iteration of the party like O'Connor were forced to adopt a *modus vivendi* with the Irish Free State to ensure career prospects and a quality of life. The erosion of such members of the party faithful left the extreme doctrinaires holding an increasingly narrow base. Mary doggedly continued to argue that de Valera had betrayed the Irish people. Fianna Fáil came to power in 1932. Mary stated that she was glad to see this development as it 'did away with the murder gang and their policy'. However, the act of taking the oath of allegiance was a 'blot on the escutcheon of the Republic'.[181] When Con Healy returned to Cork having been released on the party's coming to power, Mary attended the procession and public meeting. She 'congratulated' the government on the release of prisoners but returned to the matter of the oath and what she perceived as pernicious compromise on the republican ideal: 'By getting rid of the Oath in the Constitution they were not abolishing it, and not establishing a Republic, because the Oath was in the preamble of the Treaty.'[182] Yet initially on the party's coming to power Mary did not equate Fianna Fáil with the un-mitigating treachery of the pro-Treaty Cumannn na nGaedheal party. Ó hUigínn remonstrated with her: 'I think you should cut all favourable references or seemingly favourable references to Fianna Fáil out of your pamphlet. We should not by implication or otherwise compare them favourably with their predecessors in the same office.'[183] Sinn Féin refused to publish the unnamed leaflet until she removed any references to the ability of Fianna Fáil to enable 'the Republic to function fully'. The fact that Mary considered the possibility of Fianna Fáil 'courageously' asking 'for a mandate to repudiate the "Treaty"' was a discussion that the wider Sinn Féin leadership nihilistically refused to contemplate. The standing committee summed up its position: 'One of the many reasons given for the deletions that strikes us at the moment is: that references likely to help the policy of those who advocate that Fianna Fail [sic] be given a chance, must be avoided in our publications.'[184]

By 1933 Mary's position on Fianna Fáil was more confrontational. The *Irish Press* ran a series of three articles penned by Macardle on the concept of majority rule. Macardle distinguished between actions that were permissible during revolution and behaviour and rules that must prevail in normal political times.[185] Mary responded in a series of letters to the editor of the paper. She repeated the argument she made at the time of the Treaty split that the freedom of the Irish nation was 'an inalienable right' that no generation 'may lawfully surrender' as they held that right 'only in trust'. She rejected the gradualist approach to dismantling the Treaty adopted by de Valera on assuming power.[186] Macardle retorted by asking Mary to face the reality of the policy of sterile abstentionism. It was, Macardle argued, a barren stance that did not facilitate meaningful political growth in pursuit of the republican ideal. Mary was, she argued, attempting to 'live as though the Republic still functioned, a childlike consistency in a game of make believe'.[187] Mary refused, however, to take cognisance of political realities. In amending Article 1 of its constitution earlier in the year, Cumann na mBan noted that the while the existence of the Second Dáil was: 'a matter of deep significance, to ask young girls and women to render allegiance to a Government which does not and cannot function, is simply taxing their powers of credulity beyond reasonable doubts.'[188] This decision, and Mary's refusal to accept it, aligned very much with Macardle's criticism that she was engaged in a 'game of make believe'. Earlier in the year Mary blithely declared at a meeting in Galway that no further shots need to be fired for Irish freedom if Fianna Fáil 'who claim they are Republicans are only true to their traditions and proclaim the Republican Government and hand it over to the people'.[189]

Macardle indicted Mary for refusal to acknowledge the existence of a functioning, democratically elected government. The issue of recognition of the state and its institutions came to the fore within the Sinn Féin party with the election of Father O'Flanagan as President of the party at the Ard Fheis in 1933. His acceptance of a commission to write county-histories in the Irish language for use in schools caused some members to object to his appointment.[190] Mary was one such party member fully against the election of O'Flanagan. Despite this she did not resign from the party immediately explaining that decision at a later point. She queried the backing given to O'Flanagan by Laurence Raul who was elected one of the Vice-Presidents of the party, also in 1933. She demanded how he could support:

> the appointment of an employee of the Free State govt. as president of Sinn Fein, whether he would have looked upon the matter in the same light if the job had been given by the Cosgrave govt. He said no, it would have been quite different. I thought we were up against the British machine, not merely against the particular tools in power. Evidently another mistake on my part.
>
> I found myself in such profound disagreement with the Ard Fheis on matters that seem to me vital that I was inclined to resign at once. Owing to the very difficult position of real Republicans at present, and knowing, as I could not help knowing, that my resignation would do further harm, I decided to wait until the next Ard Feis [sic].[191]

Mary resigned from the party the following year while remaining as a member of the Second Dáil. She recalled that at the Ard Fheis in 1934:

> Much personal feeling had been worked up and there was a hot and bitter discussion. Some of us, however, stuck to the point that a matter of principle was involved, and held that if the Sinn Fein organisation permitted the 1933 resolution to stand it would compromise its own principles. When the Ard Fheis refused to alter the decision of 1933, I, for one, had no choice but to resign.[192]

She was supported in her resignation by certain members of the Standing Committee, notably Caitlín Brugha, who felt that Mary was subjected to personal attacks:

> In my opinion Miss McSweeny [sic] is the symbol of Ireland unconquered, she has given all her life her great ability to the Cause of Freedom, the sneers of traitors had no power to hurt her but it is inconceiveable [sic] that petty motives should be ascribed [by] those who have worked with her & who have been so well aware of her selfless devotion to the Republic. My whole feeling about the matter is one of anger, sorrow & amazement that she above all others should be subject to such an insult.
>
> I remained on the Standing Committee last year & though reluctant to allow my name to stand this year I did so because I had expected that the President's sense of patriotism which had always been so fine would have awakened him to the need of the organization & the danger of compromise that this acceptance of Free State patronage would bring about. In conclusion I now request that my name be deleted from membership of the Standing Committee.[193]

Mary had to defend the misconceptions that emerged as to her reasons for resigning from the party. She was accused of being jealous of O'Flanagan. Responding, she emphasised the economic sacrifices that she had made in holding to her purist political stance. It did not, she stated: 'occur to the dupes of these whispers to ask what I had to be jealous about. If my Republican conscience were as accommodating as his Reverence's, I could be quite comfortable as far as this world's goods are concerned instead of being as I am. As well accuse me of jealousy of de Valera or Art O'Connor because I did my duty as I saw it.'[194] She believed that those who supported O'Flanagan voted for a personality rather than on the basis of republican principle.[195] She emphasised that she did not resign due to the decision to allow members to take jobs in the civil service. If there was 'no overt act of treason' involved, it would be 'wrong to expect Republicans to starve if the means of subsistence was offered to them'.[196] However, the situation that pertained in the case of O'Flanagan was, she contended, very different. His position was 'specially created for him and not advertised as an ordinary C. S. post would be'.[197] She returned to this matter on several occasions after 1934:

> If a young man or woman qualifies for a competitive examination, and on his qualifications obtains a position, he is but a cypher to the Free State usurping body. His republicanism has nothing to do with the matter. If on the other hand he gets his post as a favour <u>because he is a republican</u> it is the same as a pension, and I was of the opinion that pensioners were not permitted in Sinn Fein.[198]

When members of Cumann na mBan could apply for pensions under the Military Service Pensions Act, 1934, Mary refused to write corroborating references. A letter to Frank Aiken in respect of the claim of Mary Carey, Cork, drew attention to an 'incident' delaying resolution of her application:

> Mrs Carey desired that the name of Miss MacSwiney … be given as one of those who would verify the statements made in the Form of Application and this was done. The Pensions' Registration Board sent a questionnaire to Miss MacSwiney … but Miss MacSwiney instead of replying to the Board forwarded same to Mrs Carey with a note in which she implied that she would not communicate with a Dept. of the Free State Government.

The letter writer requested that the questionnaire be forwarded to 'an alternative source'.[199] When there was a proposal to dismiss Seán Breathnach and R. O'Driscoll from the Sinn Féin party for voting at elections, Mary vehemently protested. Both men were members in Cork and were 'indefatigable' republicans over the years. The two men were 'guilty of a breach in principle'. However, the majority of Ard Fheis, she stated, 'compromised what again to my mind is also a principle'. She continued referring to the election of O'Flanagan despite his government commission:

> There are men in Cork, who became of their uncompromising allegiance to the Republic and their membership of Sinn Fein [sic] have refused to apply for or to take pensions to which they were entitled. Their attitude has not altered because of the recent decision of the Ard Feis [sic], giving its blessing to jobs, but their respect for Sinn Fein has dwindled to vanishing point.[200]

Mary did not retreat into political inactivity following her resignation from Sinn Féin: 'I have not been idle since I left … I have frequently written to the papers, and frequently made speeches … I have no intention of giving up my work for the Republic, as long as there is any life left in me.'[201]

In 1935 there was a discussion about the establishment of a new league of republican bodies to include the IRA council. Mary wrote to Moss Twomey of the necessity for a 'live political organisation'. However, by this she did not mean the establishment of a new organisation rather she desired closer co-operation between existing republican bodies. It was vital 'to decide what can be done to unite all of us, all over Ireland, who seem to stand for the same cause'. She clarified her understanding of 'that cause'.[202] As she had enunciated when she resigned as a member of Cumann na mBan, she protested: 'against any and every attempt to make that stand conditional on the acceptance of any economic or social programme, other than the general principle, clearly stated, that our Republic must be built on Social Justice, based on the practical application of Christian principles …'[203] Allegiance to the Second Dáil and the continuity that represented was the imperative. While she welcomed a possible influx of younger members into Sinn Féin, she was adamant that there could be no changes to the constitution of the party as she believed had occurred in Cumann na mBan in 1933 under the influence of younger delegates. On the matter of 'control' she proposed:

> The de jure position of Dail Eireann [sic] is acknowledged by all Republicans, but until Dail Eireann is in a position to function freely as the government of the Republic, or a new Government of the Republic has been validly chosen, involving the immediate dissolution of the Second Dail, the control of the Army will remain in the hands of the Army Council. On all other matters there will be the closest co-operation between the Republican Bodies which accept the basis of common agreement.[204]

At a meeting of the Second Dáil on 7 December 1935 it was decided to convene a conference to discuss the 'present national situation' and to ask the Army Council to co-operate in calling it. However, Mary stated that she believed that the idea was not 'even put forward' to the latter body.[205] The issue of unity between Sinn Féin and the IRA continued into 1936 with various individuals writing to Mary on this necessity. Caitlín Brugha stated that she and Ó hUigíinn were the 'two really virile members' of the Second Dáil. What is to happen, she wrote, 'when in a few years we will all have left this vale of tears … The I.R.A. will then have things in their own hands & can do whatever they like. At present so far as I can see they are ready to cooperate & I would like to suggest that they should be made responsible with Dail E to maintain the Republic.'[206]

Brugha referred to an abortive conference on the matter which Mary had not attended. The latter was indicted by the Sinn Féin standing committee for 'abstaining from Irish affairs' after she resigned from the party which she vehemently denied: 'No one who really knows me would think of suggesting that I was neglecting my duty to my country because of any personal grievance, either about persons or policies'. She was asked about 'coming forward now that Fr O' Flanagan was gone', having been expelled from the party in January 1936 for partaking in a re-enactment of the establishment of the First Dáil on Radio Éireann.[207] Mary refused to rejoin because the resolution was 'still there' that permitted the President and members of the officer board of the party to hold government jobs.[208] Moreover, she was opposed to the idea of a new republican organisation as proposed by the IRA rather than the creation of unity between existing republican bodies:

> ... they think that a new body will be able to rally the young people more effectively. They have carried their foolish attitude to Dail Eireann to the extent of ignoring any mention of the establishment of the Government of the Republic in 1919, the greatest act, and fact, in Irish history. That being so they have put it out of the power of people like myself, who do believe in the importance of Dail Eireann, to help them in any way whatever.[209]

Mary believed that unity amongst republican organisations would permit co-operation in contesting the 1936 by elections in Galway and Wexford. She proposed Moss Twomey as a candidate in Galway as he was 'the most important officer of the I.R.A. – the body against which the full force of the present coercion is directed'. Again, a lack of political realities infused her thinking, a refusal to accept that the Republic was 'increasingly abstract and elusive':[210] 'If this election is well worked and with enthusiasm by a united Republican effort it will kill coercion at once, and show Fianna Fail that the people did not elect them for this. As it is an abstentionist election there can be no valid objection to this united effort.'[211]

Mary continued to be involved in prisoner aid in the last decade of her political life. A local relief committee to aid the dependents of prisoners was established in Cork in the context of the passing of the Public Safety Act, 1931, Mary acting as chair. In the late 1920s and 1930s the IRA engaged in sporadic acts of violence. Members of the Garda Síochána were targeted as were perceived spies within the organisation itself. Intimidation of jurors and jury tampering also featured on the arsenal of activities.[212] The Public Safety Act established a Military Tribunal in November 1931 while under new constitutional powers organisations deemed to be anti-State could be proscribed.[213] Many high-profile members of the republican opposition found themselves before the Military Tribunal including Sighle Humphreys who was arrested for issuing jury-tampering leaflets. Humphreys had been in Mountjoy Jail with Mary in November 1922.[214]

In early January 1932 Mary received an official request to act on the National Executive of the Irish National Aid Committee. She believed the Cork relief committee would amalgamate with the INAC and requested the opinion of the Sinn Féin Standing Committee before she agreed. She felt, she wrote, that there was 'no danger of any "bogus unity" campaign' arising out of the establishment of the Committee'.[215] However, the view of the Standing Committee was that it: 'would be difficult for a member of Sinn Féin to act on a Committee in any sort of harmony with persons who, while ostensibly speaking in public on behalf of the prisoners, are really making election speeches on a behalf of a political party.'[216] In the lead up to the general election in February 1932 the IRA withdrew the General Order forbidding members to work in Irish Free State or Northern Irish elections.[217] While IRA men could therefore canvass for Fianna Fáil, members of Sinn Féin could not. For that reason, the latter party declined to send a representative to the Prisoners' Reception Committee in March 1932 despite the release of IRA prisoners and the lifting of the Public Safety Act, 1931, being welcome news to Mary and other members of the Sinn Féin.[218] Instead, the party focused on the welfare of former prisoners. In May 1932 the Tomás MacCurtain branch of Sinn Féin in Cork set up a committee to alleviate distress amongst republicans in the city with attempts made to find employment for them.[219]

Indeed, Sinn Féin's reticence to be officially involved in the context of the release of IRA prisoners in March 1932 proved to be prescient. As McConville states, the immediate relief of IRA prisoners by the new Fianna Fáil government was misleading news for the IRA.[220] In the immediate aftermath of the party's election success the IRA maintained a profile as a very public organisation, parading openly at local commemorations and at the Easter and Bodenstown pilgrimages. The rise of the Blueshirts increased recruitment to the IRA. Conversely the perception of links between Fianna Fáil and the IRA motivated individuals to join the Blueshirts.[221] In the context of the street fighting between the Blueshirts and the IRA, Fianna Fáil re-established the Military Tribunal while legislation allowed for internment.[222] The party came into increasing conflict with the IRA from 1934 and there were continued arrests. The IRA was declared an illegal organisation in June 1936.[223]

On 29 April 1936 Seán, a member of Cork Corporation, was arrested a series of raids conducted across Cork city and county by the Garda Síochána. The final count of imprisoned men was 31.[224] All men had IRA affiliations.[225] Seán's arrest galvanised Mary into action. Tom Barry wrote of the Cork arrests noting the treatment of relatives of men who had acquired the status of martyrs in the city during the War of Independence. He referred to the: 'spectacle of Seán MacSwiney (brother of Terry) being led through the streets handcuffed like a criminal: to Tomás MacCurtain (son of another Lord Mayor who died for Ireland) with rifles and Thompson guns pointed at their backs …'[226] Both Seán and Tomás were handcuffed together.[227] Mary and Eílís MacCurtain wrote to the Cork Corporation denouncing the proposal to erect statutes to the two dead Lord Mayors as an act of hypocrisy and mockery given that their relatives were now imprisoned for the same beliefs as they had died for.[228] In June 1936 de Valera opened the new city hall in Cork, a replacement for the building burned by the Black and Tans on 11 December 1920 during the burning of Cork. Two years later, at an event to mark the 18th anniversary of the murder of MacCurtain Mary delivered a lecture. She stated those who opened the new city hall 'were men who no longer gave real fervour to the Republic, allegiance to which caused the destruction of the old City Hall'. She instead 'formally opened the Hall in the name of the living Republic'.[229]

Following the arrest of Seán, Mary wrote to de Valera in a tone of both incredulity and anger. She referred to Fianna Fáil's volte-face in their treatment of the IRA: 'When Frank Aiken rushed up to Arbour Hill to announce their release to the Republican prisoners of 1932, could he have imagined that in 1936 he would be handcuffing together and gaoling – in that same Arbour Hill – the brother of Traolac [sic] Mac Suibne, and the son of

Tomás MacCurtáin?'[230] She denounced Aiken as Minister for Justice for torturing the prisoners by placing them in solitary confinement which, she declared, 'few young people can stand without injury'. Mary then turned to pleading with de Valera, not for release of the prisoners including her brother, but on the wider issue of the republic: 'Come back to the Republic before it is too late, before you are driven to do things which filled your soul, as well as mine with horror when they were done by your predecessors.'[231]

As IRA prisoners were released in 1937 having served their sentence, Mary often formed part of the various welcoming committees.[232] Seán was released on 14 May having undergone a ten-day hunger strike.[233] Mary continued to berate de Valera for his continued attack on the republican forces: '[p]oor, foolish, foolish Dev. how the mighty are fallen'.[234] With this letter Mary exemplified the nature of the conflict between Sinn Féin and Fianna Fáil identified by McConville:

> There was no room for the respect and even curious friendliness that political opponents from different traditions sometimes grant each other. Bitterness and deep anger would infuse this fraternal conflict, accompanied by accusations of inexcusable treachery and irredeemable bad faith. This was more than a contest for power; it was a grasping for the mantle and claim to the spirit of Irish republicanism.[235]

De Valera's reply was curt and underscored Mary's by now lack of political relevance: 'I had refrained from replying to your previous letter because to reply to it in full would have meant engaging in a futile controversy on matters of past history at a time when the problems of the present and the future claim all my attention.'[236]

Mary refused to accept the quiet and subversive revolution that, under de Valera, changed Ireland's constitutional status from dominion to republic in all but name. She discountenanced his pragmatic political approach; in her viewpoint what he achieved still entailed compromise. Macardle commended his maturity in the context of the abdication of King Edward VIII in December 1936. While there were some, she declared, who wanted the Republic 're-declared' and the connection with Great Britain severed there and them, de Valera was more far-sighted:

> That would have given us an unrecognised republic once again and have thrown into chaos our relations with all States to which our ministers were accredited formally by the King. It would not have been a step towards a free, reunited Ireland in a good and stable relationship with her neighbours – Mr de Valera's unchanging goal.[237]

Mary was one such individual who called for the declaration of the republic on the abdication of the British monarch. Her many critics referred to her refusal to accept changing political realities. Macardle, a one-time friend, had earlier accused her of refusing to engage with the 'problems of today'. She represented Mary as living in the past, trapped in a period where 'dying in jail' had political resonance.[238] Such accusations were levelled at Mary again in the context of the abdication crisis. An editorial in the *Irish Press* was scathing at her backward glance:

> She suffers from the delusion that the world has not moved on from a certain date in 1921 or 1922. We know that cases of political obsession of this kind are not uncommon, but it is a pity that a woman of the intelligence and power of mind of Miss MacSwiney could not rise

> above mere personal prejudices and preconceptions, could not view the course of events with unclouded eyes, and could not face and understand the actual conditions of the world in which she is living.

To describe Mary's stance as one based on 'personal prejudices' was to fail to understand the fact that she would not betray the sacrifice of her brother's death. For many in the 1930s Terence's martyrdom had faded into the realms of the past but that was not the case for Mary. The editorial reminded her that the people of Ireland had 'entrusted the conduct of their affairs to the present Government and its head'. Noting that if what she desired, namely the declaration of republic on the abdication of the monarch was carried out, she would be accepting partition.[239]

In keeping with his focus on present-day issues de Valera issued the draft of his new constitution, Bunreacht na hÉireann, in March 1937. Mary was approached by Caitlín Brugha to help 'to show up the proposed Free State constitution in its claim to be Republican'. Brugha noted that it was unlikely that the issue of British control of the three ports, Cobh, Berehaven and Lough Swilly, under the terms of the Treaty would be mentioned.[240] Mary believed that the Second Dáil should issue a statement on the Bunreacht na h-Éireann 'before the nations of the world'.[241] Notably, she also objected to the constitution because it furnished the 'power to discriminate against women in their economic life. Equal pay for equal work is the only just solution'.[242] Sinn Féin, Cumann na mBan and Mná na Poblachta were amongst the republican organisations that viewed the draft constitution as, in the words of Brian Ó hUigínn, 'a repudiation and abandonment of the whole Republican position since 1916'. Any republican who voted for it was committing 'an act of treason'. He noted that Mary's letter challenging the editor of the *Irish Press* to publish her views on the constitution in an unabridged form was not published.[243] Silence, rather than engagement with the republican opposition, indicated how denuded of power they had become. Undaunted, Mary addressed the constitution at length at a meeting in Daunt Square, Cork, on 1 July to demand the release of IRA prisoners. She urged listeners to 'vote for no camouflage' but instead to stand by the IRA to achieve the full freedom of Ireland.[244] Referring to her claim that the monarch was 'camouflaged' in the constitution and in Fianna Fáil policy, the *Irish Press* in an editorial entitled 'Miss MacSwiney Again' challenged her to 'point out where in the whole sphere of government and administration in Ireland the name or authority of the English King can be found'.[245] The context for the editorial was her letter to the paper which she signed 'Yours for the truth'.[246]A further framework may have been her statements at a republican meeting in Fermoy where she emphasised that de Valera had gone to the League of Nations in Geneva not as President of the Republic but as the leader of a dominion state.[247] The *Irish Press* continued to sneer at Mary as the year advanced. Later in September, in response to her criticism that Irish currency was 'pegged to that of Great Britain' and notes and coins minted in England, the paper suggested that she had not 'ever devoted a half an hour to the study of currency problems'.[248] Representing Mary as obtuse was the paper's signal to her political irrelevancy.

Mary's health deteriorated further throughout the second half of the 1930s. After a 'serious illness' in the summer of 1935 she was under medical advice to curtail her political work.[249] The stagnation of the fourth Sinn Féin party was reflected in the age of those at leadership level as other older members were beset with illnesses. There was no injection of younger members of a sufficient calibre to assume leadership positions. As Maillot states of the later 1930s and early 1940s: '[f]or much of the period, most news items concerning Sinn Féin were to be found in the obituary section'.[250] Given the moribund status of the party it was not surprising that in December 1938 the remaining members of the Second Dáil reached an agreement with the IRA reassigning their authority to the Army Council. This move was also to give legitimacy to the Seán Russell's bid to launch an IRA bombing campaign in Britain.[251] In April 1938 Mary had described the 'present age in Ireland ... as an age of political sham' in her Easter commemorative address in Glasnevin.[252] In a sense only failing health and the bleak reality of the state of the Sinn Féin party allowed her to finally embrace a reality that had long been the case; the republic would not be achieved in her lifetime.

Yet, despite stagnation and disillusionment on a political level her personal life was enhanced when Terence and Muriel's daughter, Máire Óg, came to Cork to live in Belgrave place and to attend school in St Ita's. Although Muriel denied it, the MacSwiney sisters claimed that on his deathbed Terence appointed Mary joint-guardian with Muriel of his daughter.[253] In late 1923 Muriel left Ireland, travelling across Germany, Switzerland, and France, placing her daughter in a series of boarding schools.[254] What needs to be remembered is that Muriel had lost her husband as Mary had lost her brother in October 1920. The two women responded to that traumatic event in different ways. Mary's inner strength emerged to allow her to focus on a political career to achieve a republic. Muriel, who, as discussed, already suffered from depression, manifested her trauma in a different way. She was only 28 when Terence died. By the time she left Ireland in 1923 she was a self-declared atheist. Living in continental Europe allowed her a freedom that would not have been accorded to her in an Ireland that was staunchly Catholic and patriarchal. Her membership of the Irish Communist Party and her anti-Catholicism would have ensured that she clashed with Mary, particularly over the upbringing of her daughter.[255]

Mary ensured that she kept in touch with her niece.[256] In her memoir, Máire Óg wrote of her loneliness in this period of her life as she moved from school to school, only seeing her mother during holiday periods. The birth of Muriel's second daughter Alix in 1926 may have compounded Máire Óg sense of isolation. In 1932 Mary, despite her refusal to recognise the institutions of the state, applied to de Valera for a passport to allow her to travel to Germany. During the Treaty debates Mary had declared: '[w]e are all to be British citizens with a British passport, with the seal of the Foreign Office for anyone going out of the country'.[257] While in America in 1925 she asserted that she had no passport and would never apply for one.[258] Yet, when it came to family, Mary was willing to transcend her political principles to, as she saw it, rescue her niece from, in the words of Dolan, 'the peripatetic and erratic life provided by her mother'.[259] Máire Óg recalled a furtive escape from Germany, across the Austrian border and from there to Geneva where Mary brought her to the home of Seán Lester, the representative of the Irish Free State at the League of Nations.[260] Back in Ireland a bitter custody battle with the judge uniquely for the time asking Máire Óg for her viewpoint and ruling that she would have a more stable life with Mary.

Máire Óg was adamant that she wanted to live with her aunts in Cork; it was, she declared, 'my own decision'.[261] However, a court case for custody ensued immediately after MacSwiney returned to Cork with her niece. The case continued throughout the summer of 1932. Judge Meredith made the decision to ask Máire Óg what her wishes were. Granting Mary custody, an order was made that her niece was not to be involved in any republican matters. The latter was made a ward of court under the protection of an Garda Síochána. This decision meant that for some time in the summer of 1932 a Garda escort accompanied Mary and her niece.[262] Máire Óg noted how difficult this must have been for her aunt on a political level but emphasised that Mary was willing to compromise when it meant her happiness. It showed, she wrote, 'how she once again put my welfare before her political principles'.[263]

Muriel continued throughout her life to argue that Mary had, with the connivance of the government, kidnapped her daughter.[264] This may have been her way of coping with yet another loss in her life; the estrangement of a daughter following the trauma of witnessing her husband die on hunger strike. Muriel wrote to the Military Service Pension Board on the matter in 1974:

> Alas since the Irish government has been reinstalled in Dublin, 1921, [sic] several cases of official abduction of children from their lawful parents have occurred. I made an exhaustive investigation several years later into all these cases, difficult because of the secrecy, altho' not in every case.[265]

Attending St Ita's Máire Óg settled into Cork. Her memoir includes school photos with friends and family photos with her aunts both in Cork and in Ballyferriter, Co. Kerry. These were 'happy years of stability and safety'; she could see a 'future' for herself. Her aunt was, she wrote, 'the first person to give me true love'.[266] These were also happy years for Mary; Máire Óg was the child of her beloved brother Terence. A circle was closed as the centrality of family bonds prevailed at the end of her life as at the beginning.

On 23 January 1942 Seán MacSwiney died at Glenvera Private Hospital, Sydney Place, Cork, very close to Belgrave Place.[267] He was only 53 but it is possible that his imprisonments during the revolutionary campaigns and into the 1930s coupled with numerous hunger strikes had impacted on his health. Less than two months later, on 8 March 1942 Mary passed away from heart failure surrounded by her sister and her beloved niece.[268]

Mary's funeral was private at her own request, her body reposing in St Patrick's Church before being laid to rest in St Joseph's Cemetery. Her coffin was draped with the Tricolour.[269] Although there is no extant explicit statement of her reasons for desiring a private funeral, Mary did not recognise the Irish Free State, despite the constitutional changes engineered by de Valera. She could not countenance government representation as she was laid to rest surrounded by her family. The same situation prevailed when Annie died in 1952; there was no official government representation. The Lord Mary of Cork wrote to Máire Óg: 'I quite understand the position regarding the funeral and I have explained it all to Mr. de Valera. We were sorry not to be able to show the deep respect we had for your aunt of which our non-attendance at the funeral deprived us.'[270]

If Mary had no official government representation at her funeral, the *Irish Press*, the organ of the Fianna Fáil party, was effusive in its praise on her death, no doubt a reflection of the bedrock of friendship that had sustained Mary and de Valera through the turbulent years of the civil war. She was the paper declared a 'gallant fighter for her cause'. Of the many women who gave active service to the campaign for independence, 'there was none who gave their services with a more single-minded [sic] generosity than this intrepid Cork woman'.[271] Crucially the paper recognised the way in which Terence's death defined Mary's life after October 1920: 'The tremendous drama of Brixton Gaol transformed and moulded her whole life. Thereafter, she had one set purpose in view, one goal to achieve: to bring to fulfilment the dream which had given her brother the strength to endure until his death the long agony of nights and days.'[272]

Notes

Introduction

1. Annie MacSwiney, 'Diary of Week of Terry's Greatest Torture', in Margaret Lucey, BMH WS 1561.
2. Letter to [de Valera] from Mary MacSwiney, [Dec. 1921], de Valera Papers, P150/656, UCDA.
3. Charlotte Fallon, *Soul of Fire: A Biography of Mary MacSwiney* (Cork, 1986).
4. First names will be used throughout the study for all members of the MacSwiney family to avoid confusion.
5. Full details of primary sources are listed in the bibliography.
6. http://www.census.nationalarchives.ie/pages/1911/Cork/Blackrock/Knockrea/401536/
7. Joan Scott, 'Gender: A useful category of analysis', in *American Historical review*, vol. 91, no. 5 (1986), p. 1,056.
8. Letter to 'Nan' [Annie] MacSwiney from Madame Sr F. Xavier, [1954], Mary MacSwiney Papers, P48a/458, UCDA.
9. Agnes Maillot, *In the Shadow of History: Sinn Féin, 1926–70* (Manchester 2015), p. 87.
10. See Sinéad McCoole, *Easter Widows: Seven Women Who Lived in the Shadow of the 1916 Rising* (Dublin, 2014).
11. Quoted in Síobhra Aiken, *Spiritual Wounds: Trauma, Testimony and the Irish Civil War* (Dublin, 2022), p. 110.
12. Paul Lerner and Mark S. Micale, 'Trauma, psychiatry, and history: A conceptual and historiographical introduction', in Mark S. Micale and Paul Lerner (eds), *Traumatic Pasts: History, Psychiatry, and Trauma in the Modern Age, 1870–1930* (Cambridge, 2001), p. 6.
13. Graham Dawson, 'The meaning of "moving on": From trauma to the history and memory of emotions in "post-conflict" Northern Ireland', in *Irish University Review*, vol. 47, no. 1 (2017), pp 82–3.
14. Quoted in ibid., p. 83.
15. *Freeman's Journal*, 13 Oct. 1917.
16. William Murphy, 'Dying, death and hunger strikes: Cork and Brixton, 1920', in James Kelly and Mary Ann Lyons (eds), *Death and Dying in Ireland, Britain and Europe: Historical Perspectives* (Dublin, 2013), p. 300.
17. G. B. Griffiths, Medical Report, 25 Sept. 1920, HO144/10308.
18. Telegram from Treadwell to the Chief Secretary, Sir John Anderson, 23 Sept. 1920, HO144/10308.
19. Mary MacSwiney, 'Peace Negotiations – Ratification of the Plenipotentiarie', Dáil Éireann Debates, 14 Sept. 1921.
20. Mary MacSwiney, 'Debate on the Treaty', Dáil Éireann Debates, 21 Dec. 1921.
21. Ibid.
22. *Belfast Newsletter*, 13 Feb. 1923.
23. Quoted in the *Freeman's Journal*, 12 Mar. 1923.
24. Ibid., 14 Mar. 1923.
25. Ibid., 17 Feb. 1923.
26. *Offaly Independent*, 24 Jan. 1925.
27. *Cork Examiner*, 12 Feb. 1926.
28. *Belfast Newsletter*, 26 June 1923.
29. Brian Feeney, *Sinn Féin: A Hundred Turbulent Years* (Dublin, 2002), p. 171.
30. *Cork Examiner*, 23 Feb. 1923.

31. Kathleen Lynn Diary, 12 Jan. 1926, RCPI.
32. Máire Comerford interview with Dr Margaret Ward, 1975. I am very grateful to Margaret Ward for sharing this source.
33. Mary MacSwiney, 'Testimony', in *Evidence on Conditions in Ireland: Comprising the Complete Testimony, Affidavits and Exhibits Presented Before the American Commission on Conditions in Ireland* (Washington, 1921), p. 317.
34. MacSwiney, 'Testimony', p. 305.
35. MacSwiney, 'Debate on the Treaty', Dáil Éireann Debates, 21 Dec. 1921.
36. Mary MacSwiney, Castle File, No. 3742, National Archives, Kew, London.

Chapter 1: A Republican Family Unit

1. Charlotte Fallon, *Soul of Fire: A Biography of Mary MacSwiney* (Cork, 1986), p. 11.
2. Ciaran O'Neill, 'Bourgeois Ireland, or, on the benefits of keeping one's hands clean', in James Kelly (ed.), *The Cambridge History of Ireland, III* (Cambridge, 2018), p. 535.
3. Letter to 'Nan' [Annie] MacSwiney from Madame Sr F. Xavier, [1954], Mary MacSwiney Papers, P48a/458, UCDA.
4. Mary MacSwiney, 'Testimony', in *Evidence on Conditions in Ireland: Comprising the Complete Testimony, Affidavits and Exhibits Presented Before the American Commission on Conditions in Ireland* (Washington, 1921), p. 199.
5. Ibid., p. 199.
6. Annie MacSwiney, 'Typescript biographical text of Mary MacSwiney', p. 1, Mary MacSwiney Papers, P48a/462, UCDA. This was written in 1954.
7. http://www.census.nationalarchives.ie/reels/nai000522231/
8. *Slater's Directory, Cork City and County*, 1870.
9. MacSwiney, 'Typescript biographical text of Mary MacSwiney', p. 1.
10. *Slater's Directory, Cork City and County*, 1870; 1881.
11. *Cork Examiner*, 18 Feb. 1881; 4 May 1881.
12. *Cork Examiner*, 1 June 1881.
13. *New York Times*, 27 Dec. 1884.
14. Quoted in Liam Ó Dochartaigh, 'An bárd 'gus an fó', in *Comhar*, vol. 34, no. 1 (Jan. 1975), p.6.
15. MacSwiney, 'Typescript biographical text of Mary MacSwiney', p 3.
16. Colin Barr, 'The Re-Energising of Irish Catholicism, 1790–1880', in James Kelly (ed.), *The Cambridge History of Ireland, III* (Cambridge, 2018), p. 301.
17. Robert Doyle, 'The Pope's Irish Battalion, 1860', in *History Ireland*, vol. 18, no. 5 (Sept./Oct., 2010). https://historyireland.com/the-popes-irish-battalion-1860/
18. Letter to 'Nan' [Annie MacSwiney] from Madame Sr F. Xavier, [1954], Mary MacSwiney Papers, P48a/458, UCDA. The Elementary Education Act, 1870, established semi-state funded board schools to meet the need where existing voluntary school provision was inadequate.
19. England and Wales, Marriage Registration Index, 1837-2005, https://search-findmypast-ie.dcu.idm.oclc.org/record?id=BMD%2FM%2F1871%2F2%2FAZ%2F000184&parentid=BMD%2FM%2F1871%2F2%2FAZ%2F000184%2F213, accessed 7 Jan. 2023; 'Typescript biographical text of Mary MacSwiney', p. 4.
20. MacSwiney, 'Typescript biographical text of Mary MacSwiney', p. 5.
21. Ibid., p 7; *Slater's Directory, Cork City and County* 1881.
22. Patrick Maume, 'Daniel Corkery: A reassessment', in *Studia Hibernica*, no. 26 (1992), pp 148–9.
23. Andy Bielenberg and David Johnson, 'The production and consumption of tobacco in Ireland, 1800–1914', in *Irish Economic and Social History*, vol. 25 (1998), p. 1.
24. MacSwiney, 'Typescript biographical text of Mary MacSwiney', p. 7; *Slater's Directory, Cork City and County* 1881.
25. MacSwiney, 'Typescript biographical text of Mary MacSwiney', p. 7.
26. Mary MacSwiney, Draft Memoir, no date, Mary MacSwiney Papers, P48a/3002, UCDA.
27. MacSwiney, 'Typescript biographical text of Mary MacSwiney', p. 8.
28. MacSwiney, 'Testimony', p. 200.
29. Ibid., p. 194.

30. MacSwiney, 'Typescript biographical text of Mary MacSwiney', p. 2.
31. John Borgonov, *The Dynamics of War and Revolution: Cork City, 1916–1918* (Cork, 2013), p. 7.
32. See for example, *Cork Examiner*, 15 Apr. 1882; 9 May 1882.
33. William Murphy, *Political Imprisonment and the Irish, 1912–1921* (Oxford, 2014), p. 8.
34. *Cork Examiner*, 1 Oct. 1880.
35. Deirdre Raftery and Susan M. Parkes, *Female Education in Ireland 1700–1900: Minerva or Madonna* (Dublin, 2007), p. 11.
36. MacSwiney, 'Typescript biographical text of Mary MacSwiney', p. 7.
37. Judith Harford, 'The movement for the Higher Education of women in Ireland: Gender equality or denominational rivalry', in *History of Education*, vol. 34 no. 5 (Sept 2005), p. 514.
38. Ibid., p. 514–15; See *Cork Examiner*, 3 Aug. 1887 for the advertisement for the soon to be opened St Angela's High School. This advertisement ran throughout the month.
39. Of nine children, seven survived into adulthood: Mary, Kit, Margaret, Peter, Annie, Terence and Seán. Two brothers, John Joseph and Eugene, died in early infanthood, the latter from meningitis. MacSwiney, 'Typescript biographical text of Mary MacSwiney', p. 10.
40. Letter to 'Nan' [Annie] MacSwiney from Madame Sr F. Xavier, [1954], Mary MacSwiney Papers, P48a/458, UCDA; MacSwiney, 'Typescript biographical text of Mary MacSwiney', p. 9.
41. MacSwiney, 'Typescript biographical text of Mary MacSwiney', pp 14–5, p. 18.
42. Roger Cooter, *Surgery and Society in Peace and War* (London, 1993), p. 112.
43. Julie Anderson, '"Jumpy stump": Amputation and trauma in the First World War', in *First World War Studies*, vol. 6, no. 1 (2015), pp 11–12.
44. Joanna Bourke, *Dismembering the Male: Men's Bodies, Britain and the Great War* (London, 1999), p. 51; Anderson, '"Jumpy Stump": Amputation and trauma', p. 10.
45. *Cork Examiner*, 11 Aug. 1890.
46. Bielenberg and Johnson, 'The production and consumption of tobacco in Ireland', p. 10.
47. 'Notes by Miss Mary MacSwiney, sister of Terence MacSwiney, on his early life', no date, Erskine Childers Papers, Ms 48,064, NLI.
48. *Cork Examiner*, 6 July 1883.
49. MacSwiney, 'Typescript biographical text of Mary MacSwiney', p. 7, p. 11; 'Murphy, Daniel (1815–1907)', in *Australian Dictionary of Biography*, http://adb.anu.edu.au/biography/murphy-daniel-4274/text6911, accessed 25 Apr. 2020.
50. MacSwiney, 'Typescript biographical text of Mary MacSwiney', p. 12.
51. Letter to Mrs Mary MacSwiney from John MacSwiney, 23 Sept. 1895, Terence MacSwiney Papers, P48b/1, UCDA.
52. Letter to Kit MacSwiney from Mary MacSwiney, 14 Jan. 1898, Terence MacSwiney Papers, P48b/2, UCDA.
53. Terence MacSwiney Diary, 8 Apr 1905, Terence MacSwiney Papers, Ms 35,030, NLI.
54. MacSwiney, 'Typescript biographical text of Mary MacSwiney', p. 9.
55. Frank O'Connor, *An Only Child* (Belfast, 1993), p. 3.
56. MacSwiney, 'Typescript biographical text of Mary MacSwiney', pp 12–14.
57. Letter to Étienette Beuque from Annie MacSwiney, 1 Mar. 1925, Papers of Terence MacSwiney's Biographers, P48c/23, UCDA.
58. Notes by Miss Mary MacSwiney, sister of Terence MacSwiney, on his early life', no date, Erskine Childers Papers, Ms 48,064, NLI.
59. MacSwiney, 'Testimony', p. 184; Peter MacSwiney, *Evidence on Conditions in Ireland: Comprising the Complete Testimony, Affidavits and Exhibits Presented Before the American Commission on Conditions in Ireland* (Washington, 1921), p. 889.
60. Notes by Miss Mary MacSwiney, sister of Terence MacSwiney, on his early life', no date, Erskine Childers Papers, Ms 48,064, NLI.
61. MacSwiney, 'Typescript biographical text of Mary MacSwiney', pp 16-17.
62. MacSwiney, 'Testimony', p. 200.
63. Terence MacSwiney Diary, 7 July 1904, Terence MacSwiney Papers, Ms35,030, NLI.
64. Maume, 'Daniel Corkery', p. 154.
65. Notes by Miss Mary MacSwiney, sister of Terence MacSwiney, on his early life', no date, Erskine Childers Papers, Ms 48,064, NLI.

66. Notes by Miss Mary MacSwiney, sister of Terence MacSwiney, on his early life', no date, Erskine Childers Papers, Ms 48,064, NLI.
67. Moirin Chavasse, *Terence MacSwiney* (Dublin, 1961), p. 25.
68. Terence MacSwiney Diary, 20 July 1903, Terence MacSwiney Papers, Ms 35,029, NLI.
69. Letter to Mrs Mary MacSwiney from John MacSwiney, 23 Sept. 1895, Terence MacSwiney Papers, P48b/1, UCDA.
70. MacSwiney, 'Typescript biographical text of Mary MacSwiney', p. 25.
71. Letter to Revd Mother, Hillside Convent, Farnborough from M. Punnett, Principal, Cambridge Teacher Training College, 20 Aug. 1900, Mary MacSwiney Papers P48a/3, UCDA.
72. Postcard to Mary MacSwiney from Oscar Browning, Secretary, King's College, Cambridge, July 1902 informing her of her success in the practical part of the Teacher Training Syndicate Examination, Mary MacSwiney Papers, P48a/2, UCDA; Notice from the Royal University of Ireland, c.1902, informing Mary MacSwiney that the examiners recommended that her name appear on the pass list, Mary MacSwiney Papers, P48a/4, UCDA.
73. MacSwiney, 'Typescript biographical text of Mary MacSwiney', p. 12.
74. Letter to 'Nan' [Annie] MacSwiney from Madame Sr F. Xavier, [1954], Mary MacSwiney Papers, P48a/458, UCDA.
75. MacSwiney, 'Typescript biographical text of Mary MacSwiney', pp 19–21.
76. http://www.census.nationalarchives.ie/reels/nai000518807/
77. http://www.census.nationalarchives.ie/reels/nai000518808/
78. http://www.census.nationalarchives.ie/reels/nai000518811/
79. http://www.census.nationalarchives.ie/reels/nai000518807/
80. Terence MacSwiney Diary, 8 Apr. 1905, Terence MacSwiney Papers, Ms 35,030, NLI.
81. Letter to Mary MacSwiney from Kit MacSwiney, 30 June 1904, Terence MacSwiney Papers, P48b/3, UCDA.
82. Terence MacSwiney Diary, 7 July 1904, Terence MacSwiney Papers, Ms 35,030, NLI.
83. MacSwiney, 'Typescript biographical text of Mary MacSwiney', p. 31, p. 33.
84. Ibid., p. 34.
85. Letter to Mary MacSwiney from Kit MacSwiney, 30 June 1904, Terence MacSwiney Papers, P48b/3, UCDA.
86. Terence MacSwiney Diary, 3 Dec. 1905, Terence MacSwiney Papers, Ms 35,031, NLI.
87. MacSwiney, 'Typescript biographical text of Mary MacSwiney', p. 36.
88. Terence MacSwiney Diary, 30 July 1906, Terence MacSwiney Papers, Ms 35,031, NLI.
89. Terence MacSwiney Diary, 3 May 1910, Terence MacSwiney Papers, Ms 35,033, NLI.
90. MacSwiney, 'Typescript biographical text of Mary MacSwiney', p. 40; National University of Ireland Calendar, 1913.
91. Margaret Ward, *Fearless Woman: Hanna Sheehy Skeffington, Feminism and the Irish Revolution* (Dublin, 2019), p. 67.
92. *Cork Examiner*, 9 Nov. 1911.
93. Ibid.
94. Ward, *Fearless Woman,* p. 100.
95. *Cork Examiner*, 9 Nov. 1911.
96. Mary MacSwiney, Draft Memoir, no date, Mary MacSwiney Papers, P48a/3002, UCDA.
97. *Cork Examiner*, 11 Nov. 1911.
98. Sandra McAvoy, 'Relief work and refugees: Susanne Rouviere Day (1876–1964) on war as women's business', in *Women's History Review*, vol. 27, no. 3 (2018), p. 398.
99. Account of a meeting of the MWFL at Cork City Hall on 26 Feb. 1914 at which MacSwiney gave a talk entitled 'The basis of the franchise', in *Irish Citizen*, 2 Mar. 1914.
100. *Irish Citizen*, 28 Mar. 1914.
101. *Cork Examiner*, 9 Nov. 1911.
102. McAvoy, 'Relief work and refugees', p. 399.
103. Quoted in ibid.
104. *Irish Citizen*, 23 May 1914.
105. *Fianna Fáil*, 17 Oct. 1914.
106. Terence MacSwiney Diary, 19 Sept 1902–12 Dec. 1903, Terence MacSwiney Papers, Ms 35,029, NLI.

107. Mary MacSwiney, Draft Memoir, no date, Mary MacSwiney Papers, P48a/3002, UCDA.
108. Con Murphy, BMH WS 24.
109. Patrick Higgins, BMH WS 25.
110. Patrick Maume, '*Life that is Exile*': *Daniel Corkery and the Search for Irish Ireland* (Belfast, 1993), p. 5.
111. Daniel Corkery, *The Threshold of Quiet* ((Dublin, 1946), p. 4, p. 11.
112. Letter to Peg MacSwiney from Terence MacSwiney, 30 Jan. 1914, Terence MacSwiney Papers, P48b/4, UCDA.
113. Patrick Higgins, BMH WS 25.
114. Daniel Corkery, 'Terence MacSwiney: Lord Mayor of Cork', in *Studies: An Irish Quarterly Review*, vol. 9, no. 36 (Dec. 1920), p. 520, p. 512.
115. R. F. Foster, *Vivid Faces: The Revolutionary Generation in Ireland 1890–1923* (London, 2014), p. 50.
116. Maume, '*Life that is Exile*', p. 23, p. 25.
117. Foster, *Vivid Faces*, p. 51.
118. Eithne Nic Suibhne, BMH WS 0119.
119. Corkery, 'Terence MacSwiney', p. 517.
120. Corkery, 'Foreword', in Chavasse, *Terence MacSwiney*, p. 12.
121. Corkery, 'Terence MacSwiney', p. 516.
122. Liam de Róiste, BMH 1698.
123. Maume, 'Daniel Corkery', pp 153–4.
124. Borgonovo, *The Dynamics of War and Revolution* (Cork, 2013), p. 254, note 79; Daniel Corkery, 'Literary Career' in P. S. O'Hegarty, *A Short Memoir of Terence MacSwiney* (Dublin, 1922), p. 26.
125. Letter to Peg MacSwiney from Terence MacSwiney, 30 Jan. 1914, Terence MacSwiney Papers, P48b/4, UCDA.
126. Liam de Róiste Diary, 8 Dec. 1914, CCCA.
127. De Róiste, BMH WS 1698.
128. Quoted in Borgonovo, *The Dynamics of War*, p. 18.
129. William Murphy, 'Rooney, William (Ó Maolruanaidh, Liam)', in James McGuire and James Quinn (eds), *Dictionary of Irish Biography* (Cambridge, 2009), (http://dib.cambridge.org/viewReadPage.do?articleId=a7797).
130. De Róiste, BMH WS 1699. Later in his statement de Róiste states that on 3 September 1903 this aim was adopted, replacing the initial stated object to 'endeavour to restore Ireland to its rightful position of Sovereign Independence'. At a later meeting the initial aim 'was restored'.
131. De Róiste, BMH WS 1698.
132. Ibid.
133. Letter to Étienette Beuque from Annie MacSwiney, 4 Oct. 1925, Papers of Terence MacSwiney's Biographers, P48c/26, UCDA.
134. *Cork Examiner*, 13 May 1911; Diarmuid Ó Donneabhain, BMH WS 79.
135. Michael Ó Cuill, BMH WS 89.
136. P. J. Murphy, BMH WS 869.
137. De Róiste, 5 Dec. 1905, BMH WS 1698.
138. Borgonovo, *The Dynamics of War*, p. 21.
139. MacSwiney, 'Testimony', p. 201.
140. Terence MacSwiney Diary, 19 Sept 1902–12 Dec. 1903, p. 19 Terence MacSwiney Papers, Ms 35,029, NLI.
141. Mary MacSwiney, Draft Memoir, no date, Mary MacSwiney Papers, P48a/3002, UCDA.
142. Ibid.
143. Michael Laffan, 'Griffith, Arthur Joseph', in James McGuire and James Quinn (eds), *Dictionary of Irish Biography* (Cambridge, 2009), https://www.dib.ie/biography/griffith-arthur-joseph-a3644#:~:text=Griffith%2C%20Arthur%20Joseph%20(1871–,Mary%20Griffith%20(née%20Whelan), accessed 29 Apr. 2024.
144. http://www.census.nationalarchives.ie/pages/1911/Cork/Blackrock/Knockrea/401536/
145. MacSwiney, Draft Memoir, no date, Mary MacSwiney Papers, P48a/3002, UCDA.
146. http://www.census.nationalarchives.ie/reels/nai001896165/

147. A. M. Fahy, 'Place and class in Cork', in Patrick O' Flanagan and Cornelius G. Buttimer, *Cork History and Society* (Dublin, 1993), pp 808–9.
148. Typescript draft article by W. F. P. Stockley on Seán MacSwiney following his death, 22 Jan. 1942, Mary MacSwiney Papers, P48a/460, UCDA.
149. MacSwiney, 'Typescript biographical text of Mary MacSwiney', p. 40.
150. MacSwiney, Draft Memoir, no date, Mary MacSwiney Papers, P48a/3002, UCDA.
151. Ibid.
152. *Cork Examiner*, 14 Nov. 1914.
153. *Skibbereen Eagle*, 12 Dec. 1914.
154. Letter to the Editor of the *Irish Citizen* from Mary MacSwiney, 21 Nov. 1914. A brief editorial response to MacSwiney's 'I-told-you-so' noted that Sylvia Pankhurst and the East London Federation of Suffragettes, the United Suffragists and the Women's Freedom League were taking a 'different line' to the war than Christabel Pankhurst. V. D. Farrington, the organising secretary of the MWFL, noted the regret of the members at MacSwiney's decision to resign membership but also stated that the question of 'banishing' the *Irish Citizen* was dropped. *Irish Citizen*, 28 Nov. 1914.
155. Letter to the Editor of the *Irish Citizen* from Mary MacSwiney, 21 Nov. 1914.
156. Liam Murphy, BMH WS 19.
157. Peter Hart, *The IRA and its Enemies: Violence and Community in Cork, 1916–1923* (Oxford, 1998), p. 45.
158. Margaret Ward, *Unmanageable Revolutionaries: Women and Irish Nationalism, 1880–1980* (Dublin, 2021), p. 169.
159. Senia Pašeta, *Irish Nationalist Women, 1900–1918* (Cambridge, 2014), p. 6.
160. Some Cork members of Cumann na mBan date the foundation of the Cork branch to 1913. See, for example, Peg Duggan BMH 1576.
161. Patrick Higgins, BMH WS 25.
162. MacSwiney, Draft Memoir, no date, Mary MacSwiney Papers, P48a/3002, UCDA; MacSwiney, 'Typescript biographical text of Mary MacSwiney', p. 45.
163. MacSwiney, Draft Memoir, no date, Mary MacSwiney Papers, P48a/3002, UCDA.
164. Letter to [Mary MacSwiney] from Tomás MacCurtain, 24 May 1914, Mary MacSwiney Papers, P48a/8/2, UCDA.
165. *Cork Examiner*, 5 June 1914; Borgonovo, *The Dynamics of War*, p. 141, p. 23.
166. Copy of a report of a meeting of the National Volunteers held under the auspices of the Irish Women's Council, 9 June 1914, presided over by Mary MacSwiney, Mary MacSwiney Papers, P48a/14, UCDA.
167. *Cork Examiner*, 5 June 1914.
168. Ibid.
169. Sarah Richardson, *The Political Worlds of Women: Gender and Politics in Nineteenth Century Britain* (Abingdon, 2013), p. 127.
170. *Cork Examiner*, 5 June 1914; MacSwiney, 'Typescript biographical text of Mary MacSwiney', p. 44.
171. Lil Conlon, Manuscript of *Cumann na mBan and the Women of Ireland, 1913–25*, chapter 1, p. 2, Cork Public Museum.
172. *Cork Examiner*, 9 June 1914.
173. Ward, *Fearless Woman*, p. 182.
174. Mary MacSwiney, *Irish Citizen*, 25 July 1914.
175. Letter to Mary MacSwiney from Rosamond Jacob, 24 May 1914, Mary MacSwiney Papers, P48a/8/7, UCDA.
176. Letter to Mary MacSwiney from the Secretary, Department of Agriculture and Technical Instruction for Ireland, 22 Mar. 1915, Mary MacSwiney Papers, P48a/8/24, UCDA.
177. Conlon, Manuscript of *Cumann na mBan*, chapter 1, p. 3, Cork Public Museum.
178. *Cork Examiner*, 28 July 1914.
179. MacSwiney, 'Testimony', p. 211.
180. Conlon, Manuscript of *Cumann na mBan*, chapter 1, p. 4, Cork Public Museum.
181. Peg Duggan BMH WS 1576; Margaret Lucey, BMH WS1561.
182. Borgonovo, *The Dynamics of War*, p. 26.
183. Peg Duggan BMH WS 1576.

184. De Róiste Diary, 23 Jan. 1915, CCCA.
185. Margaret Lucey, BMH WS1561.
186. Report from the Department of Agriculture and Technical Instruction for Ireland, 24 July 1915, Mary MacSwiney Papers, P48a/8/30, UCDA.
187. Margaret Skinnider, *Doing My Bit for Ireland* (New York, 1917), p. 6.
188. See, for example, letter to the editor from Edward Sheehan, Chairman, Cork Consumers' League, on the increased price of bread, *Cork Examiner*, 8 Feb. 1915.
189. Liam de Róiste, *Evening Echo* Series, 16 Sept. 1954.
190. *Cork Examiner*, 12 Aug. 1914; *Cork Examiner*, 15 Aug. 1914; John Borgonovo, '"A Soviet in embryo": Cork's food crisis and the people's food committee, 1917–18, in *Saothar*, vol. 34 (2009), p. 21.
191. *Cork Examiner*, 18 Jan. 1915.
192. Conlon, Manuscript of *Cumann na mBan*, chapter 1, p. 4, Cork Public Museum.
193. Borgonovo, '"A Soviet in embryo": Cork's food crisis', p. 21, pp 24–6.
194. *Cork Examiner*, 7 Sept. 1914; 27 Nov. 1914.
195. Borgonovo, '"A Soviet in embryo": Cork's food crisis', p. 22.
196. *Cork Examiner*, 7 Sept. 1914; 27 Nov. 1914.
197. Ibid., 28 Aug. 1914.
198. Ibid., 30 Sept. 1914. MacSwiney's apologies for non-attendance at the meeting were recorded.
199. Ibid., 11 Jan. 1915.
200. MacSwiney, 'Typescript biographical text of Mary MacSwiney', p. 54.
201. Ibid., p. 58; Ward, *Fearless Woman*, p. 290.
202. MacSwiney, 'Typescript biographical text of Mary MacSwiney', p. 56, p. 58.
203. De Róiste Diary, 8 Nov. 1914, CCCA.
204. Florence O'Donoghue, 'Typescript history of the Irish Volunteers in Cork to 1916', p. 57, Florence O'Donoghue Papers, Ms31,437/2, NLI.
205. *Fianna Fáil*, 26 Sept. 1914.
206. Corkery, 'Terence MacSwiney', pp 515–6, p. 158.
207. Florence O'Donoghue. 'Typescript history of the Irish Volunteers in Cork to 1916', p. 57, Florence O'Donoghue Papers, Ms31,437/2, NLI; Corkery, 'Terence MacSwiney', p. 518.
208. Corkery, 'Terence MacSwiney', p. 518.

Chapter 2: Cork: 1916

1. Annie MacSwiney, 'Typescript biographical text of Mary MacSwiney', p. 82, Mary MacSwiney Papers, P48a/462, UCDA. Rainfall across Ireland in April and May 1916 was unusual during the period 1881–1924. Sandra Spillane, 'Weather Easter 1916' http://edepositireland.ie/bitstream/handle/2262/76136/WeatherofEaster1916.pdf?sequence=1&isAllowed=y
2. Letter to Florence O'Donoghue from Annie MacSwiney, 9 Apr. 1954, Florence O'Donoghue Papers, Ms 31,282/2/20, NLI.
3. Charlotte Fallon, *Soul of Fire: A Biography of Mary MacSwiney* (Cork, 1984), pp 29–30.
4. Letter to Terence MacSwiney from Annie MacSwiney, 12 July 1916, Terence MacSwiney Papers, P48b/8, UCDA.
5. Terence MacSwiney became second in command of the Cork Volunteers following the split in September 1914.
6. Letter to Muriel MacSwiney from Seán MacSwiney, 30 June 1918, Fred Cronin Papers, Ms 29,526/10, NLI.
7. Letter to Peter MacSwiney from Seán MacSwiney, 19 May 1918, Fred Cronin Papers, Ms 29,526/10, NLI.
8. Sheila Wallace, Application for a Military Service Pension, 6 Dec. 1935, MSP34Ref29324 Sheila Wallace, MSPC.
9. Letter to the Secretary, Military Service Pension Board, from Martin Corry, 26 Dec. 1937, MSP34Ref29324 Sheila Wallace, MSPC. Brunswick Street is now named St Augustine Street.
10. Letter to the Military Service Pension Board from Seán O'Hegarty, 4 June 1937, MSP34Ref29324 Sheila Wallace, MSPC.

11. Ibid.
12. Letter to the Military Service Pension Board from Margaret Lucy, 19 Mar. 1938, WMSP34REF5979 Annie Walsh, MSPC.
13. https://www.census.nationalarchives.ie/reels/nai001854230/
14. *The Irish Volunteer*, 5 Feb. 1916.
15. Handwritten notes by Mary MacSwiney on Terence's first arrest and imprisonment, no date, Papers of Terence MacSwiney's biographers, P48c/275, UCDA.
16. Liam de Róiste Diary, 27 Jan. 1916; 15 Feb. 1916; 14 Jan. 1916, Liam de Róiste, BMH WS 1698, part 2.
17. William Murphy, *Political Imprisonment and the Irish, 1912–1921* (Oxford, 2014), p. 94.
18. De Róiste Diary, 3 Feb. 1916, Liam de Róiste, BMH WS 1698, part 2.
19. De Róiste Diary, 27 Jan. 1916, Liam de Róiste, BMH WS 1698, part 2.
20. MacSwiney, 'Typescript biographical text of Mary MacSwiney', p. 64.
21. L. Ginnell, 'Imprisonment without trial, House of Commons debates, 17 Feb. 1916, *Hansard,* vol. 80, col. 220.
22. *The Irish Volunteer*, 4 Mar. 1916.
23. De Róiste Diary, 15 Feb. 1916, Liam de Róiste, BMH WS 1698, part 2.
24. Ibid.
25. MacSwiney, 'Typescript biographical text of Mary MacSwiney', p. 69.
26. Liam Ruiséal, 'The position in Cork', *Capuchin Annual*, 1966, p. 375.
27. De Róiste Diary, 15 Feb.1916; 21 Feb. 1916, Liam de Róiste, BMH WS 1698, part 2.
28. MacSwiney, 'Typescript biographical text of Mary MacSwiney', p. 71.
29. Mark Duncan, 'Thomas Kent and Cork's rising', in *Century Ireland* https://www.rte.ie/centuryireland/index.php/articles/the-kent-family-corks-rising-experience, accessed 7 Nov. 2022.
30. Charles Townshend, *The Republic: The Fight for Irish Independence* (London, 2013), p. 33.
31. John Borgonovo, 'The War of Independence in Cork and Kerry', *The Irish Revolution Project* https://www.ucc.ie/en/theirishrevolution/collections/mapping-the-irish-revolution/the-war-of-independence-in-cork-and-kerry/, accessed 7 Nov. 2022.
32. John Borgonovo, *Florence and Josephine O'Donoghue's War of Independence* (Dublin, 2006), p. 20.
33. Duncan, 'Thomas Kent and Cork's rising'.
34. Letter to the Military Service Pensions Board from Breeid Martin, 8 Dec. 1954, WMSP34REF64289 Breeid Martin, MSPC.
35. Eithne NicSuibhne, BMH WS 0119.
36. MacSwiney, 'Typescript biographical text of Mary MacSwiney', p. 71.
37. Ibid., p. 76.
38. *Irish Freedom,* Nov. 1911.
39. Nora Daly Dore, BMH WS 154.
40. Ibid.
41. John Borgonovo, *The Dynamics of War and Revolution: Cork City, 1916–1918* (Cork, 2013), p. 41.
42. Francis J. Costello, *Enduring the Most: The Life and Death of Terence MacSwiney* (Dingle, 1996), p. 61.
43. Ibid.
44. Letter to Florence O'Donoghue from Annie MacSwiney, 6 Apr. 1954, Florence O'Donoghue Papers, Ms 31,282/2/14, NLI.
45. Costello, *Enduring the Most*, pp 61–2.
46. Patrick Higgins, BMH WS 25.
47. Florence O'Donoghue, 'Typescript history of the Irish Volunteers in Cork to 1916', p. 115, Florence O'Donoghue Papers, Ms 31,437/2, NLI.
48. Ruiséal, 'The position in Cork', pp 375–6.
49. Patrick Higgins, BMH WS 25.
50. Cornelius Murphy, BMH WS 24
51. De Róiste Diary, 20 Apr. 1916, Liam de Róiste, BMH WS 1698, part 2.
52. De Róiste Diary, 21 Apr. 1916, Liam de Róiste, BMH WS 1698, part 2.
53. Gerry White and Brendan O'Shea, '*Baptised in Blood': The Formation of the Cork Brigade of the Irish Volunteers 1913–1916* (Cork, 2005), p. 99.
54. MacSwiney, 'Typescript biographical text of Mary MacSwiney', pp 76–7.

55. Ibid., pp 78–9.
56. Ibid., p. 81.
57. Eithne NicSuibhne, BMH WS 0119.
58. MacSwiney, 'Typescript biographical text of Mary MacSwiney', p. 82; Letter to Florence O'Donoghue from Annie MacSwiney, 23 Mar. 1954, Florence O'Donoghue Papers, Ms 31,282/2/10, NLI.
59. Letter to Florence O'Donoghue from Annie MacSwiney, 9 Apr. 1954, Florence O'Donoghue Papers, Ms 31,282/2/20, NLI.
60. Borgonovo, *The Dynamics of War*, p. 41; White and O'Shea, *'Baptised in Blood'*, p. 99.
61. White and O'Shea, *'Baptised in Blood'*, p. 102.
62. Borgonovo, *The Dynamics of War*, p. 41.
63. Charles Townshend, *Easter 1916: The Irish Rebellion* (London, 2015), p. 235.
64. White and O'Shea, *'Baptised in Blood'*, p. 103.
65. De Róiste Diary, 23 Apr. 1916, Liam de Róiste, BMH WS 1698, part 2.
66. De Róiste Diary, 24 Apr. 1916, Liam de Róiste, BMH WS 1698, part 2.
67. Transcript of interview with Seán O'Hegarty conducted and transcribed by Florence O'Donoghue relating to events in Cork during the Easter Rising, Florence O'Donoghue Papers, Ms 31,334/4, NLI.
68. Letter to Florence O'Donoghue from Annie MacSwiney, 27 Mar. 1954, Florence O'Donoghue Papers, Ms 31,282/2/12, NLI.
69. Ruiséal, 'The Position in Cork', p. 378.
70. Transcript of interview with Seán O'Hegarty conducted and transcribed by Florence O'Donoghue relating to events in Cork during the Easter Rising, Florence O'Donoghue Papers, Ms 31,334/4, NLI.
71. Patrick Higgins, BMH WS 25.
72. Ibid.
73. Costello, *Enduring the Most*, pp 66–7.
74. Patrick Higgins, BMH WS 25.
75. Nora Daly Dore, BMH WS154.
76. De Róiste Diary, 6 May 1916, Liam de Róiste, BMH WS 1698, part 2.
77. Copy translation from Irish to English of account by Tomás MacCurtain of Easter week in Cork,16 Aug. 1916, Florence O'Donoghue Papers, Ms 31,140/2, NLI.
78. Margaret Lucey, summary of evidence before the MSPB, 19 July 1937, MSP34REF29731 Madge Lucey, MSPC.
79. Peg Duggan, BMH WS 1576.
80. MacSwiney, 'Typescript biographical text of Mary MacSwiney', p. 90.
81. Michael Leahy, BMH WS 94.
82. MacSwiney, 'Typescript biographical text of Mary MacSwiney', p. 96.
83. Borgonovo, *The Dynamics of War*, p. 47.
84. De Róiste Diary, 9 May 1916, Liam de Róiste, BMH WS 1698, part 2.
85. Borgonovo, 'The War of Independence in Cork and Kerry', https://www.ucc.ie/en/theirishrevolution/collections/mapping-the-irish-revolution/the-war-of-independence-in-cork-and-kerry/ accessed 18 Apr. 2023.
86. Costello, *Enduring the Most*, p. 76.
87. Letter from Annie MacSwiney to Terence MacSwiney, 12 July 1916, Terence MacSwiney Papers P48b/8, UCDA.
88. MacSwiney, 'Typescript biographical text of Mary MacSwiney', p. 64.
89. Lil Conlon, Manuscript of *Cumann na mBan*, p. 20, Cork Public Museum.
90. Ibid., p. 2.
91. MacSwiney, 'Typescript biographical text of Mary MacSwiney', p. 99.
92. Kathleen McDonnell from Bandon, Co. Cork, travelled to Dublin with the MacSwiney sisters. Her husband, William Keyes McDonnell, was also interned in Richmond Barracks. MacSwiney, 'Typescript biographical text of Mary MacSwiney', p. 96.
93. MacSwiney, 'Typescript biographical text of Mary MacSwiney', p. 99.
94. Ibid., p. 100.

95. Letter to Mary MacSwiney from Brigadier General Byers, 25 June 1916, Mary MacSwiney Papers, P48a/109/7, UCDA.
96. Visiting Orders issued to Mary MacSwiney by Colonel Commandant Heygate Lambert, 25 June 1916, Mary MacSwiney Papers, P48a/109/9/1-2, UCDA.
97. Townshend, *The Republic.* The title of chapter 1 is 'The imagined state: 1918–1919'.
98. Letter to Mary MacSwiney from Nancy Wyse Power, 28 July 1916, Mary MacSwiney Papers, P48a/23, UCDA.
99. Joseph Barrett to Mary MacSwiney, 3 July 1916, Mary MacSwiney Papers, P48a/109/10, UCDA.
100. MacSwiney, Typescript biographical text of Mary MacSwiney', p. 100.
101. Letter to Mary MacSwiney from Daniel Cohalan, 16 Aug. 1916, Mary MacSwiney Papers, P48a/25/7, UCDA.
102. Letter to the Home Office from Mary MacSwiney, received 5 July 1916, HO144/10308.
103. Letter to the Home Secretary, Herbert Samuel, from Mary MacSwiney, [received 5 July 1916], HO144/10308.
104. Note, July 1915, HO144/10308.
105. Minute, 7 July 1916, HO144/10308.
106. Letter to Herbert Samuel from Mary MacSwiney, received 5 July 1916, HO144/10308.
107. Letter to Herbert Samuel from Mary MacSwiney, 19 July 1916, HO144/10308.
108. Confidential letter, to M. L. Waller, Home Office, from Colonel Lambert, Frongoch 8 July 1916, HO144/10308.
109. Based in England, suffrage activist, Kate Kelly corresponded with the families of men imprisoned after 1916.
110. Letter to Kate Kelly from Mary MacSwiney, 26 July [1916], Letters to Kate Kelly regarding political prisoners, 1916–1924, MS 8,411/5, NLI.
111. Letter to Art O'Brien from the honorary secretaries, INAA, 30 June 1916, Art Ó Briain Papers, Ms8,435/31, NLI.
112. Muriel MacSwiney, 'Testimony', in *Evidence on Conditions in Ireland: Comprising the Complete Testimony, Affidavits and Exhibits Presented Before the American Commission on Conditions in Ireland* (Washington, 1921), p. 270.
113. Letter to Herbert Samuel from Mary MacSwiney, received 5 July 1916, HO144/10308.
114. Costello, *Enduring the Most*, p. 67. Michael Murphy stated that some of the men refused to hand over their weapons and 'kept them ever afterwards'. Michael Murphy, BMH WS1547.
115. Terence MacSwiney Diary during his detention in Richmond Barracks, 25 May 1916, Florence O'Donoghue Papers, Ms31,139/3, NLI.
116. Peter Hart, *The IRA and its Enemies: Violence and Community in Cork, 1916–1923* (Oxford, 1998), p. 48.
117. Townshend, *Easter 1916*, p. 234.
118. Ibid.
119. Borgonovo, *The Dynamics of War*, p. 42.
120. De Róiste Diary, 25 Apr. 1916, Liam de Róiste, BMH WS 1698, part 2.
121. Ibid.
122. Liam De Róiste Diary, 30 Apr. 1916, CCCA.
123. Costello, *Enduring the Most*, pp 71–2.
124. Kathleen Clarke, *Revolutionary Women* (Dublin, 2008), pp 158–9.
125. Ibid., p. 159.
126. MacSwiney, 'Typescript biographical text of Mary MacSwiney', p. 96.
127. Clarke, *Revolutionary Women*, p. 159.
128. Ibid., p. 117.
129. Ibid., p. 71.
130. *Fianna Fáil*, 5 Dec. 19145.
131. Clarke, *Revolutionary Women*, p. 159.
132. Letter to Florence O'Donoghue from Annie MacSwiney, 9 Apr. 1954, Florence O'Donoghue Papers, Ms 31,282/2/20, NLI.
133. Letter to Peter MacSwiney from Mary MacSwiney, received 30 June 1916, John Devoy Papers, MS 18,007/38/1, NLI.
134. Ibid.

135. Quoted in Ruiséal, 'The position in Cork', p. 379.
136. Mary MacSwiney, Report on her arrest and dismissal from St Angela's College, Mary MacSwiney Papers, P48a/7/6, UCDA; Peg Duggan, BMH WS 1576.
137. Letter to Annie MacSwiney from Mary MacSwiney 2 May 1915, de Valera Papers, P150/656, UCDA.
138. MacSwiney, 'Typescript biographical text of Mary MacSwiney', pp 84–5.
139. Ibid., p. 89.
140. Ibid., pp 89–90.
141. MacSwiney, Report on her dismissal from St Angela's College, 1916, Mary MacSwiney Papers, P48a/7/6, UCDA.
142. Letter to Mary MacSwiney from Sister M. Elizabetts, Ursuline Convent Blackrock, Cork, 28 Mar. 1916, Mary MacSwiney Papers, P48a/72, UCDA.
143. MacSwiney, 'Typescript biographical text of Mary MacSwiney', pp 74–5.
144. Mary MacSwiney, Report on her dismissal from St Angela's College, 1916, P48a/7/6, Mary MacSwiney Papers, UCDA.
145. Report by District Inspector C. F. Walsh on interned rebels from the city of Cork, 10 Oct. 1916, CSO/RP/1918/16628/A125.
146. Mary MacSwiney, Report on her dismissal from St Angela's College, 1916, P48a/7/6, Mary MacSwiney Papers, UCDA.
147. MacSwiney, 'Typescript biographical text of Mary MacSwiney', p. 63.
148. Mary MacSwiney, Report on her dismissal from St Angela's College, 1916, P48a/7/6, Mary MacSwiney Papers, UCDA.
149. Ibid.
150. MacSwiney, 'Typescript biographical text of Mary MacSwiney', p. 90 (a).
151. Ibid., pp 92–5.
152. Mary MacSwiney, Report on her dismissal from St Angela's College, 1916, P48a/7/6, Mary MacSwiney Papers, UCDA.
153. MacSwiney, 'Typescript biographical text of Mary MacSwiney', p. 61.
154. R. F. Foster, *Vivid Faces: The Revolutionary General in Ireland 1890–1923* (London, 2014), p. 31.
155. Mary MacSwiney, Report on her dismissal from St Angela's College, 1916, P48a/7/6, Mary MacSwiney Papers, UCDA.
156. Quoted in Foster, *Vivid Faces*, p. 40.
157. Letter to the most Reverend Dr Mannix from Mary MacSwiney, 28 Jan. 1928, Mary MacSwiney Papers, P48a/25/21, UCDA.
158. Ibid.
159. Foster, *Vivid Faces*, p. 41.
160. Letter to A Chara from Mary MacSwiney, 27 Sept. 1928, Mary MacSwiney Papers, P48a/25/23, UCDA.
161. Foster, *Vivid Faces*, p. 56.
162. Letter to Terence MacSwiney from Peter MacSwiney, 25 Aug. 1916, Terence MacSwiney Papers, P48b/9, UCDA.
163. Fundraising leaflet for St Ita's College, *c.*1927, Ephemera Collection, NLI.
164. Letter to the most Revd Dr Mannix from Mary MacSwiney, 28 Jan, 1928, Mary MacSwiney Papers, P48a/25/21, UCDA.
165. Foster, *Vivid Faces*, p. 38.
166. Muriel MacSwiney, BMH WS 637.
167. Máire MacSwiney Brugha, *History's Daughter: A Memoir from the Only Child of Terence MacSwiney* (Dublin, 2006), p. 13.
168. P. S. O'Hegarty, *A Short Memoir of Terence MacSwiney* (Dublin, 1922), p. 33; report by District Inspector C. F. Walsh on interned rebels from the city of Cork, 10 Oct. 1916, CSO/RP/1918/16628/A125.
169. Letter to Florence O'Donoghue from Annie MacSwiney, 27 Mar. 1954, Florence O'Donoghue Papers, Ms, 31,282/2/12, NLI.
170. MacSwiney, 'Typescript biographical text of Mary MacSwiney', p. 103.
171. Letter to the most Revd Dr Mannix from Mary MacSwiney, 28 Jan. 1928, Mary MacSwiney Papers, P48a/25/21, UCDA.

172. Mary MacSwiney, 'Testimony', in *Evidence on Conditions in Ireland: Comprising the Complete Testimony, Affidavits and Exhibits Presented Before the American Commission on Conditions in Ireland* (Washington, 1921), p. 15.
173. *Cork Examiner*, 2 Sept. 1916.
174. Newspaper clipping [1916] advertising the opening of St Ita's, Mary MacSwiney Papers, P48a/26/4, UCDA.
175. Seán Neeson, 'A great Irish school, 1916–1954', in *Capuchin Annual*, 1965, p. 244; UCC Calendar 1920–21 which includes the names of past graduates.
176. UCC Calendar 1920–21 which includes the names of past graduates.
177. Letter to Mary MacSwiney from unidentified writer, 24 July [1916] Mary MacSwiney Papers, P48a25/4, UCDA.
178. *Cork Examiner*, 28 July 1917.
179. MacSwiney, 'Typescript biographical text of Mary MacSwiney', p. 103.
180. Letter to Art O'Brien from Mary MacSwiney, 19 Sept. 1916, Art Ó Briain Papers, Ms 8,444/1, NLI.
181. MacSwiney, 'Typescript biographical text of Mary MacSwiney', pp 103–4.
182. Fundraising leaflet for St Ita's College, *c.*1927, Ephemera Collection, NLI.
183. Mary Kotsonouris, 'Gavan Duffy, Louise', in James McGuire (ed.), *Dictionary of Irish Biography*, https://www.dib.ie/biography/duffy-louise-gavan-a2813. Gavan Duffy and McHugh met while studying in UCD; both were committed members of the Gaelic League. Patrick Buckley, 'Blythe, Ernest (de Blaghd, Earnán)' in James McGuire (ed.), *Dictionary of Irish Biography*, https://www.dib.ie/biography/blythe-ernest-de-blaghd-earnan-a0753; Foster, *Vivid Faces*, p. 38.
184. Letter to Louise Gavan Duffy from Annie MacSwiney, 4 Sept. 1941, correspondence in possession of Catherine and Cathal Brugha.
185. Letter to Art O'Brien from Mary MacSwiney, 19 Sept. 1916, Art Ó Briain Papers, Ms 8,444/1, NLI.
186. Liam de Róiste Diary, 29 Dec. 1916, Liam de Róiste, BMH WS 1698, part 2.
187. Letter to Mary MacSwiney from Louise Gavan Duffy, no date, Mary MacSwiney Papers, P48a/25/12, UCDA.
188. Letter to Mary MacSwiney from Louise Gavan Duffy, 6 Apr. [ny], Mary MacSwiney Papers, P48a/25/1, UCDA.
189. *Cork Examiner*, 5 Aug. 1920.
190. Ibid.
191. Letter to Mary MacSwiney from Louise Gavan Duffy, 9 May [ny], Mary MacSwiney Papers, P48a/25/2, UCDA; letter to Mary MacSwiney from Louise Gavan Duffy, 6 Apr. [ny], Mary MacSwiney Papers, P48a/25/1, UCDA.
192. Letter to Terence MacSwiney from Muriel MacSwiney, 11 Apr. 1918, Terence MacSwiney Papers, P48b/125, UCDA.
193. Letter to Muriel MacSwiney from Terence MacSwiney, 4 July 1918, Terence MacSwiney Papers, P48b/50, UCDA.
194. Letter to Muriel MacSwiney from Terence MacSwiney, 4 Aug. 1918, Terence MacSwiney Papers, P48b/68, UCDA.
195. *Cork Examiner*, 12 Sept. 1916.
196. Memo on the establishment of St Ita's school by the Irish Self-Determination League [1922], Art Ó Bríain Papers, Ms 8,440/19, NLI.
197. *Cork Examiner*, 5 Aug. 1920.
198. Letter to Louise Gavan Duffy from Annie MacSwiney, 4 Sept. 1941, correspondence in possession of Catherine and Cathal Brugha.
199. Memo on the establishment of St Ita's school by the Irish Self-Determination League [1922], Art Ó Bríain Papers, Ms 8,440/19, NLI.
200. Gerard Fealy and Judith Harford, '"Nervous energy and administrative ability": The early lady principals and lay superintendents in Ireland', in *Journal of Educational Administration an History*, vol. 39, no. 1 (2007), p. 271.
201. *Cork Examiner*, 5 Aug. 1920.
202. Letter to A Chara from Mary MacSwiney, 27 Sept. 1928, Mary MacSwiney Paper, P48a/25/23, UCDA.

203. *Irish Press*, 9 Mar. 1942.
204. *Cork Examiner*, 7 Nov. 1916.
205. MacSwiney, 'Testimony', in *Evidence on Conditions in Ireland*, p. 195.
206. Maume, 'Daniel Corkery: A reassessment', p. 148.
207. Letter to 'My Lord' from Mary MacSwiney, *c.*1917, Mary MacSwiney Papers, P48a/27, UCDA.
208. Ibid.
209. Letter to Mary MacSwiney from Daniel Cohalan, 16 Aug. 1916, Mary MacSwiney Papers, P48a/25/7, UCDA.
210. Letter to Mary MacSwiney from Daniel Cohalan, 29 Aug. 1916, Mary MacSwiney Papers, P48a/25/7, UCDA.
211. Letter to Mary MacSwiney from Daniel Cohalan, 16 June 1917, correspondence in possession of Catherine and Cathal Brugha.
212. *Cork Examiner*, 16 Dec. 1919.
213. Patrick Pearse, *The Murder Machine* (Dublin, 1916).
214. David Limond, '"A work for other hands": Patrick Pearse and St Ita's College', in *History Ireland*, vol. 14 (Mar./Apr. 2006), https://www.historyireland.com/a-work-for-other-hands-patrick-pearse-and-st-itas-college/#:~:text=St%20Ita's%20(named%2C%20like%20the,a%20more%20remote%20site%20in
215. Townshend, *The Republic*, p. xix.
216. Foster, *Vivid Faces*, p. 458.
217. De Róiste Diary, 29 Mar. 1916, Liam de Róiste, BMH WS 1698, part 2.
218. *Cork Examiner*, 25 Nov. 1917.
219. W. F. Stockley and T. J. Murphy, 'St Ita's School, Cork', [1926], Mary MacSwiney Papers, P48a/29, UCDA.
220. Quoted in Foster, *Vivid Faces*, p. 35.
221. Conlon, Manuscript of *Cumann na mBan and the Women of Ireland, 1913–25*, p. 49, Cork Public Museum.
222. Minutes of meeting of executive council of Cumann na mBan, no date [1924], Mary MacSwiney Papers, P48a/8/29, UCDA.
223. *Cork Examiner*, 19 Aug. 1922.
224. O'Hegarty, *A Short Memoir of Terence MacSwiney*, p. 7. Cork *Examiner*, 16 Dec. 1919.
225. Foster, *Vivid Faces*, p. 34.
226. *Cork Examiner*, 25 Mar. 1919.
227. Leeann Lane, *Dorothy Macardle* (Dublin, 2019), pp 12–13.
228. Conlon, Manuscript of *Cumann na mBan*, p. 62, Cork Public Museum.
229. Quoted in ibid., p. 64, Cork Public Museum.
230. Alice Cashel, BMH WS 0336.
231. Neeson, 'A great Irish school', p. 246.
232. Memo on the establishment of St Ita's school by the Irish Self-Determination League [1922], Art Ó Bríain Papers, Ms 8,440/19, NLI.
233. Costello, *Enduring the Most*, p. 97; Letter to Terence MacSwiney from Muriel MacSwiney, 4 Apr. 1918, Terence MacSwiney Papers, P48b/128, UCDA.
234. Muriel MacSwiney BMH WS 637.
235. Letter to the Secretary Military Service Pensions Board from Joseph Baker, 12 Feb. 1937; Agnes Gallagher, Typescript account of participation during the revolutionary period [1935?], WMSP34REF3344, Agnes Gallagher, MSPC.
236. Agnes Gallagher, sworn statement made before advisory committee, 23 July 1937, WMSP34REF3344, Agnes Gallagher MSPC.
237. Letter to the Home Secretary from Mary MacSwiney, 11 July 1916, HO 144/10308.
238. Letter to Mary MacSwiney from the Home Office, 14 July 1917, HO 144/10308.
239. Letter to Kate Kelly from Mary MacSwiney, 26 July [1916], Letters to Kate Kelly regarding political prisoners, 1916–1924, Ms 8,411/5, NLI.
240. Liam de Roiste Diary, 25 December 1916; 29 December 1916, Liam de Roiste, BMH WS 1698, part 2.
241. Letter to Art O'Brien form Mary MacSwiney, 7 Jan. 1917, Art Ó Briain Papers, Ms 8,444/1, NLI.

242. Margaret Ward, *Unmanageable Revolutionaries: Women and Irish Nationalism, 1880–1980* (Dublin, 2021), pp 215–19.
243. Letter from Mary MacSwiney to Peter MacSwiney, received 30 June 1916, John Devoy Papers, MS 18,007/38/1, NLI.
244. Letter to Peter MacSwiney from Mary MacSwiney, received 30 June 1916, John Devoy Papers, MS 18,007/38/1, NLI.
245. Hart, *The IRA and its Enemies*, p. 59.
246. Letter to Peter MacSwiney from Mary MacSwiney, received 30 June 1916, John Devoy Papers, MS 18,007/38/1, NLI.

Chapter 3: Cork: May 1916–August 1920

1. Charles Townshend, *The Republic: The Fight for Irish Independence* (London, 2013), p. 19.
2. Quoted in Townshend, *The Republic*, p. 19.
3. John Borgonovo, *The Dynamics of War and Revolution: Cork City, 1916-1918* (Cork, 2013) p. 54, p. 52, p. 53.
4. Annie MacSwiney, 'Typescript biographical Text of Mary MacSwiney', p 104, p. 107, Mary MacSwiney Papers, P48a/462, UCDA.
5. Lil Conlon, Manuscript of *Cumann na mBan and the Women of Ireland, 1913-25*, p. 35, Cork Public Museum
6. *Cork Examiner*, 16 Apr. 1917.
7. Conlon, Manuscript of *Cumann na mBan,* pp 30-1, Cork Public Museum. Conlon states that the mass was held in the North Cathedral.
8. Conlon, Manuscript of *Cumann na mBan*, pp 72-3, Cork Public Museum.
9. Conlon, Manuscript of *Cumann na mBan*, p. 49, Cork Public Museum.
10. Conlon, Manuscript of *Cumann nna mBan*, p. 54, Cork Public Museum.
11. Letter marked 'secret' to the Under Secretary of State, Home Office from Dublin Castle, 16 Jan. 1917, HO144/10308.
12. See Caoimhe Nic Dháibhéid, 'The Irish National Aid Association and the Radicalization of Public Opinion in Ireland, 1916-1918' in *The Historical Journal*, vol. 55, no. 3, (Sept. 2012), p. 705, p. 719.
13. Conlon, Manuscript of *Cumann na mBan* p. 20, Cork Public Museum.
14. Nic Dháibhéid, 'The Irish National Aid Association', p. 709.
15. *Cork Examiner*, 7 June 1916.
16. *Cork Examiner*, 8 June 1916.
17. Letter from the secretary of the Dublin Committee for the Prevention of Relief and Distress to the Secretaries of the INAA, 19 June 1916. INA&VDF Papers, Ms 245,321/245
18. Nic Dháibhéid, 'The Irish National Aid Association', p. 709.
19. Liam de Róiste, Diary, 5 July 1916, Liam de Róiste, BMH WS 1698, part 2; *Cork Examiner*, 30 June 1916.
20. Aodh Quinlivan, *Forgotten Lord Mayor: Donal Óg O'Callaghan 1920-1924* (Cork, 2020), p. 19.
21. See, for example, letter from Tadg O' Shea to Michael Collins, 28 Oct. 1917, INA&VDF Papers, Ms 24, 321/6/27, NLI.
22. Liam de Róiste Diary, 29 June 1916, CCCA.
23. Letter to Peter MacSwiney from Mary MacSwiney, received 30 June 1916, John Devoy Papers, MS 18,007/38/1, NLI.
24. Nic Dháibhéid, 'The Irish National Aid Association', p. 707.
25. Letter to Peter MacSwiney from Mary MacSwiney, received 30 June 1916, John Devoy Papers, MS 18,007/38/1, NLI.
26. Nic Dháibhéid, 'The Irish National Aid Association', p. 711
27. Nancy Wyse Power, BMH WS 587.
28. Letter to Peter MacSwiney from Mary MacSwiney, received 30 June 1916, John Devoy Papers, MS 18,007/38/1, NLI.
29. Letter to Peter MacSwiney from Mary MacSwiney, received 30 June 1916, John Devoy Papers, MS 18,007/38/1, NLI.

30. Kitty O'Doherty, BMH WS 355.
31. Nic Dháibhéid, 'The Irish National Aid Association', pp 711-2.
32. Nic Dháibhéid, 'The Irish National Aid Association', pp 721, p. 722.
33. Letter from Michael Collins to D [onal] O'Callaghan, 7 Mar. 1917, INA&VDF Papers, Ms 23,464, NLI.
34. Nic Dháibhéid, 'The Irish National Aid Association', pp 721, p. 722.
35. *Cork Examiner*, 17 Aug.1916.
36. *Cork Examiner*, 20 Apr. 1918.
37. Letter to Michael Collins from Tadg O'Shea, 30 Sept 1917, INA&VDF Papers, MS 24, 321/6/23, NLI.
38. Borgonovo, *The Dynamics of War and Revolution*, p. 48.
39. Letter from Mary MacSwiney to Peter MacSwiney, received 30 June 1916, John Devoy Papers, MS 18,007/38/1, NLI.
40. Letter to Michael Collins from Tadg O'Shea, 3 Sept. 1919, INA&VDF Papers, Ms, 24,321/6/18, NLI.
41. Letter to Michael Collins from Tadg O'Shea, 5 Nov. 1919, INA&VDF Papers, Ms, 24,321/6/29, NLI.
42. *Cork Examiner*, 20 Apr. 1918.
43. William Murphy, *Political Imprisonment and the Irish, 1912-1921* (Oxford, 2014), p. 93.
44. *Cork Examiner*, 23 Feb. 1917.
45. Letter to Aunt Kate from Terence MacSwiney, 30 Oct. 1914, Terence MacSwiney Papers, P48b/6, UCDA.
46. Letter to Aunt Kate from Terence MacSwiney, 30 Oct. 1914, Terence MacSwiney Papers, P48b/6, UCDA.
47. Letter to Aunt Kate from Terence MacSwiney, 27 Oct. 1914, Terence MacSwiney Papers, P48b/6, UCDA.
48. Letter to Aunt Kate from Terence MacSwiney, 27 Oct. 1914, Terence MacSwiney Papers, P48b/6, UCDA.
49. Muriel MacSwiney, BMH WS 637.
50. Letter to Muriel Murphy from Terence MacSwiney, 28 Apr. 1917, Terence MacSwiney Papers, P48b/17. UCDA.
51. Muriel MacSwiney, BMH WS 637.
52. Letter to Muriel Murphy from Terence MacSwiney, 28 Apr. 1917, Terence MacSwiney Papers, P48b/17. UCDA.
53. Letter to Muriel Murphy from Terence MacSwiney, 16 Dec. 1916, Terence MacSwiney Papers, P48b/16, UCDA.
54. See for example, letter to Muriel Murphy from Terence MacSwiney, 16 May. 1917, Terence MacSwiney Papers, P48b/19, UCDA.
55. Letter to Muriel Murphy from Terence MacSwiney, 28 Apr. 1917, Terence MacSwiney Papers, P48b/17. UCDA.
56. Letter to Muriel MacSwiney from Terence MacSwiney, 30 Aug. 1918, Terence MacSwiney Papers, P48b/80, UCDA.
57. Marriage notices, *Cork Examiner*, 16 June 1917.
58. Francis J. Costello, *Enduring the Most: The Life and Death of Terence MacSwiney* (Dingle, 1996), p. 91.
59. *Evening Herald*, 25 June 1917.
60. Ibid.
61. Muriel MacSwiney, BMH WS 637.
62. Letter to Muriel MacSwiney from Terence MacSwiney, 24 July 1917, Terence MacSwiney Papers, P48b/23, UCDA.
63. Letter to Muriel MacSwiney from Terence MacSwiney, 1 Dec. 1917, Terence MacSwiney Papers, P48b/27, UCDA.
64. Letter to Muriel MacSwiney from Terence MacSwiney, 13 May 1918, Terence MacSwiney Papers, P48b/34, UCDA.
65. Letter to Muriel MacSwiney from Terence MacSwiney, 15 Aug. 1918, Terence MacSwiney Papers, P48b/77, UCDA.

66. *Cork Examiner*, 1 Nov. 1917.
67. 'The Lord Mayor of Cork', issued by Art O' Brien, 1920, Art Ó Briain Papers, Ms 8,448/5, NLI.
68. Liam de Róiste Diary, 29 Sept. 1917, CCCA.
69. Murphy, *Political Imprisonment and the Irish*, p. 92.
70. *Freeman's Journal*, 13 Oct. 1917
71. 'The Lord Mayor of Cork', issued by Art O' Brien, 1920, Art Ó Briain Papers, Ms 8,448/5, NLI.
72. Ibid.
73. Ibid.
74. Muriel MacSwiney, BMH WS 637.
75. Letter to Muriel MacSwiney from Terence MacSwiney, [1918], Terence MacSwiney Papers, P48b/29, UCDA.
76. Letter to Muriel MacSwiney from Terence MacSwiney, 3 Feb. 1918, Terence MacSwiney Papers, P48b/31, UCDA.
77. Letter to Muriel MacSwiney from Terence MacSwiney, 14 July. 1918, Terence MacSwiney Papers, P48b/55, UCDA.
78. Letter to Muriel MacSwiney from Terence MacSwiney, 14 July. 1918, Terence MacSwiney Papers, P48b/55, UCDA.
79. Letter to Muriel MacSwiney from Terence MacSwiney, 4 Aug. 1918, Terence MacSwiney Papers, P48a/68. UCDA.
80. Letter to Muriel MacSwiney from Terence MacSwiney, 15 Aug 1918, Terence MacSwiney Papers, P48b/77, UCDA.
81. Peg Duggan BMH WS 1576.
82. Laurence Garvey BMH WS 1062.
83. Peg Duggan BMH WS 1576.
84. Letter to the Military Service Pensions Board from Nora Martin, 4 Jan. 1943; letter to Nora Martin from the Military Service Pensions Board, 19 Jan. 1943, MSP34REF52674 Eileen Barry, MSPC.
85. Conlon, Manuscript of *Cumann na mBan*, p. 29, Cork Public Museum.
86. Peg Duggan BMH WS 1576.
87. Conlon, Manuscript of *Cumann na mBan*, p. 3, Cork Public Museum.
88. Margaret Lucey, BMH WS 1561
89. Peg Duggan BMH WS 1576.
90. Peg Duggan BMH WS 1576.
91. Cumann na mBan Minute Book, Cork District Council, 3 Feb. 1918, Cork Public Museum.
92. Cumann na mBan Minute Book, Cork District Council, 3 Mar. 1918, Cork Public Museum.
93. Secretary's Report for the Year 1919, Cumann na mBan Minute Book, 1918-1919, Cork Public Museum.
94. John Borgonovo, *Florence and Josephine O'Donoghue's War of Independence* (Dublin, 2006), p. 37.
95. Letter to Tomás MacCurtain from Mary MacSwiney, 13 Apr. 1918, Mary MacSwiney Papers, P48a/36/2, UCDA.
96. Cumann na mBan Minute Book, Cork District Council, 15 Sept. 1918, Cork Public Museum.
97. Cumann na mBan Minute Book, Cork District Council, 3 Nov. 1918, Cork Public Museum.
98. Liam de Róiste Diary, 2 Dec. 1918, CCCA.
99. Letter from the Cumann na mBan Executive to the Irish Volunteers, 8 Jan. 1919, Florence O'Donoghue Papers, Ms 31, 152/3, NLI.
100. Memo to the Secretary of the Dáil Courts from the Secretary of Dáil Éireann, 9 Mar. 1920, Dáil Éireann Collection, DE 2/38, NAI. As Borgonovo states no further files relating to the case are extant. Borgonovo, *The Dynamics of War*, p. 152.
101. Margaret Lucey, BMH WS 1561; Leaflet outlining the rules and constitution of Cumann na mBan, 1917, Cumann na mBan Leaflets and Circulars, MS 49, 918/1, NLI.
102. List of Delegates to the Mansion House Conference, 19 Apr. 1917, EPH D96, NLI.
103. Michael Laffan, *The Resurrection of Ireland: The Sinn Féin Party, 1916-1923* (Cambridge, 1999), p. 82, p. 84.
104. Laffan, *The Resurrection of Ireland*, p. 86.
105. *Cork Examiner*, 16 Apr. 1916. On 16 April 1917 the *Freeman's Journal* noted that 201 local government boards had rejected Plunkett's call to send delegates to the conference.

106. *Irish Independent*, 16 April 1917.
107. Laffan, *The Resurrection of Ireland*, p. 91.
108. Ibid., p. 90.
109. Ibid., p. 91
110. Ibid., p. 92.
111. Ibid., p. 93.
112. De Róiste Diary, 3 Dec. 1916, Liam de Róiste, BMH WS 1698, part 2.
113. Laffan, *The Resurrection of Ireland*, p. 94.
114. Ibid.
115. Mary MacSwiney, 'Debate on the Treaty', Dáil Éireann Debates, 21 Dec. 1921.
116. Laffan, *The Resurrection of Ireland*, p. 96.
117. MacSwiney, 'Typescript Biographical Text of Mary MacSwiney, ' p 43.
118. Letter from Count Plunkett to Mary MacSwiney, 26 May 1917, Mary MacSwiney Papers, P48a/368, UCDA.
119. Laffan, *The Resurrection of Ireland*, p. 87.
120. Charlotte Fallon, *Soul of Fire: A Biography of Mary MacSwiney* (Cork, 1986), p. 39.
121. Conlon, Manuscript of *Cumann na mBan*, p. 31, Cork Public Museum; Letter to Count Plunkett from Mary MacSwiney, 30 May [1917]. Count Plunkett Papers, MS 11,383/632, NLI.
122. Letter to Count Plunkett from Mary MacSwiney, 30 May [1917]. Count Plunkett Papers, MS 11,383/6/32, NLI.
123. Conlon, Manuscript of *Cumann na* mBan, p. 33, Cork public Museum.
124. Murphy, *Political Imprisonment and the Irish*, p. 63.
125. Conlon, Manuscript of *Cumann na* mBan, p. 33, Cork public Museum.
126. *Cork Examiner*, 11 June 1917.
127. *Cork Examiner*, 19 June 1917.
128. Laffan, *The Resurrection of Ireland*, p. 121.
129. Liam de Roiste Diary, 9 Jan. 1917, Liam de Roiste, BMH WS 1698, part 2.
130. Frank O'Connor described him as an 'idealist', one of the 'last of the romantics', contrasting him with Michael Collins's 'hard sense'. Frank O'Connor, *The Big Fellow: A Life of Michael Collins* (London, 1937), p. 158.
131. Laffan, *The Resurrection of Ireland*, p, 121; Townshend, *The Republic*, p. 20.
132. Liam de Roiste Diary, 1 Jan. 1916, CCCA.
133. Conlon, Manuscript of *Cumann na mBan*, p. 9, Cork public Museum.
134. Liam de Roiste Diary; 5 Jan. 1916; Liam de Roiste, BMH WS1698, part 2.
135. Laffan, *The Resurrection of Ireland*, p. 132.
136. Townshend, *The Republic*, p. 11.
137. Townshend, *The Republic*, p. 15.
138. Borgonovo, *The Dynamics of War*, pp. 190-1.
139. Borgonovo, *The Dynamics of War*, pp. 193.
140. Letter to Peter MacSwiney from Mary MacSwiney, received 30 June 1916, John Devoy Papers, MS 18,007/38/1, NLI.
141. Borgonovo, *The Dynamics of War*, p. 186, p. 187.
142. Letter to Peter MacSwiney from Mary MacSwiney, received 30 June 1916, John Devoy Papers, MS 18,007/38/1, NLI.
143. *Freeman's Journal*, 11 Apr. 1918.
144. Minutes of the Cumann na mBan Convention, 1918, Ceannt and O'Brennan Papers, Ms 41,494/1/2, NLI.
145. Quoted in Peter Hart, *The IRA and its Enemies: Violence and Community in Cork, 1916-1923* (Oxford, 1998), p. 60.
146. Townshend, *The Republic*, p. 30.
147. *Cork Examiner*, 23 Apr. 1918.
148. *Cork Examiner*, 24 Apr., 1918; Borgonovo, *The Dynamics of War*, p. 194.
149. Borgonovo, *The Dynamics of War*, p. 194.
150. Margaret Lucey, BMH WS 1561.
151. *Cork Examiner*, 24 Apr.1918.
152. *Cork Examiner*, 24 Apr. 1918.

153. Townshend, *The Republic*, p. 3.
154. *Cork Examiner*, 24. Apr 1918.
155. *Cork Examiner*, 24 Apr. 1918.
156. Borgonovo, *The Dynamics of War*, pp 194-5.
157. *Cork Examiner*, 29 Apr. 1918.
158. *The Irishman*, 15 June 1918.
159. Senia Pašeta, *Irish Nationalist Women, 1900-1918* (Cambridge, 2014), p. 245.
160. Conlon, Manuscript of *Cumann na mBan*, pp 47-8, Cork Cumann na mBan.
161. Laffan, *The Resurrection of Ireland*, p.143.
162. Townshend, *The Republic*, p. 15.
163. Laffan, *The Resurrection of Ireland*, p.143; Townshend, *The Republic*, p. 15.
164. *Freeman's Journal*, 28 Sept. 1918; *Strabane Chronicle*, 5 Oct. 1918.
165. The Lord Mayor of Cork', issued by Art O' Brien, 1920, Art Ó Briain Papers, Ms 8,448/5, NLI.
166. Typescript draft article by W. F. P. Stockley on Seán MacSwiney following his death 22 January 1942, Mary MacSwiney Papers, P48a/460, UCDA.
167. Letter to Peter MacSwiney from Seán MacSwiney, 21 Apr. 1918, Fred Cronin Papers, Ms 49,526/10, NLI.
168. Letter to Terence MacSwiney from Peter MacSwiney, 17 Feb. 1919, Fred Cronin Papers, Ms 49,526/9, NLI.
169. Letter to Peter MacSwiney from P. H. O' Meara, 10 Sept. 1918, Joseph McGarrity Papers, Ms 17,517/22, NLI.
170. Letter to Peter MacSwiney from Seán MacSwiney, 11 Sept. 1918, Joseph McGarrity Papers, Ms 17650/4/10, NLI.
171. Letter to Mary MacSwiney from Peter MacSwiney, 9 Jan. 1919, Fred Cronin Papers, Ms 49,526/9, NLI.
172. See, for example, letter from Thomas Mulvey, Under-Secretary of State, Canada, to Mary MacSwiney, 17 Mar. 1919, informing her of her brother's release. He refers to her letter of 4 Nov. 1918. Fred Cronin Papers, Ms 49,526/10/6, NLI.
173. Letter to Mary and Annie MacSwiney from Seán MacSwiney, 18 Mar. 1919, Fred Cronin Papers, Ms 49,526/10, NLI.
174. Letter to Máire Óg from Peter MacSwiney, 12 Mar. 1919, Fred Cronin Papers, Ms 49526/9, NLI.
175. Letter to Mary and Annie MacSwiney from Seán MacSwiney, 18 Mar. 1919, Fred Cronin Papers, Ms 49,526/10, NLI.
176. Letter to Mary MacSwiney from Peter MacSwiney, 15 Jan. 1919, Fred Cronin Papers, Ms 49,526/9, NLI.
177. *Cork Examiner*, 11 Dec. 1918.
178. *Cork Examiner*, 12 Dec. 1918.
179. Letter to Hanna Sheehy Skeffington from Rosamond Jacob [1918], Sheehy Skeffington Papers, Ms 24, 108, NLI.
180. Margaret Ward, *Fearless Woman: Hanna Sheehy Skeffington, Feminism and the Irish Revolution* (Dublin, 2019), pp 291-5.
181. Terence MacSwiney, 'Womanhood' in Gabriel Doherty, Fiona Brennan and Neil Buttimer (eds.), *The Art and Ideology of Terence MacSwiney: Caught in the Living Flame* (Cork, 2022), p. 745.
182. *Cork Examiner*, 12 Dec. 1918.
183. Letter to Terence MacSwiney from Mary MacSwiney, 8 Dec. 1918, Terence MacSwiney Papers, P48b13, UCDA.
184. MacSwiney, 'Typescript Biographical Text of Mary MacSwiney', p. 109.
185. MacSwiney, 'Typescript Biographical Text of Mary MacSwiney', p. 112.
186. Cumann na mBan Minute Book, Cork District Council, 3 Mar. 1918; 5 May 1918; 2 June 1918, Cork Public Museum.
187. Cumann na mBan Minute Book, Cork District Council, 1 Dec. 1918, Cork Public Museum; Conlon, *Cumann na mBan*, p. 56.
188. Cumann na mBan Minute Book, Cork District Council, 1 Dec. 1918, Cork Public Museum.
189. Conlon, Manuscript of *Cumann na mBan*, p. 57, Cork Public Museum.

190. Costello, *Enduring the Most*, p. 103. Five of the Sinn Féin nominees were elected for two seats so the party only returned sixty-eight candidates. Laffan, *The Resurrection of Ireland*, p. 164.
191. Michael Murphy, BMH WS 1547.
192. Michael Murphy, BMH WS 1547.
193. Letter to Terence MacSwiney from Mary MacSwiney, 24 Jan. 1919, Fred Cronin Papers, Ms 49,526/6, NLI.
194. *Cork Examiner*, 17 Feb. 1919.
195. Letter to Terence MacSwiney from Mary MacSwiney, 24 Feb. 1919, Fred Cronin Papers, Ms 49,526/6, NLI.
196. Letter to Mary and Annie MacSwiney from Seán MacSwiney, 18 Mar. 1919, Fred Cronin Papers, Ms 49,526/10, NLI.
197. Letter to Peter MacSwiney from Seán MacSwiney, 6 Jan. 1919, Fred Cronin Papers, Ms 49,526/10, NLI.
198. Muriel MacSwiney, 'Testimony' in *Evidence on Conditions in Ireland: Comprising the Complete Testimony, Affidavits and Exhibits Presented Before the American Commission on Conditions in Ireland* (Washington, 1921), p. 276.
199. David McCullagh, *De Valera: Rise, 1882-1932* (Dublin, 2017), p. 159.
200. MacSwiney, 'Typescript Biographical Text of Mary MacSwiney', p. 116.
201. Hart, *The IRA and its Enemies*, p. 50.
202. Hart, *The IRA and its Enemies*, p. 50.
203. Borgonovo, *Florence and Josephine O'Donoghue's War of Independence*, p. 1.
204. Liam de Róiste Diary, 11 May 1919, CCCA.
205. See for example, Liam de Róiste Diary, 4 Dec. 1919, 21 Feb. 1920, CCCA.
206. De Róiste Diary, 25 Dec. 1919, CCCA.
207. De Róiste Diary, 18 Mar. 1920, CCCA.
208. Ibid.
209. MacSwiney, 'Typescript biographical text of Mary MacSwiney', p. 117
210. Dave Hannigan, *Terence MacSwiney: The Hunger Strike that Rocked a Nation* (Dublin, 2010), p. 9.
211. MacSwiney, 'Typescript biographical text of Mary MacSwiney', p. 117; Letter to Florence O'Donoghue from Annie MacSwiney, 23 Mar. 1954, Florence O'Donoghue Papers, Ms 31,282/2/10, NLI.
212. MacSwiney, 'Typescript biographical text of Mary MacSwiney', p. 118.
213. De Róiste Diary, 19 Apr. 1920, CCCA.
214. Hart, *The IRA and its Enemies*, p. 79; Robert Lynch, *The Partition of Ireland, 1918-1925* (Cambridge, 2019), p. 90.
215. *Cork Examiner*, 31 Mar. 1920.
216. Quoted in Costello, *Enduring the Most*, p. 116.
217. MacSwiney, Typescript biographical text of Mary MacSwiney', p. 122, p. 123.
218. Liam de Róiste Diary, 25 Mar, 23 Mar. 1920, CCCA.
219. Liam de Róiste Diary, 26 Mar. 1920, CCCA.
220. R. F. Foster, *Vivid Faces: The Revolutionary Generation in Ireland 1890-1923* (London, 2014), p. 3.
221. Liam de Róiste Diary, 17 May 1920, CCCA.
222. MacSwiney, Typescript biographical text of Mary MacSwiney', p. 123.
223. MacSwiney, Typescript biographical text of Mary MacSwiney', pp 133-4.
224. MacSwiney, 'Typescript biographical text of Mary MacSwiney', p. 134.
225. Letter to Florence O'Donoghue from Annie MacSwiney, 23 Mar. 1954, Florence O'Donoghue Papers, Ms 31,282/2/10, NLI.
226. Hart, *The IRA and its Enemies*, p. 68.
227. Mary McAuliffe, 'The Homefront as Battlefront: Women Violence and the Domestic Space during the War in Ireland 1919-1921' in Linda Connolly (ed.), *Women and the Irish Revolution 1917-23: Violence, Feminism Nationalism* (Dublin, 2020).
228. Florence O'Donoghue, *Tomás MacCurtain* (Tralee, 1958), p. 173.
229. MacSwiney, Typescript biographical text of Mary MacSwiney', p. 134.
230. MacSwiney, Typescript biographical text of Mary MacSwiney', p. 135.
231. Muriel MacSwiney BMH WS 637.

232. MacSwiney, Typescript biographical text of Mary MacSwiney', p. 90.
233. Costello, *Enduring the Most*, p. 120; O'Connor, *The Big Fellow*, p. 158.
234. Liam de Róiste Diary, 1 July 1920, CCCA. *Cork Examiner*, 1 July 1920.
235. Liam de Róiste Diary, 10 July 1920 CCCA; MacSwiney, Typescript biographical text of Mary MacSwiney', pp 129-130.
236. MacSwiney, Typescript biographical text of Mary MacSwiney', pp 129-130.
237. Liam de Róiste Diary, 10 July 1920, CCCA.
238. *Cork Examiner*, 12 July 1920.
239. Liam de Róiste Diary, 19 July 1920, CCCA.
240. Liam de Róiste Diary, 19 July 1920, CCCA.
241. MacSwiney, Typescript biographical text of Mary MacSwiney', pp 136-7.
242. Liam de Róiste Diary, 19 July 1920, CCCA.
243. MacSwiney, Typescript biographical text of Mary MacSwiney', p. 124-5.
244. *Cork Examiner*, 8 May 1918.
245. Cumann na mBan Minute Book, Cork District Council, May 1919, Cork Public Museum.
246. Madge Lucey, Summary of Evidence before the MSPB, 19 July 1937, MSP24REF29731, Madge Lucey, MSPC.
247. Liam de Róiste Diary, 15 Apr. 1920, CCCA.
248. Letter from Mary MacSwiney to Eithne Ní Chumaill [Eithne Coyle] , 13 June 1933, Mary MacSwiney Papers, P48a/10/4, UCDA.

Chapter 4: 1920: Trauma and the Brixton Hunger Strike, 1920

1. Joan Didion, *The Year of Magical Thinking* (London, 2012), p. 4.
2. Liam de Róiste Diary, 22 July 1920, CCCA.
3. De Róiste Diary, 28 Mar. 1920, CCCA.
4. Anne Dolan, 'Death in the archives, witnessing war in Ireland, 1919–1921', in *Past and Present* (2021), pp 3–4.
5. Ibid., p. 5.
6. Ian Miller, *A History of Force Feeding: Hunger Strikes, Prisons and Medical Ethics, 1909–1974* (London, 2016), p. 116.
7. Letter to Father Dominic from Donal O' Callaghan, 5 Oct. 1920, Terence MacSwiney Papers, P48b/418, UCDA.
8. Orla M. Muldoon, *The Social Psychology of Trauma: Connecting the Personal and the Political* (Cambridge, 2024), p. 8.
9. Annie MacSwiney, 'Diary of week of Terry's greatest torture', in Margaret Lucey, BMH WS 1561.
10. Diaramid Ferriter, *Between Two Hells: The Irish Civil War* (London, 2021), p. 8.
11. MacSwiney, 'Diary of week of Terry's greatest torture.'
12. Ferriter, *Between Two Hells*, p. 9.
13. Ibid., p. 14.
14. Síobhra Aiken, *Spiritual Wounds: Trauma, Testimony and the Irish Civil War* (Dublin, 2022), p. 9.
15. These are Anne Dolan's words in the context of witnessing death during the War of Independence. Dolan, 'Death in the archives', p. 13.
16. Muldoon, *The Social Psychology of Trauma,* p. ix.
17. Aiken, *Spiritual Wounds*, p. 10.
18. Muldoon, *The Social Psychology of Trauma.*
19. W. D. Higson, Medical Report, 18 Aug. 1920, HO144/10308; Michael O'Donoghue, BMH WS 1741.
20. John Borgonovo, *Florence and Josephine O'Donoghue's War of Independence* (Dublin, 2006), p. 34.
21. De Róiste Diary, 9 Aug. 1920, CCCA.
22. Mary MacSwiney, 'Testimony', in *Evidence on Conditions in Ireland: Comprising the Complete Testimony, Affidavits and Exhibits Presented Before the American Commission on Conditions in Ireland* (Washington, 1921), p. 205, p. 307.
23. Francis J. Costello, *Enduring the Most: The Life and Death of Terence MacSwiney* (Dingle, 1995), p. 140.

24. *Evening Herald*, 13 Aug. 1920; *Irish Independent*, 13 Aug. 1920.
25. MacSwiney, 'Testimony', pp 306–7.
26. *The Liberator (Tralee)*, 14 Aug. 1920; *Evening Echo*, 13 Aug. 1920; William Murphy, *Political Imprisonment and the Irish, 1912–1922* (Oxford, 2014), pp 175–6.
27. De Róiste Diary, 11 Aug. 1920, CCA.
28. MacSwiney, 'Testimony', p. 308. Annie's recollection of events, written in the 1950s, does not fully align with the testimony Mary gave in America in 1920. The former stated that the sisters viewed their brother in the 'internment corner' of the lorry that had transported him from Cork Jail. Annie MacSwiney 'At the City Hall', Terence MacSwiney Papers, P48b/421, UCDA.
29. Muriel MacSwiney BMH WS 637.
30. MacSwiney, 'Testimony', p. 308.
31. *Freeman's Journal*, 17 Aug. 1920; Costello, *Enduring the Most*, p. 144.
32. *Freeman's Journal*, 17 Aug. 1920.
33. Costello, *Enduring the Most*, p. 141.
34. Michael Murphy, BMH WS 1547.
35. *Freeman's Journal*, 17 Aug. 1920.
36. Copy proceedings of court martial, Victoria barracks, Cork 16 Aug. 1920, HO144/10308.
37. *Cork Examiner*, 18 Aug. 1920; Murphy, *Political Imprisonment and the Irish*, p. 175.
38. Murphy, *Political Imprisonment and the Irish*, p. 173, pp 175–6.
39. MacSwiney, 'Testimony', p. 310.
40. *Evening Herald*, 20 Aug. 1920.
41. Memo to Michael Collins from Art O'Brien, 20 Aug 1920, DE/2/4, NAI.
42. Mary MacDiarmada, *Art O'Brien and Irish Nationalism in London, 1900–1925* (Dublin, 2020), p. 87.
43. *Times*, 20 Aug. 1920.
44. Ian Miller, *A History of Force Feeding*, p. 106.
45. Frank Gallagher, *Days of Fear: A Diary of a Hunger Strike* (Cork, 1967), p. 33.
46. Seán Prendergast, BMH WS 802.
47. MacSwiney, 'Testimony', p. 312.
48. *Times*, 20 Aug. 1920.
49. *Freeman's Journal*, 17 Aug. 1920.
50. Thomas Treacy, BMH WS 1093, p. 61.
51. Maurice Crowe, BMH WS 517, p. 9.
52. Statement by Fr Dominic on Terence MacSwiney, [n.d], Papers of Terence MacSwiney's Biographers, P48c/277, UCDA.
53. Home Office Minute, 18 Aug. 1920, HO144/10308.
54. Memo from Art O'Brien to Michael Collins, 25 Sept. 1920, DE/2/4, NAI.
55. W. D. Higson, Medical Report on Terence MacSwiney, 18 Aug. 1920, HO144/10308.
56. Home Office Minute, 18 Aug. 1920, HO144/10308.
57. Annie MacSwiney 'At the City Hall'.
58. W. D. Higson, Medical Report, 20 Aug. 1920, HO 144/10308.
59. *Freeman's Journal*, 20 Aug. 1920.
60. Ibid.
61. Miller, *A History of Force Feeding*, p. 98.
62. *The Sun and the New York Herald*, 1 Sept. 1920.
63. G. B. Griffiths, Medical Report, 6 Sept. 1920, HO 144/10308.
64. Memo to Michael Collins from Art O'Brien, DE/2/4, 20 Aug. 1920, NAI.
65. *Freeman's Journal*, 21 Aug. 1920.
66. Quoted in ibid.
67. Statement by Fr Dominic on Terence MacSwiney, [n.d], Papers of Terence MacSwiney's Biographers P48c/277, 20 Aug. 1920, UCDA; Memo to Michael Collins from Art O'Brien, DE/2/4, NAI.
68. Murphy, *Political Imprisonment and the Irish*, p. 177.
69. Minute re meeting between Sir Ernley Blackwell, Mary MacSwiney and Art O'Brien, 20 Aug. 1920, HO144/10308.
70. Letter from Mary MacSwiney to Sir Edward Shortt, 20 Aug. 1920, HO144/10308.

71. Margaret Ward, *Fearless Woman: Hanna Sheehy Skeffington, Feminism and the Irish Revolution* (Dublin, 2019), pp 220–5.
72. MacDiarmada, *Art O'Brien*, p. 15.
73. Ibid., p. 83.
74. Ibid., p. 103.
75. Memo to Michael Collins from Art O'Brien, 23 Aug 1920, DE/2/4, NAI.
76. G. B. Griffiths, copy of notes after interview with Mary MacSwiney, 18 Sept. 1920, HO144/10308.
77. Annie MacSwiney, 'Typescript biographical text of Mary MacSwiney', p. 100, Mary MacSwiney Papers, P48a/462, UCDA.
78. Quoted in the *Freeman's Journal*, 21 Aug. 1920.
79. MacSwiney, 'Testimony', pp 313–14.
80. G. B. Griffiths, Medical Report on Terence MacSwiney, 23 Oct. 1920, HO144/10308.
81. Letter to Mary MacSwiney from Sir Edward Shortt, 21 Aug. 1920, HO144/10308. Statement by Terence MacSwiney to Sir Edward Shortt, 21 Aug. 1920, HO144/10308.
82. Quoted in Dave Hannigan, *Terence MacSwiney: The Hunger Strike that Rocked a Nation* (Dublin, 2010), p. 117.
83. Ibid., p. 118.
84. MacSwiney, 'Testimony', p. 315.
85. Ibid.
86. G. B. Griffiths, Medical Report, 18 Oct. 1920, HO 144/10308.
87. Terence MacSwiney, *Rossa* (Dublin, 2015) in Gabriel Doherty, Fiona Brennan and Neil Buttimer (eds), *The Art and Ideology of Terence MacSwiney: Caught in the Flame* (Cork, 2022), p. 883, pp 885–6.
88. Letter from Mary MacSwiney to the Home Office, 20 Sept. 1920, Terence MacSwiney Papers, P48b/429, UCDA.
89. Murphy, *Political Imprisonment and the Irish*, p. 178.
90. Quoted in the *New York Tribune*, 5 Sept. 1920.
91. Prime Minister's Statement, *Times*, 26 Aug. 1920.
92. *Times*, 26 August 1920.
93. Quoted in *Irish Independent*, 26 Aug. 1920.
94. Murphy, *Political Imprisonment and the Irish*, p. 179.
95. Mary MacSwiney, 'Testimony', p. 313.
96. Letter to Sir Edward Shortt from Mary MacSwiney, 20 Aug. 1920, HO144/10308.
97. Letter to Muriel MacSwiney from Terence MacSwiney, 3 Nov. 1917, Terence MacSwiney Papers, Ms 35,034, NLI.
98. Letters to Muriel MacSwiney from Terence MacSwiney, 8 Nov. 1917; 15 Nov. 1917, Terence MacSwiney Papers, Ms 35,034, NLI.
99. Muriel MacSwiney, 'Testimony', in *Evidence on Conditions in Ireland: Comprising the Complete Testimony, Affidavits and Exhibits Presented Before the American Commission on Conditions in Ireland* (Washington, 1921), p. 270.
100. Letter to C. A. Hunt from S. M. Power, 1 Mar. 1919, HO144/10308.
101. Muriel MacSwiney, 'Testimony', p. 277, p. 278, p. 280.
102. Liam de Róiste Diary, 20 May 1920, CCCA.
103. Muriel MacSwiney BMH WS 637.
104. MacSwiney, 'Diary of week of Terry's greatest torture.'
105. G. B. Griffiths, copy of notes after interview with Mary MacSwiney, 18 Sept. 1920, HO144/10308.
106. Ernest Blythe, BMH WS 0939.
107. Liam de Róiste Diary, 26 May 1920, CCCA.
108. MacSwiney, 'Typescript biographical text of Mary MacSwiney', p. 90.
109. Peter Hart, *The IRA and its Enemies: Violence and Community in Cork, 1916–1923* (Oxford, 1998), p. 69, note 1,172.
110. Letter to Mrs Malony from Annie MacSwiney, 18 Oct. 1920, Terence MacSwiney Papers, P48b/623, UCDA.
111. *Daily Express*, 8 Sept. 1920.
112. Medical report, G. B. Griffiths, 25 Sept. 1920, HO144/10308.
113. G. B. Griffiths, copy of notes after interview with Mary MacSwiney, 18 Sept. 1920, HO144/10308.
114. Aiken, *Spiritual Wounds*, p. 111.

115. Mary MacSwiney, 'Testimony', p. 306.
116. Lucy McDiarmid, *At Home in the Revolution: What Women Said and Did in 1916* (Dublin, 2015), pp 148–9.
117. Statement by Mary MacSwiney, 'The Lord Mayor of Cork', Art Ó Brían Papers, Ms 8,448/5, NLI.
118. MacSwiney, 'Typescript biographical text of Mary MacSwiney', pp 59–60.
119. Aiken, *Spiritual Wounds*, p. 36.
120. MacSwiney, 'Typescript biographical text of Mary MacSwiney', pp 59–60.
121. Seán Prendergast, BMH WS 802.
122. Michael O'Donoghue, BMH WS 1741.
123. Statement by Mary MacSwiney, 'The Lord Mayor of Cork', Art Ó Brían Papers, Ms 8,448/5, NLI.
124. Ibid.
125. Letter to Mary MacSwiney from Sir Edward Shortt, 21 Aug. 1920, HO144/10308.
126. Statement by Terence MacSwiney to Sir Edward Shortt, 21 Aug. 1920, HO144/10308.
127. Letter to Mary MacSwiney from Sir Edward Shortt, 1 Aug. 1920, HO144/10308.
128. Aiken, *Spiritual Wounds*, p. 112.
129. Letter to J. J. Hearn from Liam Mellows, 1 Sept. 1920, J. J. Hearn Papers Ms 15,986/13, NLI.
130. Hannigan, *Terence MacSwiney*, pp 110–1.
131. Copy translation from Irish to English of Tomás MacCurtain's diary, Florence O'Donoghue Papers, Ms, 31,140/1, NLI. The original is in the Cork Public Museum.
132. Memo from Art O'Brien to Michael Collins, 4 Sept. 1920, DE/2/4, NAI.
133. *New York Tribune*, 4 Sept. 1920.
134. Ibid., 8 Sept. 1920.
135. *The Sun and New York Herald*, 10 Sept. 1920.
136. Costello, *Enduring the Most*, p. 193.
137. Medical report, G. B. Griffiths, 12 Sept. 1920, HO 144/10308.
138. *New York Tribune*, 12 Sept. 1920.
139. Medical Report, G. B. Griffiths, 23 Sept. 1920, HO 144/10308.
140. Ibid., 29 Sept. 1920, HO 144/10308.
141. *Cork Examiner*, 28 Aug. 1920.
142. Hannigan, *Terence MacSwiney*, pp 76–7.
143. De Róiste Diary, 3 Sept. 1920, CCCA.
144. *The Sun and New York Herald*, 5 Sept. 1920.
145. *Evening Star* (Washington DC), 1 Oct. 1920.
146. De Róiste Diary, 21 Aug. 1920, CCCA.
147. Charlotte Fallon, *Soul of Fire: A Biography of Mary MacSwiney* (Dublin, 1986), p. 47.
148. *Daily Chronicle*, 6 Sept. 1920.
149. *Freeman's Journal*, 11 Sept. 1920.
150. *The Sun and New York Herald*, 10 Sept. 1920.
151. *Freeman's Journal*, 11 Sept. 1920.
152. *Daily Mail*, 10 Sept. 1920.
153. *Evening Star* (Washington D.C.), 15 Sept. 1920.
154. *Morning Post*, 15 Sept. 1920.
155. Letter to the Home Office from Mary MacSwiney, 20, Sept. 1920, HO 144/10308.
156. Bernadette Whelan, *United States Foreign Policy and Ireland: From Empire to Independence, 1913–29* (Dublin, 2006), pp 180–1.
157. Quoted in Whelan, *United States Foreign Policy and Ireland*, p. 183.
158. Ibid., p. 257.
159. Ibid., p. 258.
160. Ibid., p. 184.
161. Mel Farrell, *Party Politics in a New Democracy: The Irish Free State, 1922–37* (Basingstoke, 2017), p. 28.
162. G. B. Griffiths, Medical Report on Terence MacSwiney, 4 Sept. 1920, HO144/10308.
163. Costello, *Enduring the Most*, p. 190.
164. *New York Tribune*, 4 Sept. 1920.

165. Memo to Michael Collins from Art O'Brien, 11 Sept. 1920, DE/2/4, NAI.
166. Ibid.
167. Memo to the Lord Mayor of Cork from Art O'Brien, 15 Sept. 1920, Art Ó Brían Papers, Ms 8,425/20, NLI.
168. Letter to the Home Office from Geoffrey Whiskard, 22 Sept. 1920, HO144/10308.
169. Costello, *Enduring the Most*, p. 187.
170. Memo to Michael Collins from Art O'Brien, 11 Sept. 1920, DE/2/4, NAI.
171. Petition dictated by Terence MacSwiney to the British Government, 20 Aug. 1920, HO 144/10308.
172. Medical Report, G. B. Griffiths, 12 Sept. 1920, HO 144/103038.
173. Ibid., 26 Sept. 1920, HO 144/10308.
174. Joseph Lennon, 'The starvation of a man: Terence MacSwiney and famine memory', in Oona Frawley (ed.), *Memory Ireland: The Famine and the Troubles, vol. 3* (Syracuse, 2014), p. 71.
175. De Róiste Diary, 21 Aug. 1920, CCCA.
176. *Irish Independent*, 30 Aug. 1920.
177. De Róiste Diary, 6 Aug. 1920, CCCA.
178. Medical Report, G. B. Griffiths, 22 Sept. 1920; 24 Sept. 1920; 28 Sept. 1920, HO 144/10308.
179. Ibid., 22 Sept. 1920, HO 144/10308.
180. Ibid., 14 Oct. 1920, HO 144/10308.
181. Máire MacSwiney Brugha, *History's Daughter: A Memoir from the Only Child of Terence MacSwiney* (Dublin, 2006), p. 29.
182. MacDiarmada *Art O'Brien*, p. 103; Patrick Moylett BMH WS 796.
183. Memo to Michael Collins from Art O'Brien, 9 Oct. 1920, DE2/4, NAI.
184. W. D. Higson, Medical Report on Terence MacSwiney, 26 Aug. 1920, HO144/10308.
185. Typescript draft article by W. F. P. Stockley on Seán MacSwiney following his death, 1942, Mary MacSwiney Papers, P48a/460, UCDA.
186. *Topeka State Journal*, 6 Oct. 1920.
187. Hannigan, *Terence MacSwiney*, pp 192–3.
188. *Irish Press*, 23 Oct. 1920.
189. Margaret Lucey, BMH WS 1561.
190. Miller, *A History of Force Feeding*, p. 92.
191. MacSwiney, 'Diary of week of Terry's greatest torture.'
192. Ibid., p. 6.
193. Ibid., Tuesday.
194. Medical Report, W. D. Higson, 21 Oct. 1920, HO 144/10308.
195. Letter to Mrs Malony from Annie MacSwiney, 18 Oct. 1920, Terence MacSwiney Papers, P48b/623, UCDA.
196. Miller, *A History of Force Feeding*, p. 92.
197. Ibid., p. 108.
198. Ibid., p. 115.
199. D. M. T. Fessler, 'The implications of starvation induced psychological changes for the ethical treatment of hunger strikes', in *Journal of Child Ethics* (Sept. 2003) p. 244.
200. Seán Prendergast, BMH WS 802.
201. Miller, *A History of Force Feeding* p. 92.
202. Gallagher, *Days of Fear*, pp 44–5.
203. Seán Prendergast, BMH WS 802.
204. Ibid.
205. Memo to Michael Collins, from Art O'Brien, 20 Sept. 1920, DE 2/4, NAI.
206. William Murphy, 'Dying, death and hunger strikes: Cork and Brixton, 1920', in James Kelly and Mary Ann Lyons (eds), *Death and Dying in Ireland, Britain and Europe: Historical Perspectives* (Dublin, 2013), p. 307.
207. Statement by Mary MacSwiney, 23 Oct. 1920, Art Ó Brían Papers, Ms8447/13, NLI; *Topeka State Journal*, 23 Oct. 1920.
208. MacSwiney, 'Diary of week of Terry's greatest torture', p. 6.
209. Lennon, 'The starvation of a man', pp 61–2.
210. MacSwiney, 'Diary of week of Terry's greatest torture', p. 7.
211. Ibid., p. 8.

212. *Evening Star* (Washington DC), 22 Oct. 1922.
213. MacSwiney, 'Diary of week of Terry's greatest torture', p. 14.
214. Statement by Mary MacSwiney, 23 Oct. 1920, Art Ó Brían Papers, Ms 8,447/13, NLI; *Topeka State Journal*, 23 Oct. 1920.
215. Edward Shortt, 'Alderman McSwiney(death)', *Hansard*, 25 Oct. 1920.
216. Edward Shortt, Statement, 20 Aug. 1920, HO 144/10308.
217. Medical Report, G. B. Griffiths, 19 Oct. 1920, HO 144/10308.
218. Statement by Mary MacSwiney, 23 Oct. 1920, Art Ó Brían Papers, Ms 8,447/13, NLI.
219. Ibid.
220. Ibid.
221. *Topeka State Journal*, 23 Oct. 1920.
222. MacSwiney, 'Diary of week of Terry's greatest torture', p. 14.
223. Statement by Mary MacSwiney, 23 Oct. 1920, Art Ó Brían Papers, Ms8447/13, NLI.
224. Ibid.
225. MacSwiney, 'Diary of week of Terry's greatest torture', p. 15; Statement by Mary MacSwiney, 23 Oct. 1920, Art Ó Brían Papers, Ms 8,447/13, NLI.
226. C. B. Griffiths, Note, 23 Oct. 1920, HO 144/10308.
227. MacSwiney, 'Diary of week of Terry's greatest torture', Terence MacSwiney Papers, P48b/421, UCDA. This file contains an additional page that was omitted in the Bureau of Military History Witness Statement of Margaret Lucey.
228. Ibid.
229. Ibid.
230. Bulletin on the health of Terence MacSwiney issued by the Irish Self Determination League, 24 Oct. 1920, 11am, Art Ó Briain Papers, Ms 8,448/5, NLI.
231. Bulletin on the health of Terence MacSwiney issued by the Irish Self Determination League, 23 Oct. 1920, 1pm, Art Ó Briain Papers, Ms 8,448/5, NLI.
232. MacSwiney, 'Diary of week of Terry's greatest torture', Terence MacSwiney Papers, P48b/421, UCDA.
233. *The Laurens Advertiser* (Laurens SC), 27 Oct. 1920.
234. MacSwiney, 'Diary of week of Terry's greatest torture', p. 18.
235. Ibid.
236. Ibid.
237. Ibid,; *Irish Independent*, 26 Oct. 1920.
238. Edward Shortt, 'Alderman McSwiney', *Hansard*, 21 Oct. 1920.
239. Quoted in the *Freeman's Journal*, 25 Oct 1920.
240. MacSwiney, 'Diary of week of Terry's greatest torture'; *Irish Independent*, 27 Oct. 1920.
241. MacSwiney, 'Diary of week of Terry's greatest torture.'
242. *Irish Independent*, 28 Oct. 1920.
243. MacSwiney, 'Diary of week of Terry's greatest torture,' p. 19.
244. Quoted in *Irish Independent*, 29 Oct. 1920.
245. Letter to Étienette Beuque from Mary MacSwiney, 11–16 June 1937, Papers of Terence MacSwiney's Biographers, P48c/50, UCDA.
246. MacSwiney, 'Testimony', p. 303.
247. The attendance list states: 'Mrs MacSwiney (the widow), is seriously indisposed after the strain of yesterday and is confined to bed.' Attendance list for mass held for Terence MacSwiney in Southwark Cathedral, [November, 1920], Papers of Terence MacSwiney's Biographers, P48c/440, UCDA.
248. Medical Report, G. B. Griffiths, 13 Oct. 1920, HO 144/10308.
249. MacDiarmada, *Art O'Brien*, p. 105.
250. Memo to Michael Collins from Art O'Brien, 25 Sept. 1920, DE 2/4, NAI.
251. *Cork Examiner*, 26 Oct. 1920.
252. *Evening Echo*, 28 Oct. 1920.
253. *Irish Independent*, 26 Oct. 1920.
254. MacSwiney, 'Diary of week of Terry's greatest torture', p. 21.
255. *Evening Herald*, 28 Oct. 1920.
256. MacSwiney, 'Diary of week of Terry's greatest torture'; *Evening Herald*, 28 Oct. 1920; Murphy, *Political Imprisonment*, p. 189.

257. MacSwiney, 'Diary of week of Terry's greatest torture.'
258. MacSwiney, 'Diary of week of Terry's greatest torture'; Murphy, *Political Imprisonment*, p. 189.
259. *Evening Herald*, 28 Oct. 1920.
260. MacSwiney, 'Diary of week of Terry's greatest torture'.
261. Murphy, 'Death and dying in Ireland', p. 304.
262. Letter to the Home Office from Geoffrey Whiskard, 22 Sept. 1920, HO144/10308.
263. *Topeka State Journal*, 4 Sept. 1920.
264. De Róiste Diary, 30 Oct. 1920, CCCA.
265. MacSwiney, 'Diary of week of Terry's greatest torture', p. 23; Murphy, *Political Imprisonment*, p. 190.
266. MacSwiney, 'Diary of week of Terry's greatest torture', p. 25.
267. *Evening Echo*, 29 Oct. 1920.
268. MacSwiney, 'Diary of week of Terry's greatest torture', p. 25.
269. *Evening Herald*, 29 Oct. 1920.
270. Ibid.
271. *Evening Echo*, 29 Oct. 1920.
272. De Róiste Diary, 30 Oct. 1920, CCCA.
273. *Evening Herald*, 29 Oct. 1920.
274. MacSwiney, 'Diary of week of Terry's greatest torture', p. 25.
275. Ibid., pp 26–7.
276. MacSwiney, 'Diary of week of Terry's greatest torture', pp 27–8.
277. Costello, *Enduring the Most*, p. 229.
278. MacSwiney, 'Diary of week of Terry's greatest torture', pp 27–8.
279. *Cork Examiner*, 30 Oct. 1920.
280. Ibid., 21 Sept. 1920.
281. Miller, *A History of Force Feeding*, p. 91.
282. Michael O'Donoghue, BMH WS 1741.
283. De Róiste Diary, 6 Oct. 1920, CCCA
284. *New York Tribune*, 18 Oct. 1920.
285. Terence MacSwiney, 'The revolutionist', in Doherty et al (eds), *The Art and Ideology of Terence MacSwiney*, p. 649; Lennon, 'The starvation of a man', p. 85.
286. http://www.census.nationalarchives.ie/pages/1911/Cork/Blackrock/Knockrea/401536/
287. Quoted in *Irish Press*, 23 Oct. 1923.
288. Letter to Mary and Annie MacSwiney from Terence MacSwiney, 8 Mar. 1917, Terence MacSwiney Papers, P48b/10, UCDA.
289. Costello, *Enduring the Most*, p. 98.
290. MacSwiney, 'Testimony', pp 307–8.
291. Ibid.
292. Ibid., p. 312.
293. Frank O'Connor, *An Only Child* (Belfast, 1993), p. 187.
294. Statement by Fr Dominic on Terence MacSwiney, [n.d], Papers of Terence MacSwiney's Biographers, P48c/277, UCDA.
295. Murphy, *Political Imprisonment and the Irish*, p. 174.
296. 'Prime Minister's Statement', *Times*, 26 Aug. 1920.
297. Details of the telegram were given in 'Prime Minister's Statement', *Times*, 26 Aug. 1920
298. MacSwiney, 'Testimony', p. 317.
299. Dolan, 'Death in the archives', p. 5, p. 6, p. 30.
300. MacSwiney, 'Diary of week of Terry's greatest torture'.
301. Murphy, 'Dying, death and hunger strikes: Cork and Brixton, 1920', p. 304.
302. Ibid., p. 297.
303. See also the literary critic, Paige Reynolds, 'Modernist martyrdom: The funerals of Terence MacSwiney', in *Modernism/Modernity* vol. 9, no. 4 (Nov. 2002).
304. Murphy, 'Dying, death and hunger strikes: Cork and Brixton, 1920', p. 307.
305. Murphy, *Political Imprisonment and the Irish*, p. 88.
306. Miller, *A History of Force Feeding*, pp 92–3.
307. Murphy, *Political Imprisonment and the Irish*, pp 174–5, p. 183.

308. Joanna Bourke, 'Fear and anxiety: Writing about emotion in modern history', in *History Workshop*, no. 55 (2003), p. 122.
309. Medical Report, G. B. Griffiths, 20 Sept. 1920, HO 144//10308.
310. Ibid., 21 Oct 1920; 23 Oct. 1920.
311. Letter to Edward Troup form John Webster, Senior Official Analyst to the Home Office, 19 Oct. 1920, HO 144/10308.
312. Bourke, 'Fear and anxiety', p. 121.
313. Letter to Frank Aiken from Nora Murphy, 8 Nov. 1932, 1D86, Joseph Murphy, MSPC.
314. Timothy Miller, application for a Dependent's Allowance or Gratuity, 29 Nov. 1923, 1D86 Joseph Murphy, MSPC.
315. Gallagher, *Days of Fear*, p. 26.
316. Roger Luckhurst, *The Trauma Question* (London, 2008), p. 7.
317. Ibid. p. 9.
318. Ibid.
319. Aiken, *Spiritual Wounds*, p. 90.
320. Statement by Mary MacSwiney, 23 Oct. 1920, Art Ó Brían Papers, Ms 8,447/13, NLI.
321. Mary MacSwiney, 'Is self-sacrifice a crime', Terence MacSwiney Papers, P48b/436, UCDA.
322. Typescript report of a speech delivered by Mary MacSwiney at a meeting held under the auspices of the Irish Self-Determination League and the Roger Casement Sinn Féin Club in Essex Hall, London, 25 Oct. [1922], Mary MacSwiney Papers, P48a/113, UCDA.
323. Letter to Mrs Maloney from Annie MacSwiney, 18 Oct. 1920, Terence MacSwiney Papers, P48b/623, UCDA.
324. *Washington Herald*, 18 Oct. 1920.
325. Letter to Mrs Maloney from Annie MacSwiney, 18 Oct. 1920, Terence MacSwiney Papers, P48b/623, UCDA.
326. Memo from Art O'Brien to Michael Collins, 9 Oct. 1920, DE/2/4, NAI.
327. Ibid., 20 Oct. 1920, DE/2/4, NAI.
328. Annie MacSwiney to Mrs Maloney, 18 Oct. 1920, Terence MacSwiney Papers, P48b/623, UCDA.
329. MacSwiney, 'The revolutionist', p. 651.
330. Ernest Blythe, BMH WS 939.
331. David Fitzpatrick, *Ernest Blythe in Ulster: The Making of a Double Agent?* (Cork, 2018), p. 135.

Chapter 5: America: December 1920–August 1921

1. Letter to de Valera from Mary MacSwiney, 20 July, 1921, Mary MacSwiney Papers, P48a/115/47, UCDA.; David McCullagh, *De Valera: Rise 1882–1932* (Dublin, 2017), p. 188.
2. David Fitzpatrick, *Harry Boland's Irish Revolution* (Cork, 2003), p. 193.
3. Paul Lerner and Mark S. Micale, 'Trauma, psychiatry, and history: A conceptual and historiographical introduction', in Mark S. Micale and Paul Lerner (eds), *Traumatic Pasts: History, Psychiatry, and Trauma in the Modern Age, 1870–1930* (Cambridge, 2001), p. 20.
4. *Cork Examiner*, 9 Nov. 1920.
5. Ronan Fanning, *Éamon de Valera: A Will to Power* (Dublin, 2015), p. 83; McCullagh, *De Valera: Rise*, p. 171.
6. Report on lecture entitled 'Ireland in America' delivered by Mary MacSwiney at the Cork Opera House, 16 Oct. 1921, *Cork Examiner*, 17 Oct. 1921.
7. Quoted in Mary MacDiarmada, *Art O'Brien and Irish Nationalism in London, 1900–1925* (Dublin, 2020), p. 103.
8. Proposal re involvement of St Ita's in a memorial to Terence MacSwiney, 1921, Mary MacSwiney Papers, P48a/28, UCDA.
9. Letter to Louise Gavan Duffy from Annie MacSwiney, 4 Sept. 1941, correspondence in possession of Catherine and Cathal Brugha.
10. Proposal re involvement of St Ita's in a memorial to Terence MacSwiney, 1921, Mary MacSwiney Papers, P48a/28, UCDA.
11. Liam de Róiste Diary, 6 Oct. 1920, CCCA.

12. W. F. Stockley and T. J. Murphy, 'St Ita's School, Cork', [1926], Mary MacSwiney Papers, P48a/29, UCDA.
13. Letter from Mary MacSwiney to Eileen and John J. Hearne, 6 Oct. 1921, John J. Hearne Papers, Ms. 15,989/2, NLI.
14. De Róiste Diary, 4 Nov. 1920, CCCA; *Skibbereen Eagle*, 6 Nov. 1920.
15. De Róiste Diary, 9 Oct. 1920, CCCA.
16. De Róiste Diary, 11 Nov. 1920, 13 Nov. 1920, CCCA.
17. De Róiste Diary, 14 Nov. 1920, CCCA.
18. De Róiste Diary, 20 Nov. 1920, CCCA.
19. Quoted in Francis M. Carroll, *America and the Making of an Independent Ireland* (New York, 2021), p. 95; Bernadette Whelan, *United States Foreign Policy and Ireland: From Empire to Independence, 1913–29* (Dublin, 2006), p. 263.
20. Whelan, *United States Foreign Policy and Ireland*, p. 263.
21. Carroll, *America and the Making of an Independent Ireland*, p. 89, p. 90, p. 94.
22. Ibid., p. 95.
23. Mary MacSwiney, 'Testimony', in *Evidence on Conditions in Ireland: Comprising the Complete Testimony, Affidavits and Exhibits Presented Before the American Commission on Conditions in Ireland* (Washington, 1921), p. 259.
24. Draft obituary for Annie MacSwiney, 1954, Maire Comerford Papers, Ms 24,896, NLI.
25. Typescript report on Mary MacSwiney's reception by Americans and her appearance in Washington DC before the Commission on Conditions in Ireland, [1921], Mary MacSwiney Papers, P48a/160, UCDA.
26. Typescript of report in the *Boston Globe*, 20 Dec. 1920, of a meeting on 19 Dec. 1920, Mary MacSwiney Papers, P48a/162, UCDA.
27. *Irish Independent*, 13 Nov. 1920. Muriel arrived in Dublin from London on 19 Nov. 1920. *Cork Examiner*, 20 Nov. 1920.
28. For examples, see Papers of Terence MacSwiney's biographers P48c/438**,** UCDA.
29. *The Liberator (Tralee)*, 18 Nov. 1920
30. De Róiste Diary, 14 Aug. 1920, CCCA.
31. *Cork Examiner*, 25 Nov. 1920.
32. *Irish Independent*, 26 Nov. 1920.
33. *The Liberator (Tralee)*, 27 Nov. 1920.
34. *Cork Examiner*, 4 Dec. 1920.
35. *New York Tribune*, 4 Dec. 1920.
36. Ibid., 6 Dec. 1920.
37. *Evening Star (Washington DC)*, 8 Dec. 1920.
38. *Evening World (New York NY)*, 4 Dec. 1920
39. Letter to Muriel MacSwiney from Mary F. McWhorter, 4 Dec. 1920, Mary MacSwiney Papers, P48a/114/2/1, UCDA.
40. Letter to Muriel MacSwiney from Peter MacSwiney, 27 Aug. 1920, Art Ó Briain Papers, Ms 8,447/13, NLI.
41. Síobhra Aiken, *Spiritual Wounds: Trauma, Testimony and the Irish Civil War* (Dublin, 2022), p. 110.
42. *New York Tribune*, 6 Dec. 1920.
43. Typescript of report in the *Boston Globe*, 20 Dec. 1920, of a meeting on 19 Dec. 1920, Mary MacSwiney Papers, P48a/162, UCDA.
44. Charlotte Fallon, *Soul of Fire: A Biography of Mary MacSwiney* (Cork, 1986), p. 57.
45. *Evening Star (Washington DC)*, 8 Dec. 1920.
46. MacSwiney, 'Testimony', pp 185–6.
47. Ibid., p. 186.
48. Ibid., p. 244.
49. *The Herald and News (Newberry SC)*, 14 Dec. 1920.
50. Ibid.
51. MacSwiney, 'Testimony', p. 262.
52. Report on Mary MacSwiney's reception in America and her appearance in Washington DC before the Commission on Conditions in Ireland, [1921], Mary MacSwiney Papers, P48a/160, UCDA.
53. *Topeka State Journal*, 9 Dec. 1920.

54. Ibid., 8 Feb. 1921; 16 Feb. 1921. Mary served on the governing body as one of four nominated graduate members from Feb. 1920–Feb. 1923.
55. *Washington Herald*, 13 Dec. 1920.
56. Fanning, *Éamon de Valera*, p. 84; Diarmaid Ferriter, *Judging Dev: A Reassessment of the Life and Legacy of Eamon de Valera* (Dublin, 2007), p. 34.
57. McCullagh, *De Valera: Rise*, p. 173. Fanning, *Éamon de Valera*, pp 84–5.
58. Bill Kissane, *The Politics of the Irish Civil War* (Oxford, 2005), pp 44–5.
59. Fanning, *Éamon de Valera*, p. 87.
60. McCullagh, *De Valera: Rise*, p. 187.
61. MacSwiney, 'Testimony', pp 255–6.
62. Quoted in Francis J. Costello, *Enduring the Most: The Life and Death of Terence MacSwiney* (Dingle, 1995), p. 51.
63. Letter to Eileen and John J. Hearn from Mary MacSwiney, 6 Oct. 1921, John J. Hearn Papers, Ms 15,989/2, NLI.
64. *Irish Independent*, 10 Dec. 1920.
65. Ibid., 11 Nov. 1920.
66. *Evening Star (Washington DC)*, 8 Dec. 1920.
67. *Washington Herald*, 8 Dec. 1920.
68. See, for example, Muriel MacSwiney, 'Testimony', in *Evidence on Conditions in Ireland: Comprising the Complete Testimony, Affidavits and Exhibits Presented Before the American Commission on Conditions in Ireland* (Washington, 1921), p. 301.
69. Muriel MacSwiney, 'Testimony', p. 278, p. 280.
70. Ibid., p. 278.
71. Ibid., p. 260.
72. Quoted in McCullagh, *De Valera: Rise*, p. 184.
73. Anne Dolan, 'Killing and Bloody Sunday, November 1920', in *The Historical Journal*, vol. 49, no. 3 (2006), pp 795–6.
74. Cumann na mBan leaflet enclosed in letter to Mary MacSwiney from the Honorary Secretary, Cumann na mBan headquarters, 29 Jan. 1921, Mary MacSwiney Papers, P48a/115/1, UCDA.
75. Letter 'To the bishops who have attacked the Irish Republican Army' from Annie MacSwiney 30 Dec. 1920, Mary MacSwiney Papers, P48a/192/2, UCDA. A handwritten note indicates that the letter was not published.
76. Letter to Harry Boland from Mary MacSwiney, 26 Jan. [1921], de Valera Papers, P150/655, UCDA.
77. De Róiste Diary, 12 Dec. 1920, CCCA.
78. Donal Óg O'Callaghan, 'Testimony', in *Evidence on Conditions in Ireland: Comprising the Complete Testimony, Affidavits and Exhibits Presented Before the American Commission on Conditions in Ireland* (Washington, 1921), p. 829.
79. O'Callaghan, 'Testimony', p. 816.
80. *Who Burnt Cork City* (Dublin, 1921), p. 16.
81. Charles Townshend, *The Republic: The Fight for Irish Independence* (London, 2013), pp 217–8.
82. *Who Burnt Cork* City, p. 16.
83. Lil Conlon, Manuscript of *Cumann na mBan and the Women of Ireland, 1913–25*, p. 137, Cork Public Museum.
84. *Washington Herald*, 14 Dec. 1920.
85. *Who Burnt Cork City*, p. 16.
86. O'Callaghan, 'Testimony', p. 828.
87. *Who Burnt Cork City*, p. 27.
88. Ibid., p. 28.
89. Conlon, Manuscript of *Cumann na mBan*, p. 136, Cork Public Museum.
90. Bob Powell, 'History and family memory: The "burning of Cork", 11 and 12 December 1920', in *Folk Life, Journal of Ethnological Studies*, vol. 60, no. 2 (2022), p. 171. The findings of the Strickland Inquiry were not published.
91. O'Callaghan, 'Testimony', p. 832.
92. Ibid., p. 836.
93. John Borgonovo (ed.), *Florence and Josephine O'Donoghue's War of Independence* (Dublin, 2006), p. 142.

94. *Who Burnt Cork City*, p. 19.
95. Letter to Mr O'Mara from Mary MacSwiney, Washington, no date [Dec 1920], Mary MacSwiney Papers, P48a/115/17, UCDA.
96. *Topeka State Journal*, 16 Feb. 1921; 8 Feb. 1921.
97. Report on a lecture entitled 'Ireland in America' delivered by Mary MacSwiney at the Cork Opera House, 16 Oct. 1921, *Cork Examiner*, 17 Oct. 1921.
98. Letter to de Valera from Mary MacSwiney, 20 July, 1921, Mary MacSwiney Papers, P48a/115/47, UCDA.
99. Costello, *Enduring the Most*, p. 109. Terence and de Róiste clashed over issues to do with the collection of the loan in Cork, the latter believing that MacSwiney was encroaching on his prerogatives. De Róiste Diary, 20 May. 1920; 26 May 1920; 8 June 1920; 10 June 1920, CCCA.
100. Letter to de Valera from Mary MacSwiney, 20 July 1921, Mary MacSwiney Papers, P48a/155/47, UCDA.
101. Report relating to Mary MacSwiney's reception in America and her appearance in Washington DC before the Commission on Conditions in Ireland, [1921], Mary MacSwiney Papers, P48a/160, UCDA.
102. Typescript of report in the *Boston Globe*, 20 Dec. 1920, of a meeting on 19 Dec. 1920, Mary MacSwiney Papers, P48a/162, UCDA.
103. *Irish Independent*, 12 Jan. 1921.
104. *The Liberator (Tralee)*, 30 Dec. 1920.
105. *Irish Independent*, 1 Jan. 1921.
106. *The Abbeville Press and Banner (SC)*, 3 Jan. 1921; *Irish Independent*, 12 Jan. 1921.
107. Letter to Fred Cronin from Art O'Brien, Fred Cronin Papers, Ms 49,526/13/7, NLI.
108. *Abilene Weekly Reflector*, 6 Jan. 1921.
109. Letter to Mary MacSwiney from the Honorary Secretary, Cumann na mBan headquarters, 29 Jan. 1921, Mary MacSwiney Papers, P48a/115/1/1 UCDA.
110. Joanne Mooney Eichacker, *Irish Republican Women in America: Lecture Tours, 1916–1925* (Dublin, 2003), p. 109.
111. Letter to de Valera from Mary MacSwiney, 24 July 1921, Mary MacSwiney Papers, P48a/115/47, UCDA.
112. Letter to James O'Mara from Mary MacSwiney, 26 Jan.–2 Feb. 1921, James O'Mara Papers, Ms 21,549/1, NLI.
113. Mooney Eichacker, *Irish Republican Women in America*, no. 4, p. 295.
114. McCullagh, *De Valera: Rise*, p. 167. Letter to 'A Chara' [James O'Mara] from Mary MacSwiney, no date [Mar. 1921], Mary MacSwiney Papers, P48a/115/8, UCDA.
115. Letter to 'A Chara' [James O'Mara] from Mary MacSwiney, no date [Mar. 1921], Mary MacSwiney Papers, P48a/115/8, UCDA.
116. Typescript speech by Mary MacSwiney, Galveston, Texas, 23 Feb. 1921, Mary MacSwiney Papers P48a/163, UCDA.
117. See, for example, *Mary MacSwiney: Address at the Civic Auditorium, San Francisco*, issued by the Irish Press and Publicity Bureau, San Francisco, [Mar. 1921], Mary MacSwiney Papers P48a/173, Mary MacSwiney Papers, UCDA.
118. See from example, 'Souvenir of Miss MacSwiney's visit to Pottsville', 15 July 1921, Mary MacSwiney Papers, P48a/174, UCDA. This pamphlet comprised the lyrics of 'The Star-Spangled Banner' and 'Soldiers of Erin' on facing pages.
119. Letter to James O'Mara from Catherine Flanagan, 3 Feb. 1921, Mary MacSwiney Papers, P48a/115/3, UCDA.
120. Letter to Mr J. C. Walsh, Director, Benjamin Franklin Bureau, Chicago, from Francis P. Jones, 25 May 1921, Mary MacSwiney Papers, P48a/115/28, UCDA.
121. McCullagh, *De Valera: Rise*, p. 166.
122. Report on a lecture entitled 'Ireland in America' delivered by Mary MacSwiney at the Cork Opera House, 16 Oct. 1921, *Cork Examiner*, 17 Oct. 1921.
123. Ibid. Geddes was the British Ambassador in the US from 1920–4.
124. *Freeman's Journal*, 22 Aug. 1921.
125. Report on lecture entitled 'Ireland in America' delivered by Mary MacSwiney at the Cork Opera House, 16 Oct. 1921, *Cork Examiner*, 17 Oct. 1921.

126. Fanning, *Éamon de Valera*, p. 70.
127. MacSwiney, 'Testimony', p. 215.
128. *Topeka State Journal*, 16 Feb. 1921.
129. *The Herald and News (Newberry, SC)*, 14 Dec. 1920.
130. Whelan, *United States Foreign Policy and Ireland*, p. 316, p. 320.
131. Fanning, *Éamon de Valera*, p. 79.
132. Letter to Mary MacSwiney from Revd J. P. O'Connor, 8 Apr. 1921, Mary MacSwiney Papers, P48a/115/21, UCDA.
133. Typescript speech by Mary MacSwiney, Galveston, Texas, 23 Feb. 1921, Mary MacSwiney Papers, P48a/163, UCDA.
134. De Róiste Diary, 21 Apr. 1921, CCCA.
135. *Freeman's Journal*, 22 Aug. 1921.
136. MacSwiney, 'Testimony', p. 226.
137. Telegram to Joseph McGarrity from Mary MacSwiney, 26 Mar. 1921, Joseph McGarrity Papers, Ms 17,461/2, NLI.
138. *Bamberg Herald (SC)*, 16 Dec. 1920.
139. *Topeka State Journal*, 11 Feb. 1921.
140. *Irish Independent*, 23 Feb. 1921; *Topeka State Journal*, 16 Feb. 1921.
141. *Topeka State Journal*, 16 Feb. 1921.
142. *The Herald and News (Newberry S.C)*, 14 Dec. 1920.
143. *Irish Independent*, 23 Feb. 1921.
144. *Evening Echo*, 24 Feb. 1921.
145. Statement by Art O'Brien on the arrest of Seán MacSwiney, 21 Feb. 1921, Art Ó Briain Papers, Ms 8448/5, NLI.
146. Letter to Fred Cronin from Muriel MacSwiney, 11 Feb. 1921, Fred Cronin Papers, Ms 49.525/15/2, NLI.
147. *Belfast Newsletter*, 25 Feb. 1921; *Freeman's Journal*, 25 Feb. 1921; Statement by Art O'Brien on the arrest of arrest of Seán MacSwiney, 21 Feb. 1921, Art Ó Briain Papers, Ms 8,448/5, NLI.
148. *Belfast Newsletter*, 25 Feb. 1921.
149. *Irish Independent*, 23 Feb. 1921.
150. *Evening Echo*, 24 Feb. 1921.
151. Statement by Art O'Brien on the arrest of arrest of Seán MacSwiney, 21 Feb. 1921, Art Ó Briain Papers, Ms 8,448/5, NLI.
152. Letter to Fred Cronin from Annie MacSwiney, 27 Feb. 1921, Fred Cronin Papers, Ms 49.526/8/5, NLI.
153. Statement by Art O'Brien on the arrest of arrest of Seán MacSwiney, 21 Feb. 1921, Art Ó Briain Papers, Ms 8,448/5, NLI.
154. Letter to Annie MacSwiney from Lieut. Colonel O. F. Dawson, 12 Feb. 1921, Art Ó Briain Papers, Ms 8,448/5, NLI.
155. Letter to Lieut. Colonel O. F. Dawson from Annie MacSwiney, 17 Feb. 1921, Art Ó Briain Papers, Ms 8,448/5, NLI.
156. *Evening Echo*, 25 Feb. 1921.
157. Letter to Lieut. Colonel O. F. Dawson from Annie MacSwiney, 17 Feb. 1921, Art Ó Briain Papers, Ms 8448/5, NLI.
158. Quoted in *Belfast Newsletter*, 23 Feb. 1921.
159. Statement by Art O'Brien on the arrest of arrest of Seán MacSwiney, 21 Feb. 1921, Art Ó Briain Papers, Ms 8,448/5, NLI.
160. Letter to the Adjutant General from Command Headquarters, Cork, 5 Feb. 1924, 1D87 Cornelius Murphy, MSPC.
161. De Róiste Diary, 1 Feb. 1921, 3 Feb. 1921, CCCA.
162. Ibid.
163. Note from Annie MacSwiney to [Art O'Brien] no date [1921], Art Ó Briain Papers Ms 8,447/13, NLI.
164. Telegram to Padraic Fleming from Peter MacSwiney, 28 Feb. 1921, Pádraic Fleming Papers, Ms 50,115/6/4, NLI.

165. Note from Annie MacSwiney to [Art O'Brien] no date [1921], Art Ó Briain Papers Ms 8447/13, NLI.
166. Letter to Fred Cronin from Annie MacSwiney, no date [1921], Fred Cronin Papers, Ms 49,525/8/2, NLI.
167. Peter MacSwiney in *Evidence on Conditions in Ireland: Comprising the Complete Testimony, Affidavits and Exhibits Presented Before the American Commission on Conditions in Ireland* (Washington, 1921), p. 891.
168. De Róiste Diary, 1 Mar. 1921, CCCA.
169. Ibid., 2 Mar. 1921, 1 Mar. 1921, CCCA. On 11 March the curfew reverted to 9pm, de Róiste Diary, 10 Mar. 1921, CCCA.
170. Terence MacSwiney Diary, 17 Apr. 1903, Terence MacSwiney Papers, Ms 35,029, NLI.
171. Letter to the Committee of St Ita's School from Mary MacSwiney, 11 May 1921, Mary MacSwiney Papers, P48a/115/21, UCDA.
172. *Topeka State Journal*, 16 Feb. 1921.
173. Letter to Fred Cronin from Art O'Brien, 5 Feb. 1921, Fred Cronin Papers, Ms 49,526/13/7, NLI.
174. De Róiste Diary, 25 Feb. 1921, CCCA.
175. Borgonovo, *Florence and Josephine O'Donoghue's War of Independence*, p. 142.
176. De Róiste Diary, 28 Feb. 1921, CCCA.
177. *Evening Herald*, 4 Mar. 1921.
178. *Topeka State Journal*, 17 Feb. 1921.
179. Letter to James O'Mara from Catherine Flanagan, 3 Feb. 1921, Mary MacSwiney Papers, P48a/115/3, UCDA.
180. Letter to James O'Mara from J. C. Walsh, AARIR, no date, Mary MacSwiney Papers, P48a/115/4, UCDA.
181. Letter to James O'Mara from Mary MacSwiney, 26 Jan.–2 Feb. 1921, James O'Mara Papers, Ms 21,549/1, NLI.
182. Letter to James O'Mara from Mary MacSwiney, 25 Feb. 1921, James O'Mara Papers, Ms 21,549/1, NLI.
183. Letter to Harry Boland from Mary MacSwiney, 12 Feb. 1921, Mary MacSwiney Papers, P48a/115 (6), UCDA.
184. Ibid.
185. Ibid.
186. Letter to James O'Mara from Mary MacSwiney, 26 Jan.–2 Feb. 1921, James O'Mara Papers, Ms 21,549/1, NLI.
187. Fitzpatrick, *Harry Boland's Irish Revolution*, p. 206.
188. Letter to Harry Boland from Mary MacSwiney, 12 Feb. 1921, Mary MacSwiney Papers, P48a/115/6, UCDA.
189. Letter to James O'Mara from Mary MacSwiney, 26 Jan.–2 Feb. 1921, James O'Mara Papers, Ms 21,549/1, NLI.
190. Letter to James O' Mara from Mary MacSwiney, 25 Feb. 1921, Mary MacSwiney Papers, P48a/115/12, UCDA.
191. Letter to James O'Mara from Mary MacSwiney, 26 Jan.–2 Feb. 1921, James O'Mara Papers, Ms 21,549/1, NLI.
192. Letter to de Valera from Mary MacSwiney, 20 May 1921, Mary MacSwiney Papers, P48a/115/27, UCDA. For details on de Valera's desire to retrench on expenditure in America see Fitzpatrick, *Harry Boland's Irish Revolution*, pp 204–6.
193. Letter to de Valera from James O'Mara, 29 Apr. 1921, Joseph McGarrity Papers, Ms 17,522/36, NLI; Letter to James O'Mara from de Valera, 3 Feb. 1921, quoted in McCullagh, *De Valera: Rise*, p. 188.
194. Letter to James O'Mara from de Valera, 24 Mar. 1921, James O'Mara Papers, Ms 21,5549/3, NLI.
195. Letter to de Valera from James O'Mara, 29 Apr. 1921, Joseph McGarrity Papers, Ms 17,522/36, NLI.
196. Letter to Harry Boland from James O'Mara, 29 Apr. 1921, Joseph McGarrity Papers, Ms 17,522/35, NLI.
197. Letter to de Valera from Mary MacSwiney, 20 July 1921, Mary MacSwiney Papers, P48a/155/47, UCDA.
198. Ibid.

199. Letter to James O'Mara from Mary MacSwiney, 25 Feb. 1921, Mary MacSwiney Papers, P48a/115/12, UCDA.
200. Whelan, *United States Foreign Policy and Ireland*, p. 330.
201. De Róiste Diary, 21 Apr. 1921, CCCA.
202. Whelan, *United States Foreign Policy and Ireland*, p. 331.
203. Ibid., p. 332.
204. De Róiste Diary, 22 Mar. 1921, CCCA.
205. Letter to de Valera from Mary MacSwiney, 20 May 1921, Mary MacSwiney Papers, P48a/115/27, UCDA.
206. Whelan, *United States Foreign Policy and Ireland*, p. 335.
207. De Róiste Diary, 16 Apr. 1921, CCCA.
208. Whelan, *United States Foreign Policy and Ireland*, p. 335.
209. Quoted in ibid.
210. *Irish Independent*, 13 Nov. 1920.
211. De Róiste Diary, 8 Apr. 1921; 18 Apr. 1921, CCCA.
212. De Róiste Diary, 3 May 1921, CCCA.
213. De Róiste Diary, 10 May 1921; 13 May 1921, CCCA; *Cork Examiner*, 14 May 1921.
214. De Róiste Diary, 11 May 1921; 13 May 1921, CCCA.
215. *Irish Independent*, 14 May 1921.
216. De Róiste Diary, 5 May 1921, CCCA.
217. *Irish Independent*, 14 May 1921.
218. Michael J. Burke, BMH WS 1424; William Murphy, *Political Imprisonment and the Irish, 1912–1921* (Oxford, 2014), p. 206.
219. Jason Knirck, *Women of the Dáil: Gender, Republicanism and the Anglo-Irish Treaty* (Dublin, 2006), pp 78–9.
220. Letter to Mary MacSwiney from Vivien Pierce, 11 July 1921, Mary MacSwiney Papers, P48a/115/44, UCDA.
221. Letter to James O'Mara from Catherine Flanagan, 3 Feb. 1921, Mary MacSwiney Papers, P48a/115/3, UCDA.
222. Letter to James O'Mara from Catherine Flanagan, 23 Feb. 1921, Mary MacSwiney Papers, P48a/115/10, UCDA.
223. Letter to Harry Boland from Mary MacSwiney, 12 Feb. 1921, Mary MacSwiney Papers, P48a/115/6, UCDA.
224. Letter to James O'Mara from Mary MacSwiney, no date, Mary MacSwiney Papers, P48a/115/17. UCDA.
225. Letter to James O'Mara from Mary MacSwiney, 26 Jan.–2 Feb. 1921, James O'Mara Papers, Ms 21,549/1, NLI.
226. Letter to James O'Mara from Frank P. Walsh, 11 Apr. 1921, James O'Mara Papers, Ms 21,549/4, NLI.
227. Katherine H. Adams and Michael L. Keene, *Alice Paul and the American Suffrage Campaign* (Illinois, 2007), p. 243.
228. Letter to de Valera from Mary MacSwiney, 24 July 1921, Mary MacSwiney Papers, P48a/115/47, UCDA.
229. Letter to de Valera from Mary MacSwiney, 20 July 1921, Mary MacSwiney Papers, P48a/115/47, UCDA.
230. Ibid.
231. Letter to Harry Boland from Mary MacSwiney, 19 July [1921], de Valera Papers, P150/655, UCDA.
232. Mary MacSwiney, 'The Truce', no date, Mary MacSwiney Papers, P48a/446, UCDA.
233. Letter to de Valera from Mary MacSwiney, 20 July 1921, Mary MacSwiney Papers, P48a/115/47, UCDA.
234. Ibid.
235. Letter to de Valera from Mary MacSwiney, 24 July 1921, Mary MacSwiney Papers, P48a/115/47, UCDA.
236. Ibid.
237. *Freeman's Journal*, 21 Jan. 1921.

238. Letter to de Valera from Mary MacSwiney, 24 July 1921, Mary MacSwiney Papers, P48a/115/47, UCDA.
239. Ibid.
240. Ibid.
241. Ibid.
242. Letter to Archbishop Hayes, New York, from Mary Donegan, 6 July 1921, Mary MacSwiney Papers, P48a/115/42, UCDA.
243. Letter to de Valera from Mary MacSwiney, 28 July 1921, Mary MacSwiney Papers, P48a/115/47, UCDA.
244. Letter to Mary MacSwiney from Harry Boland, 26 July 1921, Mary MacSwiney Papers, P48a/115/50, UCDA.
245. Letter to Mary Donegan from Mary MacSwiney, 31 July 1921, Mary MacSwiney Papers, P48a/115/52, UCDA.
246. Letter to de Valera from Mary MacSwiney, 4 Aug. 1921, Mary MacSwiney Papers, P48a/115/47, UCDA.
247. Letter to Mary MacSwiney from Harry Boland, 26 July 1921, Mary MacSwiney Papers, P48a/115/50, UCDA.
248. Letter to Harry Boland from Mary MacSwiney, 4 Aug. 1921, Mary MacSwiney Papers, P48a/115/57, UCDA.
249. Ibid.
250. Quoted in Fitzpatrick, *Harry Boland's Irish Revolution*, p. 198.
251. Typescript section of Agnes O'Mara diary, Apr. 1921, James O'Mara Papers, Ms 21,549/4, NLI.
252. Letter to Mary MacSwiney from Harry Boland, 26 July 1921, Mary MacSwiney Papers, P48a/115/50, UCDA.
253. Quoted in Fitzpatrick, *Harry Boland's Irish Revolution*, p. 194. Boland claimed afterwards that he had been misquoted.
254. Ibid., pp 194–5.
255. Letter to Mary MacSwiney from Harry Boland, 26 July 1921, Mary MacSwiney Papers, P48a/115/50, UCDA.
256. Letter to de Valera from Mary MacSwiney, 4 Aug. 1921, Mary MacSwiney Papers, P48a/115/47, UCDA.
257. Letter to A Chara from Mary MacSwiney, no date [Mar. 1921], Mary MacSwiney Papers, P48a115/8, UCDA.
258. Telegram to Revd Peter C. Yorke, D. D. St Peter's Church, San Francisco, California, from Joseph Scott, 5 Mar. 1921, Mary MacSwiney Papers, P48a/115/14, UCDA.
259. Letter to James O'Mara from Catherine Flanagan, 3 Feb. 1921, Mary MacSwiney Papers, P48a/115/3, UCDA.
260. Letter to James O'Mara from Catherine Flanagan, 15 Mar. 1921, James O'Mara Papers, Ms 21, 549/3, NLI.
261. Letter to James O'Mara from Mary MacSwiney, no date, Mary MacSwiney Papers, P48a/115/17, UCDA.
262. Letter to Harry Boland from Mary MacSwiney, 12 Feb. 1921, Mary MacSwiney Papers, P48a/115/6, UCDA.
263. Letter to the Committee of St Ita's School from Mary MacSwiney, 11 May 1921, Mary MacSwiney Papers, P48a/115/21, UCDA.
264. Letter to Fred Cronin from Annie MacSwiney, 24 Jan. 1921, Fred Cronin Papers, Ms 49,596/8, NLI.
265. Letter to the Committee of St Ita's School from Mary MacSwiney, 11 May 1921, Mary MacSwiney Papers, P48a/115/21, UCDA.
266. Letter to de Valera from Mary MacSwiney, 4 Aug. 1921, Mary MacSwiney Papers, P48a/115/47, UCDA.
267. Letter to de Valera from Mary MacSwiney, 20 May 1921, Mary MacSwiney Papers, P48a/115/37, UCDA.
268. Letter to Mary MacSwiney from Harry Boland, 26 July 1921, Mary MacSwiney Papers, P48a/115/50, UCDA.
269. Letter to Fred Cronin from Art O'Brien offering to assume responsibility for the Cork funeral

expenses as well as those relating to the London funeral, 5 Feb. 1921; letter to Seán O'Hegarty from Art O'Brien, Fred Cronin Papers, Ms 49,526/13/7-8, NLI.
270. Letter to Muriel MacSwiney from Fred Cronin, Fred Cronin Papers, Ms 49,526/15/3, NLI.
271. Statement entitled Mrs Muriel MacSwiney in account with Frederick J. Cronin, 29 Nov. 1920–Oct. 1921, Fred Cronin Papers, Ms 49,526/15/5, NLI.
272. Letter to Fred Cronin from Muriel MacSwiney, 11 Feb. 1921, Fred Cronin Papers, Ms 49,526/15/2, NLI.
273. Letter to Fred Cronin from Muriel MacSwiney, 4 Nov. 1920, Fred Cronin Papers, Ms 49,526/15/1, NLI.
274. *Freeman's Journal*, 25 Feb. 1921.
275. Letter to Fred Cronin from Muriel MacSwiney, 11 Feb. 1921, Fred Cronin Papers, Ms 49,526/15/2, NLI.
276. *Freeman's Journal*, 25 Feb. 1921.
277. Letter to Fred Cronin from Annie MacSwiney, 24 Jan. 1921, Fred Cronin Papers, Ms 49,526/8, NLI.
278. *Cork Examiner*, 3 Oct. 1921.

Chapter 6: Truce to Treaty Split

1. *Evening Echo*, 13 Aug. 1921. Other papers cited the date as 15 August, *Cork Examiner*, 15 Aug. 1921.
2. David Fitzpatrick, *Harry Boland's Irish Revolution* (Cork, 2003), p. 224; letter to de Valera from Mary MacSwiney, 20 May 1921, Mary MacSwiney Papers, P48a/115/27, UCDA.
3. The other two members were Laurence Ginnell, who was in South Africa, and Alderman Tom Clarke who was ill. *Freeman's Journal*, 17 Aug. 1921.
4. *Waterford News and Star*, 19 Aug. 1921.
5. *Cork Examiner*, 20 Aug. 1921.
6. *Irish Independent*, 4 Oct. 1921.
7. *Irish Independent*, 22 Aug. 1921; *Freeman's Journal*, 22 Aug. 1921.
8. *Freeman's Journal*, 22 Aug. 1921.
9. Letter to Harry Boland from Mary MacSwiney, 1 Dec. 1921, de Valera Papers, P150/655, UCDA.
10. Mary MacSwiney, 'Debate on the Treaty', Dáil Éireann Debates, 17 Dec 1921.
11. Mary MacSwiney, 'The Truce', no date, Mary MacSwiney Papers, P48a/446, UCDA.
12. Letter to de Valera from Mary MacSwiney, 7 Sept. [1921], de Valera Papers, P150/655, UCDA.
13. Letter to Eileen and John J. Hearn form Mary MacSwiney, 6 Oct. 1921, John J. Hearn Papers, Ms. 15,989/2, NLI.
14. Letter to [de Valera] from Mary MacSwiney, [Dec. 1921], de Valera Papers, P150/656, UCDA.
15. Mary MacSwiney, 'Debate on the Treaty', Dáil Éireann Debates, 14 Dec. 1921.
16. *Freeman's Journal*, 24 Aug. 1921.
17. *Evening Echo*, 23 Aug. 1921.
18. National University of Ireland, Cork, Governing Body Minutes, 21 Oct. 1921, UCC College Archives.
19. Letter to Eileen and John J. Hearn form Mary MacSwiney, 6 Oct. 1921, John J. Hearn Papers, Ms. 15,989/2, NLI.
20. Mary MacSwiney, 'Ratification of Plenipotentiaries', Dáil Éireann Debates. 14 Sept. 1921.
21. Ibid.
22. Liam de Róiste Diary, 16 Sept. 1921, CCCA.
23. Ibid., 30 Nov. 1921, CCCA.
24. Quoted in the *Freeman's Journal*, 28 Oct. 1921.
25. *Evening Echo*, 28 Oct. 1921.
26. *Irish Independent*, 26 Oct. 1921.
27. Letter to Harry Boland from Mary MacSwiney, 1 Dec. 1921, de Valara Papers, P150/655, UCDA.
28. *Freeman's Journal*, 9 Sept. 1921; Marie Coleman, 'Mac Eoin, Seán', in James McGuire (ed.), *Dictionary of Irish Biography*, https://www.dib.ie/biography/mac-eoin-Seán-a5033.

29. Bill of speakers for the republican aeridheacht in Youghal, 2 Oct. 1921, *Cork Examiner*, 30 Sept. 1921.
30. *Freeman's Journal*, 3 Oct. 1921.
31. *Cork Examiner*, 3 Oct. 1921.
32. Ibid.
33. *Freeman's Journal*, 3 Oct. 1921.
34. De Róiste Diary, 3 Oct. 1921, CCCA.
35. Mícheál Ó Fathartaigh and Liam Weeks, *Birth of a State: The Anglo-Irish Treaty* (Dublin, 2021). p. 94.
36. Mel Farrell, '"Stepping stone to freedom": Pro-Treaty rhetoric and strategy during the Dáil Debates', in Liam Weeks and Mícheál Ó Fathartaigh (eds), *The Treaty: Debating and Establishing the Irish State* (Dublin, 2018), p. 21.
37. Letter to Eileen and John J. Hearn form Mary MacSwiney, 6 Oct. 1921, John J. Hearn Papers, Ms. 15,989/2, NLI.
38. De Róiste Diary, 4 Oct. 1921, CCCA.
39. *Cork Examiner*, 3 Oct. 1921.
40. Report on lecture entitled 'Ireland in America' delivered by Mary MacSwiney at the Cork Opera House, 16 Oct. 1921, *Cork Examiner*, 17 Oct. 1921.
41. *Cork Examiner*, 10 Oct. 1921.
42. Ibid.
43. Ibid.
44. Ibid.
45. De Róiste Diary, 23 Aug. 1921, CCCA.
46. *Cork Examiner*, 3 Oct. 1921.
47. Ibid., 10 Oct. 1921.
48. Mary MacSwiney, 'Peace negotiations – Ratification of plenipotentiaries', Dáil Éireann Debates, 14 Sept. 1921.
49. *Cork Examiner*, 10 Oct. 1921.
50. Ibid., 17 April 1922.
51. Ernest Blythe, BMH WS 939.
52. Una Stack, BMH WS 418
53. *Cork Examiner*, 17 Oct. 1921.
54. Ibid.
55. *Evening Echo*, 11 Oct. 1921.
56. *Freeman's Journal*, 12 Oct. 1921.
57. Ibid., 14 Oct. 1921.
58. Bill advertising the event, *Cork Examiner*, 13 Oct..
59. *Cork Examiner*, 17 Oct. 1921. Professor of English at UCC, William Stockley was elected in 1921 as a Sinn Féin TD for the NUI constituency.
60. Patrick Maume, 'Ethchingham, Seán R.', in James McGuire (ed.), *Dictionary of Irish Biography*, https://www.dib.ie/biography/etchingham-sean-r-a2955.
61. Letter to [de Valera] from Mary MacSwiney, [Dec. 1921], de Valera Papers, P150/656, UCDA.
62. Mary MacSwiney, 'Debate on the Treaty', Dáil Éireann Debates, 17 Dec. 1921.
63. Ronan Fanning, *Éamon De Valera: A Will to Power* (London, 2015), p. 114.
64. Letter to [de Valera] from Mary MacSwiney, [Dec. 1921], de Valera Papers, P150/656, UCDA.
65. Ibid.
66. Ibid.
67. Ibid.
68. Elizabeth McGinley, née Brenan, BMH WS 860.
69. Dorothy Macardle, *The Irish Republic* (London, 1968), p. 539.
70. Quoted in Fanning, *Éamon De Valera*, p. 124.
71. Liam Weeks and Mícheál Ó Fathartaigh, 'Introduction', in Weeks and Ó Fathartaigh (eds), *The Treaty*, p. 7.
72. Macardle, *The Irish Republic*, p. 542.
73. David McCullagh, *De Valera: Rise, 1882–1932* (Dublin, 2017), p. 248.
74. McCullagh, *De Valera: Rise*, p. 248.

75. Kathleen Clarke, *Revolutionary Women* (Dublin, 2008), p. 258.
76. Letter to de Valera from Mary MacSwiney, [Dec. 1921], de Valera Papers, P150/656, UCDA.
77. Ibid.
78. McCullagh, *De Valera: Rise*, p. 252.
79. Mary MacSwiney, 'Debate on the Treaty', Dáil Éireann Debates, 14 Dec.1921.
80. Ibid.
81. Richard Mulcahy, 'Debate on the Treaty', Dáil Éireann Debates, 14 Dec. 1921.
82. Mary MacSwiney, 'Debate on the Treaty', Dáil Éireann Debates, 17 Dec. 1921.
83. Ibid.
84. Ibid.
85. De Róiste Diary, 13 Dec. 1921, CCCA.
86. Ibid., 17 Dec. 1921, CCCA.
87. Padraig de Burca and John F. Boyle, *Free State or Republic: Pen Pictures of the Historic Treaty Session of Dáil Éireann* (Dublin, 2002), pp 25–6.
88. Mary MacSwiney, 'Debate on the Treaty', Dáil Éireann Debates, 21 Dec.1921.
89. Seán T. O'Kelly, 'Debate on the Treaty', Dáil Éireann Debates, 22 Dec. 1921.
90. Kathleen Lynn Diary, 21 Dec.; 22 Dec., RCPI.
91. Letter to Mary MacSwiney from James E. Campion, Roger Casement branch of the AARIR of Boston, 27 Dec. 1921, Mary MacSwiney Papers, P48a/115/69, UCDA.
92. Macardle, *The Irish Republic*, p. 567.
93. Piaras Béaslaí, 'Debate on the Treaty', Dáil Éireann Debates, 17 Dec. 1921.
94. De Róiste Diary, 27 Dec. 1921, CCCA.
95. Caoimhe Nic Dháibhéid, 'The politics of emotions', in Darragh Gannon and Fearghal McGarry (eds), *Ireland 1922* (Dublin, 2022), p. 4.
96. Countess Markievicz, 'Election of President', Dáil Éireann Debates, 10 Jan. 1922.
97. Ó Fathartaigh and Weeks, *Birth of a State*, p. 99.
98. De Róiste Diary, 6 Jan. 1922, CCCA.
99. Mary MacSwiney, 'Debate on the Treaty', Dáil Éireann Debates, 6 Jan. 1922; De Róiste Diary, 6 Jan. 1922, CCCA.
100. Mary MacSwiney, 'Debate on the Treaty', Dáil Éireann Debates, 17 Dec. 1921.
101. Ibid.
102. Seán Etchingham, 'Debate on the Treaty'; Mary MacSwiney, 'Debate on the Treaty', Dáil Éireann Debates, 17 Dec. 1921.
103. De Róiste Diary, 5 Jan. 1922, CCCA.
104. Jason Knirck, *Women of the Dáil: Gender, Republicanism and the Anglo-Irish Treaty* (Dublin, 2006), p. 78.
105. Mary MacSwiney, 'Debate on the Treaty', Dáil Éireann Debates, 22 Dec. 1922.
106. Seán McGarry, 'Debate on the Treaty', Dáil Éireann Debates, 3 Jan. 1922.
107. Alexander McCabe, 'Debate on the Treaty'; Mary MacSwiney, 'Debate on the Treaty', Dáil Éireann Debates, 4 Jan. 1922.
108. Letter to [de Valera] from Mary MacSwiney, [Dec. 1921], de Valera Papers, P150/656, UCDA.
109. Ibid.
110. Mary MacSwiney, 'Debate on the Treaty', Dáil Éireann Debates, 21 Dec. 1921.
111. Ibid.
112. Ibid.
113. Anne Dolan and William Murphy, *Michael Collins: The Man and the Revolution* (Cork, 2018), p. 178.
114. Mary MacSwiney, 'Debate on the Treaty', Dáil Éireann Debates, 21 Dec. 1921.
115. Letter to Joseph Scott from Mary MacSwiney 27 Mar. 1922, Mary MacSwiney Papers, P48a/116/6, UCDA.
116. Mary MacSwiney, 'Debate on the Treaty', Dáil Éireann Debates, 21 Dec. 1921; Seán MacSwiney, 'Debate on The Treaty', Dáil Éireann Debates, 19 Dec. 1921.
117. De Róiste Diary, 31 Aug. 1921, CCCA.
118. Ó Fathartaigh and Weeks, *Birth of a State*, p. 101.
119. Ibid., p. 103.
120. Mary MacSwiney, 'Debate on the Treaty', Dáil Éireann Debates, 21 Dec. 1921

121. Weeks and Ó Fathartaigh, 'Introduction', in Weeks and Ó Fathartaigh, *The Treaty*, p. 5.
122. Michael Laffan, *The Resurrection of Ireland: The Sinn Féin Party, 1916–1923* (Cambridge, 1999), p. 358.
123. Mary MacSwiney, 'Debate on the Treaty', Dáil Éireann Debates, 21 Dec. 1921.
124. Terence MacSwiney, *Principles of Freedom*, in Gabriel Doherty, Fiona Brennan and Neil Buttimer (eds), *The Art and Ideology of Terence MacSwiney: Caught in the Living Flame* (Cork, 2022), p. 709.
125. Mary MacSwiney, 'Debate on the Treaty', Dáil Éireann Debates, 21 Dec. 1921.
126. McCullagh, *De Valera: Rise*, pp 256–7.
127. J. J. (Scelig) O'Kelly BMH WS 0384.
128. Fitzpatrick, *Harry Boland's Irish Revolution*, p. 265.
129. *Irish Independent*, 24 Sept. 1921.
130. *Belfast Newsletter*, 4 Jan. 1922. Markievicz and Kate O'Callaghan were also on the committee.
131. *Evening Echo*, 4 Jan. 1922.
132. Ibid., 3 Jan. 1922.
133. McCullagh, *De Valera: Rise*, p. 249.
134. Mary MacSwiney, 'Debate on the Treaty', Dáil Éireann Debates, 16 Dec. 1921.
135. McCullagh, *De Valera: Rise*, p. 250.
136. Mary MacSwiney, 'Debate on the Treaty', Dáil Éireann Debates, 9 Jan. 1922.
137. Letter to de Valera from Mary MacSwiney, 29 Dec. 1921, de Valera Papers, P150/656, UCDA.
138. McCullagh, *De Valera: Rise*, p. 257.
139. Ibid., p. 263.
140. Mary MacSwiney, 'Debate on the Treaty', Dáil Éireann Debates, 7 Jan. 1922.
141. Éamon de Valera, 'Debate on the Treaty', Dáil Éireann Debates, 7 Jan. 1922.
142. McCullagh, *De Valera: Rise*, p. 264.
143. Fitzpatrick, *Harry Boland's Revolution*, p. 286.
144. McCullagh, *De Valera: Rise*, pp 266–7.
145. Mary MacSwiney, 'Debate on the Treaty', Dáil Éireann Debates, 9 Jan. 1922.
146. *Freeman's Journal*, 9 Jan. 1922.
147. McCullagh, *De Valera: Rise*, pp 266–7.
148. *Evening Herald*, 11 Jan. 1922.
149. McCullagh, *De Valera: Rise*, p. 268.
150. Quoted in Gerard Keown, 'The Irish Race Conference, 1922, reconsidered', in *Irish Historical Studies*, vol. 32, no. 127 (May 2001), p. 365; Darragh Gannon, 'Global Ireland', in Darragh Gannon and Fearghal McGarry (eds), *Ireland 1922* (Dublin, 2022), p. 27.
151. Paul Murray, 'The Irish Race Congress, 21–28 January 1922', in *History Ireland*, vol. 9, no. 4 (Winter, 2001), https://www.historyireland.com/the-irish-race-congress-21-28-january-1922/; Keown, 'The Irish Race Conference', p. 367.
152. Fitzpatrick, *Harry Boland's Irish Revolution*, p. 271.
153. Robert Brennan, BMH WS 0779.
154. Helene O'Keeffe, 'Irish Race Congress only highlighted our deep divisions', *Irish Revolution Project*, UCC, https://www.ucc.ie/en/theirishrevolution/feature-articles/irish-race-congress-only-highlighted-our-deep-divisions.html, accessed, 5 July 2024.
155. Ibid.
156. Provisional Government, General Report on the Race Conference, DFA ES Box 11 File 77, NAI.
157. Keown, 'The Irish Race Conference', p. 370.
158. O'Keeffe, 'Irish Race Congress only highlighted our deep divisions'.
159. *Cork Examiner*, 27 Jan. 1922; 30 Jan. 1922.
160. Mary Daly, 'The Irish Free State and the Great Depression of the 1930s: The interaction of the global and the local', in *Irish Economic and Social History*, vol. 38 (2011), p. 20; *Ubi Arcano Dei Consilio* (1922), para 12.
161. Letter to Cork District Council, Cumann na mBan from Eilis Nic Eachnaidh and Sígle Nic Amhlaoibh, 13 Jan. 1922, Lil Conlon Collection, Cork Public Museum.
162. Cal McCarthy, *Cumann na mBan and the Irish Revolution* (Cork, 2014), p. 185.
163. Lil Conlon, Manuscript of *Cumann na mBan and the Women of Ireland*, Cork Public Museum, p. 211.

164. Copy attendance of the Cumann na mBan executive, 1920–1921, Ceannt and O'Brennan Papers, Ms 41, 494//1/3, NLI.
165. De Burca and Boyle (eds), *Free State or Republic*, pp 8–9.
166. *Irish Independent*, 6 Feb. 1922.
167. De Róiste Diary, 4 Jan. 1922, CCCA.
168. *Irish Independent*, 6 Feb. 1922.
169. Mary McAuliffe, '"An idea has gone abroad that all women were against the Treaty", Cumann na Saoirse, and Pro-Treaty Women, 1922–2', in Weeks and Ó Fathartaigh, *The Treaty*, pp 162–5.
170. *Evening Echo*, 6 Feb. 1922.
171. Farrell, 'Stepping Stones to Freedom', p. 21.
172. Macardle, *The Irish Republic*, p. 292, pp 321–2.
173. Michael Hopkinson, *Green Against Green: The Irish Civil War* (Dublin, 2004), p. 7.
174. Minutes of Cumann na mBan Special Convention, 5 Feb. 1922, Material relating to Constance Markievicz, Padraic Pearse and others, Ms 49,851/10, NLI.
175. Ibid.
176. *Irish Independent*, 6 Feb. 1922.
177. *Freeman's Journal*, 7 Feb. 1922.
178. Eunan O'Halpin and Daithí Ó Corráin, *The Dead of the Irish Revolution* (London, 2020), p. 539.
179. Margaret Ward, *Unmanageable Revolutionaries: Women and Irish Nationalism, 1880–1980* (Dublin, 2021), pp 288-9.
180. Minutes of Cumann na mBan Special Convention, 5 Feb. 1922, Material relating to Constance Markievicz, Padraic Pearse and others, Ms 49,851/10, NLI.
181. Ibid.
182. *Irish Independent*, 6 Feb. 1922. The IRA did not take a position on the Treaty until 25 March while Sinn Féin held their meeting on 22–23 February.
183. Ward, *Unmanageable Revolutionaries*, p. 178.
184. Marie Coleman, 'Women activists during the Civil War', in Darragh Gannon and Fearghal McGarry (eds), *Ireland 1922* (Dublin, 2022), p. 54.
185. Minutes of Cumann na mBan Special Convention, 5 Feb. 1922, Material relating to Constance Markievicz, Padraic Pearse and others, Ms 49,851/10, NLI; *Irish Independent*, 6 Feb. 1922.
186. Mel Farrell, *Party Politics in a New Democracy: The Irish Free State, 1922–1937* (London, 2017), p. 62.
187. John Borgonovo, 'Cumann na mBan and the Civil War', in John Crowley, Donal Ó Drisceoil and Mike Murphy (eds), *Atlas of the Irish Revolution* (Cork, 2017), p. 688.
188. Lil Conlon, *Cumann na mBan and the Women of Ireland, 1913–25* (Kilkenny, 1969), p. 274.
189. Laffan, *The Resurrection of Ireland*, p. 365. Laffan bases this statement on the unpublished PhD thesis by Brian S. Murphy, 'Politics and ideology: Mary MacSwiney and Irish republicanism, 1972–1942' (Cork, 1994). This thesis is now closed to researchers.
190. Laffan, *The Resurrection of Ireland*, p. 361.
191. De Róiste Diary, 31 Jan. 1922, CCCA.
192. Conlon, Manuscript of *Cumann na mBan*, p. 212.
193. De Róiste Diary, 31 Jan. 1922, CCCA.
194. Letter to May Conlon from Mary MacSwiney, 10 Feb. 1922, Lil Conlon Collection, Cork Public Museum.
195. Conlon, Manuscript of *Cumann na mBan*, p. 214.
196. Minutes of Cork District Council, Cumann na mBan, 12 Feb. 1922, Cumann na mBan Collection, Cork Public Museum.
197. Ibid.
198. Letter to Mary MacSwiney from District Council, Cork Cumann na mBan, 13 Feb. 1922, Lil Conlon Collection, Cork Public Museum.
199. Rough note from Shandon branch, Cumann na mBan to the Cork District Council, 12 Feb. 1922, Lil Conlon Collection, Cork Public Museum.
200. McAuliffe, 'An idea has gone abroad that all women were against the Treaty', p. 160; Lily Cooney, BMH WS 805.
201. Conlon, Manuscript of *Cumann na mBan*, p. 213, Cork Public Museum.

202. Minutes of District Council meeting, Cork Cumann na mBan, 12 Feb. 1922, Cumann na mBan Collection, Cork Public Museum.
203. Letter to the Secretary, Cork District Council of Cumann na mBan from Leslie de Barra, 12 Jan. 1922, Lil Conlon Collection, Cork Public Museum.
204. *Cork Examiner*, 15 Feb. 1922.
205. Ibid., 16 Feb. 1922; *Limerick Leader*, 3 Feb. 1922.
206. *Cork Examiner*, 16 Feb. 1922.
207. Letter to Miss Conlon from J. J. Walsh, 18 Feb. 1922; 21 Feb. 1921, Lil Conlon Collection, Cork Public Museum.
208. Letter to the editor, *Cork Examiner*, from Mary MacSwiney, 14 Mar. 1922.
209. *Evening Echo*, 13 Mar. 1922.
210. *Freeman's Journal*, 14 Mar. 1922.
211. *Cork Examiner*, 6 Mar. 1922.
212. Conlon, Manuscript of *Cumann na mBan*, p. 216, Cork Public Museum.
213. McAuliffe, 'An idea has gone abroad that all women were against the Treaty', p. 173.
214. De Róiste Diary, 25 Jan. 1922; 28 Jan. 1922, CCCA.
215. Ibid., 15 Feb. 1922,CCCA.
216. McCullagh, *De Valera: Rise*, pp 268–9.
217. Ibid., p. 270.
218. *Cork Examiner*, 15 Feb. 1922.
219. *Belfast Newsletter*, 20 Feb.1922.
220. *Skibbereen Eagle*, 25 Feb. 1922.
221. Ibid.
222. *Cork Examiner*, 20 Feb. 1922.
223. Ibid.
224. *Cork Examiner*, 22 Feb. 1922.
225. *Freeman's Journal*, 22 Feb. 1922.
226. *Irish Independent*, 22 Feb. 1922.
227. Fitzpatrick, *Harry Boland's Revolution*, pp 286–7; Farrell, *Party Politics*, p. 61.
228. Laffan, *The Resurrection of Ireland*, p. 373.
229. Arthur Griffith, 'Ratification of ministerial appointments', Dáil Éireann Debates, 28 Feb. 1922.
230. Cumann na Saoirse 'Points for canvassers' [1922], Ephemera Collection, EPH B9, NLI.
231. Mary MacSwiney, 'Ratification of ministerial appointments', Dáil Éireann Debates, 28 Feb. 1922.
232. Laffan, *The Resurrection of Ireland*, p. 374.
233. Diarmaid Ferriter, *Between Two Hells: The Irish Civil War* (London, 2021), p. 35.
234. Mary MacSwiney, 'Army Officers' statement – Report of Committee', Dáil Éireann Debates, 17 May 1922.
235. Fitzpatrick, *Harry Boland's Irish Revolution*, p. 289.
236. Letter to Joseph McGarrity from Mary MacSwiney, 29 Apr. 1922, Joseph McGarrity Papers, Ms 17,654/3/1, NLI.
237. Ibid.
238. Ibid.
239. See for example report of a meeting in Castlebar, *Irish Independent*, 3 May 1922.
240. McCullagh, *De Valera: Rise*, p. 249.
241. Deirdre MacMahon, 'Ireland, the Empire, and the Commonwealth', in Kevin Kenny (ed.), *Ireland and the British Empire* (Oxford, 2004), p. 207, p. 209.
242. *Cork Examiner*, 17 Apr. 1922.
243. Ibid., 29 Apr. 1922.
244. Michael Gallagher, 'The Pact General Election of 1922', in *Irish Historical Studies*, vol. 22, no. 84 (Sept. 1979), p. 405.
245. Mary MacSwiney, 'Army Officers' statement – Report of Committee', Dáil Éireann Debates, 17 May 1922.
246. McCullagh, *De Valera: Rise*, p. 250.
247. Ibid., pp 258–9.
248. George Gavan Duffy, 'Questions', Dáil Éireann Debates, 1 Mar. 1922.

249. Mary MacSwiney, 'Questions', Dáil Éireann Debates, 1 Mar. 1922.
250. Letter to Joseph McGarrity from Mary MacSwiney, 29 Apr. 1922, Joseph McGarrity Papers, Ms 17,654/3/1, NLI.
251. *Irish Independent*, 22 Apr. 1922.
252. Letter to Joseph McGarrity from Mary MacSwiney, 29 Apr. 1922, Joseph McGarrity Papers, Ms 17,654/3/1, NLI.
253. McCullagh, *De Valera: Rise*, p. 279; Laffan, *The Resurrection of Ireland*, pp 386–7.
254. McCullagh, *De Valera: Rise*, pp 280–1.
255. Gallagher, 'The Pact General Election of 1922', p. 405; Farrell, *Party Politics*, p. 62.
256. McCullagh, *De Valera: Rise*, p. 279.
257. Mary MacSwiney, 'The National Situation – Army Officers' Deputation', Dáil Debates, 3 May 1922.
258. Mary MacSwiney, 'Army Officers' Statement – Report of Committee' Dáil Éireann Debates, 17 May 1922.
259. Ibid.
260. Ibid.
261. Ferriter, *Between Two Hells*, p. 38.
262. Mary MacSwiney, 'Army Officers' Statement – Report of Committee' Dáil Éireann Debates, 17 May 1922.
263. Ibid.
264. Ibid.
265. Ibid.
266. McCullagh, *De Valera: Rise*, p. 251.
267. Mary MacSwiney, 'Army Officers' Statement – Report of Committee' Dáil Debates, 17 May 1922.
268. W.T. Cosgrave, 'Army Officers' Statement – Report of Committee', Dáil Debates, 17 May 1922.
269. Seán O'Hegarty, 'The National Situation – Army Officers' Deputation', Dáil Debates, 3 May 1922.
270. Mary MacSwiney, 'Army Officers' Statement – Report of Committee', Dáil Debates, 17 May 1922.
271. W.T. Cosgrave, 'Army Officers' Statement – Report of Committee', Dáil Debates, 17 May 1922.
272. Harry Boland, 'Army Officers' Statement – Report of Committee', Dáil Debates, 17 May 1922.
273. McCullagh, *De Valera: Rise*, p. 253.
274. Quoted in Ferriter, *Between Two Hells*, p. 19.
275. Letter to Joseph McGarrity from Mary MacSwiney, 29 Apr. 1922, Joseph McGarrity Papers, Ms 17,654/3/1, NLI.
276. Mary MacSwiney to Joseph McGarrity, 29 Apr. 1922, Ms 17,654/3/1, Joseph McGarrity Papers, NLI.
277. *Freeman's Journal*, 2 June 1922.
278. *Evening Echo*, 10 June 1922.
279. *Skibbereen Eagle*, 17 June 1922.
280. McCullagh, *De Valera: Rise*, p. 281.
281. *Skibbereen Eagle*, 17 June 1922.
282. *Sunday Independent*, 18 June 1922; *Cork Examiner*, 19 June 1922.
283. *Evening Echo*, 19 June 1922.
284. *Irish Independent*, 19 June 1922.
285. *Belfast Newsletter*, 19 June 1922.
286. *Irish Independent*, 19 June 1922.
287. *Cork Examiner*, 19 June 1922.
288. *Evening Echo*, 19 June 1922.
289. McCullagh, *De Valera: Rise*, p. 284.
290. *Irish Independent* 22 June 1922.
291. *Belfast Newsletter*, 17 Oct. 1921.
292. Ibid., 9 Jan. 1922.
293. *Irish Independent*, 9 Jan 1922.
294. Quoted in Ferriter, *Between Two Hells*, p. 21.

295. McCullagh, *De Valera: Rise*, p. 254; Fitzpatrick, *Harry Boland's Irish Revolution*, p. 265.
296. De Róiste Diary, 24 Feb. 1921, CCCA.
297. *Freeman's Journal*, 9 Jan. 1922.
298. McCullagh, *De Valera: Rise*, p. 259.
299. Quoted in David McCullagh, 'Éamon de Valera's Civil War', in Darragh Gannon and Fearghal McGarry (eds), *Ireland 1922* (Dublin, 2022), p. 103.
300. Ibid., p. 103.
301. Nic Dháibhéid, 'The politics of emotions', p. 7.
302. Cathal Brugha, 'Debate on the Treaty', Dáil Éireann Debates, 7 Jan. 1922.
303. De Róiste Diary, 9 Jan. 1922, CCCA.
304. *Sligo Champion*, 4 Mar. 1922.
305. *Evening Echo*, 13 Mar. 1922.
306. Letter to the editor, *Freeman's Journal* from Seán Mac Eoin, 14 Mar. 1922.
307. *Skibbereen Eagle*, 18 Mar. 1922.
308. *Belfast Newsletter*, 3 Mar. 1922.
309. Memo to the 'Southern Command' from Mary MacSwiney, [Mar. 1923], de Valera papers, P150/657, UCDA.
310. Arthur Griffith, 'Irish Women and the Franchise', Dáil Éireann Debates, 2 Mar. 1922.
311. George Gavan Duffy, 'Questions', Dáil Éireann Debates, 1 Mar. 1922.
312. *Irish Independent*, 5 Jan. 1922.
313. W. T. Cosgrave, 'Questions', Dáil Éireann Debates, 1 Mar. 1922.
314. Mary MacSwiney, 'Questions', Dáil Éireann Debates, 1 Mar. 1922.
315. W. T. Cosgrave, 'Questions', Dáil Éireann Debates, 1 Mar. 1922.
316. Mary MacSwiney, Questions of Refund, Dáil Éireann Debates, 11 May 1922.

Chapter 7: The Civil War

1. Guy Beiner, 'Between trauma and triumphalism: The Easter Rising, the Somme, and the crux of deep memory in modern Ireland', in *The Journal of British Studies*, vol. 46, no. 2 (Apr. 2007), p. 375.
2. Letter to John J. Hearn from Mary MacSwiney, 2 May 1922, John J. Hearn Papers, Ms 15,989/4, NLI.
3. Síobhra Aiken, *Spiritual Wounds: Trauma, Testimony and the Irish Civil War* (Dublin, 2022), p. 6.
4. Quoted in ibid., p. 37.
5. Ibid., p. 37.
6. Diarmaid Ferriter, *Between Two Hells: The Irish Civil War* (London, 2021), p. 34.
7. *Cork Examiner*, 26 Apr. 1922.
8. *Belfast Newsletter*, 29 June 1922.
9. Tom Garvin, 'O'Hegarty, Patrick Sarsfield', in James McGuire, *Dictionary of Irish Biography*, https://www.dib.ie/biography/ohegarty-patrick-sarsfield-p-s-a6801; P.S. O'H[egarty], 'An Irish Constitution and British interference', in *The Separatist*, 10 June 1922.
10. David McCullagh, *De Valera I: Rise, 1882–1932* (Dublin, 2017), p. 282.
11. Quoted in ibid., p. 283. See also Mel Farrell, *Party Politics in a New Democracy: The Irish Free State, 1922–1937* (London, 2017), p. 66.
12. Anne Dolan and William Murphy, *Michael Collins: The Man and the Revolution* (Cork, 2018), p. 162.
13. Diarmaid Ferriter, *The Transformation of Ireland, 1900–2000* (London, 2004), p. 254; Michael Laffan, *The Resurrection of Ireland: The Sinn Féin Party, 1916–1923* (Cambridge, 1999), p. 411.
14. Bill Kissane, *The Politics of the Irish Civil War* (Oxford, 2005), p. 74.
15. Quoted in Fergus O'Farrell, *Cathal Brugha* (Dublin, 2018), p. 86.
16. Quoted in Daithí Ó Corráin and Gerard Hanley, *Cathal Brugha: 'An Indomitable Spirit'* (Dublin, 2022), p. 161.
17. Dorothy Macardle, *Tragedies of Kerry* (Dublin, 1924), p. 44.
18. O'Farrell, *Cathal Brugha*, p. 91; Ferriter, *Between Two Hells*, p. 47.
19. *The Nationalist (Tipperary)*, 12 July 1922.
20. Message of condolences, *Cork Examiner*, 7 Aug. 1922.

21. Letter to Harry Boland from Mary MacSwiney, 12 Feb. 1921, Mary MacSwiney Papers, P48a/115/6, UCDA.
22. David Fitzpatrick, 'Boland, Henry James ('Harry') in James McGuire (ed.), *The Dictionary of Irish Biography*, https://www.dib.ie/biography/boland-henry-james-harry-a0763
23. Quoted in McCullagh, *De Valera: Rise*, p. 294.
24. *Cork Examiner*, 24 July 1922.
25. Ibid.
26. *Evening Echo*, 5 Aug. 1922; *Cork Examiner*, 7 Aug. 1922.
27. Robert Brennan, BMH WS 0779.
28. Ferriter, *Between Two Hells*, pp 49–50.
29. McCullagh, *De Valera: Rise*, p. 294.
30. Lil Conlon, *Cumann na mBan and the Women of Ireland, 1913–25* (Kilkenny, 1969), p. 276.
31. *Poblacht na hÉireann*, 6 Sept. 1922.
32. Letters to Edward Byrne, Archbishop of Dublin, from Conn Murphy, 26 Jan. 1923; 29 Jan. 1923, Archbishop Byrne Papers, AB7/b/ Political Prisoners (uncatalogued), DDA.
33. *Freeman's Journal*, 19 Feb. 1923.
34. Letter to Louise Gavan Duffy from Annie MacSwiney, 4 Sept. 1941, correspondence in possession of Catherine and Cathal Brugha.
35. *Nenagh Guardian*, 19 Aug. 1922.
36. *Irish Independent*, 9 Sept. 1922.
37. *Connacht Tribune*, 16 Sept. 1922.
38. *Irish Independent*, 16 Sept. 1922.
39. *Freeman's Journal*, 28 Sept. 1922.
40. Richard Mulcahy, 'Precedent for ministerial business', Dáil Éireann Debates, 27 Sept. 1922.
41. Andy Bielenberg and James S. Donnelly, *Cork Fatality Register, 1919–1923* https://www.ucc.ie/en/theirishrevolution/collections/cork-fatality-register/register-index/1922-117/.
42. *Evening Echo*, 26 Sept. 1922.
43. Letter to the editor from Clodhopper, *Evening Echo*, 27 Sept. 1922.
44. Laffan, *The Resurrection of Ireland*, p. 411.
45. Liam de Róiste Diary, 8 June 1922, CCCA.
46. Letter to the editor, *Cork Examiner*, from 'Free State', 2 Oct. 1922.
47. De Róiste Diary, 31 Aug. 1922, CCCA.
48. Ibid., 3 Sept. 1922, 6 Sept. 1922, CCCA.
49. Ibid., 29 Oct. 1922, CCCA.
50. Letter to the editor, *Cork Examiner*, from 'Justice', 4 Oct. 1922.
51. Ibid., from 'A Poor Woman', 7 Oct. 1922.
52. Laffan, *The Resurrection of Ireland*, pp 420–1.
53. Dorothy Macardle, *The Irish Republic* (London, 1968), p. 734.
54. McCullagh, *De Valera: Rise*, p. 299.
55. Macardle, *The Irish Republic*, p. 734.
56. Laffan, *The Resurrection of Ireland*, p. 422.
57. Ibid., p. 426; *Freeman's Journal*, 27 Oct. 1922.
58. *Freeman's Journal*, 27 Oct. 1922.
59. References to the Council are made in the document giving details of six women on hunger strike sent to the Secretary of the Executive Council by the Secretary Department of Defence, 23 Apr. 1923, Department of the Taoiseach Files, S1369/3 'Civil War Prisoners, 1922: Prison Treatment', NAI.
60. Letter to de Valera from Mary MacSwiney, 10 Sept. 1922, Valera papers, P150/657, UDCA.
61. McCullagh, *De Valera: Rise*, pp 298–303.
62. Laffan, *The Resurrection of Sinn Féin*, p. 381.
63. Letter to Mary MacSwiney from de Valera, 11 Sept. 1922, de Valera papers, P150/657, UCDA.
64. Quoted in Ronan Fanning, *Éamon de Valera: A Will to Power* (London, 2015), p. 138.
65. Letter to Mary MacSwiney from de Valera, 11 Sept. 1922, de Valera papers, P150/657, UCDA.
66. Ibid.
67. Ibid.

68. Letter to Joseph McGarrity from de Valera, 10 Sept. 1922, quoted in Laffan, *The Resurrection of Ireland*, p. 425.
69. Letter to Mary MacSwiney from de Valera, 11 Sept. 1922, de Valera papers, P150/657, UCDA.
70. Letter to de Valera from Mary MacSwiney, [Sept. 1922], de Valera papers, P150/657, UCDA.
71. Mary MacSwiney, 'A plea for real peace', in *Poblacht na h-Éireann*, 25 Oct. 1922.
72. Máire Comerford, *On Dangerous Ground: A Memoir of the Irish Revolution* (Dublin, 2021), p. 277.
73. McCullagh, *De Valera: Rise*, p. 309.
74. Ferriter, *Between Two Hells*, p. 80.
75. McCullagh, *De Valera: Rise*, p. 301.
76. Letter to de Valera from Mary MacSwiney, [Sept./Oct. 1922], de Valera Papers, P150/657, UCDA.
77. McCullagh, *De Valera: Rise*, p. 301.
78. *Evening Echo*, 4 Nov. 1922; 6 Nov. 1922.
79. Ibid.
80. De Róiste Diary. 4 Nov. 1922, CCCA.
81. Letter to [Archbishop Byrne] from Mary MacSwiney, 5 Nov. [1922}, Mary MacSwiney Papers, P48a/194/1, UCDA.
82. Seán McConville, *Irish Political Prisoner 1920–1962: A Pilgrimage of Desolation* (London, 2014), pp 249–50.
83. *Cork Examiner*, 9 Nov. 1922.
84. *Belfast Newsletter*, 14 Nov. 1922.
85. Letter to [de Valera] from Mary MacSwiney, [Nove. 1922], de Valera Papers, P150/657, UCDA.
86. *Freeman's Journal*, 13 Nov. 1922.
87. *Belfast Newsletter*, 8 Nov. 1922.
88. Ferriter, *Between Two Hells*, p. 79.
89. *Freeman's Journal*, 21 Nov. 1922.
90. Ferriter, *Between Two Hells*, p. 79.
91. Letter to the editor, *Irish Independent*, from Brighid O'Mullane, 10 Nov. 1922.
92. *Freeman's Journal*, 8 Nov. 1922.
93. See *Irish Times*, 9 and 18 Nov. 1922.
94. Telegram to W. T. Cosgrave from Michael A. Kelly, New York City, received 8 Nov. 1922, Department of the Taoiseach Papers, S1369/9 'Miss Mary McSwiney [sic]: Imprisonment and Hunger Strike', NAI.
95. *Evening Herald*, 9 Nov. 1922.
96. *Evening Echo*, 11 Nov. 1922.
97. Ferriter, *Between Two Hells*, p. 82.
98. *Irish Independent*, 28 Nov. 1922.
99. *Belfast Newsletter*, 28 Nov. 1922.
100. Letter to Cosgrave from Susan Mitchell, 16 Nov. 1922, Department of the Taoiseach Papers, S1369/9 'Miss Mary McSwiney [sic]: Imprisonment and Hunger Strike', NAI.
101. *Freeman's Journal*, 15 Nov. 1922.
102. Telegram to W. T. Cosgrave from Father O'Gorman, received 18 Nov. 1922, Department of the Taoiseach Papers, S1369/9 'Miss Mary McSwiney [sic]: Imprisonment and Hunger Strike', NAI.
103. *Evening Herald*, 15 Nov. 1922.
104. *Belfast Telegraph*, 16 Nov. 1922.
105. Quoted in Ferriter, *Between Two Hells*, p. 86.
106. Statement by W. T. Cosgrave, 13 Nov. 1922, Department of the Taoiseach Papers, S1369/9 'Miss Mary McSwiney [sic]: Imprisonment and Hunger Strike', NAI.
107. Letter to de Valera from Joseph Connolly, 17 Dec. 1922, de Valera Papers, P150/1818, UCDA.
108. Letter to [Archbishop Byrne] from Mary MacSwiney, 5 Nov. 1922, Department of the Taoiseach Papers, S1369/9 'Miss Mary McSwiney [sic]: Imprisonment and Hunger Strike', NAI.
109. Letter to Cardinal Logue from W. T. Cosgrave, 15 Nov. 1922, Department of the Taoiseach Papers, S1369/9 'Miss Mary McSwiney [sic]: Imprisonment and Hunger Strike', NAI.
110. Quoted in Ferriter, *Between Two Hells*, p. 84.
111. Daithí Ó Corráin, 'Upholding the commandments and the will of the majority, the Catholic

hierarchy, the October 1922 pastoral, and the Irish Civil War', in *Archivium Hibernicum*, lxxvi (2023), p. 101.
112. Liam de Róiste Diary, 7 Feb. 1922.
113. Kissane, *The Politics of the Irish Civil War*, p. 89.
114. Michael Hopkinson, *Green Against Green: The Irish Civil War* (Dublin, 2004), p. 182.
115. Kissane, *The Politics of the Irish Civil War*, p. 88.
116. Ferriter, *Transformation*, p. 27.
117. Annie MacSwiney, 'Diary of week of Terry's greatest torture' in Margaret Lucey, BMH WS 1561.
118. Letter to the editor, *Evening Herald*, from Brighid O'Mullane, 10 Nov. 1922.
119. *Freeman's Journal*, 8 Nov. 1922.
120. 'A message from Mountjoy, to the people of Ireland' in *Herald*, 15 Nov. 1922.
121. Francis J. Costello, *Enduring the Most: The Life and Death of Terence MacSwiney* (Dingle, 1995), p. 174; MacSwiney, 'Diary of week of Terry's greatest torture'; 'A message from Mountjoy, to the people of Ireland' in *Herald*, 15 Nov. 1922.
122. Letter to [Archbishop Byrne] from Mary MacSwiney, 5 Nov. [1922], Mary MacSwiney Papers, 48a/194/1, UCDA.
123. Ibid.
124. Ibid.
125. Ibid.
126. Letter to Annie MacSwiney from Mary MacSwiney, [Nov. 1922], Mary MacSwiney Papers, P48a/194/7, UCDA.
127. Letter to [Archbishop Byrne] from Mary MacSwiney, 5 Nov. [1922], Mary MacSwiney Papers, 48a/194/1, UCDA.
128. Letter to [Archbishop Byrne] from Mary MacSwiney, 9 Nov. 1922, Mary MacSwiney Papers, P48a/194/3, UCDA.
129. Ibid.
130. Letter to Mary MacSwiney from Edward Byrne, Archbishop of Dublin, 8 Nov. 1922, Mary MacSwiney Papers, P48a/194/2, UCDA.
131. Letter to [de Valera] from Mary MacSwiney, [Nov 1922], de Valera Papers, P150/657, UCDA.
132. Letter to [Archbishop Byrne] from Mary MacSwiney, 9 Nov. 1922, Mary MacSwiney Papers, P48a/194/3, UCDA.
133. Letter to Mary MacSwiney from the Director of Intelligence informing her that Annie's visit 'cannot be allowed', 19 Nov. 1922, Mary MacSwiney Papers, P48a/194/9, UCDA.
134. Kathleen Lynn Diary, 8 Nov. 1922, RCPI.
135. *Éire*, 10 Feb. 1923.
136. *Irish Times*, 21 Nov. 1922; *Irish Independent*, 22 Nov. 1922.
137. Letter to Edward Byrne, Archbishop of Dublin from Annie MacSwiney, Nov. 1922, Archbishop Byrne Papers, AB7/b/Political Papers (uncatalogued), DDA.
138. Letter to de Valera from Mary MacSwiney, 19 Nov. 1922, de Valera Papers, P150/657, UCDA.
139. Letter to Edward Byrne from Mary MacSwiney, 15 Nov. 1922, Mary MacSwiney Papers, P48a/194/7, UCDA.
140. Ibid.
141. Letter to Archbishop Byrne from Dorothy Macardle and signed by 16 other women including Mary MacSwiney, 17 Nov. 1922, Archbishop Byrne Papers, AB7/b/Political Papers (uncatalogued), DDA.
142. Letter to W. T. Cosgrave from Edward Byrne, received 20 Nov. 1922, Department of the Taoiseach Papers, S1369/9 'Miss Mary McSwiney [sic]: Imprisonment and Hunger Strike', NAI.
143. Letter to Cardinal Logue from W. T. Cosgrave, 15 Nov. 1922, Department of the Taoiseach Papers, S1369/9 'Miss Mary McSwiney [sic]: Imprisonment and Hunger Strike', NAI.
144. William Murphy, *Political Imprisonment and the Irish, 1912–1921* (Oxford, 2014), p. 10.
145. Letter to the Director of Intelligence from Mary MacSwiney, 20 Nov. 1922, Mary MacSwiney Papers, P48a/194/11, UCDA.
146. Ibid.
147. Provisional Government Memo, Nov. 1922, Department of the Taoiseach Papers, S1369/9 'Miss Mary McSwiney [sic]: Imprisonment and Hunger Strike', NAI.

148. Cathal O'Shannon, 'General Prisons Board', Dáil Éireann Debates, 28 Nov. 1922; *Cork Examiner*, 29 Nov. 1922.
149. *Cork Examiner*, 29 Nov. 1922; Kevin O'Higgins, 'General Prisons Board', Dáil Éireann Debates, 28 Nov. 1922.
150. Letter to de Valera from Mary MacSwiney, 19 Nov. 1922, de Valera Papers, P150/657, UCDA.
151. Letter to W. T. Cosgrave from Edward Byrne, 16 Nov. 1922, Department of the Taoiseach Papers, S1369/9 'Miss Mary McSwiney [sic]: Imprisonment and Hunger Strike', NAI.
152. Letter to Edward Byrne from W. T. Cosgrave, 18 Nov. 1922, Department of the Taoiseach Papers, S1369/9 'Miss Mary McSwiney [sic]: Imprisonment and Hunger Strike', NAI.
153. G. B. Griffiths, Medical Report, 22 Sept. 1920, HO 144//10308.
154. Letter to de Valera from Mary MacSwiney [November] 1922, de Valera Papers, P150/657, UCDA.
155. *Freeman's Journal*, 13 Nov. 1922.
156. Letter to [Archbishop Byrne] from Mary MacSwiney, 5 Nov. 1922, Department of the Taoiseach Papers, S1369/9 'Miss Mary McSwiney [sic]: Imprisonment and Hunger Strike', NAI.
157. Dorothy Macardle, Jail Journal, 26 Dec. 1922, de Valera Papers, P150/1658, UCDA.
158. Murphy, *Political Imprisonment and the Irish,* p. 182.
159. Letter to Pauline Henley from Mary MacSwiney, 22–27 Sept. 1920, Pauline Henley Collection, IE/BL/PC/PH/10, UCC.
160. Macardle, JJ, 23 Nov. 1922; 26 Nov. 1922.
161. *Evening Herald*, 10 Nov. 1922.
162. Report to the Director General Medical Services from M. H. O'Connor, 10 Nov. 1922, Department of the Taoiseach Papers, S1369/9 'Miss Mary McSwiney [sic]: Imprisonment and Hunger Strike', NAI.
163. *Evening Echo*, 15 Nov. 1922; *Belfast Newsletter*, 16 Nov. 1922.
164. Quoted in *Straight Talk*, 22 Nov. 1922; MacSwiney's letter was dated 16 Nov. 1922.
165. Copy receipt of a telephone message from Dr Higson to O. F. N. Treadwell, 24 Aug. 1920, HO144/10308.
166. Report by Major-General M. Hayes, Director General, Army Medical Services [11 Nov. 1922], Department of the Taoiseach Papers, S1369/9 'Miss Mary McSwiney [sic]: Imprisonment and Hunger Strike', NAI.
167. Síobhra Aiken, '"The women who had been straining every nerve": Gender-specific medical management in the Irish Revolution (1916–1923)', in Melania Terrazas Gallego (ed.), *Trauma and Identity in Contemporary Irish Culture* (Bern, 2019), p. 133.
168. Report by M. H. O'Connor to the Director General, Army Medical Services, 8 Nov. 1922, Department of the Taoiseach Papers, S1369/9 'Miss Mary McSwiney [sic]: Imprisonment and Hunger Strike', NAI.
169. P. S. O'Hegarty, *The Victory of Sinn Féin: How it Won it and How it Used it* (Dublin, 1924), p. 102, p. 105, p. 108.
170. De Róiste Diary, 14 Nov. 1922, CCCA.
171. Letters to Cosgrave from Liam de Róiste, 16 Nov. 1922; 17 Nov. 1922, Department of the Taoiseach Papers, S1369/9 'Miss Mary McSwiney [sic]: Imprisonment and Hunger Strike', NAI; de Róiste Diary, 14 Nov. 1922, CCCA.
172. See Leeann Lane, *Dorothy Macardle* (Dublin, 2019), chapter 2 and chapter 3.
173. Dorothy Macardle, JJ, Nov. 1922, de Valera Papers, P150/1658, UCDA.
174. *Poblacht na hÉireann*, 1 Dec. 1922.
175. *Éire*, 10 Feb. 1923.
176. *Cork Examiner*, 1 Dec. 1922.
177. Ibid.
178. De Róiste Diary, 24 Nov. 1922, CCCA.
179. *Freeman's Journal*, 23 Nov. 1922.
180. *Cork Examiner*, 4 Dec. 1922.
181. *Irish Independent*, 28 Nov. 1922.
182. Letter to de Valera from Mary MacSwiney, 19 Dec. 1922, de Valera Papers, P150/657, UCDA.
183. Ibid.
184. Letter to Eileen Hearn from Mary MacSwiney, 21 Dec. 1922, John J. Hearn Papers, Ms 15,989/5, NLI.

185. Letter to Art O'Brien from Mary MacSwiney, 20 Dec. 1922, Art Ó Bríain Papers, Ms 8,440/19, NLI.
186. Kissane, *The Politics of the Irish Civil War*, p. 87.
187. Hopkinson, *Green against Green*, p. 189.
188. Lane, *Dorothy Macardle*, p. 36.
189. Macardle, *The Irish Republic*, p. 744, pp 750–1.
190. Letter to de Valera from Mary MacSwiney, 27 Jan. 1923, de Valera Papers, P150/657, UCDA.
191. Ibid.
192. *Éire*, 10 Feb. 1923.
193. Ibid. Máire Comerford, *On Dangerous Ground: A Memoir of the Irish Revolution* (Dublin, 2021), pp 279–80.
194. *Éire*, 10 Feb. 1923.
195. Ibid.
196. Letter to de Valera from Mary MacSwiney, 27 Jan. 1923, de Valera Papers, P150/657, UCDA.
197. *Poblacht na hÉireann*, 3 Feb. 1923.
198. Letter to Mary MacSwiney from de Valera, 18 Dec. 1922, de Valera Papers, P150/657, UCDA.
199. Memo to Eamon Donnelly from de Valera, 21 Dec. 1922, Department of the Taoiseach Papers, S1297, 'Sinn Féin: Re-organisation 1922–23', NAI.
200. Farrell, *Party Politics*, p. 75.
201. McCullagh, *De Valera: Rise*, pp 323–4.
202. Laffan, *The Resurrection of Ireland*, pp 426–7. See also Farrell, *Party Politics*, p. 61.
203. Farrell, *Party Politics*, p. 74.
204. Statement to the Organising Committee of Sinn Féin from de Valera, 31 May 1923, de Valera Papers, P150/1818, UCDA.
205. 'Plan' enclosed in letter to de Valera from Mary MacSwiney, 19 Dec. 1922, de Valera Papers, P150/656, UCDA.
206. Fanning, *Éamon de Valera*, pp 131–2.
207. Hopkinson, *Green against Green*, p. 100.
208. Memo to de Valera from Eamon Donnelly, 20 Dec. 1922, Department of the Taoiseach Papers, S1297, 'Sinn Féin: Re-organisation 1922–23', NAI.
209. Circular letter from Cumann na mBan headquarters, 14 Feb. 1922, Mary MacSwiney Papers, P 48a/38/3, UCDA.
210. Laffan, *The Resurrection of Ireland*, p. 427.
211. Circular to all Sinn Féin branches from de Valera and Austin Stack, 1 Jan. 1923, Department of the Taoiseach Papers, S1297, 'Sinn Féin: Re-organisation 1922–23', NAI.
212. Letter to Mary MacSwiney from de Valera, 8 Dec. 1922, de Valera Papers, P150/657, UCDA.
213. Ibid.
214. Margaret Ward, *Fearless Woman: Hanna Sheehy Skeffington, Feminism and the Irish Revolution* (Dublin, 2019), p. 334.
215. Memo to Mary MacSwiney from de Valera, 6 Feb. 1923, de Valera Papers, P150/657, UCDA.
216. Letter to de Valera from Mary MacSwiney, 27 Jan. 1923, de Valera Papers, P150/657, UCDA.
217. Fanning, *Éamon de Valera*, p. 140.
218. Gavin M. Foster, *The Irish Civil War and Society: Politics, Class and Conflict* (London, 2015), p. 4.
219. Margaret Ward, *Unmanageable Revolutionaries: Women and Irish Nationalism, 1880–1980* (Dublin, 2021), p. 309.
220. De Róiste Diary, 18 Aug. 1922 CCCA.
221. Hopkinson, *Green Against Green*, p. 230.
222. Letter to de Valera from Mary MacSwiney, [Jan. 1923], de Valera Papers P150/657, UCDA.
223. Letter to Mary MacSwiney from Eamon de Valera, 5 Feb. 1923, de Valera Papers, P150/657, UCDA.
224. Letter de Valera from Mary MacSwiney, 14 Feb. 1923, de Valera Papers, P150/657, UCDA.
225. McCullagh, *De Valera: Rise*, p. 310.
226. Letter to Mary MacSwiney from de Valera, 12 Feb. 1923, de Valera Papers, P150/657, UCDA.
227. Laffan, *The Resurrection of Ireland*, p. 424.
228. Letter to de Valera from Mary MacSwiney, 9 Feb. 1923, correspondence in possession of Catherine and Cathal Brugha.

229. *Belfast Newsletter*, 12 Feb. 1923.
230. *Freeman's Journal*, 12 Feb. 1923.
231. De Róiste Diary, 20 Jan. 1922, CCCA.
232. Letter to de Valera from Mary MacSwiney, 10 Feb. 1923, de Valera Papers, P150/657, UCDA.
233. Letter to Mary MacSwiney from Eamon de Valera, 12 Feb. 1923, de Valera Papers, P150/657, UCDA.
234. Ferriter, *Between Two Hells*, p. 68.
235. *Belfast Newsletter*, 12 Feb. 1923.
236. *Irish Independent*, 17 Feb. 1923.
237. Kathleen Lynn Diary, 17 Feb. 1923, RCPI.
238. *Belfast Newsletter*, 13 Feb. 1923.
239. *Irish Independent*, 3 Jan. 1923.
240. Memo to de Valera from Mary MacSwiney [Feb.] 1923, de Valera Papers, P150/657, UCDA.
241. Letter to de Valera from Mary MacSwiney, 13 Feb. 1923, correspondence in possession of Catherine and Cathal Brugha.
242. *Belfast Newsletter*, 13 Feb. 1923.
243. Ibid.
244. Ibid.
245. Ibid.; *Poblacht na hEireann*, 16 Feb. 1923.
246. *Belfast Newsletter*, 13 Feb. 1923.
247. Macardle, JJ, Feb 1923, de Valera Papers, P150/1658, UCDA.
248. Letter to de Valera from Mary MacSwiney, 27 Jan. 1923, de Valera Papers, P150/657, UCDA.
249. Letter to the Editor, *Irish Independent*, from C[harlotte] Despard, 24 Feb. 1923.
250. Macardle, JJ, 17 Feb. 1923.
251. Letter to Mary MacSwiney from de Valera, 14 Feb. 1923, correspondence in possession of Catherine and Cathal Brugha.
252. Note to de Valera from [P. J. Ruttledge], 13 Feb. 1923, correspondence in possession of Catherine and Cathal Brugha.
253. Memo to de Valera from [P. J. Ruttledge], 14 Feb. 1923, correspondence in possession of Catherine and Cathal Brugha.
254. Copy letter to de Valera from Mary MacSwiney, 10 Feb. 1923, Archbishop Byrne Papers, AB7/b/Political Papers (uncatalogued), DDA.
255. Letter to de Valera from Mary MacSwiney, 13 Feb. 1923, correspondence in possession of Catherine and Cathal Brugha.
256. Letter to de Valera from Mary MacSwiney, 15 Feb. 1923, de Valera Papers, P150/657, UCDA.
257. Ibid.
258. See Fanning, *Éamon de Valera*; McCullagh, *De Valera: Rise*.
259. Letter to de Valera from Mary MacSwiney, 15 Feb. 1923, de Valera Papers, P150/657, UCDA.
260. T. Ryle Dwyer, *De Valera's Darkest Hour, 1919–1932* (Dublin, 1982), p. 136.
261. Letter to de Valera from Mary MacSwiney, 15 Feb. 1923, de Valera Papers, P150/657, UCDA.
262. Ibid.
263. *Irish Independent*, 17 Feb. 1923; letter to de Valera from Mary MacSwiney, 10 Feb. 1923, Archbishop Byrne Papers, AB7/b/Political Papers (uncatalogued), DDA.
264. *The United Irishman*, 22 Feb. 1922.
265. *Freeman's Journal*, 17 Feb. 1923.
266. Ibid., 22 Feb. 1923.
267. Memo to Mary MacSwiney from de Valera, 19 Feb. 1923, de Valera Papers, P150/657, UCDA.
268. *Freeman's Journal*, 19 Feb. 1923.
269. Ferriter, *Between Two Hells*, p. 65.
270. *Freeman's Journal*, 15 Feb. 1923; *Belfast Newsletter*, 20 Feb. 1923; *Poblacht na hÉireann*, 23 Feb. 1923; *Cork Examiner*, 16 Feb. 1923. The papers give different numbers for the women arrested ranging from 29 to 31.
271. *Freeman's Journal*, 19 Feb. 1923.
272. *Poblacht na hÉireann*, 23 Feb. 1923.
273. *Freeman's Journal*, 26 Feb. 1923.
274. *Cork Examiner*, 23 Feb. 1923.

275. Letter to the editor, *Irish Independent*, from Charlotte Despard, 23 Feb. 1923.
276. *Evening Herald*, 20 Feb. 1923; *Irish Independent*, 20 Feb. 1923.
277. Second letter to de Valera from Mary MacSwiney, 14 Feb. 1923, de Valera Papers, P150/657, UCDA.
278. Letter to Edward Byrne from Annie MacSwiney, 28 Feb. 1923, Archbishop Byrne Papers, AB7/b/ Political Prisoners (uncatalogued), DDA. Annie began this letter to Byrne on 28 February, finishing it after her release on 1 March.
279. Letter to Edward Byrne from Annie MacSwiney, 21 Feb. 1923, Archbishop Byrne Papers, AB7/b/ Political Prisoners (uncatalogued), DDA.
280. *Freeman's Journal*, 22 Feb. 1923.
281. *Irish Independent*, 28 Feb. 1923.
282. Letter to de Valera from Mary MacSwiney, 15 Feb. 1923, de Valera Papers, P150/657, UCDA.
283. First letter to de Valera from Mary MacSwiney, 14 Feb. 1923, de Valera Papers, P150/657, UCDA.
284. Letter to de Valera from Mary MacSwiney, 24 Jan. 1923, de Valera Papers, P150/657, UCDA; *Belfast Newsletter*, 20 Feb. 1923; *Poblacht na hÉireann*, 23 Feb. 1923.
285. *Poblacht na hÉireann*, 23 Feb. 1923; *Cork Examiner*, 23 Feb. 1923.
286. Letter to Mary MacSwiney from de Valera, 14 Feb. 1923, de Valera Papers, P150/657, UCDA.
287. Second letter to de Valera from Mary MacSwiney, 14 Feb. 1923, de Valera Papers P150/657, UCDA.
288. Ibid.
289. *Cork Examiner*, 1 Mar. 1923; *Irish Independent*, 1 Mar. 1923.
290. Letter to de Valera from Mary MacSwiney, 5 Apr. 1923, de Valera Papers, P150/657, UCDA.
291. Joanne Mooney Eichacker, *Irish Republican Women in America: Lecture Tours, 1916–1925* (Dublin, 2003), pp 168–9, p. 156.
292. *Belfast Newsletter*, 15 Nov. 1922.
293. *Evening Herald*, 24 Feb. 1923.
294. Anne Dolan, 'MacSwiney, Muriel Francis', in James McGuire (ed.), *Dictionary of Irish Biography*, https://www.dib.ie/biography/macswiney-muriel-frances-a5296#; John Gibney, 'Revolutionary diplomacy', in Darragh Gannon and Fearghal McGarry (eds), *Ireland 1922* (Dublin, 2022), p. 326.
295. *Evening Herald*, 24 Feb. 1923.
296. Gibney, 'Revolutionary diplomacy', p. 327.
297. Cited in ibid., p. 327.
298. Mooney Eichacker, *Irish Republican Women*, p. 157.
299. Máire MacSwiney Brugha, *History's Daughter: A Memoir from the Only Child of Terence MacSwiney* (Dublin, 2006), pp 23–4.
300. Ibid., p. 25.
301. Ibid., p. 31, p. 43.
302. Dolan, 'MacSwiney, Muriel Francis'.
303. MacSwiney Brugha, *History's Daughter*, p. 29.
304. Gibney, 'Revolutinary Diplomacy'.
305. *Freeman's Journal*, 27 Feb. 1923.
306. Kathleen Lynn Diary, 26 Feb. 1923, RCPI.
307. Quoted in the *Freeman's Journal*, 12 Mar. 1923.
308. *Irish Independent*, 14 Mar. 1923.
309. *Belfast Newsletter*. Nunc Dimittis or the Song of Simeon takes its name from the first line of the gospel of Luke, second chapter, verses 29–36: 'Now let depart'.
310. *Freeman's Journal*, 14 Mar. 1923.
311. *Belfast Newsletter*, 10 Apr. 1923.
312. *Freeman's Journal*, 3 Apr. 1923.
313. *Belfast Newsletter*, 14 Mar. 1923.
314. Farrell, *Party Politics*, p. 76.
315. *Belfast Newsletter*, 9 Mar. 1923.
316. Macardle, *The Irish Republic*, p. 770.
317. *Belfast Newsletter*, 10 Apr. 1923.
318. *Irish Independent*, 9 Apr. 1923.

319. *Belfast Newsletter*, 10 Apr. 1923.
320. Second letter to de Valera from Mary MacSwiney, 10 Apr. 1923, de Valera Papers, P150/657, UCDA.
321. *Belfast Newsletter*, 10 Apr. 1923.
322. Letter to de Valera from Mary MacSwiney, 11 Apr. 1923, de Valera Papers, P150/657, UCDA.
323. Letter to P. J. Ruttledge from de Valera, 9 Apr. 1923, quoted in David McCullagh, 'Éamon de Valera's Civil War', in Darragh Gannon and Fearghal McGarry (eds), *Ireland 1922* (Dublin, 2022), p. 106.
324. *Cork Examiner*, 2 Apr. 1923.
325. *Freeman's Journal*, 3 Apr. 1923.
326. *Belfast Newsletter*, 3 Apr. 1923; *Fermanagh Herald*, 7 Apr. 1923.
327. *Belfast Newsletter*, 12 Apr. 1923. The paper noted that three women were at the conference and believed that Markievicz and Kathleen Barry, sister of Kevin Barry, were the other two in attendance.
328. *Belfast Newsletter*, 13 Apr. 1923.
329. Speech delivered by Mary MacSwiney in Cork, 17 Mar. 1934, Mary MacSwiney Papers, P48a/50/2, UCDA.
330. Letter to de Valera from Mary MacSwiney, 14 Apr. 1923, de Valera Papers, P150/657, UCDA.
331. Speech delivered by Mary MacSwiney in Cork, 17 Mar. 1934, Mary MacSwiney Papers, P48a/50/2, UCDA.
332. *Fermanagh Herald*, 21 Apr. 1923; *Nenagh Guardian*, 21 Apr. 1923.
333. Letter to de Valera from Mary MacSwiney, 14 Apr. 1923, de Valera Papers, P150/657, UCDA.
334. Letter to [P. J. Ruttledge] from Mary MacSwiney, 14 Apr. 1923, de Valera Papers, P150/657, UCDA.
335. *Cork Examiner*, 21 Apr. 1923.
336. Letter to the Archbishop of Dublin from Kitty Costello, Nell Ryan and Annie O'Neill, [April 1923], Archbishop Byrne Papers, AB7/b/ Political Prisoners (uncatalogued), DDA.
337. Patrick McCartan, 'Prisoners on hunger strike', Dáil Éireann Debates, 20 Apr. 1923.
338. Ferriter, *Between Two Hells*, p. 112.
339. McCartan, 'Prisoners on hunger strike', Dáil Éireann Debates, 20 Apr. 1923; *Freeman's Journal*, 21 Apr. 1923.
340. Patrick McCartan, 'Prisoners on hunger strike', Dáil Éireann Debates, 20 Apr. 1923.
341. *Freeman's Journal*, 21 Apr. 1923.
342. Ibid.
343. Ibid.
344. Kevin O'Higgins, 'Prisoners on hunger strike', Dáil Éireann Debates, 20 Apr. 1923; *Freeman's Journal*, 21 Apr. 1923.
345. Letter to Edward Byrne from W. T. Cosgrave, 19 Apr. 1923, Archbishop Byrne Papers, AB7/b/ Political Prisoners (uncatalogued), DDA.
346. Darrell Figgis, 'Prisoners on hunger strike', Dáil Éireann Debates, 25 Apr. 1923; *Freeman's Journal*, 26 Apr. 1923.
347. O'Higgins, 'Prisoners on Hunger Strike, Dáil Éireann Debates, 25 Apr. 1923; *Freeman's Journal*, 26 Apr. 1923.
348. Ferriter, *Between Two Hells*, p. 113.
349. Patrick McCartan, 'Prisoners on Hunger Strike, Dáil Éireann Debates, 25 Apr. 1923
350. Ibid.
351. *Irish Independent*, 23 Apr. 1923.
352. Ibid., 24 Apr. 1924.
353. Letter to Edward Byrne from Mary MacSwiney, 19 Apr. 1923, Archbishop Byrne Papers, AB7/b/ Political Prisoners (uncatalogued), DDA.
354. *Belfast Newslette*r, 27 Apr 1923.
355. *Irish Independent*, 28 Apr. 1928.
356. *Freeman's Journal*, 1 May 1923.
357. Mary MacSwiney, Statement on prison condition in Kilmainham women's prison 1923, 17 Mar. 1934, Mary MacSwiney Paper, P48a/50/2, UCDA.
358. Dorothy Macardle, 'Farewell to Kilmainham', 1 May 1923, IR 320, NLI. For a fuller discussion of this riot see Lane, *Dorothy* Macardle, pp 71–80.

359. Macardle, 'Farewell to Kilmainham'.
360. *Irish Independent*, 2 May 1923.
361. Ibid., 3 May 1923.
362. 'Prisoners on hunger strike', Dáil Éireann Debates, 3 May 1923; *Belfast Newsletter*, 4 May 1923.
363. *Belfast Newsletter*, 4 May 1923.
364. Ibid.
365. Letter to de Valera from Mary MacSwiney, 4 May 1923, correspondence in possession of Catherine and Cathal Brugha; letter to de Valera from Mary MacSwiney, 15 May 1923; Letter to de Valera from Mary MacSwiney, 11 May 1923, de Valera Papers, P150/657, UCDA.
366. Letter to de Valera from Mary MacSwiney, 4 May 1923, correspondence in possession of Catherine and Cathal Brugha.
367. Letter to de Valera from Mary MacSwiney, 15 May 1923; Letter to de Valera from Mary MacSwiney, 11 May 1923, de Valera Papers, P150/657, UCDA.
368. Letter to de Valera from Mary MacSwiney, 15 May 1923, de Valera Papers, P150/657, UCDA.

Chapter 8: Disillusionment: 1923–26

1. Sean McConville, *Irish Political Prisoners, 1920–1962: Pilgrimage of Desolation* (London, 2014), p. 142.
2. Ibid., pp 203–4.
3. Bill Kissane, *The Politics of the Irish Civil War* (Oxford, 2005), p. 66.
4. Richard Dunphy, *The Making of Fianna Fáil Power in Ireland, 1923–1948* (Oxford, 1995), p. 64.
5. *Longford Leader*, 11 Aug.1923.
6. *Irish Independent*, 7 Apr. 1924.
7. Letter to the editor, *Irish Independent*, from Mary MacSwiney, 18 May 1923.
8. Ibid., from Margaret Collins-O'Driscoll, 21 May 1923.
9. *Freeman's Journal*, 21 May 1923. This paper republished the letter sent to the *Irish Independent.*
10. Ibid.
11. Letter to de Valera from Mary MacSwiney, 12 May 1923, de Valera Papers, P150/657, UCDA.
12. Memo to A. L. from de Valera, 16 May 1923, Department of the Taoiseach Papers, S1297, 'Sinn Féin: Re-organisation 1922–23', NAI.
13. Note to A. L. from de Valera, 15 May 1923, enclosing a copy of letter sent to Father Burbage, Department of the Taoiseach Papers, S1297, 'Sinn Féin: Re-organisation 1922–23', NAI.
14. *Irish Times*, 13 Nov. 1923.
15. *Southern Star*, 11 Aug.1923.
16. *Freeman's Journal*, 6 Aug. 1923.
17. *Irish Independent*, 20 Aug. 1923.
18. *Éire*, 3 Mar. 1923.
19. *Irish Independent*, 4 June 1923.
20. Ibid., 11 June 1923.
21. John Regan, *The Irish Counter-Revolution 1921–1936* (Dublin, 2001), p. 146.
22. Lil Conlon, *Cumann na mBan and the Women of Ireland, 1913–25* (Kilkenny, 1969), p. 276.
23. *Freeman's Journal*, 11 June 1923.
24. Quoted in David McCullagh, *De Valera: Rise, 1882–1932* (Dublin, 2017), p. 320.
25. Letter to Mary MacSwiney from de Valera, 26 July 1923, de Valera Papers P150/657, UCDA.
26. Ibid., 7 August 1923, P150/657, de Valera Papers, UCDA.
27. Statement by de Valera issued to the organising committee of Sinn Féin, 17 June 1923, de Valera Papers, P150/657, UCDA.
28. Mel Farrell, *Party Politics in a New Democracy: The Irish Free State, 1922–1937* (London, 2017), p. 84.
29. Statement by de Valera issued to the organising committee of Sinn Féin, 17 June 1923, de Valera Papers, P150/657, UCDA.
30. McCullagh, *De Valera: Rise*, p. 327.
31. *Belfast Newsletter*, 18 July 1923.
32. *Irish Independent*, 23 July 1923.

33. *Freeman's Journal*, 23 July 1923.
34. *Irish Independent*, 16 Aug. 1923.
35. Farrell, *Party Politics*, p. 87.
36. *Derry Journal*, 25 July 1923.
37. *Irish Independent*, 16 Aug. 1923.
38. *Freeman's Journal*, 21 June 1923.
39. *Irish Independent*, 21 June 1923.
40. *Waterford News and Star*, 22 June 1923.
41. *Waterford News and Star*, 22 June 1923.
42. *Belfast Newsletter*, 26 June 1923.
43. McCullagh, *De Valera: Rise*, p. 336.
44. *Irish Statesman*, 8 Dec. 1923.
45. *Irish Statesman*, 22 Dec. 1923.
46. *Westmeath Independent*, 18 Aug. 1923.
47. *Irish Times*, 9 Aug. 1923. This was a report of Mary's speech in Gorey on the previous Tuesday night.
48. Ciara Meehan, *The Cosgrave Party: A History of Cumann na nGaedheal, 1923–33* (Dublin, 2010). p. 29.
49. Letter to the editor, *Irish Independent*, from 'Common Sense', 16 Aug. 1923.
50. *Freeman's Journal*, 17 Aug. 1923.
51. Letter to de Valera from Mary MacSwiney, 9 Aug. 1923, Mary MacSwiney Papers, P48a/38/1, UCDA.
52. Ibid.
53. *Leinster Leader*, 11 Aug. 1923.
54. Letter to [unclear] from Mary MacSwiney, 5 Aug. 1923, Mary MacSwiney Papers, P48a/38/2, UCDA. A copy of this letter was sent to de Valera.
55. Ibid.
56. *Irish Independent*, 29 Jan. 1924.
57. Letter to [unclear] from Mary MacSwiney, 5 Aug. 1923, Mary MacSwiney Papers, P48a/38/2, UCDA. A copy of this letter was sent to de Valera.
58. She also stated that no Dáil Minister should have a salary of more than £100 a year 'while there were men and women hungry in Ireland'. *Freeman's Journal*, 6 Aug. 1923.
59. Letter to [unclear] from Mary MacSwiney, 5 Aug. 1923, Mary MacSwiney Papers, P48a/38/2, UCDA. A copy of this letter was sent to de Valera.
60. *Southern Star*, 29 July 1923.
61. *Westmeath Independent*, 28 July 1923.
62. *The Nationalist (Tipperary)*, 1 Aug. 1923.
63. *Freeman's Journal*, 9 Aug. 1923.
64. *Irish Independent*, 11 Aug. 1923.
65. *The Liberator (Tralee)*, 23 Aug. 1923.
66. *Freeman's Journal*, 23 Aug. 1923.
67. Letter to the Editor. *Éire*, from Una Tutty, 10 Nov. 1923.
68. Letter to the Editor, *Irish Independent*, from Louie Bennett, 16 Aug. 1923.
69. *Irish Independent*, 10 Aug. 1923.
70. Letter to the editor, *Cork Examiner*, from Mary MacSwiney, 28 Aug. 1923.
71. *Belfast Newsletter*, 20 Aug. 1923.
72. *Irish Independent*, 30 Aug. 1923.
73. *Freeman's Journal*, 30 Aug. 1923.
74. *Belfast Newsletter*, 31 Aug. 1923.
75. McCullagh, *De Valera: Rise*, p. 330.
76. *Irish Independent*, 3 Sept. 1923.
77. *Cork Examiner*, 17 Sept. 1923.
78. P. J. Ruttledge, Minutes of Comhairle na dTeachtaí, 7 Aug. 1923 in J. Anthony Gaughan, *Austin Stack: Portrait of a Separatist* (Dublin, 1977), p. 331.
79. *Donegal News*, 22 Sept. 1922.
80. *Sinn Féin*, 20 Oct.1923.

81. Farrell, *Party Politics*, p. 84.
82. Kathleen Lynn Diary, 16 Oct. 1923, RCPI.
83. Mary MacSwiney, address to the Sinn Féin Ard Fheis, 16 Oct. 1923, Mary MacSwiney Papers, P48a/70, UCDA.
84. Charlotte Fallon, *Soul of Fire: A Biography of Mary MacSwiney* (Cork, 1986), p. 106.
85. *Cork Examiner*, 17 Oct. 1923.
86. Anne Dolan, 'Lemass, Noel Denis Joseph', in James McGuire (ed.), *Dictionary of Irish Biography* https://www.dib.ie/biography/lemass-noel-denis-joseph-a4785#:~:text=Despite%20his%20 mother's%20conviction%20that,near%20the%20Dublin–Wicklow%20border.
87. *Belfast Newsletter*, 17 Oct. 1923.
88. *Cork Examiner*, 17 Oct. 1923.
89. *Belfast Newsletter* 17 Oct. 1923.
90. McConville, *Irish Political Prisoners*, pp 202–3.
91. *Freeman's Journal*, 17 Oct. 1923.
92. *Belfast Newsletter*, 20 Oct. 1923.
93. Ibid., 26 Oct. 1923.
94. *Cork Examiner*, 23 Nov. 1923.
95. *Freeman's Journal*, 26 Nov. 1923.
96. Quoted in Gaughan, *Austin Stack*, p. 238.
97. Kathleen Lynn Diary, 24 Nov. 1923, RCPI.
98. Ibid., 20 Nov. 1923, RCPI.
99. McConville, *Irish Political Prisoners*, p. 204.
100. *Evening Herald*, 17 Nov. 1923.
101. *Cork Examiner*, 19 Nov. 1923.
102. McConville, *Irish Political Prisoners*, p. 205.
103. Anne-Marie McInerney, 'Barry, Dennis', in James McGuire et al (eds), *Dictionary of Irish Biography* (Dublin, 2019) https://www.dib.ie/biography/barry-denis-a10116.
104. Ibid.
105. *Cork Examiner*, 29 Nov. 1923.
106. *Sinn Féin*, 1 Dec.1923.
107. Ibid., 8 Dec. 1923.
108. McConville, *Irish Political Prisoners*, p. 206.
109. *Cork Examiner*, 28 Nov. 1923.
110. Letter to the editor, *Cork Examiner*, from Mary MacSwiney, 29 Nov. 1923.
111. Ibid.
112. Letter to the editor, *Cork Examiner*, from S[eán] O'Hegarty, 29 Nov. 1923.
113. Ibid.
114. Letter to My Lord Cardinal, my Lords Archbishops and Bishops from Mary MacSwiney, 8 Dec. 1922, Archbishop Byrne Papers, AB7/b/Political Papers (uncatalogued), DDA.
115. *Southern Star*, 11 Aug. 1923.
116. *Irish Independent*, 6 Aug. 1923.
117. *Éire*, 23 June 1923.
118. *Freeman's Journal*, 15 Aug. 1923.
119. Letter to Archbishop Byrne from Annie MacSwiney, 21 Feb. 1923, Archbishop Byrne Papers, AB7/b/ Political Prisoners (uncatalogued), DDA.
120. Ibid., 28 Feb. 1923, Archbishop Byrne Papers, AB7/b/ Political Prisoners (uncatalogued), DDA.
121. Letters to Archbishop Byrne from Anna O'Rahilly, 15 Dec. 1922; 21 Dec. 1922, Archbishop Byrne Papers, AB7/b/ Political Prisoners (uncatalogued), DDA.
122. *Belfast Newsletter*, 30 Nov. 1923.
123. *Freeman's Journal*, 30 Nov. 1923.
124. Letter to the editor, *Cork Examiner*, from Mary MacSwiney, 1 Dec. 1923.
125. Kathleen Lynn Diary, 29 Oct. 1923, 20 Oct. 1923, 27 Oct. 1923, RCPI.
126. Mary MacSwiney, 'Debate on the Treaty', Dáil Éireann Debates, 17 Dec. 1921.
127. *Éire*, 15 Dec. 1923.
128. *Freeman's Journal*, 10 Dec. 1923.

129. *Sinn Féin*, 2 Feb. 1923.
130. Minutes of Comhairle na dTeachtaí, 8 Aug. 1924, Mary MacSwiney Papers, P48a/290/56, UCDA.
131. Tom Garvin, *1922: The Birth of Irish Democracy* (Dublin, 1996), pp 11–2.
132. C. S. Andrews, *Man of No Property* (Dublin, 2001), p. 52.
133. *Cork Examiner*, 19 Nov. 1923.
134. *Freeman's Journal*, 12 Mar. 1923.
135. Michael Laffan, *The Resurrection of Ireland: The Sinn Féin Party, 1916–1923* (Cambridge, 1999), p. 439.
136. Quoted in Diarmaid Ferriter, *Between Two Hells: The Irish Civil War* (London, 2021), p. 34.
137. *Freeman's Journal*, 21 July 1924.
138. Mike Cronin, 'Projecting the nation through sport and culture: Ireland, Aonach Tailteann and the Irish Free State, 1924–32', in *Journal of Contemporary History*, vol. 38, no. 3 (July 2003), pp 396–7. The Tailteann games took place in 1924, 1926 and 1928.
139. *Sinn Féin*, 19 Jan. 1924. See also *Sinn Féin*, 5, 12, 26 Jan., 2 Feb. and 9 Feb. 1924.
140. Ibid.
141. Richard Dunphy, *The Making of Fianna Fáil Power in Ireland, 1923–1948* (Oxford, 1995), p. 64.
142. Máire MacSwiney Brugha, *History's Daughter: A Memoir from the Only Child of Terence MacSwiney* (Dublin, 2006), p. 110.
143. Circular letter to all shareholders of Cumann Idé um Oideacas from Annie MacSwiney, 21 June 1923, Mary MacSwiney Papers, P48a/25/16, UCDA.
144. Letter to the Secretary, St Ita's Educational Society from the Secretary, Irish Agricultural Organisation Society, 9 July 1923, Mary MacSwiney Papers, P48a/25/17, UCDA.
145. Letter to the Secretary of [unclear] from Annie MacSwiney, 8 Feb. 1924, Mary MacSwiney Papers, P48a/25/18, UCDA.
146. Letter to W. J. Stockley and T. J. Murphy from Mary MacSwiney, 9 Oct. 1925, Mary MacSwiney Papers, P48a/25/20, UCDA.
147. Proposal re involvement of St Ita's in a memorial to Terence MacSwiney, c.1921, Mary MacSwiney Papers, P48a/28, UCDA.
148. Letter to John and Eileen Hearn from Mary MacSwiney, 25 Jan. 1927, John J. Hearn Papers, Ms 15,989/9, NLI.
149. Rosamond Jacob Diary, 15–17 Oct. 1923, Ms 32582/44, NLI.
150. Quoted in Laffan, *The Resurrection of Ireland*, p. 438.
151. Ibid., p. 437.
152. Ronan Fanning, *Éamon de Valera: A Will to Power* (London, 2015), p. 147.
153. Earl of Longford and T. P. O'Neill, Eamon de Valera (London, 1974).
154. McCullagh, *De Valera: Rise*, p. 336; Gaughan, *Austin Stack*, pp 241–2.
155. Minutes of the meeting of the Second Dáil, 8 Aug. 1924 in Gaughan, *Austin Stack*, p. 355.
156. Mary MacSwiney, Minutes of Comhairle na dTeachtaí, 8 Aug. 1924, in Gaughan, *Austin Stack*, p. 341.
157. Gaughan, *Austin Stack*, p. 319.
158. McCullagh, *De Valera: Rise*, p. 336.
159. Minutes of Comhairle na dTeachtaí, 7 Aug. 1924, Mary MacSwiney Papers, P48a/290/56, UCDA.
160. Letter to [AL] from Mary MacSwiney, 5 Sept. 1923, Mary MacSwiney Papers, P48a/39/2, UCDA.
161. Minutes of Comhairle na dTeachtaí, 7 Aug. 1924 in Gaughan, *Austin Stack*, p. 337.
162. *Waterford News and Star*, 15 Aug. 1924.
163. Kathleen Lynn Diary, 15 Aug. 1924, RCPI.
164. *Cork Examiner*, 15 Sept. 1924; *Waterford News and Star*, 19 Sept. 1924.
165. *Cork Examiner*, 15 Sept. 1924.
166. Dorothy Macardle, 'In rebel Cork', *Sinn Féin*, 20 Sept. 1924.
167. Ibid.
168. Kathleen Lynn Diary, 15 Sept. 1924, RCPI.
169. Letter to Mary MacSwiney from the Hon. Secretaries, Sinn Féin, 20 Oct. 1924, Mary MacSwiney Papers, P48a/40/9, UCDA.

170. Letter to J. Harris from Mary MacSwiney, 21 Oct. 1924, Mary MacSwiney Papers, P48a/40/10, UCDA.
171. *Irish Independent* 19 Mar. 1924.
172. Ibid., 29 Jan. 1924.
173. *Nenagh News*, 5 Apr. 1924.
174. Peter Pyne, 'The Third Sinn Féin Party: 1923–1926', in *Economic and Social Review*, vol. 1., no. 1 (Oct. 1969), p. 40. Donnacha Ó Beacháin offers a reassessment of Pyne's criteria for measuring the decline of the party. Donnacha Ó Beacháin, 'Was Sinn Féin dying?: A quantitative post-mortem of the party's decline and the emergence of Fianna Fáil', in *Irish Political Studies*, vol. 24, no. 3 (2009).
175. McCullagh, *De Valera: Rise*, p. 339.
176. See, for example, the report on her speech in Rathmines in support of Seán McEntee for the vacant seat in South County Dublin, *Cork Examiner*, 25 Feb. 1924.
177. *Irish Independent*, 6 Mar. 1924.
178. Minutes of Comhairle na dTeactaí, 10 July 1924, Mary MacSwiney Papers, P48a/290/46, UCDA.
179. Statement to the Acting President of Sinn Féin from D/F, 19 July 1924, Mary MacSwiney Papers, P48a/290/52; Note to all republican deputies from Mary MacSwiney, 30 July 1924, Mary MacSwiney Papers, P48a/290/54, UCDA.
180. Minutes of Comhairle na dTeachtaí, 8 Aug. 1924, Mary MacSwiney Papers, P48a/290/57, UCDA.
181. *Cork Examiner*, 14 Mar. 1924.
182. Minutes of Comhairle na dTeachtaí, 8 Aug. 1924, Mary MacSwiney Papers, P48a/290/57, UCDA.
183. Telegram from Begley to Mary MacSwiney, 27 Mar. 1925 detailing Peter MacSwiney's travel arrangements, Mary MacSwiney Papers, P48a/119/2, UCDA; letter to de Valera from Mary MacSwiney, 30 Mar. 1925, Mary MacSwiney Papers, P48a/119/47, UCDA.
184. Letter from M. Conway to Mary MacSwiney, 15 Feb. 1925, Mary MacSwiney Papers, P48a/1119/25, UCDA.
185. McCullagh, *De Valera: Rise*, p. 337.
186. Joanne Mooney Eichacker, *Irish Republican Women in America: Lecture Tours, 1916–1925* (Dublin, 2003), p. 191.
187. Letter to Mary MacSwiney from Joseph Scott, 11 Jan. 1922, Mary MacSwiney Papers, P48a/116/1. UCDA.
188. Ibid.
189. Ibid.
190. Francis M. Carroll, *America and the Making of an Independent Ireland* (New York, 2021), p. 146.
191. Letter to Mary MacSwiney from Linda Kearns, 9 Sept. 1922, Mary MacSwiney Papers, P48a/116/22, UCDA.
192. Letter to Mary MacSwiney from Louise Hunt, Secretary to Mr Villard, 6 Feb. 1925, Mary MacSwiney Papers, P48a/119/11/2, UCDA.
193. Bernadette Whelan, *United States Foreign Policy and Ireland: From Empire to Independence, 1913–29* (Dublin, 2006), p. 469, pp 467–510.
194. Letter to Mary MacSwiney from Joseph Scott, 2 Feb. 1925, Mary MacSwiney Papers, P48a/119/15, UCDA.
195. Ibid., 13 July 1925, Mary MacSwiney Papers, P48a/121/4, UCDA.
196. Letter to Andrew Gallagher from Mary MacSwiney, 24 July 1925, Mary MacSwiney Papers, P48a/121/5, UCDA.
197. *Liberator (Tralee)*, 27 Jan. 1925.
198. Letter to Luke Dillion from Mary MacSwiney, 23 Jan. 1925, Mary MacSwiney Papers, P48a/119/3, UCDA.
199. Letter to Mary MacSwiney from Seán T. O'Kelly, 19 Feb. 1925, Mary MacSwiney Papers, P48a/119/27, UCDA; letter to Mary MacSwiney from Seán T. O'Kelly, 25 March 1925, Mary MacSwiney Papers, P48a/119/44, UCDA.
200. Letter to Mary MacSwiney from Seán T. O'Kelly, 28 Mar. 1925, Mary MacSwiney Papers, P48a/119/46, UCDA.

201. Letter to de Valera from Mary MacSwiney, 30 Mar. 1925, Mary MacSwiney Papers, P48a/119/47, UCDA.
202. Letter to Mary MacSwiney from Joe Begley, 23 Apr. 1925, Mary MacSwiney Papers, P48a/120/18/2, UCDA.
203. Letter to Mary MacSwiney from Joe Begley, 7 May 1925, Mary MacSwiney Papers, P48a/120/30, UCDA.
204. Letter to de Valera from Mary MacSwiney, 31 Mar. 1925, Mary MacSwiney Papers, P48a/119/47, UCDA.
205. Letter to Mary MacSwiney from Seán T. O'Kelly, 19 Apr. 1925, Mary MacSwiney Papers, P48a/120/7, UCDA.
206. Letter to Mr Villiard from Mary MacSwiney, 28 Jan. 1925, Mary MacSwiney Papers, P48a/119/11; letter to all friends of the Irish Republic from Mary MacSwiney, 6 Feb. 1925, Mary MacSwiney Papers, P48a/119/16, UCDA.
207. Letter to Seán T. O'Kelly from Mary MacSwiney, 17 Mar. 1925, Mary MacSwiney Papers, P48a/119/38, UCDA.
208. Letter to Mary MacSwiney from Stephen J. Donahue, 25 Jan. 1925, Mary MacSwiney Papers, P48a/119/6, UCDA.
209. Letter to Carrie Chapman Catt from Mary MacSwiney, 6 Feb. 1925, Mary MacSwiney Papers, P48a/119/18.
210. Letter to Mary MacSwiney from Seán T. O'Kelly, 19 Feb. 1922, Mary MacSwiney Papers, P48a/119/27, UCDA.
211. Letter to Joe Begley from Mary MacSwiney, 25 Apr. 1925, Mary MacSwiney Papers, P48a/120/21, UCDA.
212. Letter to de Valera from Mary MacSwiney, 30 Mar. 1925, Mary MacSwiney Papers, P48a/119/47, UCDA.
213. Letter to de Valera from Mary MacSwiney, 27 June 1925, Mary MacSwiney Papers, P48a/120/42, UCDA.
214. McCullagh, *De Valera: Rise*, p. 341.
215. Letter to Seán T. O'Kelly from Mary MacSwiney, 17 Mar. 1925, Mary MacSwiney Papers, P48a/119/38, UCDA.
216. Letter to de Valera from Mary MacSwiney, 27 June 1925, Mary MacSwiney Papers, P48a/120/42, UCDA.
217. Letter to Seán T. O'Kelly from Mary MacSwiney, Mary MacSwiney Papers, P48a/121/12, UCDA.
218. Letter to Mary MacSwiney from W. B. McKinley, 2 Oct. 1925, Mary MacSwiney Papers, P48a/121/16/11, UCDA.
219. McCullagh, *De Valera: Rise*, p. 336, pp 340–2.
220. Ibid., pp 342–3.
221. Quoted in ibid., pp 344–5.
222. Ibid., p. 343; Fanning, *Éamon de Valera*, p. 151.
223. Letter to 'Gentlemen' from Mary MacSwiney, 9 Dec. 1925, Mary MacSwiney Papers, P48a/41/3, UCDA.
224. Quoted in McCullagh, *De Valera: Rise*, p. 346; Gaughan, *Austin Stack*, p. 249.
225. Letter from Mary MacSwiney to 'Gentlemen', 9 Dec. 1925, Mary MacSwiney Papers, P48a/41 (3), UCDA. This letter was written in response to the protest issued by the Conference of Border Nationalists at Omagh, 7 Dec. 1925, with which she agreed.
226. Dorothy Macardle, *The Irish Republic* (London, 1968), pp 814–17.
227. Fanning, *Éamon de Valera*, p. 151.

Chapter 9: 'Holding the Republican Fort': 1926–42

1. Letter to Eamon Donnelly from Mary MacSwiney, 2 Apr.1927, Mary MacSwiney Papers, P48a/43/15, UCDA.
2. Síobhra Aiken, *Spiritual Wounds: Trauma, Testimony and the Irish Civil War* (Dublin, 2022), p. 2.
3. Ibid., p. 3.

4. Ibid., p. 4.
5. Quoted in David McCullagh, *De Valera: Rise, 1882–1932* (Dublin, 2017), p. 343.
6. Letter to addressed to Irish Americans from Mary MacSwiney, 12 Apr. 1926, Joseph McGarrity Papers, Ms 17,461/7, NLI.
7. Ibid.
8. Letter to Annie MacSwiney from Eamon Donnelly, 16 June 1925, Mary MacSwiney Papers, P48a/41/2, UCDA.
9. Letter to John J. Hearn from Mary MacSwiney, 7 Apr. 1926, John J. Hearn Papers, Ms 15,989/6, NLI.
10. Ibid.; speech delivered in Blarney, Co. Cork, May 1927, *Irish Independent*, 30 May 1927.
11. Agnès Maillot, *In the Shadow of History: Sinn Féin, 1926–70* (Manchester, 2015), p. 30.
12. Letter to John J. Hearn from Mary MacSwiney, 9 Sept. 1926, John J. Hearn Papers, Ms 15, 989/8, NLI.
13. Letter to Mary MacSwiney from Dorothy Macardle, 27 Apr. 1926, Mary MacSwiney Papers, P48a371/3, UCDA.
14. Letter to Eamon Donnelly from Mary MacSwiney, 2 Apr. 1927, Mary MacSwiney Papers, P48a/43/15, UCDA; Mary MacSwiney, *An Phoblacht*, 2 July 1926.
15. Máire MacSwiney Brugha, *History's Daughter: A Memoir from the Only Child of Terence MacSwiney* (Dublin, 2006), p. 145.
16. Ibid., p. 122.
17. McCullagh, *De Valera: Rise*, p. 344.
18. Quoted in ibid., p. 345.
19. Letter to the Honorary Secretaries, Sinn Féin, from Mary MacSwiney, 14 Jan. 1926, Mary MacSwiney Papers, P48a/42/1, UCDA.
20. Ibid.
21. Letter to Mary MacSwiney from de Valera, 10 Feb. 1926, Mary MacSwiney Papers, P48a/42/13, UCDA.
22. McCullagh, *De Valera: Rise*, p. 347.
23. *Donegal News*, 6 Feb. 1926.
24. McCullagh, *De Valera: Rise*, p. 347.
25. Ibid., p. 348.
26. Mary MacSwiney, 'No compromise', n.d., Mary MacSwiney Papers, P48a/441, UCDA.
27. *Belfast Newsletter*, 13 Mar. 1926.
28. *An Phoblacht*, 16 Apr. 1926.
29. Maillot, *In the Shadow of History*, p. 25.
30. Kathleen Lynn Diary, 22 Mar. 1926, RCPI.
31. Statement by Seán Lemass, [Apr. 1926], Mary MacSwiney Papers, P48a/42/23, UCDA.
32. *Irish Statesman*, 17 Apr. 1926.
33. Ibid., 1 May 1926.
34. Kathleen Lynn Diary, 21 Mar. 1926, RCSI.
35. Letter to John J. Hearn from Mary MacSwiney, 9 Sept. 1926, John J. Hearn Papers, Ms 15, 989/8, NLI.
36. Letter to John J. Hearn from Mary MacSwiney, 29 Dec. 1927, John J. Hearn Papers, Ms 15, 989/11, NLI.
37. Mary MacSwiney, 'No compromise', n.d., Mary MacSwiney Papers, P48a/441, UCDA.
38. Mary MacSwiney, 'Is unity possible', [1927], Mary MacSwiney Papers, P48a/444, UCDA.
39. *An Phoblacht*, 9 Apr. 1926.
40. Letter to John J. Hearn from Mary MacSwiney, 7 Apr. 1926, John J. Hearn Papers, Ms 15,989/6, NLI.
41. Mary MacSwiney, 'No compromise', n.d., Mary MacSwiney Papers, P48a/441, UCDA.
42. Letter to John J. Hearn from Mary MacSwiney, 7 Apr. 1926, John J. Hearn Papers, Ms 15,989/6, NLI.
43. Letter to Eileen and John J. Hearn from Mary MacSwiney, 25 Jan. 1927, John J. Hearn Papers, Ms 15,989/9, NLI.
44. Kathleen Lynn Diary, 1 May 1926, RCPI.

45. Letter to Eileen and John J. Hearn from Mary MacSwiney, 25 Jan. 1927, John J. Hearn Papers, Ms 15,989/9, NLI.
46. M. A. Hopkinson, 'Breen, Daniel ("Dan")', in James McGuire (ed.), *Dictionary of Irish Biography*, https://www.dib.ie/biography/breen-daniel-dan-a0914.
47. *Cork Examiner*, 13 May 1927.
48. Letter to the editor, *Irish Independent*, from Dan Breen, 17 May 1927.
49. *An Phoblacht*, 2 July 1926.
50. Letter to Eileen and John J. Hearn from Mary MacSwiney, 25 Jan. 1927, John J. Hearn Papers, Ms 15,989/9, NLI.
51. Letter to John J. Hearn from Mary MacSwiney, 29 Dec. 1927, John J. Hearn Papers, Ms 15,989/11, NLI.
52. *Donegal News*, 20 Mar. 1926.
53. Quoted in McCullagh, *De Valera: Rise*, p. 348.
54. Maillot, *In the Shadow of History*, p. 28.
55. McCullagh, *De Valera: Rise*, p. 350.
56. Letter to Mary MacSwiney from Dáithí Ó Donnachadha, 28 Apr. 1926, Mary MacSwiney Papers, P48a/42/28, UCDA.
57. Letter to Mary MacSwiney from Art O'Connor, 13 May 1927, Mary MacSwiney Papers, P48a/42/32, UCDA.
58. Circular letter to members of the Sinn Féin Standing Committee from the joint secretaries, 15 May 1926, Mary MacSwiney Papers, P48a/42/34, UCDA.
59. Rail voucher issued by the joint secretaries, Sinn Féin, May 1926, Mary MacSwiney Papers, P48a/42/35, UCDA.
60. Letter to Dáithí Ó Donnachadha from Mary MacSwiney, 8 June 1926, Mary MacSwiney Papers, P48a/42/40, UCDA.
61. Letter to Mary MacSwiney from Dáithí Ó Donnachadha, 12 Aug. 1926, Mary MacSwiney Papers, P48a/42/43, UCDA.
62. Kathleen Lynn Diary, 11 Feb. 1927, RCPI.
63. *An Phoblacht*, 9 July 1926.
64. Ibid., 23 July 1926.
65. Resume of Peter Golden's life, Florence O'Donoghue Papers, Ms 31,298/7, NLI.
66. Letter to John J. Hearn from Mary MacSwiney, 16 Apr. 1926, J. J. Hearn Papers, Ms 15,989/7, NLI.
67. *An Phoblacht*, 17 Dec. 1926.
68. Letter to Mary MacSwiney from Dáithí Ó Donnachadha, 19 Nov. 1926, Mary MacSwiney Papers, P48a/42/47, UCDA.
69. Letter to Joint Secretaries, Sinn Féin from Mary MacSwiney, 9 Dec. 1926, Mary MacSwiney Papers, P48a/42/48, UCDA.
70. Letter to Mary MacSwiney from the Honorary Secretaries, Sinn Féin, 20 Apr. 1926, Mary MacSwiney Papers, P48a/43/17, UCDA.
71. *Irish Freedom*, 1 Feb. 1927.
72. Ibid.
73. Michael Laffan, *The Resurrection of Ireland: The Sinn Féin Party, 1916–1923* (Cambridge, 1999), p. 433.
74. Letter to the joint secretaries, Sinn Féin, from Mary MacSwiney, 9 Dec. 1926, Mary MacSwiney Papers, P48a/42/48, UCDA.
75. Letter to the Standing Committee, Sinn Féin from Mary MacSwiney, 14 Feb. 1927, Mary MacSwiney Papers, P48a/43/3, UCDA.
76. Circular letter to members of the Standing Committee, Sinn Féin from the honorary secretaries, 21 June 1926, Mary MacSwiney Papers, P48a/42/41, UCDA.
77. Letter to Eamon Donnelly from Mary MacSwiney, 2 Apr. 1927, Mary MacSwiney Papers, P48a/43/15, UCDA.
78. Ibid.
79. Letter to John J. Hearn from Mary MacSwiney, 7 Apr. 1926, John J. Hearn Papers, Ms 15, 989/6, NLI.

80. Seán McConville, *Irish Political Prisoners, 1920–1962: Pilgrimage of Desolation* (London, 2014), p. 280.
81. Letter to John J. Hearn from Mary MacSwiney, 9 Sept. 1926, John J. Hearn Papers, Ms 15, 989/8, NLI.
82. Letter to John J. Hearn from Mary MacSwiney, 16 Apr. 1926, John J. Hearn Papers, Ms 15, 989/7, NLI.
83. *Irish Freedom*, 1 Feb. 1927.
84. Letter to the Standing Committee, Sinn Féin, from Mary MacSwiney, 9 Apr. 1927, Mary MacSwiney Papers, P48a/43/19, UCDA.
85. Letter to de Valera from Mary MacSwiney, 11 May 1927, Mary MacSwiney Papers, P48a/43/49, UCDA.
86. Mary MacSwiney, 'Is unity possible', [1927], Mary MacSwiney Papers, P48a/444, UCDA.
87. Ibid.
88. Ibid.
89. Letter to Michael Ua Domhnaill, Castlegregory, from Mary MacSwiney, 25 Apr. 1927, Mary MacSwiney Papers, P48a/43/31, UCDA.
90. Ibid.
91. Mary MacSwiney, 'Is unity possible', [1927], Mary MacSwiney Papers, P48a/444, UCDA.
92. *Irish Independent*, 16 May 1927.
93. Letter to Father O'Reilly from Mary MacSwiney, 28 Apr. [1927], Mary MacSwiney Papers, P48a/43/36, UCDA.
94. Letter to Mary MacSwiney from Austin Stack, 27 Apr. 1927, Mary MacSwiney Papers, P48a/43/33, UCDA.
95. Letter to the secretaries of Sinn Féin from Peadar O'Donnell, 27 Apr. 1927, Mary MacSwiney Papers, P48a/43/34, UCDA; letter to Austin Stack from Mary MacSwiney, 30 Apr. 1927, Mary MacSwiney Papers, P48a/43/38, UCDA.
96. Kathleen Lynn Diary, 2 Nov. 1928, RCPI.
97. Letter to Éamon Donnelly from Mary MacSwiney, 2 Apr. 1927, Mary MacSwiney Papers, P48a/43/15, UCDA.
98. Letter to de Valera from Mary MacSwiney, 11 May 1927, Mary MacSwiney Papers, P48a/43/49, UCDA.
99. Letter to Mary MacSwiney from de Valera, 14 May 1927, Mary MacSwiney Papers, P48a/43/50, UCDA.
100. Quoted in McCullagh, *De Valera: Rise*, p. 349.
101. *Southern Star*, 5 Mar. 1927.
102. Kathleen Clarke, *Revolutionary Women* (Dublin, 2008), p. 288.
103. *Irish Statesman*, 16 Apr. 1927.
104. *Irish Independent*, 25 Apr. 1927; Ronan Fanning, *Éamon de Valera: A Will to Power* (London, 2015), p. 157.
105. *Cork Examiner*, 23 May 1927.
106. Ibid., 6 June 1927.
107. Ibid., 12 May 1927.
108. Ibid., 13 May 1927.
109. Letter to 'All True Sinn Fein [sic] Workers' from Mary MacSwiney, 15 June 1927, Mary MacSwiney Papers, P48a/61/5, UCDA.
110. McCullagh, *De Valera: Rise*, p. 360; *Irish Independent*, 21 June 1927.
111. Fanning, *Éamon de* Valera, pp 154–5.
112. J. J. Lee, *Ireland, 1912–85: Politics and Society* (Cambridge, 1989), p. 152, p. 154; quoted in Fanning, *Éamon de Valera*, p. 155.
113. Letter to John J. Hearn from Mary MacSwiney, 29 Dec. 1927, John J. Hearn Papers, Ms 15,989/11, NLI.
114. Maillot, *In the Shadow of History*, p. 37.
115. Donnacha Ó Beacháin, *The Destiny of the Soldiers: Fianna Fáil, Irish Republicanism and the IRA, 1926–1973* (Dublin, 2010), chapter 3.
116. Mary MacSwiney, 'Republican oath', n.d., Mary MacSwiney Papers, P48a/445, UCDA.
117. Maillot, *In the Shadow of History*, p. 37.

118. Laffan, *The Resurrection of Ireland*, pp 442–3.
119. Ibid., p. 443.
120. Letter to de Valera from Mary MacSwiney, 21 Jan. 1926, correspondence in possession of Catherine and Cathal Brugha.
121. Letter to the Standing Committee, Sinn Féin, from Mary MacSwiney, 9 Apr. 1927, Mary MacSwiney Papers, P48a/43/21, UCDA.
122. Ibid.
123. Eoin Ó Broin, *Sinn Féin and the Politics of Left Republicanism* (London, 2009), p. 194.
124. Kevin Rafter, *Sinn Féin 1905–2005: In the Shadow of Gunmen* (Dublin, 2005), p. 70.
125. Ibid., p. 72.
126. Ó Broin, *Sinn Féin and the Politics of Left Republicanism*, p. 194.
127. Letter to Louise Gavan Duffy from Annie MacSwiney, 4 Sept. 1941, correspondence in possession of Catherine and Cathal Brugha.
128. Letter to John J. Hearn from Mary MacSwiney, 15 Dec. 1927, John J. Hearn Papers, Ms 15,989/10, NLI.
129. Letter to John J. Hearn from Mary MacSwiney, 18 May 1928, John J. Hearn Papers, Ms 15,989/13, NLI.
130. Letter to Seán Lemass from Mary MacSwiney, 30 Jan. 1926, Mary MacSwiney Papers, P48a/42/2, UCDA.
131. Martin Maguire, 'From state-destruction to state-building: The civil service in revolutionary Ireland', in *Irish Political Studies*, no. 1 (2024), p. 16.
132. Letter to John J. Hearn from Mary MacSwiney, 15 Dec. 1927, John J. Hearn Papers, Ms 15,989/10, NLI.
133. Letter to John J. Hearn from Mary MacSwiney, 25 Apr. 1928, John J. Hearn Papers, Ms 15,989/12, NLI.
134. Circular letter to members of the Sinn Féin Standing Committee from Mary MacSwiney, 2 Jan. 1928, Mary MacSwiney Papers, P48a/44/2, UCDA.
135. *Cork Examiner*, 21 Jan. 1929.
136. Ibid.
137. *Belfast Newsletter*, 22 Jan. 1929
138. *Evening Herald*, 21 Jan. 1929; *Belfast Newsletter*, 22 Jan. 1929.
139. *Belfast Newsletter*, 22 Jan. 1929.
140. *Evening Herald*, 21 Jan. 1929.
141. *Belfast Newsletter*, 22 Jan.1929.
142. Ibid.
143. Statement entitled 'Comhairle na Phoblachta', Dec. 1928, Mary MacSwiney Papers, P48a/44/16, UCDA.
144. Letter to the Secretary, Cumann na Poblachta from Mary MacSwiney enclosing an invitation template, 4 Oct. 1929, Mary MacSwiney Papers, P48a/45/14, UCDA.
145. Letter to John J. Hearn from Mary MacSwiney, 10 Oct. 1929, John J. Hearn Papers, Ms 15,989/15, NLI.
146. Circular letter to members of the Sinn Féin Standing Committee from the secretaries of Sinn Féin 30 Sept. 1930, Mary MacSwiney Papers, P48a/46/2, UCDA.
147. Letter to Mary MacSwiney from the honorary secretaries, Sinn Féin, 11 Mar. 1932, Mary MacSwiney Papers, P48a/48/9, UCDA.
148. Letter to Mary MacSwiney from the honorary secretaries, Sinn Féin, 25 May 1932, Mary MacSwiney Papers, P48a/48/14, UCDA.
149. Letter to Sinn Féin branches from the Standing Committee, 30 May 1932, Mary MacSwiney Papers, P48a/48/18, UCDA.
150. List of officers and members of the Standing Committee and their attendance, 1932, Mary MacSwiney Papers, P48a/48/32, UCDA.
151. List of officers and members of the Standing Committee and their attendance, 21 Oct. 1932–14 July 1933, Mary MacSwiney Papers, P48a/49/8, UCDA.
152. Letter to Mary MacSwiney from Brian Ó hUigínn, 11 June 1932, Mary MacSwiney Papers, P48a/48/21, UCDA.

153. Margaret Ward, *Unmanageable Revolutionaries: Women and Irish Nationalism, 1880–1980* (Dublin, 2021), p. 364.
154. Quoted in ibid., p. 364.
155. Ibid.
156. Report of Cumann na mBan convention, 10–11 June 1933, Mary MacSwiney Papers, P48a/17, UCDA.
157. Ward, *Unmanageable Revolutionaries*, p. 365.
158. *United Irishman*, 1 July 1933.
159. Letter to Eithne Coyle from Mary MacSwiney, 13 June 1933, Mary MacSwiney Papers, P48a/10/4, UCDA.
160. Ibid.
161. Letter to Mary MacSwiney from Eithne Coyle, 17 June 1933, Mary MacSwiney Papers, P48a/10/6, UCDA.
162. Letter to Sighle Humphries from Mary MacSwiney, 29 June 1933, Mary MacSwiney Papers, P48a/10/12, UCDA.
163. Letter to Eithne Coyle from Mary MacSwiney, 22 June 1933, Mary MacSwiney Papers, P48a/10/8, UCDA.
164. Patrick Maume, 'Humphreys, Sighle (Mary Ellen: Sighle Bean Uí Dhonnchadha)', in James McGuire (ed.), *Dictionary of Irish Biography*, https://www.dib.ie/biography/humphreys-sighle-mary-ellen-sighle-bean-ui-dhonnchadha-a4157.
165. Brian Hanley, *The IRA, 1926–1936* (Dublin, 2002), p. 31.
166. Letter to Sighle Humphreys from Mary MacSwiney, 29 June 1933, Mary MacSwiney Papers, P48a/10/12, UCDA.
167. Letter to Mary MacSwiney from Sighle Humphreys, 29 June 1933, Mary MacSwiney Papers, P48a/10/15, UCDA.
168. Ibid.
169. Ward, *Unmanageable Revolutionaries*, p. 369.
170. Letter to Mary MacSwiney from the honorary secretaries, Sinn Féin, 18 Jan. 1932, Mary MacSwiney Papers, P48a/48/7, UCDA.
171. Letter to Mary MacSwiney from Eileen Tubbert, 26 July 1933, Mary MacSwiney Papers, P48a/10/17, UCDA.
172. Letter to Mary MacSwiney from Eileen Tubbert, 27 July 1933, Mary MacSwiney Papers, P48a/10/18, UCDA.
173. Letter to Mary MacSwiney from Caitleen O'Moore, 29 July 1933, Mary MacSwiney Papers, P48a/10/20, UCDA.
174. Letter to Eileen Tubbert from Mary MacSwiney, 29 June 1933, Mary MacSwiney Papers, P48a/1011, UCDA.
175. *Irish Independent*, 8 Dec. 1933.
176. Constitution of Mná na Poblachta [October 1933], Mary MacSwiney Papers, P48a/11/5, UCDA.
177. Letter to Mary MacSwiney from Eileen Tubbert, 1 Nov. 1933, Mary MacSwiney Papers, P48a/11/3, UCDA.
178. Letter to Eileen Tubbert from Mary MacSwiney, 6 Dec. 1933, Mary MacSwiney Papers, P48a/11/11, UCDA.
179. *Irish Press*, 23 Mar. 1936.
180. *Irish Independent*, 5 Feb. 1937.
181. *Connacht Sentinel*, 15 Mar. 1932.
182. *Evening Herald*, 17 Mar. 1932.
183. Letter to Mary MacSwiney from Brian Ó hUigínn, 11 June 1932, Mary MacSwiney Papers, P48a/48/21, UCDA.
184. Letter to Mary MacSwiney from the Sinn Féin Standing Committee, 14 June 1932, Mary MacSwiney Papers, P48a/48/22, UCDA.
185. Dorothy Macardle, *Irish Press*, 18, 19, 20 Oct. 1933.
186. Mary MacSwiney, *Irish Press*, 2 Nov. 1933.
187. Dorothy Macardle, Letter to the editor, *Irish Press*, 7 Nov. 1933.
188. *Irish Press*, 14 June 1933.
189. *Connacht Tribune*, 8 July 1933.

190. Patrick Maume, 'O'Flanagan, Michael', in James McGuire (ed.), *Dictionary of Irish Biography*, https://www.dib.ie/biography/oflanagan-michael-a6756.
191. Letter to the members of the Standing Committee of Sinn Féin from Mary MacSwiney, 16 Dec. 1933, Mary MacSwiney Papers, P48a/49/19, UCDA.
192. Letter to the honorary secretary, Sinn Féin, Cork, from Mary MacSwiney, 10 Dec. 1937, Mary MacSwiney Papers, P48a/53/3, UCDA.
193. Letter to the members of the Standing Committee of Sinn Féin from Caitlín Brugha, 18 Oct. 1934, Mary MacSwiney Papers, P48a/50/8, UCDA.
194. Letter to J. J. Kelly from Mary MacSwiney, 20 Nov. 1933, Mary MacSwiney Papers, P48a/59/32, UCDA.
195. Ibid.
196. Letter to [unclear] from Mary MacSwiney, 23 Oct. 1934, Mary MacSwiney Papers, P48a/50/9, UCDA.
197. Letter to [unclear] from Mary MacSwiney, 13 Mar. 1936, Mary MacSwiney Papers, P48a/52/3, UCDA.
198. Letter to the honorary secretary, Sinn Féin, Cork, from Mary MacSwiney, 10 Dec. 1937, Mary MacSwiney Papers, P48a/53/3, UCDA.
199. Letter to Frank Aiken from Joseph O'Connor, 6 Apr. 1933, DP1503, Mary Carey, MSPC.
200. Letter to the members of the Standing Committee of Sinn Féin from Mary MacSwiney, 16 Dec. 1933, Mary MacSwiney Papers, P48a/49/19. UCDA.
201. Letter to [unclear] from Mary MacSwiney, 13 Mar. 1936, Mary MacSwiney Papers, P48a/52/3, UCDA.
202. Letter to M. T. from Mary MacSwiney, 16 Nov. 1935, Mary MacSwiney Papers, P48a/51/6, UCDA.
203. Ibid.
204. Enclosure in letter to M. T. from Mary MacSwiney, 16 Nov. 1935, Mary MacSwiney Papers, P48a/51/7, UCDA.
205. Note by Mary MacSwiney [1936], Mary MacSwiney Papers, P48a/51/8, UCDA.
206. Letter to Mary MacSwiney from Caitlín Brugha, 24 Feb. 1936, Mary MacSwiney Papers, P48a/52/2, UCDA.
207. Maume, 'O'Flanagan, Michael'.
208. Letter to the honorary secretaries, Sinn Féin Standing Committee, from Mary MacSwiney, 14 Mar. 1936, Mary MacSwiney Papers, P48a/52/3, UCDA.
209. Enclosures in a letter to the honorary secretaries, Sinn Féin Standing Committee, from Mary MacSwiney, 14 March 1936, Mary MacSwiney Papers, P48a/52/3, UCDA.
210. McConville, *Irish Political Prisoners, 1920–1962*, p. 276.
211. Letter to the honorary secretaries, Sinn Féin Standing Committee, from Mary MacSwiney, 24 July 1936, Mary MacSwiney Papers, P48a/52/7, UCDA.
212. McConville, *Irish Political Prisoners, 1920–1962*, p. 285.
213. Ibid., p. 286.
214. Ibid.
215. Letter to the honorary secretaries, Sinn Féin from Mary MacSwiney, 7 Jan. 1932, Mary MacSwiney Papers, P48a/48/2, UCDA.
216. Letter to Mary MacSwiney from the honorary secretaries, Sinn Féin, 16 Jan. 1932, Mary MacSwiney Papers, P48a/48/6, UCDA.
217. McConville, *Irish Political Prisoners, 1920–1962*, p. 286.
218. Letter to Mary MacSwiney from the honorary secretaries, Sinn Féin, 9 Mar. 1932, Mary MacSwiney Papers, P48a/48/8, UCDA; Hanley, *The IRA*, pp 15–16.
219. Letters to members of the Tomas MacCurtain branch, Sinn Féin from the honorary secretary, 28 May 1932, Mary MacSwiney Papers, P48a/48/16, UCDA.
220. McConville, *Irish Political Prisoners, 1920–1962*, p. 287.
221. Hanley, *The IRA*, pp 15–16; Mike Cronin, *The Blueshirts and Irish Politics* (Dublin, 1997), p. 130.
222. McConville, *Irish Political Prisoners, 1920–1962*, p. 289.
223. Hanley, *The IRA*, pp 17–18.
224. *Irish Independent*, 30 Apr. 1936; *Irish Press*, 15 May 1936.
225. *Irish Press*, 30 Apr. 1936

226. Letter to the editor, *Irish Press*, from Tom Barry, 4 May 1936.
227. Letter to Cork Corporation from Mary MacSwiney, printed in the *Irish Press*, 6 May 1936.
228. *Irish Press*, 6 May 1936.
229. *Southern Star*, 28 Mar. 1938.
230. Letter to de Valera from Mary MacSwiney, 11 May 1936, correspondence in possession of Catherine and Cathal Brugha.
231. Ibid.
232. *Irish Independent*, 1 Feb. 1937.
233. *Irish Press*, 15 May 1936.
234. Letter to de Valera from Mary MacSwiney, 20 June 1936, correspondence in possession of Catherine and Cathal Brugha.
235. McConville, *Irish Political Prisoners, 1920–1962*, p. 287.
236. Letter to Mary MacSwiney from de Valera, 22 June 1936, correspondence in possession of Catherine and Cathal Brugha.
237. Dorothy Macardle, *Without Fanfares: Some Reflections on the Republic of Éire* (Dublin, 1946), p. 9.
238. Dorothy Macardle, Letter to the editor, *Irish Press*, 7 Nov. 1933.
239. *Irish Press*, 3 Feb. 1937.
240. Letter to Caitlín Brugha from Mary MacSwiney, 25 Feb. 1937, Mary MacSwiney Papers, P48a/53/1, UCDA.
241. Letter to Scelig from Mary MacSwiney, Nov. 1937, Mary MacSwiney Papers, P48a/60/35, UCDA.
242. Quoted in Maillot, *In the Shadow of History*, p. 81.
243. Brian Ó hUigínn, Letter to the editor, *Irish Press.*
244. *Cork Examiner*, 1 July 1937.
245. *Irish Press*, 13 Sept. 1937.
246. Letter to the editor, *Irish Press*, from Mary MacSwiney, 13 Sept. 1937.
247. *Irish Independent*, 13 Sept. 1937; *Irish Press*, 13 Sept. 1937.
248. *Irish Press*, 23 Sept. 1937.
249. Letter to [unclear] from Mary MacSwiney, 13 Mar. 1936, Mary MacSwiney Papers, P48a/52/3, UCDA.
250. Maillot, *In the Shadow of History*, p. 86.
251. Ibid., pp 82–3.
252. *Irish Press*, 18 Apr. 1938.
253. See, for example, letter to Fred Cronin Papers from Annie MacSwiney, 24 Jan. 1921, Fred Cronin Papers, Ms 49,526/8, NLI.
254. Anne Dolan, 'MacSwiney, Muriel Frances', in James McGuire (ed.), *Dictionary of Irish Biography*, https://www.dib.ie/biography/macswiney-muriel-frances-a5296.
255. Ibid.
256. MacSwiney Brugha, *History's Daughter*, p. 61.
257. Mary MacSwiney, 'Debate on the Treaty', Dáil Éireann Debates, 21 Dec. 1921.
258. *New York Times*, 25 June 1925.
259. Dolan, 'MacSwiney, Muriel Frances'.
260. MacSwiney Brugha, *History's Daughter*, p. 69.
261. Ibid., p. 72.
262. Ibid., pp 75–7.
263. Ibid., p. 77.
264. Letter to the Department of Defence from Muriel MacSwiney, 15 Apr. 1953, DP19903 Terence MacSwiney, MSPC.
265. Letter to the Military Service Pensions Board from Muriel MacSwiney, 5 Feb. 1974, DP 19903, Terence MacSwiney, MSPC.
266. MacSwiney Brugha, *History's Daughter*, p. 165.
267. *Irish Press*, 23 Jan. 1942.
268. MacSwiney Brugha, *History's Daughter*, p. 165.
269. *Irish Press*, 11 Mar. 1942.
270. Letter to Máire MacSwiney Brugha from Pa McGrath, Lord Mayor of Cork, 16 Nov. 1954, correspondence in possession of Catherine and Cathal Brugha.

271. *Irish Press*, 9 Mar. 1942.
272. Ibid.

Bibliography

Primary Sources

Archives

Cork City and County Archives

Liam de Róiste Diary

Cork Public Museum

Lil Conlon Collection
Cumann na mBan Collection

Dublin Diocesan Archive

Archbishop Byrne Papers, AB7/b/ Political Prisoners (uncatalogued)

Irish Military Archives

Bureau of Military History Witness Statements
Military Service Pensions Collection

National Archives

Chief Secretary's Office Registered Papers
Dáil Éireann Collection
Department of Foreign Affairs Papers
Department of the Taoiseach Papers

National Archives, Kew, London

Home Office Papers

National Library of Ireland

Art Ó Briain Papers
Ceannt and O'Brennan Papers
Count Plunkett Papers
Fred Cronin Papers
Cumann na mBan Leaflets and Circulars
Ephemera Collection
Erskine Childers Papers
Florence O'Donoghue Papers
James O'Mara Papers
John Devoy Papers
John J. Hearn Papers
Joseph McGarrity Papers

Irish National Aid and Volunteer Dependents' Fund Papers
Letters to Kate Kelly regarding political prisoners, 1916-1924
Máire Comerford Papers
Material relating to Constance Markievicz, Padraic Pearse and Others
Pádraic Fleming Papers
Sheehy Skeffington Papers
Terence MacSwiney Papers

Royal College of Physicians Ireland

Kathleen Lynn Diaries

UCC Archives

College Calendars
Governing Body Minutes

UCC Special Collections

Pauline Henley Collection

UCD Archives

Éamon de Valera Papers
Mary MacSwiney Papers
Terence MacSwiney Papers
Papers of Terence MacSwiney's Biographers
Copy of HO144/10308.

Directories

Slater's Directory, Cork City and County

Government Debates

Dáil Éireann Debates
Hansard Debates

Material in Private Hands

Correspondence and other documents relating to the MacSwiney family in the possession of Catherine and Cathal Brugha.

Newspapers

Abilene Weekly Reflector
Boston Globe
Bamberg Herald (SC)
Belfast Newsletter
Cork Examiner
Daily Chronicle
Daily Express
Daily Mail
Éire
Evening Echo

Evening Herald
Evening Star (Washington DC)
Evening World (New York NY)
Fianna Fáil
Freeman's Journal
Irish Citizen
Irish Independent
Irish Press
Irish Times
Liberator (Tralee)
Limerick Leader
Morning Post
Nenagh Guardian
New York Times
New York Tribune
Poblacht na hÉireann,
Skibbereen Eagle
Sligo Champion
Strabane Chronicle
Sunday Independent,
The Abbeville Press and Banner (SC)
The Herald
The Herald and News (Newberry SC)
The Irishman
The Irish Volunteer
The Laurens Advertiser (Laurens SC)
The Nationalist (Tipperary)
The Sun and the New York Herald
The Times
Topeka State Journal
Washington Herald
Waterford News and Star

Published Novels, Memoirs and Contemporary Publications

Clarke, Kathleen, *Revolutionary Women* (Dublin, 2008).
Chavasse, Móirín, *Terence MacSwiney* (Dublin, 1961).
Comerford, Máire, *On Dangerous Ground: A Memoir of the Irish Revolution* (Dublin, 2021).
Corkery, Daniel, *The Threshold of Quiet* ((Dublin, 1946).
Corkery, Daniel, 'Terence MacSwiney: Lord Mayor of Cork', *Studies: An Irish Quarterly Review*, vol. 9, no. 36 (Dec. 1920).
De Burca, Padraig and John F, Boyle, *Free State or Republic: Pen Pictures of the Historic Treaty Session of Dáil Éireann* (Dublin 2002).
Didion, Joan, *The Year of Magical Thinking* (London, 2012).
Evidence on Conditions in Ireland: Comprising the Complete Testimony, Affidavits and Exhibits Presented Before the American Commission on Conditions in Ireland (Washington, 1921).
Gallagher, Frank, *Days of Fear: A Diary of a Hunger Strike* (Cork, 1967).
Macardle, Dorothy, *The Irish Republic* (London, 1968).
Macardle, *Without Fanfares: Some Reflectiosn on the Republic of Éire* (Dublin, 1946).
Macardle, Dorothy, *Tragedies of Kerry* (Dublin, 1924).
MacSwiney Brugha, Máire , *History's Daughter: A Memoir from the Only Child of Terence MacSwiney* (Dublin, 2006).
Neeson, Seán, 'A Great Irish School, 1916-1954', *Capuchin Annual* (1965).
O'Connor, Frank, *An Only Child* (Belfast, 1993).
O'Connor, Frank, *The Big Fellow: A Life of Michael Collins* (London, 1937).
Pearse, Patrick, *The Murder Machine* (Dublin, 1916).

O'Donoghue, Florence, *Tomás MacCurtain* (Tralee, 1958).
O'Hegarty, P. S., *A Short Memoir of Terence MacSwiney* (Dublin, 1922).
O'Hegarty, P. S., 'An Irish Constitution and British Interference', *The Separatist*, 10 June 1922.
Ruiséal, Liam, 'The Position in Cork', *Capuchin Annual*, 1966.
Skinnider, Margaret, *Doing My Bit for Ireland* (New York, 1917).
Who Burnt Cork City (Dublin, 1921).

Secondary Sources

Adams, Katherine H. and Michael L. Keene, *Alice Paul and the American Suffrage Campaign* (Illinois, 2007).
Aiken, Síobhra , *Spiritual Wounds: Trauma, Testimony and the Irish Civil War* (Dublin, 2022).
Anderson, Julie, '"Jumpy Stump": Amputation and Trauma in the First World War', *First World War Studies*, vol. 6, no. 1 (2015).
Barr, Colin, 'The Re-Energising of Irish Catholicism, 1790-1880' in James Kelly (ed.), *The Cambridge History of Ireland, III* (Cambridge, 2018).
Beiner, Guy, 'Between Trauma and Triumphalism: The Easter Rising, The Somme, and The Crux of Deep Memory in Modern Ireland', *The Journal of British Studies*, vol. 46, no. 2 (April 2007).
Bielenberg Andy, and David Johnson, 'The Production and Consumption of Tobacco in Ireland, 1800-1914', *Irish Economic and Social History*, vol. 25 (1998).
Borgonovo, John, 'Cumann na mBan and the Civil War' in John Crowley, Donal Ó Drisceoil and Mike Murphy (eds.), *Atlas of the Irish Revolution* (Cork, 2017).
Borgonovo, John, *The Dynamics of War and Revolution: Cork City, 1916-1918* (Cork, 2013).
Borgonovo, John, '"A Soviet in Embryo": Cork's Food Crisis and the People's Food Committee', 1917-18, *Saothar*, vo. 34 (2009).
Borgonovo, John, *Florence and Josephine O'Donoghue's War of Independence* (Dublin, 2006).
Bourke, Joanna, 'Fear and Anxiety: Writing about Emotion in Modern History' in *History Workshop*, no. 55 (2003).
Bourke, Joanna, *Dismembering the Male: Men's Bodies, Britain and the Great War* (London, 1999).
Carroll, Francis, M., *America and the Making of an Independent Ireland* (New York, 2021).
Coleman, Marie, 'Women Activists During the Civil War'. In Darragh Gannon and Fearghal McGarry (eds.), *Ireland 1922* (Dublin, 2022).
Cooter, Roger, *Surgery and Society in Peace and War* (London, 1993).
Costello, Francis J., *Enduring the Most: The Life and Death of Terence MacSwiney* (Dingle, 1996).
Cronin, Mike, 'Projecting the Nation through Sport and Culture: Ireland, Aonach Tailteann and the Irish Free State, 1924-32', *Journal of Contemporary History*, vol. 38, no. 3 (July 2003).
Cronin, Mike, *The Blueshirts and Irish Politics* (Dublin, 1997).
Daly, Mary, 'The Irish Free State and the Great Depression of the 1930s: the Interaction of the Global and the Local', *Irish Economic and Social History*, vol. 38 (2011).
Doherty, Gabriel, Fiona Brennan and Neil Buttimer (eds.), *The Art and Ideology of Terence MacSwiney: Caught in the Living Flame* (Cork, 2022).
Dolan, Anne, 'Death in the Archives, Witnessing War in Ireland, 1919-1921' in *Past and Present* (2021).
Dolan, Anne and William Murphy, *Michael Collins: the Man and the Revolution* (Cork, 2018).
Dolan, Anne, 'Killing and Bloody Sunday, November 1920' in *The Historical Journal*, vol. 49, no. 3 (2006).
Doyle, 'The Pope's Irish Battalion, 1860' in *History Ireland*, vol. 18, no. 5 (Sept./Oct., 2010).
Dunphy, Richard, *The Making of Fianna Fáil Power in Ireland, 1923-1948* (Oxford, 1995).
Fallon, Charlotte, *Soul of Fire: A Biography of Mary MacSwiney* (Cork, 1986).
Fahy, A. M., 'Place and Class in Cork' in Patrick O' Flanagan and Cornelius G. Buttimer, *Cork History and Society* (Dublin, 1993).
Fanning, Ronan, *Éamon de Valera: A Will to Power* (Dublin, 2015).
Farrell, Mel, 'Stepping Stones to Freedom.'
Farrell, Mel, *Party Politics in a New Democracy: The Irish Free State, 1922-37* (Basingstoke, 2017).

Fealy, Gerard and Judith Harford, '"Nervous Energy and Administrative Ability": The Early Lady Principals and Lay Superintendents in Ireland', *Journal of Educational Administration and History*, vol. 39, no. 1 (2007).

Ferriter, Diarmaid, *Between Two Hells: The Irish Civil War* (London, 2021).

Ferriter, Diarmaid, *Judging Dev: a reassessment of the life and legacy of Eamon de Valera* (Dublin, 2007).

Ferriter, Diarmaid, *The Transformation of Ireland, 1900-2000* (London, 2004).

Fessler, D. M. T. , 'The Implications of Starvation Induced Psychological Changes for the Ethical Treatment of Hunger Strikes', *Journal of Child Ethics*, (September 2003).

Fitzpatrick, David, *Ernest Blythe in Ulster: The Making of a Double Agent?* (Cork, 2018).

Fitzpatrick, David, *Harry Boland's Irish Revolution* (Cork, 2003).

Foster, R. F. *Vivid Faces: the Revolutionary Generation in Ireland 1890-1923* (London, 2014).

Gallagher, Michael, 'The Pact General Election of 1922', *Irish Historical Studies*, vol. 22, no. 84 (September 1979).

Gannon, Darragh, 'Global Ireland' in Darragh Gannon and Fearghal McGarry (eds.), *Ireland 1922* (Dublin, 2022).

Gaughan, J. Anthony, *Austin Stack: Portrait of a Separatist* (Dublin, 1977).

Garvin, Tom, *1922: The Birth of Irish Democracy* (Dublin, 1996).

Gibney, John, 'Revolutionary Diplomacy' in Darragh Gannon and Fearghal McGarry (eds.), *Ireland 1922* (Dublin, 2022).

Hanley, Brian, *The IRA, 1926-1936* (Dublin, 2002).

Hannigan, Dave, *Terence MacSwiney: The Hunger Strike that Rocked a Nation* (Dublin, 2010).

Harford, Judith, 'The Movement for the Higher Education of Women in Ireland: Gender Equality or Denominational Rivalry' in *History of Education*, vol. 34 no. 5 (Sept 2005).

Hart, Peter, *The IRA and its Enemies: Violence and Community in Cork, 1916-1923* (Oxford, 1998).

Hopkinson, Michael, *Green Against Green: The Irish Civil War* (Dublin, 2004).

Hopkinson, *Green Against Green*

Keown, Geard, 'The Irish Race Conference, 1922, reconsidered', *Irish Historical Studies*, vol. 32, no. 127 (May 2001).

Kissane, Bill, *The Politics of the Irish Civil War* (Oxford, 2005).

Knirck, Jason, *Women of the Dáil: Gender, Republicanism and the Anglo-Irish Treaty* (Dublin, 2006).

Laffan, Michael, *The Resurrection of Ireland: The Sinn Féin Party, 1916-1923* (Cambridge, 1999).

Lane, Leeann, *Dorothy Macardle* (Dublin, 2019).

Lee, J. J., *Ireland, 1912-85: Politics and Society* (Cambridge, 1989).

Lerner, Paul and Mark S. Micale, 'Trauma, Psychiatry, and History: A Conceptual and Historiographical Introduction' in Mark S. Micale and Paul Lerner (eds.), *Traumatic Pasts: History, Psychiatry, and Trauma in the Modern Age, 1870-1930* (Cambridge, 2001).

Lennon, Joseph, 'The Starvation of a Man: Terence MacSwiney and Famine Memory' in Oona Frawley (ed.), *Memory Ireland: the Famine and the Troubles, vol. 3* (Syracuse, 2014).

Limond, David, '"A Work for Other Hands": Patrick Pearse and St Ita's College', *History Ireland*, vol. 14 (Mar./Apr. 2006).

Lynch, Robert, *The Partition of Ireland, 1918-1925* (Cambridge, 2019).

Luckhurst, Roger, *The Trauma Question* (London, 2008).

MacDiarmada, Mary, *Art O'Brien and Irish Nationalism in London, 1900-1925* (Dublin, 2020).

MacMahon, Deirdre, 'Ireland, the Empire, and the Commonwealth' in Kevin Kenny (ed.), *Ireland and the British Empire* (Oxford, 2004).

Maguire, Martin, 'From State-Destruction to State-Building: the Civil Service in Revolutionary Ireland', *Irish Political Studies*, no. 1 (2024).

Maillot, Agnès, *In the Shadow of History: Sinn Féin, 1926-70* (Manchester, 2015).

Maume, Patrick, '*Life that is Exile*': *Daniel Corkery and the Search for Irish Ireland* (Belfast, 1993).

Maume, Patrick, 'Daniel Corkery: a Reassessment' in *Studia Hibernia*, no 26 (1992).

McAuliffe, '"An idea has Gone Abroad that All Women Were Against the Treaty" Cumann na Saoirse, and Pro-Treaty Women, 1922-2' in Liam Weeks and Mícheál Ó Fathartaigh (eds), *The Treaty: Debating and Establishing the Irish State* (Dublin, 2018).

McAuliffe, Mary, The Homefront as Battlefront: Women Violence and the Domestic Space during the War in Ireland 1919-1921 in Linda Connolly (ed.), *Women and the Irish Revolution 1917-23: Violence, Feminism Nationalism* (Dublin, 2020).

McAvoy, Sandra, 'ReliefWork and Refugees: Susanne Rouviere Day (1876–1964) on War as Women's Business', *Women's History Review*, vol. 27, no. 3 (2018).
McDiarmid, Lucy, *At Home in the Revolution: What Women Said and Did in 1916* (Dublin, 2015).
McCarthy, Cal, *Cumann na mBan and the Irish Revolution* (Cork, 2014).
McConville, Seán, *Irish Political Prisoner 1920-1962: A Pilgrimage of Desolation* (London, 2014).
McCullagh, 'Éamon de Valera's Civil War' in Darragh Gannon and Fearghal McGarry (eds.), *Ireland 1922* (Dublin, 2022).
McCullagh, David *De Valera: Rise, 1882-1932* (Dublin, 2017).
McCullagh, David, *De Valera: Rule, 1932-1975* (Dublin, 2018).
Meehan, Ciara, *The Cosgrave Party. A History of Cumann na nGaedheal, 1923-33* (Dublin, 2010).
Miller, Ian, *A History of Force Feeding: Hunger Strikes, Prisons and Medical Ethics, 1909-1974* (London, 2016).
Mooney Eichacker, Joanne, *Irish Republican Women in America: Lecture Tours, 1916-1925* (Dublin, 2003).
Muldoon, Orla M., *The Social Psychology of Trauma: Connecting the Personal and the Political* (Cambridge, 2024).
Murphy, William, 'Dying, Death and Hunger Strikes: Cork and Brixton, 1920' in James Kelly and Mary Ann Lyons (eds.), *Death and Dying in Ireland, Britain and Europe: Historical Perspectives* (Dublin, 2013).
Murphy, William, *Political Imprisonment and the Irish, 1912-1921* (Oxford, 2014).
Murray, Paul, 'The Irish Race Congress, 21-28 January 1922', *History Ireland*, vol. 9, no. 4 (Winter, 2001).
Nic Dháibhéid, Caoimhe, 'The Irish National Aid Association and the Radicalization of Public Opinion in Ireland, 1916-1918' in *The Historical Journal*, vol. 55, no. 3, (Sept. 2012).
Nic Dháibhéid, Caoimhe, 'The Politics of Emotions' in Darragh Gannon and Fearghal McGarry (eds.), *Ireland 1922* (Dublin, 2022).
Ó Beacháin, Donnacha, *The Destiny of the Soldiers: Fianna Fáil, Irish Republicanism and the IRA, 1926-1973* (Dublin, 2010).
Ó Beacháin, Donnacha, 'Was Sinn Féin Dying?: A Quantitative Post-Mortem of the Party's Decline and the Emergence of Fianna Fáil', *Irish Political Studies*, vol. 24, no. 3 (2009).
Ó Broin, Eoin, *Sinn Féin and the Politics of Left Republicanism* (London, 2009).
Ó Corráin, Daithí, 'Upholding the Commandments and the Will of the Majority, the Catholic Hierarchy, the October 1922 Pastoral, and the Irish Civil War', *Archivium Hibernicum*, lxxvi (2023).
Ó Corráin, Daithí and Gerard Hanley, *Cathal Brugha:* 'An Indomitable Spirit' (Dublin, 2022).
Ó Fathartaigh, Ó Dochartaigh, Liam, 'An Bárd 'Gus an Fó', *Comhar*, vol. 34, no. 1 (Jan. 1975).
Mícheál and Liam Weeks, *Birth of a State: the Anglo-Irish Treaty* (Dublin, 2021).
O'Farrell, Fergus, *Cathal Brugha* (Dublin, 2018).
O'Neill, Ciaran, 'Bourgeois Ireland, or, on the Benefits of Keeping One's Hands Clean' in James Kelly (ed.), *The Cambridge History of Ireland, III* (Cambridge, 2018).
Pašeta, Senia, *Irish Nationalist Women, 1900-1918* (Cambridge, 2014).
Powell, Bob, 'History and Family Memory: The "Burning of Cork", 11 and 12 December 1920' in *Folk Life, Journal of Ethnological Studies*, vo. 60, no. 2 (2022).
Pyne, Peter, 'The Third Sinn Féin Party: 1923–1926', *Economic and Social Review*, vol. 1, no. 1 (October 1969).
Quinlivan, Aodh, *Forgotten Lord Mayor: Donal Óg O'Callaghan 1920-1924* (Cork, 2020).
Rafter, Kevin, *Sinn Féin 1905-2005: In the Shadow of Gunmen* (Dublin, 2005).
Raftery Deirdre and Susan M. Parkes, *Female Education in Ireland 1700-1900: Minerva or Madonna* (Dublin, 2007).
Regan, John, *The Irish Counter-Revolution 1921–1936* (Dublin, 2001).
Reynolds, Paige, 'Modernist Martyrdom: The Funerals of Terence MacSwiney' in *Modernism/ Modernity* vol. 9, no. 4 (November 2002).
Richardson, Sarah, *The Political Worlds of Women: Gender and Politics in Nineteenth Century Britain* (Abingdon, 2013).
Townshend, *Easter 1916: the Irish Rebellion* (London, 2015).
Townshend, Charles, *The Republic: The Fight for Irish Independence* (London, 2013).

Ward, Margaret, *Unmanageable Revolutionaries: Women and Irish Nationalism, 1880-1980* (Dublin, 2021).
Ward, Margaret, *Fearless Woman. Hanna Sheehy Skeffington, Feminism and the Irish Revolution* (Dublin, 2019).
Weeks, Liam and Mícheál Ó Fathartaigh (eds.), *The Treaty: Debating and Establishing the Irish State* (Dublin, 2018).
Whelan, Bernadette, *United States Foreign Policy and Ireland: From Empire to Independence, 1913-29* (Dublin, 2006).
White, Gary and Brendan O'Shea, *'Baptised in Blood': The Formation of the Cork Brigade of the Irish Volunteers 1913-1916* (Cork, 2005).

Websites

Australian Dictionary of Biography
Century Ireland
Dictionary of Irish Biography
The Irish Revolution Irish Biography Project

Index